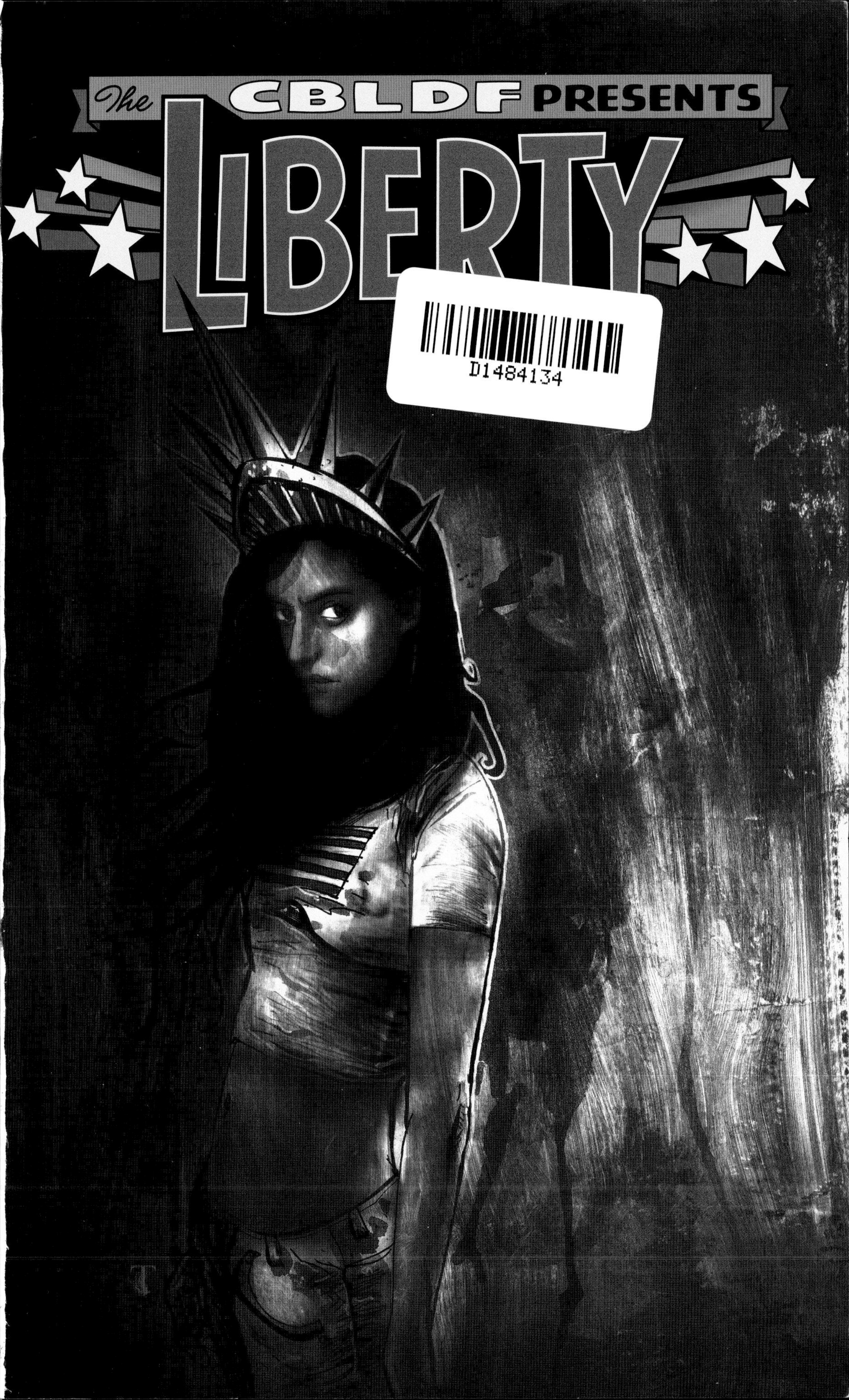
The CBLDF PRESENTS
LIBERTY

STAFF

Charles Brownstein
Executive Director

Alex Cox
Deputy Director

Robert Corn-Revere
Legal Counsel

Betsy Gomez
Editorial Director

BOARD OF DIRECTORS

Larry Marder
President

Milton Griepp
Vice President

Jeff Abraham
Treasurer

Dale Cendali
Secretary

Joe Ferrara
Jennifer L. Holm
Paul Levitz
Andrew McIntire
Chris Powell
Jeff Smith

ADVISORY BOARD

**Neil Gaiman
& Denis Kitchen**
Co-chairs

Susan Alston
Matt Groening
Chip Kidd
Jim Lee
Frenchy Lunning
Frank Miller
Louise Nemschoff
Mike Richardson
William Schanes

www.cbldf.org

CORPORATE MEMBERS:

BLACK PHOENIX ALCHEMY LAB
www.blackphoenixalchemylab.com

CBLDF thanks our Guardian Members: James Wood Bailey, Grant Geissman, Philip Harvey, Joseph H. King, Midwest Comic Book Association, and SPX

THE CBLDF PRESENTS: LIBERTY Published by Image Comics, Inc. Office of Publication: 2001 Center Street, Sixth Floor Berkeley, CA 94704. The CBLDF Presents: LIBERTY and its logos, and CBLDF logos are ™ and ©2014 the Comic Book Legal Defense Fund. BRATPACK is ™ & © 2008, 2014 Rick Veitch. HIP FLASK and ELEPHANTMEN are ™ & © 2008, 2011, 2014 Active Images. CRIMINAL is ™ & © 2008, 2014 Ed Brubaker & Sean Phillips. GOBUKAN is © 2008, 2014 J. Bone. HELLBOY is © 2008, 2014 Mike Mignola. HOUSE OF DRACULA is © 2008, 2014 Mark Millar & John Paul Leon. MARK EVANIER & SERGIO ARAGONES are © 2008, 2014 Mark Evanier & Sergio Aragones. THE BOYS is © 2008, 2014 Spitfire Productions Ltd. & Darick Robertson. THE DEADLY BOOK is © 2008, 2014 Darwyn Cooke. THE FIRST CENSOR ™ & © 2009, 2014 Jason Aaron & Moritat. CHOKER ™ & © 2009, 2014 Ben McCool & Ben Templesmith. MR. GUM, MADMAN and all related characters ™ & © 2009, 2014 Mike Allred. LOVERMAN ™ & © 2009, 2014 Paul Pope. CHANNEL ZERO ™ & © 2009, 2014 Brian Wood. ORIGIN OF THE SPECIOUS ™ & © 2009, 2014 Kathryn & Stuart Immonen. PAINKILLER JANE ™ & © 2009, 2014 Jimmy Palmiotti & Joe Quesada. JACK STAFF ™ & © 2009, 2014 Paul Grist. MARTHA WASHINGTON ™ & © 2009, 2010, 2014 Frank Miller, Inc. & Dave Gibbons. I BEG YOUR PARDON ™ & © 2009, 2014 Chynna Clugston-Flores. THE APOCALIPSTIX ™ & © 2009, 2014 Ray Fawkes & Cameron Stewart. 100 WORDS ™ & © 2009, 2014 Neil Gaiman & Jim Lee. KICK-ASS ™ & © 2009, 2014 Mark Millar & John S. Romita. BEST. DEFENSE. EVER. ™ and ©2010, 2014 Jill Thompson & Brian Azzarello. BLIND JUSTICE ™ and ©2010, 2014 Jeff Smith. BOILERPLATE ™ and ©2010, 2014 Paul Guinan and Anina Bennett. CHAIN GAME ™ and ©2010, 2014 Fábio Moon and Gabriel Bá. Charley Loves Robots ™ and ©2010, 2014 Active Images. FREEDOM'S LADY ™ and ©2010, 2014 Rob Liefeld. IT'S WHY WE FIGHT!, BEANISH, MR. SPOOK, PROFESSOR GARBANZO, MR. TEACH'M ™ and ©2010, 2014 Larry Marder. LIBERTY TREE ™ and ©2010, 2014 Paul Pope. MEGATON MAN AND THE LIBERTY ALLIANCE ™ and ©2010, 2014 Don Simpson. MILK AND CHEESE IN CBLDF-U! ™ and ©2010, 2014 Evan Dorkin. MONSTERS AT THE DOOR ™ and ©2010, 2014 Gail Simone and Amanda F. Gould. PHAETON! ™ and ©2010, 2014 Scott Morse. PURSUING LIBERTY ™ and ©2010, 2014 Terry Moore. R.E.S.P.E.C.T ™ and ©2010, 2014 Colleen Doran. Sin City ™ and ©2010, 2014 Frank Miller. THE BOYS ™ and ©2010, 2014 Garth Ennis & Darick Robertson. INTRODUCTION is ™ and © 2011, 2014 Bob Schreck, Fábio Moon & Gabriel Bá. GRENDEL is ™ and © 2011, 2014 Matt Wagner. ALAN TURING pin-up is ™ and © 2011, 2014 Frank Quitely. IT'S NOT A TRICK is ™ and © 2011, 2014 J.H. Williams III & Todd Klein. THE LIGHT AT THE END OF THE TUNNEL is ™ and © 2011, 2014 Kevin McColloch & Dave Cooper. COWBOY NINJA VIKING is ™ and © 2011, 2014 A.J. Lieberman and Riley Rossmo. LA CARICATURE is ™ and © 2011, 2014 Brandon Montclare & Joëlle Jones. PUNK ROCK, GAY, TIME MACHINE is ™ and © 2011, 2014 Steve Niles & Michael Montenat. DUNCE is ™ and © 2011, 2014 Carla Speed McNeil. THE BROKEN ARROW is ™ and © 2011, 2014 Michael Vincent Bramley & Fred Hembeck. RADIATION is ™ and © 2011, 2014 Shane Davis & Michelle Davis. FLOWERING is ™ and © 2011, 2014 Kazim Ali & Craig Thompson. SEPARATION OF CHURCH AND STATE is ™ and © 2011, 2014 J. Michael Straczynski & Kevin Sacco. THE CONVERSION is ™ and © 2011, 2014 Dara Naraghi & Christopher Mitten. GREAT, UNSUNG MOMENTS IN THE HISTORY OF FREE SPEECH is ™ and © 2011, 2014 Judd Winick & Thiago Micalopulos. BEING NORMAL is ™ and © 2011, 2014 Mark Waid & Jeff Lemire. DANGEROUS CUSTOMS is ™ and © 2011, 2014 Dave Grilli & J. Gonzo. WHICH CAME FIRST is ™ and © 2012, 2014 Jonathan Hickman. BARREN GROUND is ™ and © 2012, 2014 Andy Diggle & Ben Templesmith. FREEDOM FROM... is ™ and © 2012, 2014 Howard Chaykin & Sina Grace. FREE is ™ and © 2012, 2014 Steven T. Seagle & Marco Cinello. LUMIÈRE is ™ and © 2012, 2014 Joe Keatinge & Chynna Clugston-Flores. HUNTERS is ™ and © 2012, 2014 James Robinson & J. Bone. LAST RIGHTS is ™ and © 2012, 2014 James Asmus & Takeshi Miyazawa. MARINEMAN is ™ and © 2012, 2014 Ian Churchill. SASQUATCH is ™ and © 2012, 2014 Chris Roberson & Roger Langridge. COMMON COMIC-CONVERSATION and G-MAN are ™ and © 2012, 2014 Chris Giarrusso. STORM DOGS ™ and © 2012, 2014 David Hine & Doug Braithwaite. KING KIM is ™ and © 2012, 2014 Brandon Graham. JUST AS REAL AS YOURS is ™ and © 2012, 2014 Jim McCann & Janet Lee. UNLEASHED is ™ and © 2012, 2014 Kieron Gillen, Nate Bellegarde & Jordie Bellaire. DOUCHEBAG is ™ and © 2012, 2014 Terry Moore. THE WALKING DEAD is ™ and © 2012, 2014 Robert Kirkman, LLC. Image Comics® and its logos are registered trademarks of Image Comics, Inc. No part of this publication may be reproduced or transmitted, in any form or by any means (except for short excerpts for review purposes) without the express written permission of the individual copyright holders. All names, characters, events and locales in this publication are entirely fictional. Any resemblance to actual persons (living or dead), events or places, without satiric intent, is coincidental. PRINTED IN USA. For information regarding the CPSIA on this printed material call: 203-595-3636 and provide reference # RICH – 548741. International Rights / Foreign Licensing -- foreignlicensing@imagecomics.com
Hardcover ISBN 978-1-60706-937-9 Softcover ISBN 978-1-60706-996-6 • FIRST PRINTING

2008 LIBERTY COMICS

Edited by SCOTT DUNBIER

2009 LIBERTY COMICS

Edited by JAMIE S. RICH

2010 Liberty Annual

Edited by Larry Marder

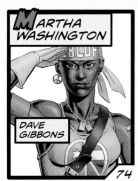

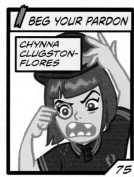

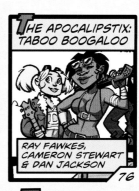

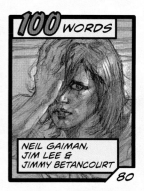

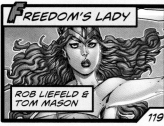

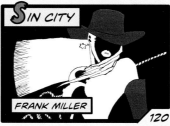

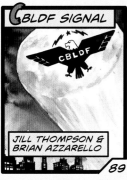

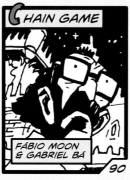

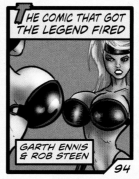

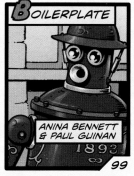

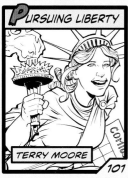

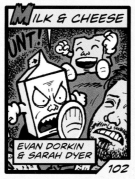

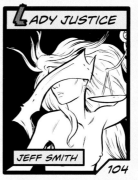

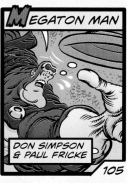

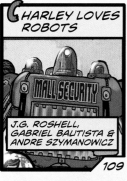

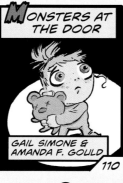

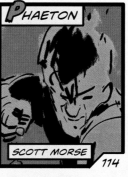

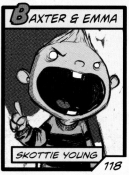

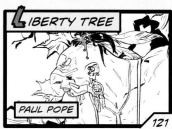

2011 LIBERTY ANNUAL

Edited by
BOB SCHRECK &
GREG TUMBARELLO

2012 LIBERTY ANNUAL

Edited by ERIC STEPHENSON

THANK YOU

The Framers of the US Constitution for drafting the concise and elegant prose that is the First Amendment, Nick Barrucci, Branwyn Bigglestone, Charles Brownstein, David Bogart, Dan Buckley, C.B. Cebulski, Jonathan Chan, Bob Chapman, Comicraft's Richard Starkings, JG Roshell & Jimmy Betancourt, Alex Cox, Diamond Comic Distributors, Sarah deLaine, Dan DiDio, Amanda Dunbier, Scott Dunbier, Dynamite Entertainment, the Gaiman Foundation, Drew Gill, Betsy Gomez, Graphitti Designs, Dave Grilli, Brian Haberlin, Sierra Hahn, Image Comics, Jim Lee, Tom Long, Heidi MacDonald, Dennis Mallonee, Larry Marder, Cory Marder, Todd Martinez, Harris Miller, Ligeia Minetta, John Nee, Diane Nelson, Randy Paterno, Jamie S. Rich, Mike Richardson, Bill Schanes, Bob Schreck, Diana Schutz, Tyler Shainline, Dezi Sienty, Philip Simon, Gail Simone, Alex Sinclair, Greg Staples, Eric Stephenson, Shannon T. Stewart, Francis Takenaga, Thomas Tull, Keith Wood, and to all the creators, retailers and friends who went above and beyond and have been so instrumental in making this book come together.

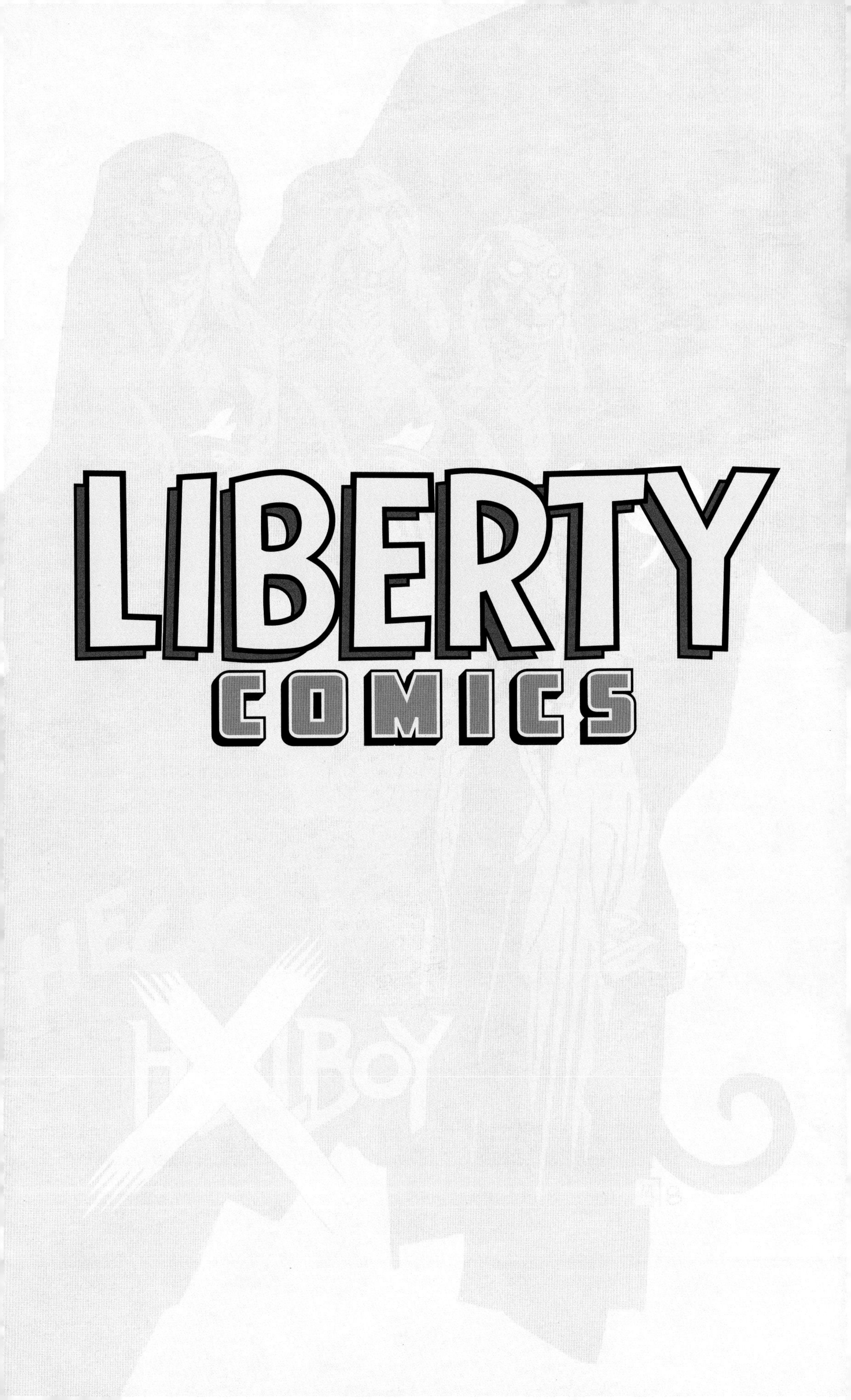

LIBERTY
COMICS

HELLBOY COVER BY *MIKE MIGNOLA*
COLORED BY *DAVE STEWART*

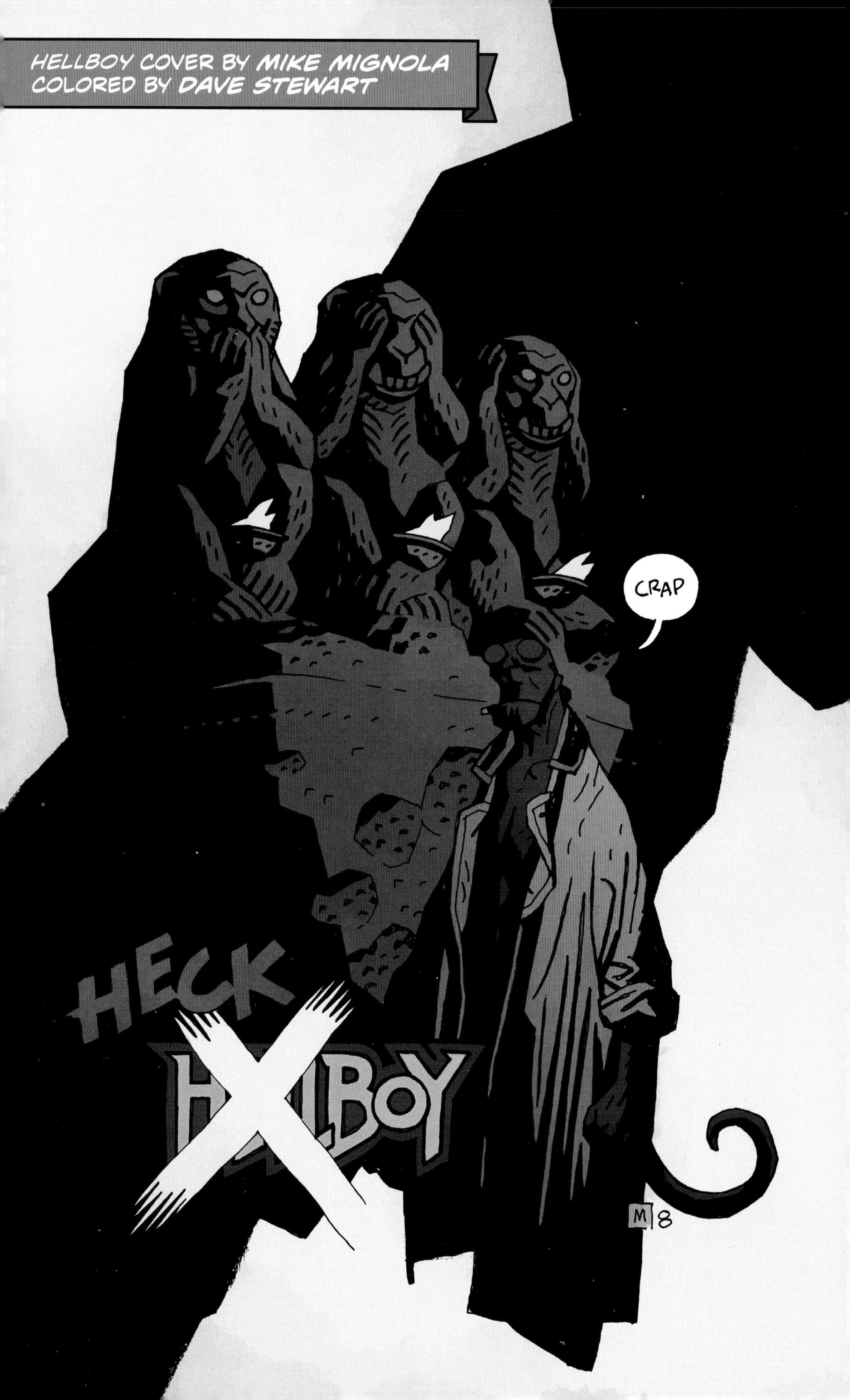
HECK
CRAP

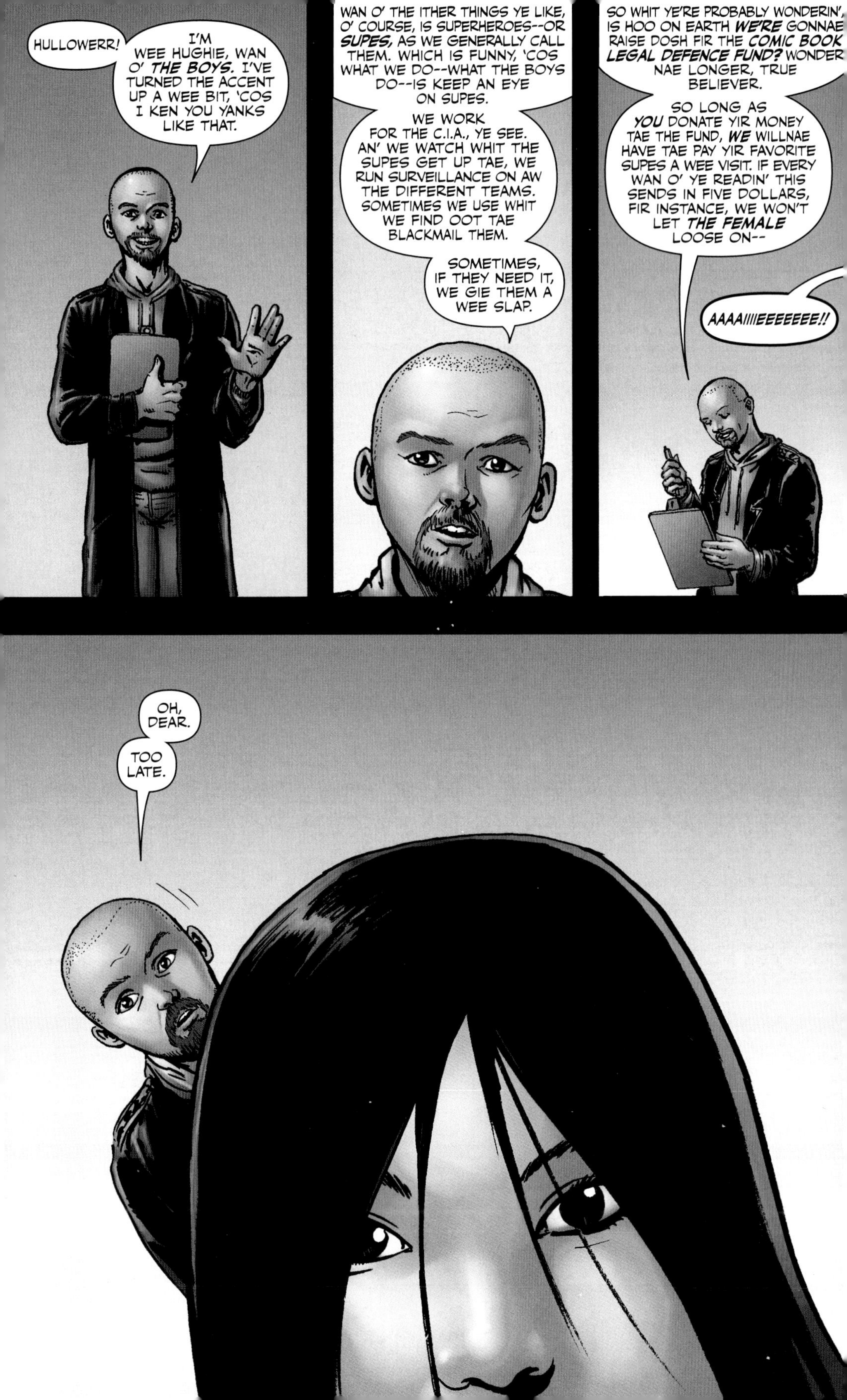
HULLOWERR!
I'M WEE HUGHIE, WAN O' THE BOYS. I'VE TURNED THE ACCENT UP A WEE BIT, 'COS I KEN YOU YANKS LIKE THAT.
WAN O' THE ITHER THINGS YE LIKE, O' COURSE, IS SUPERHEROES--OR SUPES, AS WE GENERALLY CALL THEM. WHICH IS FUNNY, 'COS WHAT WE DO--WHAT THE BOYS DO--IS KEEP AN EYE ON SUPES.
WE WORK FOR THE C.I.A., YE SEE. AN' WE WATCH WHIT THE SUPES GET UP TAE, WE RUN SURVEILLANCE ON AW THE DIFFERENT TEAMS. SOMETIMES WE USE WHIT WE FIND OOT TAE BLACKMAIL THEM.
SOMETIMES, IF THEY NEED IT, WE GIE THEM A WEE SLAP.
SO WHIT YE'RE PROBABLY WONDERIN', IS HOO ON EARTH WE'RE GONNAE RAISE DOSH FIR THE COMIC BOOK LEGAL DEFENCE FUND? WONDER NAE LONGER, TRUE BELIEVER.
SO LONG AS YOU DONATE YIR MONEY TAE THE FUND, WE WILLNAE HAVE TAE PAY YIR FAVORITE SUPES A WEE VISIT. IF EVERY WAN O' YE READIN' THIS SENDS IN FIVE DOLLARS, FIR INSTANCE, WE WON'T LET THE FEMALE LOOSE ON--
AAAAIIIIIEEEEEEE!!
OH, DEAR.
TOO LATE.

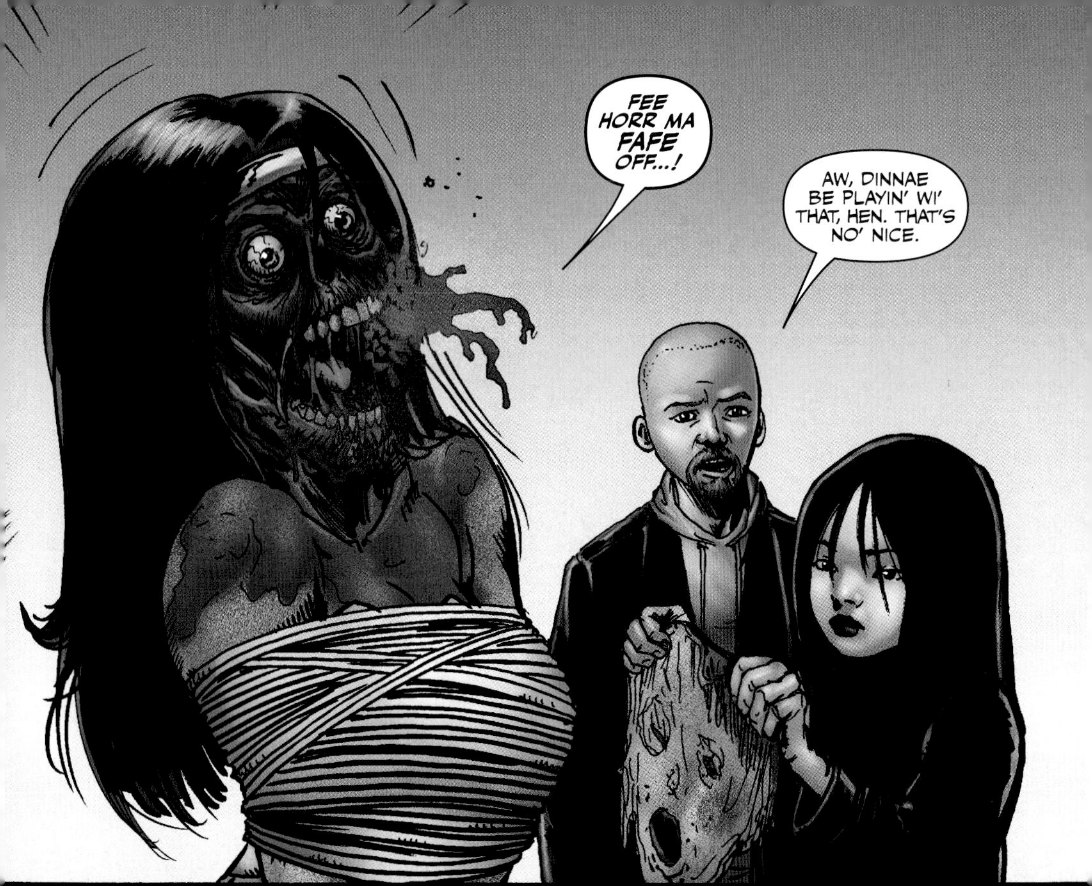
FEE HORR MA FAFE OFF...!
AW, DINNAE BE PLAYIN' WI' THAT, HEN. THAT'S NO' NICE.

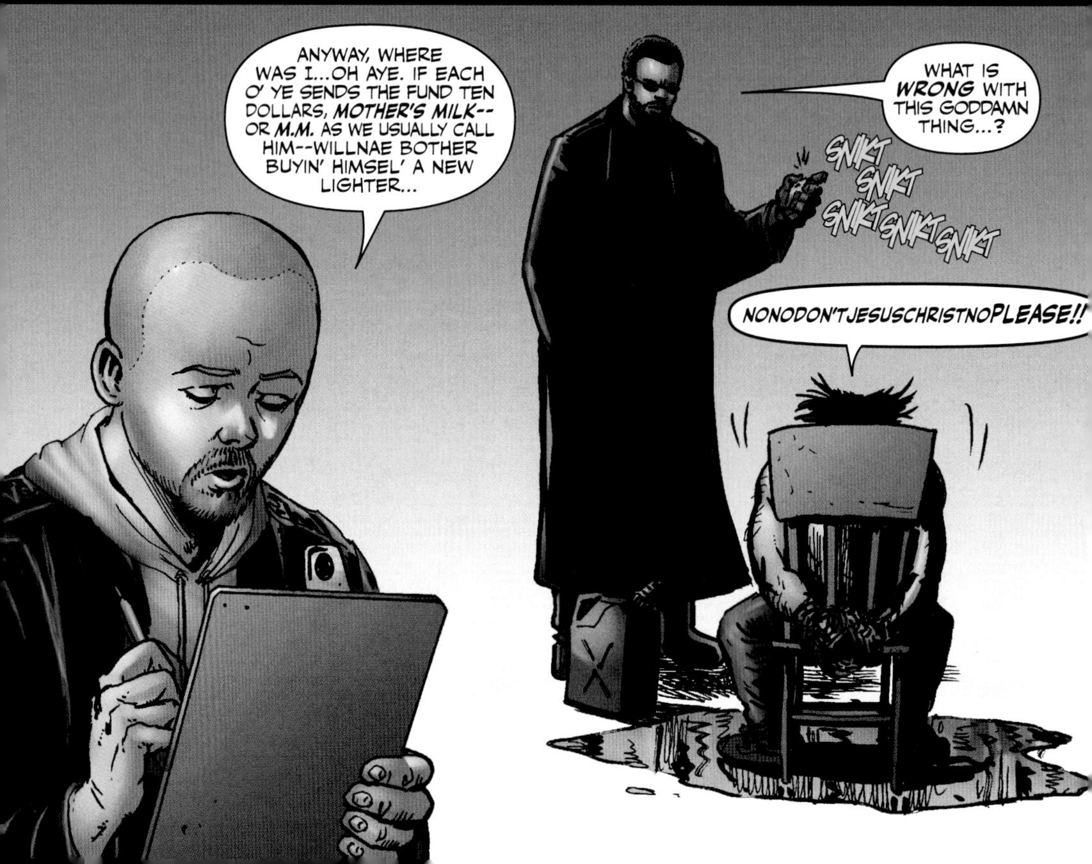
ANYWAY, WHERE WAS I...OH AYE. IF EACH O' YE SENDS THE FUND TEN DOLLARS, MOTHER'S MILK-- OR M.M. AS WE USUALLY CALL HIM--WILLNAE BOTHER BUYIN' HIMSEL' A NEW LIGHTER...
WHAT IS WRONG WITH THIS GODDAMN THING...?
SNIKT SNIKT SNIKT SNIKT SNIKT
NONODON'TJESUSCHRISTNOPLEASE!!

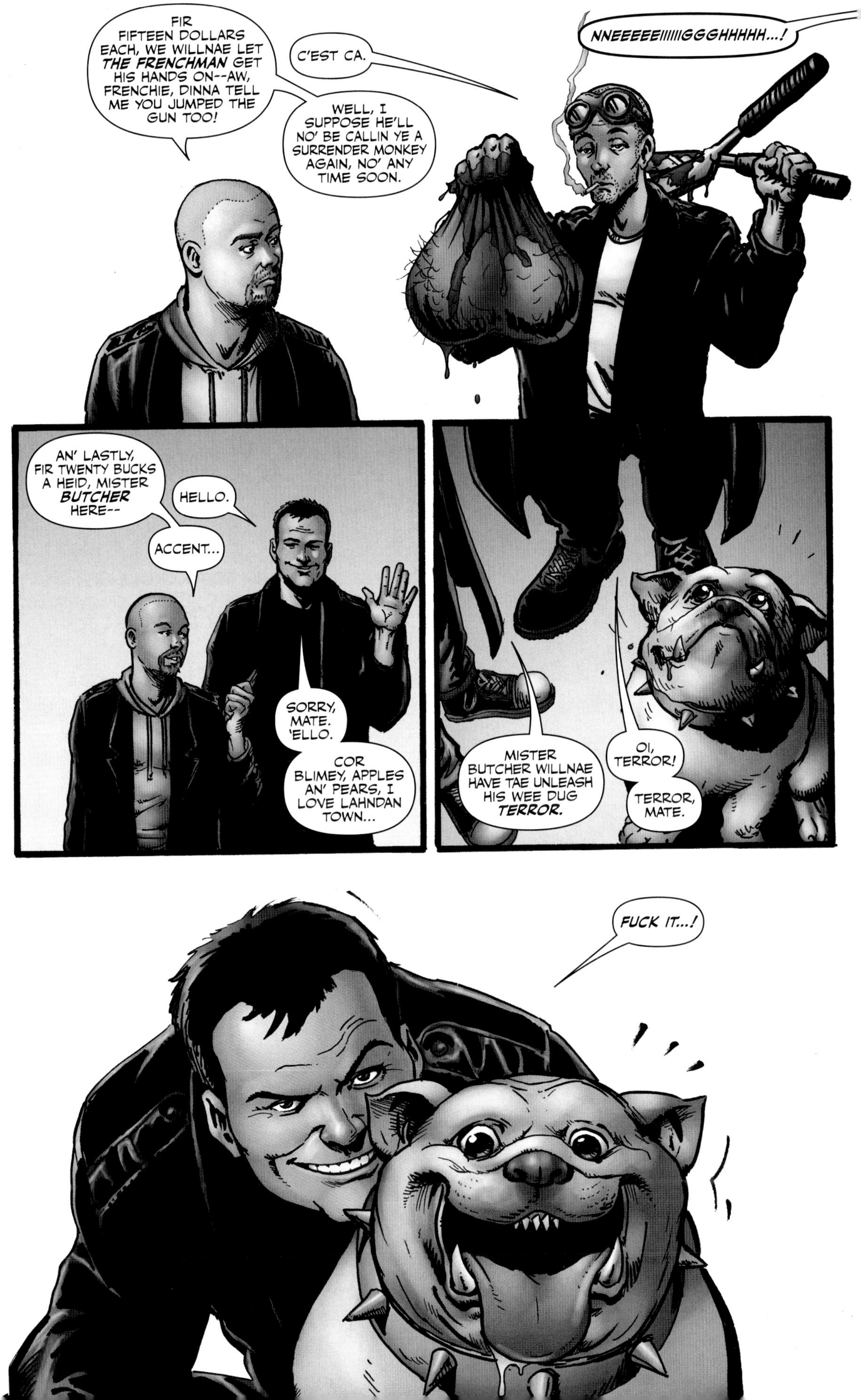
FIR FIFTEEN DOLLARS EACH, WE WILLNAE LET THE FRENCHMAN GET HIS HANDS ON--AW, FRENCHIE, DINNA TELL ME YOU JUMPED THE GUN TOO!
C'EST CA.
WELL, I SUPPOSE HE'LL NO' BE CALLIN YE A SURRENDER MONKEY AGAIN, NO' ANY TIME SOON.
NNEEEEEIIIIIIGGGHHHHH...!
AN' LASTLY, FIR TWENTY BUCKS A HEID, MISTER BUTCHER HERE--
HELLO.
ACCENT...
SORRY, MATE. 'ELLO.
COR BLIMEY, APPLES AN' PEARS, I LOVE LAHNDAN TOWN...
MISTER BUTCHER WILLNAE HAVE TAE UNLEASH HIS WEE DUG TERROR.
OI, TERROR!
TERROR, MATE.
FUCK IT...!

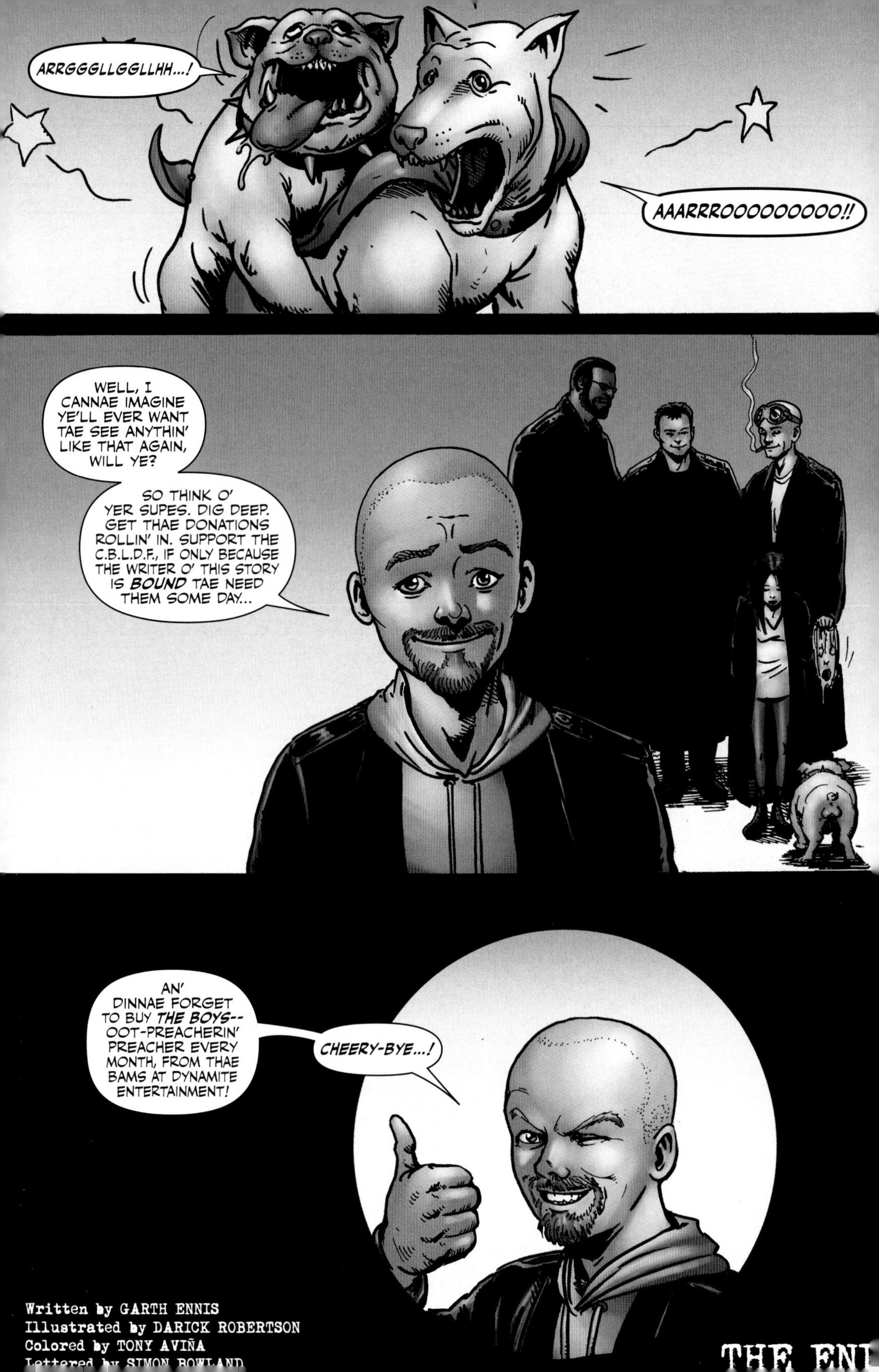
ARRGGGLLGGLLHH...!
AAARRROOOOOOOOO!!
WELL, I CANNAE IMAGINE YE'LL EVER WANT TAE SEE ANYTHIN' LIKE THAT AGAIN, WILL YE?
SO THINK O' YER SUPES. DIG DEEP. GET THAE DONATIONS ROLLIN' IN. SUPPORT THE C.B.L.D.F., IF ONLY BECAUSE THE WRITER O' THIS STORY IS *BOUND* TAE NEED THEM SOME DAY...
AN' DINNAE FORGET TO BUY *THE BOYS*-- OOT-PREACHERIN' PREACHER EVERY MONTH, FROM THAE BAMS AT DYNAMITE ENTERTAINMENT!
CHEERY-BYE...!
Written by GARTH ENNIS
Illustrated by DARICK ROBERTSON
Colored by TONY AVIÑA
Lettered by SIMON ROWLAND
THE EN

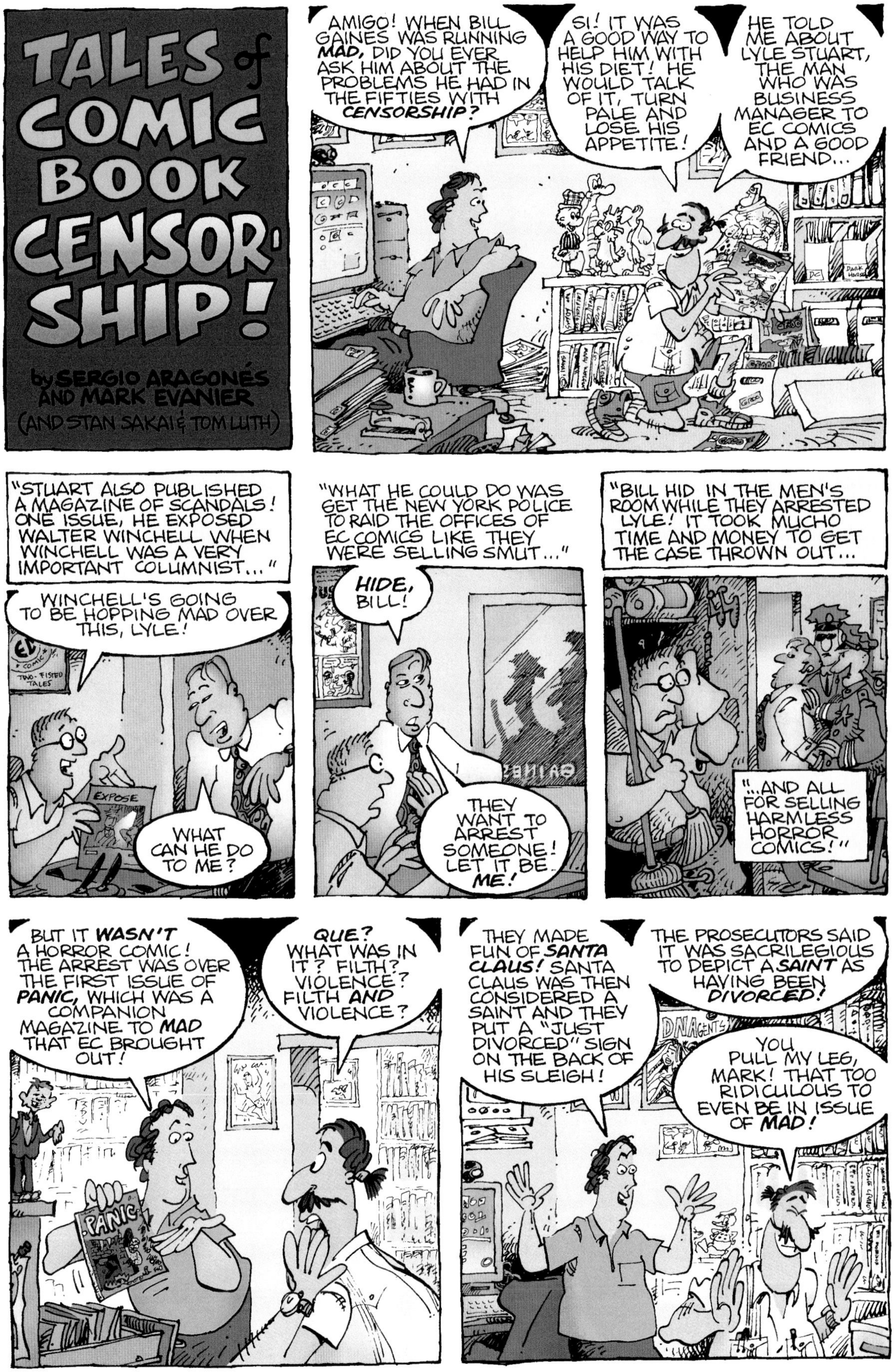
TALES of COMIC BOOK CENSORSHIP!
by SERGIO ARAGONÉS AND MARK EVANIER
(AND STAN SAKAI & TOM LUTH)
AMIGO! WHEN BILL GAINES WAS RUNNING MAD, DID YOU EVER ASK HIM ABOUT THE PROBLEMS HE HAD IN THE FIFTIES WITH CENSORSHIP?
SI! IT WAS A GOOD WAY TO HELP HIM WITH HIS DIET! HE WOULD TALK OF IT, TURN PALE AND LOSE HIS APPETITE!
HE TOLD ME ABOUT LYLE STUART, THE MAN WHO WAS BUSINESS MANAGER TO EC COMICS AND A GOOD FRIEND...
"STUART ALSO PUBLISHED A MAGAZINE OF SCANDALS! ONE ISSUE, HE EXPOSED WALTER WINCHELL WHEN WINCHELL WAS A VERY IMPORTANT COLUMNIST..."
WINCHELL'S GOING TO BE HOPPING MAD OVER THIS, LYLE!
EXPOSE
WHAT CAN HE DO TO ME?
"WHAT HE COULD DO WAS GET THE NEW YORK POLICE TO RAID THE OFFICES OF EC COMICS LIKE THEY WERE SELLING SMUT..."
HIDE, BILL!
THEY WANT TO ARREST SOMEONE! LET IT BE ME!
"BILL HID IN THE MEN'S ROOM WHILE THEY ARRESTED LYLE! IT TOOK MUCHO TIME AND MONEY TO GET THE CASE THROWN OUT...
"...AND ALL FOR SELLING HARMLESS HORROR COMICS!"
BUT IT WASN'T A HORROR COMIC! THE ARREST WAS OVER THE FIRST ISSUE OF PANIC, WHICH WAS A COMPANION MAGAZINE TO MAD THAT EC BROUGHT OUT!
QUE? WHAT WAS IN IT? FILTH? VIOLENCE? FILTH AND VIOLENCE?
PANIC
THEY MADE FUN OF SANTA CLAUS! SANTA CLAUS WAS THEN CONSIDERED A SAINT AND THEY PUT A "JUST DIVORCED" SIGN ON THE BACK OF HIS SLEIGH!
THE PROSECUTORS SAID IT WAS SACRILEGIOUS TO DEPICT A SAINT AS HAVING BEEN DIVORCED!
YOU PULL MY LEG, MARK! THAT TOO RIDICULOUS TO EVEN BE IN ISSUE OF MAD!

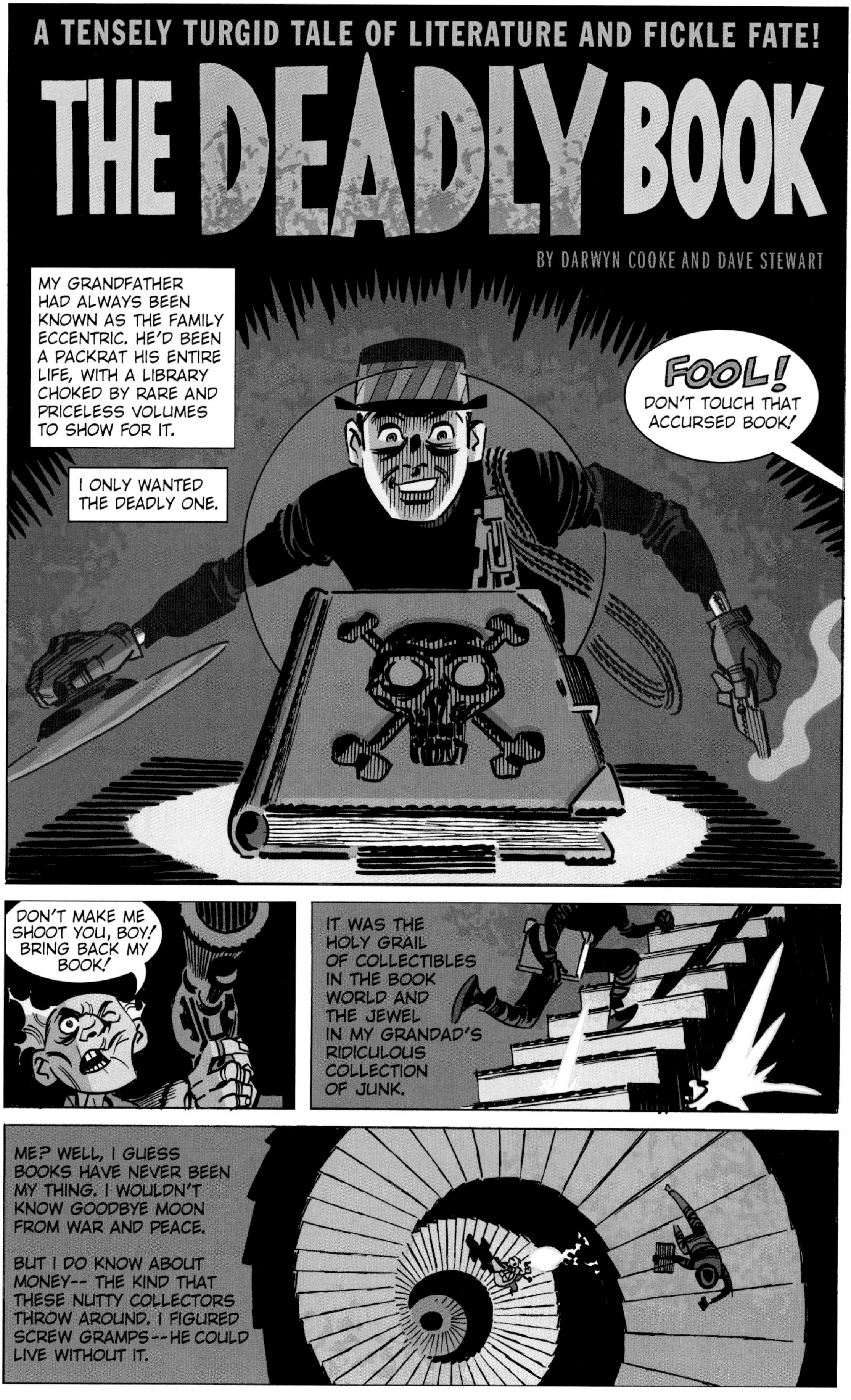
A TENSELY TURGID TALE OF LITERATURE AND FICKLE FATE!
THE DEADLY BOOK
BY DARWYN COOKE AND DAVE STEWART
MY GRANDFATHER HAD ALWAYS BEEN KNOWN AS THE FAMILY ECCENTRIC. HE'D BEEN A PACKRAT HIS ENTIRE LIFE, WITH A LIBRARY CHOKED BY RARE AND PRICELESS VOLUMES TO SHOW FOR IT.
FOOL! DON'T TOUCH THAT ACCURSED BOOK!
I ONLY WANTED THE DEADLY ONE.
DON'T MAKE ME SHOOT YOU, BOY! BRING BACK MY BOOK!
IT WAS THE HOLY GRAIL OF COLLECTIBLES IN THE BOOK WORLD AND THE JEWEL IN MY GRANDAD'S RIDICULOUS COLLECTION OF JUNK.
ME? WELL, I GUESS BOOKS HAVE NEVER BEEN MY THING. I WOULDN'T KNOW GOODBYE MOON FROM WAR AND PEACE.
BUT I DO KNOW ABOUT MONEY-- THE KIND THAT THESE NUTTY COLLECTORS THROW AROUND. I FIGURED SCREW GRAMPS--HE COULD LIVE WITHOUT IT.

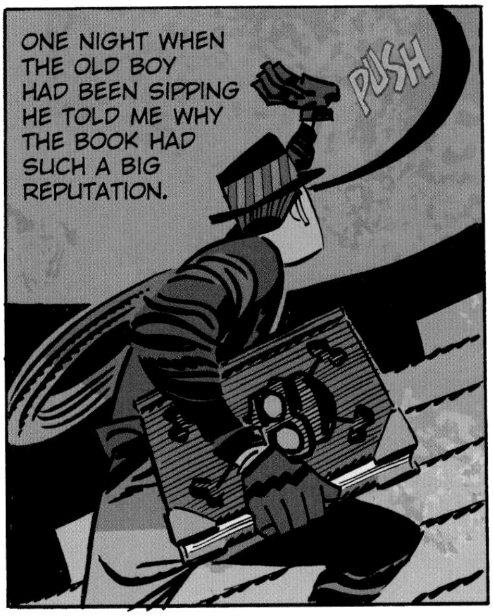
ONE NIGHT WHEN THE OLD BOY HAD BEEN SIPPING HE TOLD ME WHY THE BOOK HAD SUCH A BIG REPUTATION.
PUSH

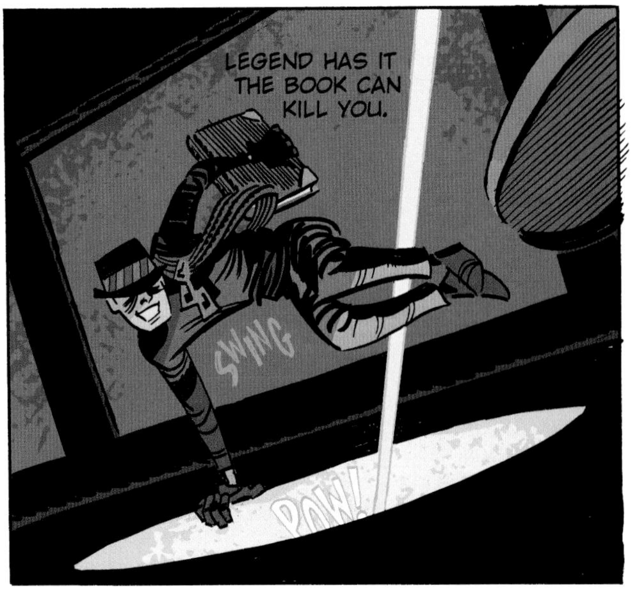
LEGEND HAS IT THE BOOK CAN KILL YOU.
SWING
POW!

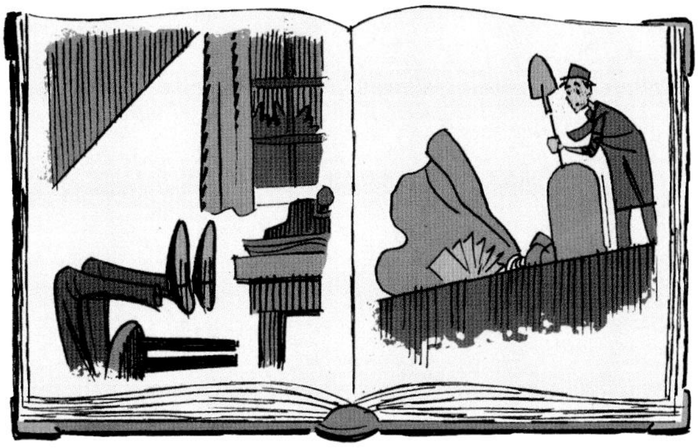

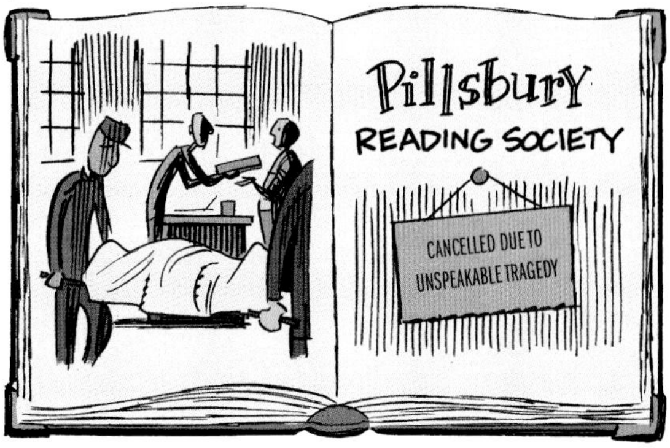
Pillsbury
READING SOCIETY
CANCELLED DUE TO
UNSPEAKABLE TRAGEDY

THE AUTHOR HAD BEEN FOUND DEAD OF UNDETERMINED CAUSES, THE LAST PAGE OF HIS OPUS STILL COILED IN THE TYPEWRITER.

HIS LOVING WIDOW WAS THE NEXT TO GO, FOUND CLUTCHING THE DREADED BOOK AT HER HAPLESS HUSBAND'S GRAVESITE.

THIRD TO DIE WAS THE AUTHOR'S AGENT. HIS UNWITTING ASSISTANT HANDED THE MANUSCRIPT OVER TO THE LOCAL ENGRAVER.

THE DEATHS HAD PIQUED LOCAL INTEREST AND THE BOOK WAS A MODEST SALES SUCCESS. UNFORTUNATELY, NO ONE EVER LIVED TO REVIEW IT.

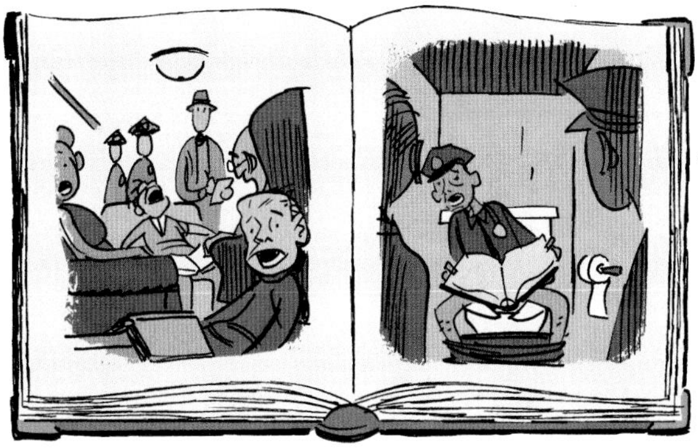

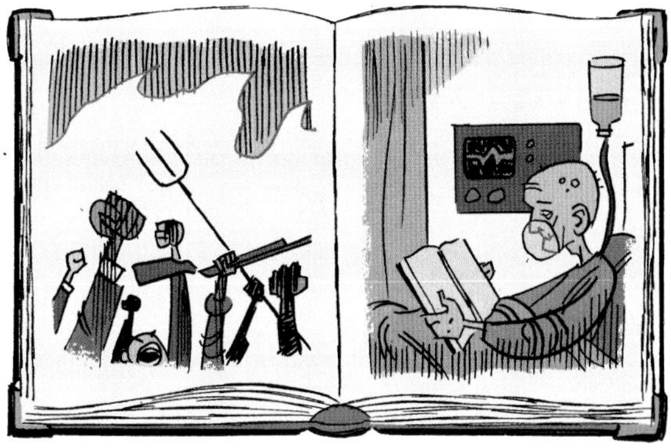

BY THIS POINT, EVEN THE POLICE WERE GETTING SUSPICIOUS OF THE DEADLY BOOK. IN THE FACE OF SUCH BAFFLING DEATHS THEY ASSUMED A CULT HAD FORMED AROUND THE BOOK.

THERE WAS ONE COP WHO FACED THE MYSTERY HEAD ON. ALTHOUGH HE DIED IN THE COURSE OF HIS INVESTIGATION, HIS VALIANT EFFORTS GAVE HIS FELLOW OFFICERS THE FINAL PIECE OF THE PUZZLE.

IT WAS THE ACT OF READING THE BOOK THAT KILLED YOU. PEOPLE WERE OUTRAGED. THEY DEMANDED THE BOOK BE BANNED AND ALL COPIES DESTROYED. EVEN PEOPLE WHO COULDN'T READ WERE INCENSED.

PUBLIC SAFETY WAS JUST THE TIP OF THE ICEBERG. THERE WERE ACTUALLY PEOPLE CHOOSING TO READ IT. MANY FELT THIS AN AFFRONT TO THEIR SPIRITUAL BELIEFS.

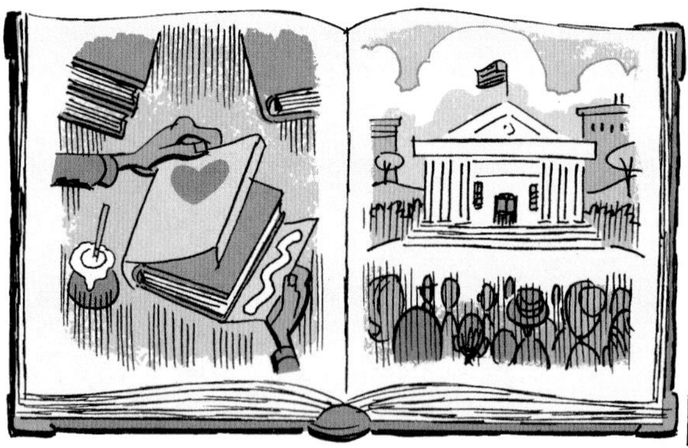

THEN THERE WERE THE PROPER VILLAINS USING THE BOOK TO KILL. MOST NOTABLE WAS THE LIBRARIAN WHO SENT IT TO ALL THE WOMEN WHO'D SPURNED HIS ATTENTIONS.

WHEN THE ISSUE FINALLY GOT ITS DAY IN COURT THE ENTIRE TOWN TURNED OUT TO HAVE A SAY. THOUSANDS SPOKE OUT TO CONDEMN THE BOOK, BUT ONLY ONE BRAVE SOUL DEFENDED IT.

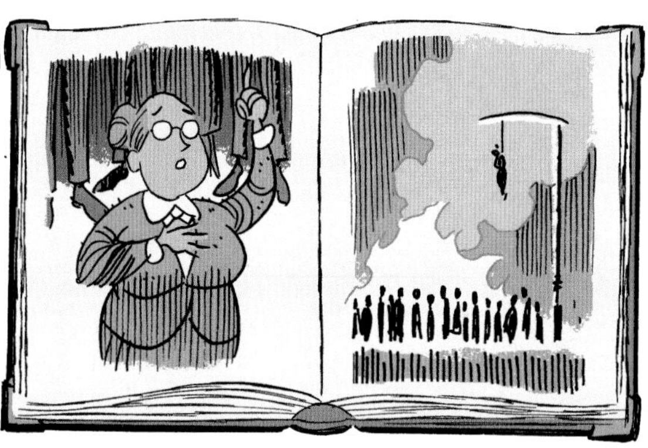

WHO ARE WE TO DESTROY A WORK OF ART WITH SO MUCH POWER? SHOULD IT NOT BE REVERED AND MADE AVAILABLE TO THOSE BRAVE ENOUGH TO KNOW ITS SECRETS?

AFTER HANGING HER, THE CROWD GATHERED UP EVERY COPY OF THE DEADLY BOOK AND BURNED THEM TO CINDERS.

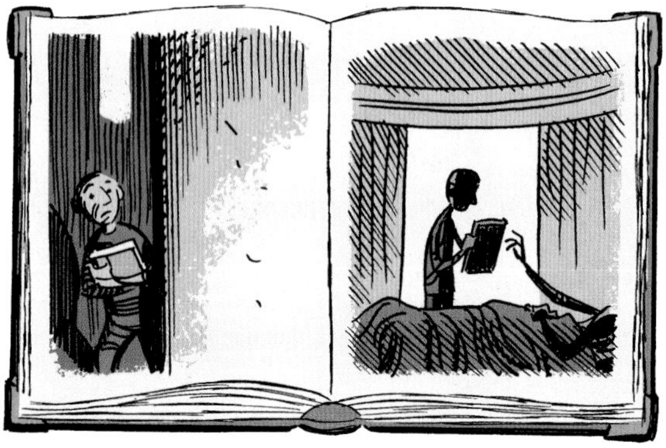

THERE WAS ONE COPY THAT SURVIVED. IT BELONGED TO THE BOOK'S ENGRAVER, A PRIDEFUL ARTISAN WHO HID HIS PROOF OF THE INFAMOUS TOME.

ON HIS DEATHBED, HE PASSED THE BOOK ON TO HIS ELDEST SON. A SIMPLETON WITH LITTLE INTEREST IN BOOKS, THE BOY SOON SOLD THE PRIZE TO COVER HIS DEBTS.

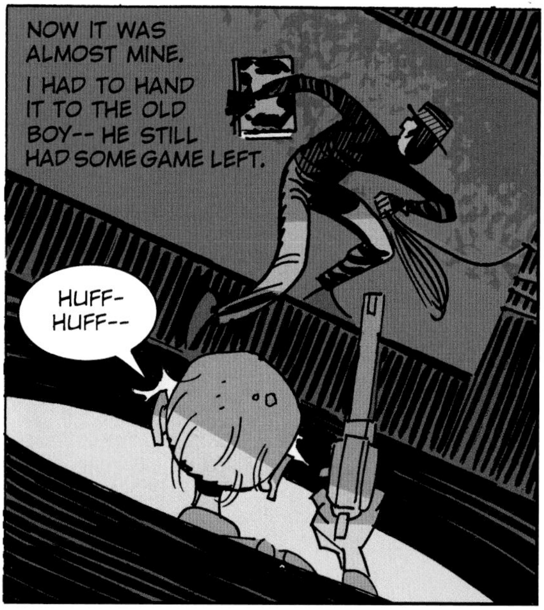
NOW IT WAS ALMOST MINE.
I HAD TO HAND IT TO THE OLD BOY-- HE STILL HAD SOME GAME LEFT.
HUFF-HUFF--

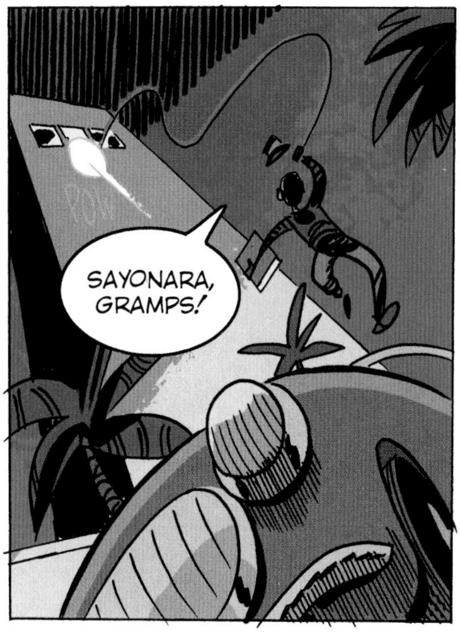
SAYONARA, GRAMPS!

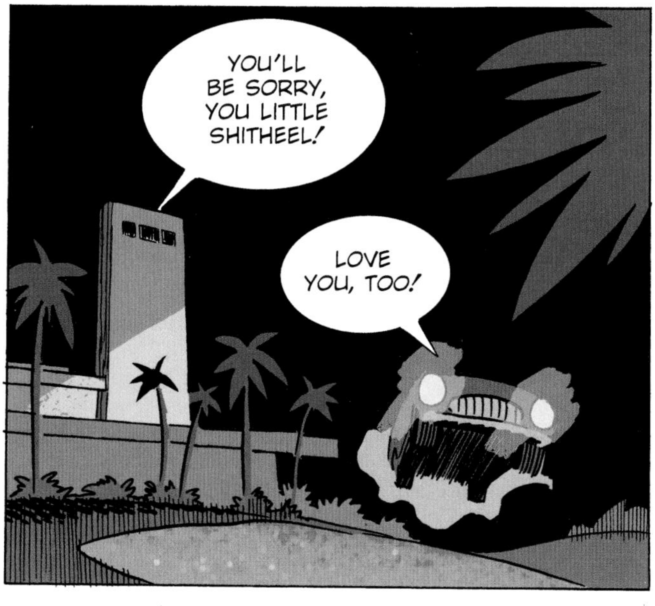
YOU'LL BE SORRY, YOU LITTLE SHITHEEL!
LOVE YOU, TOO!

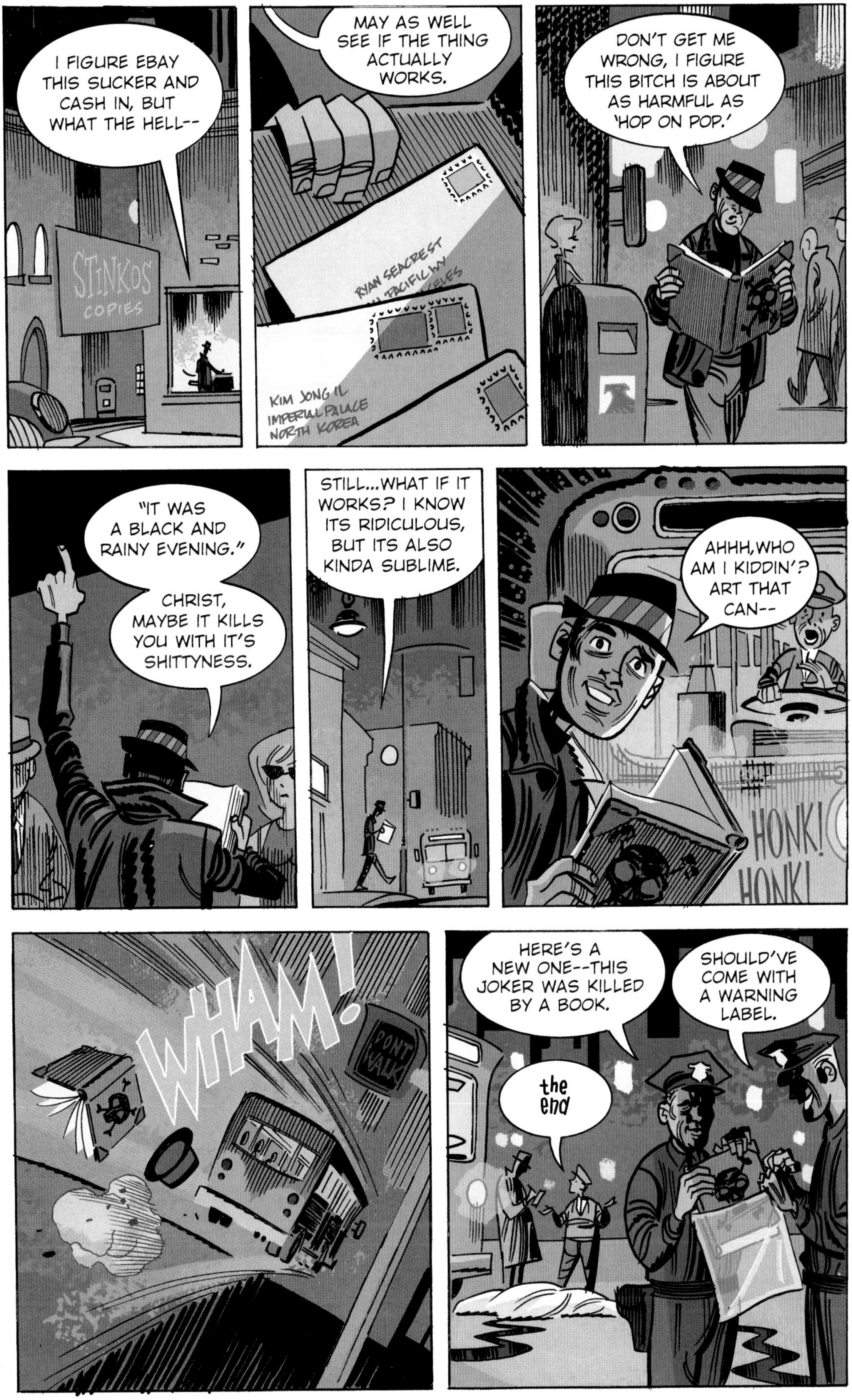
I FIGURE EBAY THIS SUCKER AND CASH IN, BUT WHAT THE HELL--
STINKO'S COPIES
MAY AS WELL SEE IF THE THING ACTUALLY WORKS.
RYAN SEACREST
KIM JONG IL IMPERIAL PALACE NORTH KOREA
DON'T GET ME WRONG, I FIGURE THIS BITCH IS ABOUT AS HARMFUL AS 'HOP ON POP.'
"IT WAS A BLACK AND RAINY EVENING."
CHRIST, MAYBE IT KILLS YOU WITH IT'S SHITTYNESS.
STILL...WHAT IF IT WORKS? I KNOW ITS RIDICULOUS, BUT ITS ALSO KINDA SUBLIME.
AHHH,WHO AM I KIDDIN'? ART THAT CAN--
HONK! HONK!
WHAM!
DONT WALK
HERE'S A NEW ONE--THIS JOKER WAS KILLED BY A BOOK.
SHOULD'VE COME WITH A WARNING LABEL.
the end

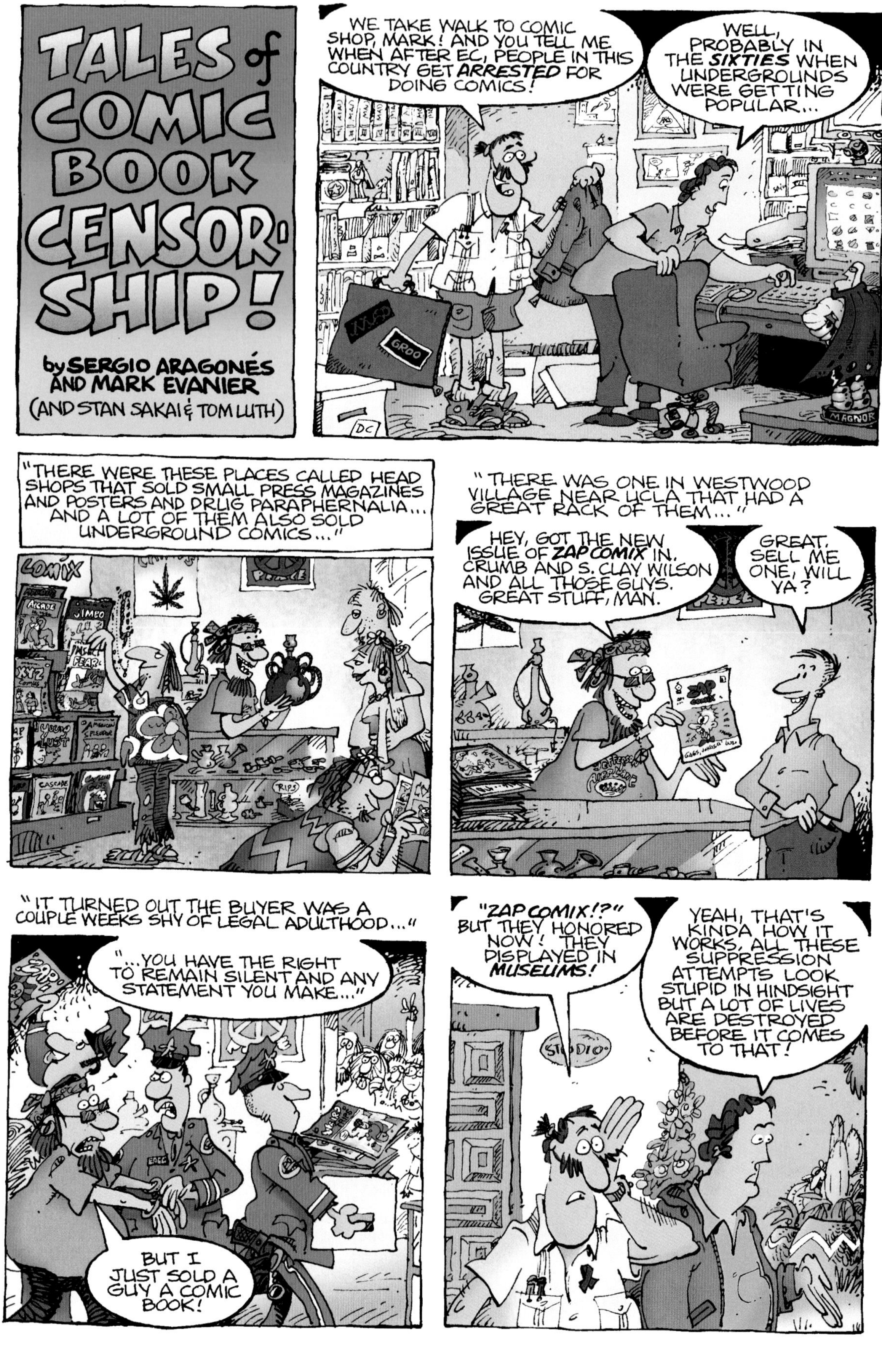
TALES of COMIC BOOK CENSORSHIP!
by SERGIO ARAGONÉS AND MARK EVANIER
(AND STAN SAKAI & TOM LUTH)
WE TAKE WALK TO COMIC SHOP, MARK! AND YOU TELL ME WHEN AFTER EC, PEOPLE IN THIS COUNTRY GET ARRESTED FOR DOING COMICS!
WELL, PROBABLY IN THE SIXTIES WHEN UNDERGROUNDS WERE GETTING POPULAR...
GROO
DC
MAGNOR
"THERE WERE THESE PLACES CALLED HEAD SHOPS THAT SOLD SMALL PRESS MAGAZINES AND POSTERS AND DRUG PARAPHERNALIA... AND A LOT OF THEM ALSO SOLD UNDERGROUND COMICS..."
COMIX
PEACE
ARCADE
JIMBO
INSECT FEAR
XYZ COMICS
YOUNG LUST
AMERICAN SPLENDOR
CASCADE
RIPS
"THERE WAS ONE IN WESTWOOD VILLAGE NEAR UCLA THAT HAD A GREAT RACK OF THEM..."
HEY, GOT THE NEW ISSUE OF ZAP COMIX IN. CRUMB AND S. CLAY WILSON AND ALL THOSE GUYS. GREAT STUFF, MAN.
GREAT. SELL ME ONE, WILL YA?
ZAP COMIX
JEFFERSON AIRPLANE
"IT TURNED OUT THE BUYER WAS A COUPLE WEEKS SHY OF LEGAL ADULTHOOD..."
"...YOU HAVE THE RIGHT TO REMAIN SILENT AND ANY STATEMENT YOU MAKE..."
BUT I JUST SOLD A GUY A COMIC BOOK!
"ZAP COMIX!?" BUT THEY HONORED NOW! THEY DISPLAYED IN MUSEUMS!
YEAH, THAT'S KINDA HOW IT WORKS. ALL THESE SUPPRESSION ATTEMPTS LOOK STUPID IN HINDSIGHT BUT A LOT OF LIVES ARE DESTROYED BEFORE IT COMES TO THAT!
STUDIO

THE HOUSE OF DRACULA

FOR FIVE CENTURIES, COUNT DRACULA WAS A SCOURGE OF ALL MANKIND. NOW RETIRED, HE LIVES ALONE IN A COUNCIL FLAT IN SOUTH LONDON.

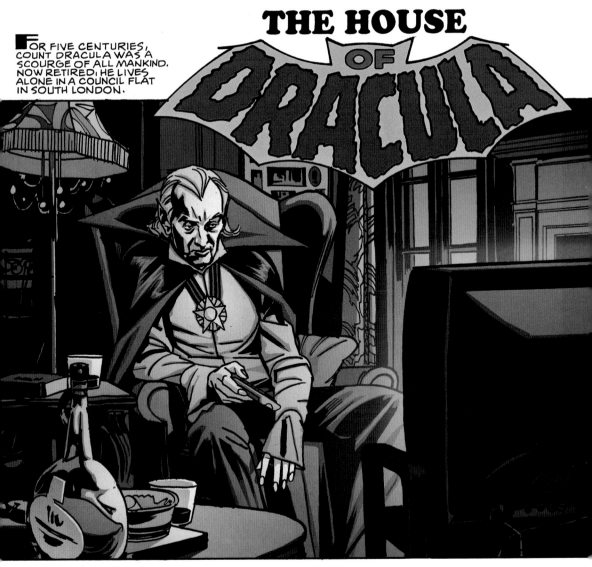

WOKE UP REALLY TIRED THIS MORNING. JOINTS WERE STIFF. AND I STILL HAVE A BIT OF A HANGOVER FROM THAT BOTTLE OF WINE ISOBEL GAVE ME THE WEEKEND BEFORE LAST.

SHAVING IS SO MUCH EASIER WITH A MACH THREE. THEY'RE MORE EXPENSIVE THAN ORDINARY BLADES, BUT I SEE THEM AS MY LITTLE TREAT TO MYSELF. I LIKE THE WAY THEY GLIDE ACROSS THE SKIN.

JUST HAD TEA AND TOAST FOR BREAKFAST. EVEN WITH THE PILLS, I FIND IT HARD TO EAT THIS EARLY IN THE DAY. MUST REMEMBER TO TELL THE DOCTOR THAT WHEN I SEE HIM LATER.

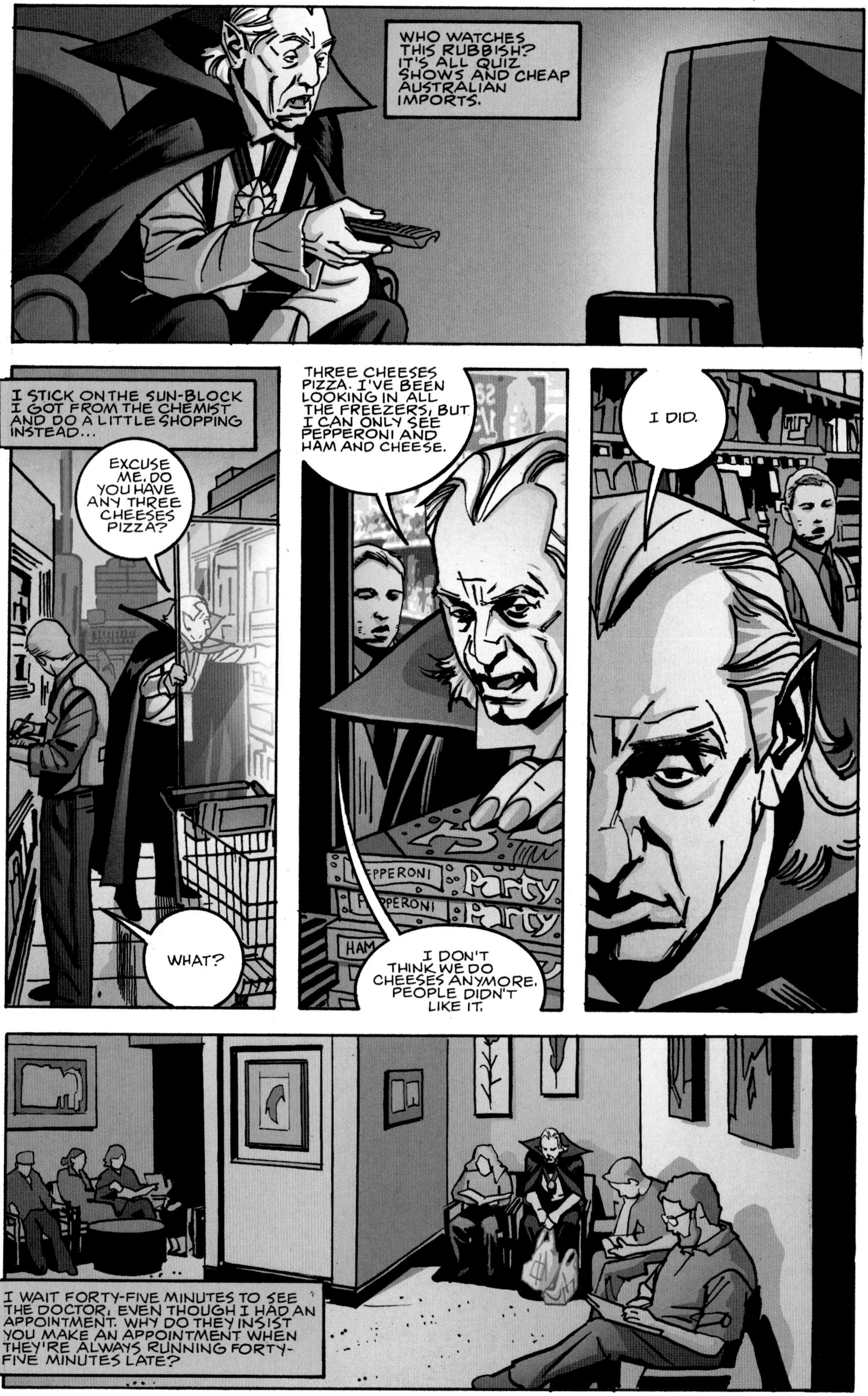
WHO WATCHES THIS RUBBISH? IT'S ALL QUIZ SHOWS AND CHEAP AUSTRALIAN IMPORTS.
I STICK ON THE SUN-BLOCK I GOT FROM THE CHEMIST AND DO A LITTLE SHOPPING INSTEAD...
EXCUSE ME. DO YOU HAVE ANY THREE CHEESES PIZZA?
WHAT?
THREE CHEESES PIZZA. I'VE BEEN LOOKING IN ALL THE FREEZERS, BUT I CAN ONLY SEE PEPPERONI AND HAM AND CHEESE.
PEPPERONI
Party
PEPPERONI
Party
HAM
I DON'T THINK WE DO CHEESES ANYMORE. PEOPLE DIDN'T LIKE IT.
I DID.
I WAIT FORTY-FIVE MINUTES TO SEE THE DOCTOR, EVEN THOUGH I HAD AN APPOINTMENT. WHY DO THEY INSIST YOU MAKE AN APPOINTMENT WHEN THEY'RE ALWAYS RUNNING FORTY-FIVE MINUTES LATE?

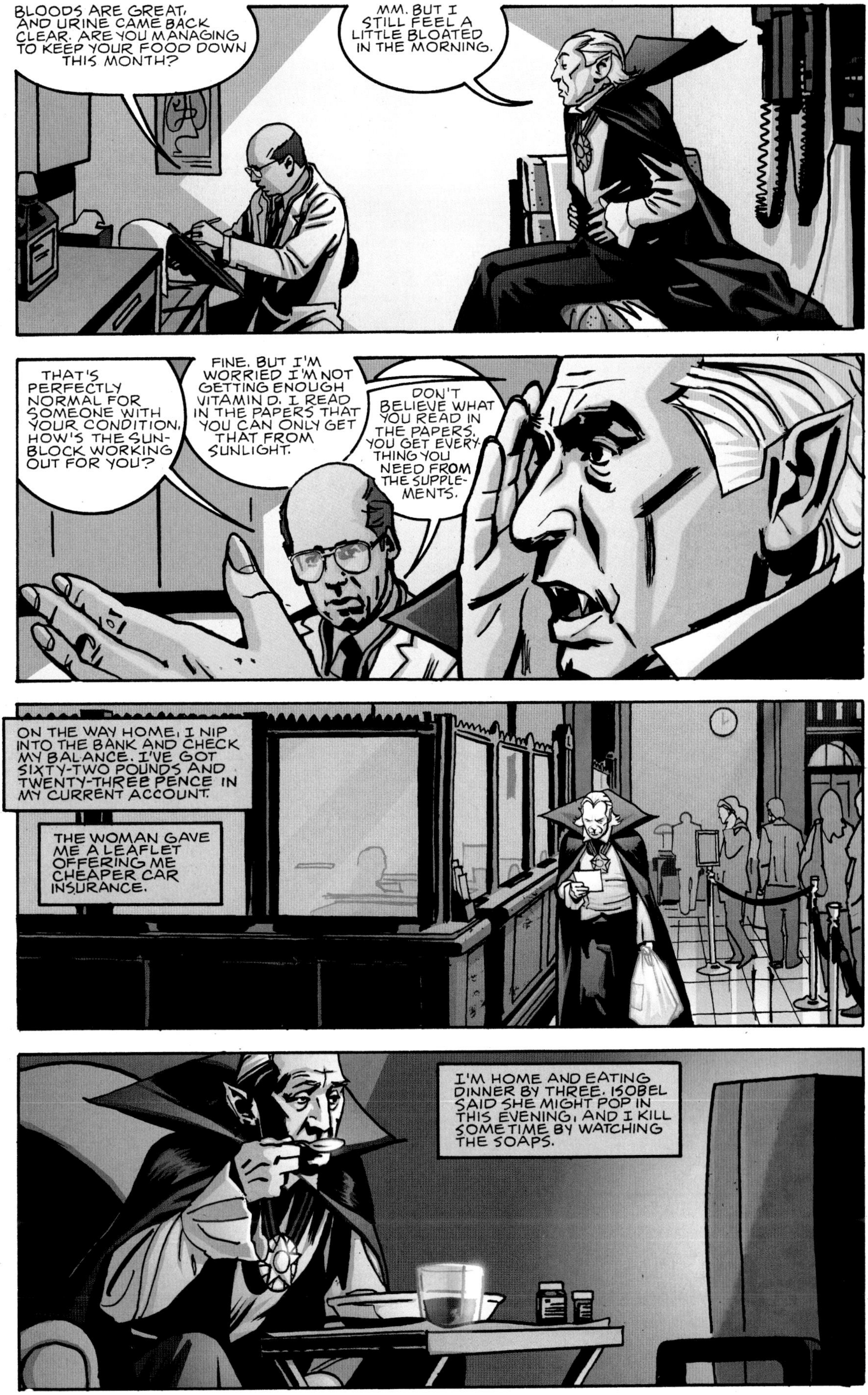
BLOODS ARE GREAT, AND URINE CAME BACK CLEAR. ARE YOU MANAGING TO KEEP YOUR FOOD DOWN THIS MONTH?
MM. BUT I STILL FEEL A LITTLE BLOATED IN THE MORNING.
THAT'S PERFECTLY NORMAL FOR SOMEONE WITH YOUR CONDITION. HOW'S THE SUN-BLOCK WORKING OUT FOR YOU?
FINE. BUT I'M WORRIED I'M NOT GETTING ENOUGH VITAMIN D. I READ IN THE PAPERS THAT YOU CAN ONLY GET THAT FROM SUNLIGHT.
DON'T BELIEVE WHAT YOU READ IN THE PAPERS. YOU GET EVERY-THING YOU NEED FROM THE SUPPLE-MENTS.
ON THE WAY HOME, I NIP INTO THE BANK AND CHECK MY BALANCE. I'VE GOT SIXTY-TWO POUNDS AND TWENTY-THREE PENCE IN MY CURRENT ACCOUNT.
THE WOMAN GAVE ME A LEAFLET OFFERING ME CHEAPER CAR INSURANCE.
I'M HOME AND EATING DINNER BY THREE. ISOBEL SAID SHE MIGHT POP IN THIS EVENING, AND I KILL SOME TIME BY WATCHING THE SOAPS.

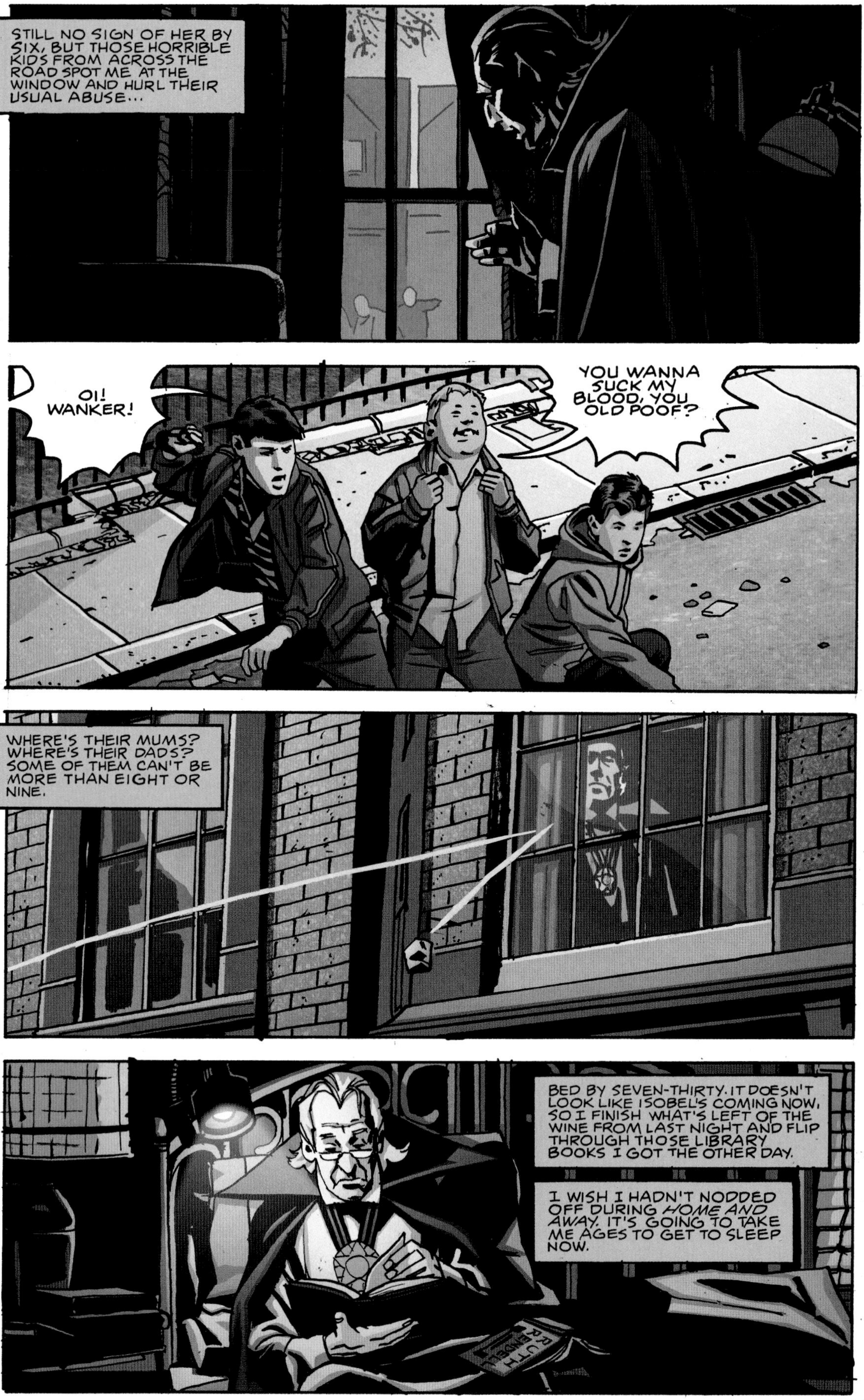
STILL NO SIGN OF HER BY SIX, BUT THOSE HORRIBLE KIDS FROM ACROSS THE ROAD SPOT ME AT THE WINDOW AND HURL THEIR USUAL ABUSE...
OI! WANKER!
YOU WANNA SUCK MY BLOOD, YOU OLD POOF?
WHERE'S THEIR MUMS? WHERE'S THEIR DADS? SOME OF THEM CAN'T BE MORE THAN EIGHT OR NINE.
BED BY SEVEN-THIRTY. IT DOESN'T LOOK LIKE ISOBEL'S COMING NOW, SO I FINISH WHAT'S LEFT OF THE WINE FROM LAST NIGHT AND FLIP THROUGH THOSE LIBRARY BOOKS I GOT THE OTHER DAY.
I WISH I HADN'T NODDED OFF DURING *HOME AND AWAY*. IT'S GOING TO TAKE ME AGES TO GET TO SLEEP NOW.
RUTH RENDELL

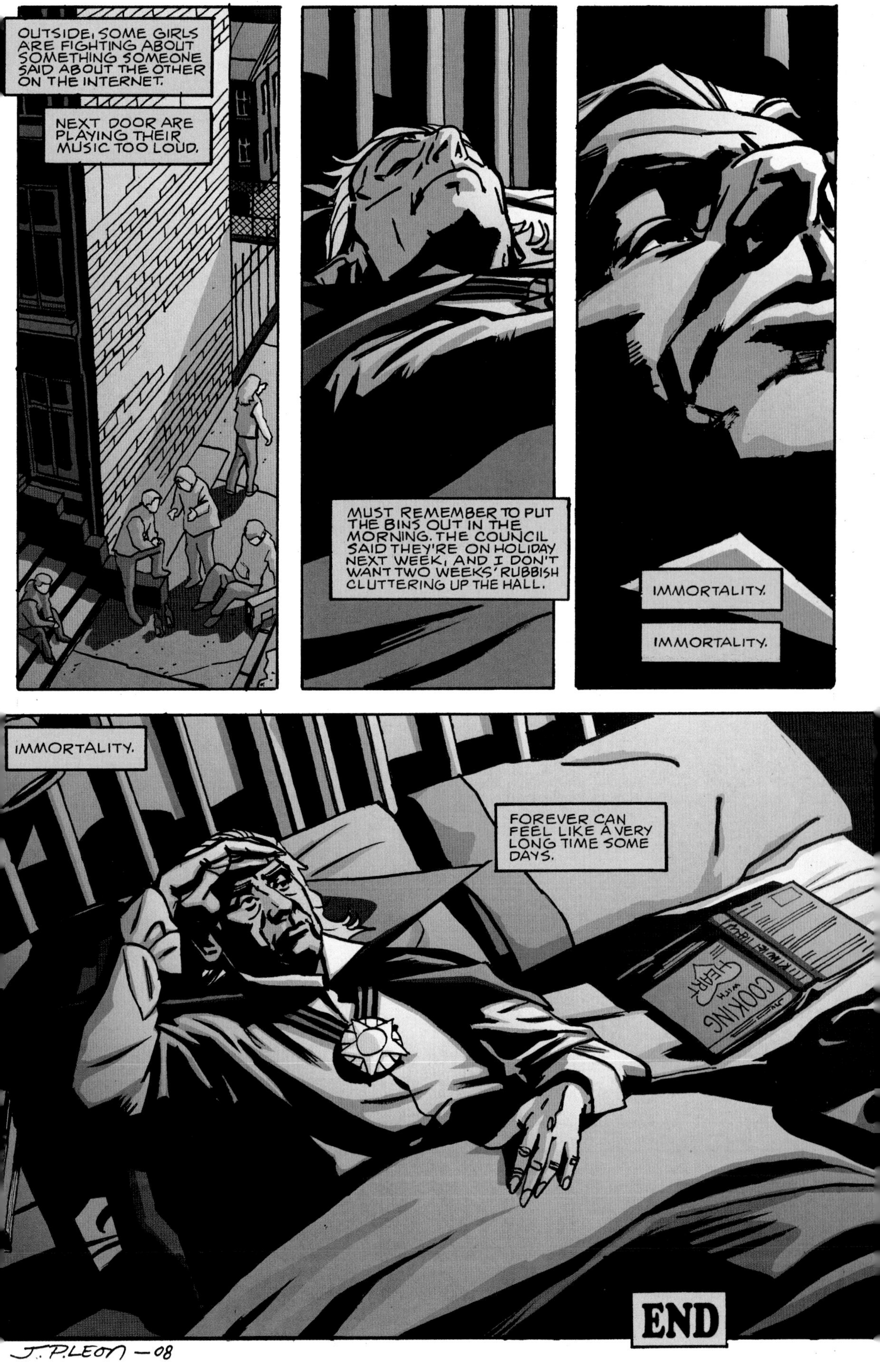
OUTSIDE, SOME GIRLS ARE FIGHTING ABOUT SOMETHING SOMEONE SAID ABOUT THE OTHER ON THE INTERNET.
NEXT DOOR ARE PLAYING THEIR MUSIC TOO LOUD.
MUST REMEMBER TO PUT THE BINS OUT IN THE MORNING. THE COUNCIL SAID THEY'RE ON HOLIDAY NEXT WEEK, AND I DON'T WANT TWO WEEKS' RUBBISH CLUTTERING UP THE HALL.
IMMORTALITY.
IMMORTALITY.
IMMORTALITY.
FOREVER CAN FEEL LIKE A VERY LONG TIME SOME DAYS.
COOKING with HEART
END
J.P.LEON -08

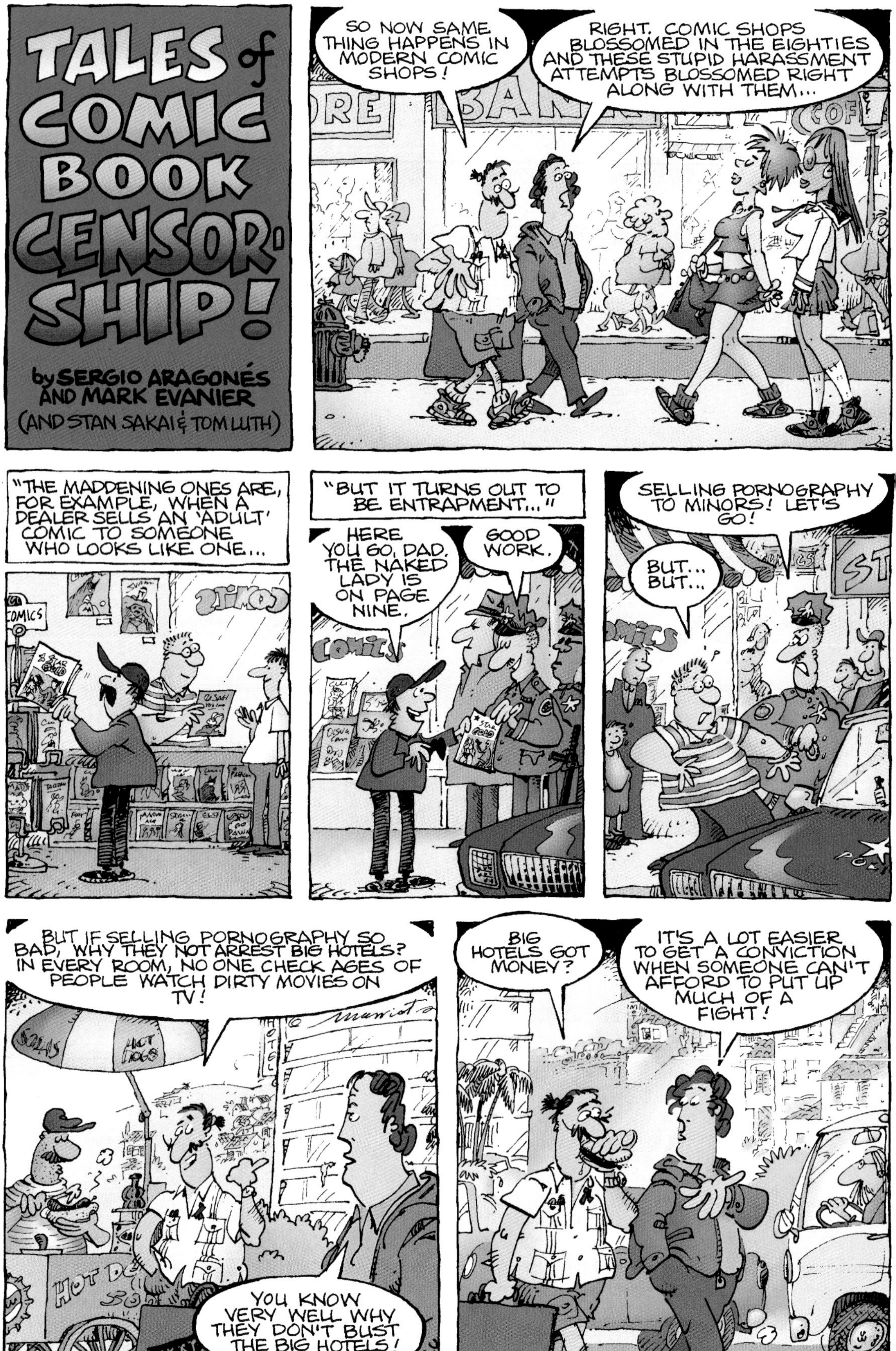
TALES of COMIC BOOK CENSORSHIP!
by SERGIO ARAGONÉS AND MARK EVANIER
(AND STAN SAKAI & TOM LUTH)
SO NOW SAME THING HAPPENS IN MODERN COMIC SHOPS!
RIGHT. COMIC SHOPS BLOSSOMED IN THE EIGHTIES AND THESE STUPID HARASSMENT ATTEMPTS BLOSSOMED RIGHT ALONG WITH THEM...
"THE MADDENING ONES ARE, FOR EXAMPLE, WHEN A DEALER SELLS AN 'ADULT' COMIC TO SOMEONE WHO LOOKS LIKE ONE...
"BUT IT TURNS OUT TO BE ENTRAPMENT..."
HERE YOU GO, DAD. THE NAKED LADY IS ON PAGE NINE.
GOOD WORK.
SELLING PORNOGRAPHY TO MINORS! LET'S GO!
BUT... BUT...
BUT IF SELLING PORNOGRAPHY SO BAD, WHY THEY NOT ARREST BIG HOTELS? IN EVERY ROOM, NO ONE CHECK AGES OF PEOPLE WATCH DIRTY MOVIES ON TV!
YOU KNOW VERY WELL WHY THEY DON'T BUST THE BIG HOTELS!
BIG HOTELS GOT MONEY?
IT'S A LOT EASIER TO GET A CONVICTION WHEN SOMEONE CAN'T AFFORD TO PUT UP MUCH OF A FIGHT!

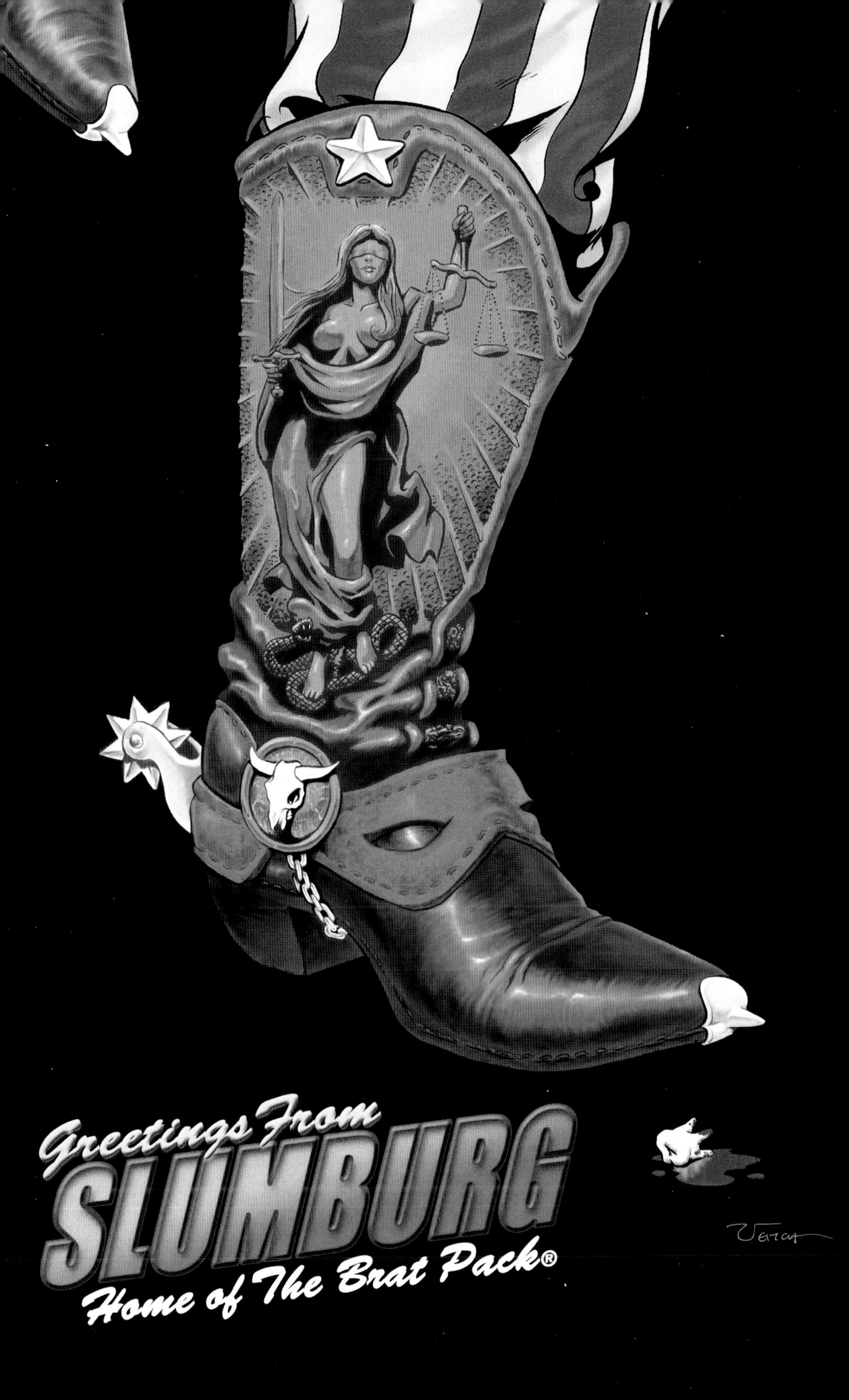
Greetings From
SLUMBURG
Home of The Brat Pack®
Veitch

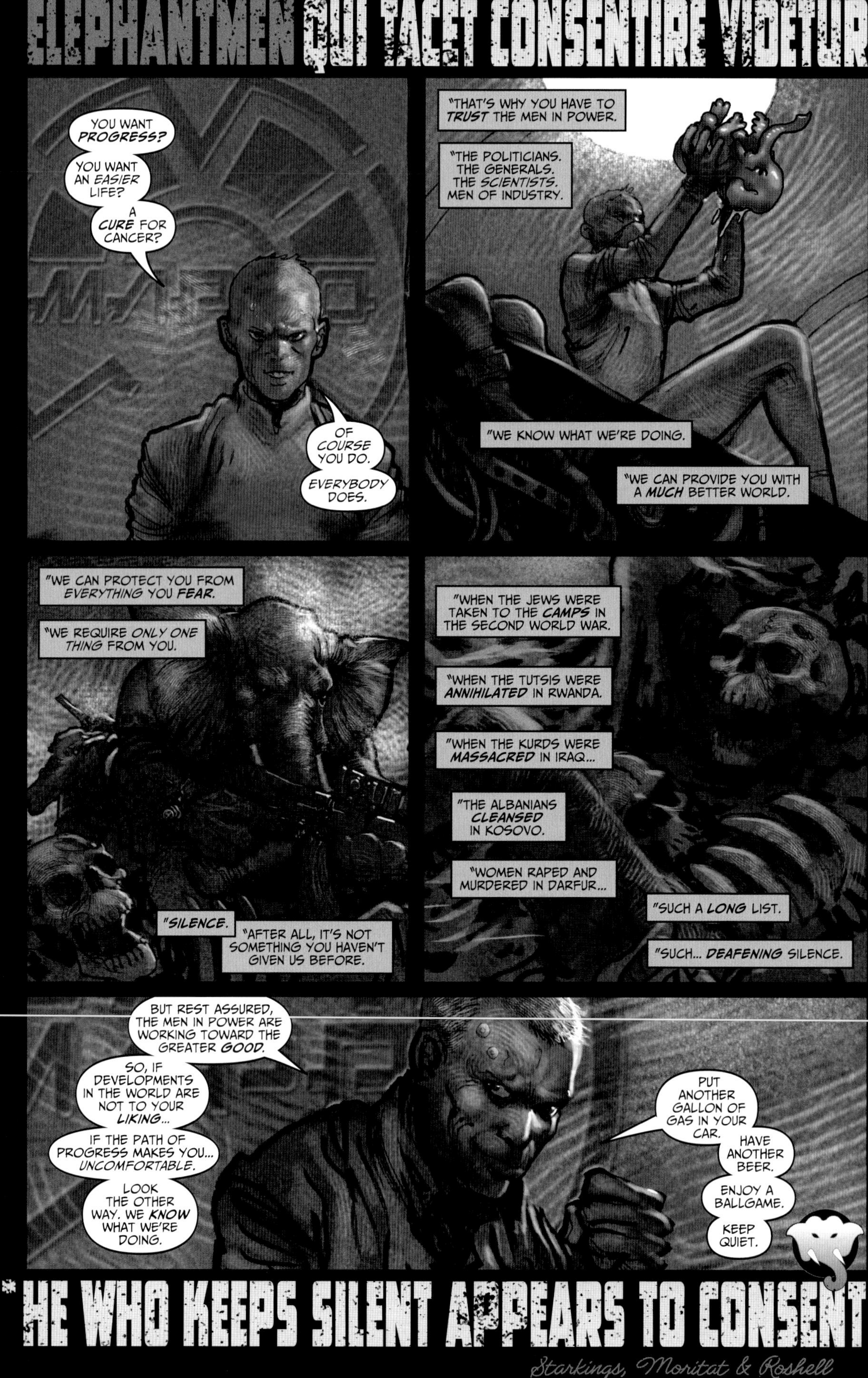
ELEPHANTMEN QUI TACET CONSENTIRE VIDETUR
YOU WANT PROGRESS?
YOU WANT AN EASIER LIFE?
A CURE FOR CANCER?
OF COURSE YOU DO.
EVERYBODY DOES.
"THAT'S WHY YOU HAVE TO TRUST THE MEN IN POWER.
"THE POLITICIANS. THE GENERALS. THE SCIENTISTS. MEN OF INDUSTRY.
"WE KNOW WHAT WE'RE DOING.
"WE CAN PROVIDE YOU WITH A MUCH BETTER WORLD.
"WE CAN PROTECT YOU FROM EVERYTHING YOU FEAR.
"WE REQUIRE ONLY ONE THING FROM YOU.
"SILENCE.
"AFTER ALL, IT'S NOT SOMETHING YOU HAVEN'T GIVEN US BEFORE.
"WHEN THE JEWS WERE TAKEN TO THE CAMPS IN THE SECOND WORLD WAR.
"WHEN THE TUTSIS WERE ANNIHILATED IN RWANDA.
"WHEN THE KURDS WERE MASSACRED IN IRAQ...
"THE ALBANIANS CLEANSED IN KOSOVO.
"WOMEN RAPED AND MURDERED IN DARFUR...
"SUCH A LONG LIST.
"SUCH... DEAFENING SILENCE.
BUT REST ASSURED, THE MEN IN POWER ARE WORKING TOWARD THE GREATER GOOD.
SO, IF DEVELOPMENTS IN THE WORLD ARE NOT TO YOUR LIKING...
IF THE PATH OF PROGRESS MAKES YOU... UNCOMFORTABLE.
LOOK THE OTHER WAY. WE KNOW WHAT WE'RE DOING.
PUT ANOTHER GALLON OF GAS IN YOUR CAR.
HAVE ANOTHER BEER.
ENJOY A BALLGAME.
KEEP QUIET.
*HE WHO KEEPS SILENT APPEARS TO CONSENT
Starkings, Moritat & Roshell

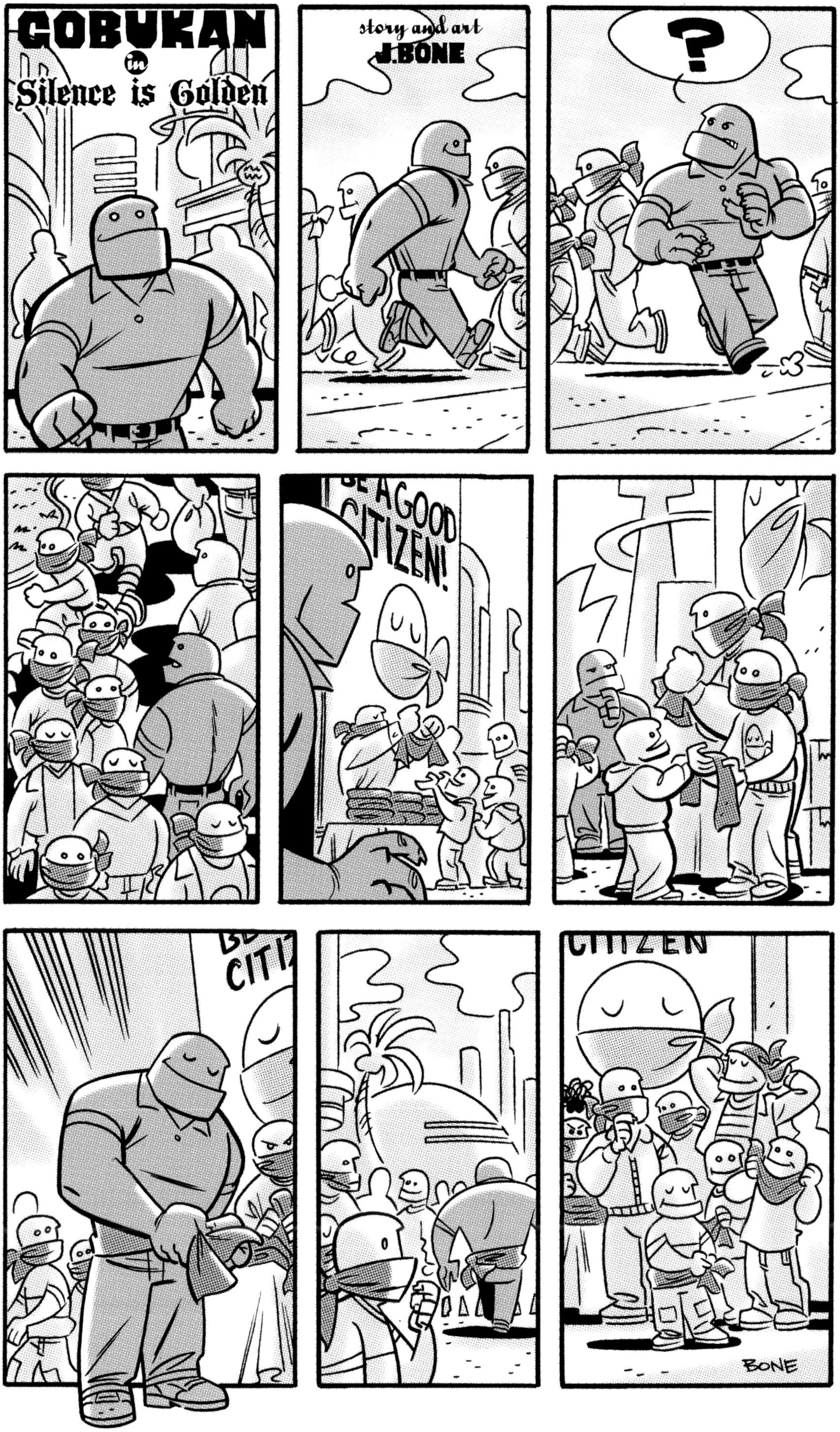
GOBUKAN
in
Silence is Golden
story and art
J.BONE
?
BE A GOOD CITIZEN!
CITIZEN
BONE

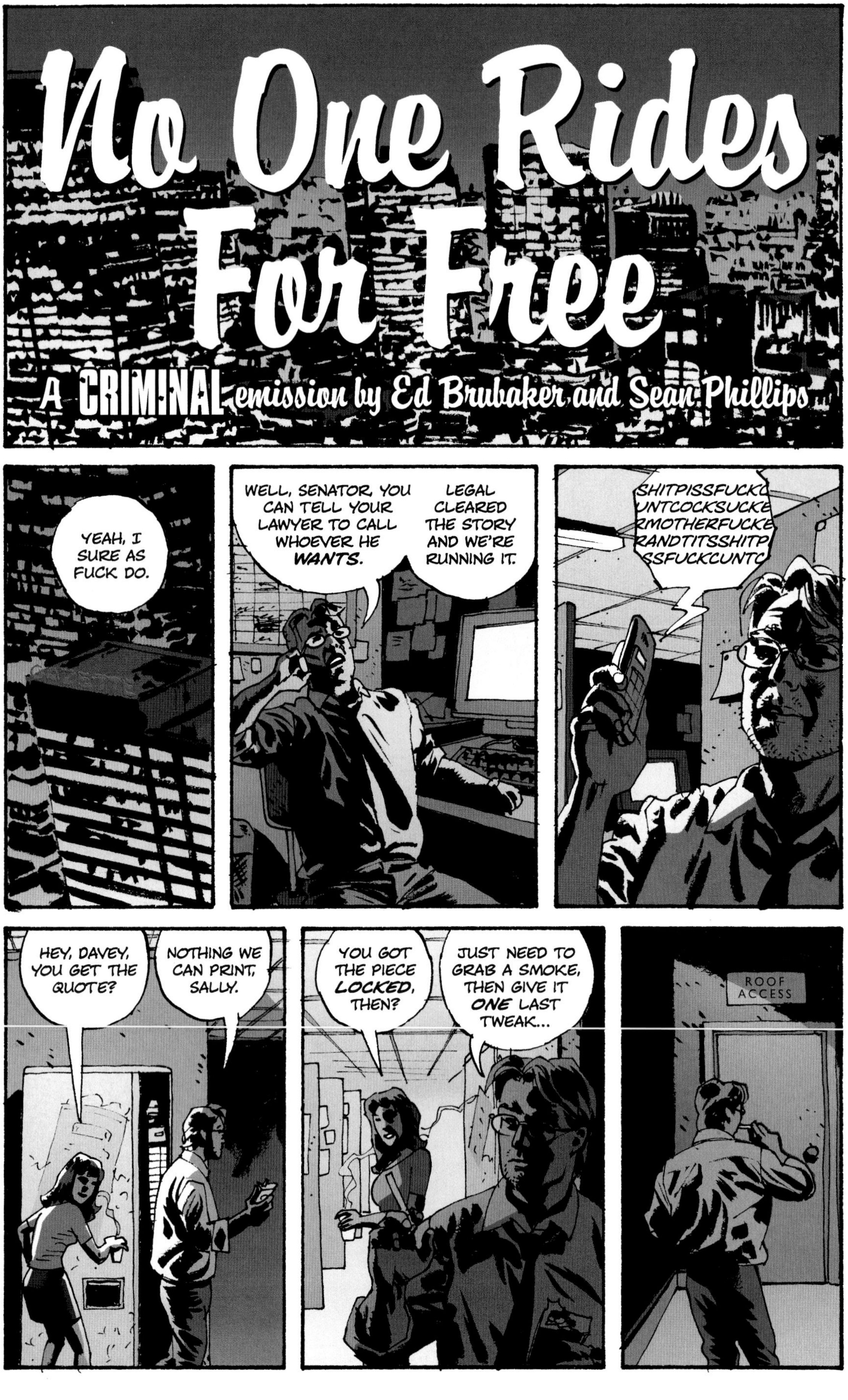
No One Rides For Free
A CRIMINAL emission by Ed Brubaker and Sean Phillips
YEAH, I SURE AS FUCK DO.
WELL, SENATOR, YOU CAN TELL YOUR LAWYER TO CALL WHOEVER HE WANTS.
LEGAL CLEARED THE STORY AND WE'RE RUNNING IT.
SHITPISSFUCKC UNTCOCKSUCKE RMOTHERFUCKE RANDTITSSHITP SSFUCKCUNTC
HEY, DAVEY, YOU GET THE QUOTE?
NOTHING WE CAN PRINT, SALLY.
YOU GOT THE PIECE LOCKED, THEN?
JUST NEED TO GRAB A SMOKE, THEN GIVE IT ONE LAST TWEAK...
ROOF ACCESS

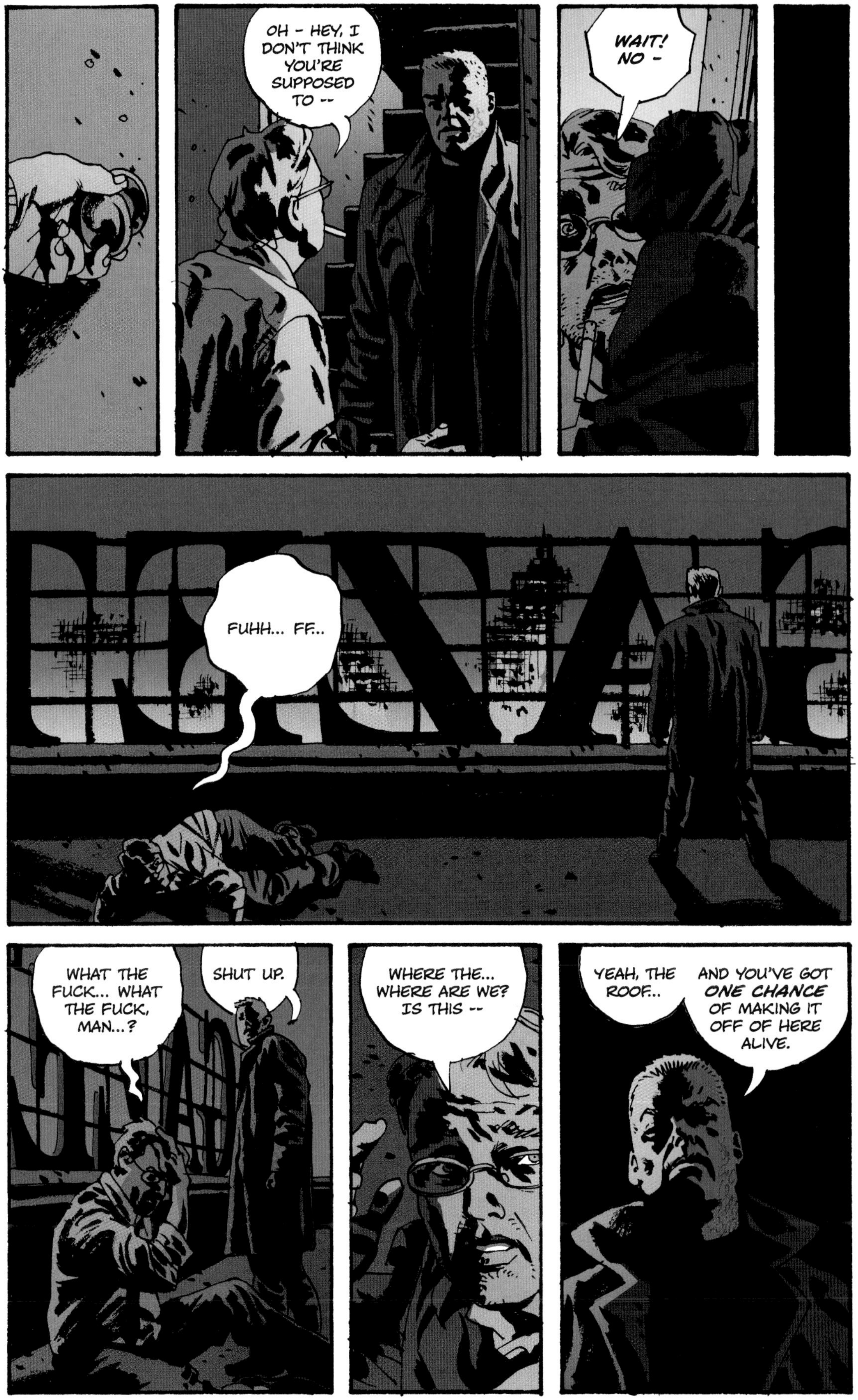
OH - HEY, I DON'T THINK YOU'RE SUPPOSED TO --
WAIT! NO -
FUHH... FF..
WHAT THE FUCK... WHAT THE FUCK, MAN...?
SHUT UP.
WHERE THE... WHERE ARE WE? IS THIS --
YEAH, THE ROOF...
AND YOU'VE GOT *ONE CHANCE* OF MAKING IT OFF OF HERE ALIVE.

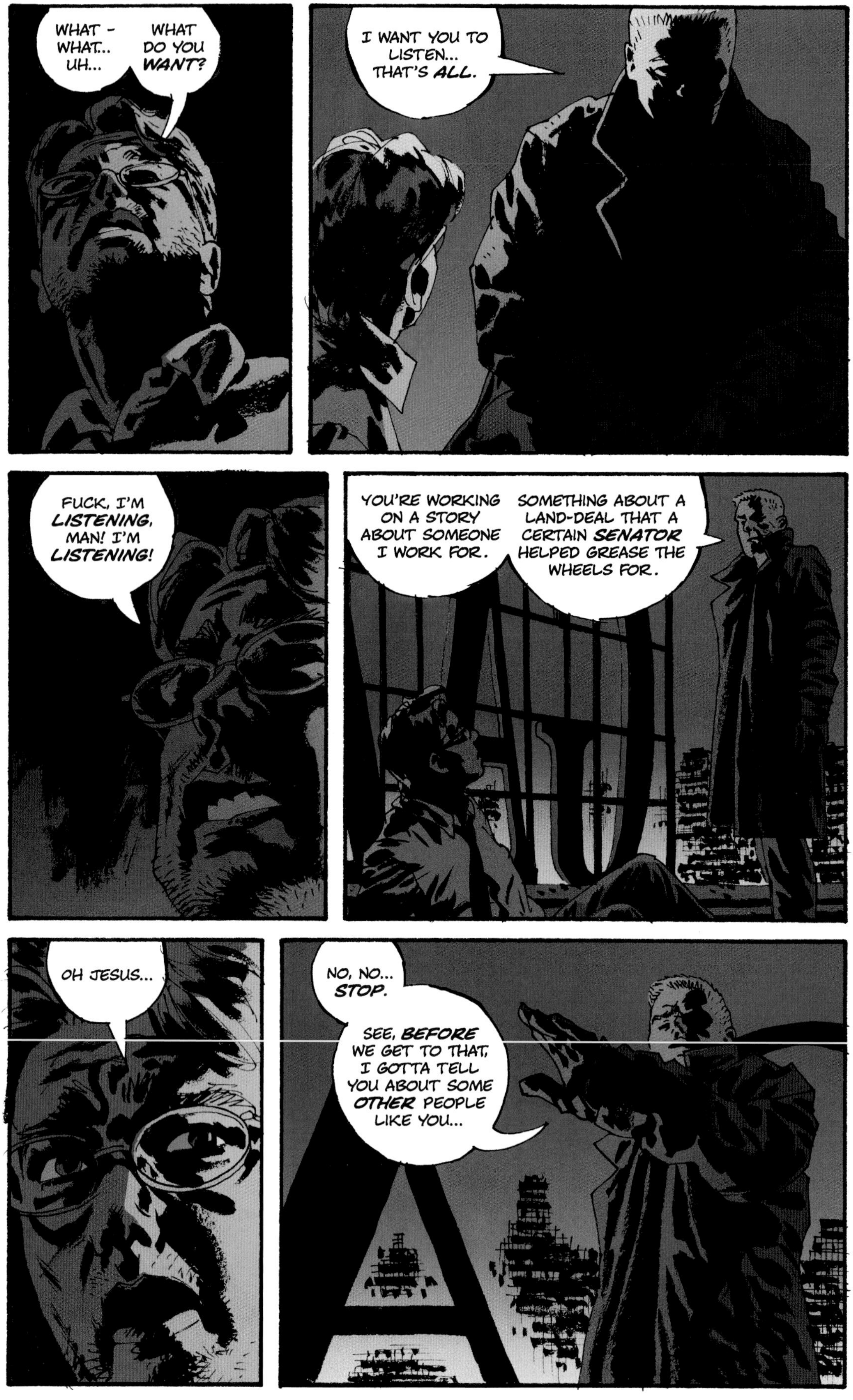
WHAT - WHAT... UH...
WHAT DO YOU *WANT?*
I WANT YOU TO LISTEN... THAT'S *ALL.*
FUCK, I'M *LISTENING,* MAN! I'M *LISTENING!*
YOU'RE WORKING ON A STORY ABOUT SOMEONE I WORK FOR.
SOMETHING ABOUT A LAND-DEAL THAT A CERTAIN *SENATOR* HELPED GREASE THE WHEELS FOR.
OH JESUS...
NO, NO... *STOP.*
SEE, *BEFORE* WE GET TO THAT, I GOTTA TELL YOU ABOUT SOME *OTHER* PEOPLE LIKE YOU...

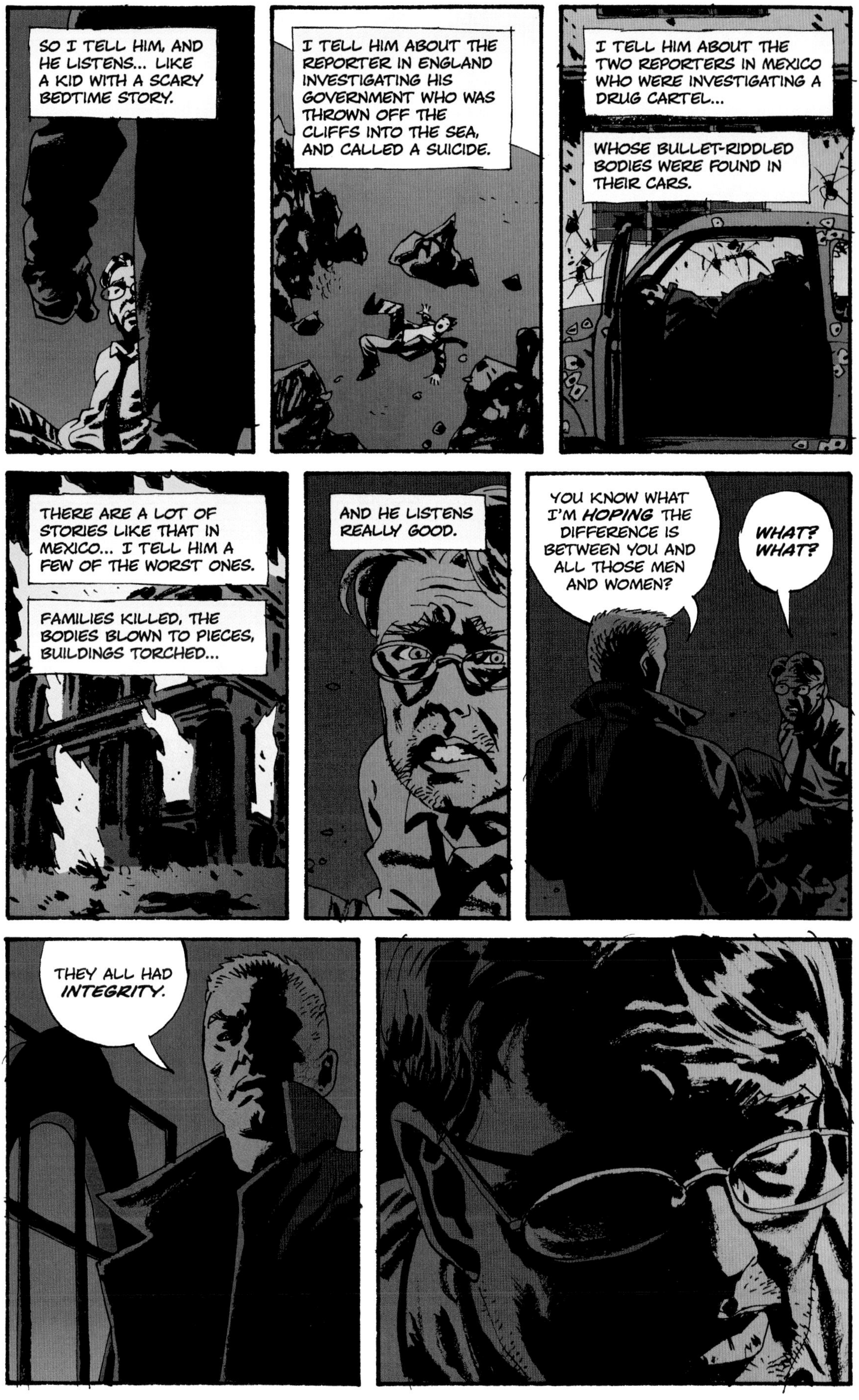
SO I TELL HIM, AND HE LISTENS... LIKE A KID WITH A SCARY BEDTIME STORY.
I TELL HIM ABOUT THE REPORTER IN ENGLAND INVESTIGATING HIS GOVERNMENT WHO WAS THROWN OFF THE CLIFFS INTO THE SEA, AND CALLED A SUICIDE.
I TELL HIM ABOUT THE TWO REPORTERS IN MEXICO WHO WERE INVESTIGATING A DRUG CARTEL...
WHOSE BULLET-RIDDLED BODIES WERE FOUND IN THEIR CARS.
THERE ARE A LOT OF STORIES LIKE THAT IN MEXICO... I TELL HIM A FEW OF THE WORST ONES.
FAMILIES KILLED, THE BODIES BLOWN TO PIECES, BUILDINGS TORCHED...
AND HE LISTENS REALLY GOOD.
YOU KNOW WHAT I'M *HOPING* THE DIFFERENCE IS BETWEEN YOU AND ALL THOSE MEN AND WOMEN?
WHAT? WHAT?
THEY ALL HAD *INTEGRITY*.

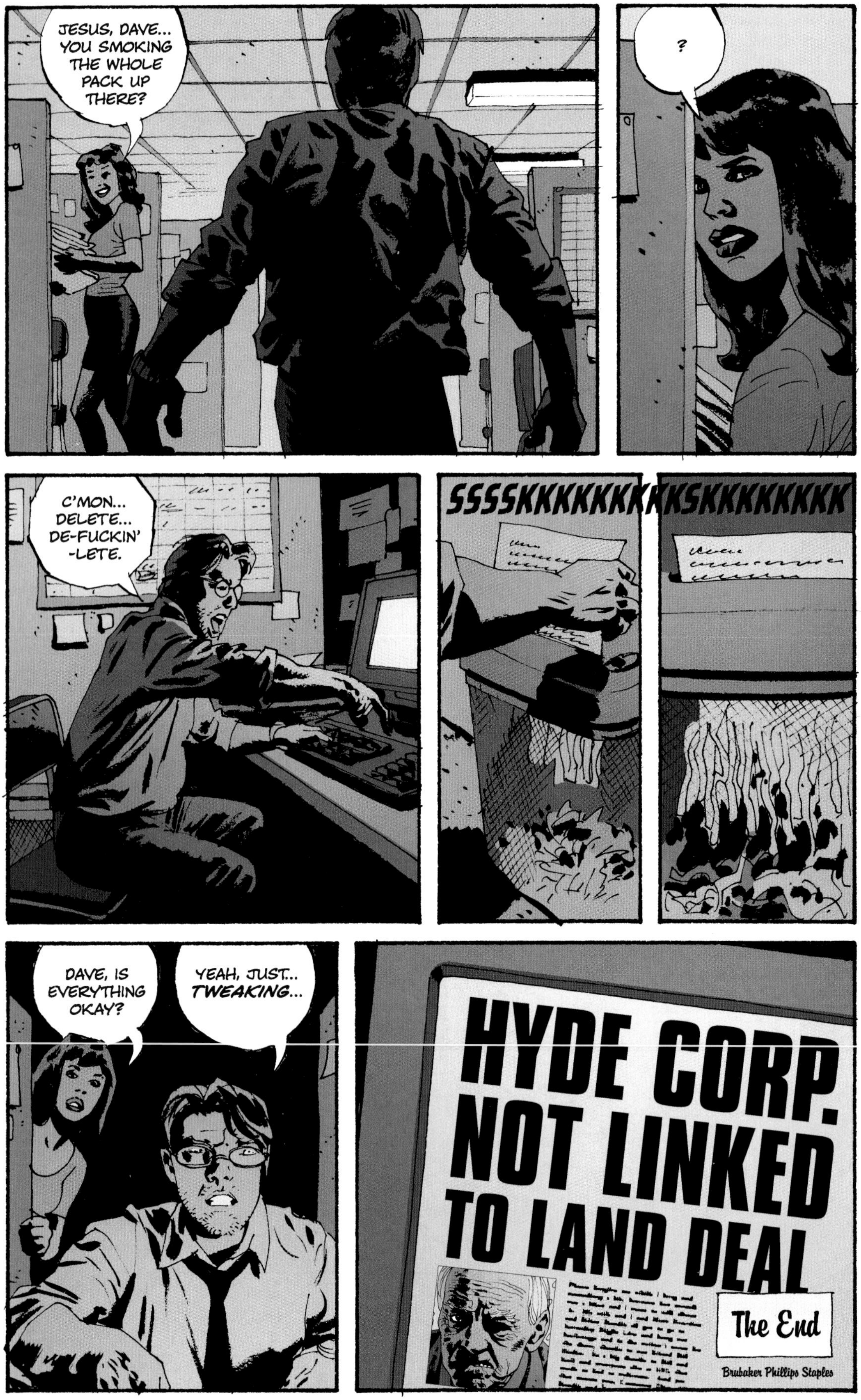
JESUS, DAVE... YOU SMOKING THE WHOLE PACK UP THERE?
?
C'MON... DELETE... DE-FUCKIN' -LETE.
SSSSKKKKKKKKKSKKKKKKK
DAVE, IS EVERYTHING OKAY?
YEAH, JUST... *TWEAKING*...
HYDE CORP. NOT LINKED TO LAND DEAL
The End
Brubaker Phillips Staples

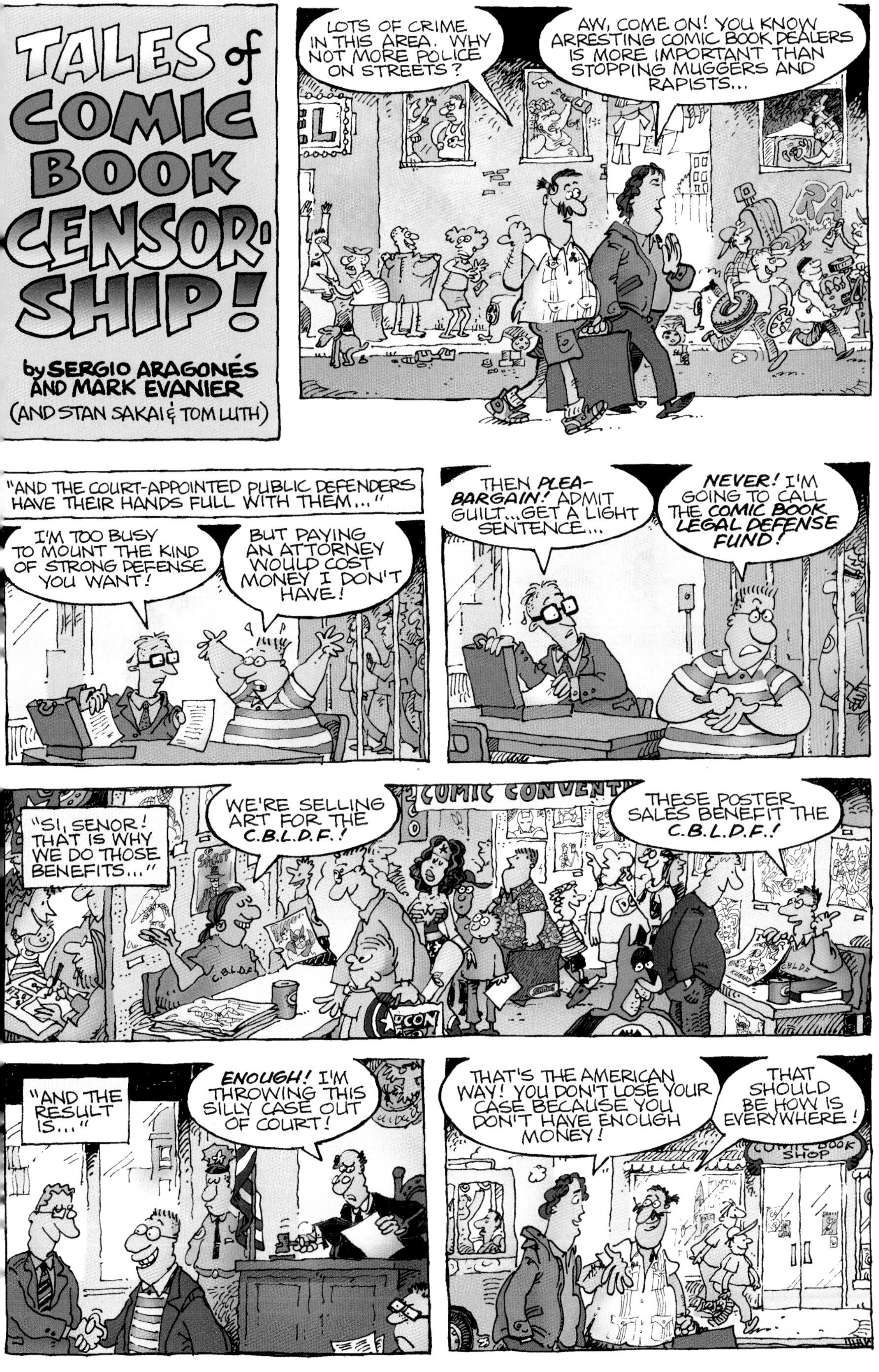
TALES of COMIC BOOK CENSORSHIP!
by SERGIO ARAGONÉS AND MARK EVANIER
(AND STAN SAKAI & TOM LUTH)
LOTS OF CRIME IN THIS AREA. WHY NOT MORE POLICE ON STREETS?
AW, COME ON! YOU KNOW ARRESTING COMIC BOOK DEALERS IS MORE IMPORTANT THAN STOPPING MUGGERS AND RAPISTS...
"AND THE COURT-APPOINTED PUBLIC DEFENDERS HAVE THEIR HANDS FULL WITH THEM..."
I'M TOO BUSY TO MOUNT THE KIND OF STRONG DEFENSE YOU WANT!
BUT PAYING AN ATTORNEY WOULD COST MONEY I DON'T HAVE!
THEN PLEA-BARGAIN! ADMIT GUILT...GET A LIGHT SENTENCE...
NEVER! I'M GOING TO CALL THE COMIC BOOK LEGAL DEFENSE FUND!
"SI, SENOR! THAT IS WHY WE DO THOSE BENEFITS..."
WE'RE SELLING ART FOR THE C.B.L.D.F.!
COMIC CONVENT
THESE POSTER SALES BENEFIT THE C.B.L.D.F.!
"AND THE RESULT IS..."
ENOUGH! I'M THROWING THIS SILLY CASE OUT OF COURT!
THAT'S THE AMERICAN WAY! YOU DON'T LOSE YOUR CASE BECAUSE YOU DON'T HAVE ENOUGH MONEY!
THAT SHOULD BE HOW IS EVERYWHERE!
COMIC BOOK SHOP

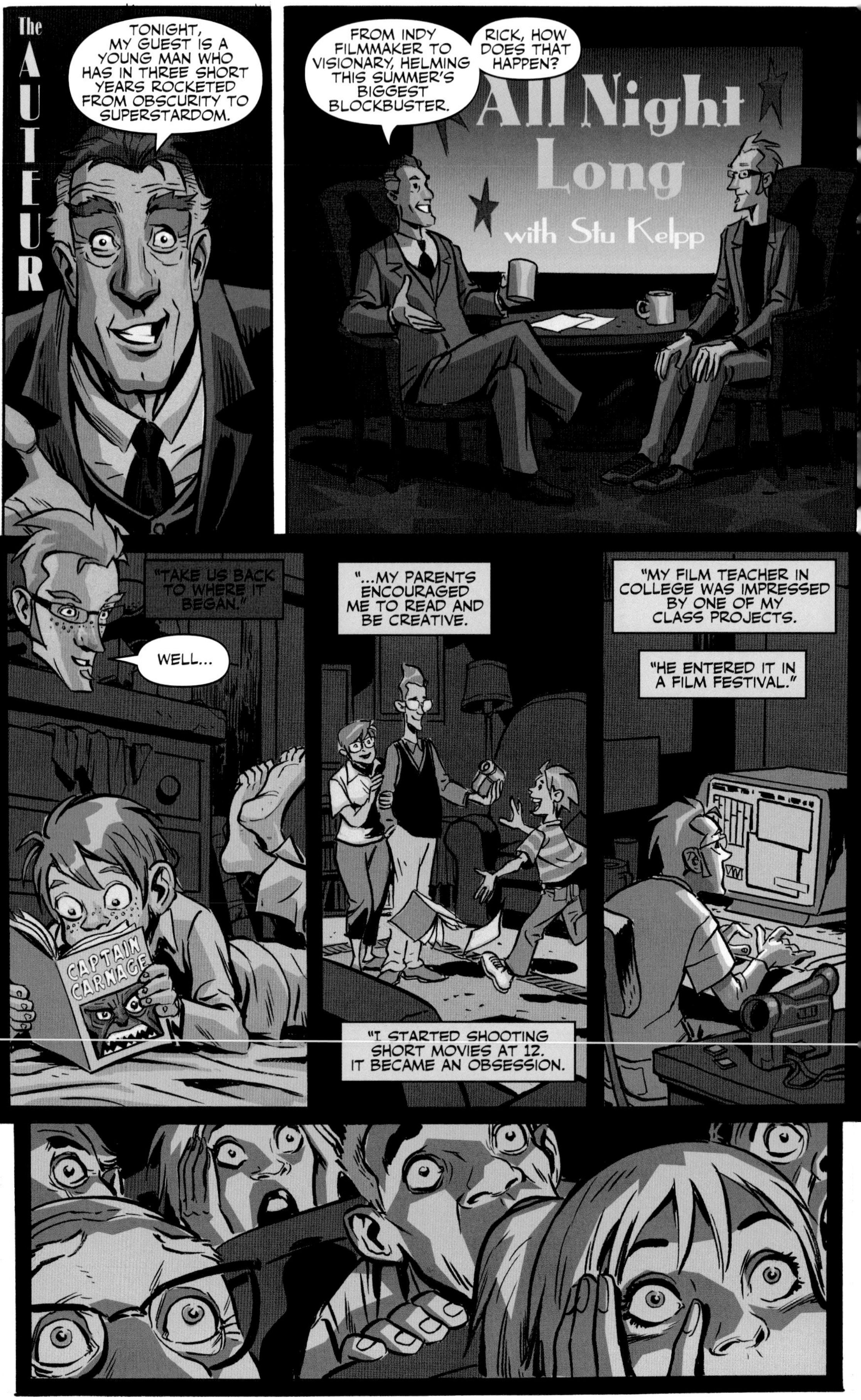
The AUTEUR
TONIGHT, MY GUEST IS A YOUNG MAN WHO HAS IN THREE SHORT YEARS ROCKETED FROM OBSCURITY TO SUPERSTARDOM.
FROM INDY FILMMAKER TO VISIONARY, HELMING THIS SUMMER'S BIGGEST BLOCKBUSTER.
RICK, HOW DOES THAT HAPPEN?
All Night Long with Stu Kelpp
"TAKE US BACK TO WHERE IT BEGAN."
WELL...
CAPTAIN CARNAGE
"...MY PARENTS ENCOURAGED ME TO READ AND BE CREATIVE.
"I STARTED SHOOTING SHORT MOVIES AT 12. IT BECAME AN OBSESSION.
"MY FILM TEACHER IN COLLEGE WAS IMPRESSED BY ONE OF MY CLASS PROJECTS.
"HE ENTERED IT IN A FILM FESTIVAL."

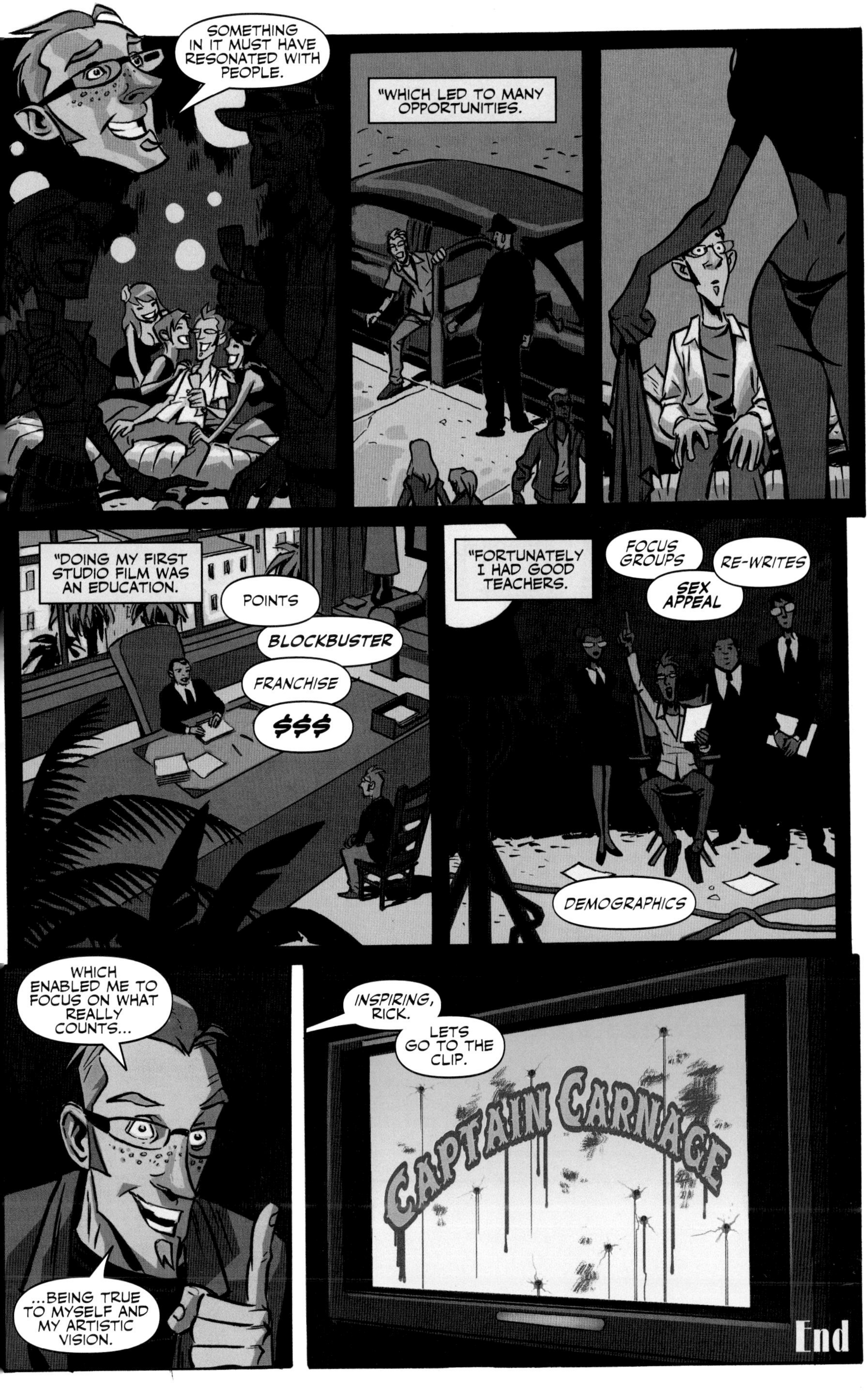
SOMETHING IN IT MUST HAVE RESONATED WITH PEOPLE.
"WHICH LED TO MANY OPPORTUNITIES.
"DOING MY FIRST STUDIO FILM WAS AN EDUCATION.
POINTS
BLOCKBUSTER
FRANCHISE
$$$
"FORTUNATELY I HAD GOOD TEACHERS.
FOCUS GROUPS
RE-WRITES
SEX APPEAL
DEMOGRAPHICS
WHICH ENABLED ME TO FOCUS ON WHAT REALLY COUNTS...
...BEING TRUE TO MYSELF AND MY ARTISTIC VISION.
INSPIRING, RICK.
LETS GO TO THE CLIP.
CAPTAIN CARNAGE
End

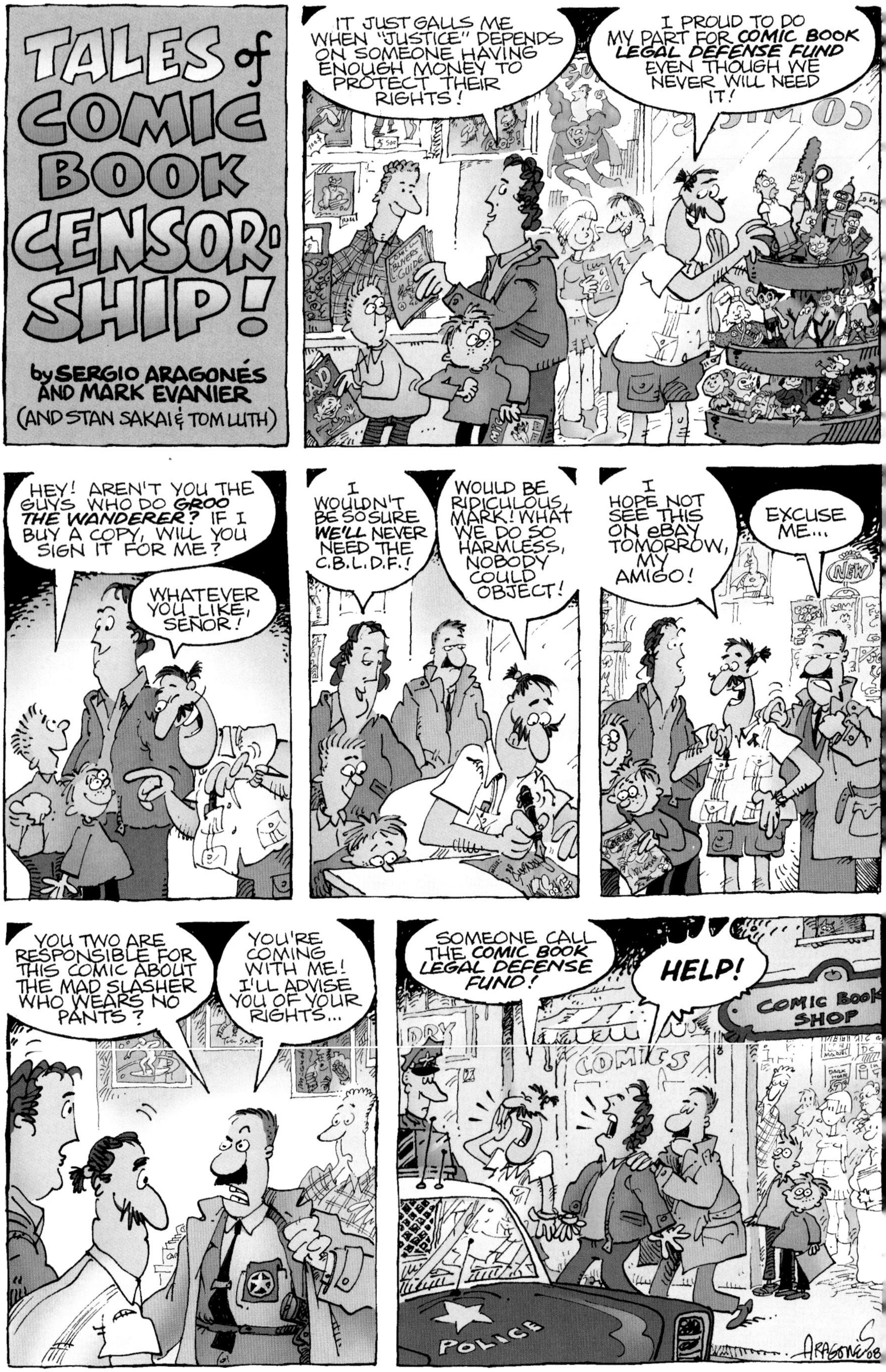
TALES of COMIC BOOK CENSORSHIP!
by SERGIO ARAGONÉS AND MARK EVANIER
(AND STAN SAKAI & TOM LUTH)
IT JUST GALLS ME WHEN "JUSTICE" DEPENDS ON SOMEONE HAVING ENOUGH MONEY TO PROTECT THEIR RIGHTS!
I PROUD TO DO MY PART FOR COMIC BOOK LEGAL DEFENSE FUND EVEN THOUGH WE NEVER WILL NEED IT!
HEY! AREN'T YOU THE GUYS WHO DO GROO THE WANDERER? IF I BUY A COPY, WILL YOU SIGN IT FOR ME?
WHATEVER YOU LIKE, SEÑOR!
I WOULDN'T BE SO SURE WE'LL NEVER NEED THE C.B.L.D.F.!
WOULD BE RIDICULOUS, MARK! WHAT WE DO SO HARMLESS, NOBODY COULD OBJECT!
I HOPE NOT SEE THIS ON eBAY TOMORROW, MY AMIGO!
EXCUSE ME...
YOU TWO ARE RESPONSIBLE FOR THIS COMIC ABOUT THE MAD SLASHER WHO WEARS NO PANTS?
YOU'RE COMING WITH ME! I'LL ADVISE YOU OF YOUR RIGHTS...
SOMEONE CALL THE COMIC BOOK LEGAL DEFENSE FUND!
HELP!
COMIC BOOK SHOP
COMICS
POLICE
ARAGONÉS 08

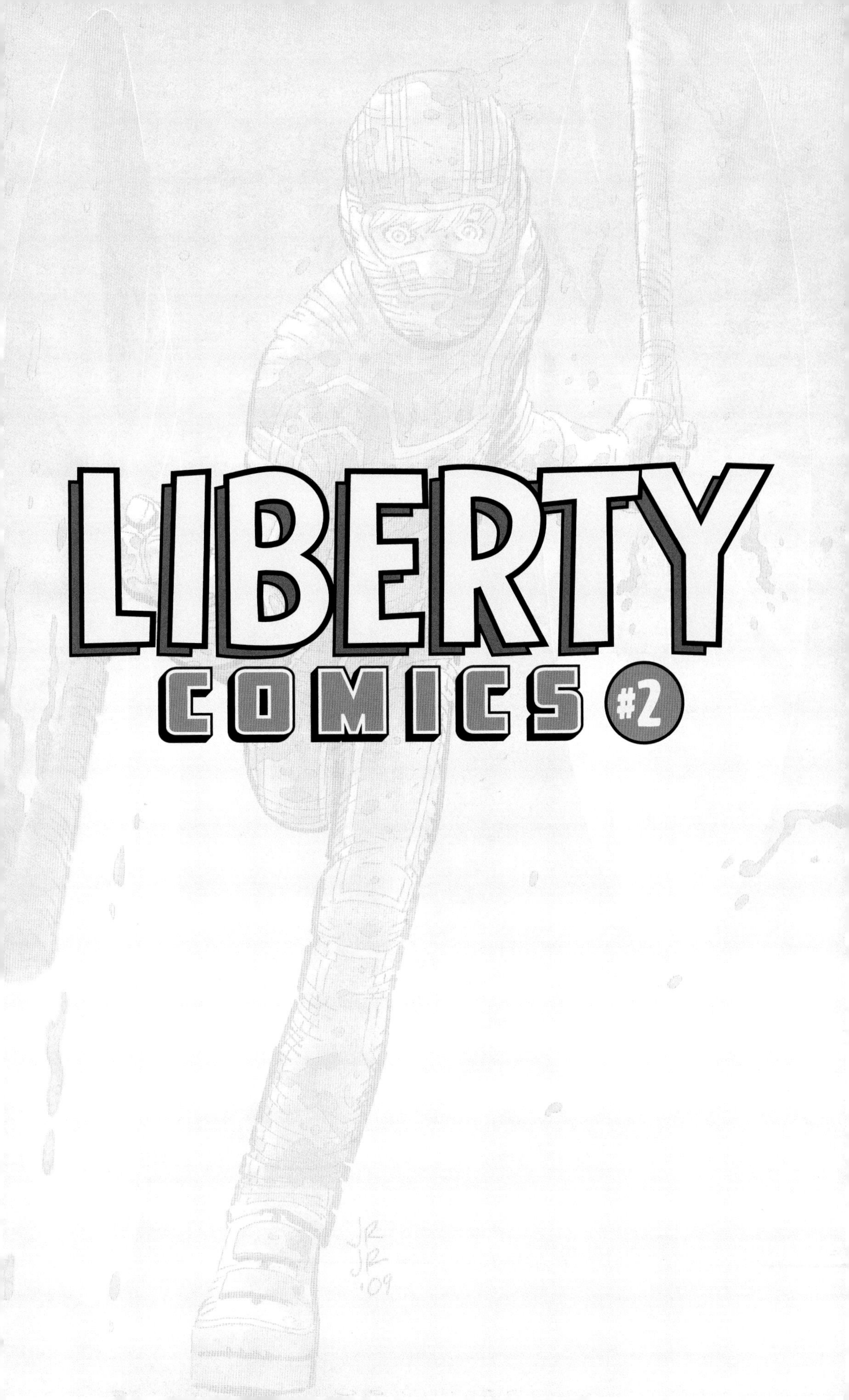
LIBERTY
COMICS #2

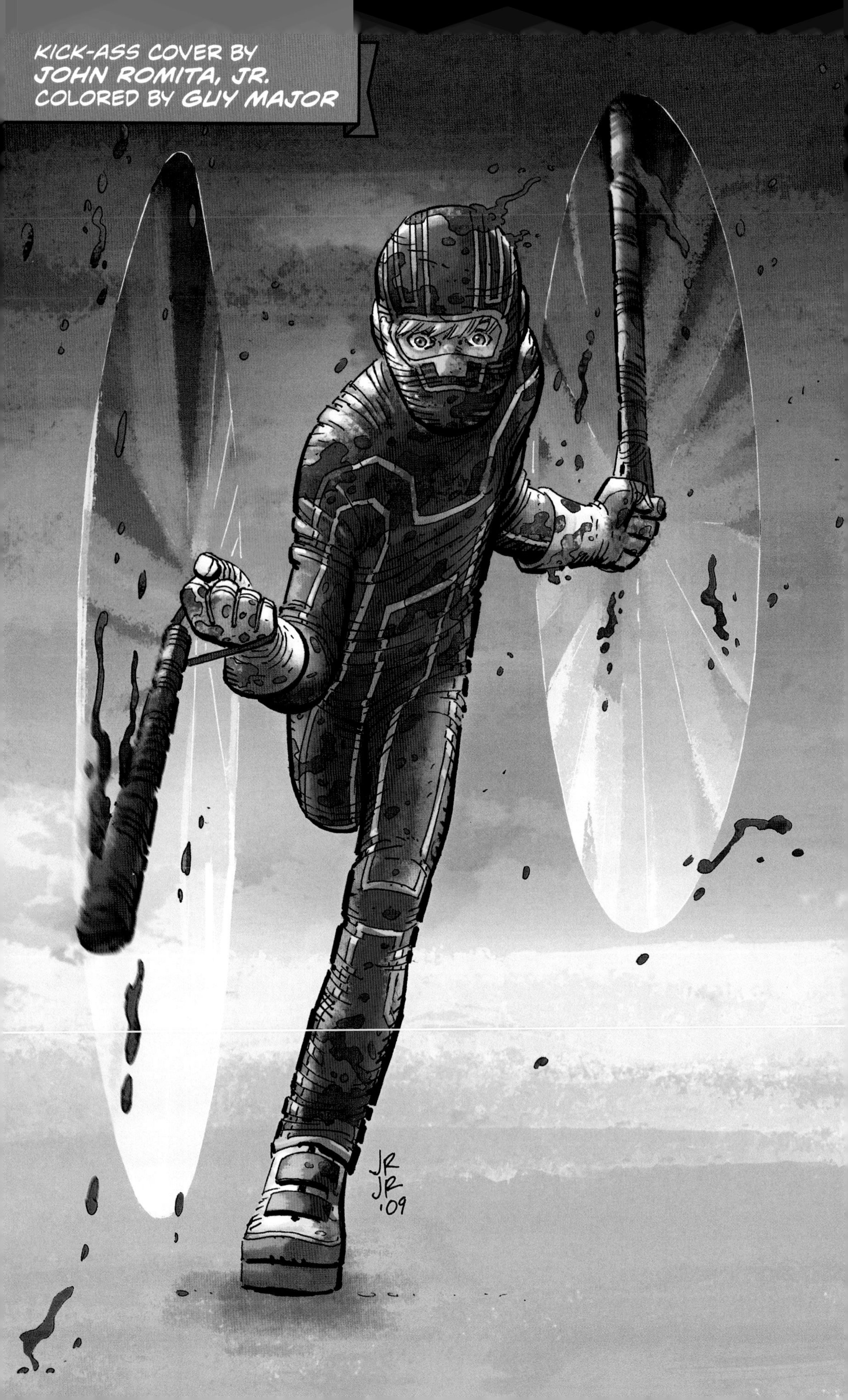
JR
JR
'09

KICK-ASS COVER BY
JOHN ROMITA, JR.
COLORED BY GUY MAJOR

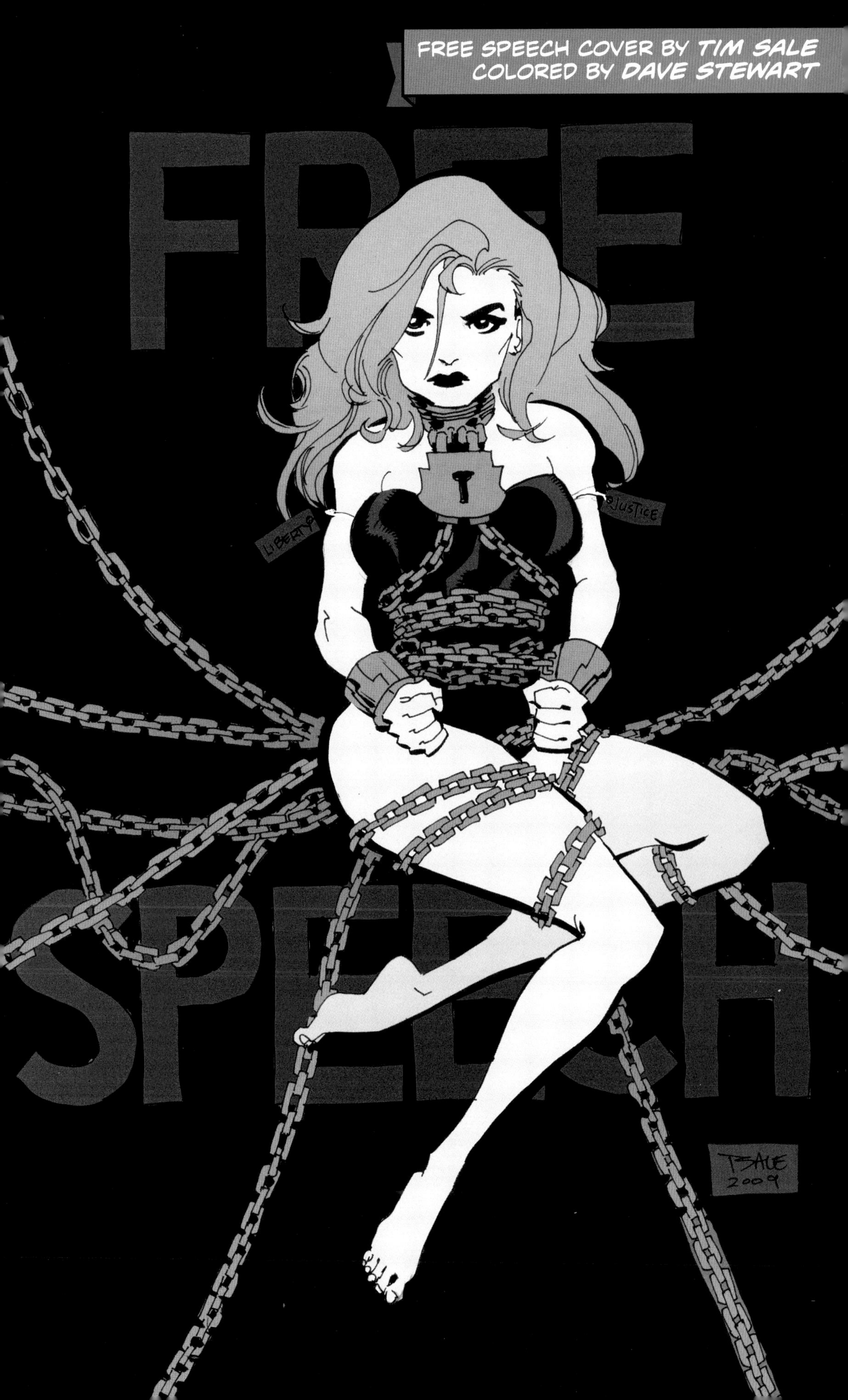
FREE
SPEECH
LIBERTY
JUSTICE
T SALE
2009

FREE SPEECH COVER BY *TIM SALE*
COLORED BY *DAVE STEWART*

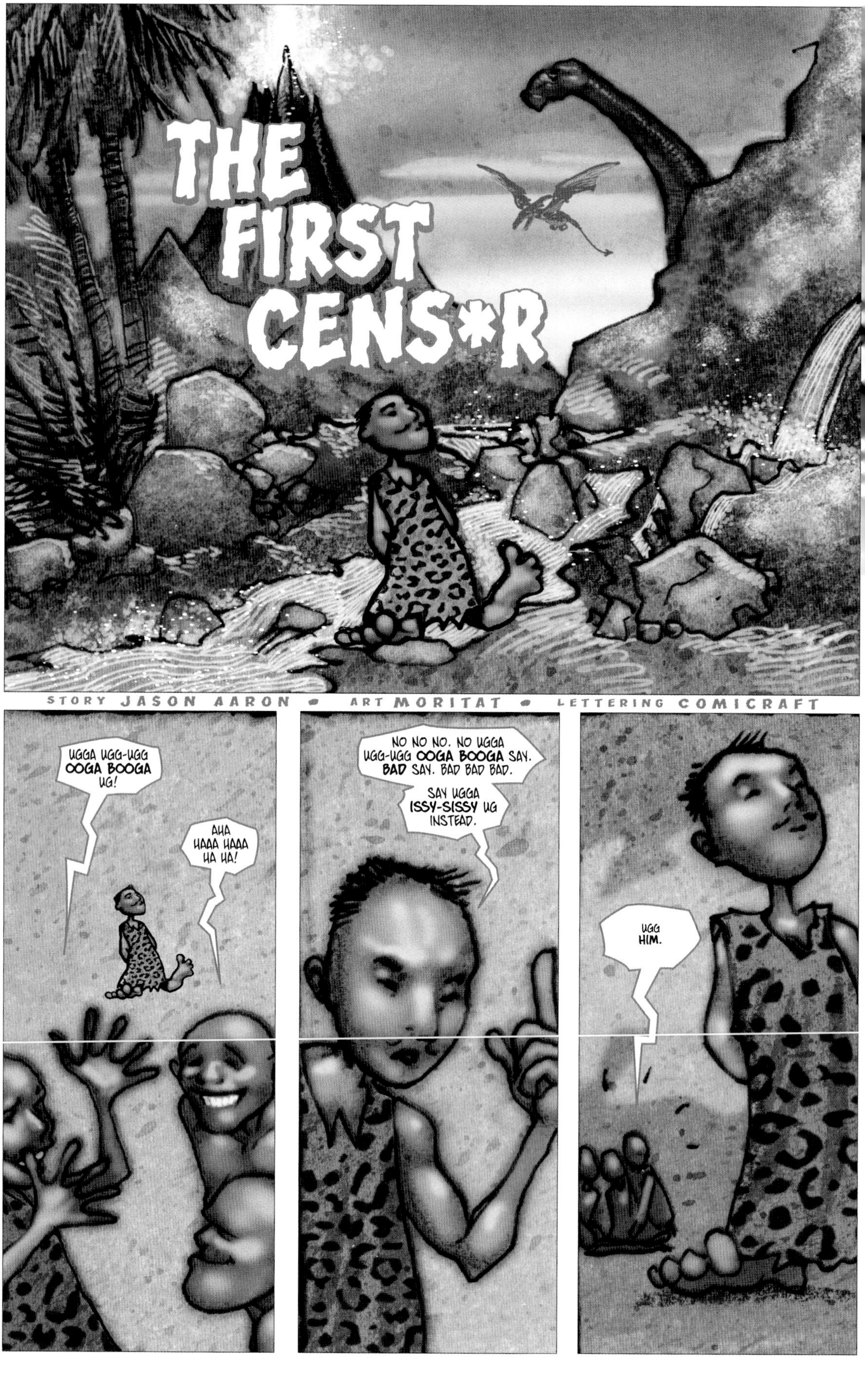
THE FIRST CENS*R
STORY JASON AARON • ART MORITAT • LETTERING COMICRAFT
UGGA UGG-UGG OOGA BOOGA UG!
AHA HAAA HAAA HA HA!
NO NO NO. NO UGGA UGG-UGG OOGA BOOGA SAY. BAD SAY. BAD BAD BAD.
SAY UGGA ISSY-SISSY UG INSTEAD.
UGG HIM.

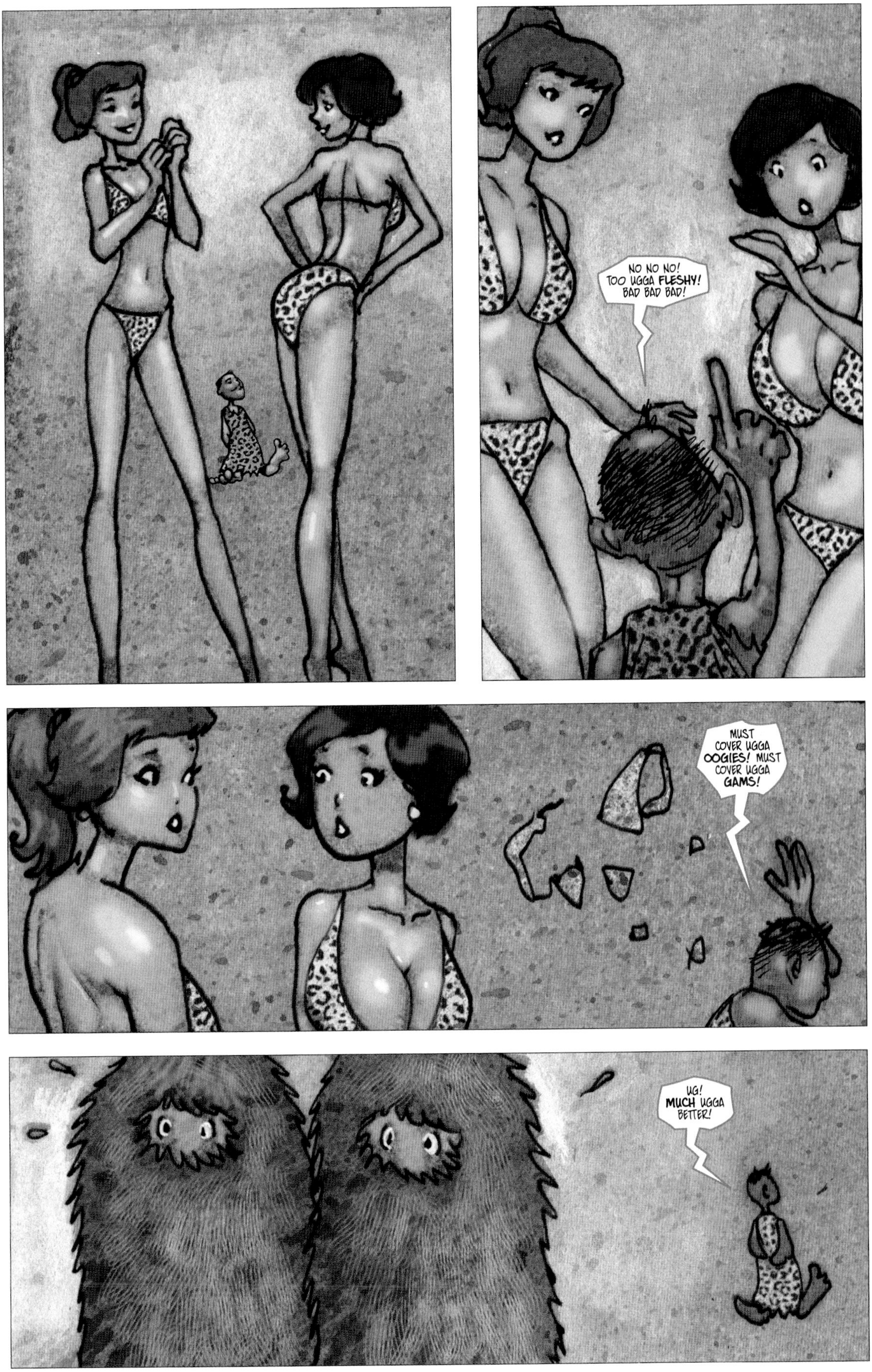
NO NO NO! TOO UGGA FLESHY! BAD BAD BAD!
MUST COVER UGGA OOGIES! MUST COVER UGGA GAMS!
UG! MUCH UGGA BETTER!

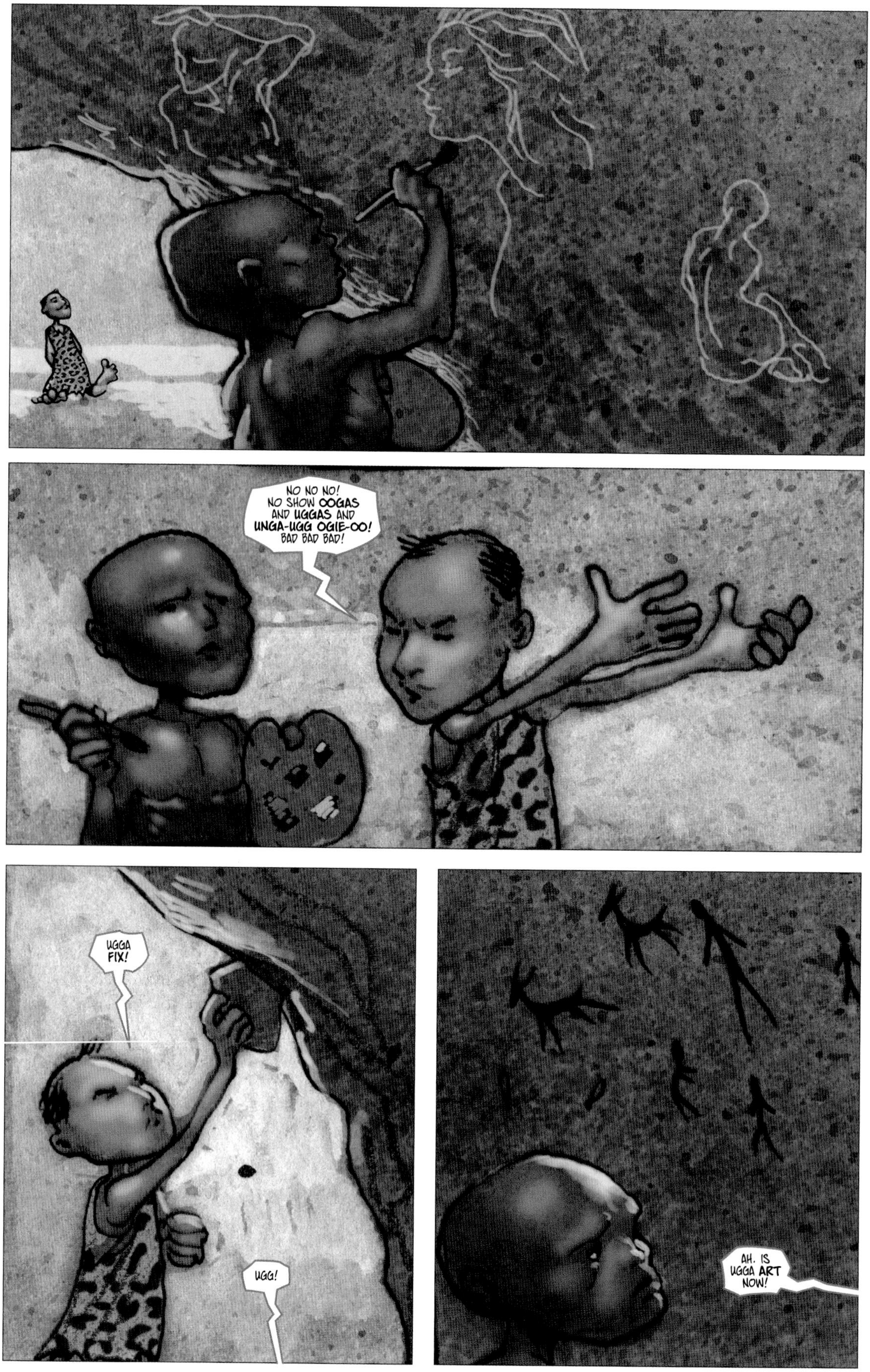
NO NO NO! NO SHOW OOGAS AND UGGAS AND UNGA-UGG OGIE-OO! BAD BAD BAD!
UGGA FIX!
UGG!
AH. IS UGGA ART NOW!

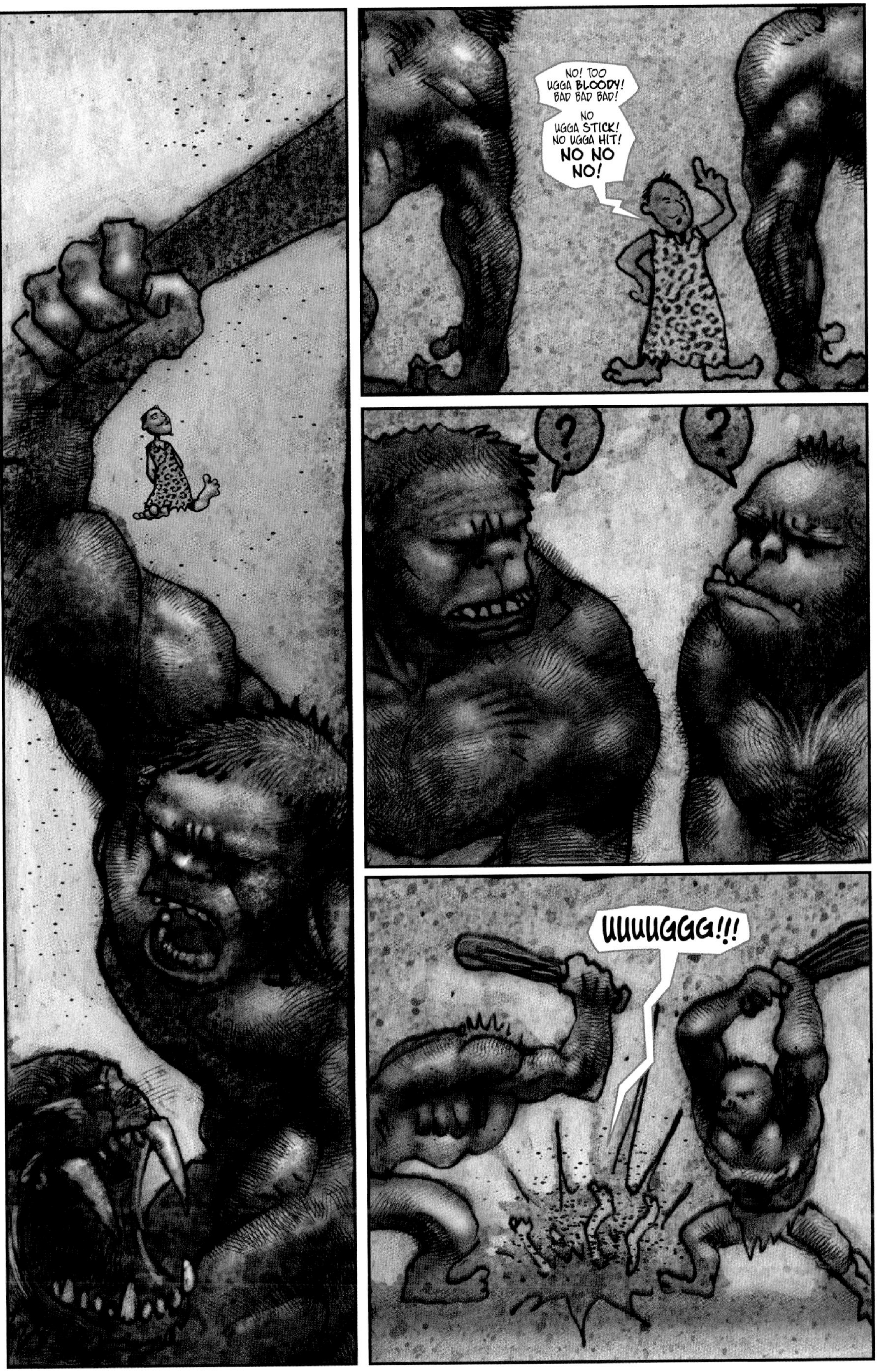
NO! TOO UGGA BLOODY! BAD BAD BAD!
NO UGGA STICK! NO UGGA HIT! NO NO NO!
?
?
UUUUGGG!!!

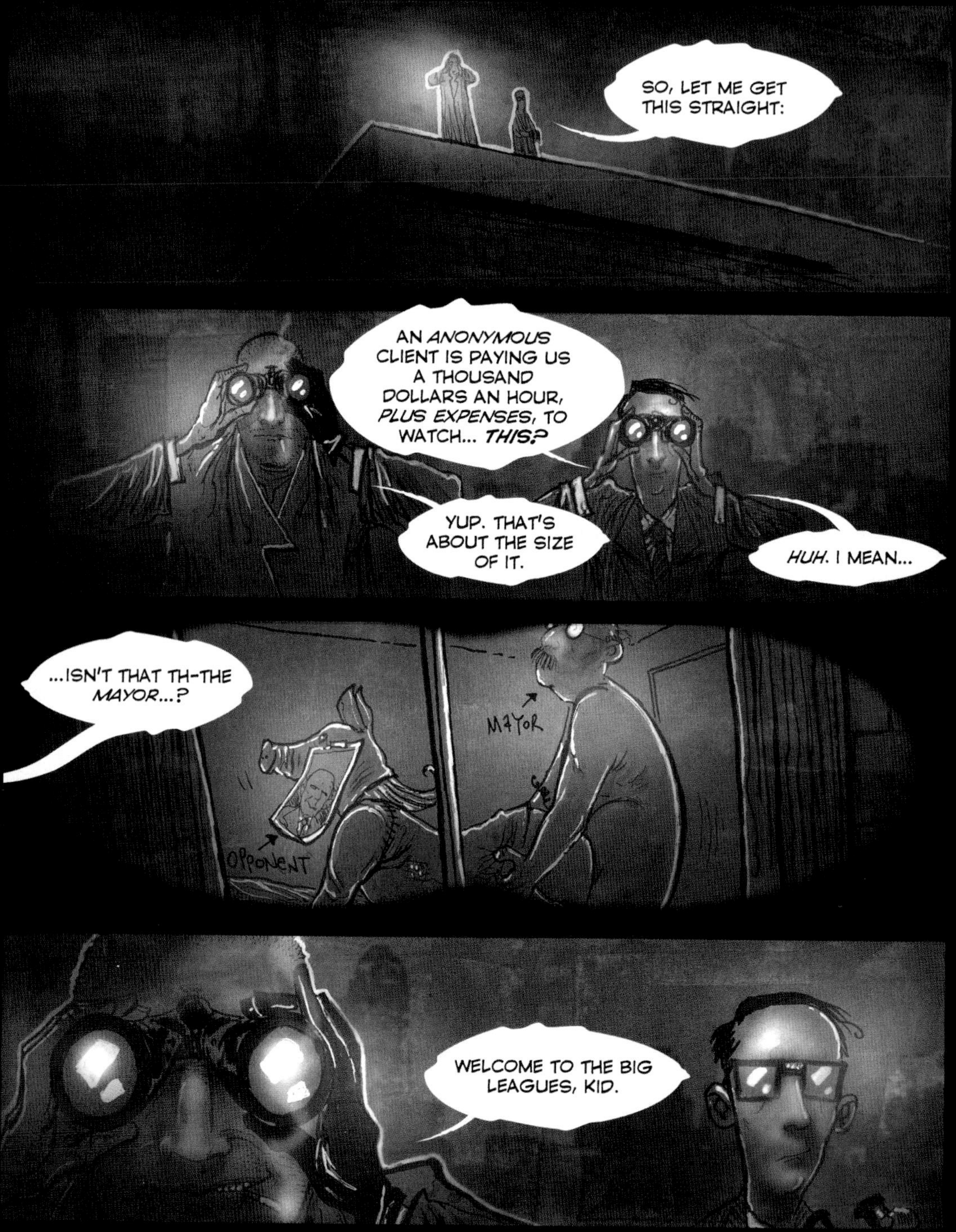
SO, LET ME GET THIS STRAIGHT:
AN *ANONYMOUS* CLIENT IS PAYING US A THOUSAND DOLLARS AN HOUR, *PLUS EXPENSES*, TO WATCH... *THIS?*
YUP. THAT'S ABOUT THE SIZE OF IT.
HUH. I MEAN...
...ISN'T THAT TH-THE *MAYOR...?*
MAYOR
OPPONENT
WELCOME TO THE BIG LEAGUES, KID.

BIG BAD CITY, BIG BAD WORLD.

WORDS: BEN MCCOOL

ART/LETTERS: BEN TEMPLESMITH

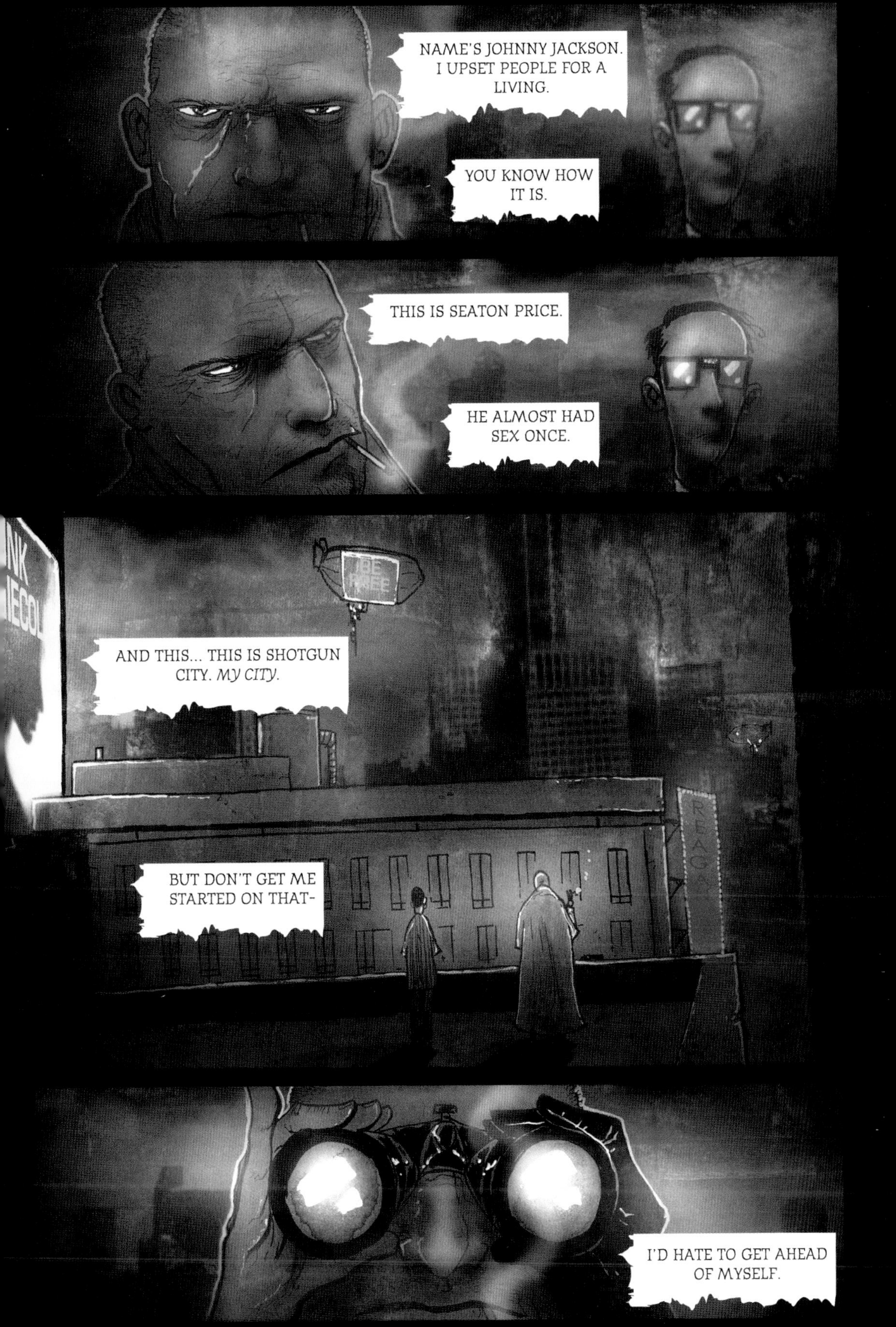
NAME'S JOHNNY JACKSON. I UPSET PEOPLE FOR A LIVING.
YOU KNOW HOW IT IS.
THIS IS SEATON PRICE.
HE ALMOST HAD SEX ONCE.
BE FREE
AND THIS... THIS IS SHOTGUN CITY. *MY CITY*.
BUT DON'T GET ME STARTED ON THAT-
I'D HATE TO GET AHEAD OF MYSELF.

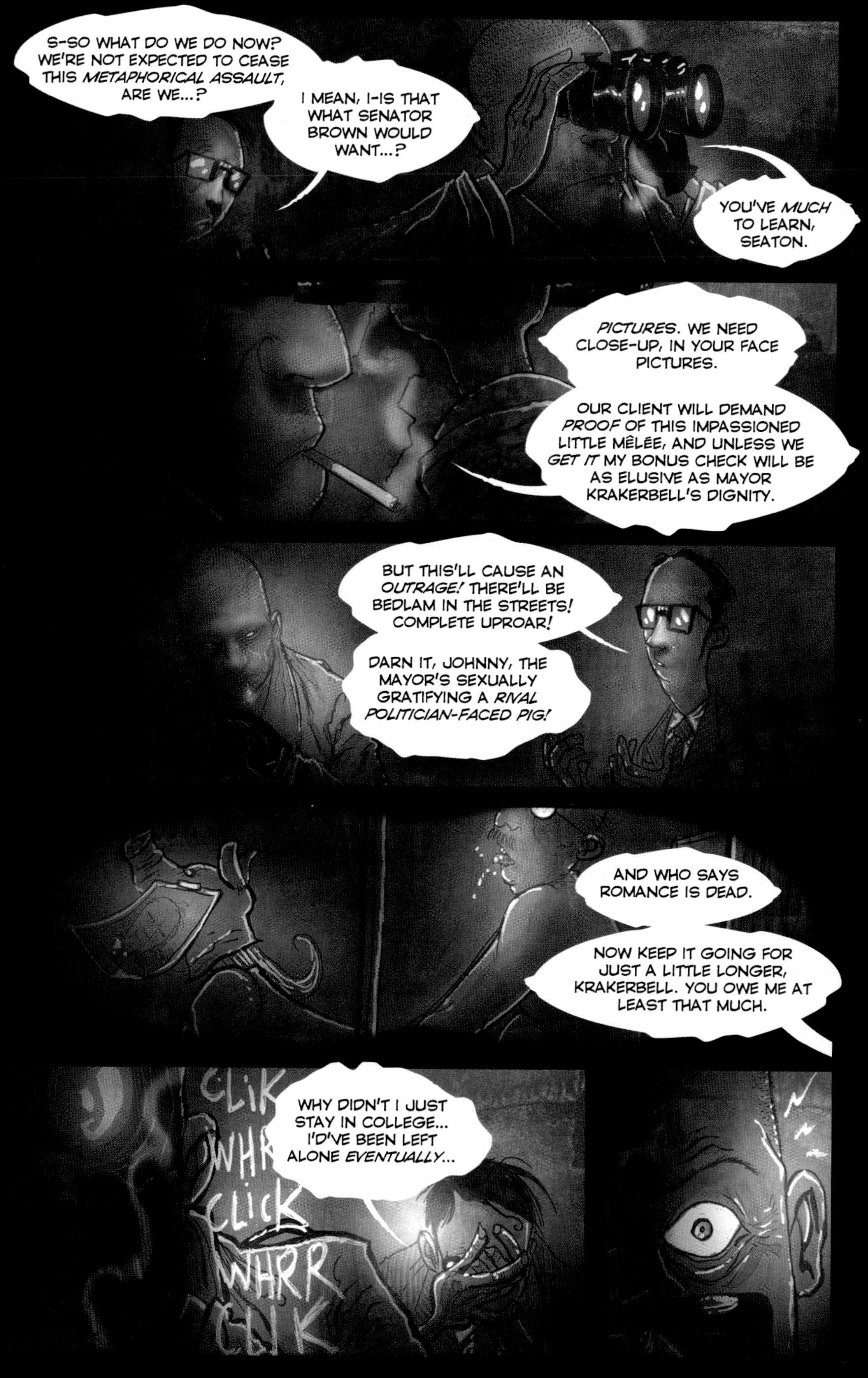
S-SO WHAT DO WE DO NOW? WE'RE NOT EXPECTED TO CEASE THIS *METAPHORICAL ASSAULT*, ARE WE...?
I MEAN, I-IS THAT WHAT SENATOR BROWN WOULD WANT...?
YOU'VE *MUCH* TO LEARN, SEATON.
PICTURES. WE NEED CLOSE-UP, IN YOUR FACE PICTURES.
OUR CLIENT WILL DEMAND *PROOF* OF THIS IMPASSIONED LITTLE MÊLÉE, AND UNLESS WE *GET IT* MY BONUS CHECK WILL BE AS ELUSIVE AS MAYOR KRAKERBELL'S DIGNITY.
BUT THIS'LL CAUSE AN *OUTRAGE!* THERE'LL BE BEDLAM IN THE STREETS! COMPLETE UPROAR!
DARN IT, JOHNNY, THE MAYOR'S SEXUALLY GRATIFYING A *RIVAL POLITICIAN-FACED PIG!*
AND WHO SAYS ROMANCE IS DEAD.
NOW KEEP IT GOING FOR JUST A LITTLE LONGER, KRAKERBELL. YOU OWE ME AT LEAST THAT MUCH.
CLIK
WHRR
CLICK
WHRR
CLIK
WHY DIDN'T I JUST STAY IN COLLEGE... I'D'VE BEEN LEFT ALONE *EVENTUALLY*...

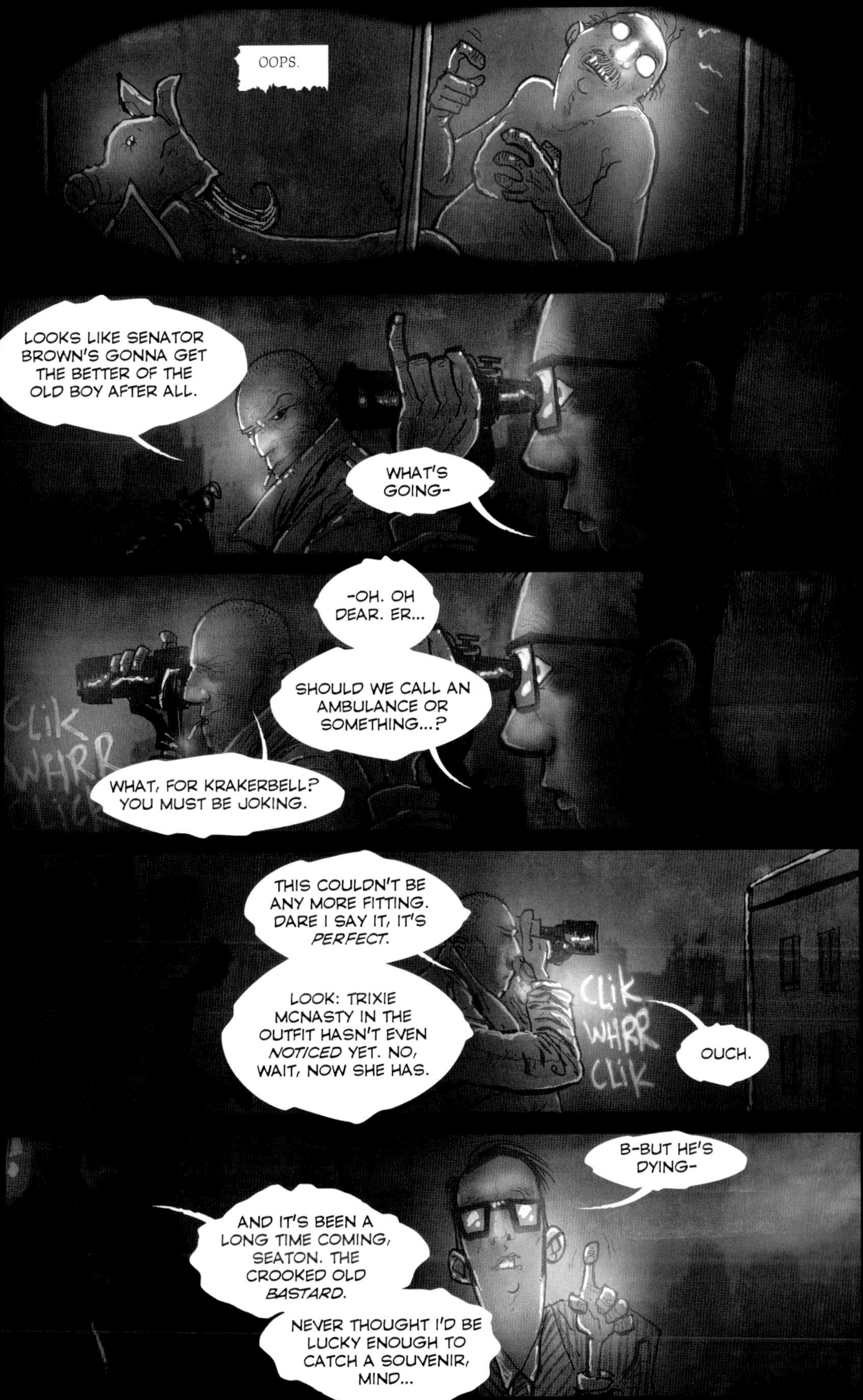
OOPS.
LOOKS LIKE SENATOR BROWN'S GONNA GET THE BETTER OF THE OLD BOY AFTER ALL.
WHAT'S GOING-
-OH. OH DEAR. ER...
SHOULD WE CALL AN AMBULANCE OR SOMETHING...?
CLIK WHRR
WHAT, FOR KRAKERBELL? YOU MUST BE JOKING.
THIS COULDN'T BE ANY MORE FITTING. DARE I SAY IT, IT'S *PERFECT*.
LOOK: TRIXIE MCNASTY IN THE OUTFIT HASN'T EVEN *NOTICED* YET. NO, WAIT, NOW SHE HAS.
CLIK WHRR CLIK
OUCH.
B-BUT HE'S DYING-
AND IT'S BEEN A LONG TIME COMING, SEATON. THE CROOKED OLD *BASTARD*.
NEVER THOUGHT I'D BE LUCKY ENOUGH TO CATCH A SOUVENIR, MIND...

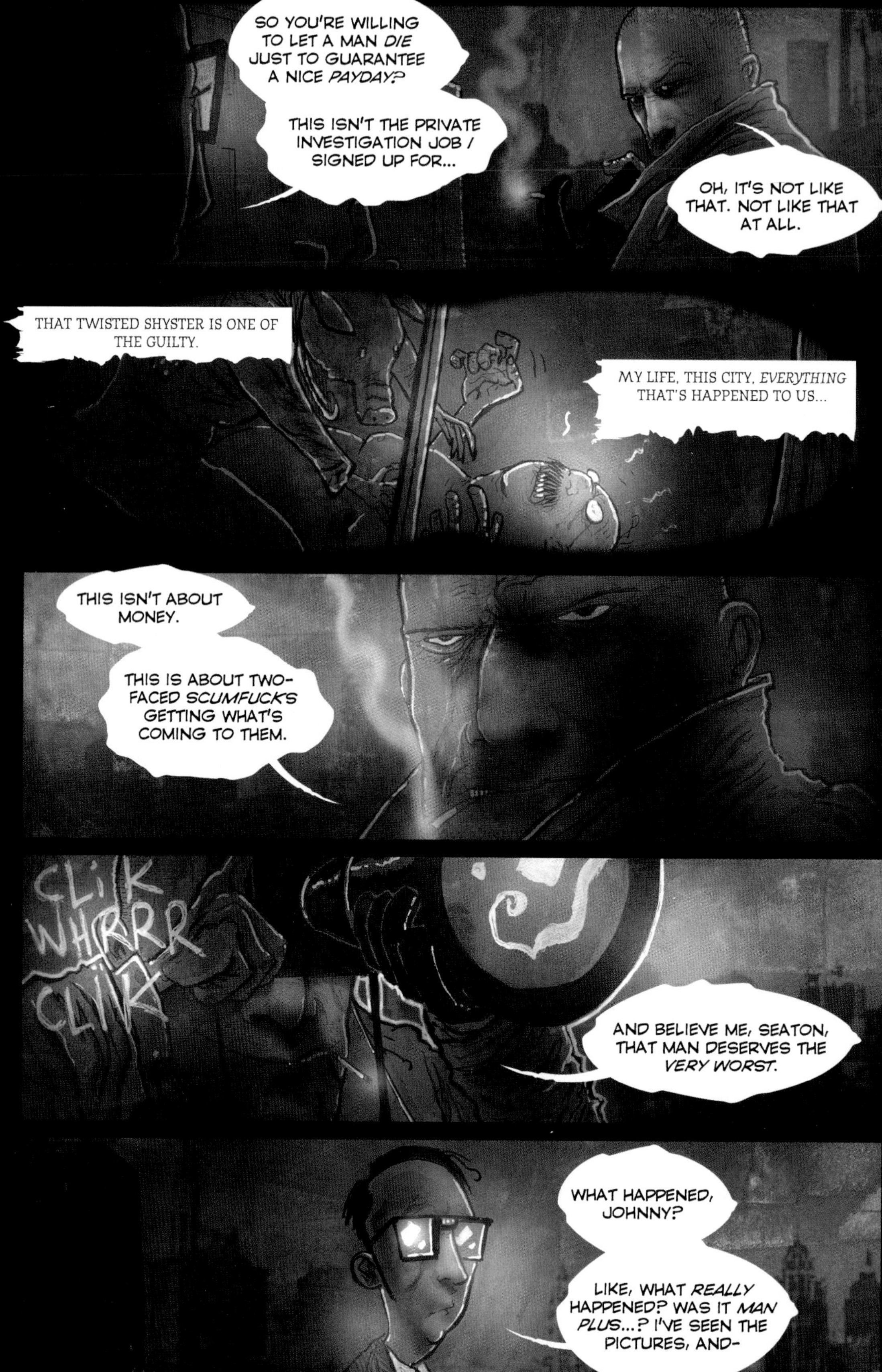

SO YOU'RE WILLING TO LET A MAN *DIE* JUST TO GUARANTEE A NICE *PAYDAY?*
THIS ISN'T THE PRIVATE INVESTIGATION JOB I SIGNED UP FOR...
OH, IT'S NOT LIKE THAT. NOT LIKE THAT AT ALL.
THAT TWISTED SHYSTER IS ONE OF THE GUILTY.
MY LIFE, THIS CITY, *EVERYTHING* THAT'S HAPPENED TO US...
THIS ISN'T ABOUT MONEY.
THIS IS ABOUT TWO-FACED *SCUMFUCKS* GETTING WHAT'S COMING TO THEM.
CLIK
WHRRR
CLIK
AND BELIEVE ME, SEATON, THAT MAN DESERVES THE *VERY WORST*.
WHAT HAPPENED, JOHNNY?
LIKE, WHAT *REALLY* HAPPENED? WAS IT *MAN PLUS*...? I'VE SEEN THE PICTURES, AND-

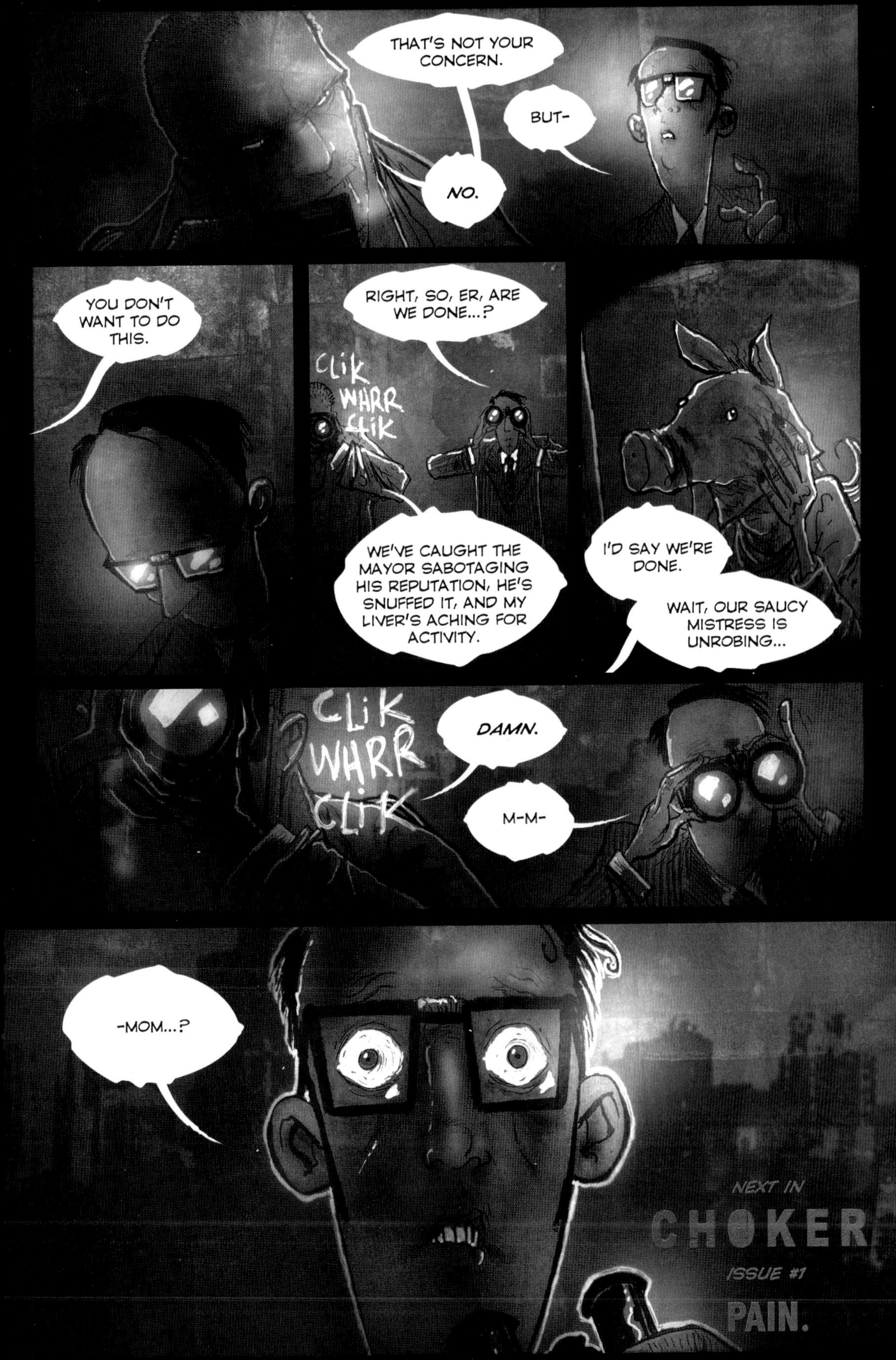
THAT'S NOT YOUR CONCERN.
BUT-
NO.
YOU DON'T WANT TO DO THIS.
RIGHT, SO, ER, ARE WE DONE...?
CLIK
WHRR
CLIK
WE'VE CAUGHT THE MAYOR SABOTAGING HIS REPUTATION, HE'S SNUFFED IT, AND MY LIVER'S ACHING FOR ACTIVITY.
I'D SAY WE'RE DONE.
WAIT, OUR SAUCY MISTRESS IS UNROBING...
CLIK
WHRR
CLIK
DAMN.
M-M-
-MOM...?
NEXT IN
CHOKER
ISSUE #1
PAIN.

EEEEE

--Oh?

Story:
Jamie S. Rich

Coloring:
Laura Allred

Art: Mike Allred
and Dave Johnson

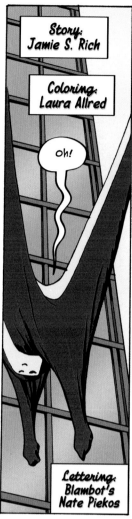

Oh!

Lettering:
Blambot's
Nate Piekos

OH!

HO!

POP

NO WORRIES, MISS, I'VE GOT YOU.

Starring
Mr. G...

NOT SO FAST THERE! DON'T SAY IT!

9m:

"Who Sell Out? You Sell Out!"

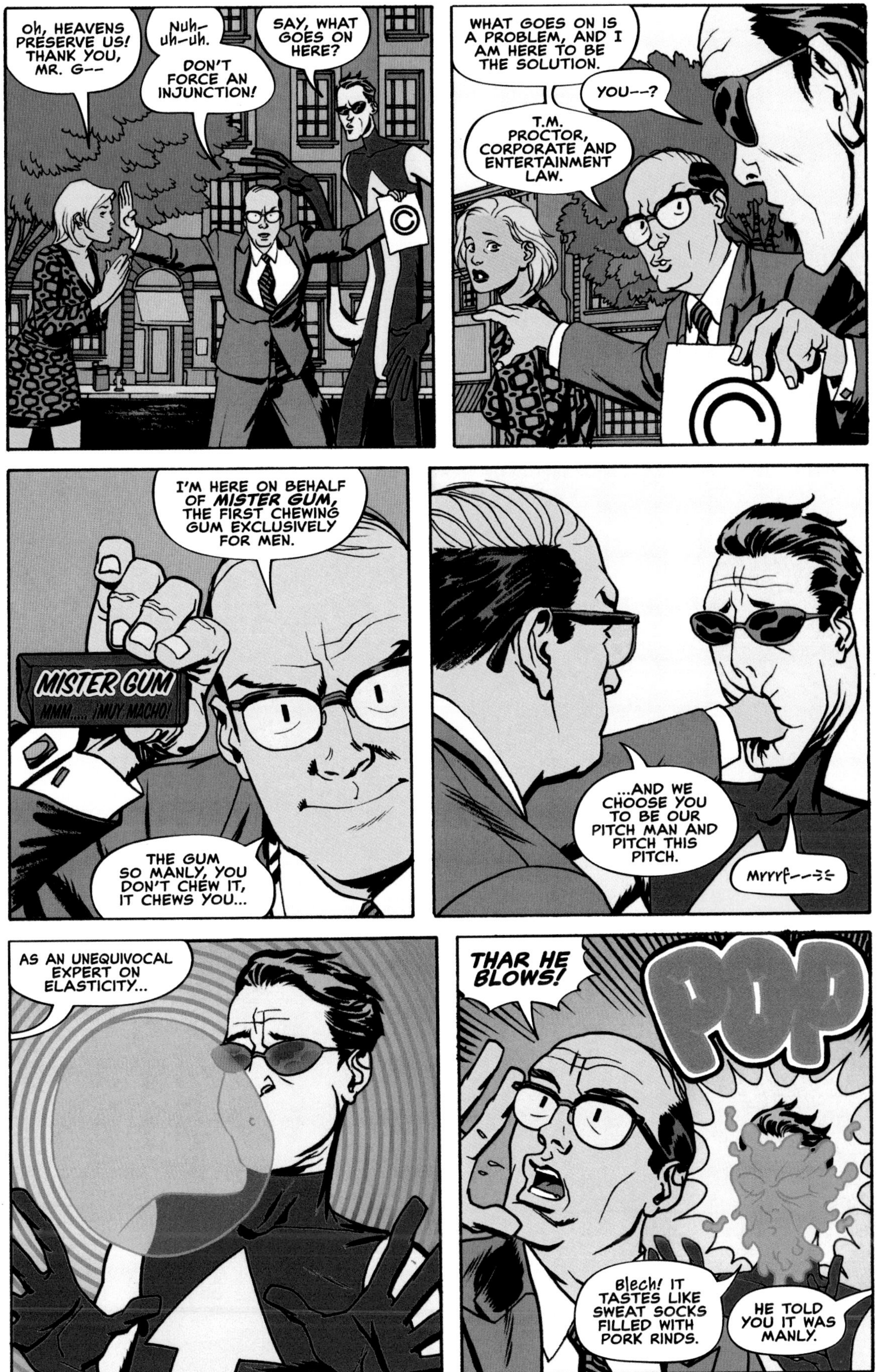
Oh, HEAVENS PRESERVE US! THANK YOU, MR. G--
Nuh-uh-uh.
DON'T FORCE AN INJUNCTION!
SAY, WHAT GOES ON HERE?
WHAT GOES ON IS A PROBLEM, AND I AM HERE TO BE THE SOLUTION.
YOU--?
T.M. PROCTOR, CORPORATE AND ENTERTAINMENT LAW.
I'M HERE ON BEHALF OF MISTER GUM, THE FIRST CHEWING GUM EXCLUSIVELY FOR MEN.
MISTER GUM
MMM.... ¡MUY MACHO!
THE GUM SO MANLY, YOU DON'T CHEW IT, IT CHEWS YOU...
...AND WE CHOOSE YOU TO BE OUR PITCH MAN AND PITCH THIS PITCH.
Mrrrf--
AS AN UNEQUIVOCAL EXPERT ON ELASTICITY...
THAR HE BLOWS!
POP
Blech! IT TASTES LIKE SWEAT SOCKS FILLED WITH PORK RINDS.
HE TOLD YOU IT WAS MANLY.

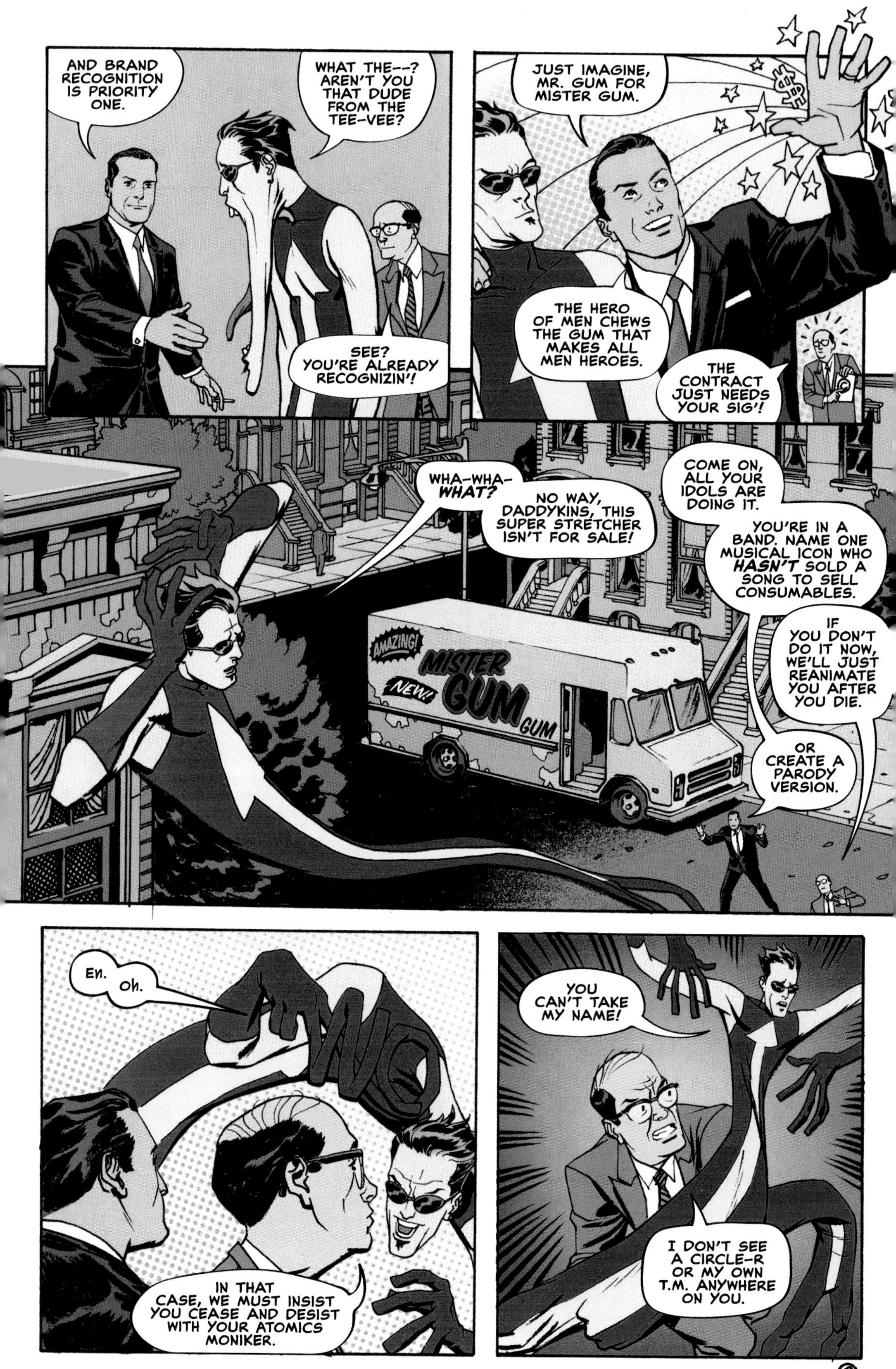
AND BRAND RECOGNITION IS PRIORITY ONE.
WHAT THE--? AREN'T YOU THAT DUDE FROM THE TEE-VEE?
SEE? YOU'RE ALREADY RECOGNIZIN'!
JUST IMAGINE, MR. GUM FOR MISTER GUM.
THE HERO OF MEN CHEWS THE GUM THAT MAKES ALL MEN HEROES.
THE CONTRACT JUST NEEDS YOUR SIG'!
WHA-WHA-WHAT?
NO WAY, DADDYKINS, THIS SUPER STRETCHER ISN'T FOR SALE!
AMAZING!
NEW!
MISTER GUM GUM
COME ON, ALL YOUR IDOLS ARE DOING IT.
YOU'RE IN A BAND. NAME ONE MUSICAL ICON WHO HASN'T SOLD A SONG TO SELL CONSUMABLES.
IF YOU DON'T DO IT NOW, WE'LL JUST REANIMATE YOU AFTER YOU DIE.
OR CREATE A PARODY VERSION.
En.
Oh.
NO
IN THAT CASE, WE MUST INSIST YOU CEASE AND DESIST WITH YOUR ATOMICS MONIKER.
YOU CAN'T TAKE MY NAME!
I DON'T SEE A CIRCLE-R OR MY OWN T.M. ANYWHERE ON YOU.

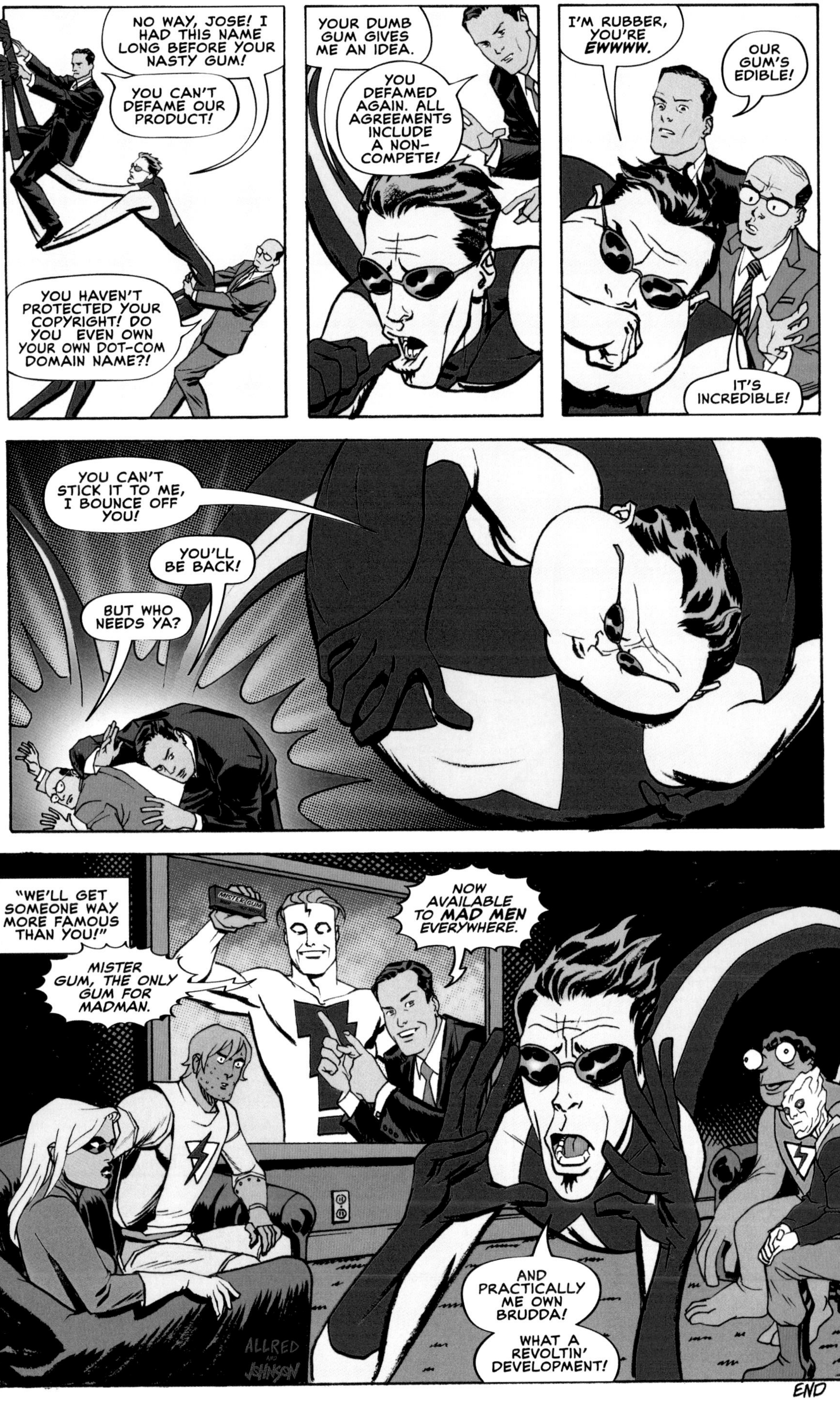
NO WAY, JOSE! I HAD THIS NAME LONG BEFORE YOUR NASTY GUM!
YOU CAN'T DEFAME OUR PRODUCT!
YOU HAVEN'T PROTECTED YOUR COPYRIGHT! DO YOU EVEN OWN YOUR OWN DOT-COM DOMAIN NAME?!
YOUR DUMB GUM GIVES ME AN IDEA.
YOU DEFAMED AGAIN. ALL AGREEMENTS INCLUDE A NON-COMPETE!
I'M RUBBER, YOU'RE *EWWWW.*
OUR GUM'S EDIBLE!
IT'S INCREDIBLE!
YOU CAN'T STICK IT TO ME, I BOUNCE OFF YOU!
YOU'LL BE BACK!
BUT WHO NEEDS YA?
"WE'LL GET SOMEONE WAY MORE FAMOUS THAN YOU!"
MISTER GUM
NOW AVAILABLE TO **MAD MEN** EVERYWHERE.
MISTER GUM, THE ONLY GUM FOR MADMAN.
AND PRACTICALLY ME OWN BRUDDA!
WHAT A REVOLTIN' DEVELOPMENT!
ALLRED AND JOHNSON

END

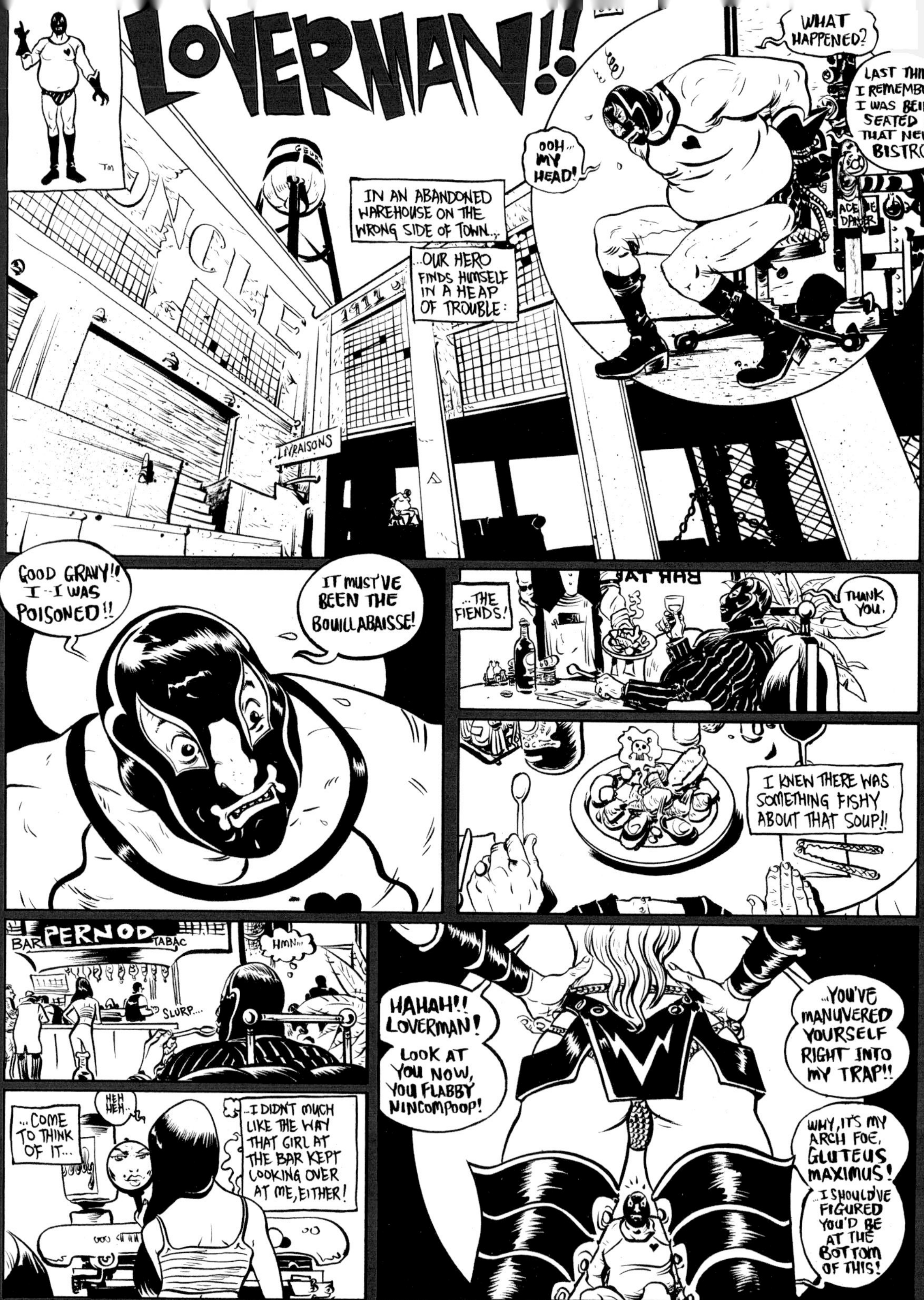
LOVERMAN!!
TM
IN AN ABANDONED WAREHOUSE ON THE WRONG SIDE OF TOWN...
...OUR HERO FINDS HIMSELF IN A HEAP OF TROUBLE:
LIVRAISONS
OOH... MY HEAD!
WHAT HAPPENED?
LAST THING I REMEMBER I WAS BEING SEATED AT THAT NEW BISTRO...
GOOD GRAVY!! I-- I WAS POISONED!!
IT MUST'VE BEEN THE BOUILLABAISSE!
...THE FIENDS!
THANK YOU.
I KNEW THERE WAS SOMETHING FISHY ABOUT THAT SOUP!!
BAR PERNOD TABAC
HMN...
SLURP...
...COME TO THINK OF IT...
HEH HEH...
...I DIDN'T MUCH LIKE THE WAY THAT GIRL AT THE BAR KEPT LOOKING OVER AT ME, EITHER!
HAHAH!! LOVERMAN!
LOOK AT YOU NOW, YOU FLABBY NINCOMPOOP!
...YOU'VE MANUVERED YOURSELF RIGHT INTO MY TRAP!!
WHY, IT'S MY ARCH FOE, GLUTEUS MAXIMUS!
...I SHOULD'VE FIGURED YOU'D BE AT THE BOTTOM OF THIS!

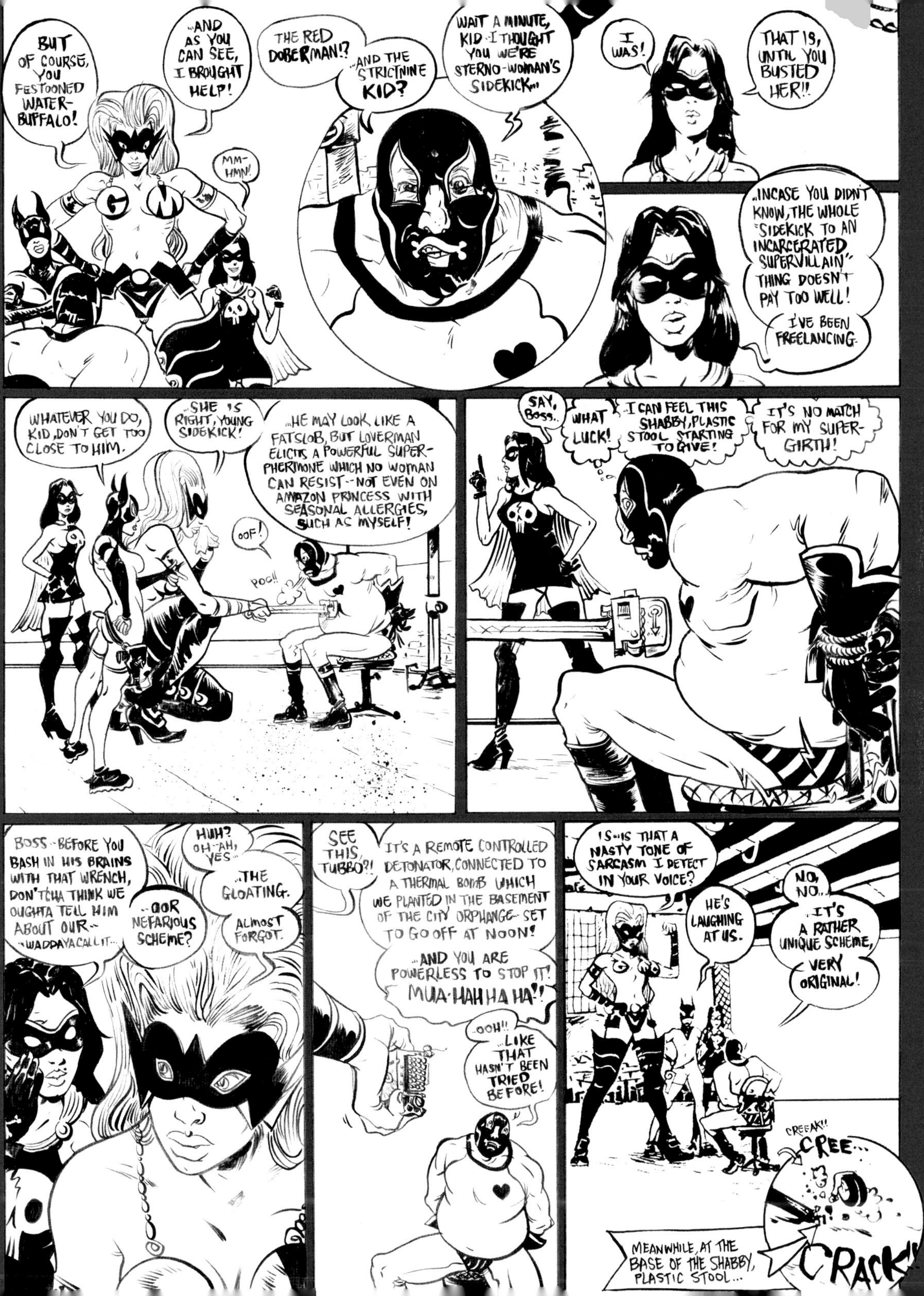
BUT OF COURSE, YOU FESTOONED WATER-BUFFALO!
...AND AS YOU CAN SEE, I BROUGHT HELP!
MM-HMN!
THE RED DOBERMAN!?
...AND THE STRICTNINE KID?
WAIT A MINUTE, KID-I THOUGHT YOU WE'RE STERNO-WOMAN'S SIDEKICK...
I WAS!
THAT IS, UNTIL YOU BUSTED HER!!
...INCASE YOU DIDN'T KNOW, THE WHOLE "SIDEKICK TO AN INCARCERATED SUPERVILLAIN" THING DOESN'T PAY TOO WELL!
I'VE BEEN FREELANCING.
WHATEVER YOU DO, KID, DON'T GET TOO CLOSE TO HIM.
...SHE IS RIGHT, YOUNG SIDEKICK!
...HE MAY LOOK LIKE A FATSLOB, BUT LOVERMAN ELICITS A POWERFUL SUPER-PHERMONE WHICH NO WOMAN CAN RESIST--NOT EVEN ON AMAZON PRINCESS WITH SEASONAL ALLERGIES, SUCH AS MYSELF!
OOF!
POC!!
SAY, BOSS..
WHAT LUCK!
...I CAN FEEL THIS SHABBY, PLASTIC STOOL STARTING TO GIVE!
IT'S NO MATCH FOR MY SUPER-GIRTH!
BOSS--BEFORE YOU BASH IN HIS BRAINS WITH THAT WRENCH, DON'T'CHA THINK WE OUGHTA TELL HIM ABOUT OUR-- ...WADDAYACALLIT...
HUH? OH--AH, YES--
...OUR NEFARIOUS SCHEME?
...THE GLOATING.
ALMOST FORGOT.
SEE THIS, TUBBO?!
IT'S A REMOTE CONTROLLED DETONATOR, CONNECTED TO A THERMAL BOMB WHICH WE PLANTED IN THE BASEMENT OF THE CITY ORPHANGE--SET TO GO OFF AT NOON!
...AND YOU ARE POWERLESS TO STOP IT! MUA-HAH HA HA!!
OOH!! ...LIKE THAT HASN'T BEEN TRIED BEFORE!
IS...IS THAT A NASTY TONE OF SARCASM I DETECT IN YOUR VOICE?
HE'S LAUGHING AT US.
NO, NO... ...IT'S A RATHER UNIQUE SCHEME, VERY ORIGINAL!
CREEAK!!
CREE...
MEANWHILE, AT THE BASE OF THE SHABBY, PLASTIC STOOL...
CRACK!

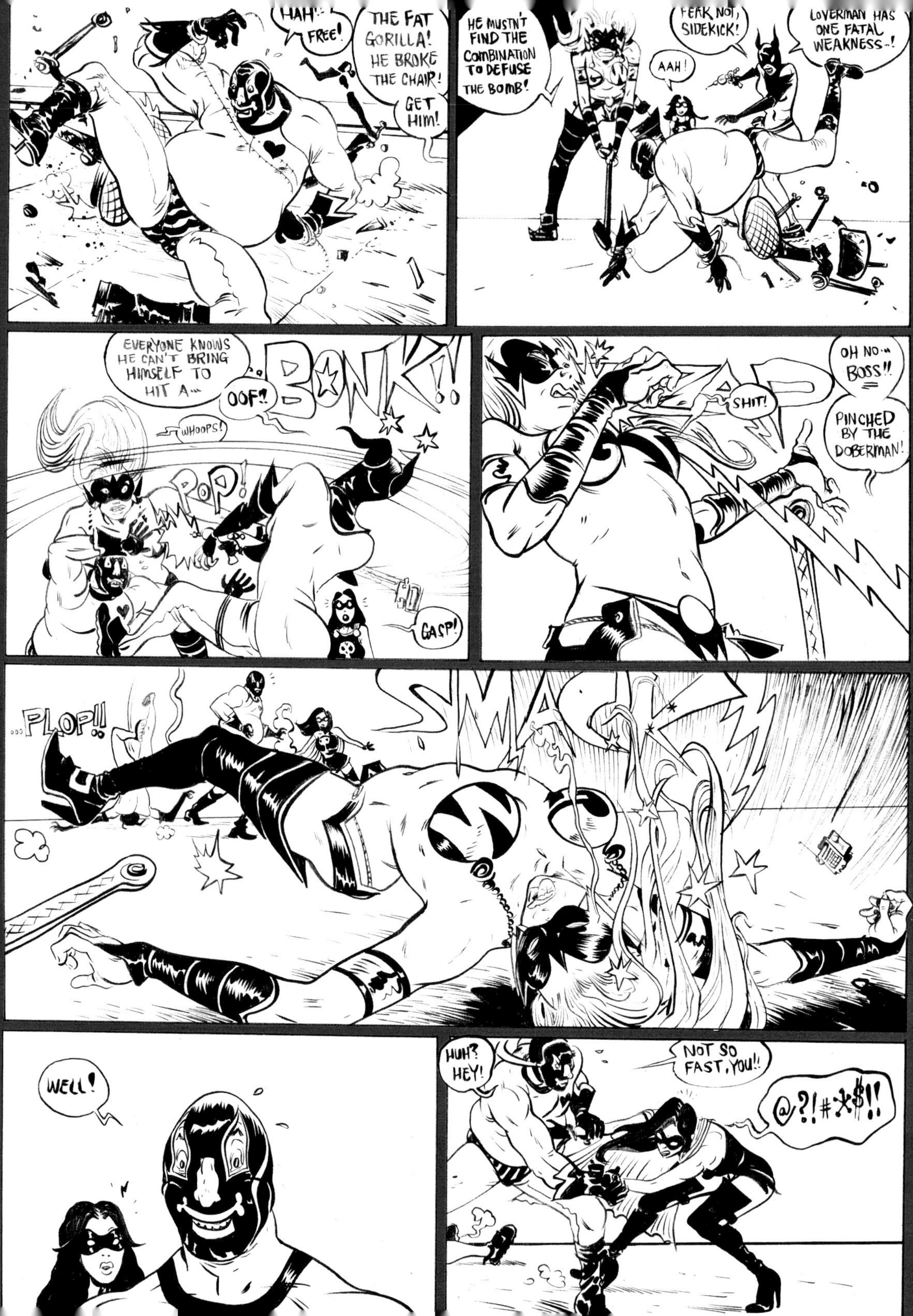
HAH!! FREE!
THE FAT GORILLA! HE BROKE THE CHAIR!
GET HIM!
HE MUSTN'T FIND THE COMBINATION TO DEFUSE THE BOMB!
FEAR NOT, SIDEKICK!
AAH!
LOVERMAN HAS ONE FATAL WEAKNESS..!
EVERYONE KNOWS HE CAN'T BRING HIMSELF TO HIT A..
OOF!!
BONK!!
WHOOPS!
POP!
GASP!
OH NO.. BOSS!!
SHIT!
PINCHED BY THE DOBERMAN!
...PLOP!!
SMACK
WELL!
HUH? HEY!
NOT SO FAST, YOU!!
@?!#✱$!!

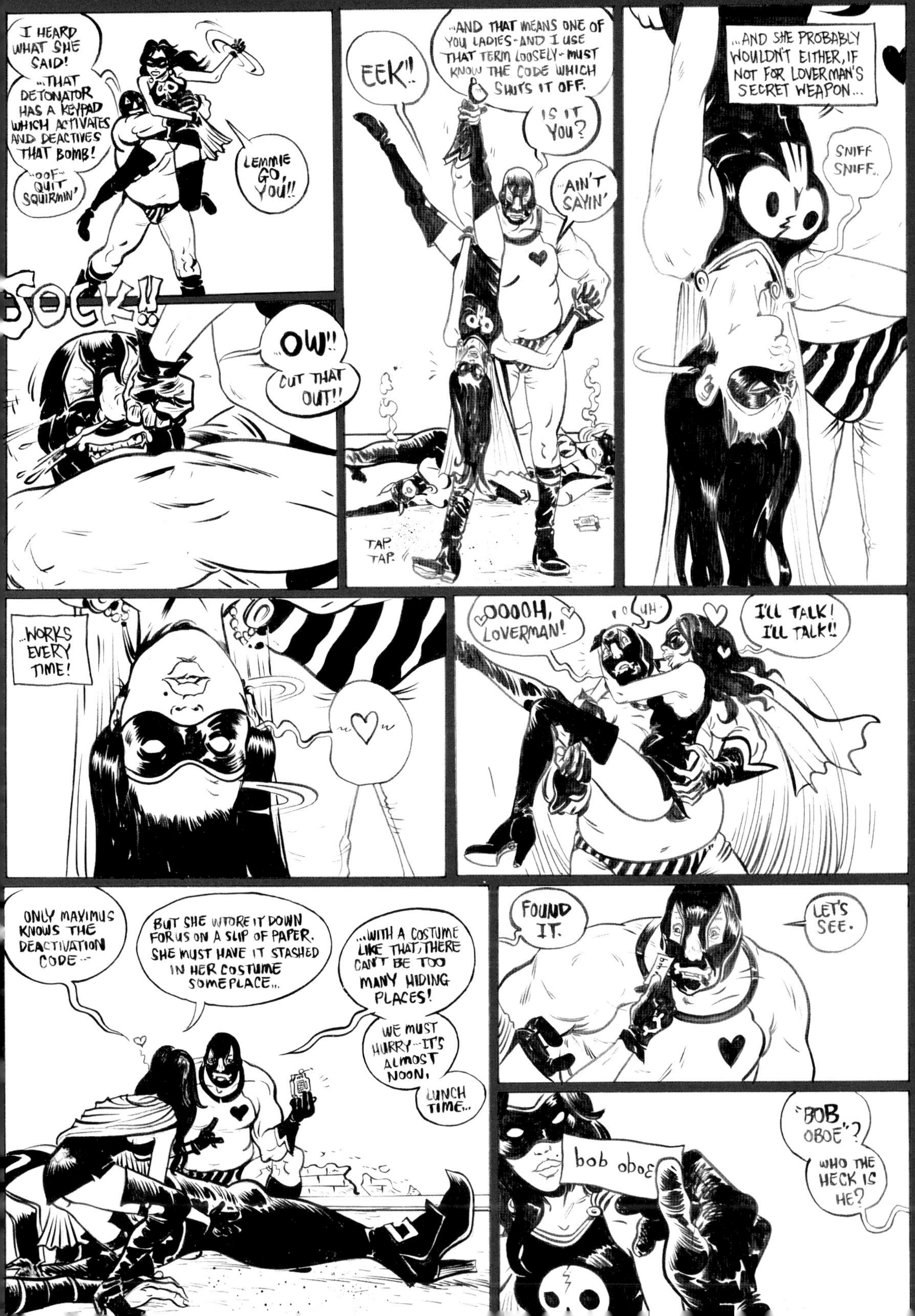
I HEARD WHAT SHE SAID!
...THAT DETONATOR HAS A KEYPAD WHICH ACTIVATES AND DEACTIVES THAT BOMB!
...OOF-- QUIT SQUIRMIN'
LEMMIE GO, YOU!!
SOCK!!
...OW!!
CUT THAT OUT!!
EEK!!
...AND THAT MEANS ONE OF YOU LADIES--AND I USE THAT TERM LOOSELY--MUST KNOW THE CODE WHICH SHUTS IT OFF.
IS IT YOU?
...AIN'T SAYIN'
TAP TAP
...AND SHE PROBABLY WOULDN'T EITHER, IF NOT FOR LOVERMAN'S SECRET WEAPON...
SNIFF SNIFF..
...WORKS EVERY TIME!
OOOOH, LOVERMAN!
UH-
I'LL TALK! I'LL TALK!!
ONLY MAXIMUS KNOWS THE DEACTIVATION CODE--
BUT SHE WROTE IT DOWN FOR US ON A SLIP OF PAPER. SHE MUST HAVE IT STASHED IN HER COSTUME SOMEPLACE...
...WITH A COSTUME LIKE THAT, THERE CAN'T BE TOO MANY HIDING PLACES!
WE MUST HURRY--IT'S ALMOST NOON.
LUNCH TIME...
FOUND IT.
LET'S SEE.
bob oboe
"BOB OBOE"?
WHO THE HECK IS HE?

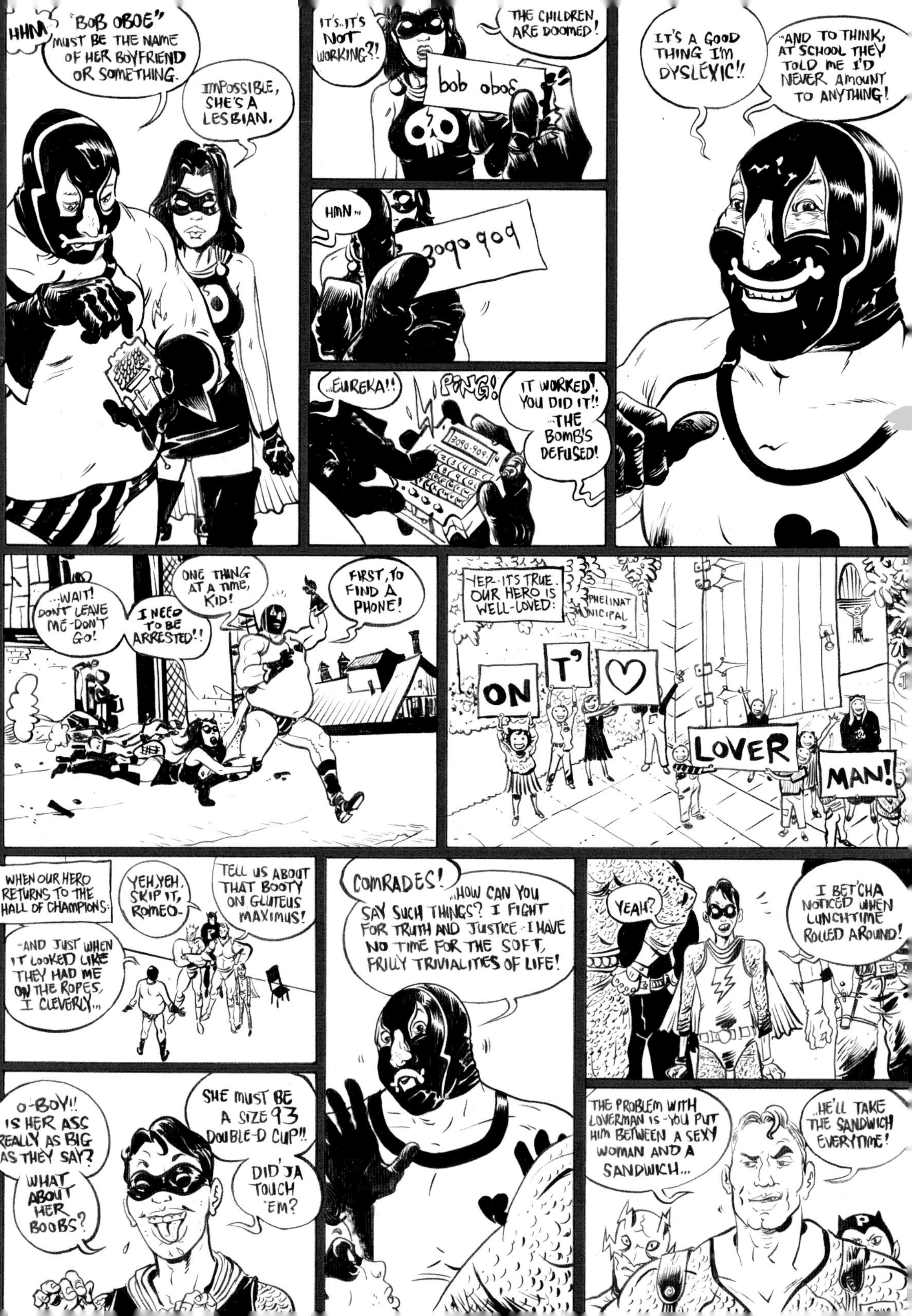
HHM..
"BOB OBOE" MUST BE THE NAME OF HER BOYFRIEND OR SOMETHING.
IMPOSSIBLE, SHE'S A LESBIAN.
IT'S.. IT'S NOT WORKING?!
THE CHILDREN ARE DOOMED!
bob oboe
HMN...
...EUREKA!!
PING!
IT WORKED! YOU DID IT!! ...THE BOMB'S DEFUSED!
IT'S A GOOD THING I'M DYSLEXIC!!
...AND TO THINK, AT SCHOOL THEY TOLD ME I'D NEVER AMOUNT TO ANYTHING!
...WAIT! DON'T LEAVE ME-DON'T GO!
I NEED TO BE ARRESTED!!
ONE THING AT A TIME, KID!
FIRST, TO FIND A PHONE!
YEP- IT'S TRUE. OUR HERO IS WELL-LOVED!
ON T' ♥ LOVER MAN!
WHEN OUR HERO RETURNS TO THE HALL OF CHAMPIONS:
...AND JUST WHEN IT LOOKED LIKE THEY HAD ME ON THE ROPES, I CLEVERLY...
YEH, YEH, SKIP IT, ROMEO-
TELL US ABOUT THAT BOOTY ON GLUTEUS MAXIMUS!
O-BOY!! IS HER ASS REALLY AS BIG AS THEY SAY?
WHAT ABOUT HER BOOBS?
SHE MUST BE A SIZE 93 DOUBLE-D CUP!!
DID'JA TOUCH 'EM?
COMRADES! ...HOW CAN YOU SAY SUCH THINGS? I FIGHT FOR TRUTH AND JUSTICE - I HAVE NO TIME FOR THE SOFT, FRILLY TRIVIALITIES OF LIFE!
YEAH?
I BET'CHA NOTICED WHEN LUNCHTIME ROLLED AROUND!
THE PROBLEM WITH LOVERMAN IS - YOU PUT HIM BETWEEN A SEXY WOMAN AND A SANDWICH...
...HE'LL TAKE THE SANDWICH EVERYTIME!

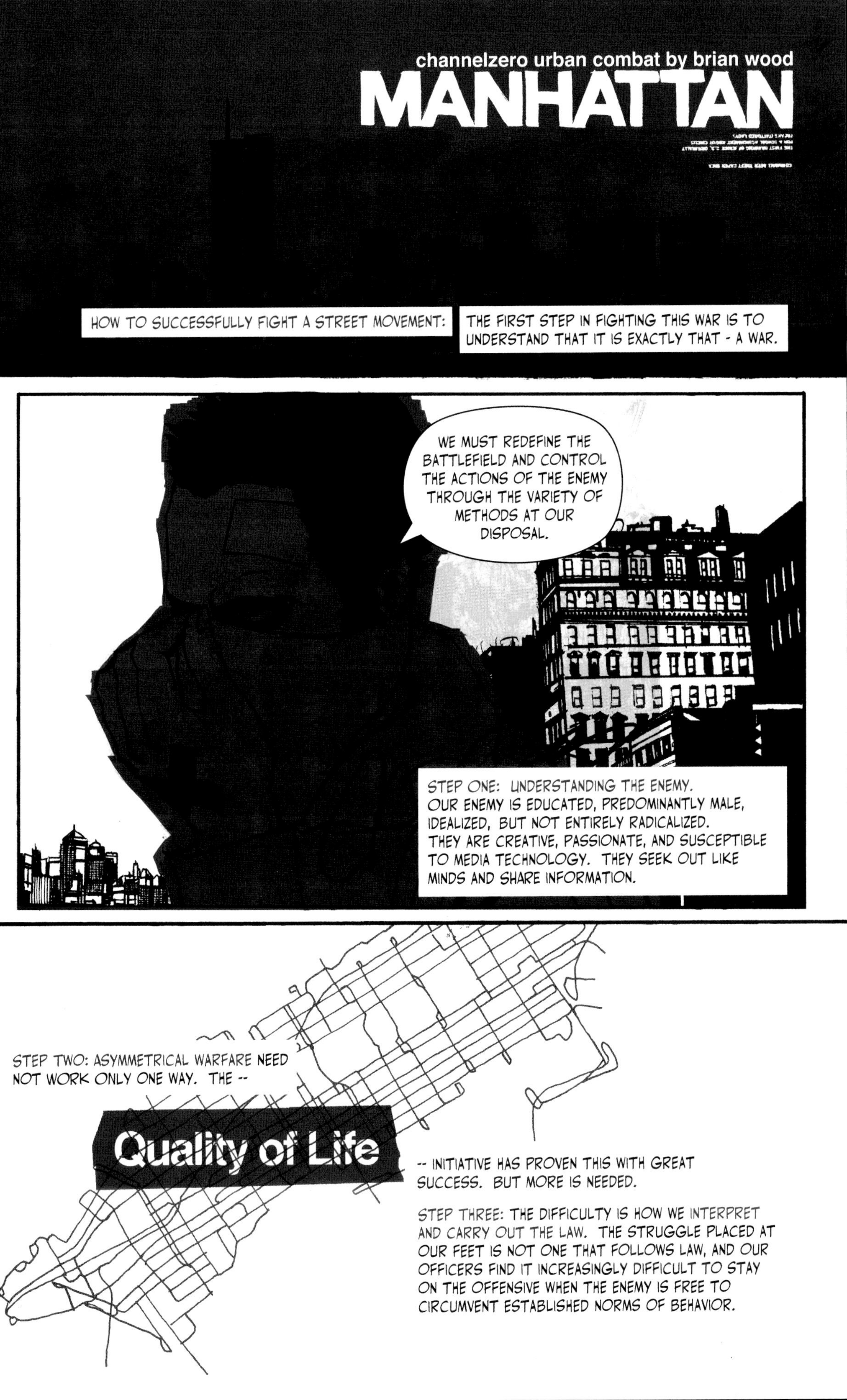
channelzero urban combat by brian wood
MANHATTAN
HOW TO SUCCESSFULLY FIGHT A STREET MOVEMENT:
THE FIRST STEP IN FIGHTING THIS WAR IS TO UNDERSTAND THAT IT IS EXACTLY THAT - A WAR.
WE MUST REDEFINE THE BATTLEFIELD AND CONTROL THE ACTIONS OF THE ENEMY THROUGH THE VARIETY OF METHODS AT OUR DISPOSAL.
STEP ONE: UNDERSTANDING THE ENEMY. OUR ENEMY IS EDUCATED, PREDOMINANTLY MALE, IDEALIZED, BUT NOT ENTIRELY RADICALIZED. THEY ARE CREATIVE, PASSIONATE, AND SUSCEPTIBLE TO MEDIA TECHNOLOGY. THEY SEEK OUT LIKE MINDS AND SHARE INFORMATION.
STEP TWO: ASYMMETRICAL WARFARE NEED NOT WORK ONLY ONE WAY. THE --
Quality of Life
-- INITIATIVE HAS PROVEN THIS WITH GREAT SUCCESS. BUT MORE IS NEEDED.
STEP THREE: THE DIFFICULTY IS HOW WE INTERPRET AND CARRY OUT THE LAW. THE STRUGGLE PLACED AT OUR FEET IS NOT ONE THAT FOLLOWS LAW, AND OUR OFFICERS FIND IT INCREASINGLY DIFFICULT TO STAY ON THE OFFENSIVE WHEN THE ENEMY IS FREE TO CIRCUMVENT ESTABLISHED NORMS OF BEHAVIOR.

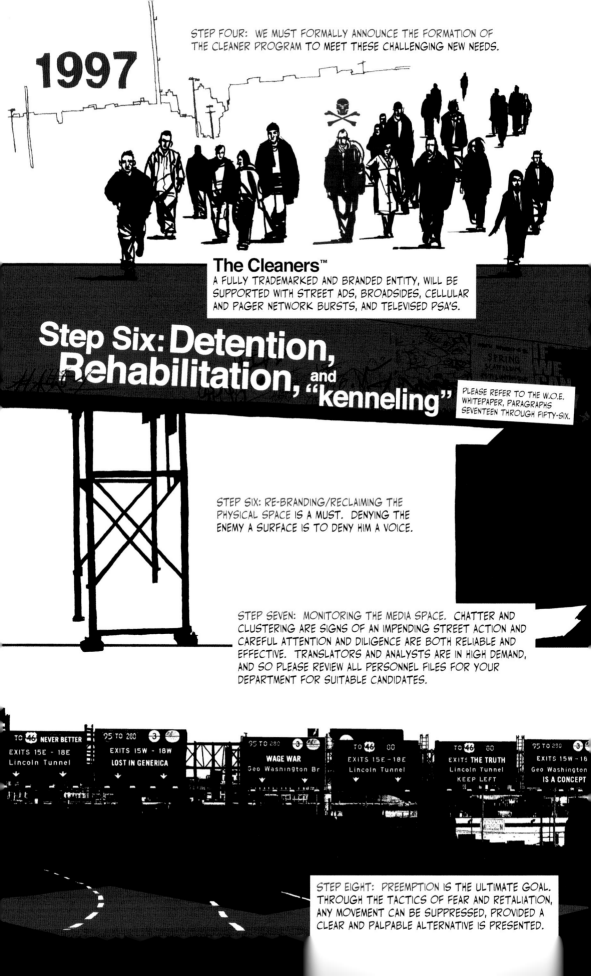

1997

STEP FOUR: WE MUST FORMALLY ANNOUNCE THE FORMATION OF THE CLEANER PROGRAM TO MEET THESE CHALLENGING NEW NEEDS.

The Cleaners™
A FULLY TRADEMARKED AND BRANDED ENTITY, WILL BE SUPPORTED WITH STREET ADS, BROADSIDES, CELLULAR AND PAGER NETWORK BURSTS, AND TELEVISED PSA'S.

Step Six: Detention, Rehabilitation, and "kenneling"

PLEASE REFER TO THE W.O.E. WHITEPAPER, PARAGRAPHS SEVENTEEN THROUGH FIFTY-SIX.

STEP SIX: RE-BRANDING/RECLAIMING THE PHYSICAL SPACE IS A MUST. DENYING THE ENEMY A SURFACE IS TO DENY HIM A VOICE.

STEP SEVEN: MONITORING THE MEDIA SPACE. CHATTER AND CLUSTERING ARE SIGNS OF AN IMPENDING STREET ACTION AND CAREFUL ATTENTION AND DILIGENCE ARE BOTH RELIABLE AND EFFECTIVE. TRANSLATORS AND ANALYSTS ARE IN HIGH DEMAND, AND SO PLEASE REVIEW ALL PERSONNEL FILES FOR YOUR DEPARTMENT FOR SUITABLE CANDIDATES.

TO 46 NEVER BETTER
EXITS 15E - 18E
Lincoln Tunnel

95 TO 280
EXITS 15W - 18W
LOST IN GENERICA

95 TO 280
WAGE WAR
Geo Washington Br

TO 46 80
EXITS 15E - 18E
Lincoln Tunnel

TO 46 80
EXITS THE TRUTH
Lincoln Tunnel
KEEP LEFT

95 TO 280
EXITS 15W - 18
Geo Washington
IS A CONCEPT

STEP EIGHT: PREEMPTION IS THE ULTIMATE GOAL. THROUGH THE TACTICS OF FEAR AND RETALIATION, ANY MOVEMENT CAN BE SUPPRESSED, PROVIDED A CLEAR AND PALPABLE ALTERNATIVE IS PRESENTED.

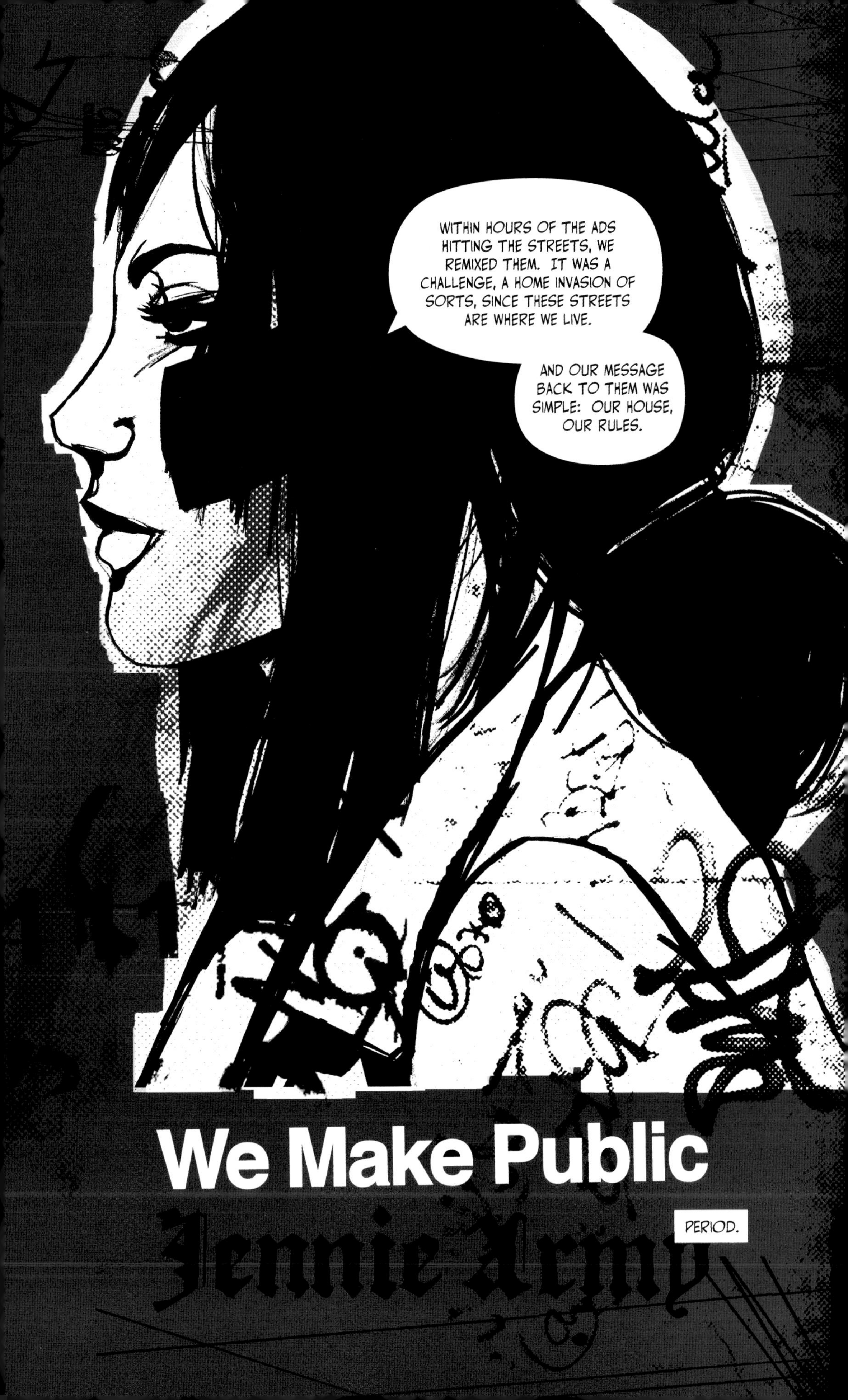

WITHIN HOURS OF THE ADS HITTING THE STREETS, WE REMIXED THEM. IT WAS A CHALLENGE, A HOME INVASION OF SORTS, SINCE THESE STREETS ARE WHERE WE LIVE.
AND OUR MESSAGE BACK TO THEM WAS SIMPLE: OUR HOUSE, OUR RULES.
We Make Public
Jennie Army
PERIOD.

THEY PUT THIS CITY IN CULTURAL LOCKDOWN.
IT'S PLASTIC, IT'S SOULLESS, IT'S THE CULTURE THEY GIVE YOU.
THE STINK OF MARKET RESEARCH AND FOCUS GROUP IS ALL OVER IT.
THE SHEEN OF DESIGN-BY-COMMITTEE REFLECTS BACK A DESPERATE AND
UGLY GRAB FOR WHAT THEY CALL MASS APPEAL, MAXIMUM MARKET PENETRATION.
MIDDLE OF THE ROAD WITH A HIGH PRO GLOW. WE CHOKE ON IT LIKE THE POLLUTION IT IS.

Is it too much to want something different?

Something more?

Something better?

CAN WE TAKE A CHANCE? CAN WE SHOW YOU WHAT WE GOT?

CAN WE NOT SHAKE OFF THE CORPORATE COLLAR AND CREATE FOR THE INDIVIDUAL, FOR THE PURE ACT OF CREATING SOMETHING THAT MAKES THE WORLD BETTER, AND NOT JUST A FEW PEOPLE RICHER?

CAN WE BE RISKY? CAN WE USE OUR BRAINS AND OUR HANDS?

Can you back off?
Can you respect our intelligence? Can you respect our ability? Our community? Our humanity?

FROM THE INFAMOUS VANDAL SQUAD TO THE RUMORED CLEANERS, WE'VE EVADED AND ADAPTED, ALWAYS FINDING OUR CANVAS, ALWAYS POOLING INFORMATION AND COMMUNICATING. YOU CALL US YOUR ENEMY, YOU SUGGEST WE'RE MERELY CRIMINALS, MALCONTENTS, DISSIDENTS, NON-CONFORMISTS.

PROTECT

SURVIVE

WE'RE IDEALISTS, OPTIMISTS, ARTISTS AND INVENTORS. WE'RE LOOKING FORWARD, NOT BACK. WE SEEK TO OPEN DOORS, NOT LOCK THEM BEHIND THE INDIVIDUAL. WE'RE FREEDOM FIGHTERS, MARTYRS, PROPHETS AND ICONOCLASTS.

WE ALWAYS SURVIVE, WE ALWAYS SUCCEED.

TRAMPOLINE HALL

The Trampoline Hall lecture series, conceptually created by author Sheila Heti, debuted at Toronto's Cameron House in 2001. On any given evening, three lectures are delivered by speakers with no expertise whatsoever in their selected subject area. 'Free speech' barely begins to describe the content of Trampoline Hall. This speech is so free it makes illegal left turns while fishing for candy in the glove box. It skinny dips in the neighbour's pool at nine in the morning. This speech wears no pants and wouldn't know where to buy pants even if it wanted to. The results are frequently arresting, often hilarious and always delightful.

On a dark October night in 2007, we were asked, along with a whole host of super-talented Toronto comic creators, to be a part of the stenographic pool for that evening's Trampoline Hall. Leah Buckareff, Waylen Miki and Jacob Zimmer spoke of Hyperbolic Crochet, Robotism and Diverse Curiosity. We listened, we wrote, we drew.

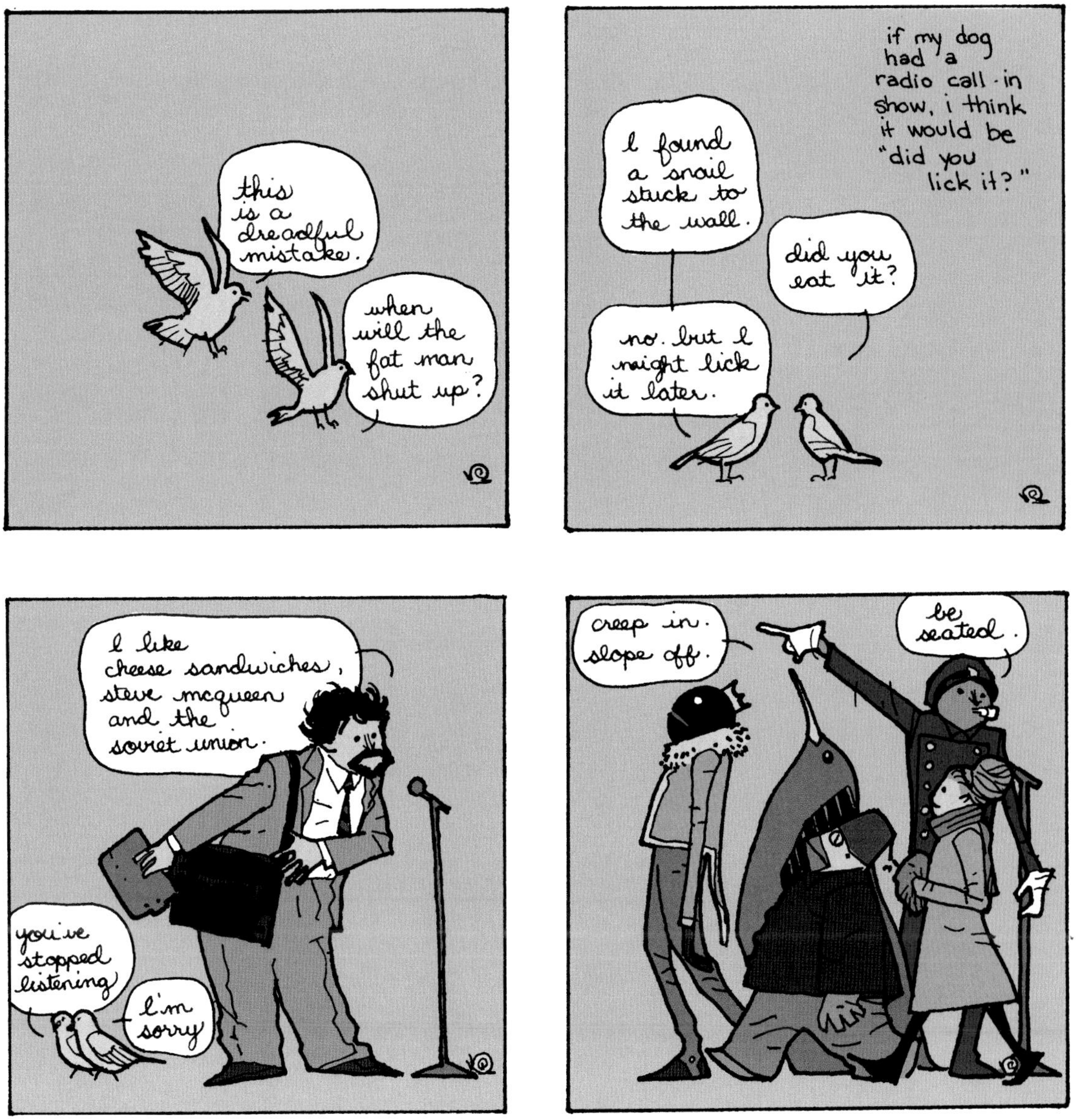
this is a dreadful mistake.
when will the fat man shut up?
if my dog had a radio call-in show, i think it would be "did you lick it?"
I found a snail stuck to the wall.
did you eat it?
no. but I might lick it later.
I like cheese sandwiches, steve mcqueen and the soviet union.
you've stopped listening
i'm sorry
creep in. slope off.
be seated.

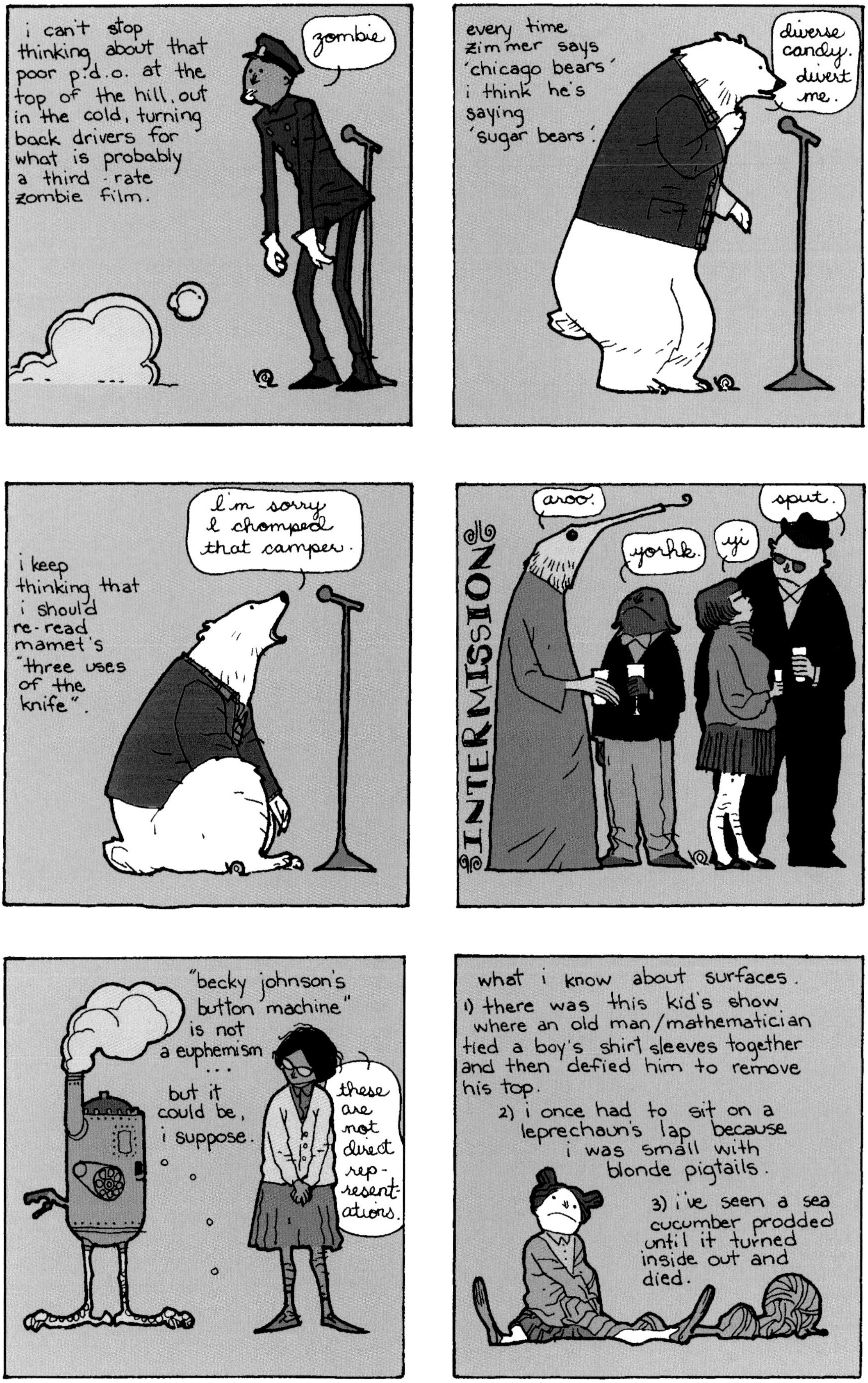
i can't stop thinking about that poor p.d.o. at the top of the hill, out in the cold, turning back drivers for what is probably a third-rate zombie film.
zombie
every time zimmer says 'chicago bears' i think he's saying 'sugar bears'.
diverse candy. divert me.
i keep thinking that i should re-read mamet's "three uses of the knife".
i'm sorry i chomped that camper.
INTERMISSION
aroo.
sput.
yorhk.
yi
"becky johnson's button machine" is not a euphemism
. . .
but it could be, i suppose.
these are not direct rep-resent-ations.
what i know about surfaces.
1) there was this kid's show where an old man/mathematician tied a boy's shirt sleeves together and then defied him to remove his top.
2) i once had to sit on a leprechaun's lap because i was small with blonde pigtails.
3) i've seen a sea cucumber prodded until it turned inside out and died.

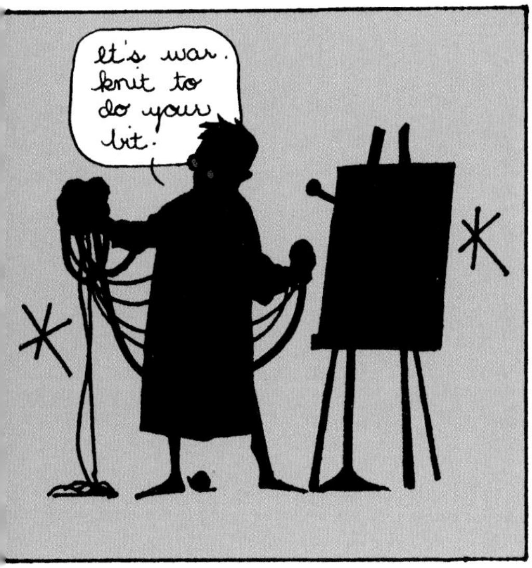
it's war. knit to do your bit.

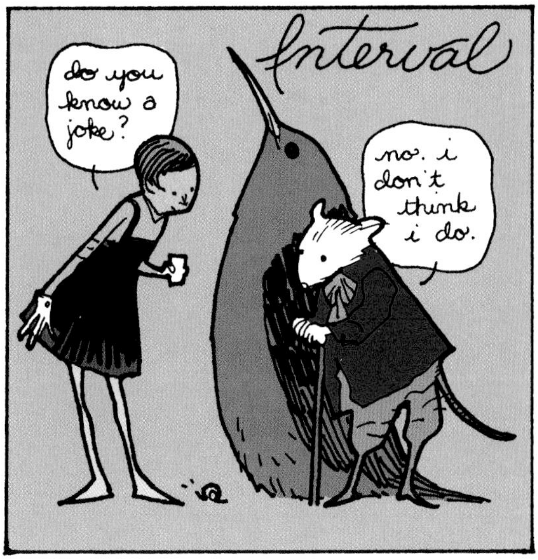
Interval
do you know a joke?
no. i don't think i do.

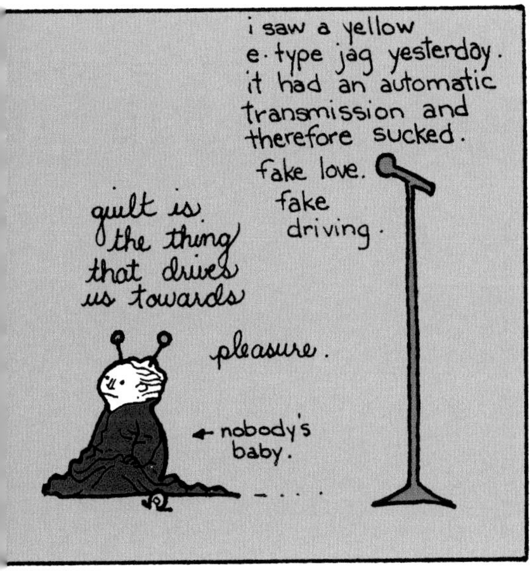
i saw a yellow e-type jag yesterday. it had an automatic transmission and therefore sucked.
fake love.
fake driving.
guilt is the thing that drives us towards
pleasure.
← nobody's baby.

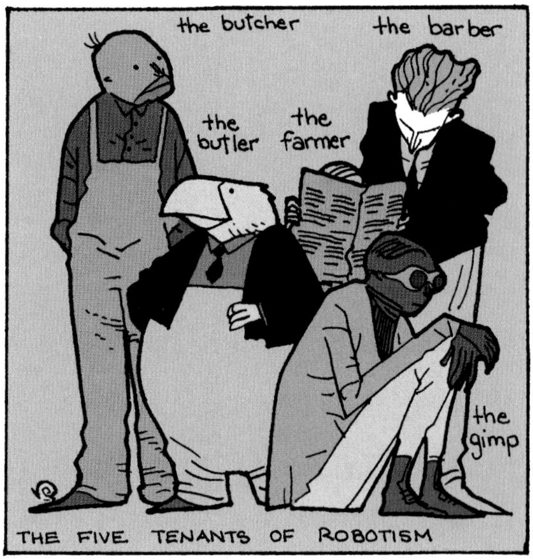
the butcher
the barber
the butler
the farmer
the gimp
THE FIVE TENANTS OF ROBOTISM

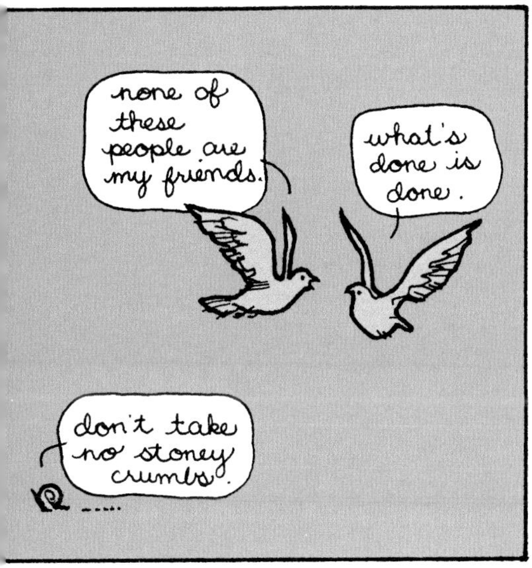
none of these people are my friends.
what's done is done.
don't take no stoney crumbs.

There's no business like the comic book business... but you've got to do something with your time, haven't you. And you could do much worse than spend some of that time perusing the following

http://www.trampolinehall.net/
http://www.sheilaheti.net/

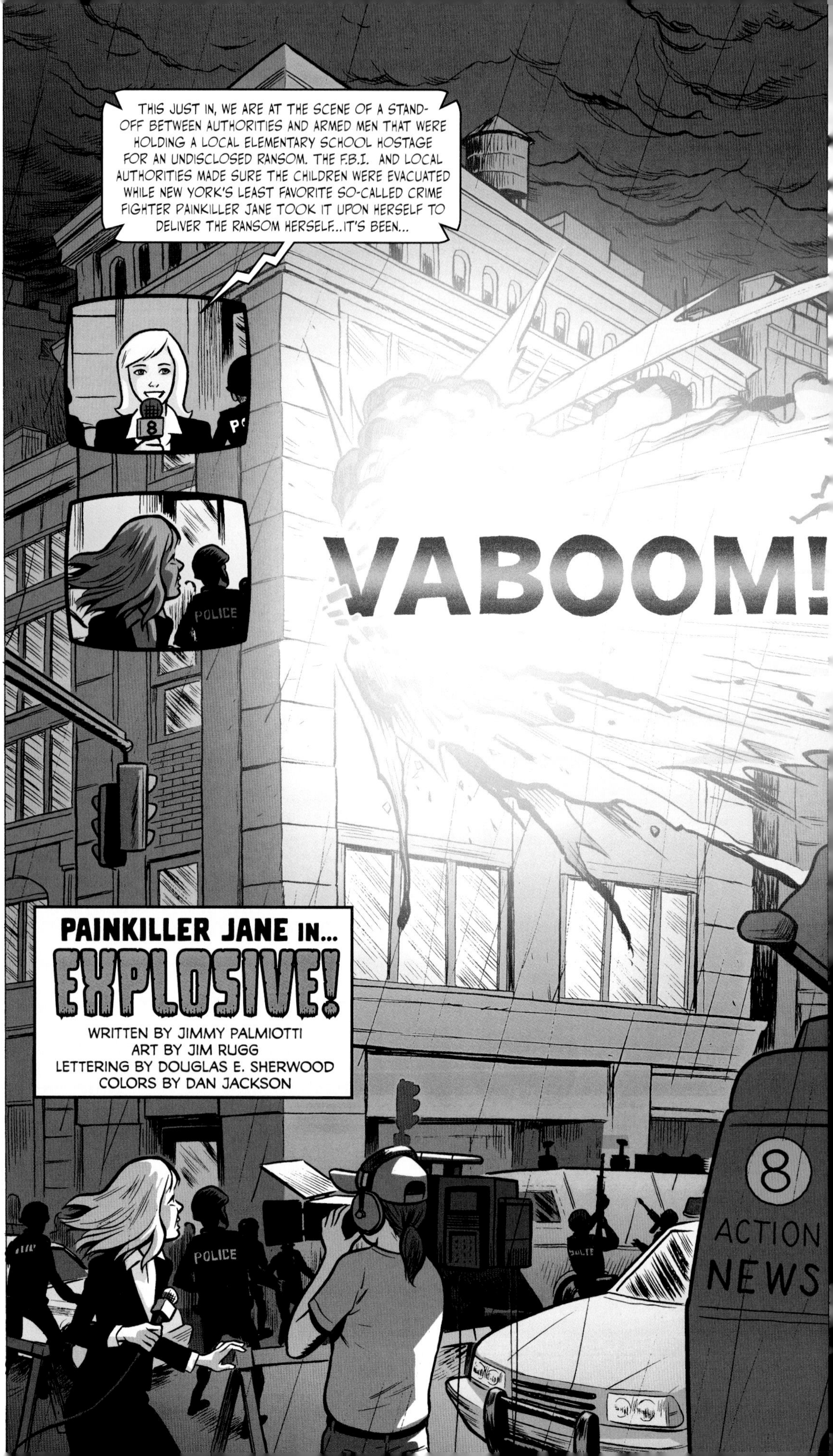
THIS JUST IN, WE ARE AT THE SCENE OF A STAND-OFF BETWEEN AUTHORITIES AND ARMED MEN THAT WERE HOLDING A LOCAL ELEMENTARY SCHOOL HOSTAGE FOR AN UNDISCLOSED RANSOM. THE F.B.I. AND LOCAL AUTHORITIES MADE SURE THE CHILDREN WERE EVACUATED WHILE NEW YORK'S LEAST FAVORITE SO-CALLED CRIME FIGHTER PAINKILLER JANE TOOK IT UPON HERSELF TO DELIVER THE RANSOM HERSELF...IT'S BEEN...
VABOOM!
PAINKILLER JANE IN...
EXPLOSIVE!
WRITTEN BY JIMMY PALMIOTTI
ART BY JIM RUGG
LETTERING BY DOUGLAS E. SHERWOOD
COLORS BY DAN JACKSON
POLICE
POLICE
8 ACTION NEWS

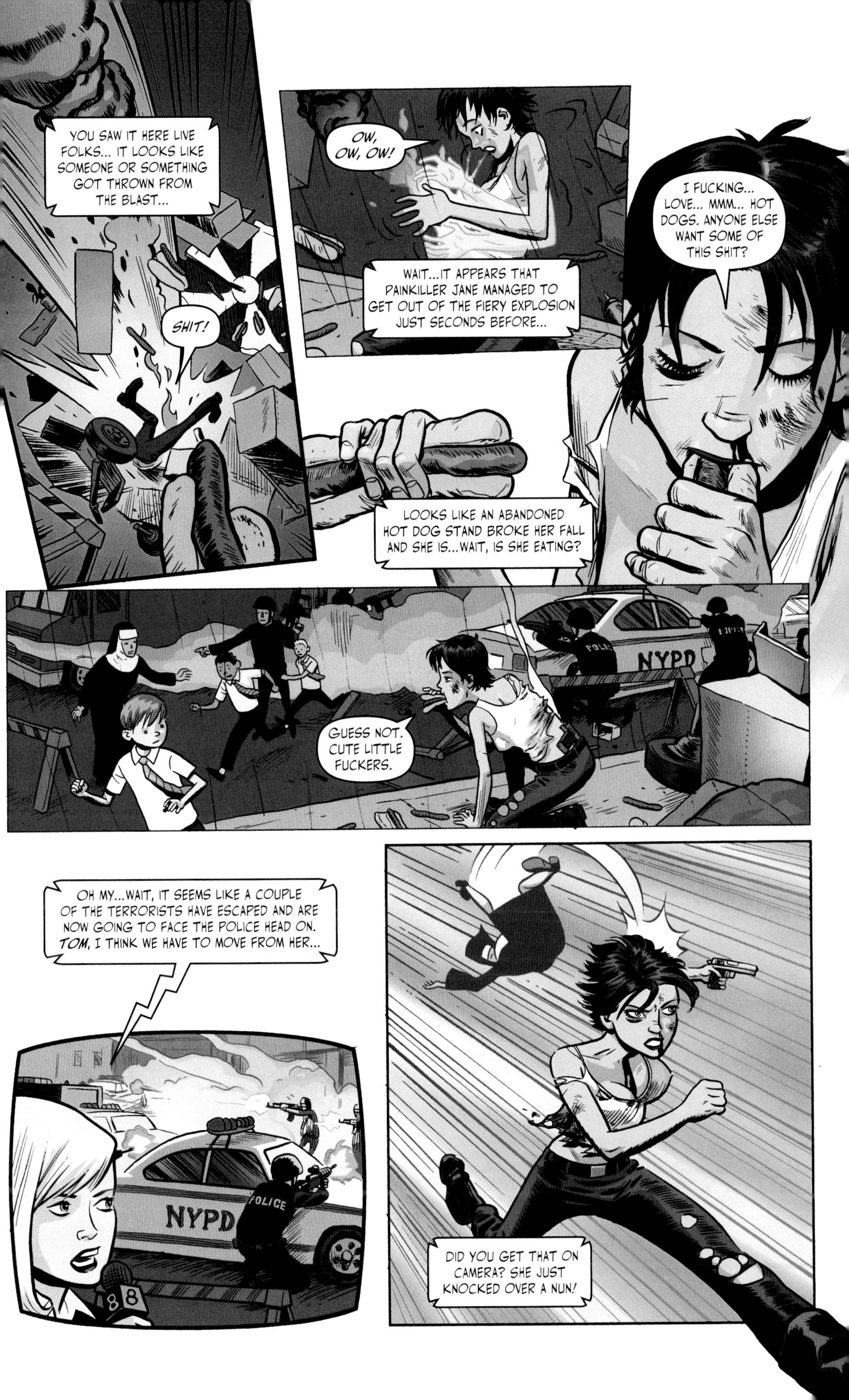
YOU SAW IT HERE LIVE FOLKS... IT LOOKS LIKE SOMEONE OR SOMETHING GOT THROWN FROM THE BLAST...
SHIT!
OW, OW, OW!
WAIT...IT APPEARS THAT PAINKILLER JANE MANAGED TO GET OUT OF THE FIERY EXPLOSION JUST SECONDS BEFORE...
I FUCKING... LOVE... MMM... HOT DOGS. ANYONE ELSE WANT SOME OF THIS SHIT?
LOOKS LIKE AN ABANDONED HOT DOG STAND BROKE HER FALL AND SHE IS...WAIT, IS SHE EATING?
NYPD
GUESS NOT. CUTE LITTLE FUCKERS.
OH MY...WAIT, IT SEEMS LIKE A COUPLE OF THE TERRORISTS HAVE ESCAPED AND ARE NOW GOING TO FACE THE POLICE HEAD ON. *TOM*, I THINK WE HAVE TO MOVE FROM HER...
NYPD
POLICE
8
DID YOU GET THAT ON CAMERA? SHE JUST KNOCKED OVER A NUN!

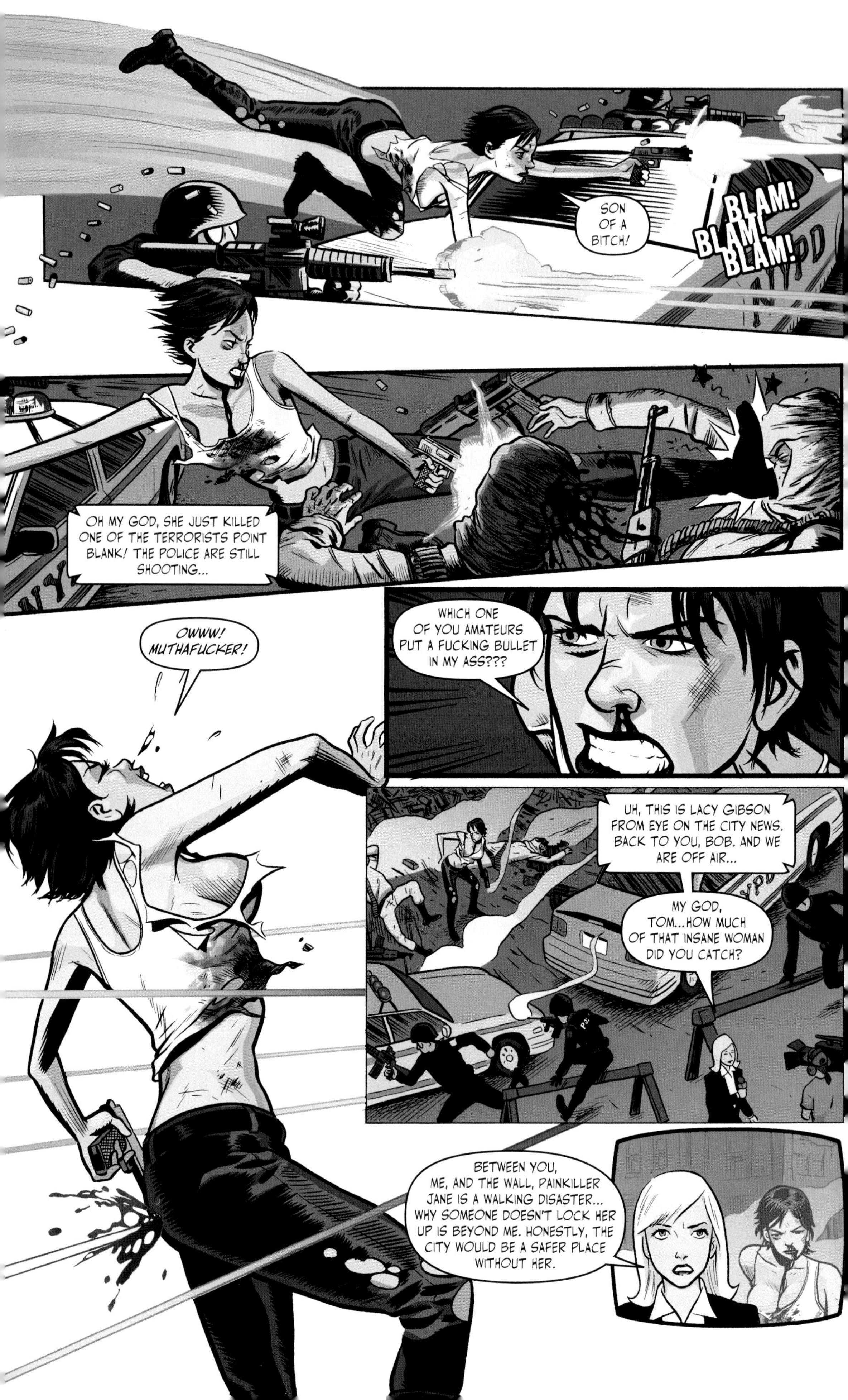
SON OF A BITCH!
BLAM! BLAM! BLAM!
OH MY GOD, SHE JUST KILLED ONE OF THE TERRORISTS POINT BLANK! THE POLICE ARE STILL SHOOTING...
OWWW! MUTHAFUCKER!
WHICH ONE OF YOU AMATEURS PUT A FUCKING BULLET IN MY ASS???
UH, THIS IS LACY GIBSON FROM EYE ON THE CITY NEWS. BACK TO YOU, BOB. AND WE ARE OFF AIR...
MY GOD, TOM...HOW MUCH OF THAT INSANE WOMAN DID YOU CATCH?
BETWEEN YOU, ME, AND THE WALL, PAINKILLER JANE IS A WALKING DISASTER... WHY SOMEONE DOESN'T LOCK HER UP IS BEYOND ME. HONESTLY, THE CITY WOULD BE A SAFER PLACE WITHOUT HER.

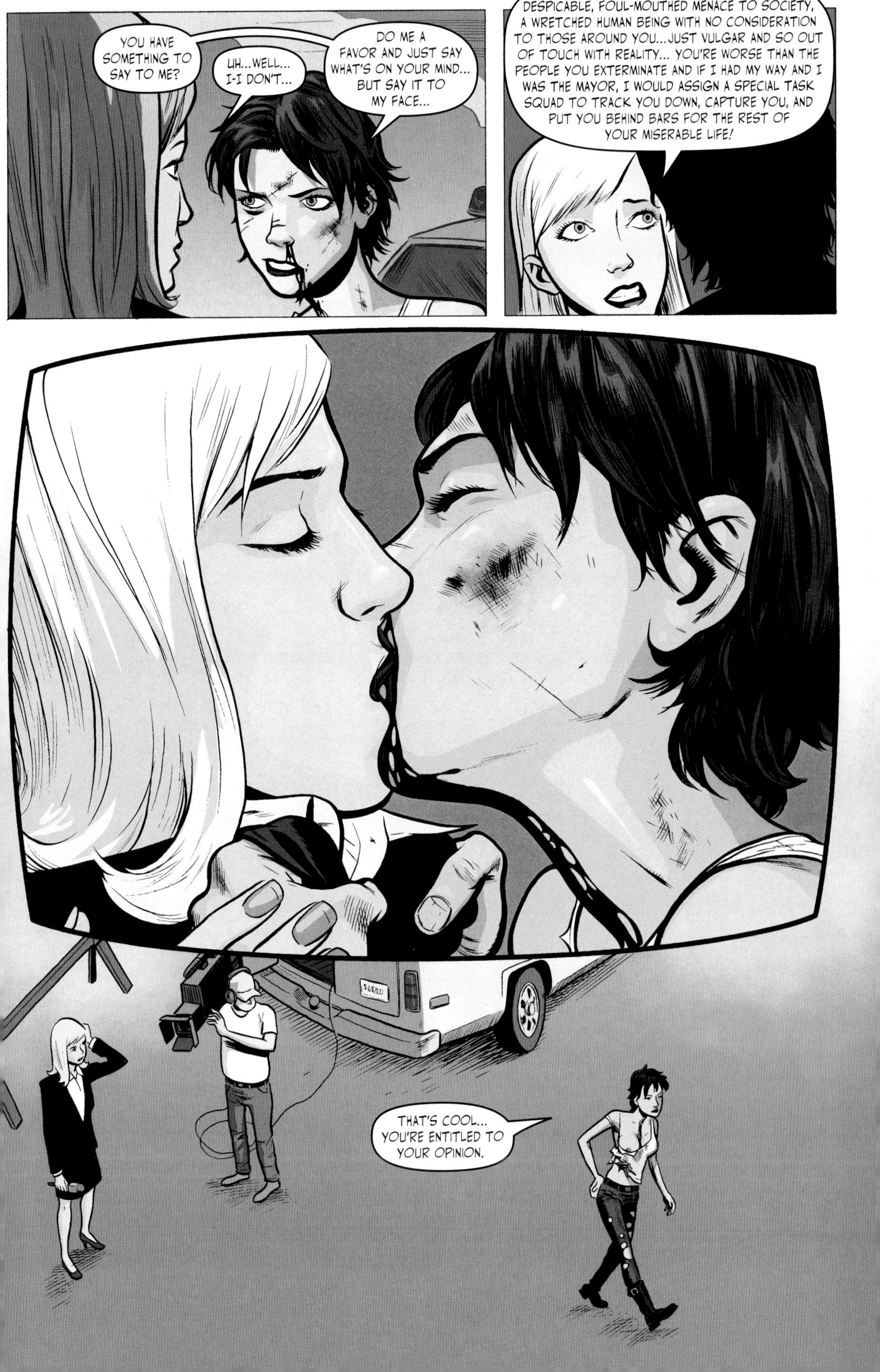
YOU HAVE SOMETHING TO SAY TO ME?
UH...WELL... I-I DON'T...
DO ME A FAVOR AND JUST SAY WHAT'S ON YOUR MIND... BUT SAY IT TO MY FACE...
O.K....I THINK YOU ARE A GOD DAMN DESPICABLE, FOUL-MOUTHED MENACE TO SOCIETY, A WRETCHED HUMAN BEING WITH NO CONSIDERATION TO THOSE AROUND YOU...JUST VULGAR AND SO OUT OF TOUCH WITH REALITY... YOU'RE WORSE THAN THE PEOPLE YOU EXTERMINATE AND IF I HAD MY WAY AND I WAS THE MAYOR, I WOULD ASSIGN A SPECIAL TASK SQUAD TO TRACK YOU DOWN, CAPTURE YOU, AND PUT YOU BEHIND BARS FOR THE REST OF YOUR MISERABLE LIFE!
THAT'S COOL... YOU'RE ENTITLED TO YOUR OPINION.

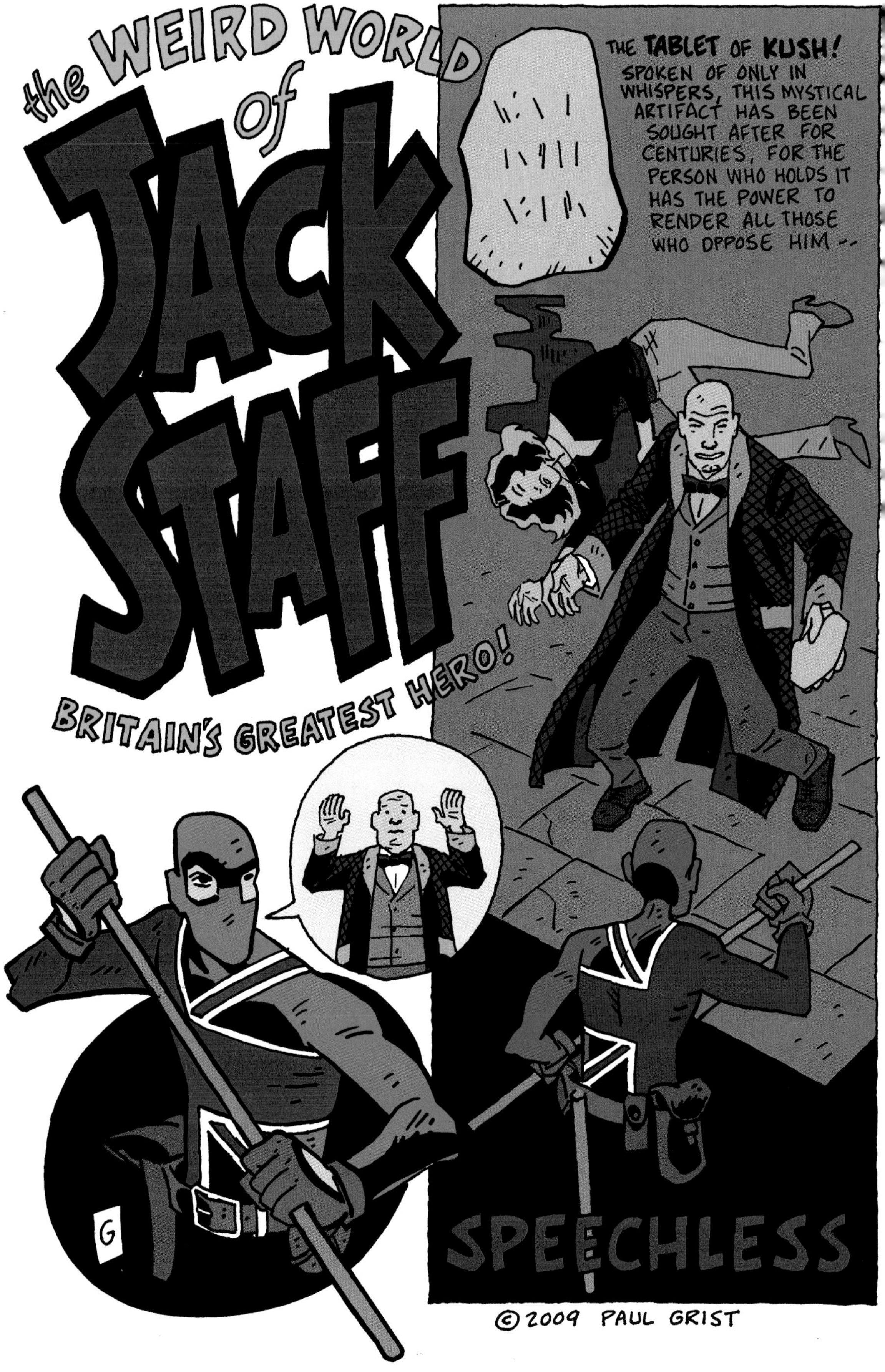
the WEIRD WORLD of
JACK STAFF
BRITAIN'S GREATEST HERO!
THE TABLET OF KUSH! SPOKEN OF ONLY IN WHISPERS, THIS MYSTICAL ARTIFACT HAS BEEN SOUGHT AFTER FOR CENTURIES, FOR THE PERSON WHO HOLDS IT HAS THE POWER TO RENDER ALL THOSE WHO OPPOSE HIM --
SPEECHLESS
G

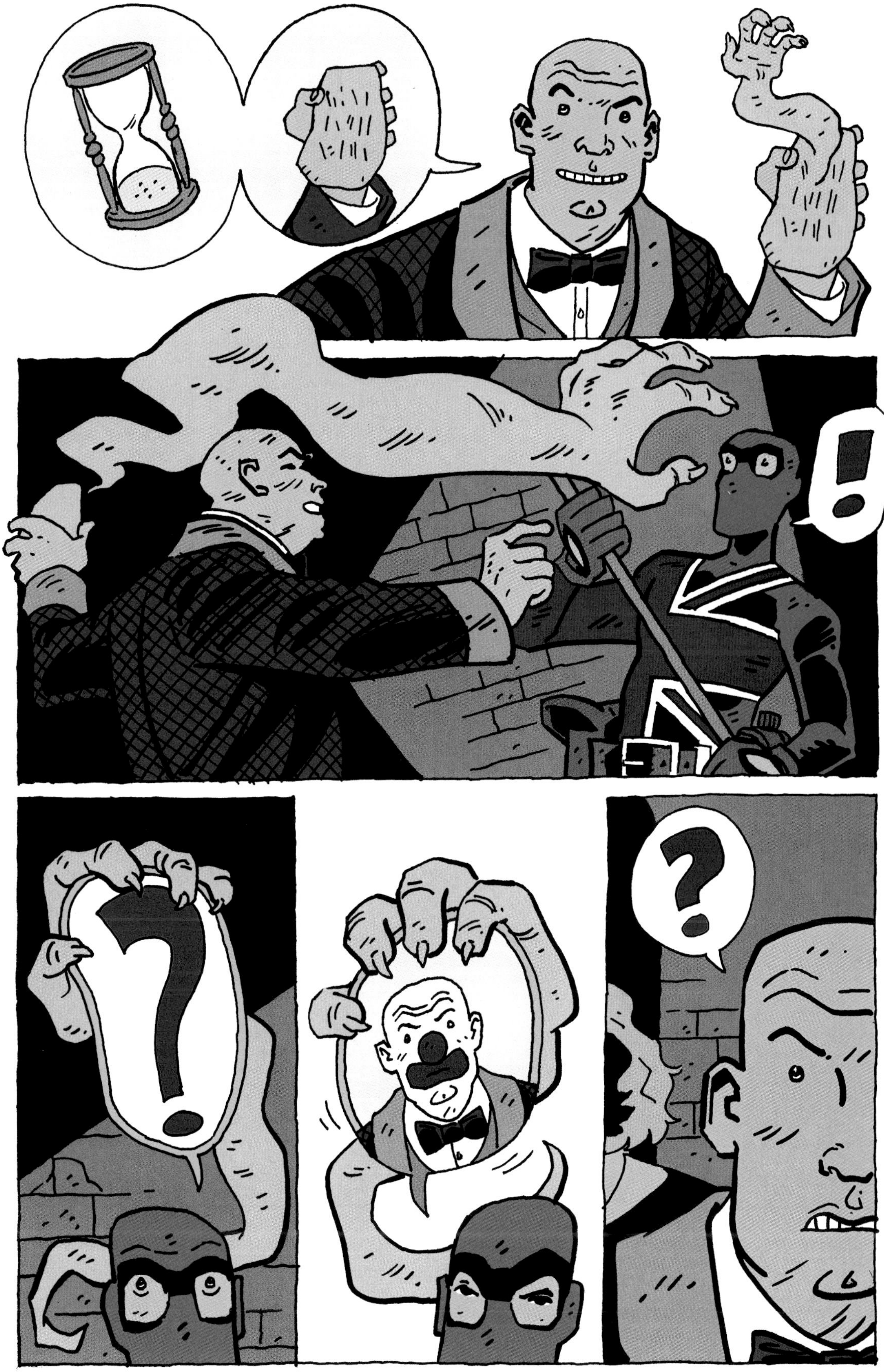

!
?
?

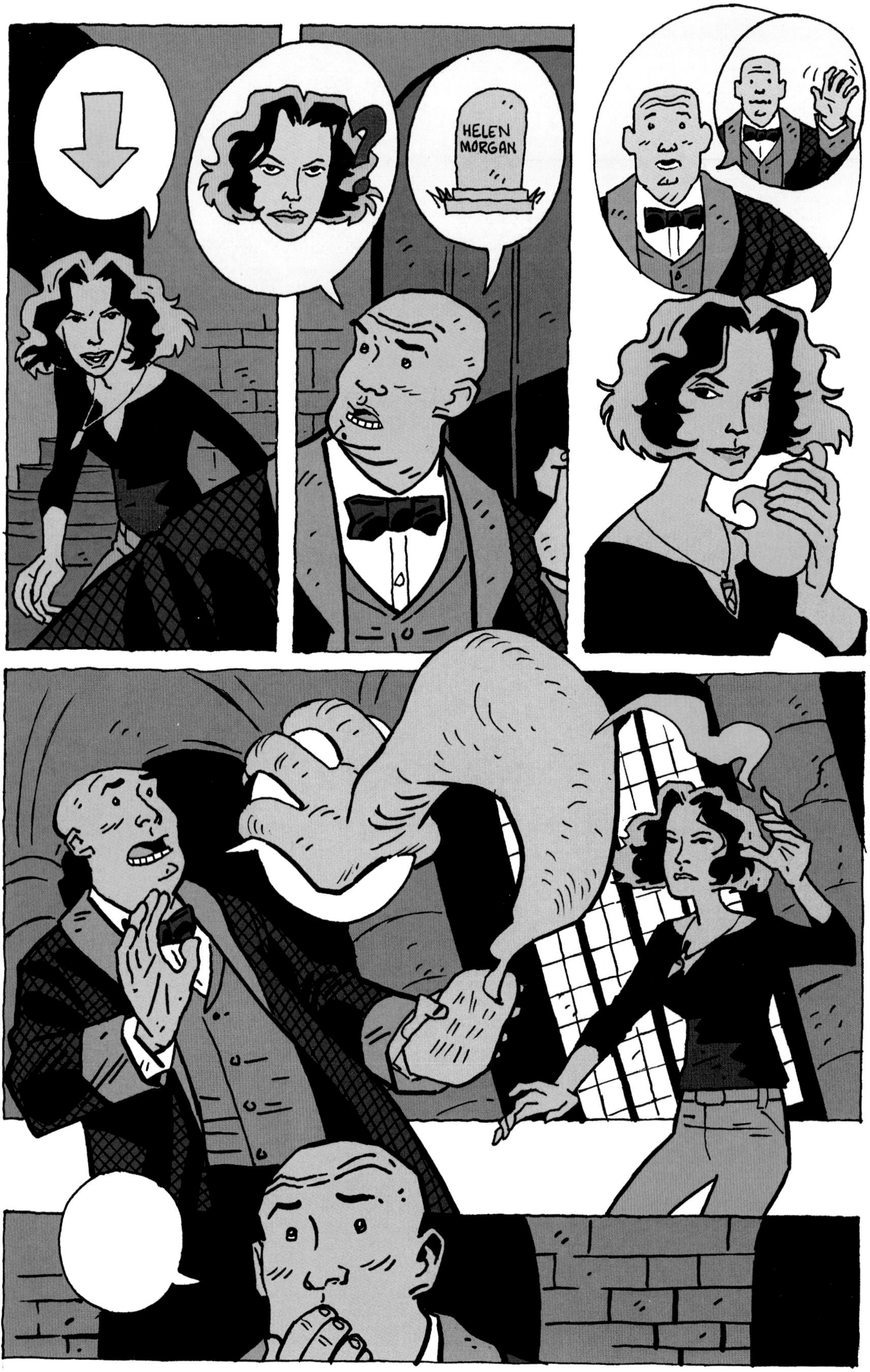
HELEN
MORGAN

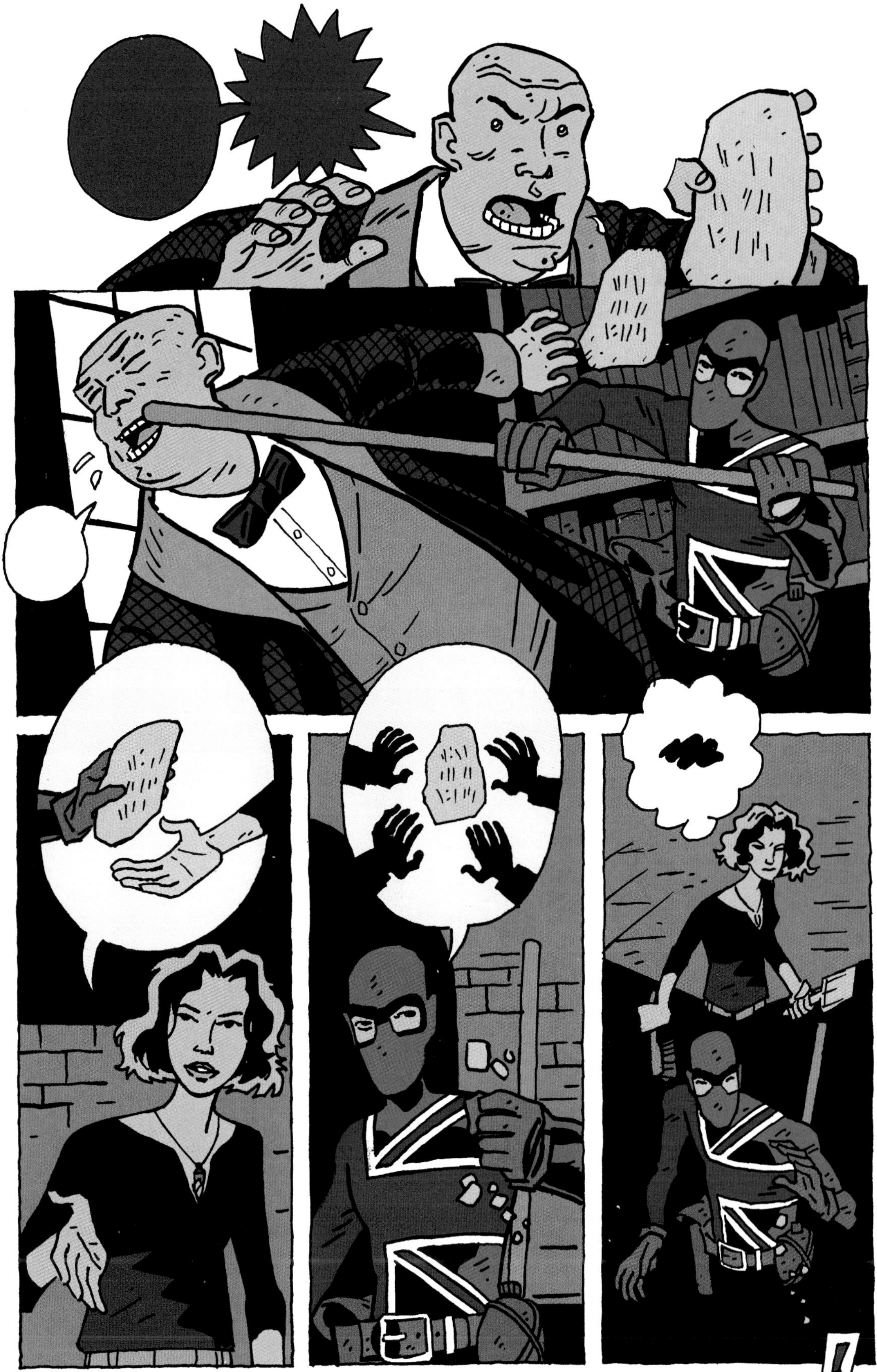
!

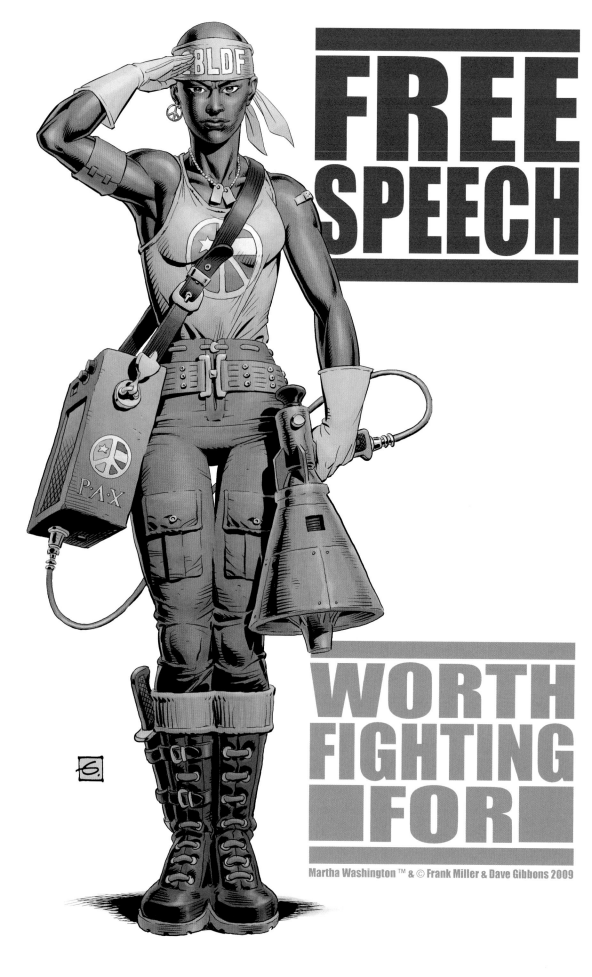

Martha Washington ™ & © Frank Miller & Dave Gibbons 2009

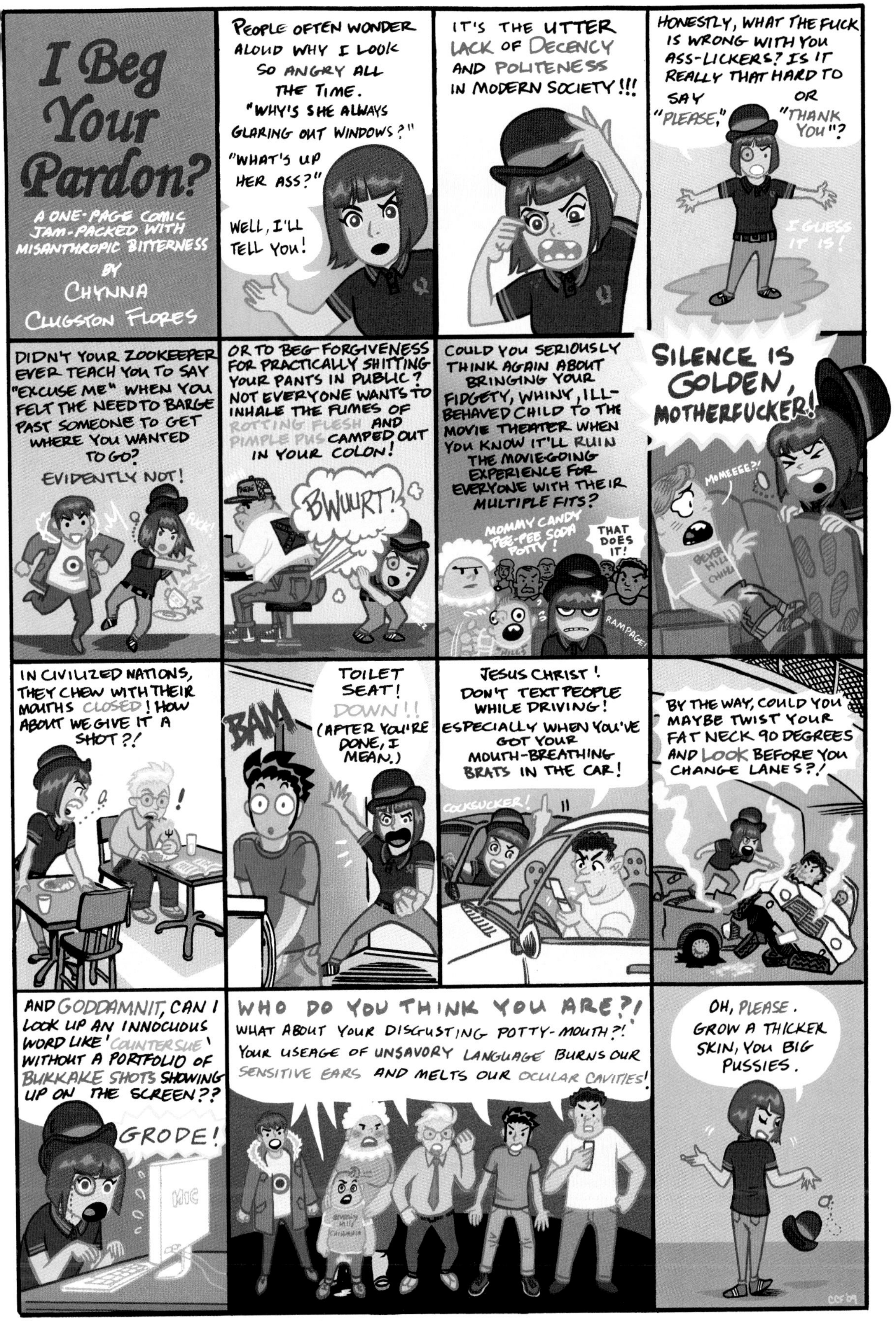

I Beg Your Pardon?
A ONE-PAGE COMIC JAM-PACKED WITH MISANTHROPIC BITTERNESS
BY
CHYNNA CLUGSTON FLORES
PEOPLE OFTEN WONDER ALOUD WHY I LOOK SO ANGRY ALL THE TIME.
"WHY'S SHE ALWAYS GLARING OUT WINDOWS?"
"WHAT'S UP HER ASS?"
WELL, I'LL TELL YOU!
IT'S THE UTTER LACK OF DECENCY AND POLITENESS IN MODERN SOCIETY!!!
HONESTLY, WHAT THE FUCK IS WRONG WITH YOU ASS-LICKERS? IS IT REALLY THAT HARD TO SAY "PLEASE," OR "THANK YOU"?
I GUESS IT IS!
DIDN'T YOUR ZOOKEEPER EVER TEACH YOU TO SAY "EXCUSE ME" WHEN YOU FELT THE NEED TO BARGE PAST SOMEONE TO GET WHERE YOU WANTED TO GO?
EVIDENTLY NOT!
FUCK!
OR TO BEG FORGIVENESS FOR PRACTICALLY SHITTING YOUR PANTS IN PUBLIC? NOT EVERYONE WANTS TO INHALE THE FUMES OF ROTTING FLESH AND PIMPLE PUS CAMPED OUT IN YOUR COLON!
UNH
BWUURT!
COULD YOU SERIOUSLY THINK AGAIN ABOUT BRINGING YOUR FIDGETY, WHINY, ILL-BEHAVED CHILD TO THE MOVIE THEATER WHEN YOU KNOW IT'LL RUIN THE MOVIE-GOING EXPERIENCE FOR EVERYONE WITH THEIR MULTIPLE FITS?
MOMMY CANDY PEE-PEE SODA POTTY!
THAT DOES IT!
RAMPAGE!
SILENCE IS GOLDEN, MOTHERFUCKER!
MOMEEEE?!
IN CIVILIZED NATIONS, THEY CHEW WITH THEIR MOUTHS CLOSED! HOW ABOUT WE GIVE IT A SHOT?!
BAM
TOILET SEAT! DOWN!! (AFTER YOU'RE DONE, I MEAN.)
JESUS CHRIST! DON'T TEXT PEOPLE WHILE DRIVING! ESPECIALLY WHEN YOU'VE GOT YOUR MOUTH-BREATHING BRATS IN THE CAR!
COCKSUCKER!
BY THE WAY, COULD YOU MAYBE TWIST YOUR FAT NECK 90 DEGREES AND LOOK BEFORE YOU CHANGE LANES?!
AND GODDAMNIT, CAN I LOOK UP AN INNOCUOUS WORD LIKE 'COUNTERSUE' WITHOUT A PORTFOLIO OF BUKKAKE SHOTS SHOWING UP ON THE SCREEN??
GRODE!
WHO DO YOU THINK YOU ARE?!
WHAT ABOUT YOUR DISGUSTING POTTY-MOUTH?! YOUR USEAGE OF UNSAVORY LANGUAGE BURNS OUR SENSITIVE EARS AND MELTS OUR OCULAR CAVITIES!
OH, PLEASE. GROW A THICKER SKIN, YOU BIG PUSSIES.
CCF 09

TOURING THE POST-NUCLEAR WASTELAND, MANDY, MEGUMI, AND DOT ARE...

THE APOCALIPSTIX IN TABOO BOOGALOO

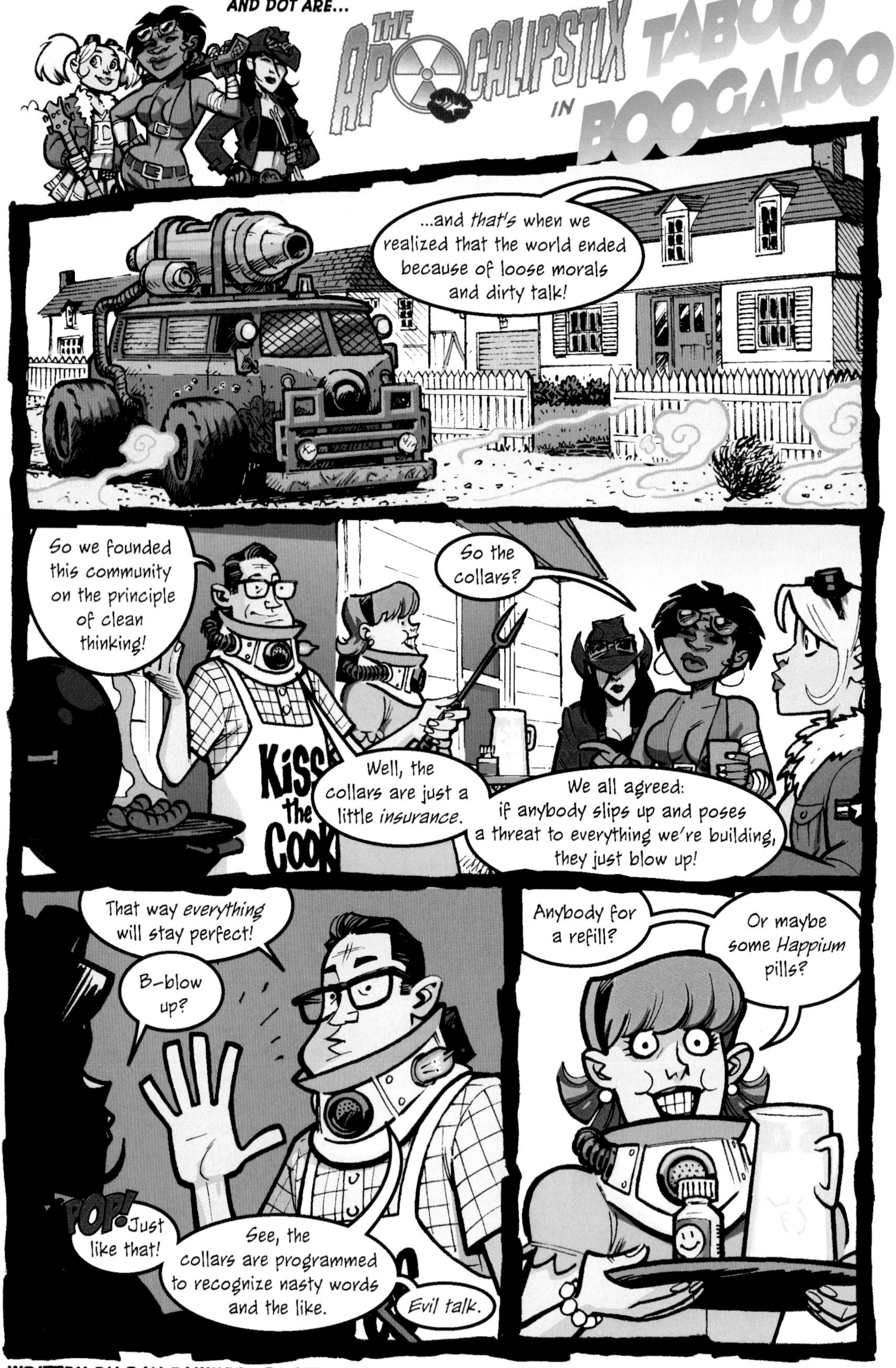
...and *that's* when we realized that the world ended because of loose morals and dirty talk!
So we founded this community on the principle of clean thinking!
So the collars?
Well, the collars are just a little *insurance*.
We all agreed: if anybody slips up and poses a threat to everything we're building, they just blow up!
That way *everything* will stay perfect!
B-blow up?
POP! Just like that!
See, the collars are programmed to recognize nasty words and the like.
Evil talk.
Anybody for a refill?
Or maybe some *Happium* pills?

WRITTEN BY RAY FAWKES, DRAWN BY CAMERON STEWART
SEE MORE OF THE APOCALIPSTIX IN BOOKS PUBLISHED BY ONI PRESS!

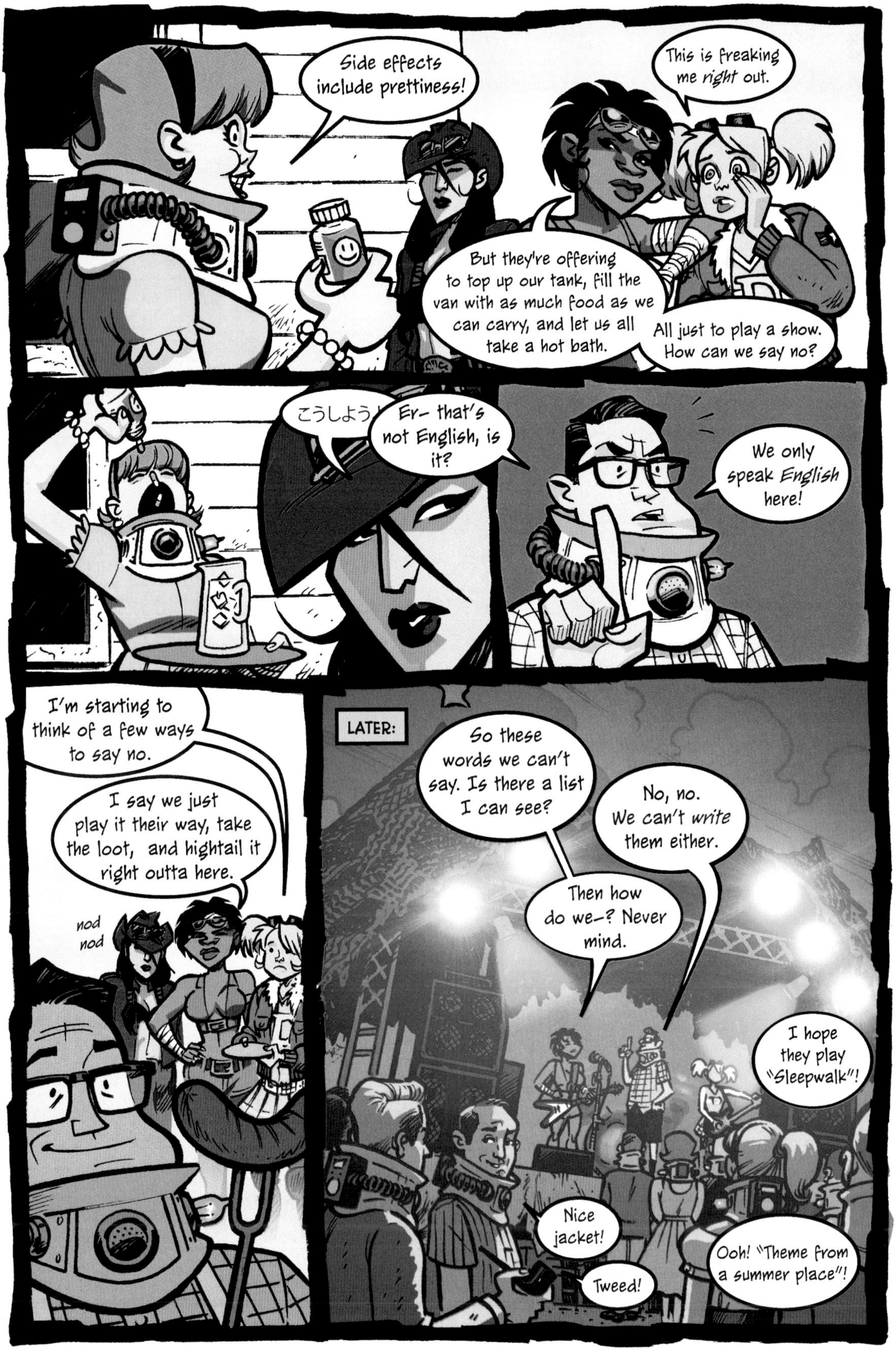
Side effects include prettiness!
This is freaking me *right* out.
But they're offering to top up our tank, fill the van with as much food as we can carry, and let us all take a hot bath.
All just to play a show. How can we say no?
こうしよう
Er- that's not English, is it?
We only speak *English* here!
I'm starting to think of a few ways to say no.
I say we just play it their way, take the loot, and hightail it right outta here.
nod nod
LATER:
So these words we can't say. Is there a list I can see?
No, no. We can't *write* them either.
Then how do we-? Never mind.
I hope they play "Sleepwalk"!
Nice jacket!
Tweed!
Ooh! "Theme from a summer place"!

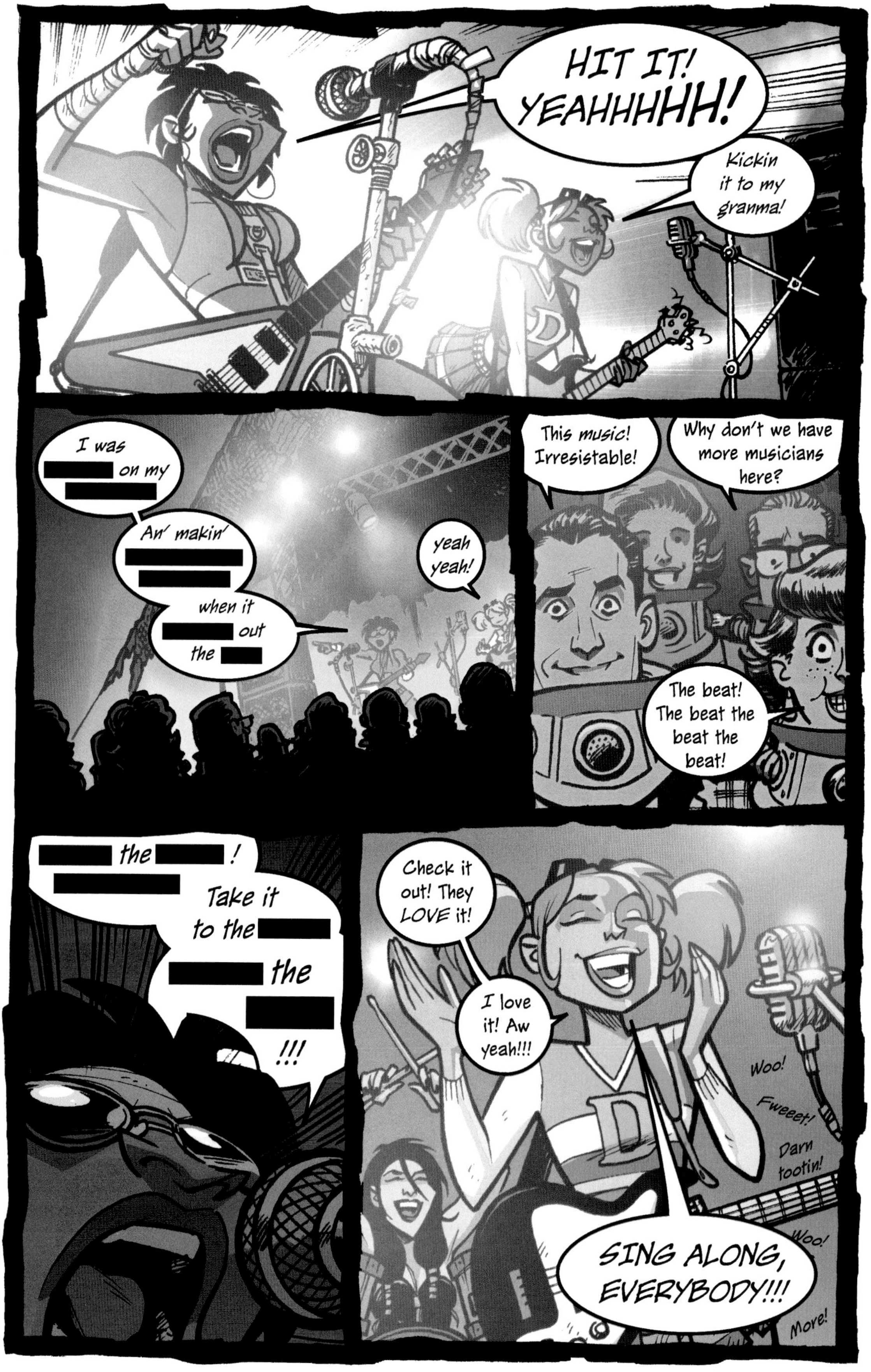
HIT IT! YEAHHHHH!
Kickin it to my granma!
I was [redacted] on my [redacted]
An' makin' [redacted]
when it [redacted] out the [redacted]
yeah yeah!
This music! Irresistable!
Why don't we have more musicians here?
The beat! The beat the beat the beat!
[redacted] the [redacted]! [redacted]
Take it to the [redacted] [redacted] the [redacted]!!!
Check it out! They LOVE it!
I love it! Aw yeah!!!
Woo!
Fweeet!
Darn tootin!
Woo!
SING ALONG, EVERYBODY!!!
More!

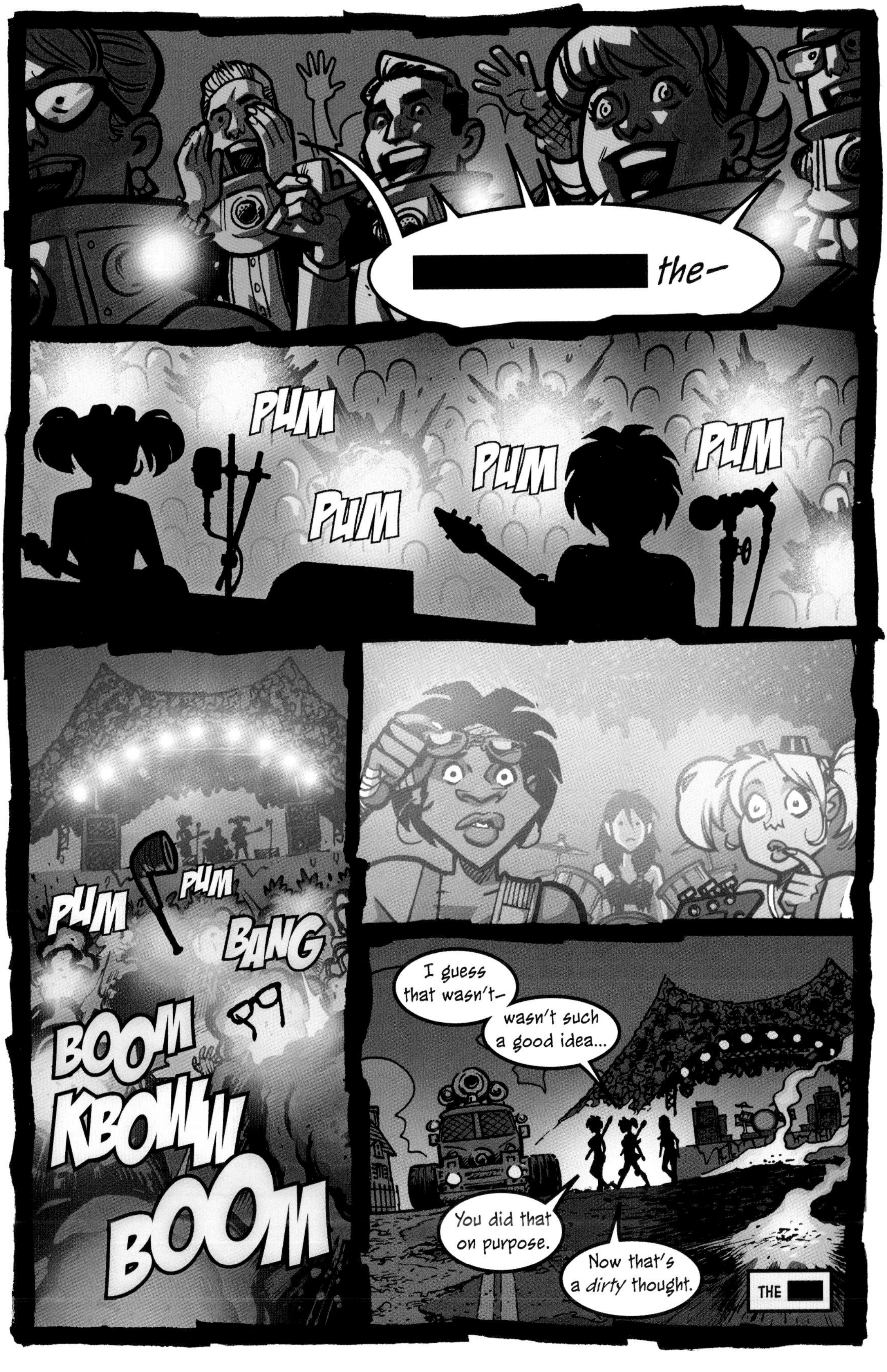

[redacted] the-
PUM
PUM
PUM
PUM
PUM
PUM
BANG
BOOM
KBOWW
BOOM
I guess that wasn't-
wasn't such a good idea...
You did that on purpose.
Now that's a *dirty* thought.
THE [redacted]

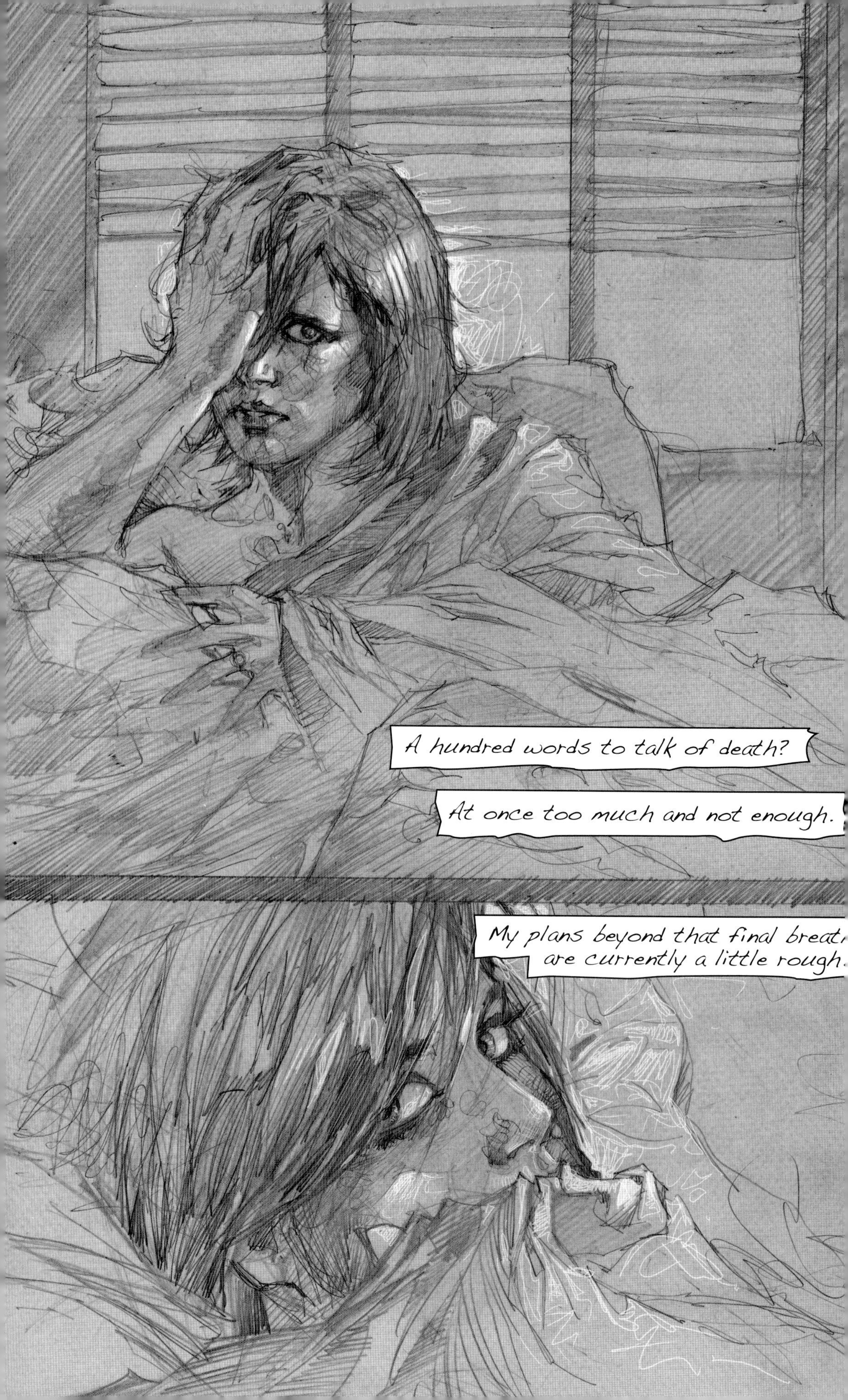
A hundred words to talk of death?
At once too much and not enough.
My plans beyond that final breat
are currently a little rough.

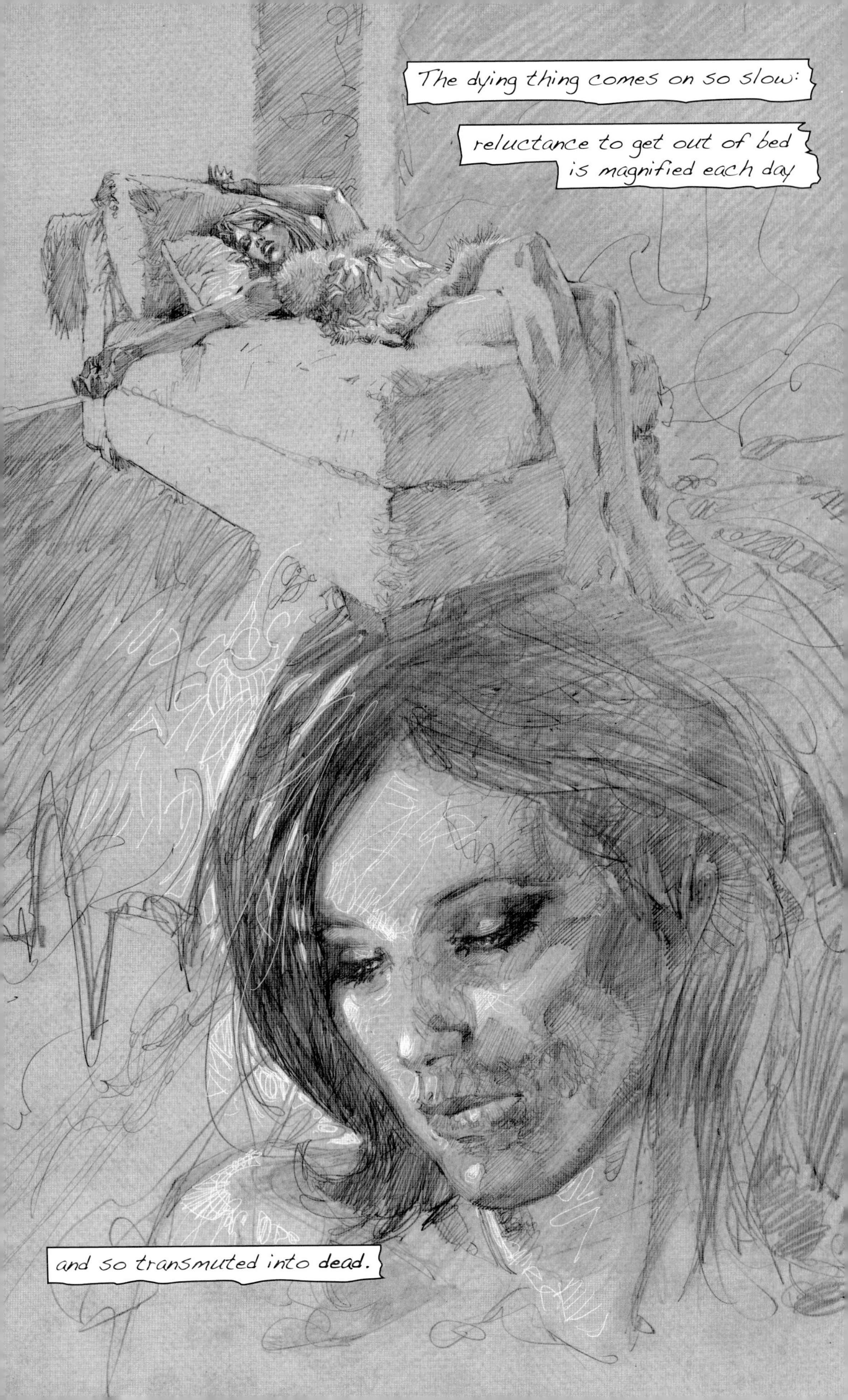
The dying thing comes on so slow:
reluctance to get out of bed is magnified each day
and so transmuted into dead.

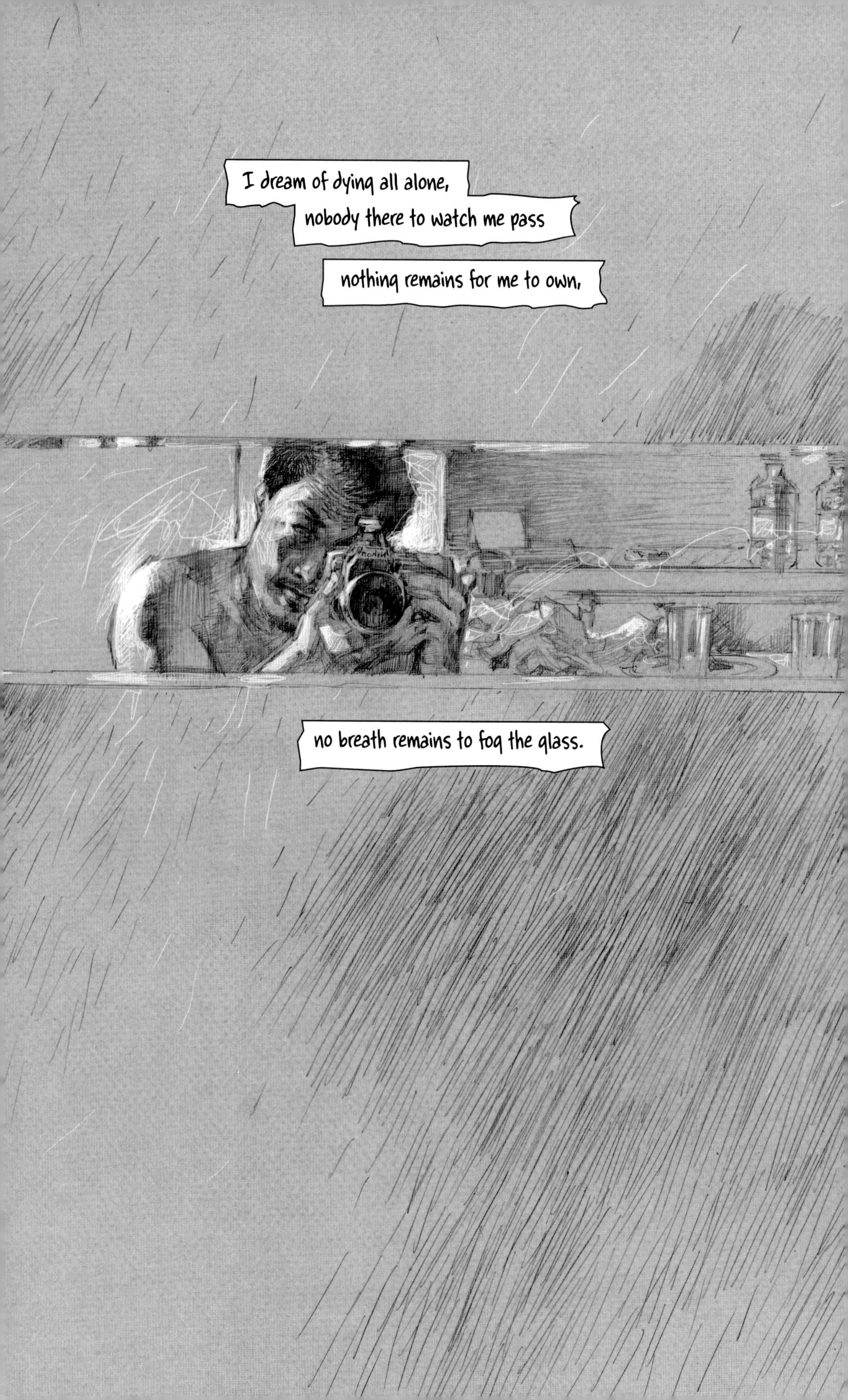
I dream of dying all alone,
nobody there to watch me pass
nothing remains for me to own,
no breath remains to fog the glass.

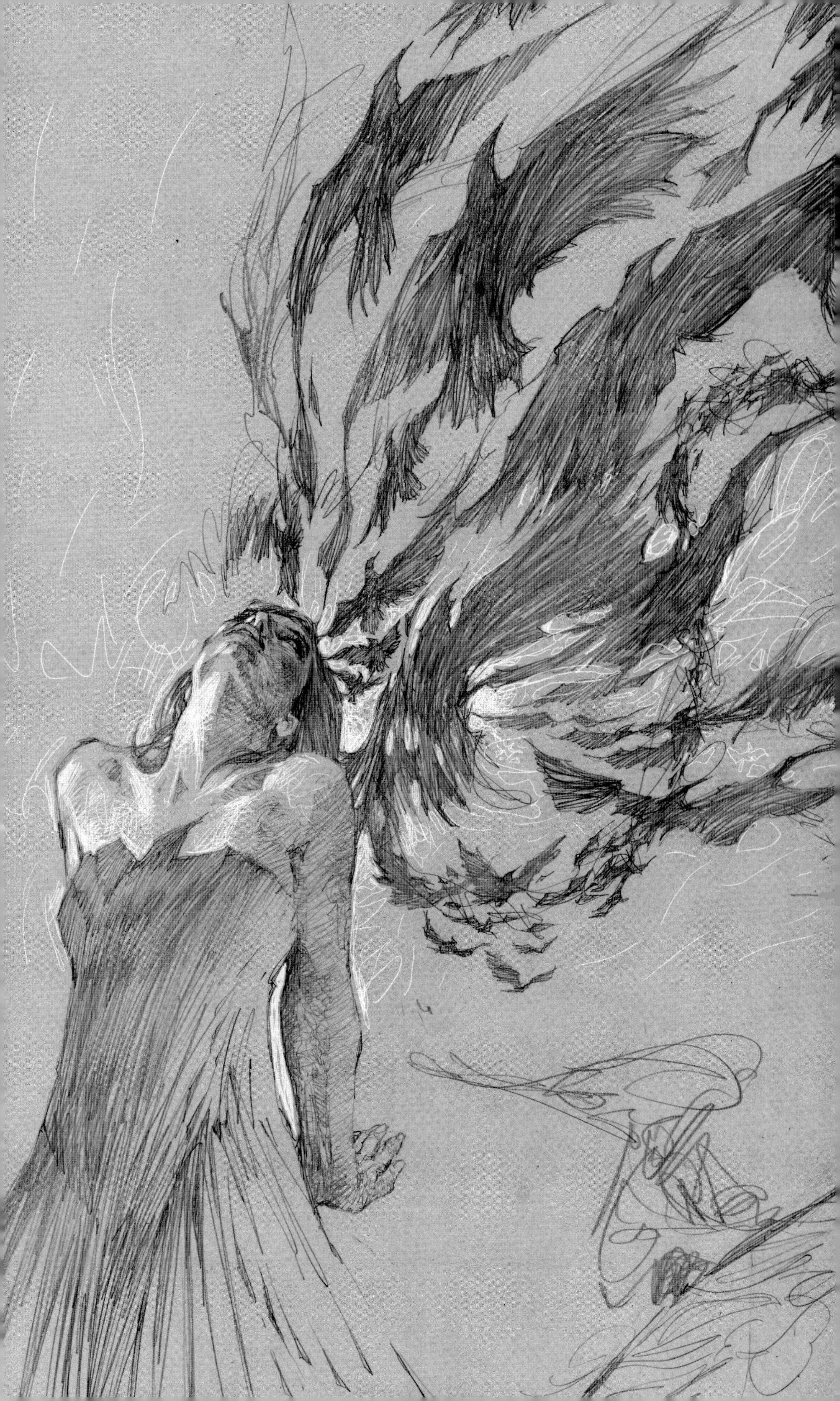

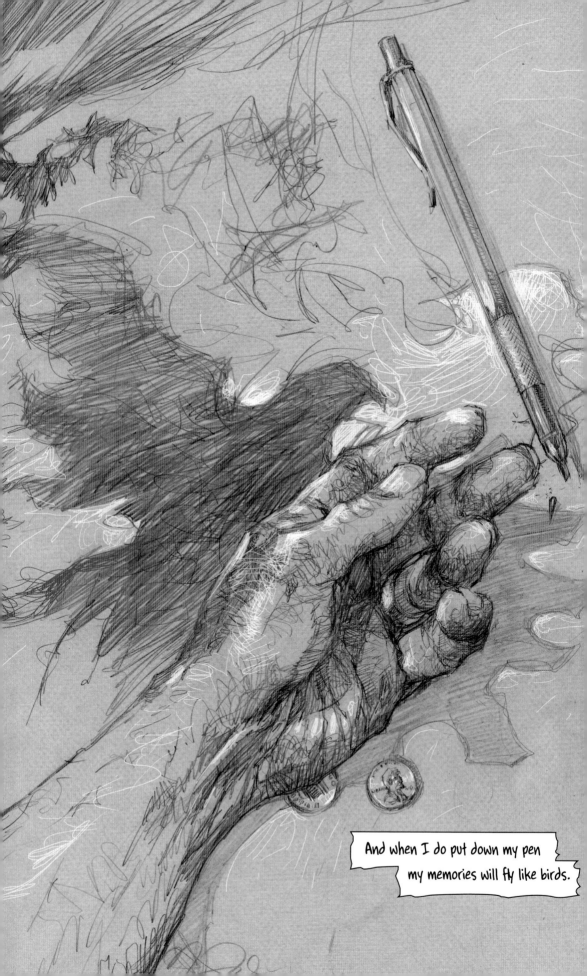

And when I do put down my pen
my memories will fly like birds.

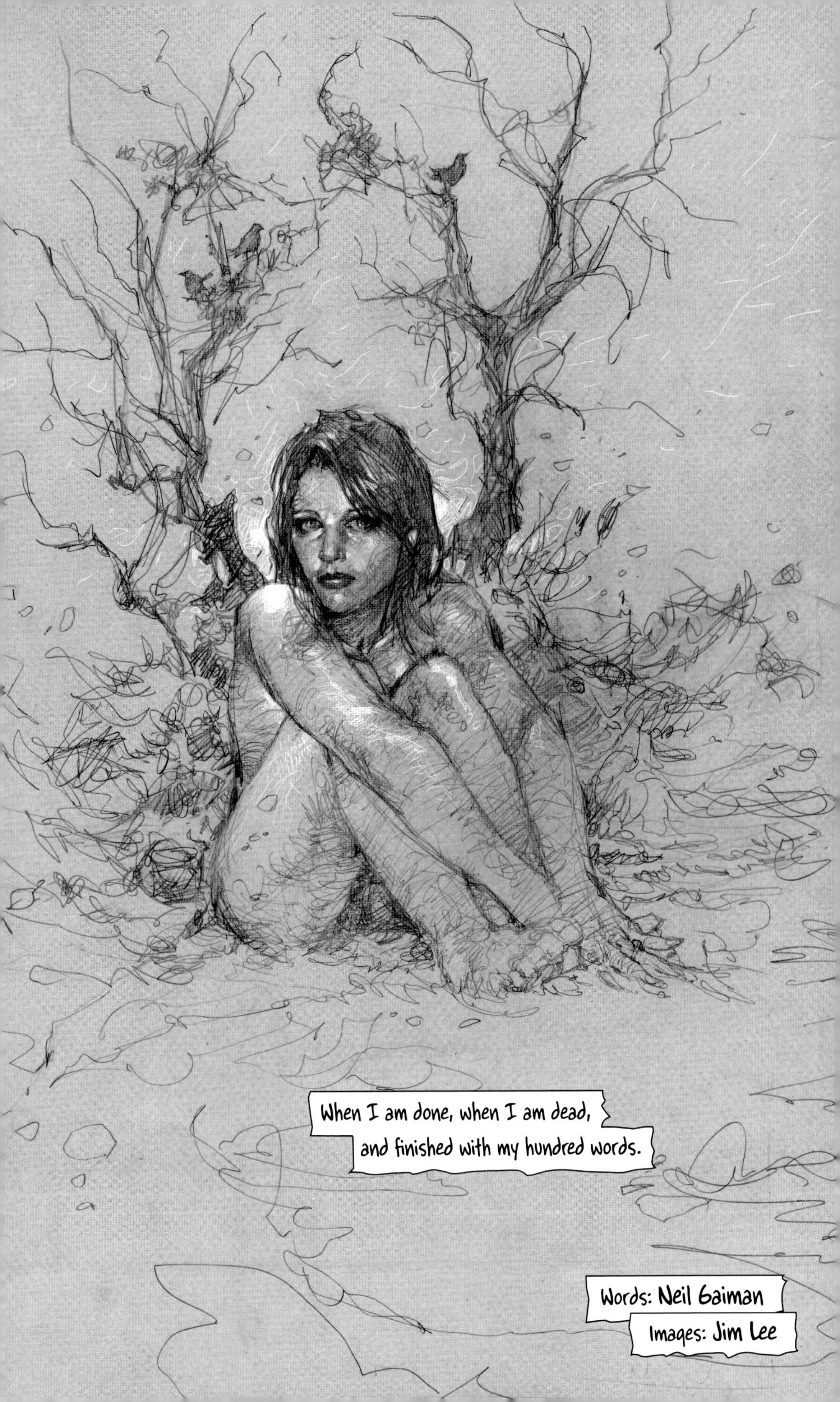
When I am done, when I am dead,
and finished with my hundred words.
Words: Neil Gaiman
Images: Jim Lee

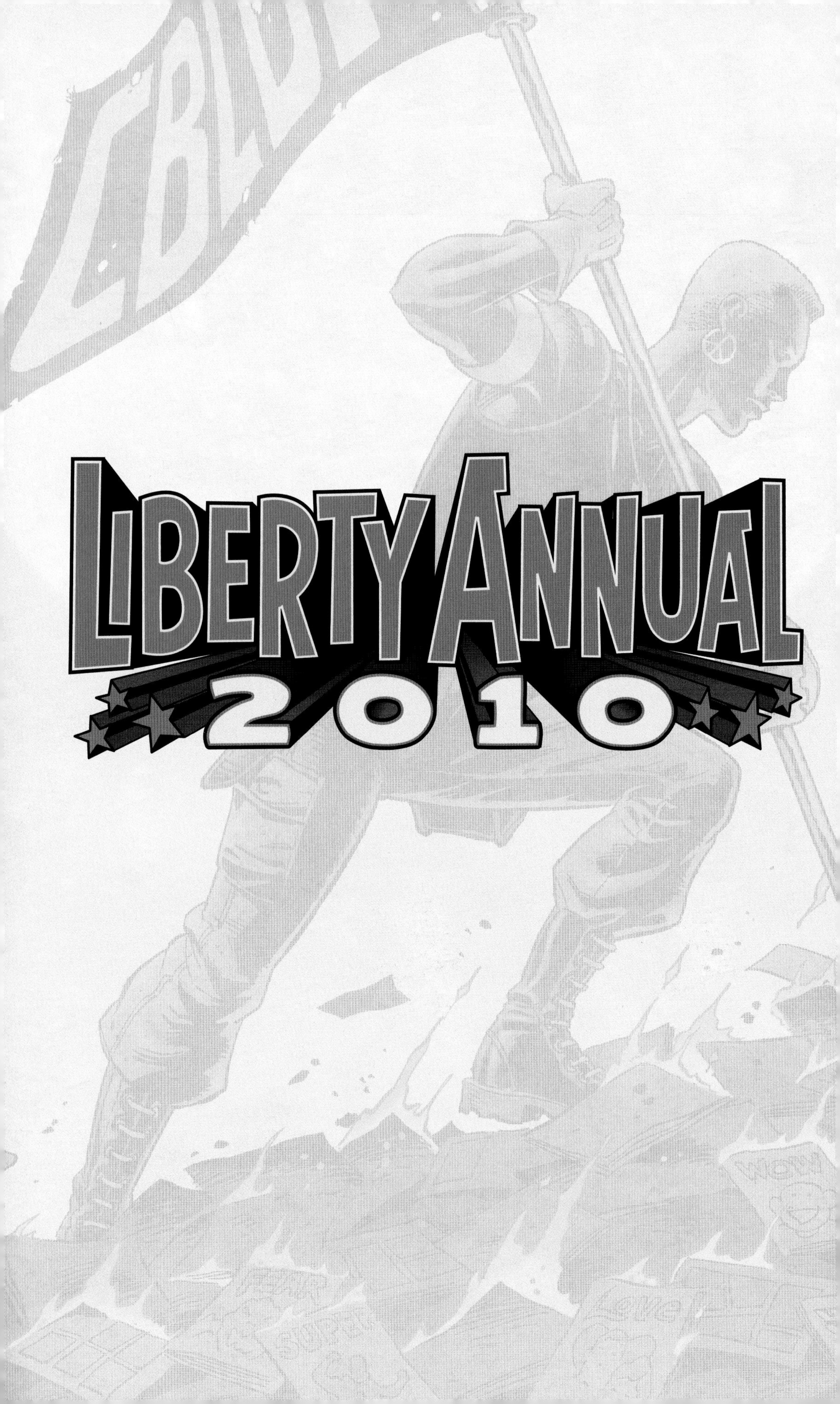
LIBERTY ANNUAL
2010

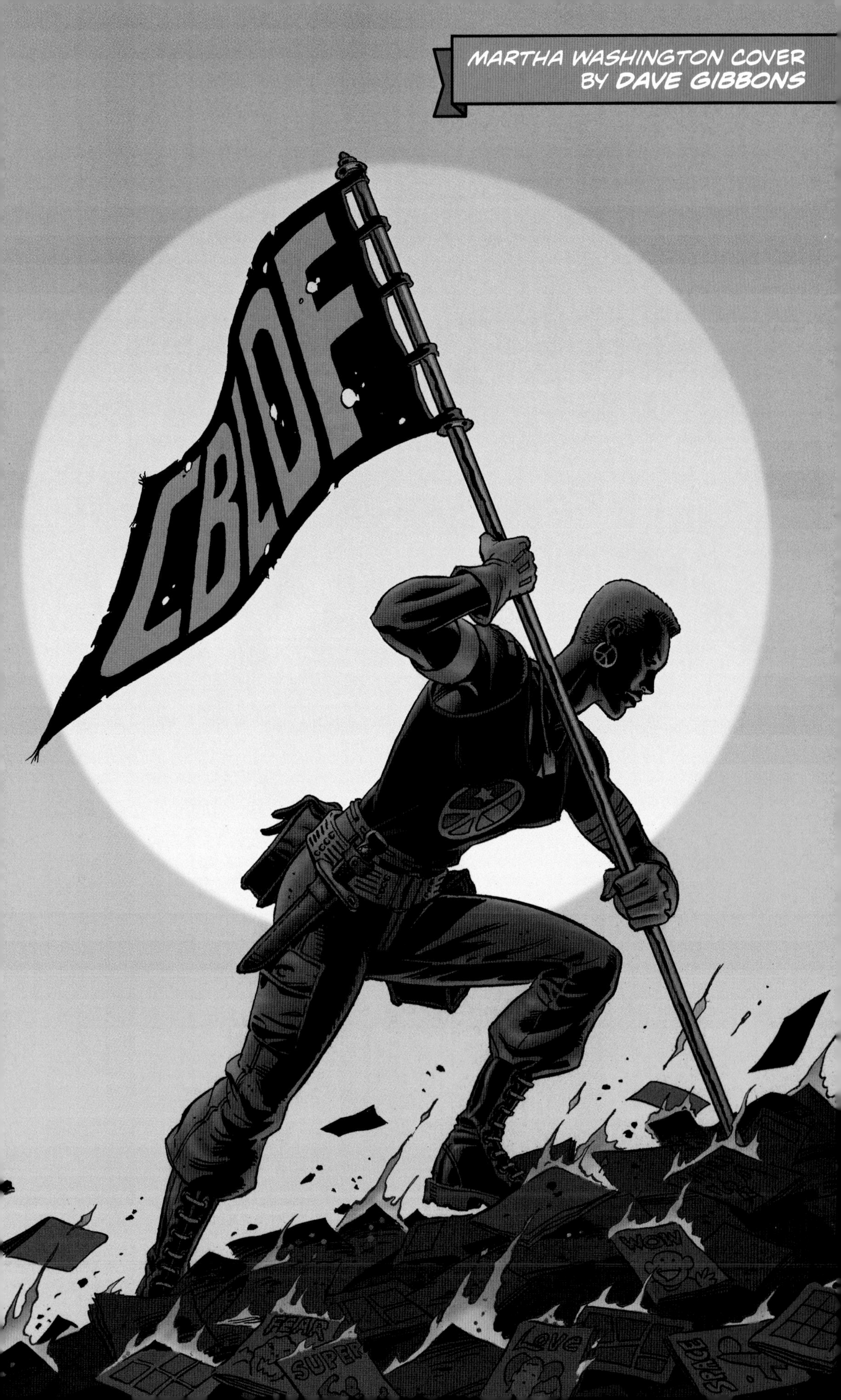
CBLDF
WOW
FEAR
SUPER
LOVE

MARTHA WASHINGTON COVER
BY DAVE GIBBONS

THE WALKING DEAD COVER BY
CHARLIE ADLARD & CLIFF RATHBURN

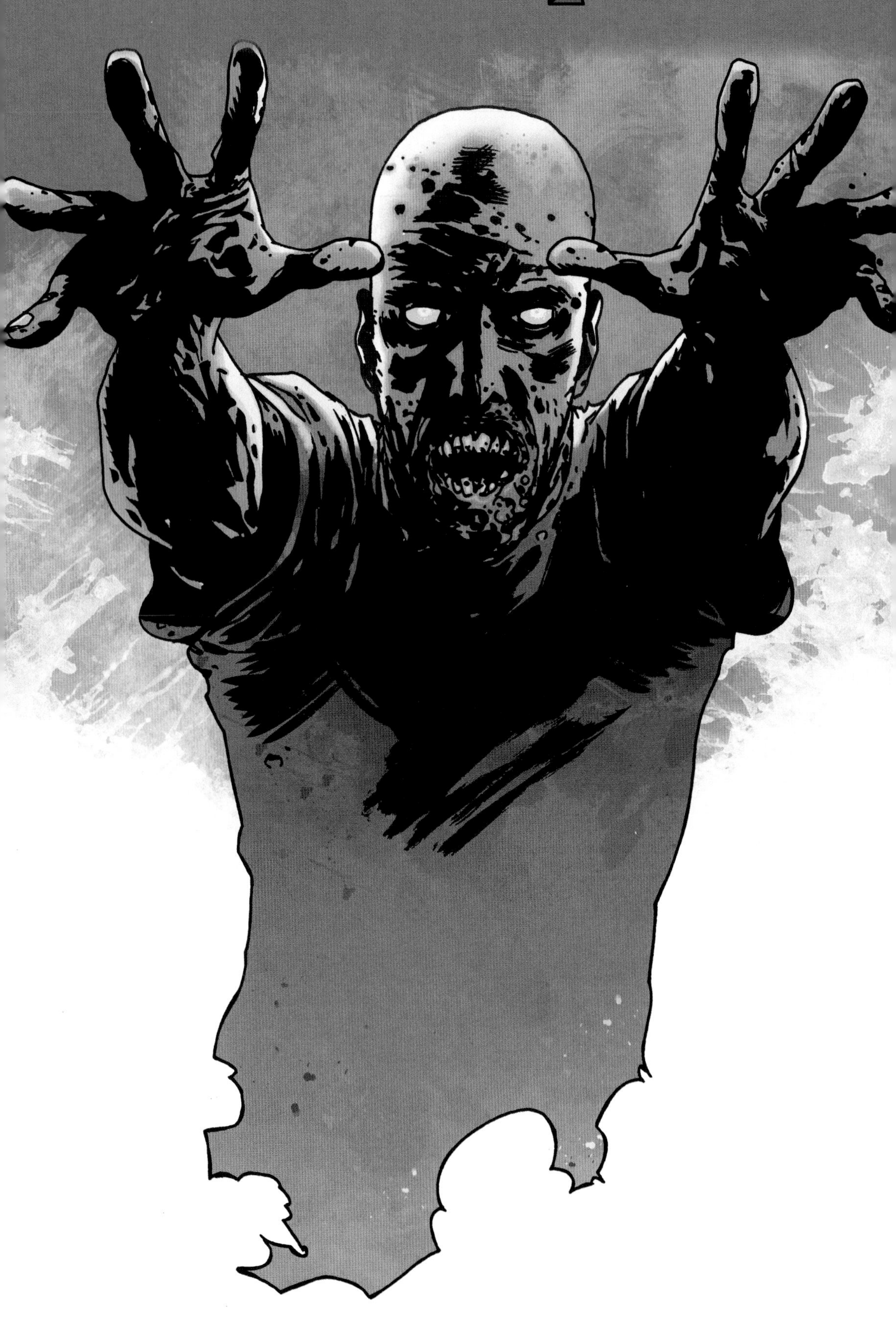

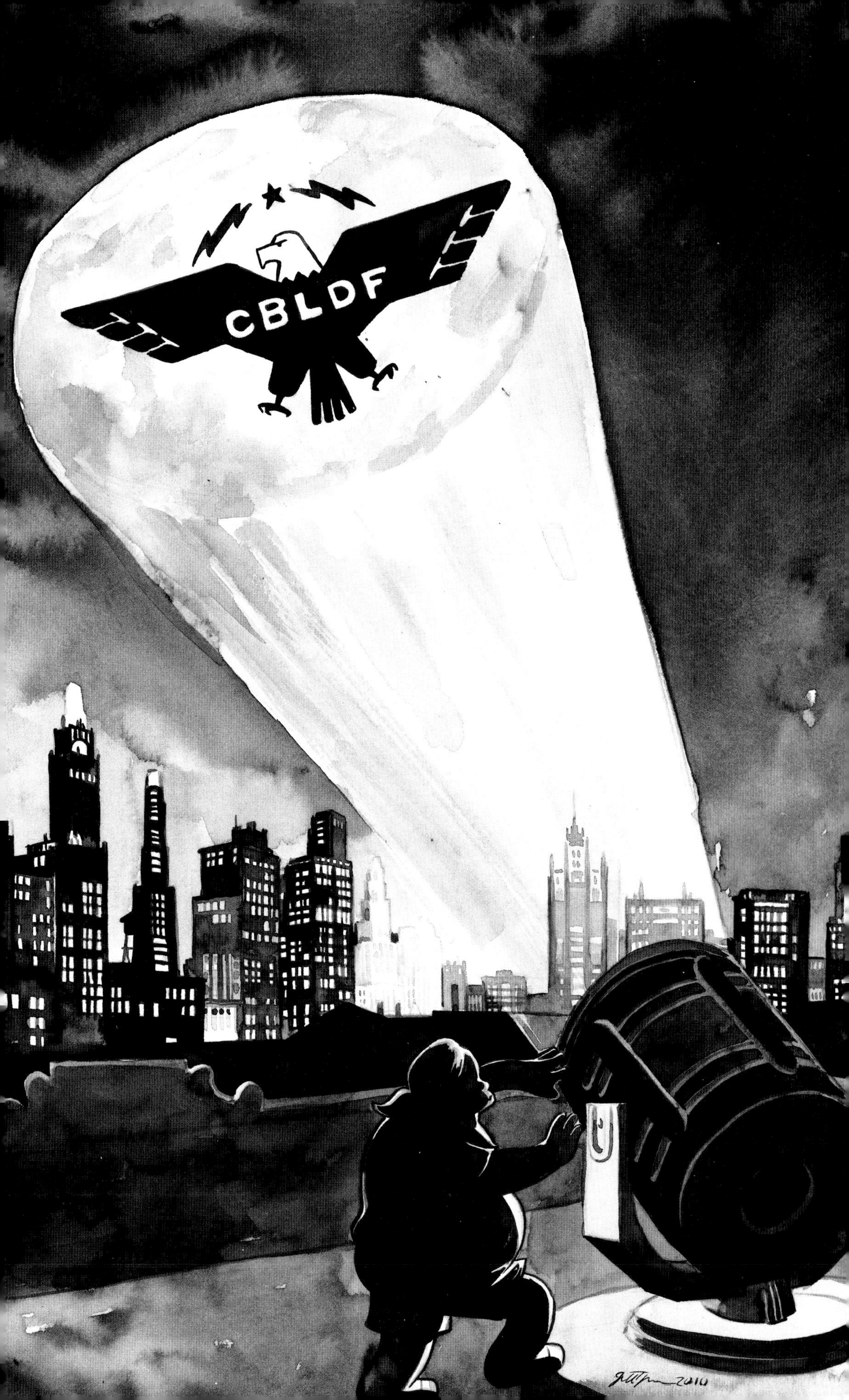
CBLDF

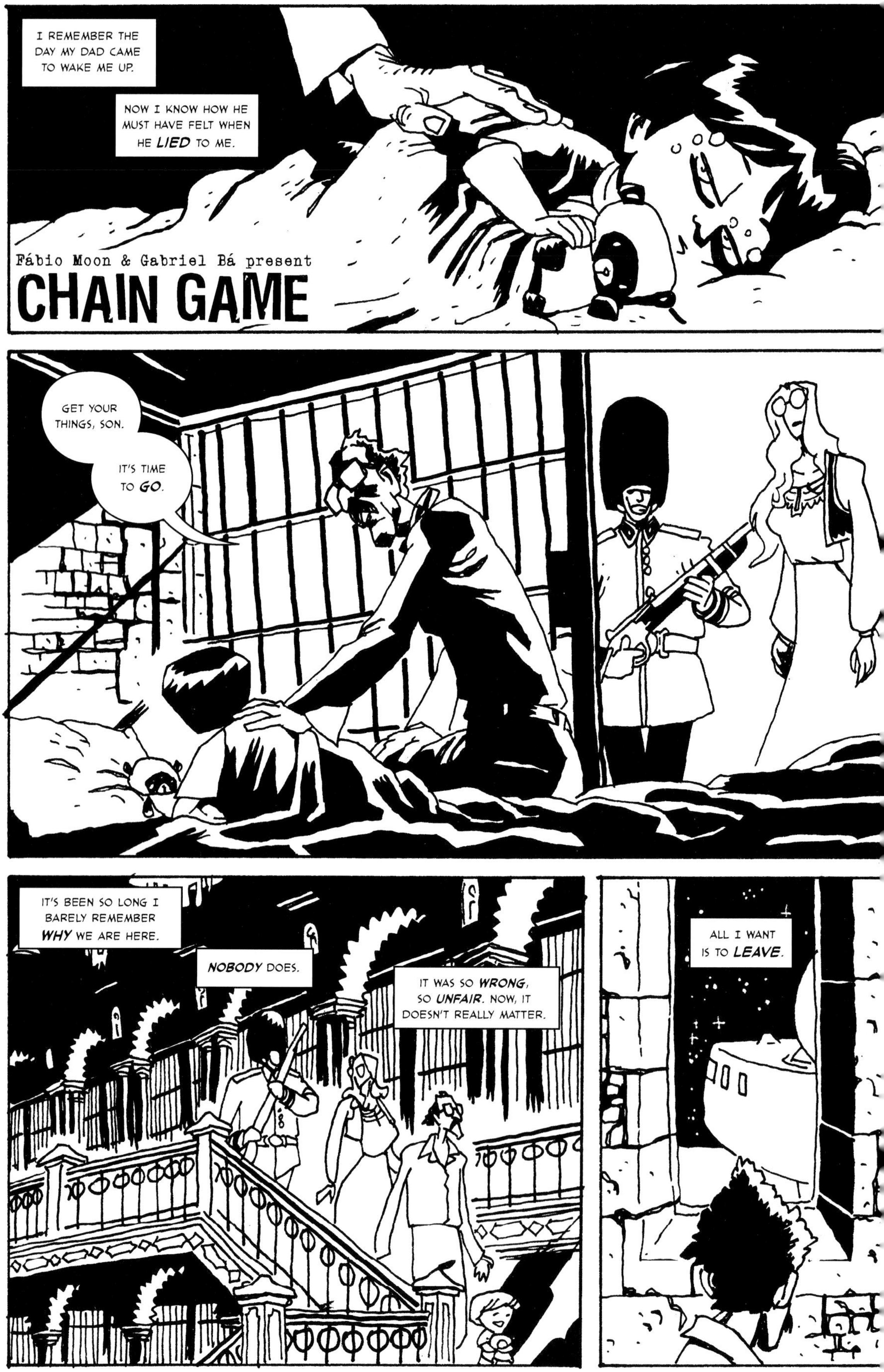

I REMEMBER THE DAY MY DAD CAME TO WAKE ME UP.
NOW I KNOW HOW HE MUST HAVE FELT WHEN HE LIED TO ME.
Fábio Moon & Gabriel Bá present
CHAIN GAME
GET YOUR THINGS, SON.
IT'S TIME TO GO.
IT'S BEEN SO LONG I BARELY REMEMBER WHY WE ARE HERE.
NOBODY DOES.
IT WAS SO WRONG, SO UNFAIR. NOW, IT DOESN'T REALLY MATTER.
ALL I WANT IS TO LEAVE.

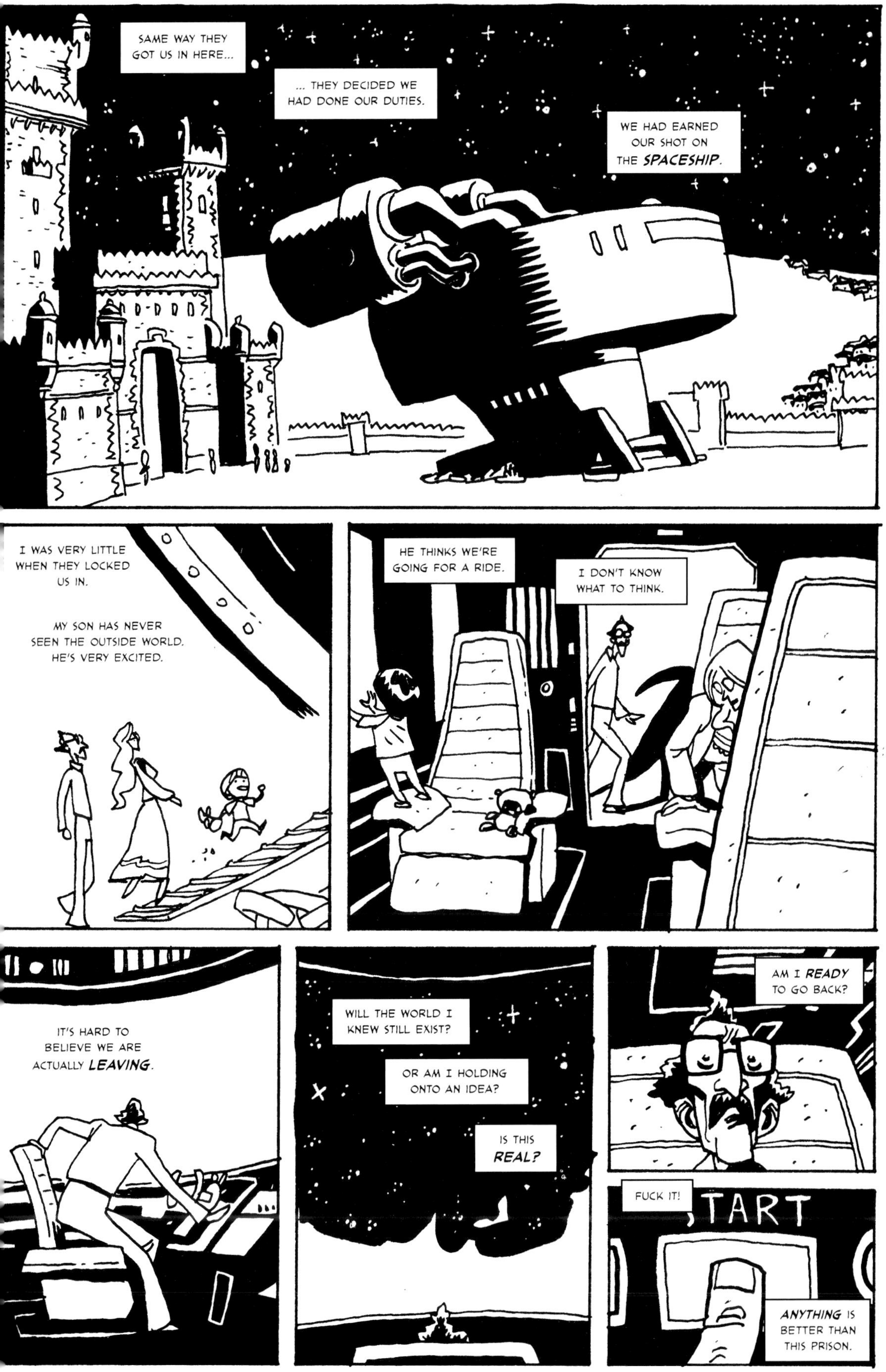
SAME WAY THEY GOT US IN HERE...
... THEY DECIDED WE HAD DONE OUR DUTIES.
WE HAD EARNED OUR SHOT ON THE SPACESHIP.
I WAS VERY LITTLE WHEN THEY LOCKED US IN.
MY SON HAS NEVER SEEN THE OUTSIDE WORLD. HE'S VERY EXCITED.
HE THINKS WE'RE GOING FOR A RIDE.
I DON'T KNOW WHAT TO THINK.
IT'S HARD TO BELIEVE WE ARE ACTUALLY LEAVING.
WILL THE WORLD I KNEW STILL EXIST?
OR AM I HOLDING ONTO AN IDEA?
IS THIS REAL?
AM I READY TO GO BACK?
FUCK IT!
TART
ANYTHING IS BETTER THAN THIS PRISON.

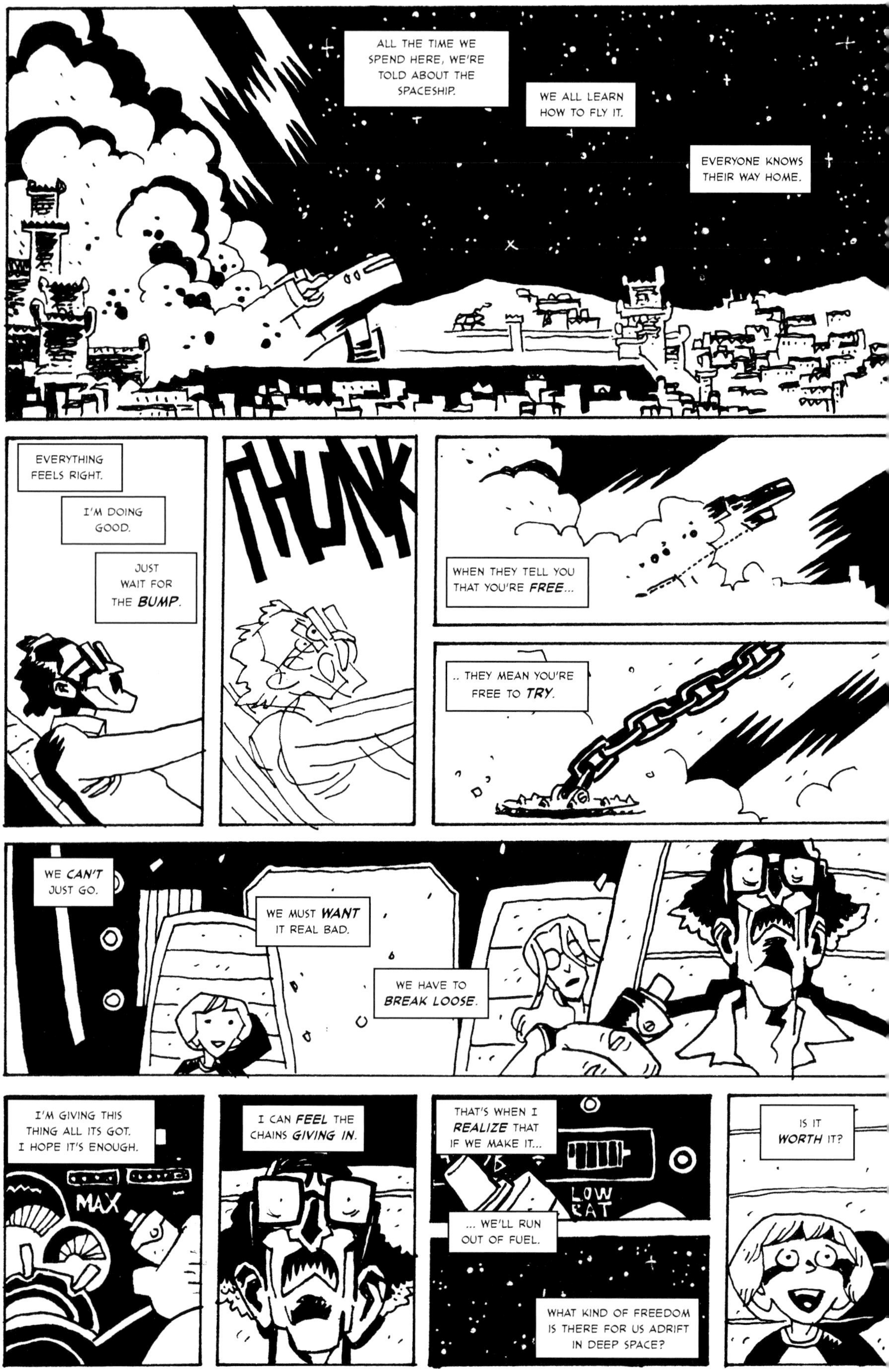
ALL THE TIME WE SPEND HERE, WE'RE TOLD ABOUT THE SPACESHIP.
WE ALL LEARN HOW TO FLY IT.
EVERYONE KNOWS THEIR WAY HOME.
EVERYTHING FEELS RIGHT.
I'M DOING GOOD.
JUST WAIT FOR THE BUMP.
THUNK
WHEN THEY TELL YOU THAT YOU'RE FREE...
.. THEY MEAN YOU'RE FREE TO TRY.
WE CAN'T JUST GO.
WE MUST WANT IT REAL BAD.
WE HAVE TO BREAK LOOSE.
I'M GIVING THIS THING ALL ITS GOT. I HOPE IT'S ENOUGH.
MAX
I CAN FEEL THE CHAINS GIVING IN.
THAT'S WHEN I REALIZE THAT IF WE MAKE IT...
LOW
... WE'LL RUN OUT OF FUEL.
WHAT KIND OF FREEDOM IS THERE FOR US ADRIFT IN DEEP SPACE?
IS IT WORTH IT?

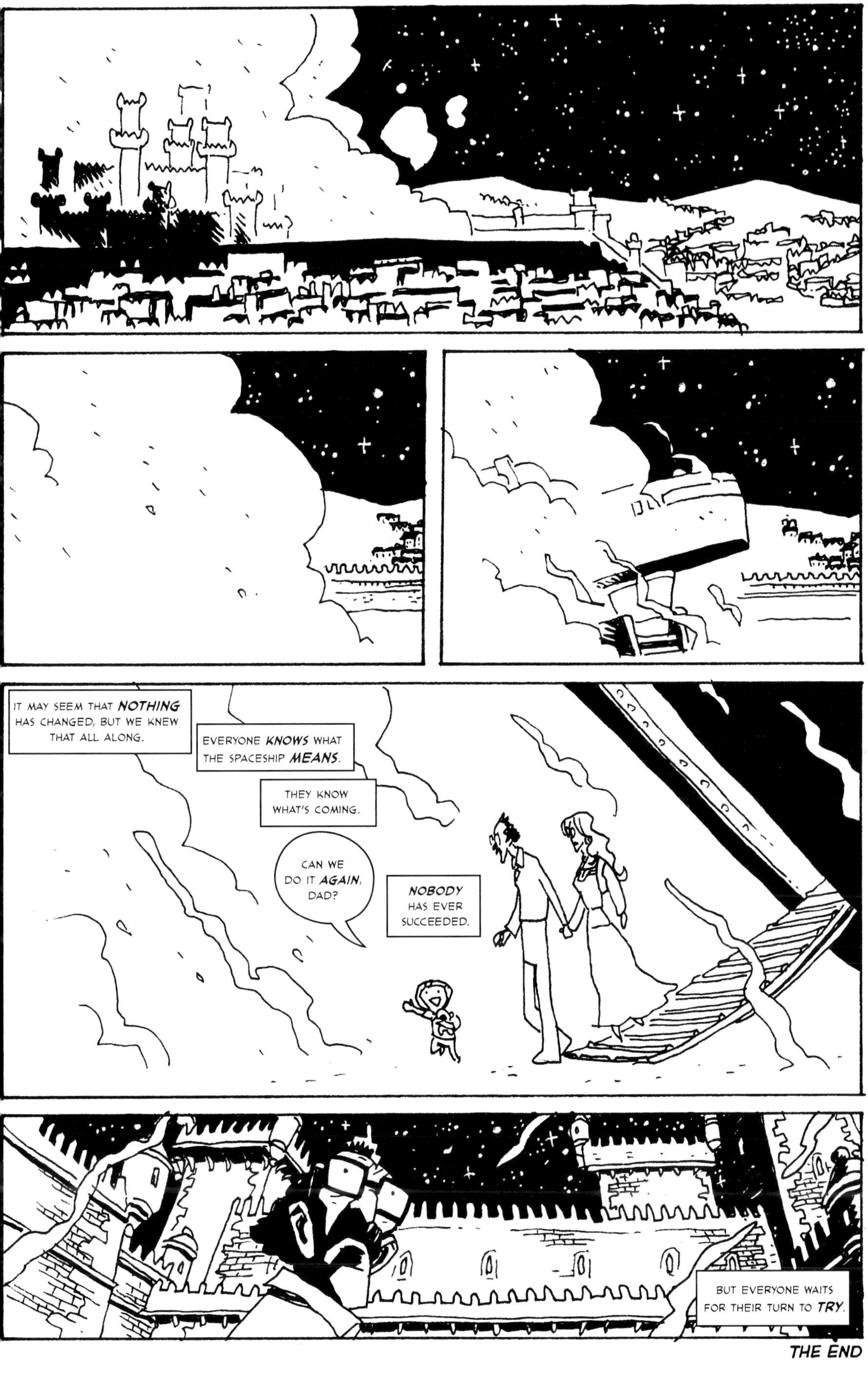
IT MAY SEEM THAT NOTHING HAS CHANGED, BUT WE KNEW THAT ALL ALONG.
EVERYONE KNOWS WHAT THE SPACESHIP MEANS.
THEY KNOW WHAT'S COMING.
CAN WE DO IT AGAIN, DAD?
NOBODY HAS EVER SUCCEEDED.
BUT EVERYONE WAITS FOR THEIR TURN TO TRY.
THE END

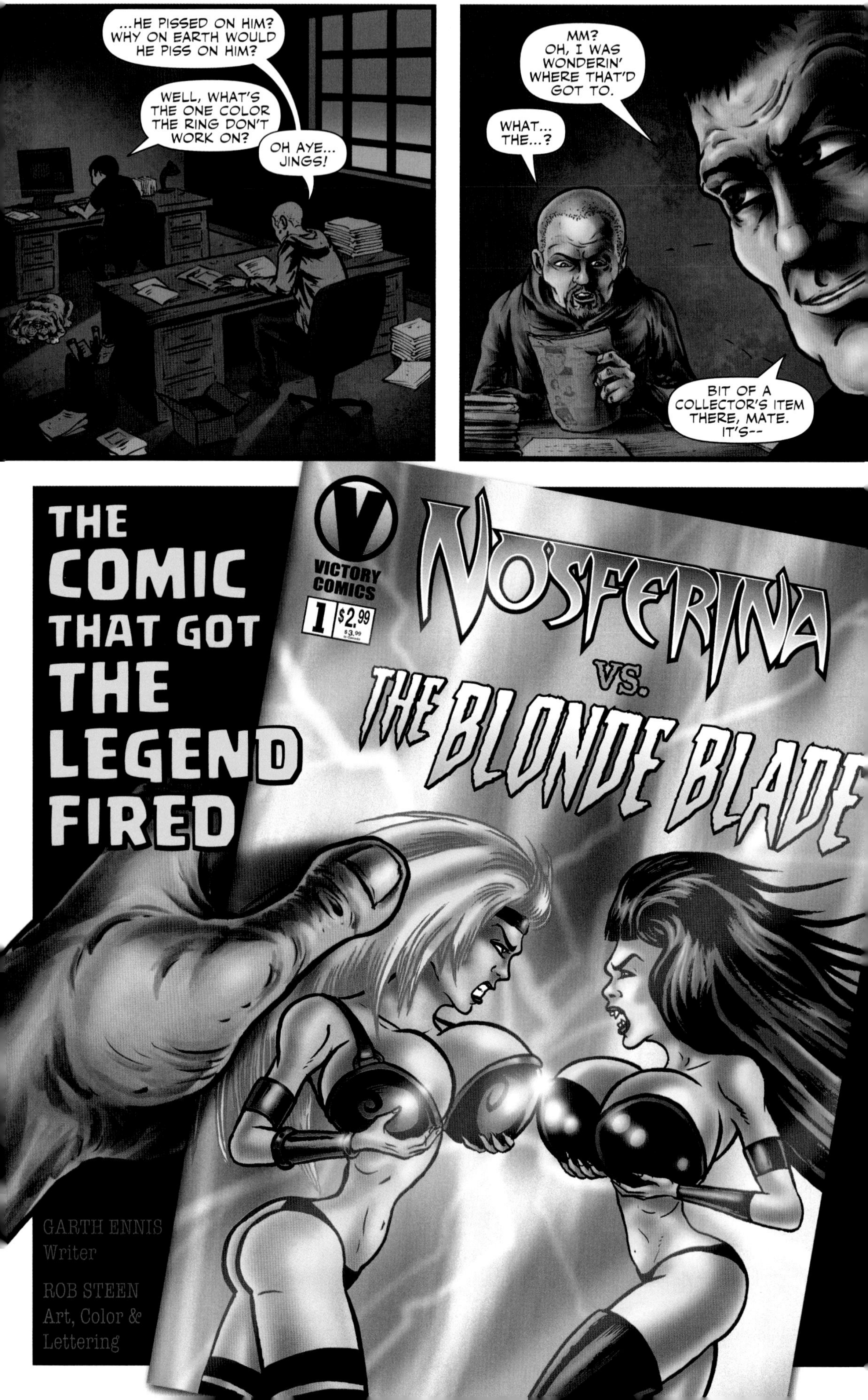
...HE PISSED ON HIM? WHY ON EARTH WOULD HE PISS ON HIM?
WELL, WHAT'S THE ONE COLOR THE RING DON'T WORK ON?
OH AYE... JINGS!
MM? OH, I WAS WONDERIN' WHERE THAT'D GOT TO.
WHAT... THE...?
BIT OF A COLLECTOR'S ITEM THERE, MATE. IT'S--
THE COMIC THAT GOT THE LEGEND FIRED
VICTORY COMICS
1 $2.99 $3.99 in Canada
NOSFERINA VS. THE BLONDE BLADE
GARTH ENNIS
Writer
ROB STEEN
Art, Color & Lettering

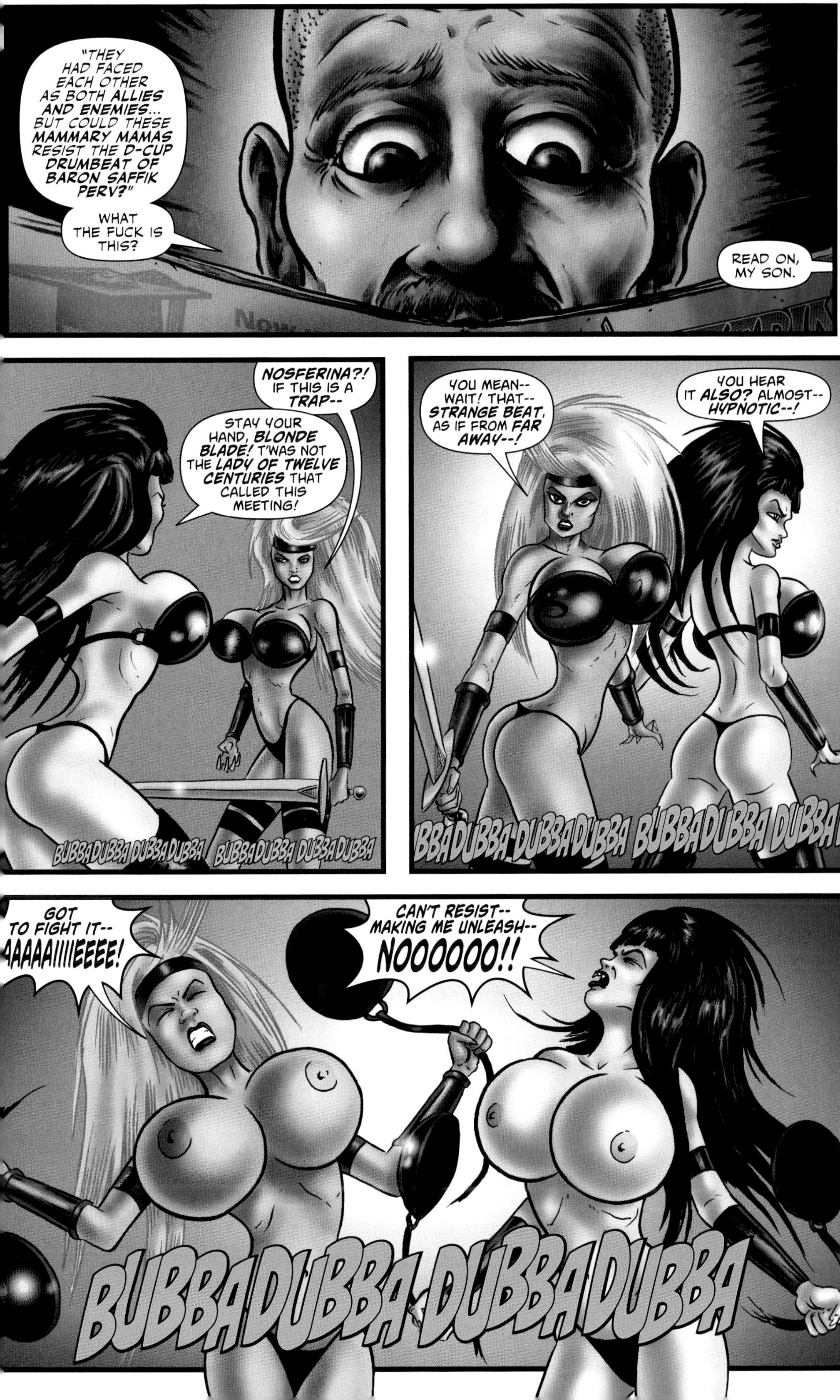
"THEY HAD FACED EACH OTHER AS BOTH **ALLIES AND ENEMIES**... BUT COULD THESE **MAMMARY MAMAS** RESIST THE **D-CUP DRUMBEAT OF BARON SAFFIK PERV?**"
WHAT THE FUCK IS THIS?
READ ON, MY SON.
NOSFERINA?! IF THIS IS A ***TRAP--***
STAY YOUR HAND, ***BLONDE BLADE!*** T'WAS NOT THE ***LADY OF TWELVE CENTURIES*** THAT CALLED THIS MEETING!
BUBBADUBBA DUBBADUBBA BUBBADUBBA DUBBADUBBA
YOU MEAN-- WAIT! THAT-- ***STRANGE BEAT,*** AS IF FROM ***FAR AWAY--!***
YOU HEAR IT ***ALSO?*** ALMOST-- ***HYPNOTIC--!***
BBADUBBA DUBBADUBBA BUBBADUBBA DUBBADU
GOT TO FIGHT IT--
AAAAAIIIIIEEEE!
CAN'T RESIST-- MAKING ME UNLEASH--
NOOOOOO!!
BUBBADUBBA DUBBADUBBA

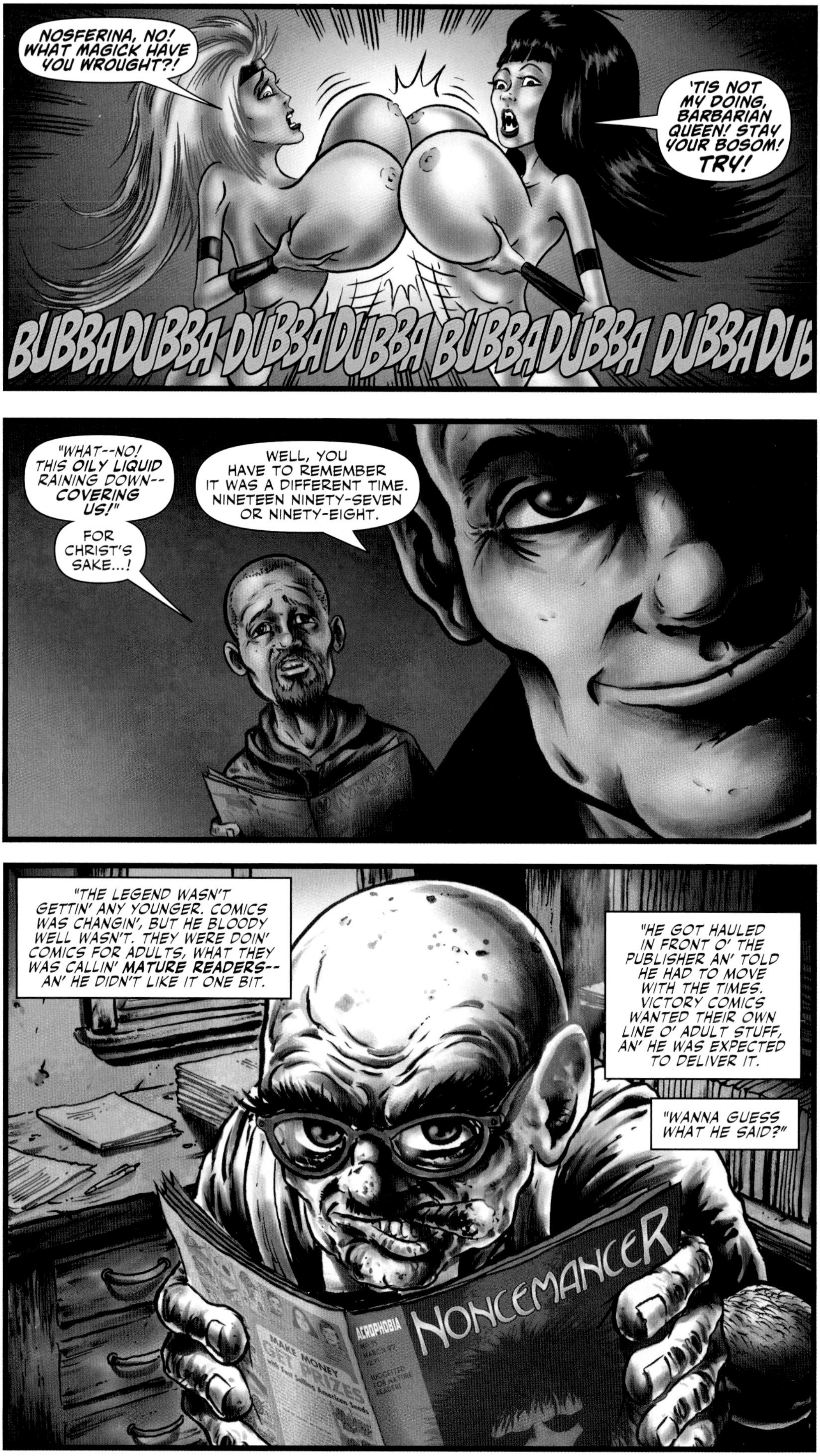
NOSFERINA, NO! WHAT MAGICK HAVE YOU WROUGHT?!
'TIS NOT MY DOING, BARBARIAN QUEEN! STAY YOUR BOSOM! TRY!
BUBBADUBBA DUBBADUBBA BUBBADUBBA DUBBADUB
"WHAT--NO! THIS OILY LIQUID RAINING DOWN-- COVERING US!"
FOR CHRIST'S SAKE...!
WELL, YOU HAVE TO REMEMBER IT WAS A DIFFERENT TIME. NINETEEN NINETY-SEVEN OR NINETY-EIGHT.
"THE LEGEND WASN'T GETTIN' ANY YOUNGER. COMICS WAS CHANGIN', BUT HE BLOODY WELL WASN'T. THEY WERE DOIN' COMICS FOR ADULTS, WHAT THEY WAS CALLIN' MATURE READERS-- AN' HE DIDN'T LIKE IT ONE BIT.
"HE GOT HAULED IN FRONT O' THE PUBLISHER AN' TOLD HE HAD TO MOVE WITH THE TIMES. VICTORY COMICS WANTED THEIR OWN LINE O' ADULT STUFF, AN' HE WAS EXPECTED TO DELIVER IT.
"WANNA GUESS WHAT HE SAID?"
NONCEMANCER
ACROPHOBIA
MAKE MONEY
GET PRIZES

"FAGGOTS..."

WELL, YEAH, BUT NOT STRAIGHT AWAY. FIRST HE PUT OUT THE SPECIAL LITTLE GEM YOU'RE HOLDIN' IN YER TREMBLIN' MITTS.

WROTE IT HIMSELF. PICKED TWO CLASSIC CHARACTERS, GOT THE LATEST SUPERSTAR ARTIST TO DRAW IT--AN' THE BLOODY THING SOLD LIKE A BASTARD...

IS IT... DYING AWAY...?

ARE WE-- FREE--?

BUBBA DUBBA DUBBA DUBBA BUBBA DUBBA DUBBA DUBBA

BUBBA DUBBA DUBBA DUBBA

STARTING UP AGAIN! NO! NO!

NOOOOOOO!!!

BUBBA DUBBA DUBBA DUBBA

THE LEGEND SAID THAT IF THEY WANTED ADULT READERS-- WELL, STUFF LIKE NOSFERINA AN' THE BLONDE BLADE'D ALWAYS HAD ADULT READERS. DIFFERENT SORT, MAYBE, AN' NOT THE KIND YOU WANNA OWN UP TO, BUT THEY WERE THERE.

HE WAS RIGHT, TOO, THAT ONE ISSUE OUTSOLD REVEREND SWEAR AN' BUSYDICK AN' BALDY DOME, 3D GLASSES ALL PUT TOGETHER.

SO... THEY FIRED HIM?

ON THE FUCKIN' SPOT.

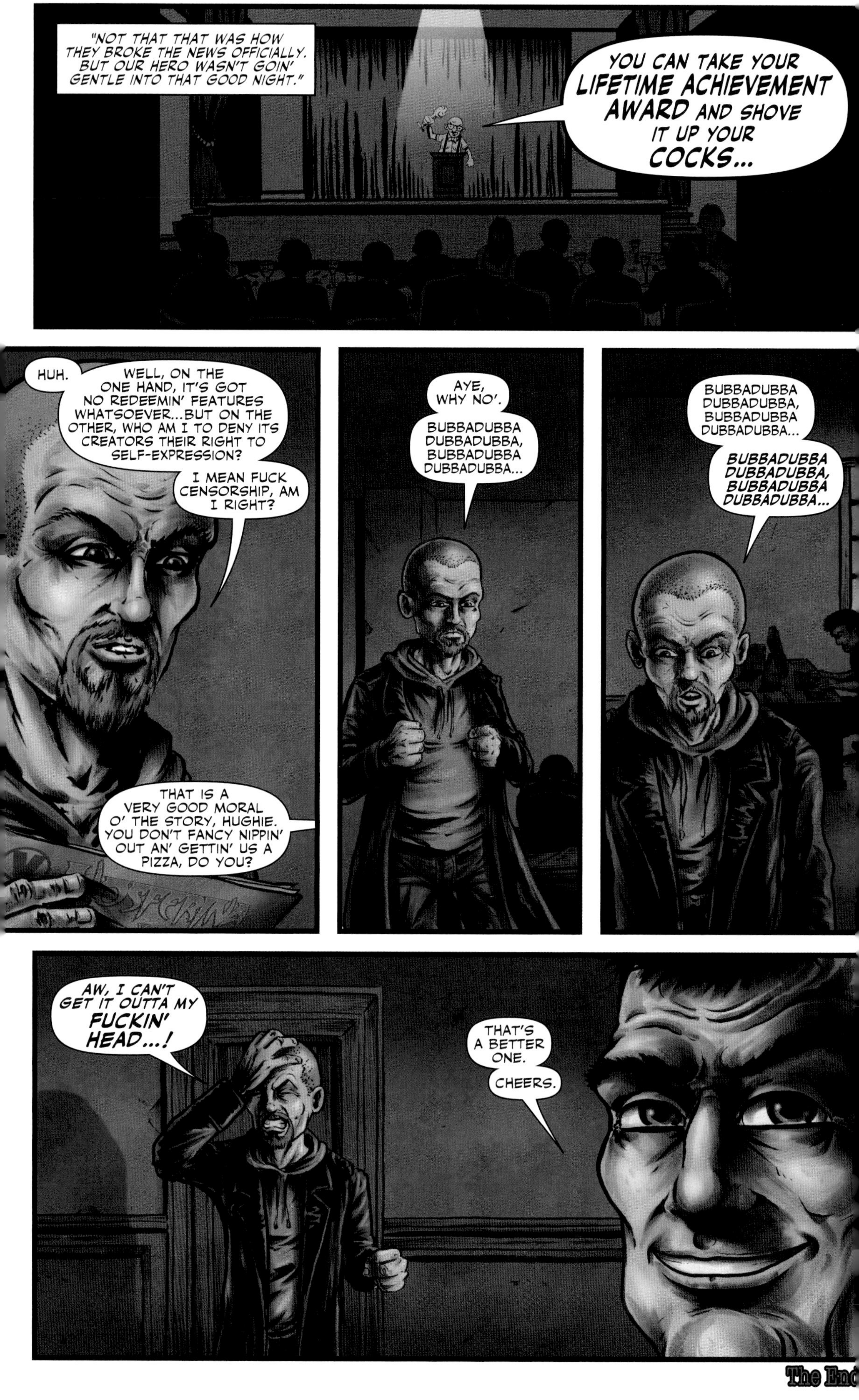
"NOT THAT THAT WAS HOW THEY BROKE THE NEWS OFFICIALLY. BUT OUR HERO WASN'T GOIN' GENTLE INTO THAT GOOD NIGHT."
YOU CAN TAKE YOUR LIFETIME ACHIEVEMENT AWARD AND SHOVE IT UP YOUR COCKS...
HUH.
WELL, ON THE ONE HAND, IT'S GOT NO REDEEMIN' FEATURES WHATSOEVER...BUT ON THE OTHER, WHO AM I TO DENY ITS CREATORS THEIR RIGHT TO SELF-EXPRESSION?
I MEAN FUCK CENSORSHIP, AM I RIGHT?
THAT IS A VERY GOOD MORAL O' THE STORY, HUGHIE. YOU DON'T FANCY NIPPIN' OUT AN' GETTIN' US A PIZZA, DO YOU?
AYE, WHY NO'.
BUBBADUBBA DUBBADUBBA, BUBBADUBBA DUBBADUBBA...
BUBBADUBBA DUBBADUBBA, BUBBADUBBA DUBBADUBBA...
BUBBADUBBA DUBBADUBBA, BUBBADUBBA DUBBADUBBA...
AW, I CAN'T GET IT OUTTA MY FUCKIN' HEAD...!
THAT'S A BETTER ONE.
CHEERS.
The End

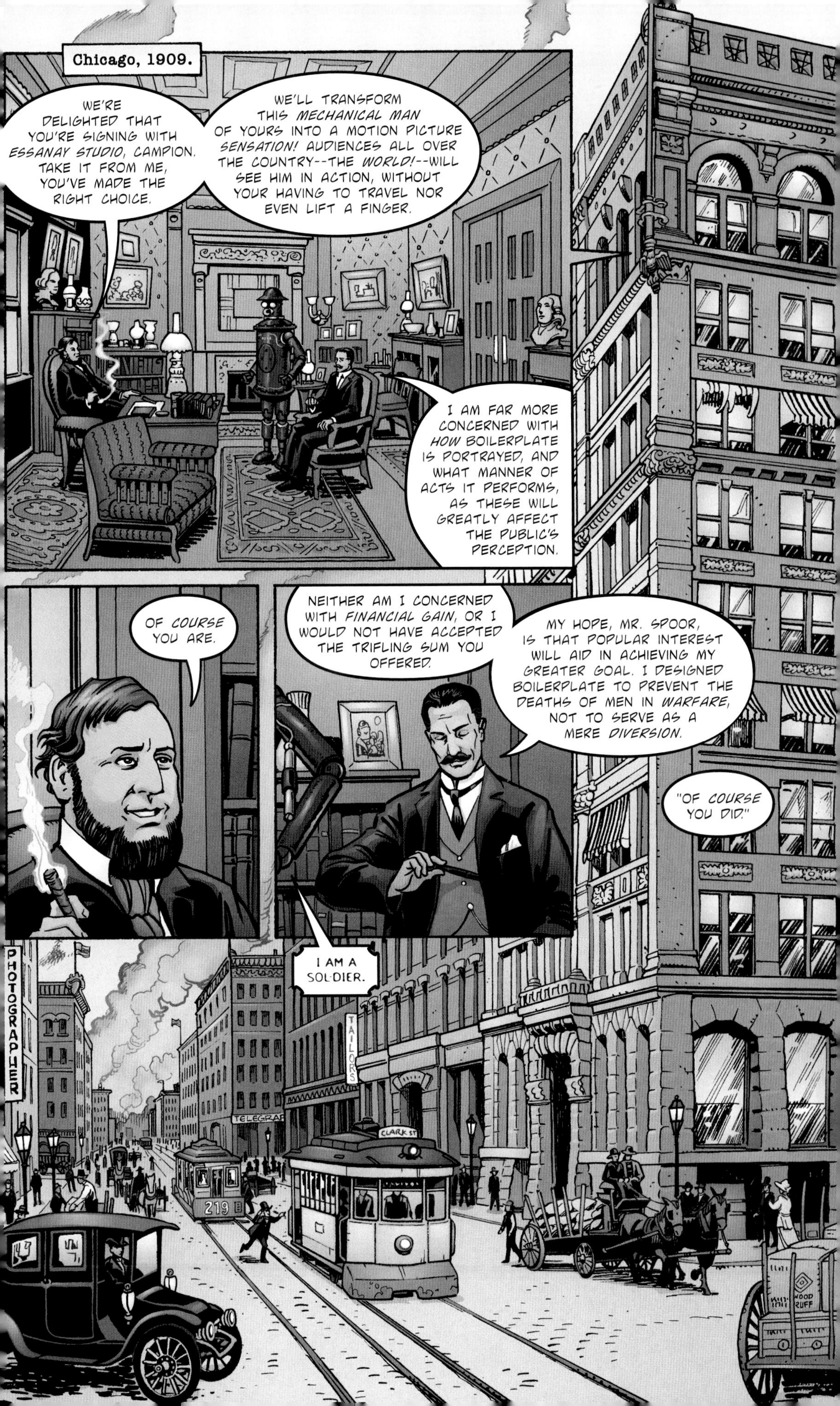

Chicago, 1909.
WE'RE DELIGHTED THAT YOU'RE SIGNING WITH *ESSANAY STUDIO*, CAMPION. TAKE IT FROM ME, YOU'VE MADE THE RIGHT CHOICE.
WE'LL TRANSFORM THIS *MECHANICAL MAN* OF YOURS INTO A MOTION PICTURE *SENSATION!* AUDIENCES ALL OVER THE COUNTRY--THE *WORLD!*--WILL SEE HIM IN ACTION, WITHOUT YOUR HAVING TO TRAVEL NOR EVEN LIFT A FINGER.
I AM FAR MORE CONCERNED WITH *HOW* BOILERPLATE IS PORTRAYED, AND WHAT MANNER OF ACTS IT PERFORMS, AS THESE WILL GREATLY AFFECT THE PUBLIC'S PERCEPTION.
OF *COURSE* YOU ARE.
NEITHER AM I CONCERNED WITH *FINANCIAL GAIN*, OR I WOULD NOT HAVE ACCEPTED THE TRIFLING SUM YOU OFFERED.
MY HOPE, MR. SPOOR, IS THAT POPULAR INTEREST WILL AID IN ACHIEVING MY GREATER GOAL. I DESIGNED BOILERPLATE TO PREVENT THE DEATHS OF MEN IN *WARFARE*, NOT TO SERVE AS A MERE *DIVERSION*.
"OF *COURSE* YOU DID."
I AM A SOL-DIER.
PHOTOGRAPHER
TAILORS
TELEGRAP
CLARK ST
219
WOOD RUFF

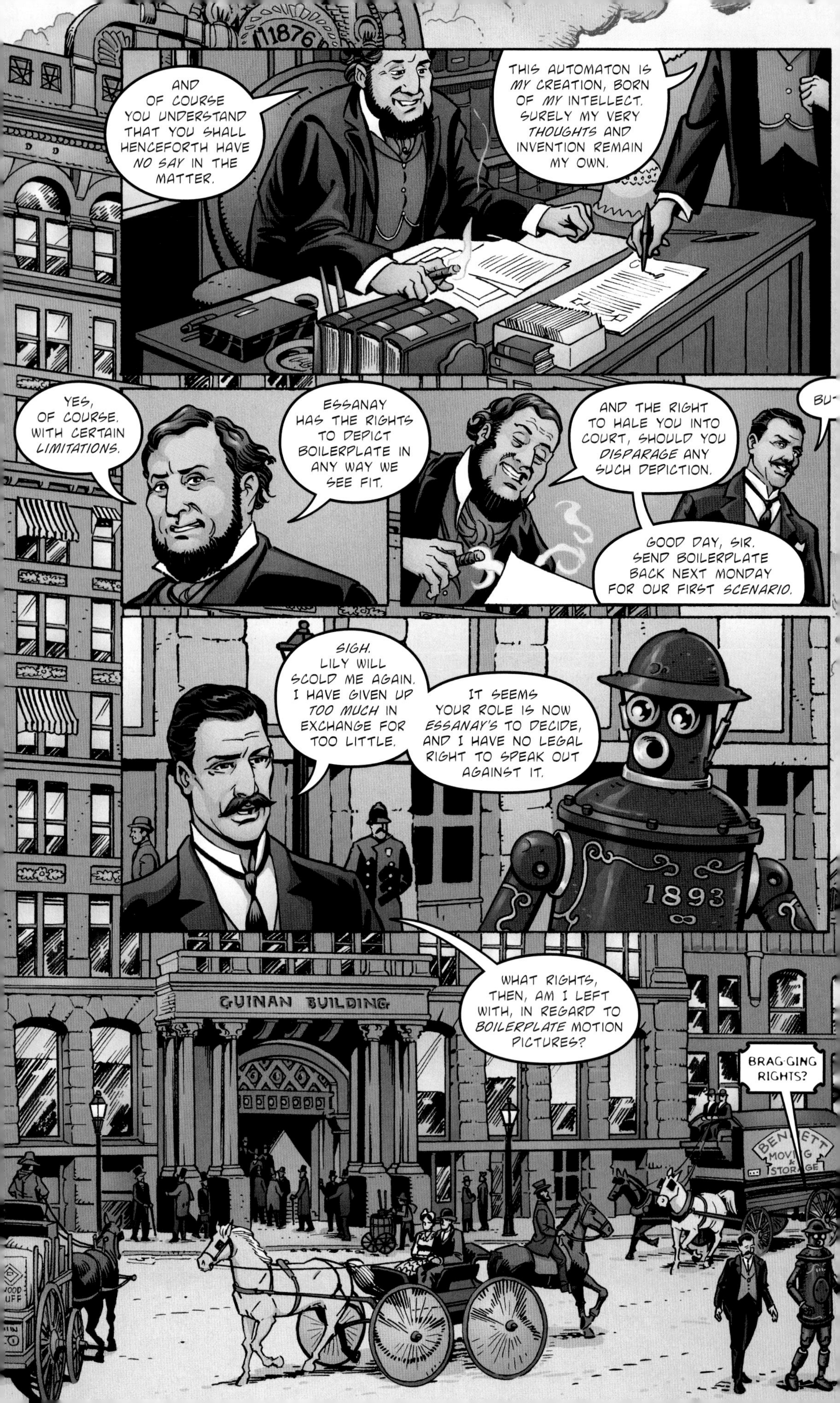

11876
AND OF COURSE YOU UNDERSTAND THAT YOU SHALL HENCEFORTH HAVE *NO SAY* IN THE MATTER.
THIS AUTOMATON IS *MY* CREATION, BORN OF *MY* INTELLECT. SURELY MY VERY *THOUGHTS* AND INVENTION REMAIN MY OWN.
YES, OF COURSE. WITH CERTAIN *LIMITATIONS*.
ESSANAY HAS THE RIGHTS TO DEPICT BOILERPLATE IN ANY WAY WE SEE FIT.
AND THE RIGHT TO HALE YOU INTO COURT, SHOULD YOU *DISPARAGE* ANY SUCH DEPICTION.
BU–
GOOD DAY, SIR. SEND BOILERPLATE BACK NEXT MONDAY FOR OUR FIRST *SCENARIO*.
SIGH. LILY WILL SCOLD ME AGAIN. I HAVE GIVEN UP *TOO MUCH* IN EXCHANGE FOR TOO LITTLE.
IT SEEMS YOUR ROLE IS NOW *ESSANAY'S* TO DECIDE, AND I HAVE NO LEGAL RIGHT TO SPEAK OUT AGAINST IT.
1893
GUINAN BUILDING
WHAT RIGHTS, THEN, AM I LEFT WITH, IN REGARD TO *BOILERPLATE* MOTION PICTURES?
BRAG·GING RIGHTS?
BENNETT MOVING & STORAGE

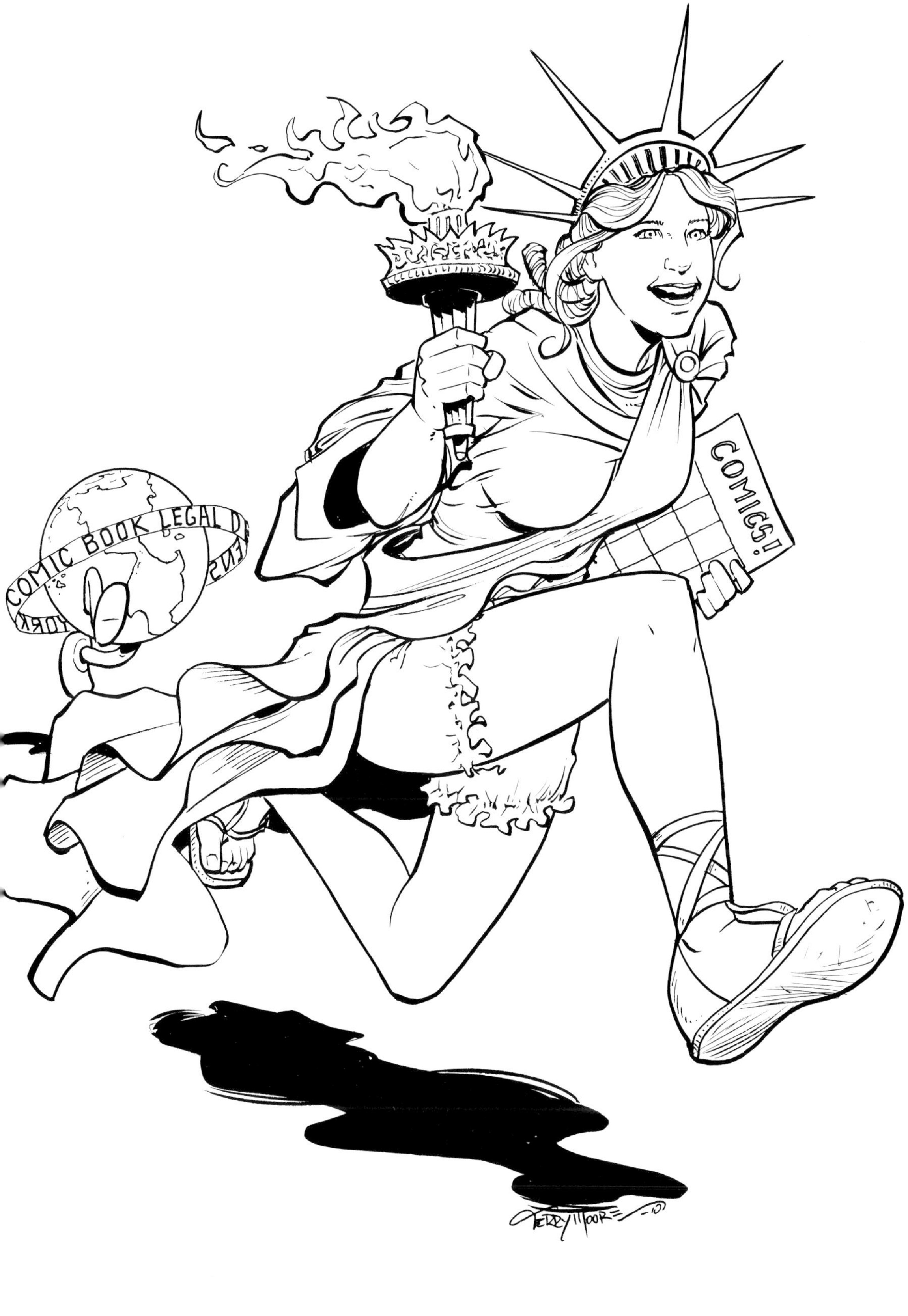
COMIC BOOK LEGAL
COMICS!
TERRY MOORE -10

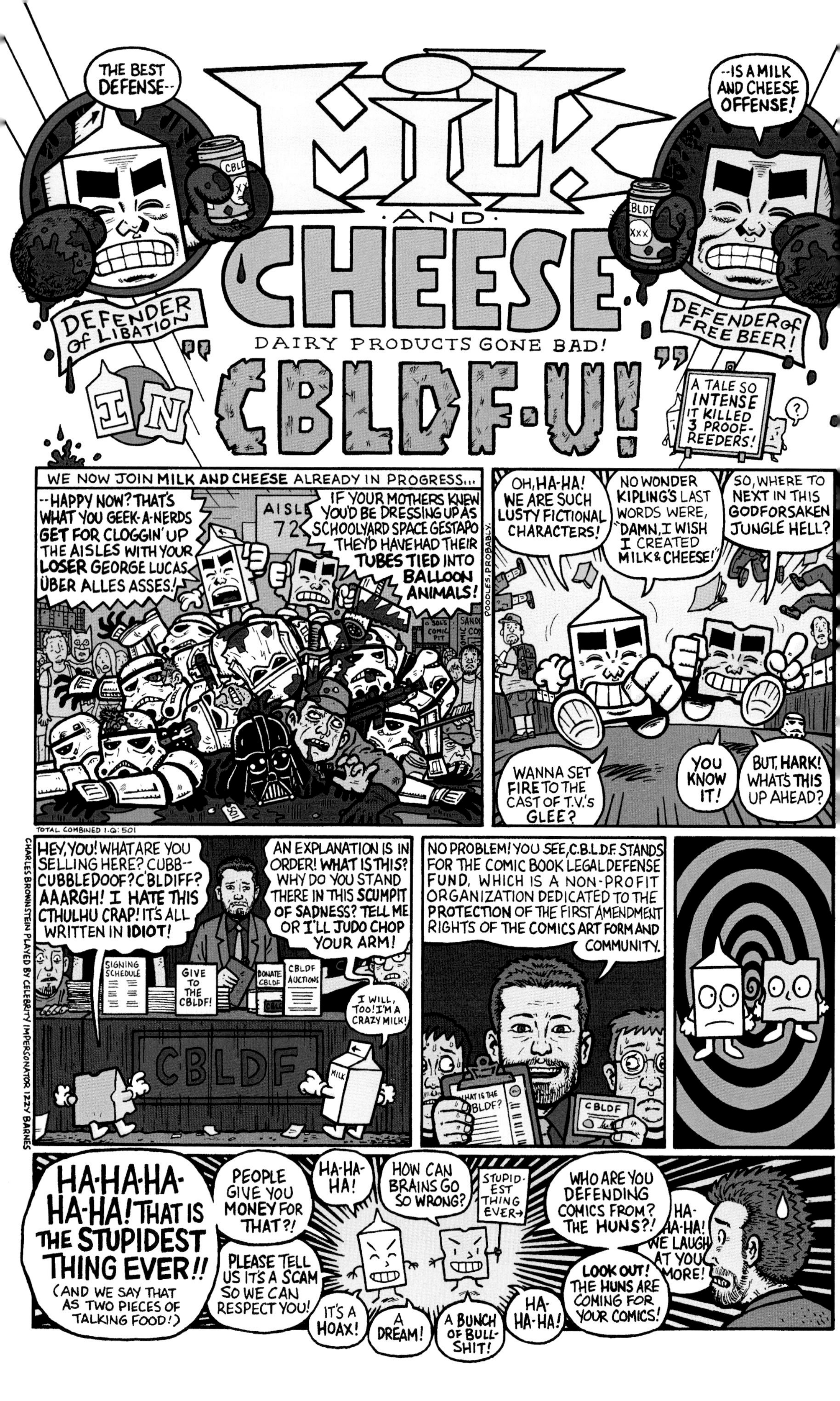

THE BEST DEFENSE--
--IS A MILK AND CHEESE OFFENSE!
MILK
·AND·
CHEESE
DEFENDER of LIBATION
DEFENDER of FREE BEER!
DAIRY PRODUCTS GONE BAD!
IN
"CBLDF-U!"
A TALE SO INTENSE IT KILLED 3 PROOF-REEDERS!
?
WE NOW JOIN MILK AND CHEESE ALREADY IN PROGRESS...
--HAPPY NOW? THAT'S WHAT YOU GEEK-A-NERDS GET FOR CLOGGIN' UP THE AISLES WITH YOUR LOSER GEORGE LUCAS ÜBER ALLES ASSES!
AISLE 72
IF YOUR MOTHERS KNEW YOU'D BE DRESSING UP AS SCHOOLYARD SPACE GESTAPO THEY'D HAVE HAD THEIR TUBES TIED INTO BALLOON ANIMALS!
SOL'S COMIC PIT
POODLES, PROBABLY.
TOTAL COMBINED I.Q.: 501
OH, HA-HA! WE ARE SUCH LUSTY FICTIONAL CHARACTERS!
NO WONDER KIPLING'S LAST WORDS WERE, "DAMN, I WISH I CREATED MILK & CHEESE!"
SO, WHERE TO NEXT IN THIS GODFORSAKEN JUNGLE HELL?
WANNA SET FIRE TO THE CAST OF T.V.'s GLEE?
YOU KNOW IT!
BUT, HARK! WHAT'S THIS UP AHEAD?
CHARLES BROWNSTEIN PLAYED BY CELEBRITY IMPERSONATOR IZZY BARNES
HEY, YOU! WHAT ARE YOU SELLING HERE? CUBB--CUBBLEDOOF? C'BLDIFF? AAARGH! I HATE THIS CTHULHU CRAP! IT'S ALL WRITTEN IN IDIOT!
AN EXPLANATION IS IN ORDER! WHAT IS THIS? WHY DO YOU STAND THERE IN THIS SCUMPIT OF SADNESS? TELL ME OR I'LL JUDO CHOP YOUR ARM!
SIGNING SCHEDULE
GIVE TO THE CBLDF!
DONATE CBLDF
CBLDF AUCTIONS
I WILL, TOO! I'M A CRAZY MILK!
CBLDF
MILK
NO PROBLEM! YOU SEE, C.B.L.D.F. STANDS FOR THE COMIC BOOK LEGAL DEFENSE FUND, WHICH IS A NON-PROFIT ORGANIZATION DEDICATED TO THE PROTECTION OF THE FIRST AMENDMENT RIGHTS OF THE COMICS ART FORM AND COMMUNITY.
WHAT IS THE CBLDF?
CBLDF
HA-HA-HA-HA-HA! THAT IS THE STUPIDEST THING EVER!! (AND WE SAY THAT AS TWO PIECES OF TALKING FOOD!)
PEOPLE GIVE YOU MONEY FOR THAT?!
HA-HA-HA!
HOW CAN BRAINS GO SO WRONG?
STUPID-EST THING EVER→
WHO ARE YOU DEFENDING COMICS FROM? THE HUNS?!
PLEASE TELL US IT'S A SCAM SO WE CAN RESPECT YOU!
HA-HA-HA! WE LAUGH AT YOU MORE!
LOOK OUT! THE HUNS ARE COMING FOR YOUR COMICS!
IT'S A HOAX!
A DREAM!
A BUNCH OF BULL-SHIT!
HA-HA-HA!

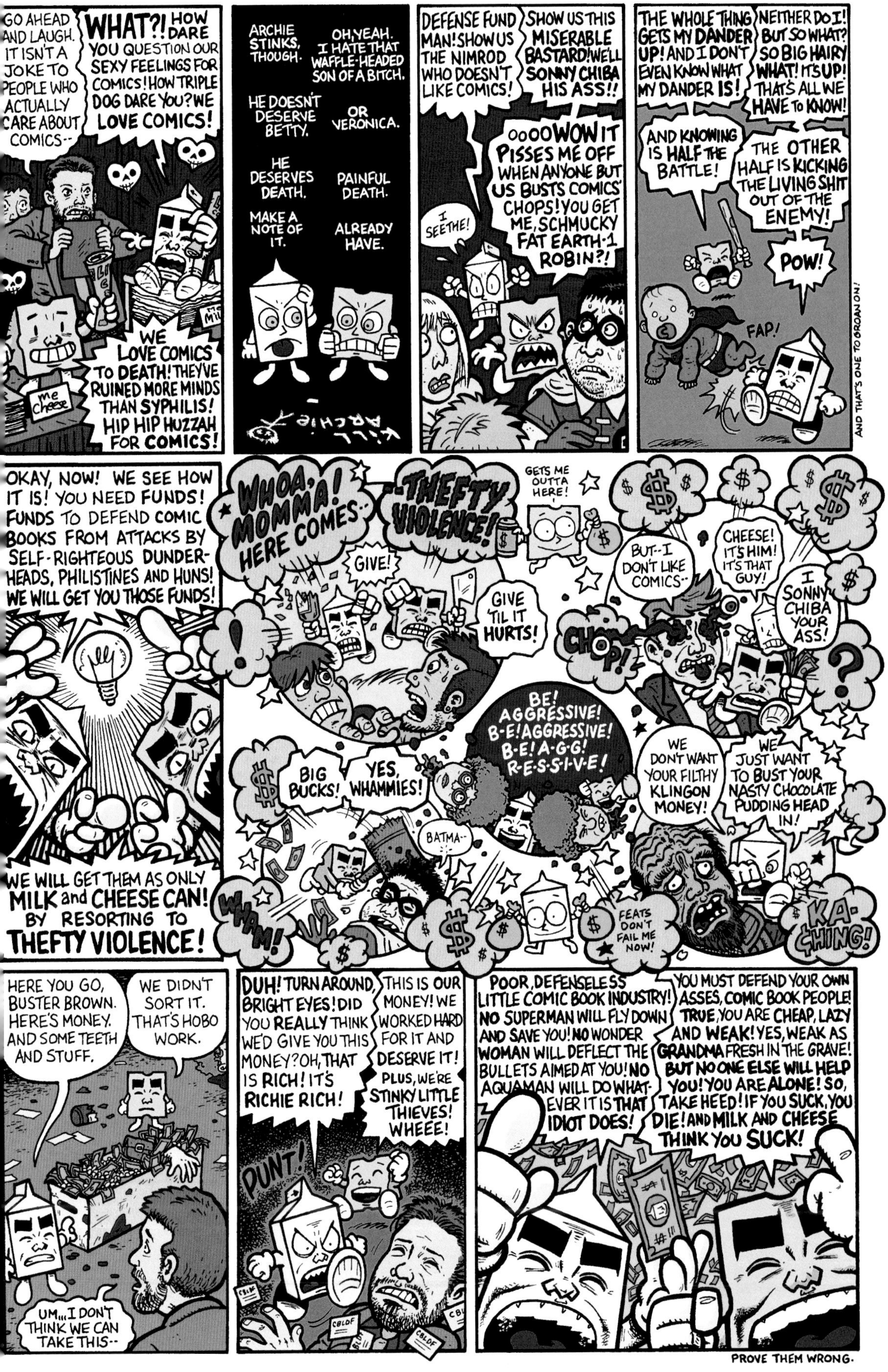

GO AHEAD AND LAUGH. IT ISN'T A JOKE TO PEOPLE WHO ACTUALLY CARE ABOUT COMICS--
WHAT?! HOW DARE YOU QUESTION OUR SEXY FEELINGS FOR COMICS! HOW TRIPLE DOG DARE YOU? WE LOVE COMICS!
WE LOVE COMICS TO DEATH! THEY'VE RUINED MORE MINDS THAN SYPHILIS! HIP HIP HUZZAH FOR COMICS!
me Cheese
ARCHIE STINKS, THOUGH.
OH, YEAH. I HATE THAT WAFFLE-HEADED SON OF A BITCH.
HE DOESN'T DESERVE BETTY.
OR VERONICA.
HE DESERVES DEATH.
PAINFUL DEATH.
MAKE A NOTE OF IT.
ALREADY HAVE.
KILL ARCHIE
DEFENSE FUND MAN! SHOW US THE NIMROD WHO DOESN'T LIKE COMICS!
SHOW US THIS MISERABLE BASTARD! WE'LL SONNY CHIBA HIS ASS!!
I SEETHE!
OOOOWOW IT PISSES ME OFF WHEN ANYONE BUT US BUSTS COMICS' CHOPS! YOU GET ME, SCHMUCKY FAT EARTH-1 ROBIN?!
THE WHOLE THING GETS MY DANDER UP! AND I DON'T EVEN KNOW WHAT MY DANDER IS!
NEITHER DO I! BUT SO WHAT? SO BIG HAIRY WHAT! IT'S UP! THAT'S ALL WE HAVE TO KNOW!
AND KNOWING IS HALF THE BATTLE!
THE OTHER HALF IS KICKING THE LIVING SHIT OUT OF THE ENEMY!
POW!
FAP!
AND THAT'S ONE TO GROAN ON!
OKAY, NOW! WE SEE HOW IT IS! YOU NEED FUNDS! FUNDS TO DEFEND COMIC BOOKS FROM ATTACKS BY SELF-RIGHTEOUS DUNDERHEADS, PHILISTINES AND HUNS! WE WILL GET YOU THOSE FUNDS!
WE WILL GET THEM AS ONLY MILK and CHEESE CAN! BY RESORTING TO THEFTY VIOLENCE!
WHOA, MOMMA! HERE COMES--
--THEFTY VIOLENCE!
GETS ME OUTTA HERE!
GIVE!
GIVE 'TIL IT HURTS!
BUT--I DON'T LIKE COMICS--
CHEESE! IT'S HIM! IT'S THAT GUY!
I SONNY CHIBA YOUR ASS!
CHOP!
BE! AGGRESSIVE! B-E! AGGRESSIVE! B-E! A-G-G! R-E-S-S-I-V-E!
BIG BUCKS!
YES, WHAMMIES!
BATMA--
WE DON'T WANT YOUR FILTHY KLINGON MONEY!
WE JUST WANT TO BUST YOUR NASTY CHOCOLATE PUDDING HEAD IN!
WHAM!
FEATS DON'T FAIL ME NOW!
KA-CHING!
HERE YOU GO, BUSTER BROWN. HERE'S MONEY. AND SOME TEETH AND STUFF.
WE DIDN'T SORT IT. THAT'S HOBO WORK.
UM... I DON'T THINK WE CAN TAKE THIS--
DUH! TURN AROUND, BRIGHT EYES! DID YOU REALLY THINK WE'D GIVE YOU THIS MONEY? OH, THAT IS RICH! IT'S RICHIE RICH!
THIS IS OUR MONEY! WE WORKED HARD FOR IT AND DESERVE IT! PLUS, WE'RE STINKY LITTLE THIEVES! WHEEE!
PUNT!
CBLDF
POOR, DEFENSELESS LITTLE COMIC BOOK INDUSTRY! NO SUPERMAN WILL FLY DOWN AND SAVE YOU! NO WONDER WOMAN WILL DEFLECT THE BULLETS AIMED AT YOU! NO AQUAMAN WILL DO WHATEVER IT IS THAT IDIOT DOES!
YOU MUST DEFEND YOUR OWN ASSES, COMIC BOOK PEOPLE! TRUE, YOU ARE CHEAP, LAZY AND WEAK! YES, WEAK AS GRANDMA FRESH IN THE GRAVE! BUT NO ONE ELSE WILL HELP YOU! YOU ARE ALONE! SO, TAKE HEED! IF YOU SUCK, YOU DIE! AND MILK AND CHEESE THINK YOU SUCK!
PROVE THEM WRONG.

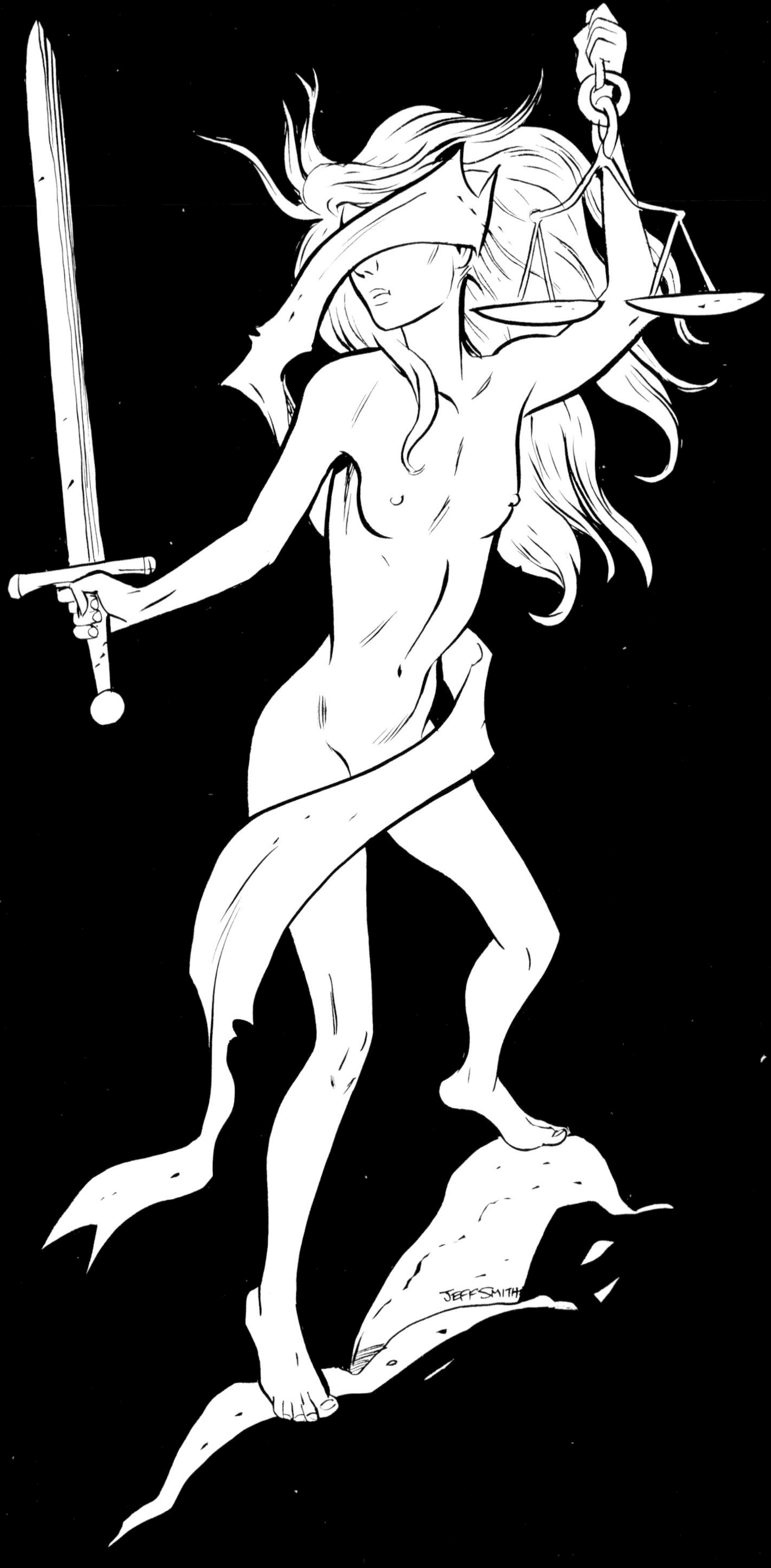
JEFF SMITH

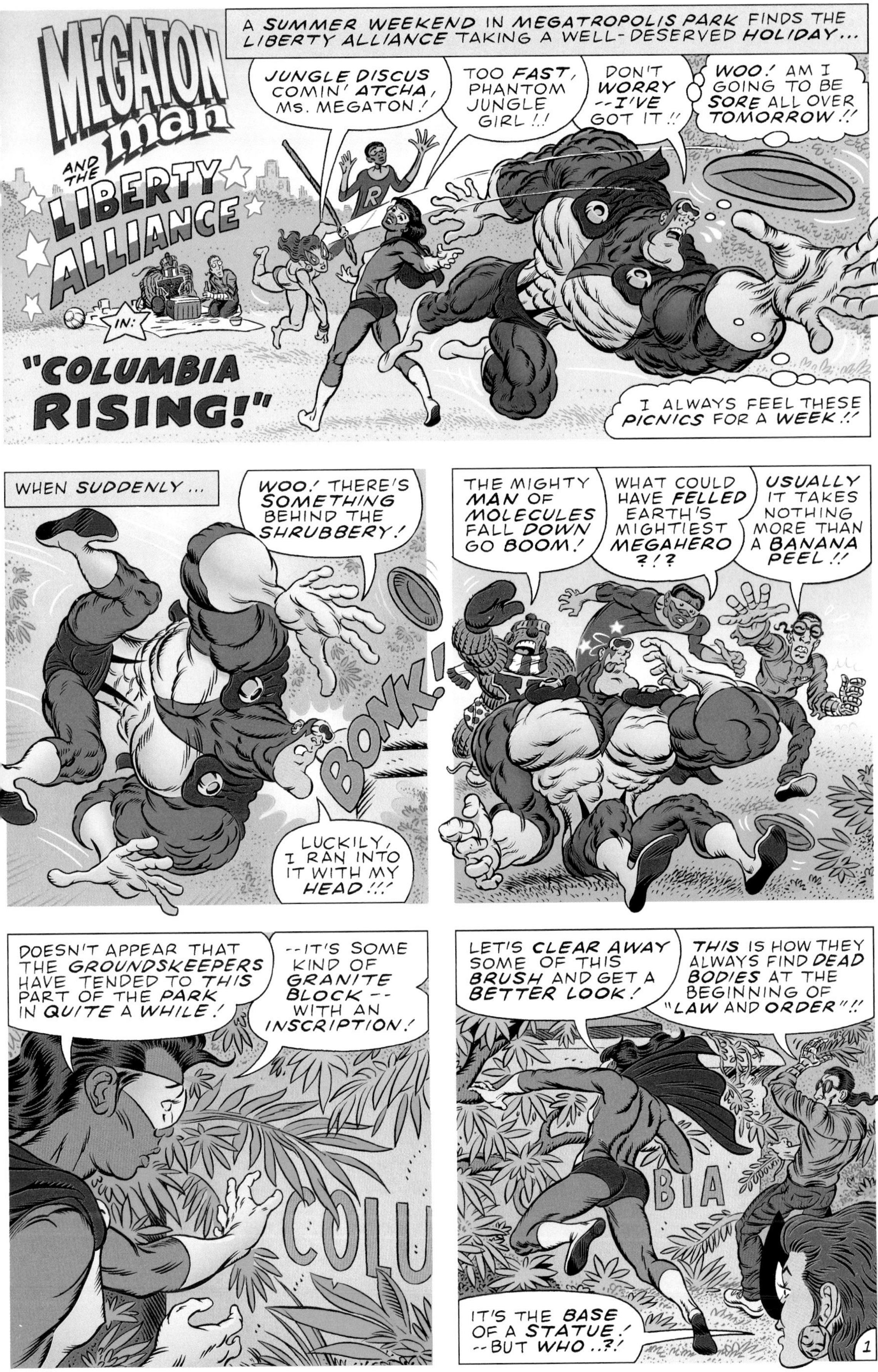
MEGATON man
AND THE LIBERTY ALLIANCE
IN:
"COLUMBIA RISING!"
A SUMMER WEEKEND IN MEGATROPOLIS PARK FINDS THE LIBERTY ALLIANCE TAKING A WELL-DESERVED HOLIDAY...
JUNGLE DISCUS COMIN' ATCHA, Ms. MEGATON!
TOO FAST, PHANTOM JUNGLE GIRL!!
DON'T WORRY --I'VE GOT IT!!
WOO! AM I GOING TO BE SORE ALL OVER TOMORROW!!
I ALWAYS FEEL THESE PICNICS FOR A WEEK!!
WHEN SUDDENLY...
WOO! THERE'S SOMETHING BEHIND THE SHRUBBERY!
BONK!
LUCKILY, I RAN INTO IT WITH MY HEAD!!!
THE MIGHTY MAN OF MOLECULES FALL DOWN GO BOOM!
WHAT COULD HAVE FELLED EARTH'S MIGHTIEST MEGAHERO ?!?
USUALLY IT TAKES NOTHING MORE THAN A BANANA PEEL!!
DOESN'T APPEAR THAT THE GROUNDSKEEPERS HAVE TENDED TO THIS PART OF THE PARK IN QUITE A WHILE!
--IT'S SOME KIND OF GRANITE BLOCK -- WITH AN INSCRIPTION!
COLU
LET'S CLEAR AWAY SOME OF THIS BRUSH AND GET A BETTER LOOK!
THIS IS HOW THEY ALWAYS FIND DEAD BODIES AT THE BEGINNING OF "LAW AND ORDER"!!
BIA
IT'S THE BASE OF A STATUE! --BUT WHO..?!

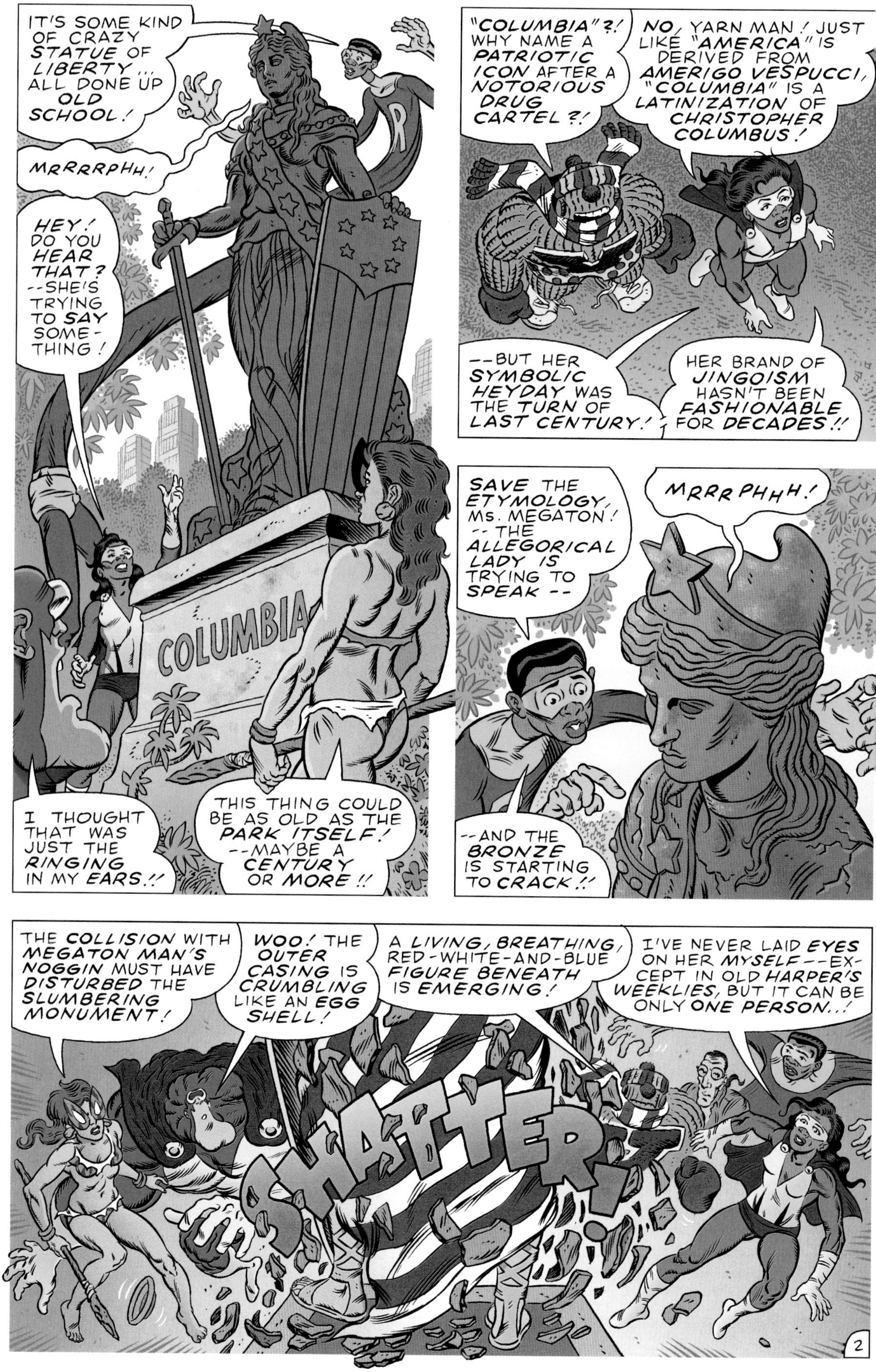
IT'S SOME KIND OF CRAZY STATUE OF LIBERTY... ALL DONE UP OLD SCHOOL!
MRRRRPHH!
HEY! DO YOU HEAR THAT? --SHE'S TRYING TO SAY SOME-THING!
COLUMBIA
I THOUGHT THAT WAS JUST THE RINGING IN MY EARS.!
THIS THING COULD BE AS OLD AS THE PARK ITSELF! --MAYBE A CENTURY OR MORE!!
"COLUMBIA"?! WHY NAME A PATRIOTIC ICON AFTER A NOTORIOUS DRUG CARTEL?!
NO, YARN MAN! JUST LIKE "AMERICA" IS DERIVED FROM AMERIGO VESPUCCI, "COLUMBIA" IS A LATINIZATION OF CHRISTOPHER COLUMBUS!
--BUT HER SYMBOLIC HEYDAY WAS THE TURN OF LAST CENTURY!
HER BRAND OF JINGOISM HASN'T BEEN FASHIONABLE FOR DECADES!!
SAVE THE ETYMOLOGY, Ms. MEGATON! --THE ALLEGORICAL LADY IS TRYING TO SPEAK --
MRRRPHHH!
--AND THE BRONZE IS STARTING TO CRACK!!
THE COLLISION WITH MEGATON MAN'S NOGGIN MUST HAVE DISTURBED THE SLUMBERING MONUMENT!
WOO! THE OUTER CASING IS CRUMBLING LIKE AN EGG SHELL!
A LIVING, BREATHING, RED-WHITE-AND-BLUE FIGURE BENEATH IS EMERGING!
I'VE NEVER LAID EYES ON HER MYSELF--EXCEPT IN OLD HARPER'S WEEKLIES, BUT IT CAN BE ONLY ONE PERSON...!
SHATTER!

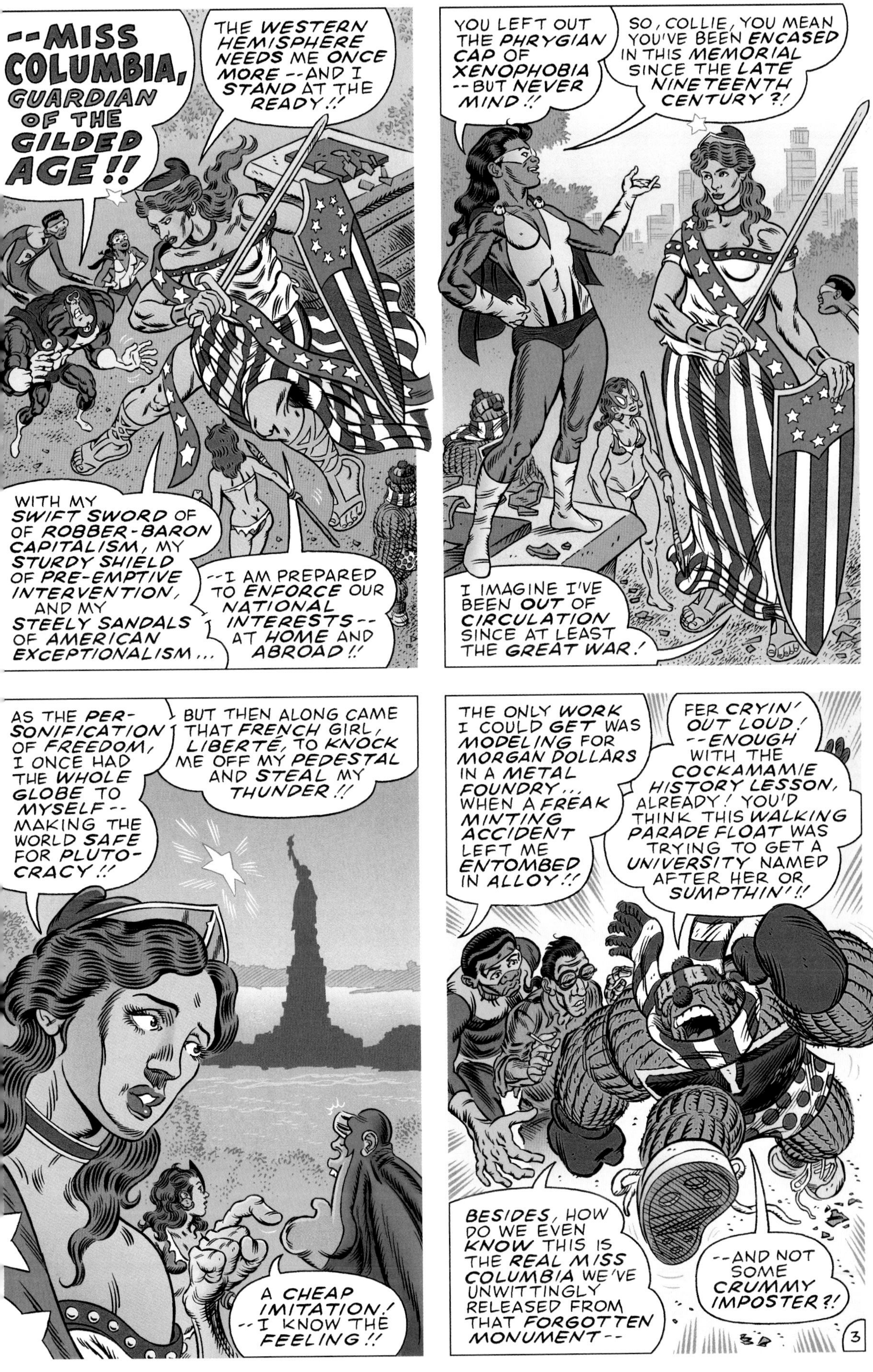
--MISS COLUMBIA, GUARDIAN OF THE GILDED AGE!!
THE WESTERN HEMISPHERE NEEDS ME ONCE MORE --AND I STAND AT THE READY!!
WITH MY SWIFT SWORD OF OF ROBBER-BARON CAPITALISM, MY STURDY SHIELD OF PRE-EMPTIVE INTERVENTION, AND MY STEELY SANDALS OF AMERICAN EXCEPTIONALISM...
--I AM PREPARED TO ENFORCE OUR NATIONAL INTERESTS-- AT HOME AND ABROAD!!
YOU LEFT OUT THE PHRYGIAN CAP OF XENOPHOBIA --BUT NEVER MIND!!
SO, COLLIE, YOU MEAN YOU'VE BEEN ENCASED IN THIS MEMORIAL SINCE THE LATE NINETEENTH CENTURY?!
I IMAGINE I'VE BEEN OUT OF CIRCULATION SINCE AT LEAST THE GREAT WAR!
AS THE PERSONIFICATION OF FREEDOM, I ONCE HAD THE WHOLE GLOBE TO MYSELF-- MAKING THE WORLD SAFE FOR PLUTOCRACY!!
BUT THEN ALONG CAME THAT FRENCH GIRL, LIBERTÉ, TO KNOCK ME OFF MY PEDESTAL AND STEAL MY THUNDER!!
A CHEAP IMITATION! --I KNOW THE FEELING!!
THE ONLY WORK I COULD GET WAS MODELING FOR MORGAN DOLLARS IN A METAL FOUNDRY... WHEN A FREAK MINTING ACCIDENT LEFT ME ENTOMBED IN ALLOY!!
FER CRYIN' OUT LOUD! --ENOUGH WITH THE COCKAMAMIE HISTORY LESSON, ALREADY! YOU'D THINK THIS WALKING PARADE FLOAT WAS TRYING TO GET A UNIVERSITY NAMED AFTER HER OR SUMPTHIN'!!
BESIDES, HOW DO WE EVEN KNOW THIS IS THE REAL MISS COLUMBIA WE'VE UNWITTINGLY RELEASED FROM THAT FORGOTTEN MONUMENT--
--AND NOT SOME CRUMMY IMPOSTER?!

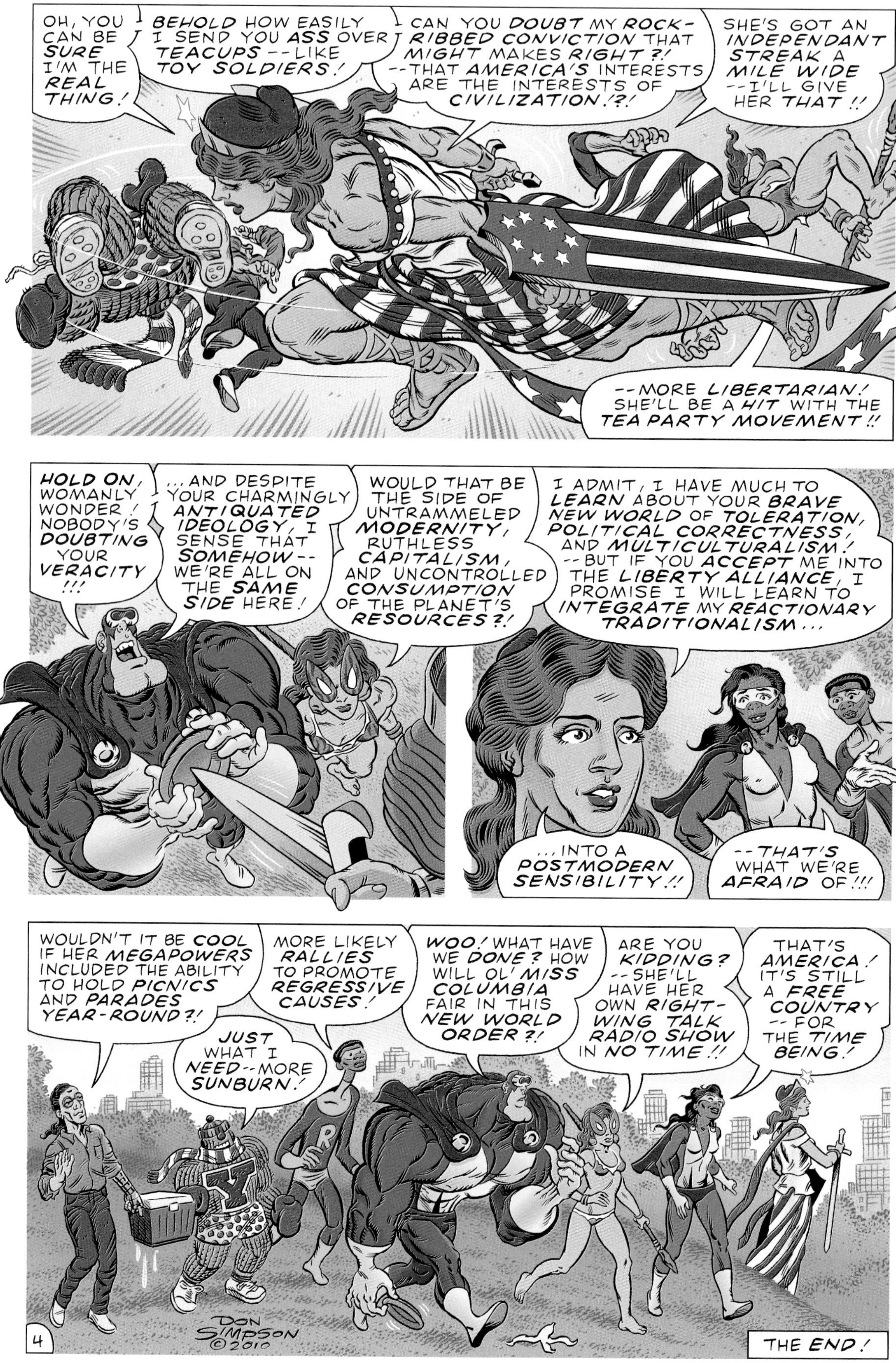
OH, YOU CAN BE SURE I'M THE REAL THING!
BEHOLD HOW EASILY I SEND YOU ASS OVER TEACUPS --LIKE TOY SOLDIERS!
CAN YOU DOUBT MY ROCK-RIBBED CONVICTION THAT MIGHT MAKES RIGHT?! --THAT AMERICA'S INTERESTS ARE THE INTERESTS OF CIVILIZATION!?!
SHE'S GOT AN INDEPENDANT STREAK A MILE WIDE --I'LL GIVE HER THAT!!
--MORE LIBERTARIAN! SHE'LL BE A HIT WITH THE TEA PARTY MOVEMENT!!
HOLD ON, WOMANLY WONDER! NOBODY'S DOUBTING YOUR VERACITY!!!
...AND DESPITE YOUR CHARMINGLY ANTIQUATED IDEOLOGY, I SENSE THAT SOMEHOW--WE'RE ALL ON THE SAME SIDE HERE!
WOULD THAT BE THE SIDE OF UNTRAMMELED MODERNITY, RUTHLESS CAPITALISM, AND UNCONTROLLED CONSUMPTION OF THE PLANET'S RESOURCES?!
I ADMIT, I HAVE MUCH TO LEARN ABOUT YOUR BRAVE NEW WORLD OF TOLERATION, POLITICAL CORRECTNESS, AND MULTICULTURALISM! --BUT IF YOU ACCEPT ME INTO THE LIBERTY ALLIANCE, I PROMISE I WILL LEARN TO INTEGRATE MY REACTIONARY TRADITIONALISM...
...INTO A POSTMODERN SENSIBILITY!!
--THAT'S WHAT WE'RE AFRAID OF!!!
WOULDN'T IT BE COOL IF HER MEGAPOWERS INCLUDED THE ABILITY TO HOLD PICNICS AND PARADES YEAR-ROUND?!
JUST WHAT I NEED--MORE SUNBURN!
MORE LIKELY RALLIES TO PROMOTE REGRESSIVE CAUSES!
WOO! WHAT HAVE WE DONE? HOW WILL OL' MISS COLUMBIA FAIR IN THIS NEW WORLD ORDER?!
ARE YOU KIDDING? --SHE'LL HAVE HER OWN RIGHT-WING TALK RADIO SHOW IN NO TIME!!
THAT'S AMERICA! IT'S STILL A FREE COUNTRY --FOR THE TIME BEING!
DON SIMPSON ©2010
THE END!

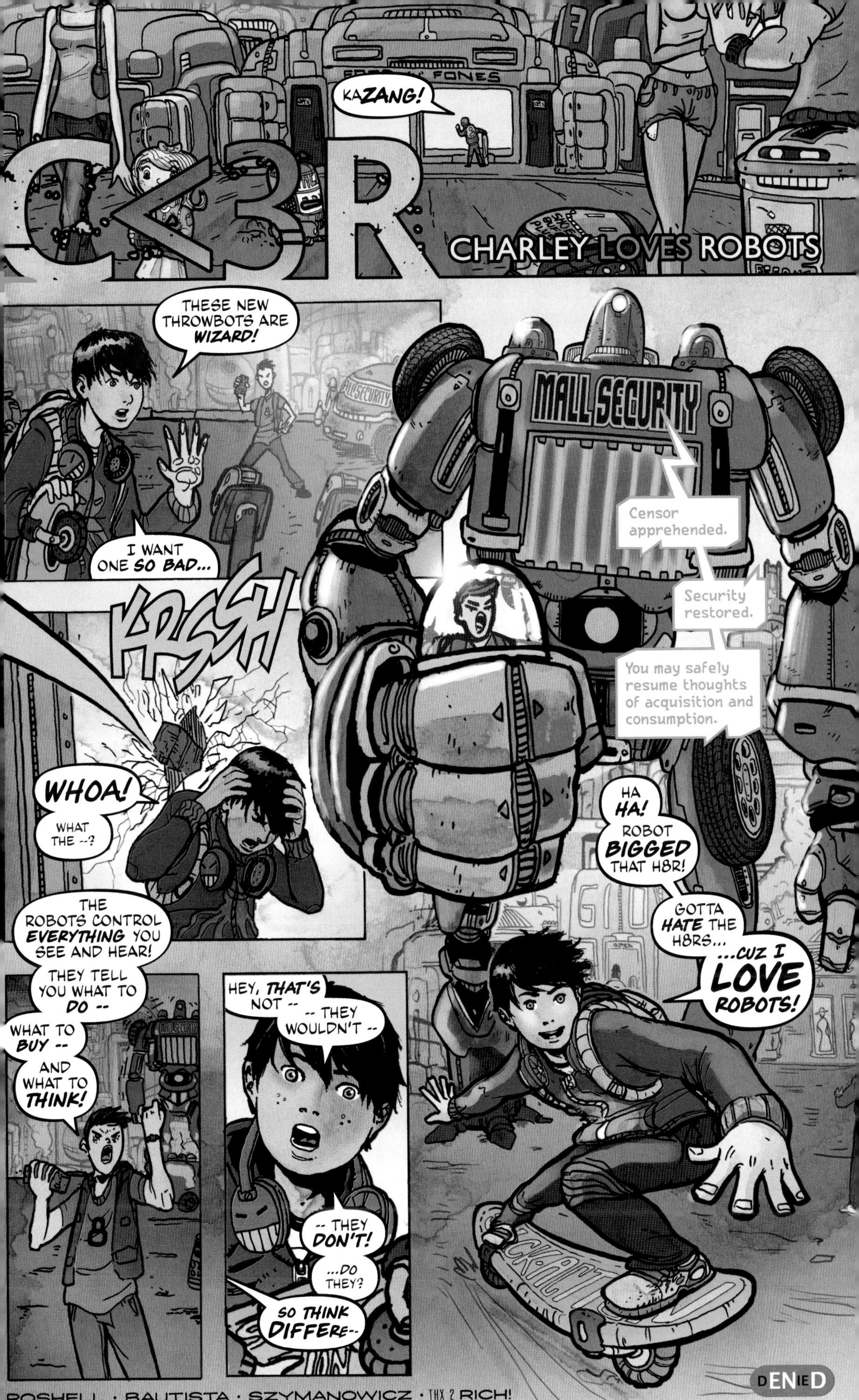
KAZANG!
C<3R
CHARLEY LOVES ROBOTS
THESE NEW THROWBOTS ARE WIZARD!
I WANT ONE SO BAD...
MALL SECURITY
Censor apprehended.
Security restored.
You may safely resume thoughts of acquisition and consumption.
KRSSH
WHOA!
WHAT THE --?
HA HA! ROBOT BIGGED THAT H8R!
GOTTA HATE THE H8RS...
...CUZ I LOVE ROBOTS!
THE ROBOTS CONTROL EVERYTHING YOU SEE AND HEAR!
THEY TELL YOU WHAT TO DO --
WHAT TO BUY --
AND WHAT TO THINK!
HEY, THAT'S NOT --
-- THEY WOULDN'T --
-- THEY DON'T!
...DO THEY?
SO THINK DIFFERE--
DENIED

ROSHELL · BAUTISTA · SZYMANOWICZ · THX 2 RICH!

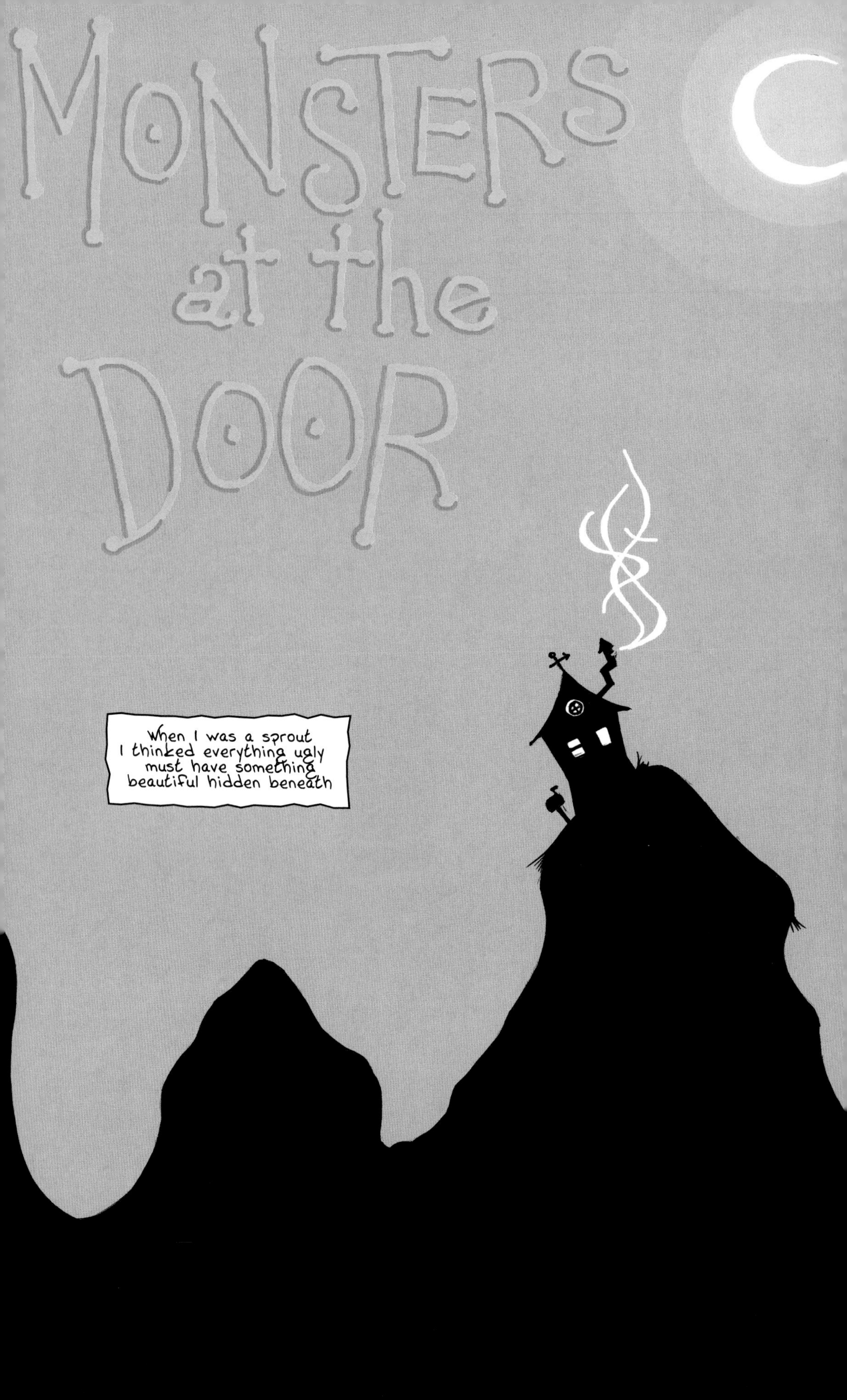
MONSTERS at the DOOR
When I was a sprout I thinked everything ugly must have something beautiful hidden beneath

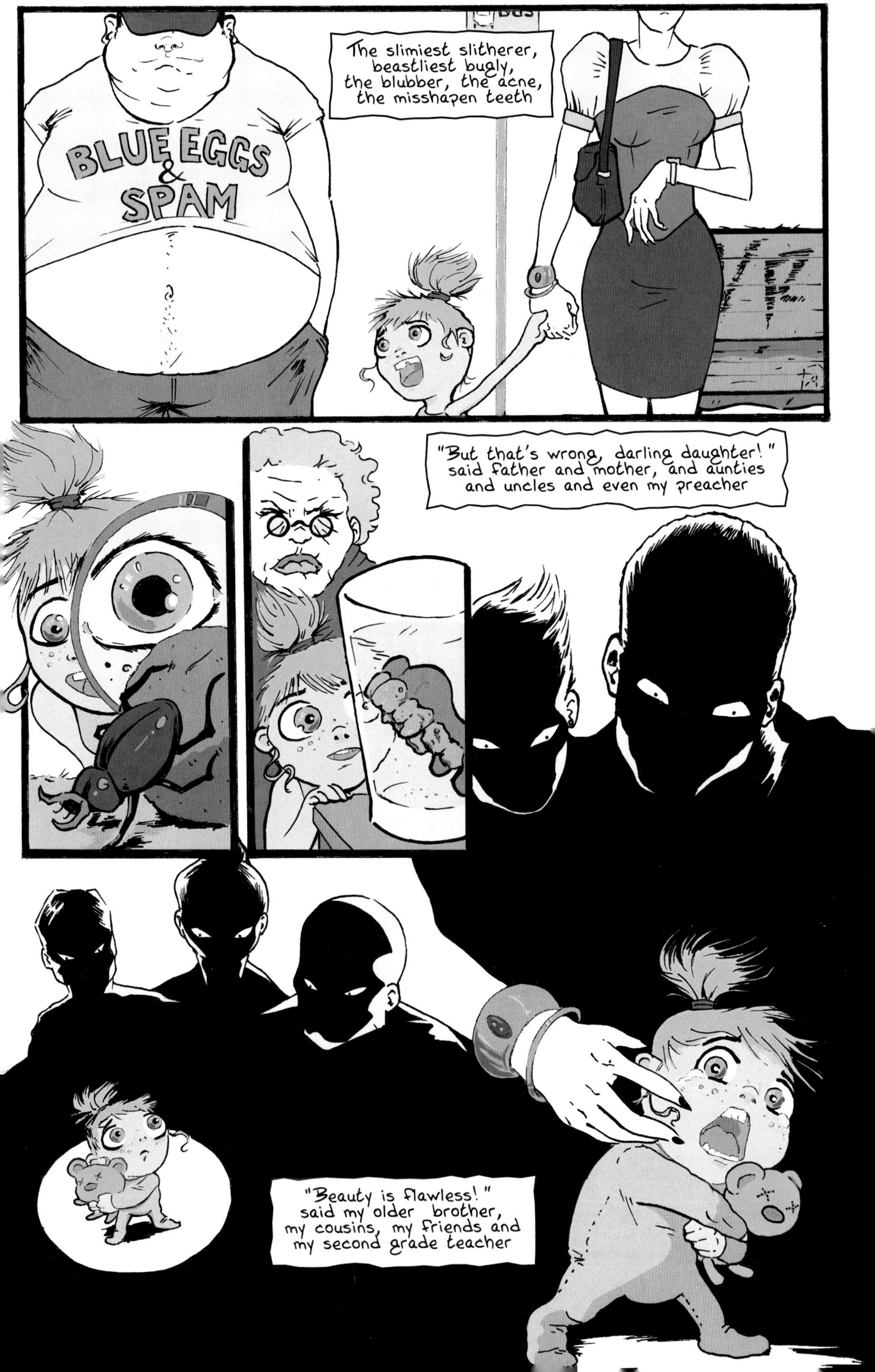
BUS
The slimiest slitherer, beastliest bugly, the blubber, the acne, the misshapen teeth
BLUE EGGS & SPAM
"But that's wrong, darling daughter!" said father and mother, and aunties and uncles and even my preacher
"Beauty is flawless!" said my older brother, my cousins, my friends and my second grade teacher

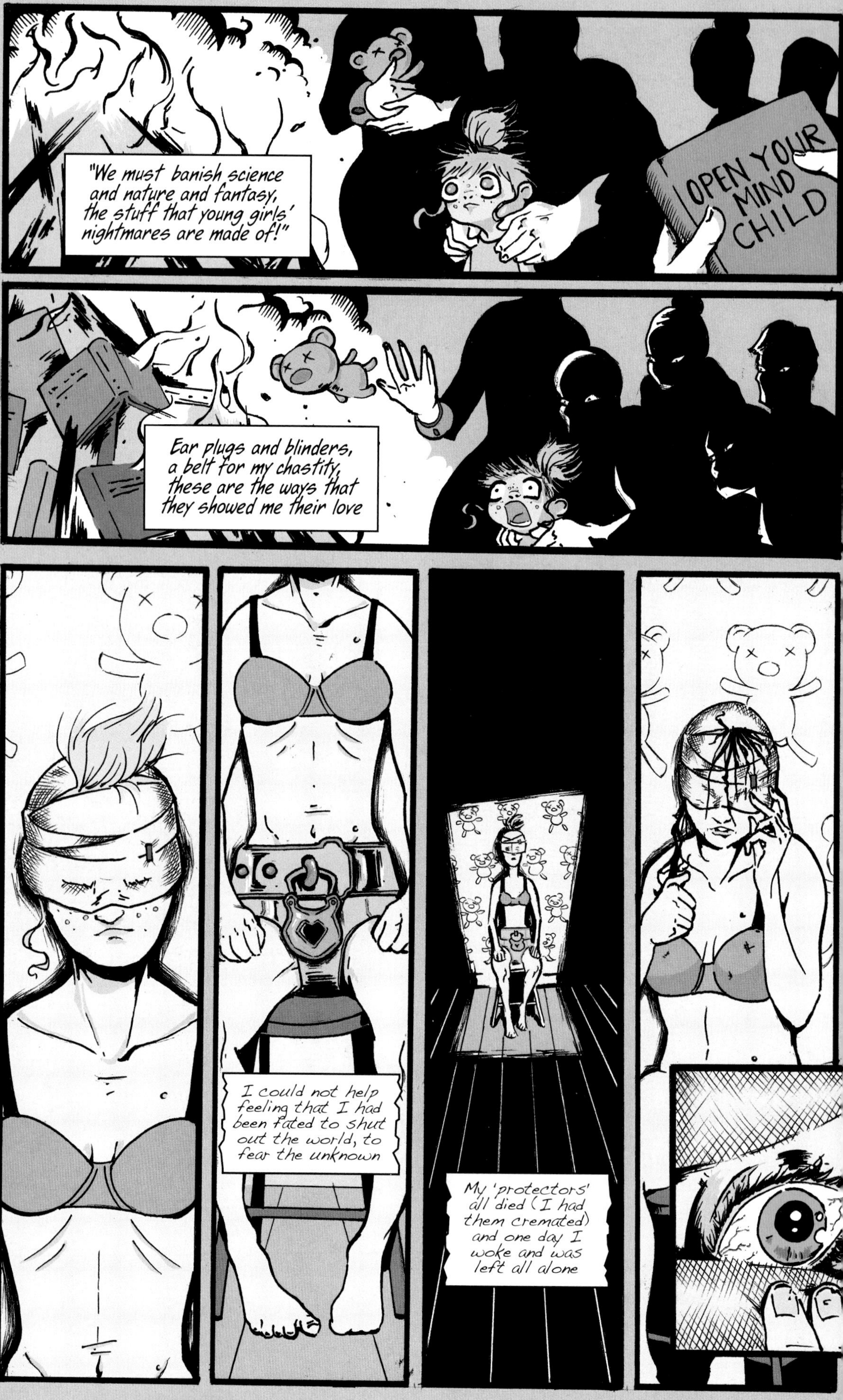
"We must banish science and nature and fantasy, the stuff that young girls' nightmares are made of!"
OPEN YOUR MIND CHILD
Ear plugs and blinders, a belt for my chastity, these are the ways that they showed me their love
I could not help feeling that I had been fated to shut out the world, to fear the unknown
My 'protectors' all died (I had them cremated) and one day I woke and was left all alone

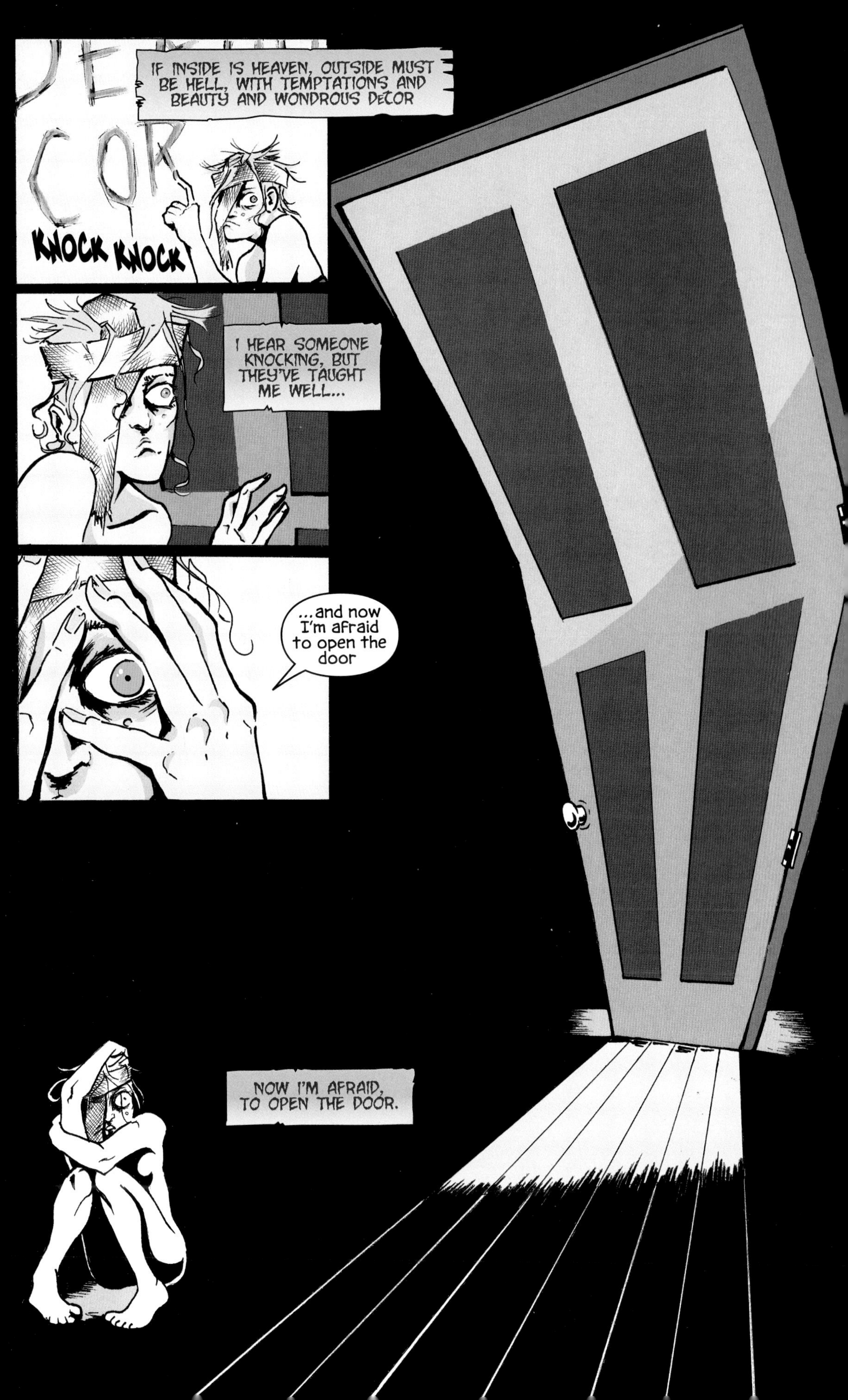
IF INSIDE IS HEAVEN, OUTSIDE MUST BE HELL, WITH TEMPTATIONS AND BEAUTY AND WONDROUS DECOR
KNOCK KNOCK
I HEAR SOMEONE KNOCKING, BUT THEY'VE TAUGHT ME WELL...
...and now I'm afraid to open the door
NOW I'M AFRAID, TO OPEN THE DOOR.

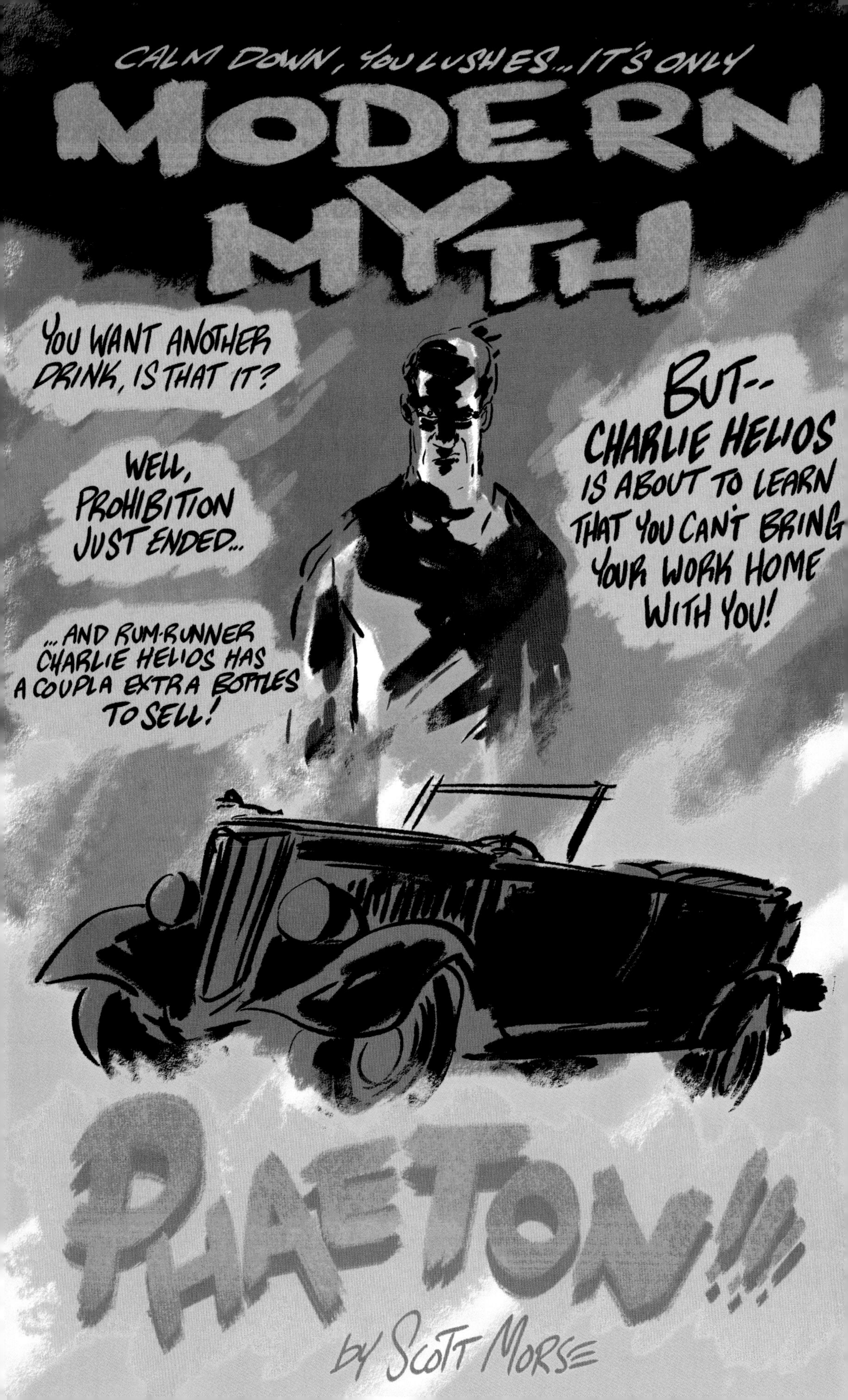
CALM DOWN, YOU LUSHES... IT'S ONLY
MODERN MYTH
YOU WANT ANOTHER DRINK, IS THAT IT?
WELL, PROHIBITION JUST ENDED...
...AND RUM-RUNNER CHARLIE HELIOS HAS A COUPLA EXTRA BOTTLES TO SELL!
BUT-- CHARLIE HELIOS IS ABOUT TO LEARN THAT YOU CAN'T BRING YOUR WORK HOME WITH YOU!
PHAETON!!!
BY SCOTT MORSE

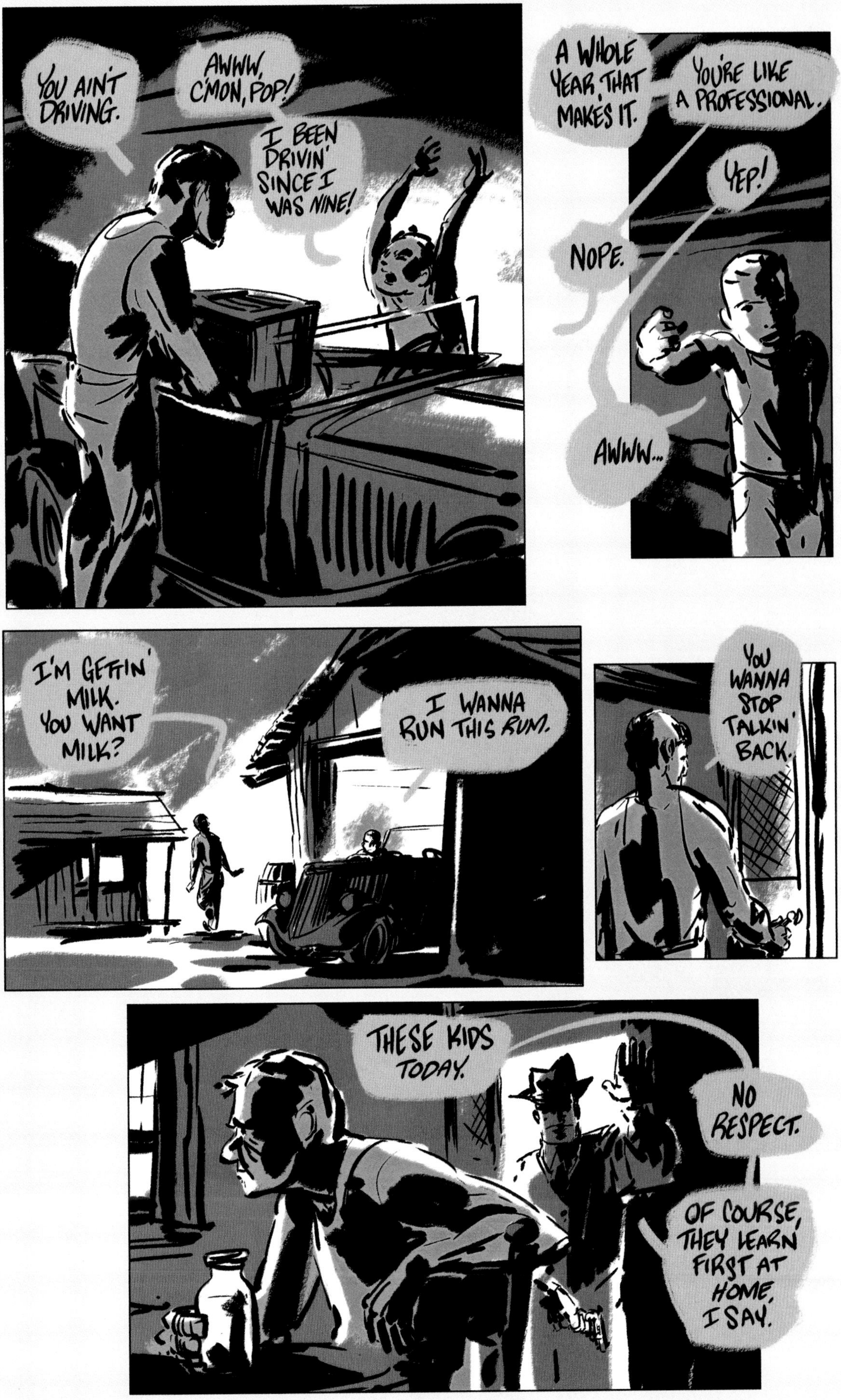
YOU AIN'T DRIVING.
AWWW, C'MON, POP!
I BEEN DRIVIN' SINCE I WAS NINE!
A WHOLE YEAR, THAT MAKES IT.
YOU'RE LIKE A PROFESSIONAL.
YEP!
NOPE.
AWWW...
I'M GETTIN' MILK. YOU WANT MILK?
I WANNA RUN THIS RUM.
YOU WANNA STOP TALKIN' BACK.
THESE KIDS TODAY.
NO RESPECT.
OF COURSE, THEY LEARN FIRST AT HOME, I SAY.

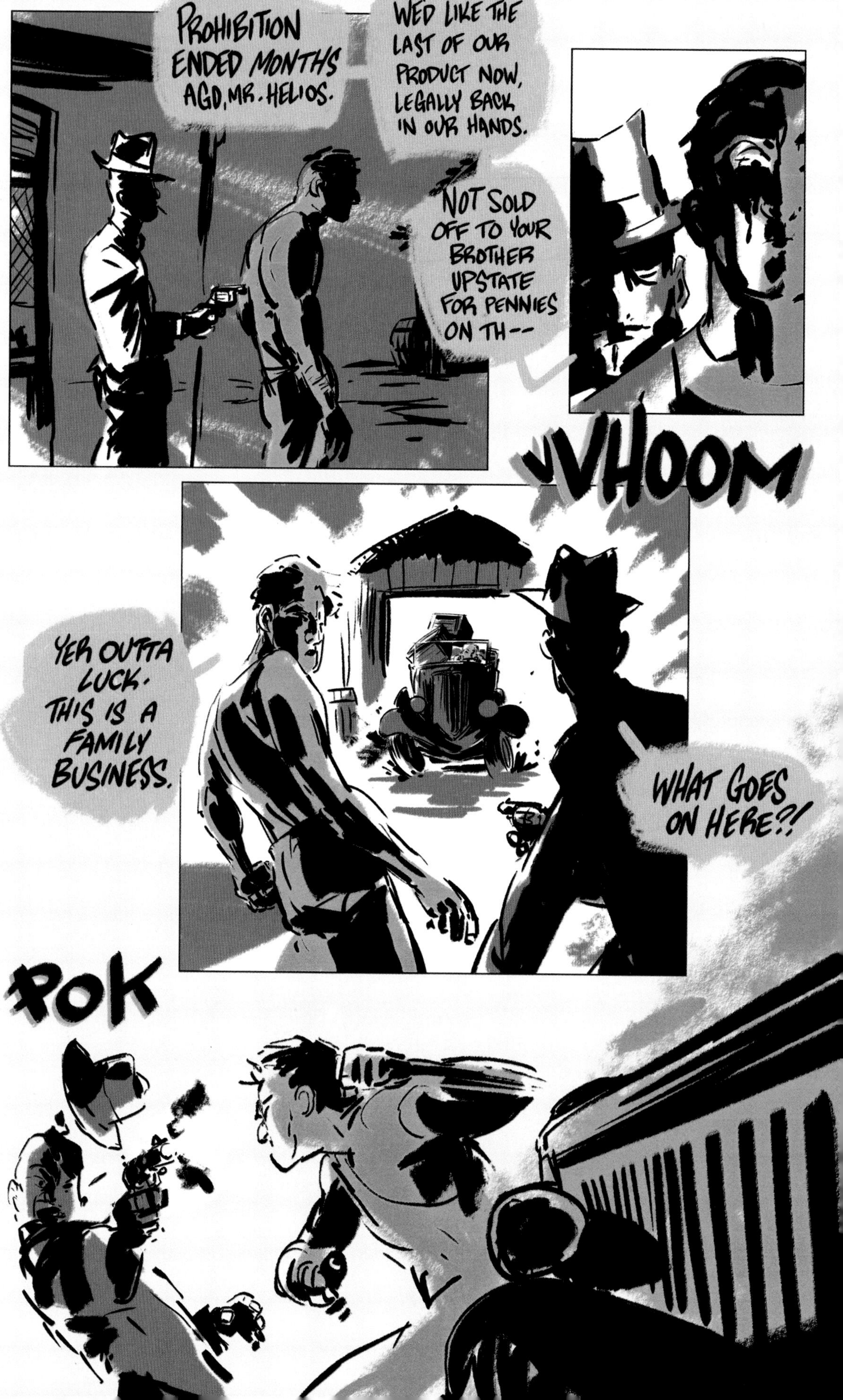
PROHIBITION ENDED MONTHS AGO, MR. HELIOS.
WE'D LIKE THE LAST OF OUR PRODUCT NOW, LEGALLY BACK IN OUR HANDS.
NOT SOLD OFF TO YOUR BROTHER UPSTATE FOR PENNIES ON TH--
VVHOOM
YER OUTTA LUCK. THIS IS A FAMILY BUSINESS.
WHAT GOES ON HERE?!
POK

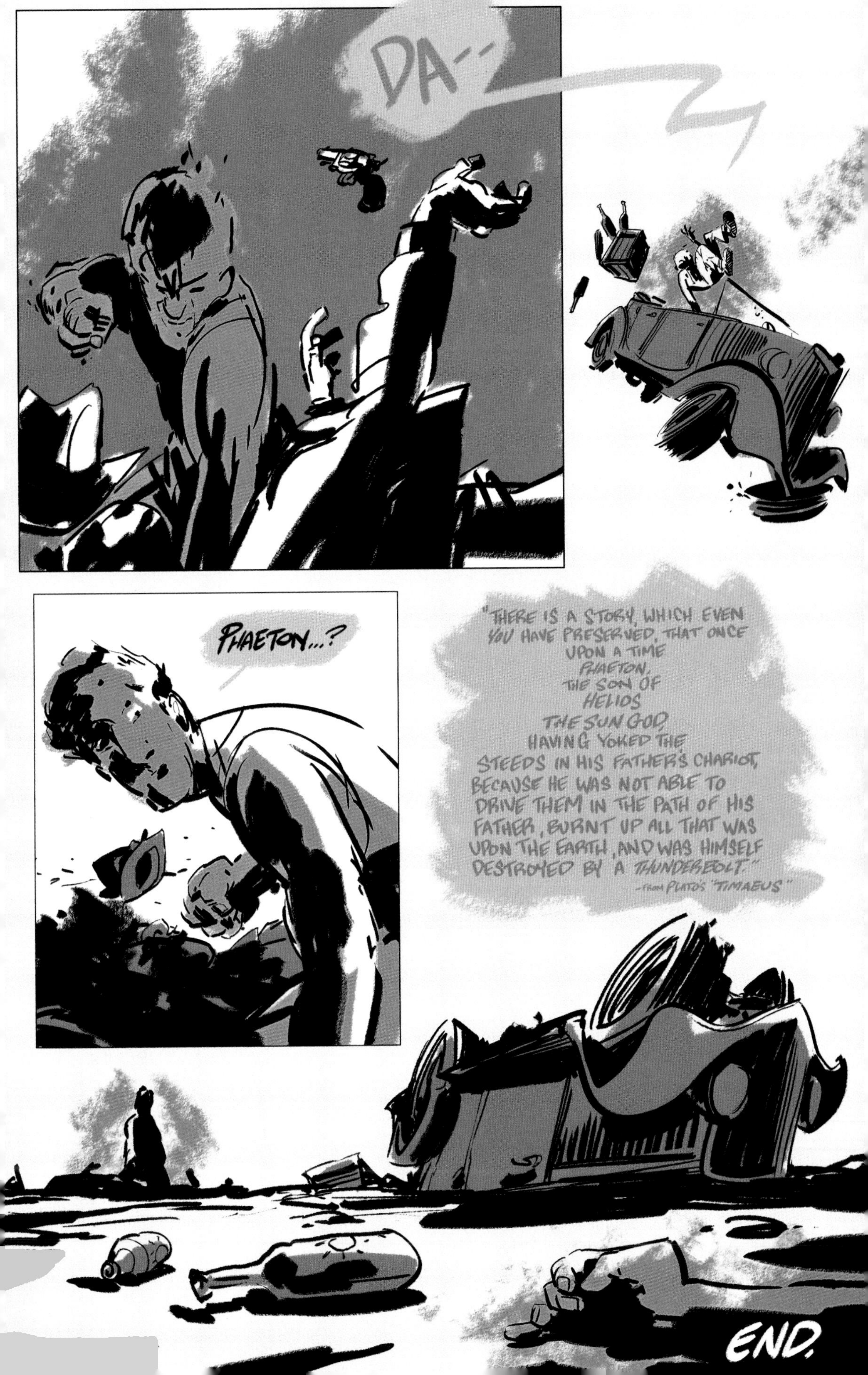
DA--
PHAETON...?
"THERE IS A STORY, WHICH EVEN YOU HAVE PRESERVED, THAT ONCE UPON A TIME PHAETON, THE SON OF HELIOS THE SUN GOD, HAVING YOKED THE STEEDS IN HIS FATHER'S CHARIOT, BECAUSE HE WAS NOT ABLE TO DRIVE THEM IN THE PATH OF HIS FATHER, BURNT UP ALL THAT WAS UPON THE EARTH, AND WAS HIMSELF DESTROYED BY A THUNDERBOLT."
-FROM PLATO'S "TIMAEUS"
END.

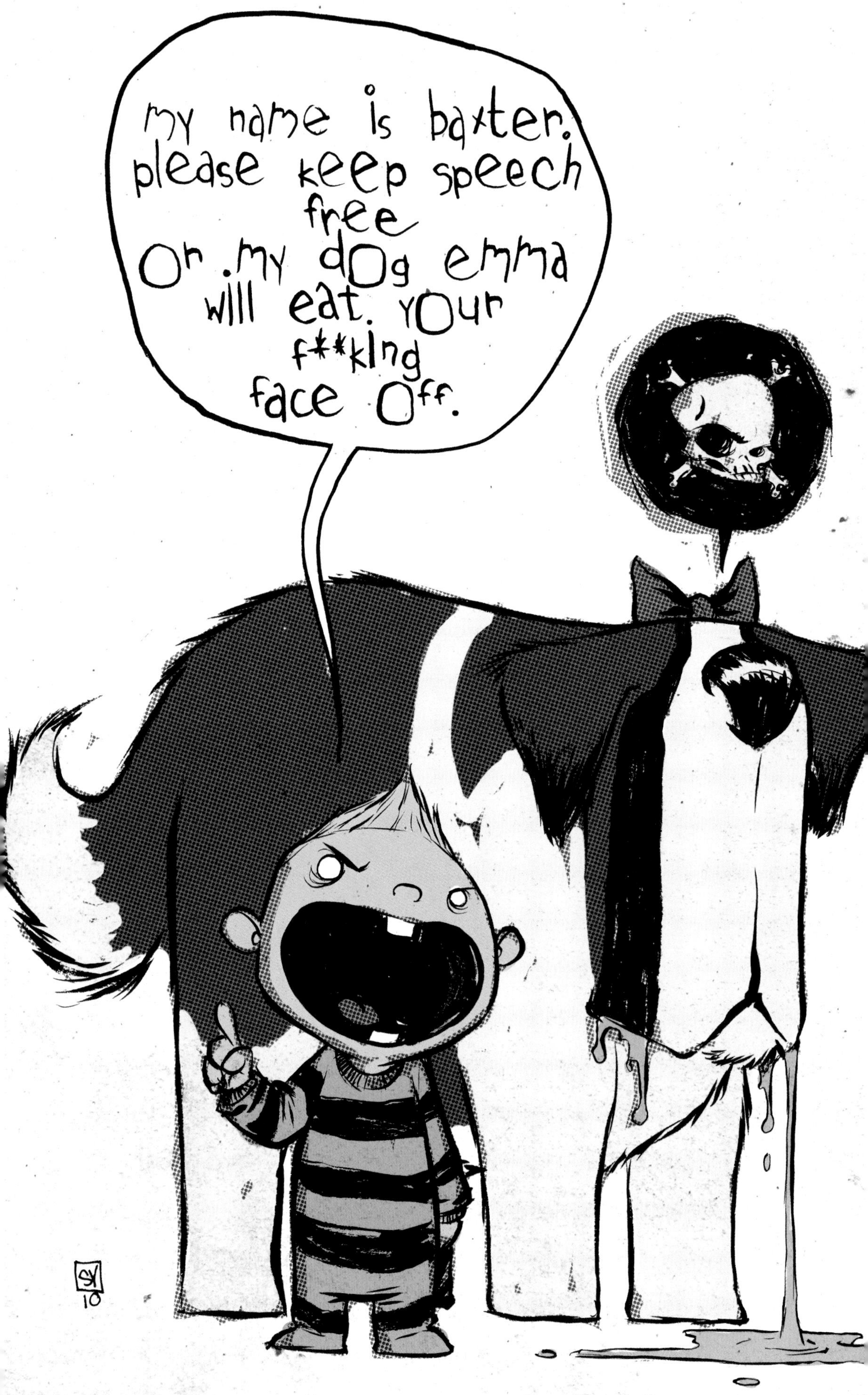
my name is baxter. please keep speech free Or my dOg emma will eat your f**kIng face Off.
SY 10

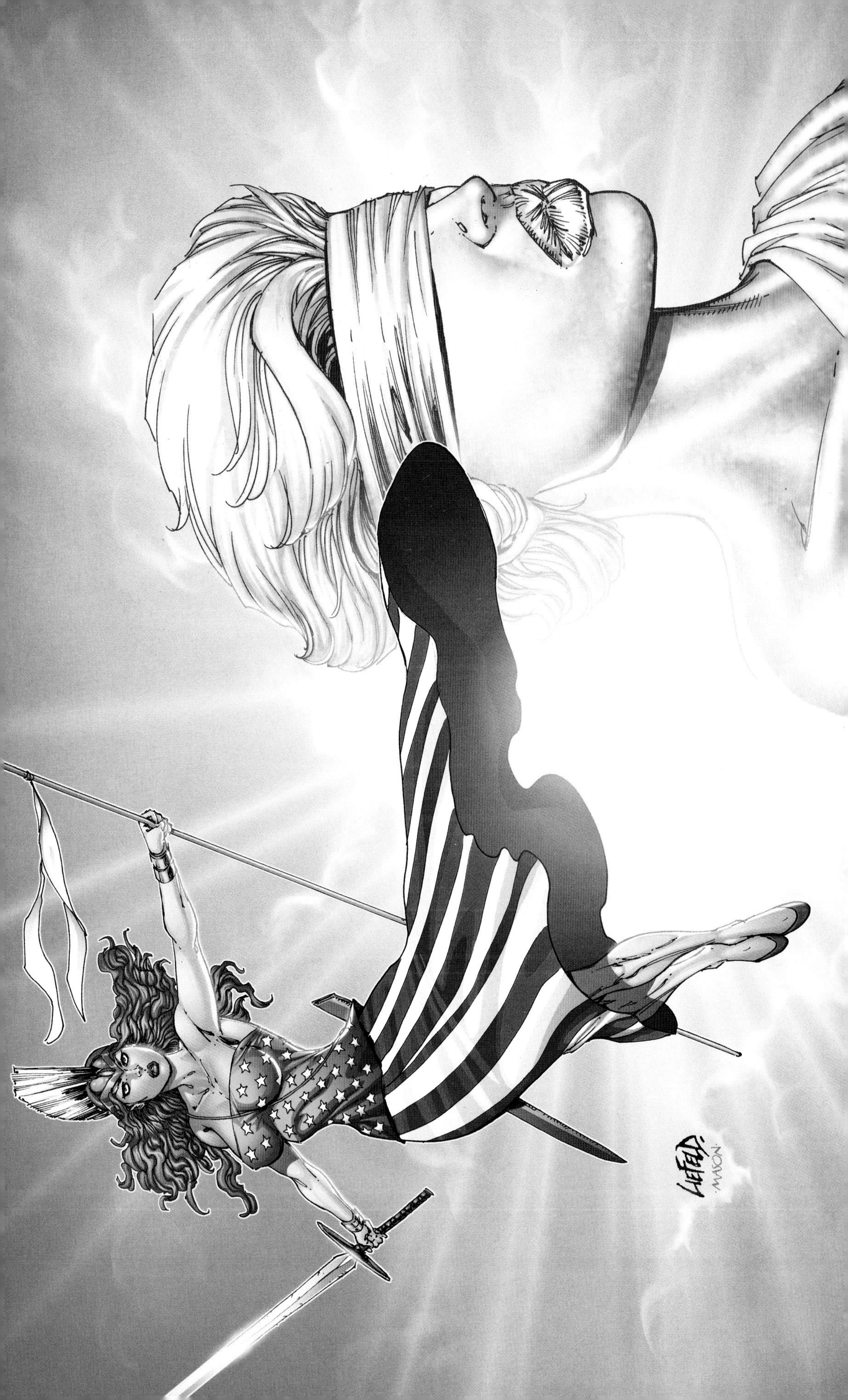

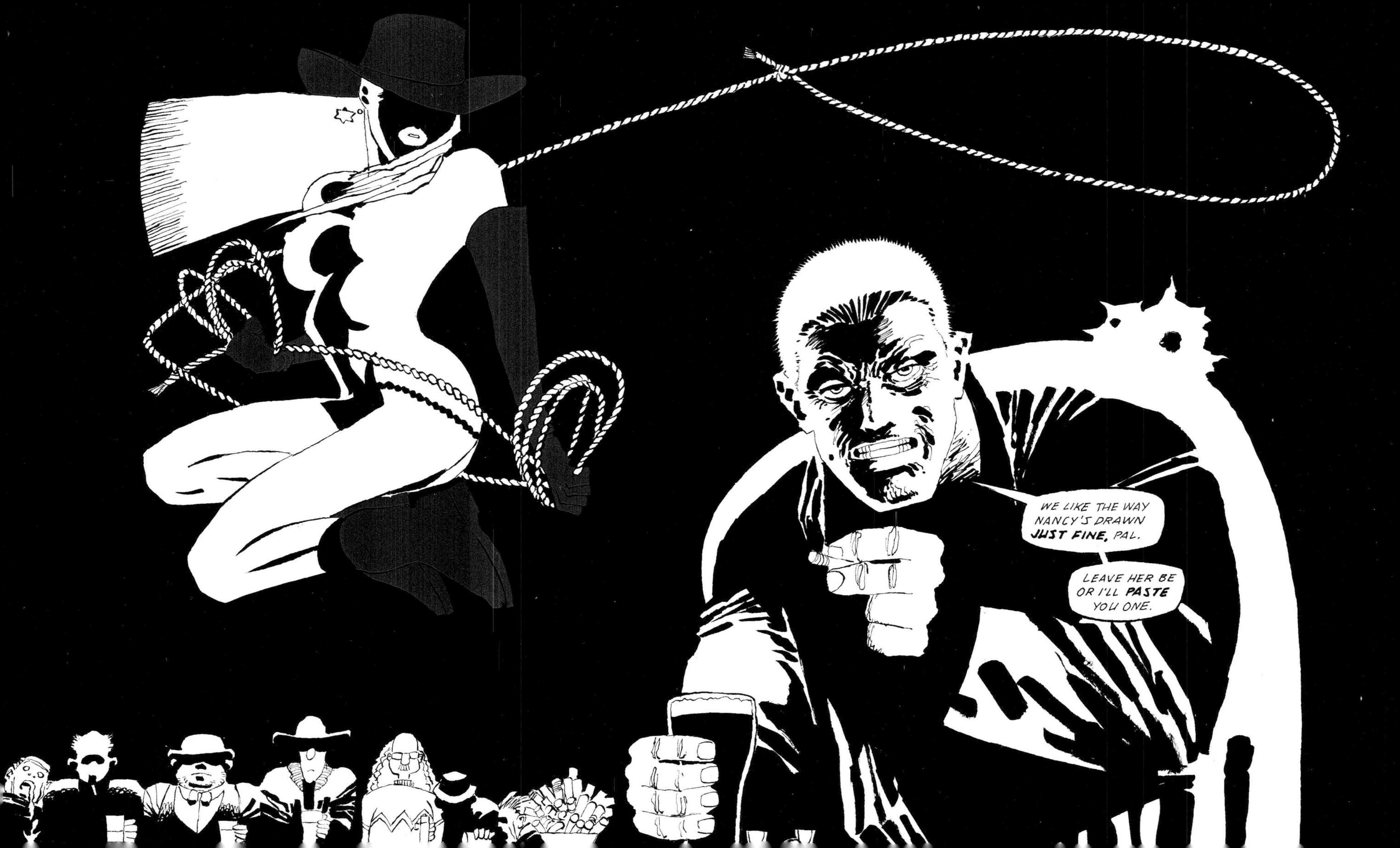
WE LIKE THE WAY NANCY'S DRAWN JUST FINE, PAL.
LEAVE HER BE OR I'LL PASTE YOU ONE.

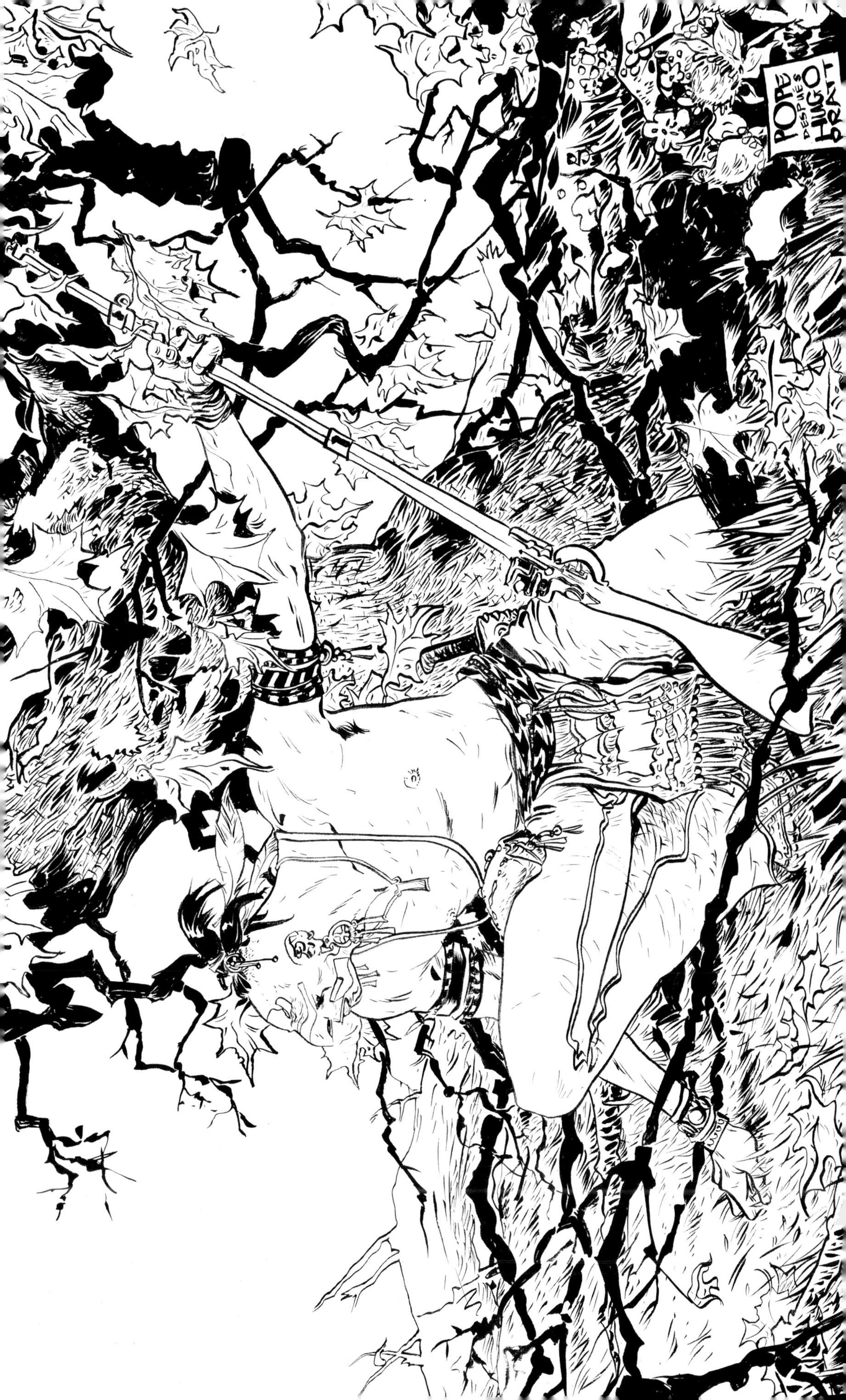
POPE DESPUÉS HUGO PRATT

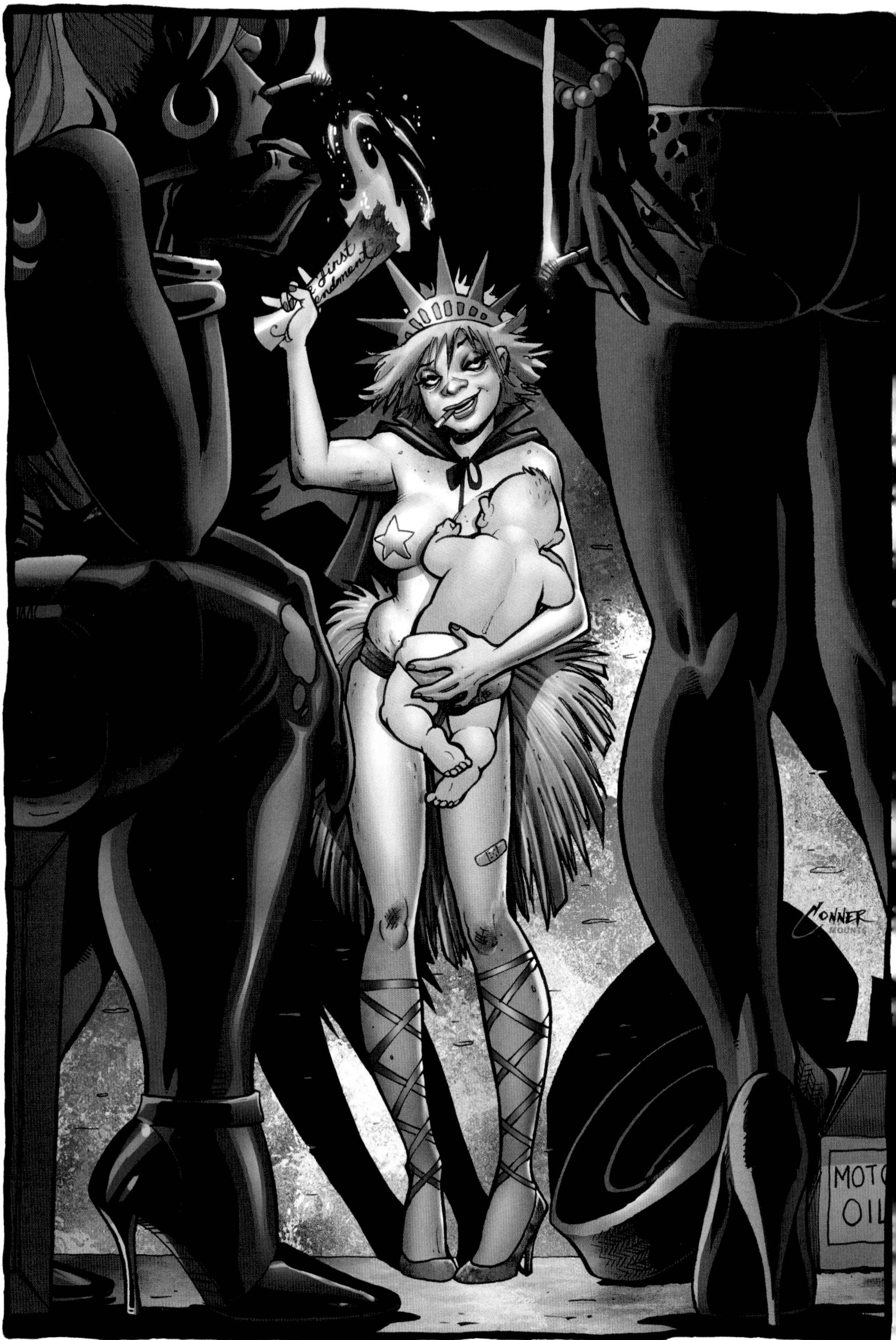
CONNER

So, this judge throws the book at a guy who drew titties in some comic book, and then later pays me shitloads of cash to dress up like this and beat his bare ass with a copy of the Bill of Rights!... Go figure!

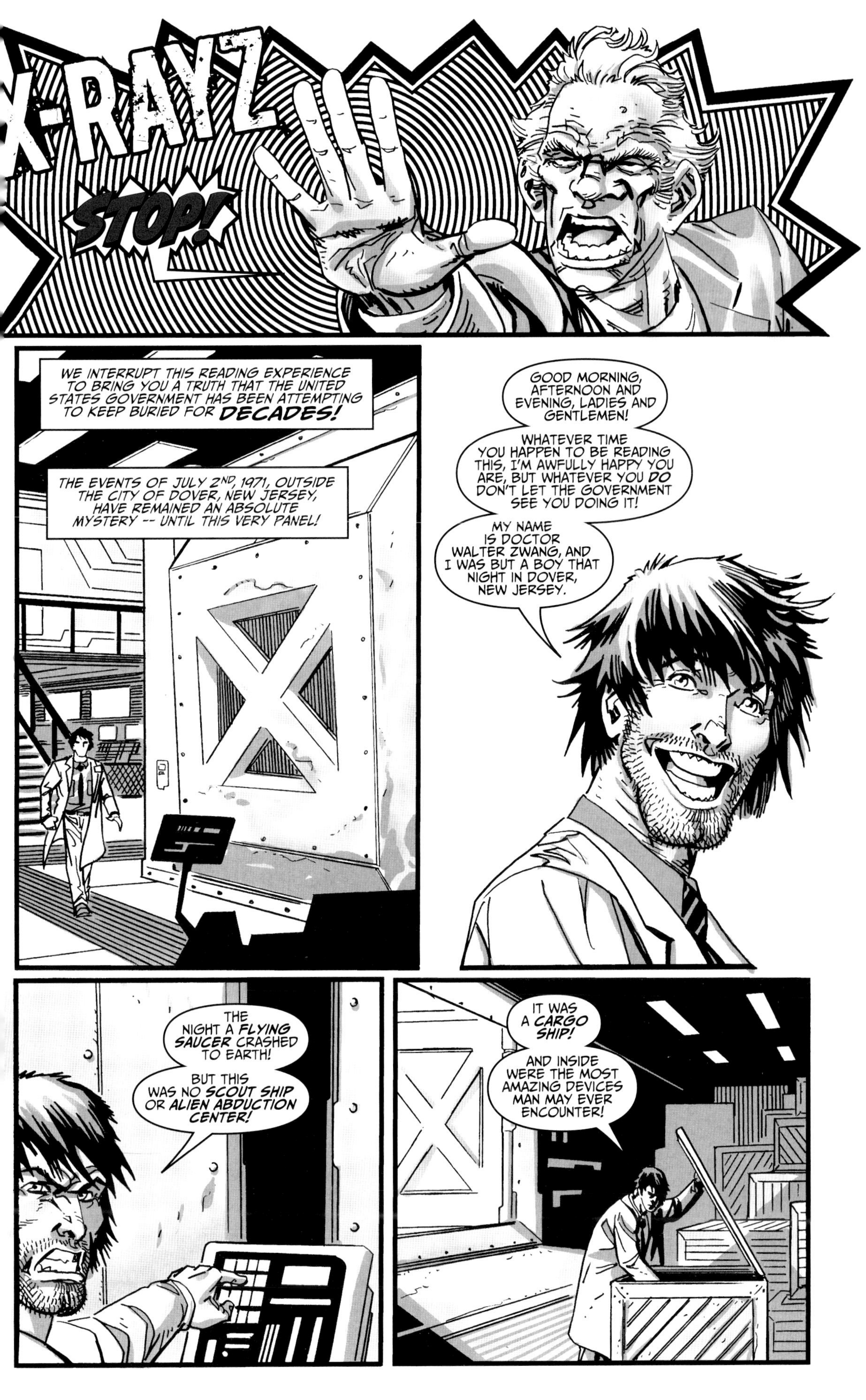
X-RAYZ
STOP!
WE INTERRUPT THIS READING EXPERIENCE TO BRING YOU A TRUTH THAT THE UNITED STATES GOVERNMENT HAS BEEN ATTEMPTING TO KEEP BURIED FOR DECADES!
THE EVENTS OF JULY 2ND, 1971, OUTSIDE THE CITY OF DOVER, NEW JERSEY, HAVE REMAINED AN ABSOLUTE MYSTERY -- UNTIL THIS VERY PANEL!
GOOD MORNING, AFTERNOON AND EVENING, LADIES AND GENTLEMEN!
WHATEVER TIME YOU HAPPEN TO BE READING THIS, I'M AWFULLY HAPPY YOU ARE, BUT WHATEVER YOU DO DON'T LET THE GOVERNMENT SEE YOU DOING IT!
MY NAME IS DOCTOR WALTER ZWANG, AND I WAS BUT A BOY THAT NIGHT IN DOVER, NEW JERSEY.
THE NIGHT A FLYING SAUCER CRASHED TO EARTH!
BUT THIS WAS NO SCOUT SHIP OR ALIEN ABDUCTION CENTER!
IT WAS A CARGO SHIP!
AND INSIDE WERE THE MOST AMAZING DEVICES MAN MAY EVER ENCOUNTER!

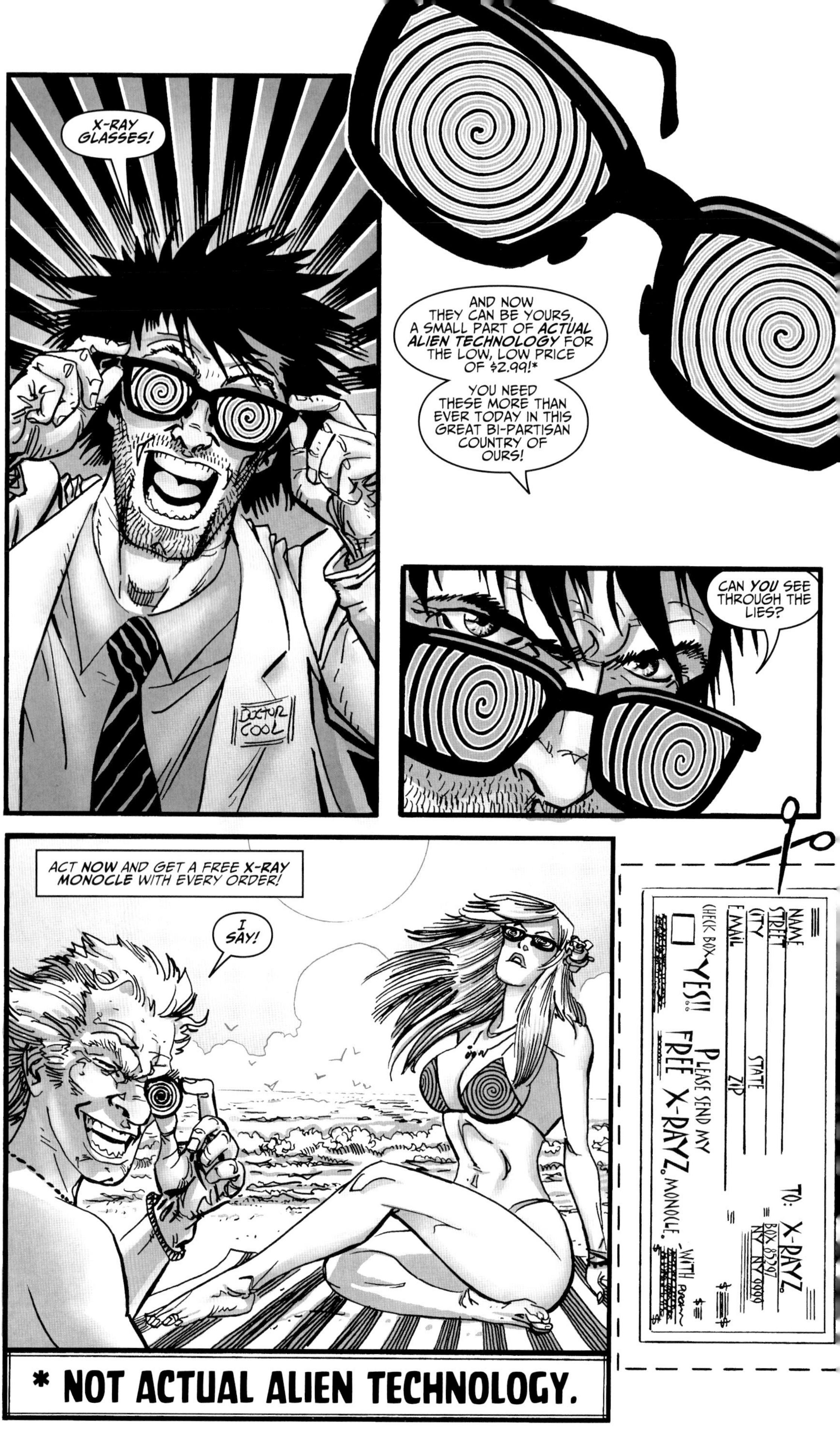
X-RAY GLASSES!
AND NOW THEY CAN BE YOURS, A SMALL PART OF ACTUAL ALIEN TECHNOLOGY FOR THE LOW, LOW PRICE OF $2.99!*
YOU NEED THESE MORE THAN EVER TODAY IN THIS GREAT BI-PARTISAN COUNTRY OF OURS!
DOCTOR COOL
CAN YOU SEE THROUGH THE LIES?
ACT NOW AND GET A FREE X-RAY MONOCLE WITH EVERY ORDER!
I SAY!
NAME
STREET
CITY
STATE
E-MAIL
ZIP
CHECK BOX
YES!!
PLEASE SEND MY FREE X-RAYZ MONOCLE
TO: X-RAYZ BOX 85297 NY NY 9999
* NOT ACTUAL ALIEN TECHNOLOGY.

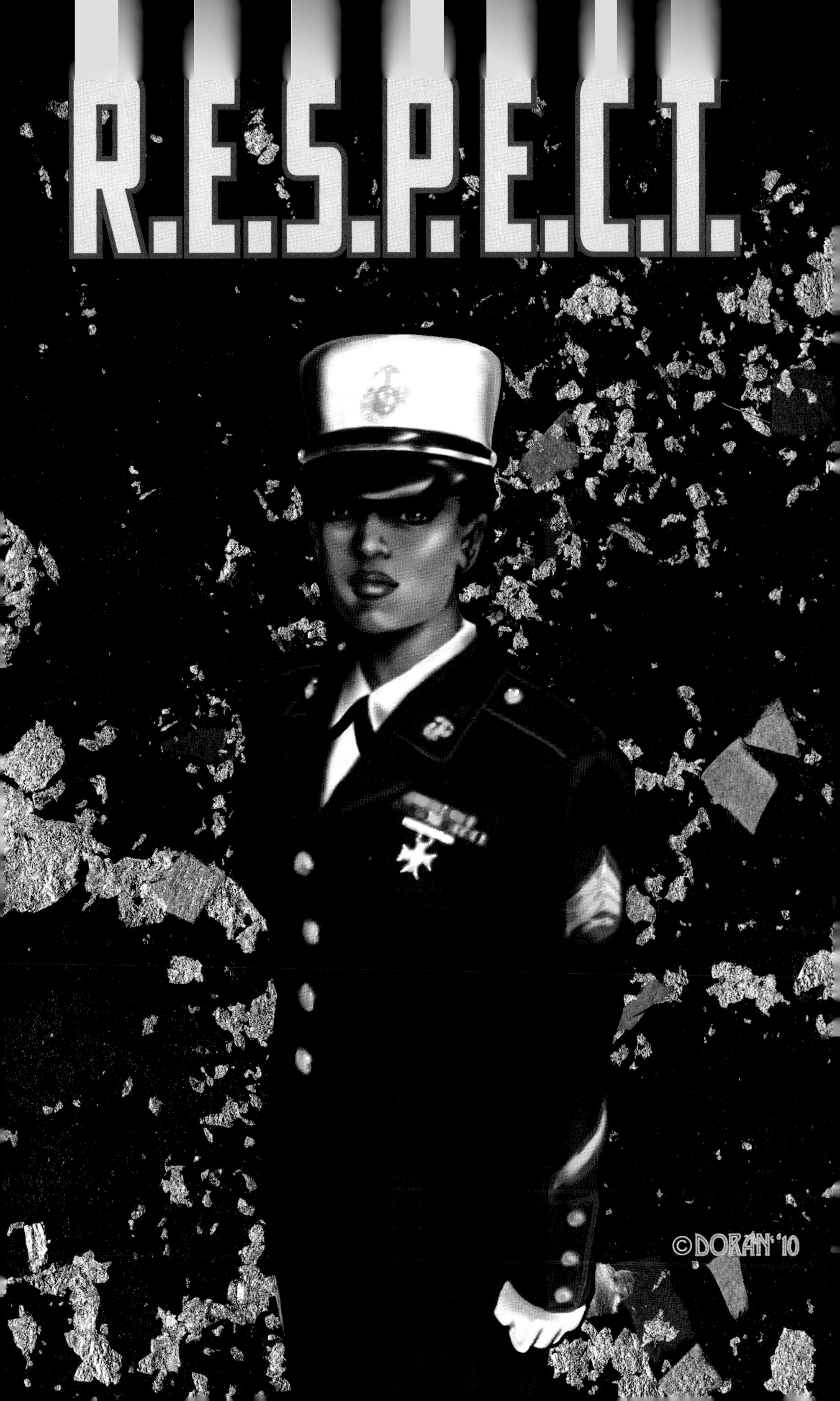
R.E.S.P.E.C.T.
©DORAN '10

The First Amendment: It's why we fight!

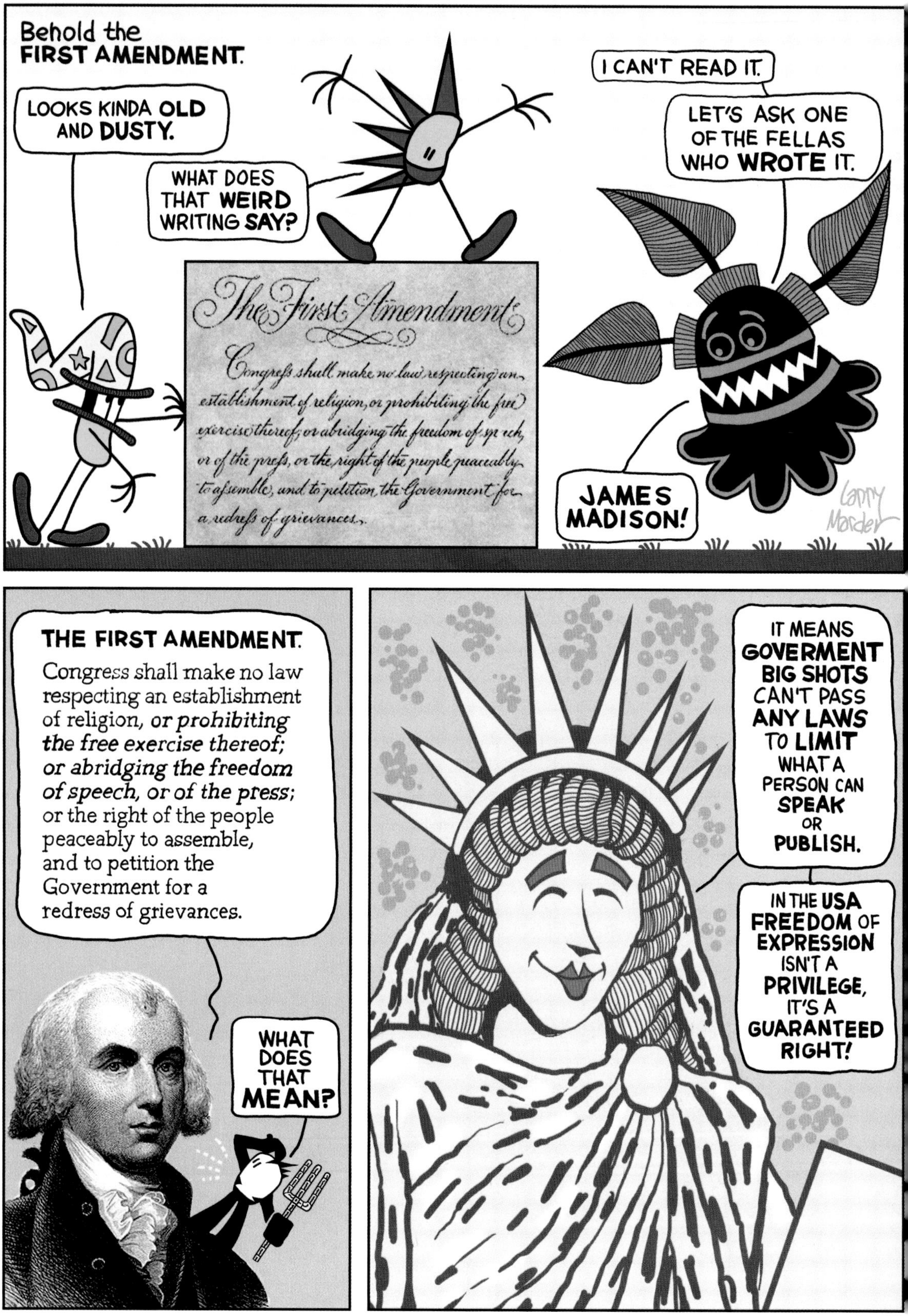

Behold the FIRST AMENDMENT.
LOOKS KINDA OLD AND DUSTY.
WHAT DOES THAT WEIRD WRITING SAY?
I CAN'T READ IT.
LET'S ASK ONE OF THE FELLAS WHO WROTE IT.
The First Amendment
Congress shall make no law respecting an establishment of religion, or prohibiting the free exercise thereof; or abridging the freedom of speech, or of the press, or the right of the people peaceably to assemble, and to petition the Government for a redress of grievances.
JAMES MADISON!
Larry Marder
THE FIRST AMENDMENT.
Congress shall make no law respecting an establishment of religion, *or prohibiting the free exercise thereof; or abridging the freedom of speech, or of the press;* or the right of the people peaceably to assemble, and to petition the Government for a redress of grievances.
WHAT DOES THAT MEAN?
IT MEANS GOVERMENT BIG SHOTS CAN'T PASS ANY LAWS TO LIMIT WHAT A PERSON CAN SPEAK OR PUBLISH.
IN THE USA FREEDOM OF EXPRESSION ISN'T A PRIVILEGE, IT'S A GUARANTEED RIGHT!

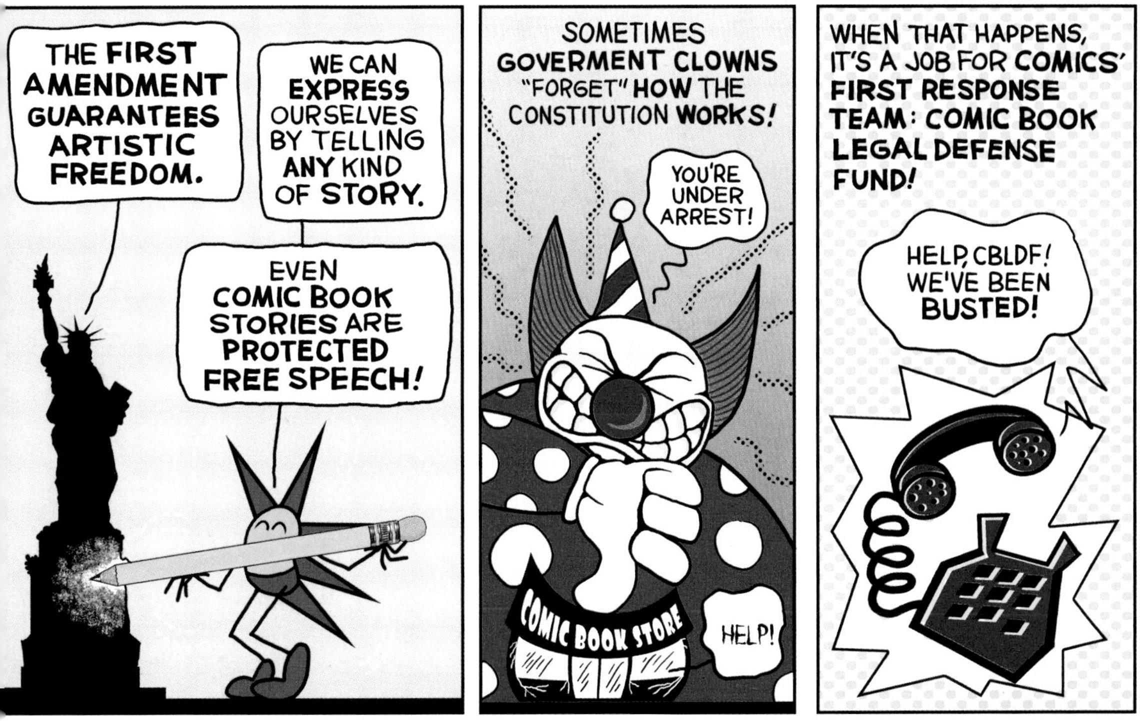
THE FIRST AMENDMENT GUARANTEES ARTISTIC FREEDOM.
WE CAN EXPRESS OURSELVES BY TELLING ANY KIND OF STORY.
EVEN COMIC BOOK STORIES ARE PROTECTED FREE SPEECH!
SOMETIMES GOVERMENT CLOWNS "FORGET" HOW THE CONSTITUTION WORKS!
YOU'RE UNDER ARREST!
COMIC BOOK STORE
HELP!
WHEN THAT HAPPENS, IT'S A JOB FOR COMICS' FIRST RESPONSE TEAM: COMIC BOOK LEGAL DEFENSE FUND!
HELP, CBLDF! WE'VE BEEN BUSTED!

CBLDF Mission

Comic Book Legal Defense Fund is a non-profit organization dedicated to the protection of the First Amenment rights of the comics art form and its community of retailers, creators, publishers, librarians, and readers.

The CBLDF provides legal referrals, representation, advice, assistance, and education in furtherance of these goals.

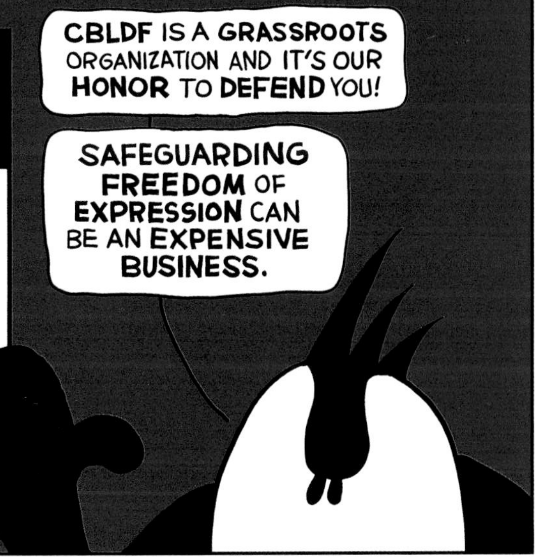
CBLDF IS A GRASSROOTS ORGANIZATION AND IT'S OUR HONOR TO DEFEND YOU!
SAFEGUARDING FREEDOM OF EXPRESSION CAN BE AN EXPENSIVE BUSINESS.

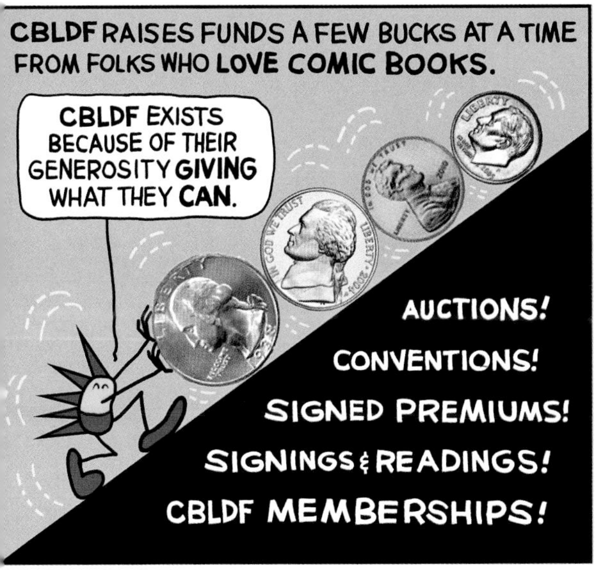
CBLDF RAISES FUNDS A FEW BUCKS AT A TIME FROM FOLKS WHO LOVE COMIC BOOKS.
CBLDF EXISTS BECAUSE OF THEIR GENEROSITY GIVING WHAT THEY CAN.
AUCTIONS!
CONVENTIONS!
SIGNED PREMIUMS!
SIGNINGS & READINGS!
CBLDF MEMBERSHIPS!

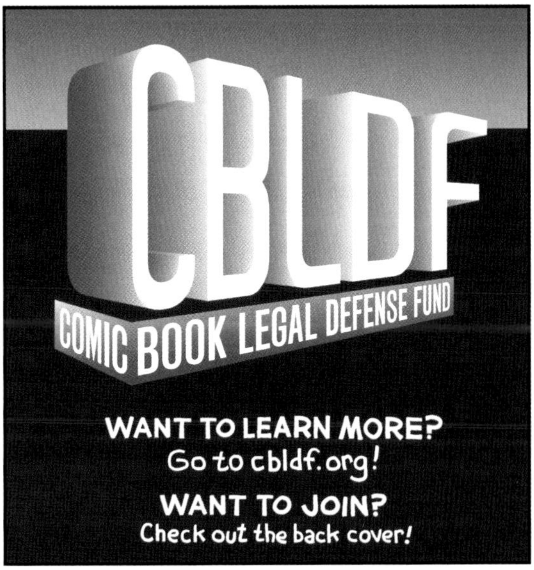
CBLDF
COMIC BOOK LEGAL DEFENSE FUND
WANT TO LEARN MORE?
Go to cbldf.org!
WANT TO JOIN?
Check out the back cover!

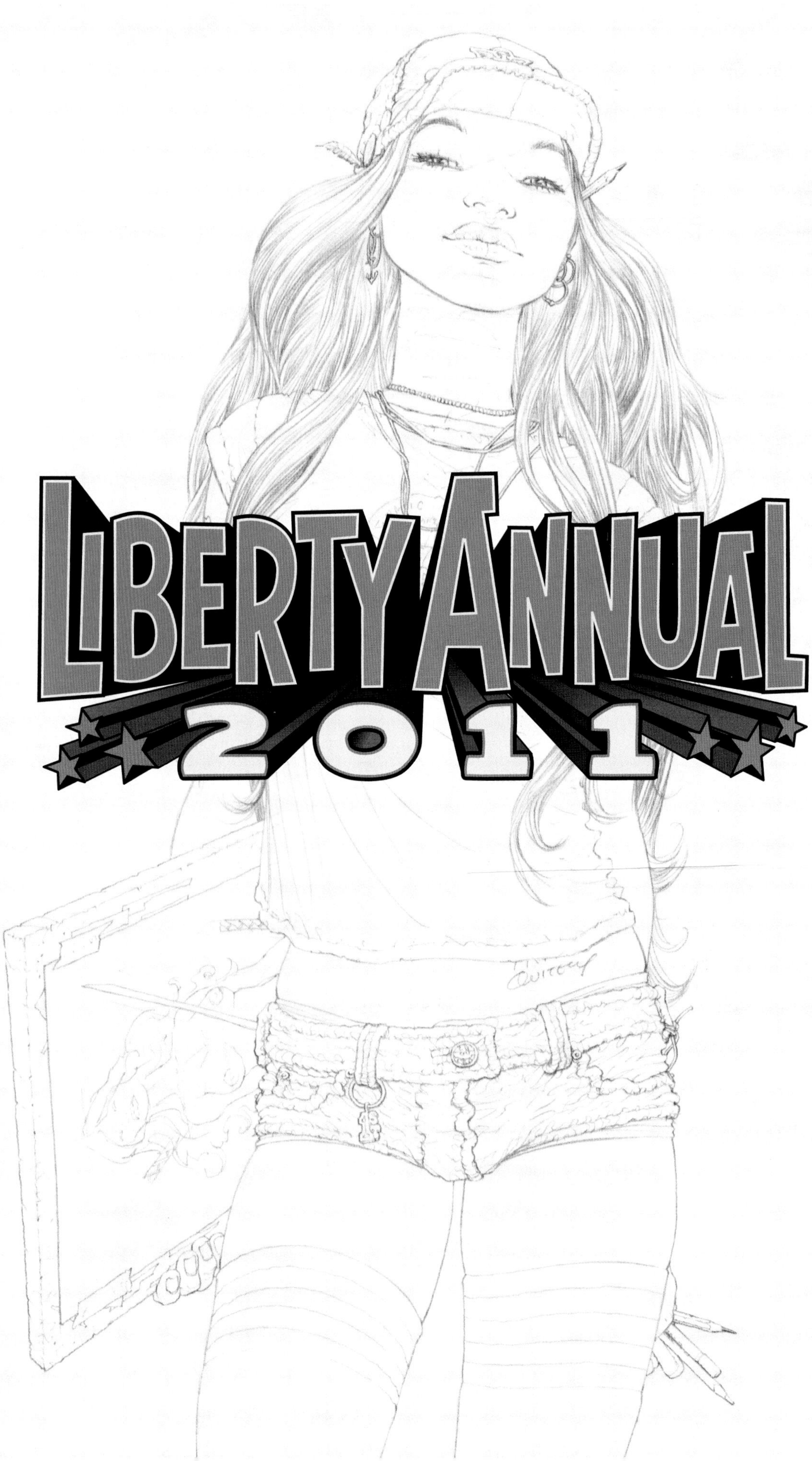
LIBERTY ANNUAL
2011

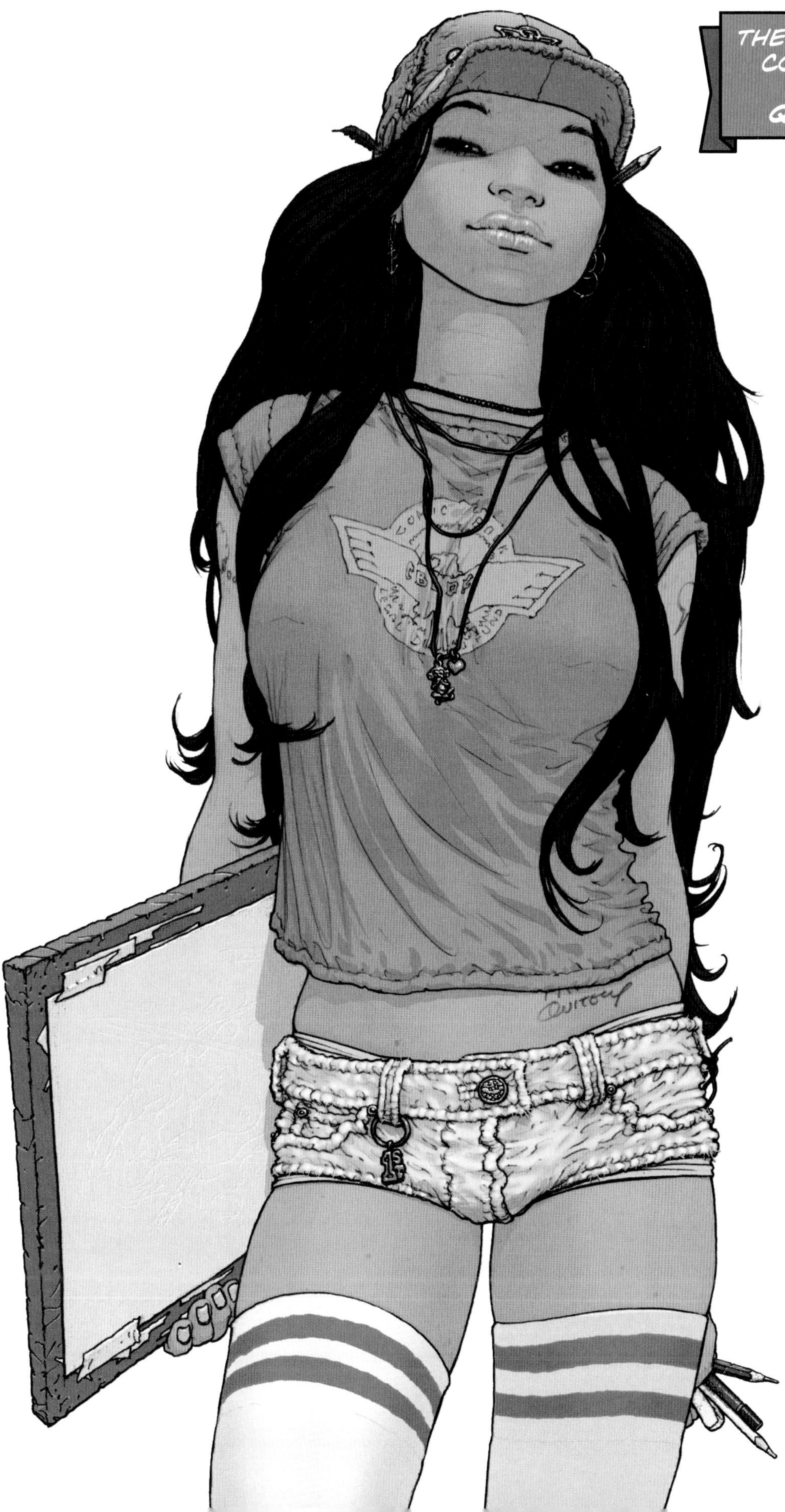

THE ARTIST COVER BY FRANK QUITELY

BUY SPEECH COVER BY JOHN CASSADAY COLOR BY DAVE STEWART

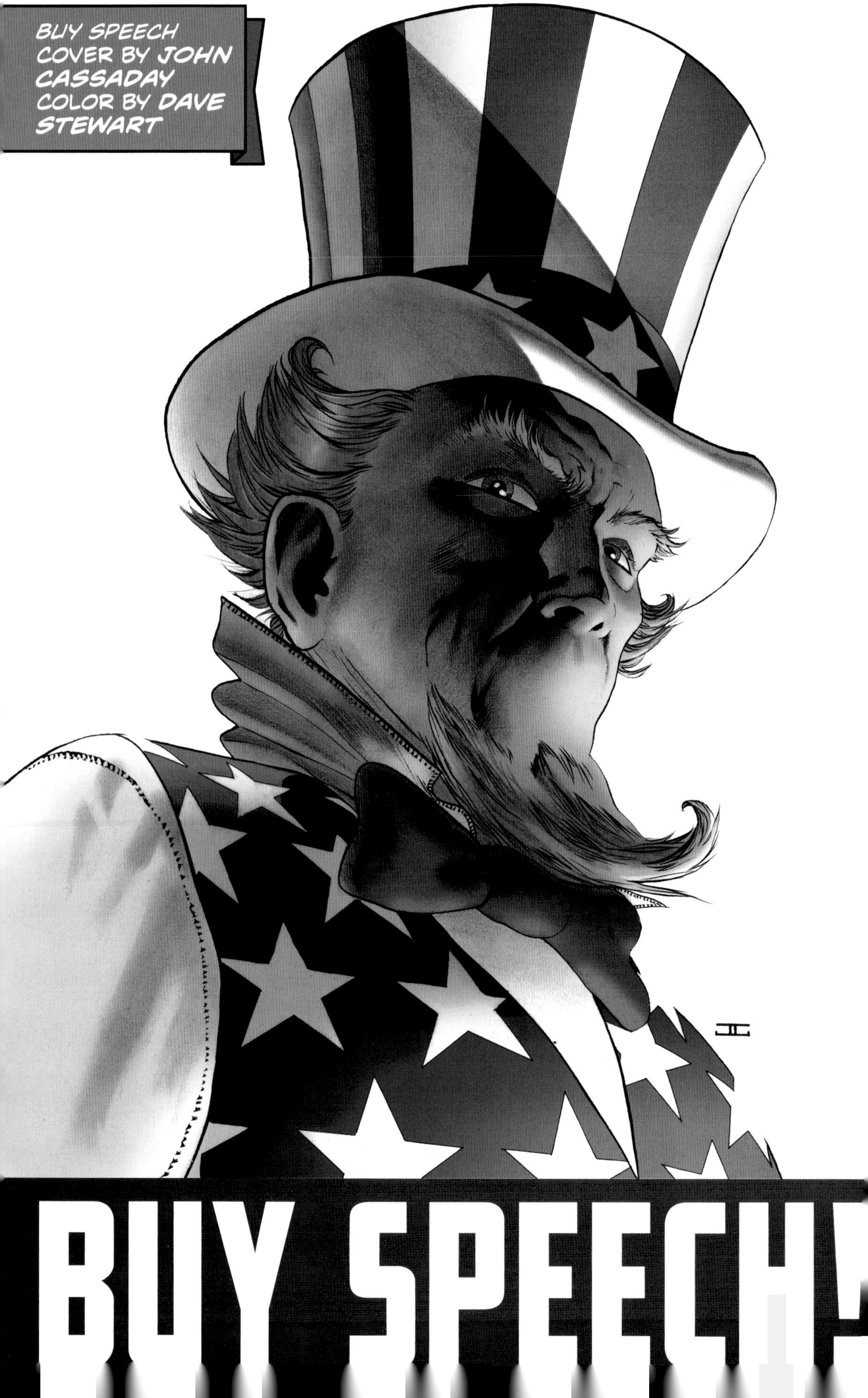
BUY SPEECH!

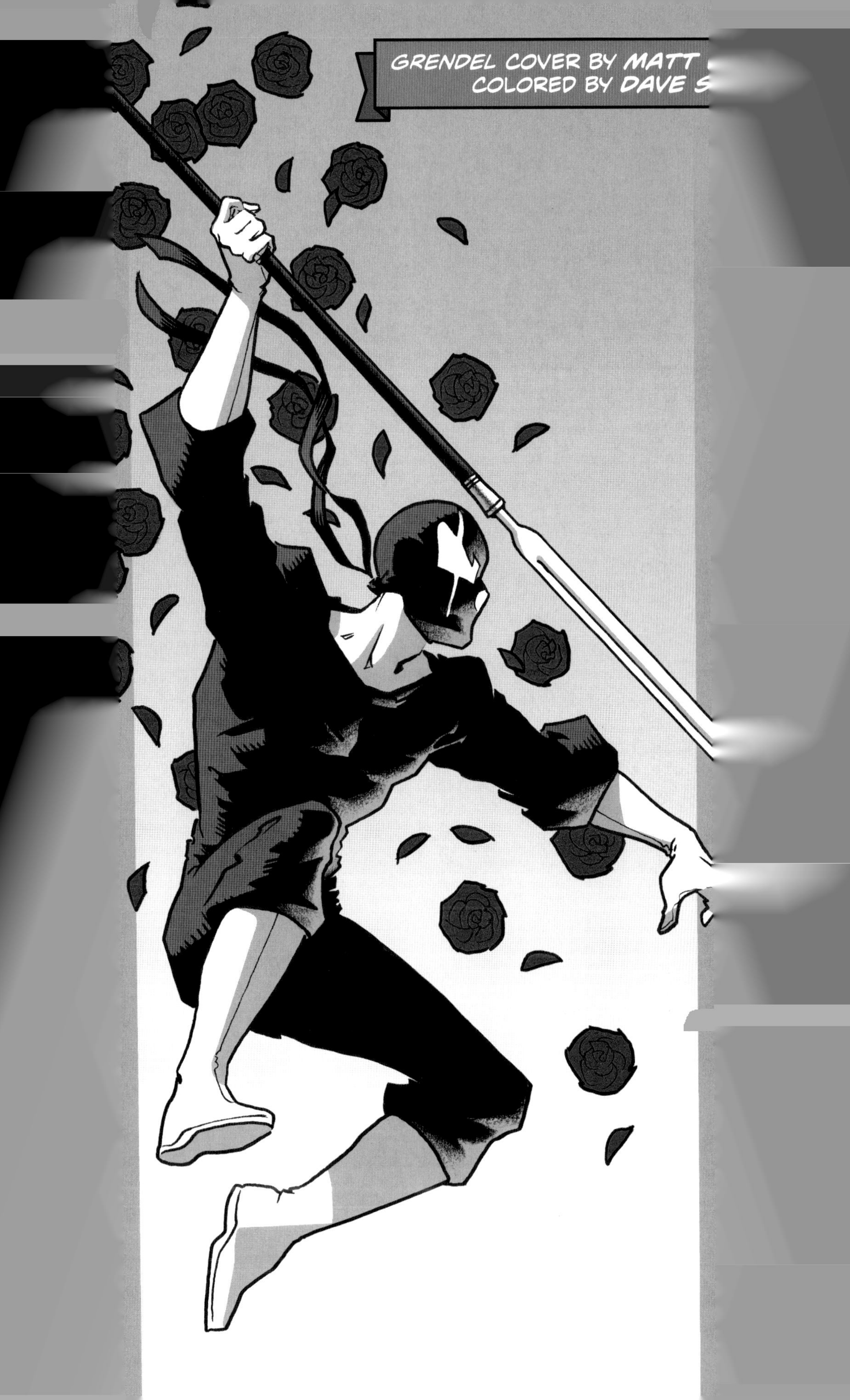
GRENDEL COVER BY MATT
COLORED BY DAVE S

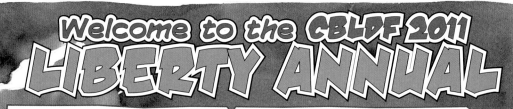

Welcome to the CBLDF 2011 LIBERTY ANNUAL

When the CBLDF's Executive Director (an old pal) Charles Brownstein called to see if I would man the helm of this year's annual fundraising comic book, I immediately said, "YES!" Well... first I had to assure everyone at my day job that all my Legendary Comics commitments would be met while I was moonlighting for the fund, but that was settled in mere minutes.

So here we are, so many months later and on the racks begging for your support of this worthy cause. I tried to broaden the scope of topics and the definition of free speech and in doing so, I thought we could juxtapose the freedoms we so often take for granted in America with that of the lack of those freedoms in other countries and cultures.

Also, growing up with the added confusion of discovering I was bi-sexual, made me ultra-sensitive to the horrible bullying and subsequent suicides of gay, lesbian and transgender youth in recent months... and so, herein we embrace Dan Savage's **IT GETS BETTER** theme through our most favorite medium, **COMICS!** Bullying someone to stay quiet about who and what they are at their very core is definitely the cruelest form of censorship.

I would like to thank all of the wonderful, talented people who wrote, drew, colored, lettered, (and some even bled), creating these amazing tales and were so giving of their time and skills. A special thanks to Sean Konot for doing a great job on the lion's share of the lettering. Also to John Hill and Drew Gill for the 11th hour design work. Thanks also to the fine folks at Marvel Comics & DC Comics for their help, support and participation. And, of course, a **BIG THANK YOU** to the great team at Image Comics for getting this book to the printer!

It is my sincere hope that you find a healthy mix of fun, thought-provoking, ire-inciting and, dare I say, gut-wrenching stories in this anthology, and that it was worthy of the price of admission.
ENJOY!

Schreck

(Oh, and my assistant, Greg, helped out a little, too!)

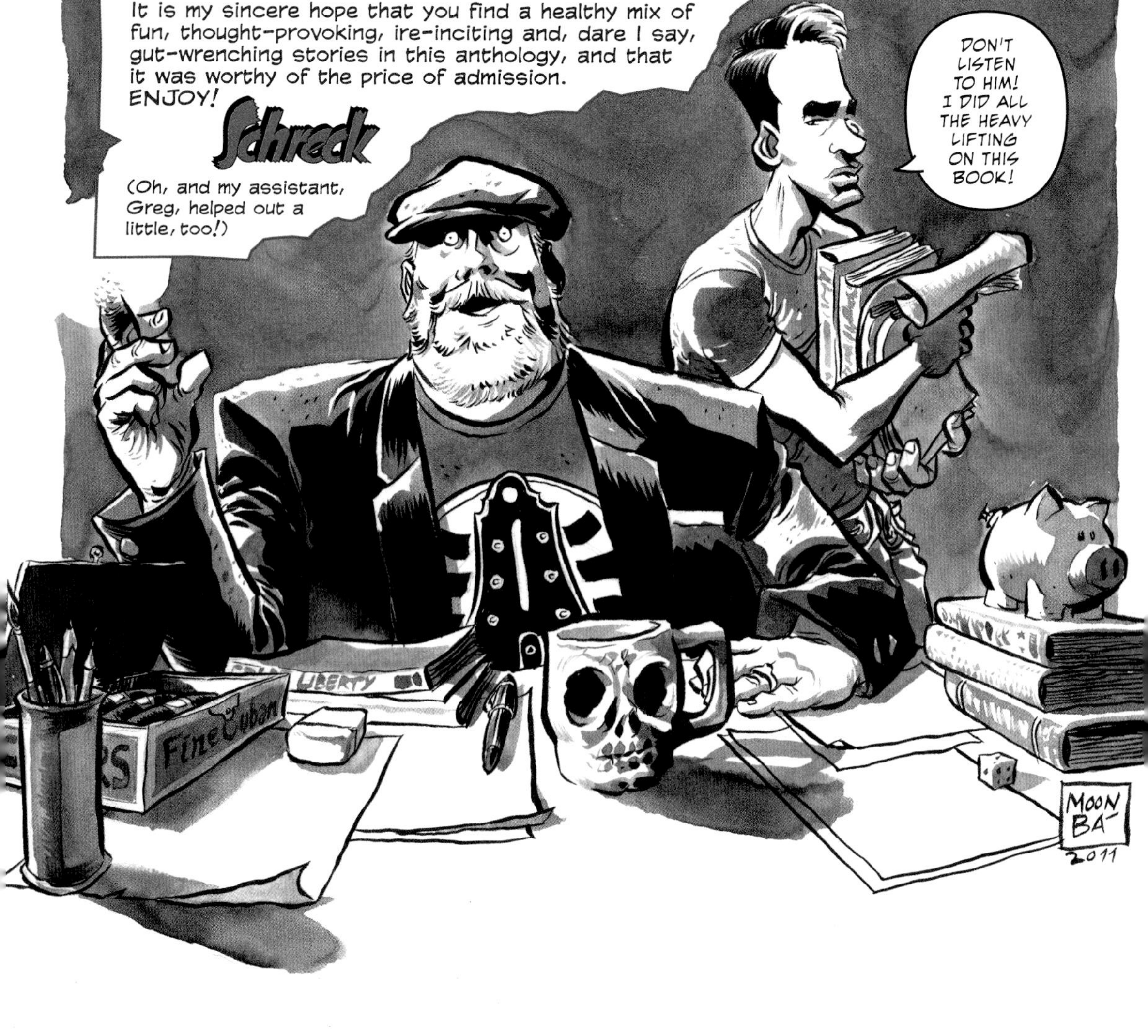
DON'T LISTEN TO HIM! I DID ALL THE HEAVY LIFTING ON THIS BOOK!
LIBERTY
Fine Cuban
MOON BA 2011

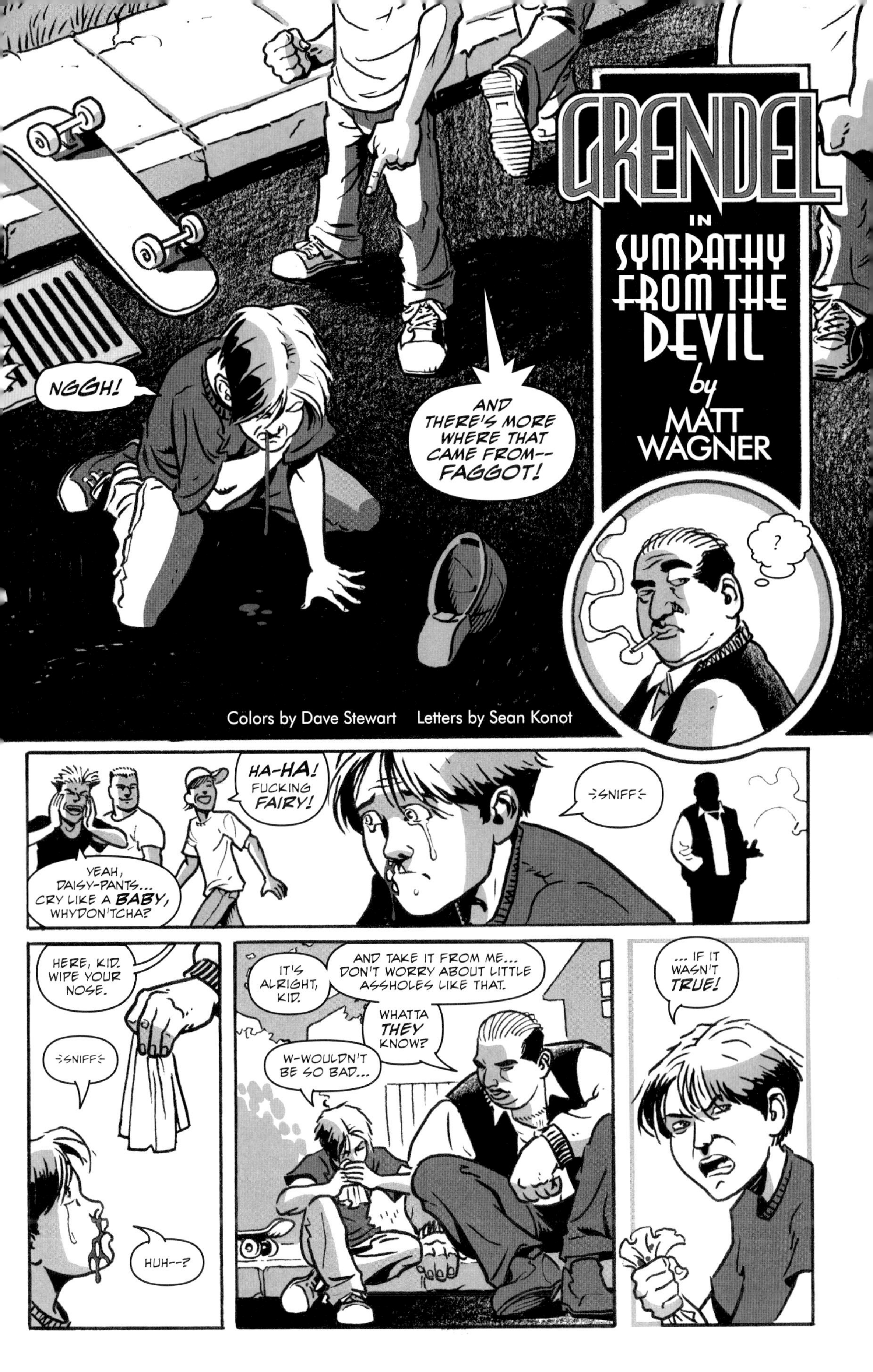
GRENDEL
IN
SYMPATHY FROM THE DEVIL
by
MATT WAGNER
NGGH!
AND THERE'S MORE WHERE THAT CAME FROM-- FAGGOT!
?
Colors by Dave Stewart Letters by Sean Konot
HA-HA! FUCKING FAIRY!
YEAH, DAISY-PANTS... CRY LIKE A BABY, WHYDON'TCHA?
>SNIFF<
HERE, KID. WIPE YOUR NOSE.
>SNIFF<
HUH--?
IT'S ALRIGHT, KID.
AND TAKE IT FROM ME... DON'T WORRY ABOUT LITTLE ASSHOLES LIKE THAT.
WHATTA THEY KNOW?
W-WOULDN'T BE SO BAD...
... IF IT WASN'T TRUE!

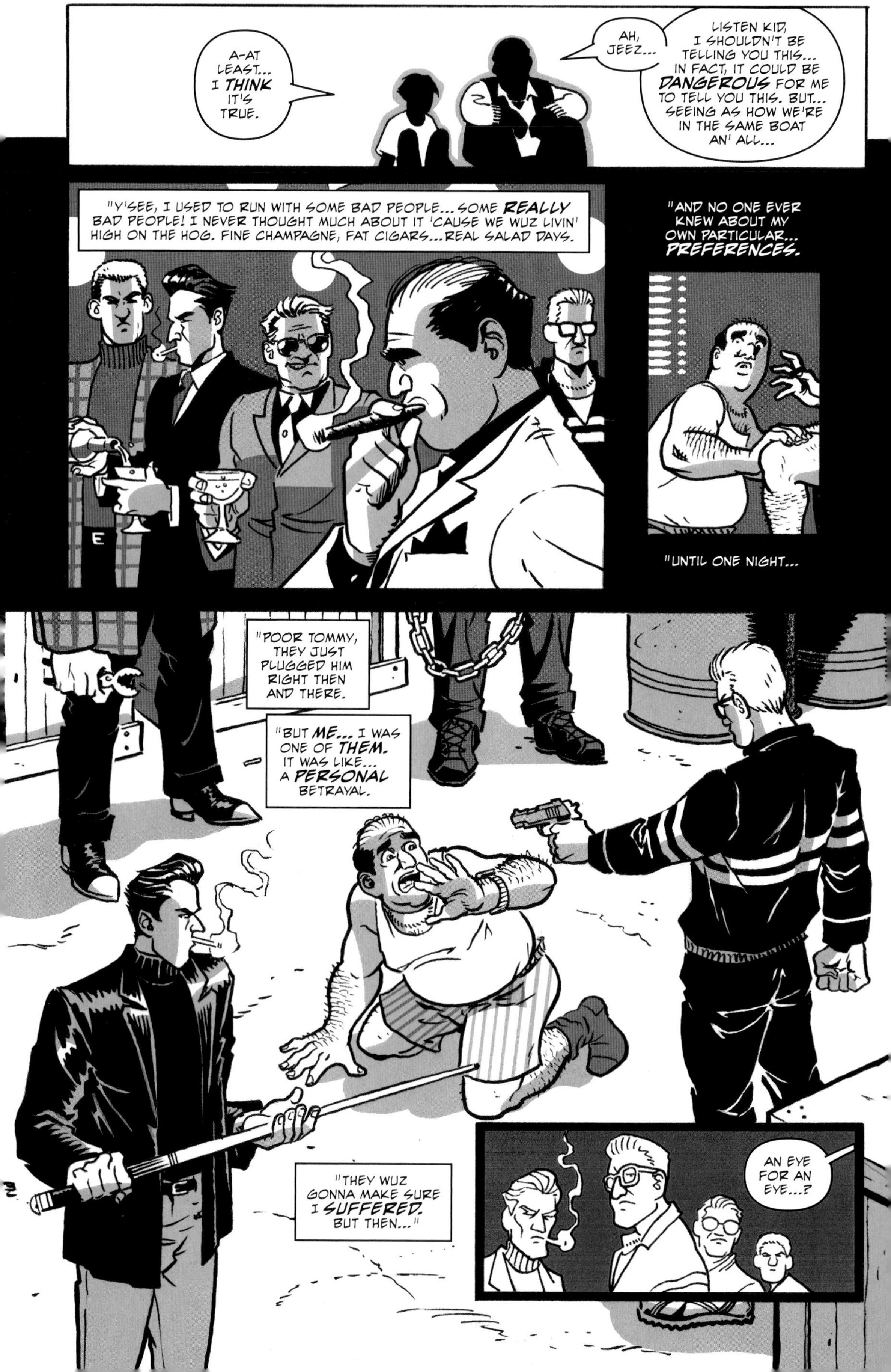
A-AT LEAST... I THINK IT'S TRUE.
AH, JEEZ...
LISTEN KID, I SHOULDN'T BE TELLING YOU THIS... IN FACT, IT COULD BE DANGEROUS FOR ME TO TELL YOU THIS. BUT... SEEING AS HOW WE'RE IN THE SAME BOAT AN' ALL...
"Y'SEE, I USED TO RUN WITH SOME BAD PEOPLE... SOME REALLY BAD PEOPLE! I NEVER THOUGHT MUCH ABOUT IT 'CAUSE WE WUZ LIVIN' HIGH ON THE HOG. FINE CHAMPAGNE, FAT CIGARS...REAL SALAD DAYS.
"AND NO ONE EVER KNEW ABOUT MY OWN PARTICULAR... PREFERENCES.
"UNTIL ONE NIGHT...
"POOR TOMMY, THEY JUST PLUGGED HIM RIGHT THEN AND THERE.
"BUT ME... I WAS ONE OF THEM. IT WAS LIKE... A PERSONAL BETRAYAL.
"THEY WUZ GONNA MAKE SURE I SUFFERED. BUT THEN..."
AN EYE FOR AN EYE...?

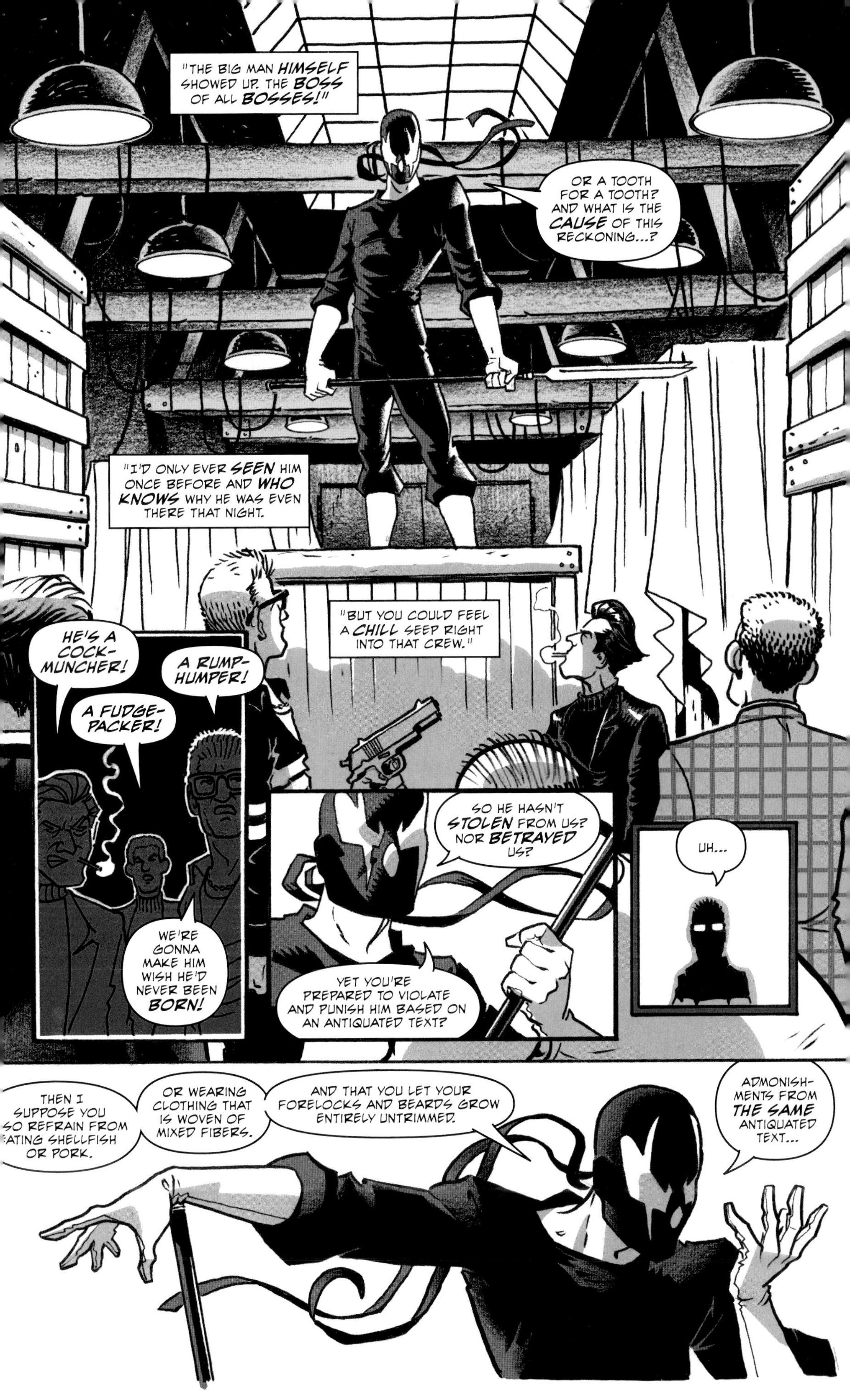
"THE BIG MAN HIMSELF SHOWED UP. THE BOSS OF ALL BOSSES!"
OR A TOOTH FOR A TOOTH? AND WHAT IS THE CAUSE OF THIS RECKONING...?
"I'D ONLY EVER SEEN HIM ONCE BEFORE AND WHO KNOWS WHY HE WAS EVEN THERE THAT NIGHT.
"BUT YOU COULD FEEL A CHILL SEEP RIGHT INTO THAT CREW."
HE'S A COCK-MUNCHER!
A RUMP-HUMPER!
A FUDGE-PACKER!
WE'RE GONNA MAKE HIM WISH HE'D NEVER BEEN BORN!
SO HE HASN'T STOLEN FROM US? NOR BETRAYED US?
YET YOU'RE PREPARED TO VIOLATE AND PUNISH HIM BASED ON AN ANTIQUATED TEXT?
UH...
THEN I SUPPOSE YOU SO REFRAIN FROM EATING SHELLFISH OR PORK.
OR WEARING CLOTHING THAT IS WOVEN OF MIXED FIBERS.
AND THAT YOU LET YOUR FORELOCKS AND BEARDS GROW ENTIRELY UNTRIMMED.
ADMONISHMENTS FROM THE SAME ANTIQUATED TEXT...

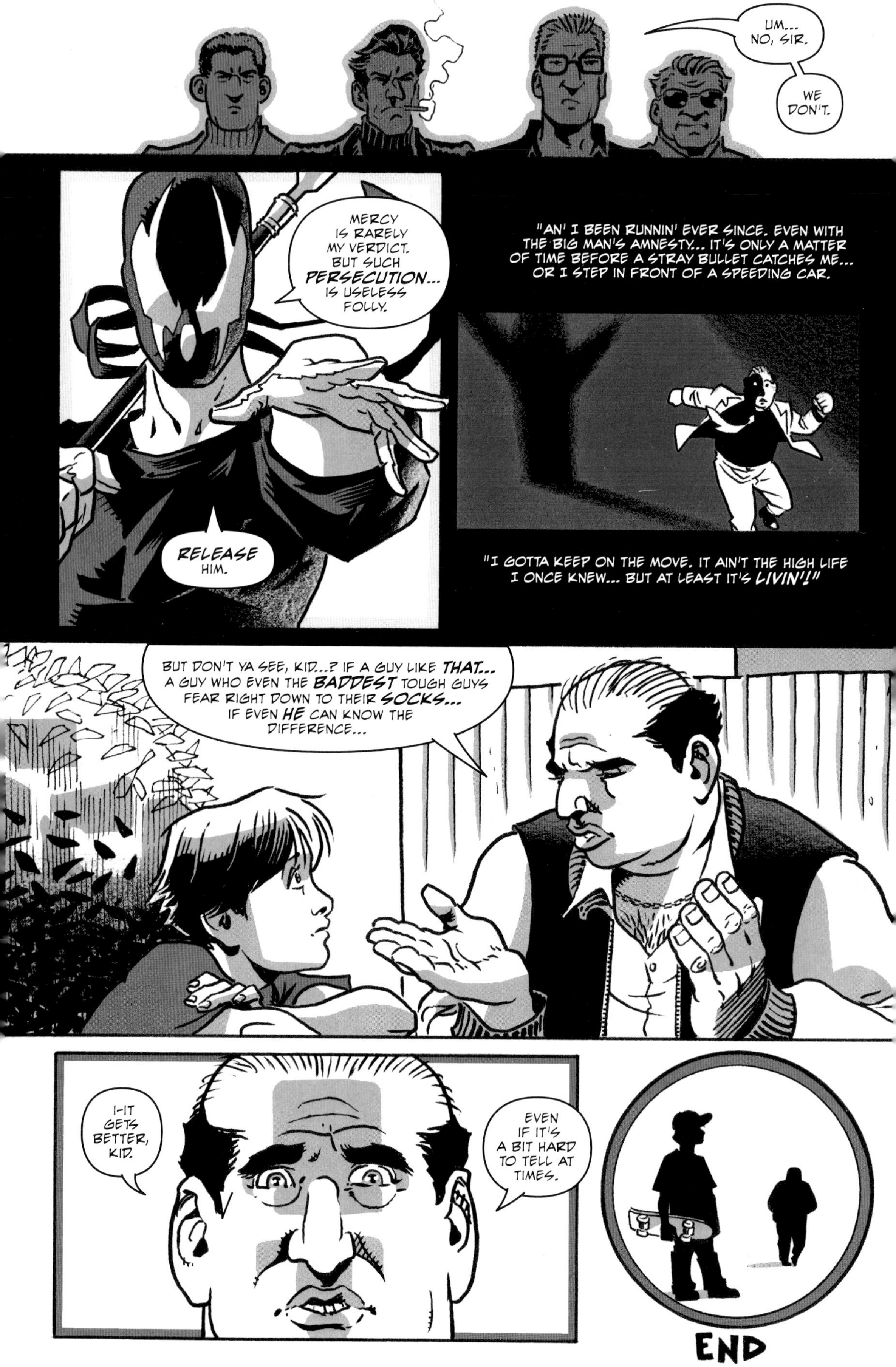
UM... NO, SIR.
WE DON'T.
MERCY IS RARELY MY VERDICT. BUT SUCH PERSECUTION... IS USELESS FOLLY.
RELEASE HIM.
"AN' I BEEN RUNNIN' EVER SINCE. EVEN WITH THE BIG MAN'S AMNESTY... IT'S ONLY A MATTER OF TIME BEFORE A STRAY BULLET CATCHES ME... OR I STEP IN FRONT OF A SPEEDING CAR.
"I GOTTA KEEP ON THE MOVE. IT AIN'T THE HIGH LIFE I ONCE KNEW... BUT AT LEAST IT'S LIVIN'!"
BUT DON'T YA SEE, KID...? IF A GUY LIKE THAT... A GUY WHO EVEN THE BADDEST TOUGH GUYS FEAR RIGHT DOWN TO THEIR SOCKS... IF EVEN HE CAN KNOW THE DIFFERENCE...
I-IT GETS BETTER, KID.
EVEN IF IT'S A BIT HARD TO TELL AT TIMES.
END

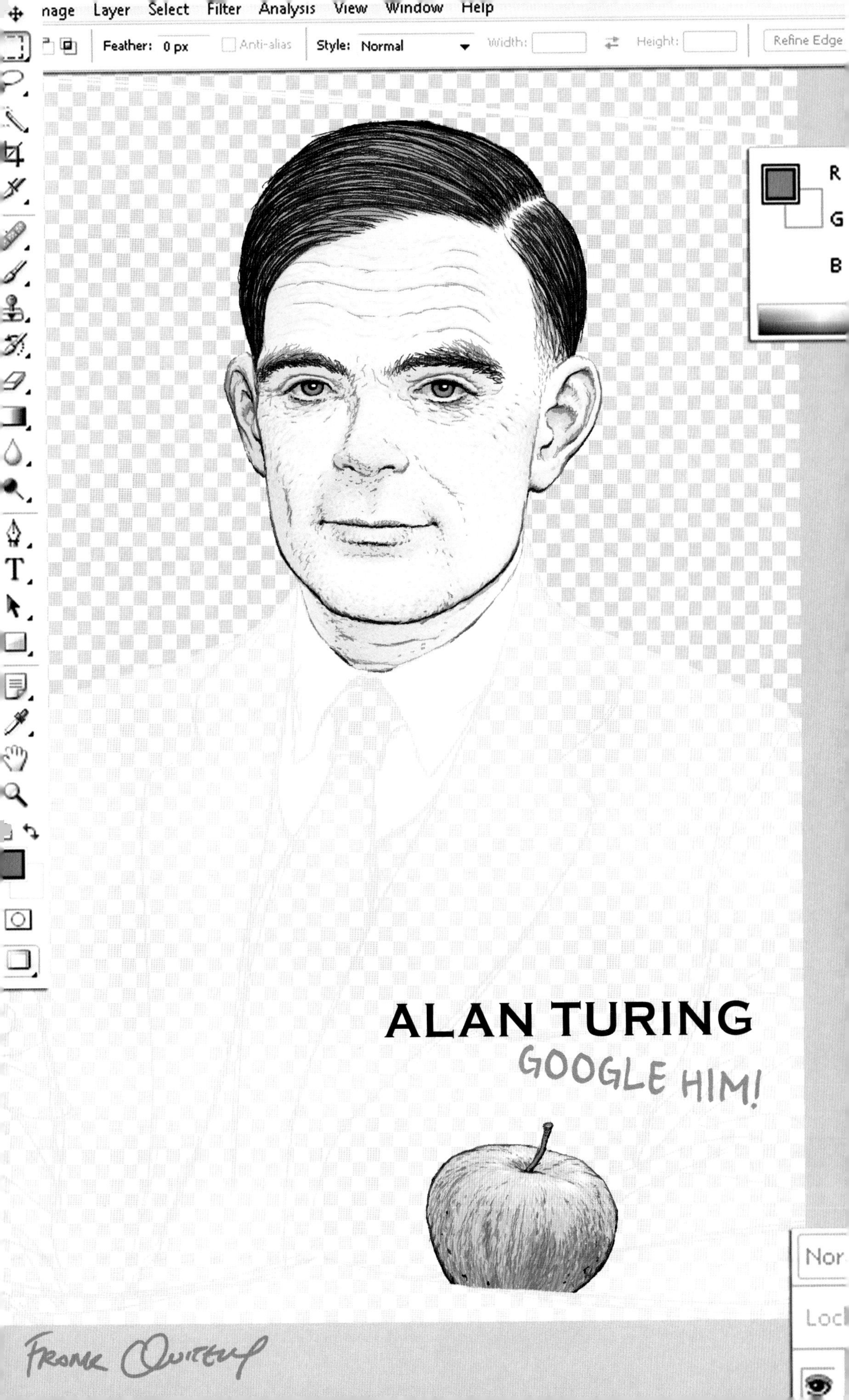

Image Layer Select Filter Analysis View Window Help
Feather: 0 px
Anti-alias
Style: Normal
Width:
Height:
Refine Edge
R
G
B
ALAN TURING
GOOGLE HIM!
Nor
Loc
FRANK QUITELY

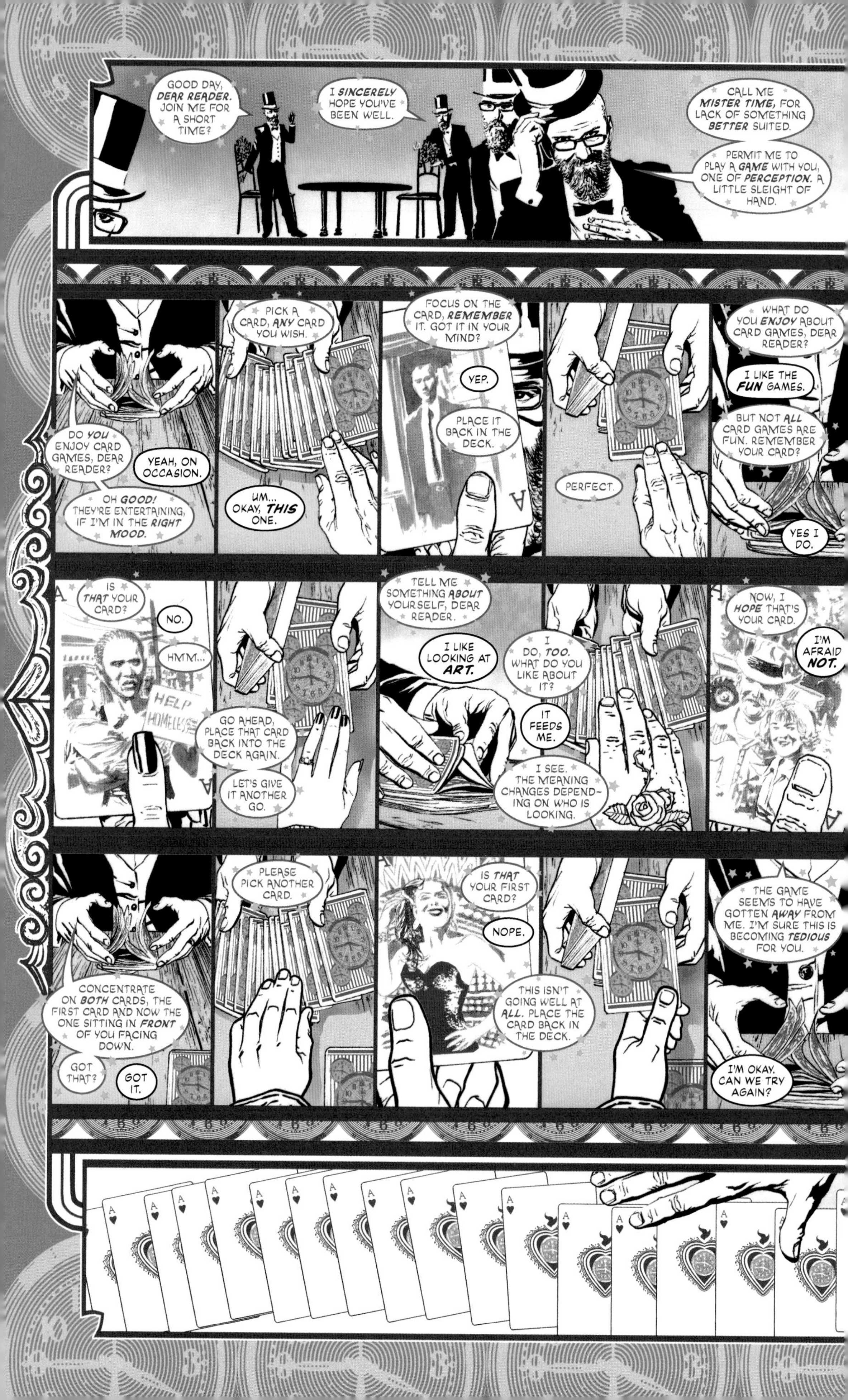
GOOD DAY, DEAR READER. JOIN ME FOR A SHORT TIME?
I SINCERELY HOPE YOU'VE BEEN WELL.
CALL ME MISTER TIME, FOR LACK OF SOMETHING BETTER SUITED.
PERMIT ME TO PLAY A GAME WITH YOU, ONE OF PERCEPTION. A LITTLE SLEIGHT OF HAND.
DO YOU ENJOY CARD GAMES, DEAR READER?
YEAH, ON OCCASION.
OH GOOD! THEY'RE ENTERTAINING, IF I'M IN THE RIGHT MOOD.
PICK A CARD, ANY CARD YOU WISH.
UM... OKAY, THIS ONE.
FOCUS ON THE CARD, REMEMBER IT. GOT IT IN YOUR MIND?
YEP.
PLACE IT BACK IN THE DECK.
PERFECT.
WHAT DO YOU ENJOY ABOUT CARD GAMES, DEAR READER?
I LIKE THE FUN GAMES.
BUT NOT ALL CARD GAMES ARE FUN. REMEMBER YOUR CARD?
YES I DO.
IS THAT YOUR CARD?
NO.
HMM...
HELP HOMELESS
GO AHEAD, PLACE THAT CARD BACK INTO THE DECK AGAIN.
LET'S GIVE IT ANOTHER GO.
TELL ME SOMETHING ABOUT YOURSELF, DEAR READER.
I LIKE LOOKING AT ART.
I DO, TOO. WHAT DO YOU LIKE ABOUT IT?
IT FEEDS ME.
I SEE. THE MEANING CHANGES DEPENDING ON WHO IS LOOKING.
NOW, I HOPE THAT'S YOUR CARD.
I'M AFRAID NOT.
CONCENTRATE ON BOTH CARDS, THE FIRST CARD AND NOW THE ONE SITTING IN FRONT OF YOU FACING DOWN.
GOT THAT?
GOT IT.
PLEASE PICK ANOTHER CARD.
IS THAT YOUR FIRST CARD?
NOPE.
THIS ISN'T GOING WELL AT ALL. PLACE THE CARD BACK IN THE DECK.
THE GAME SEEMS TO HAVE GOTTEN AWAY FROM ME. I'M SURE THIS IS BECOMING TEDIOUS FOR YOU.
I'M OKAY. CAN WE TRY AGAIN?

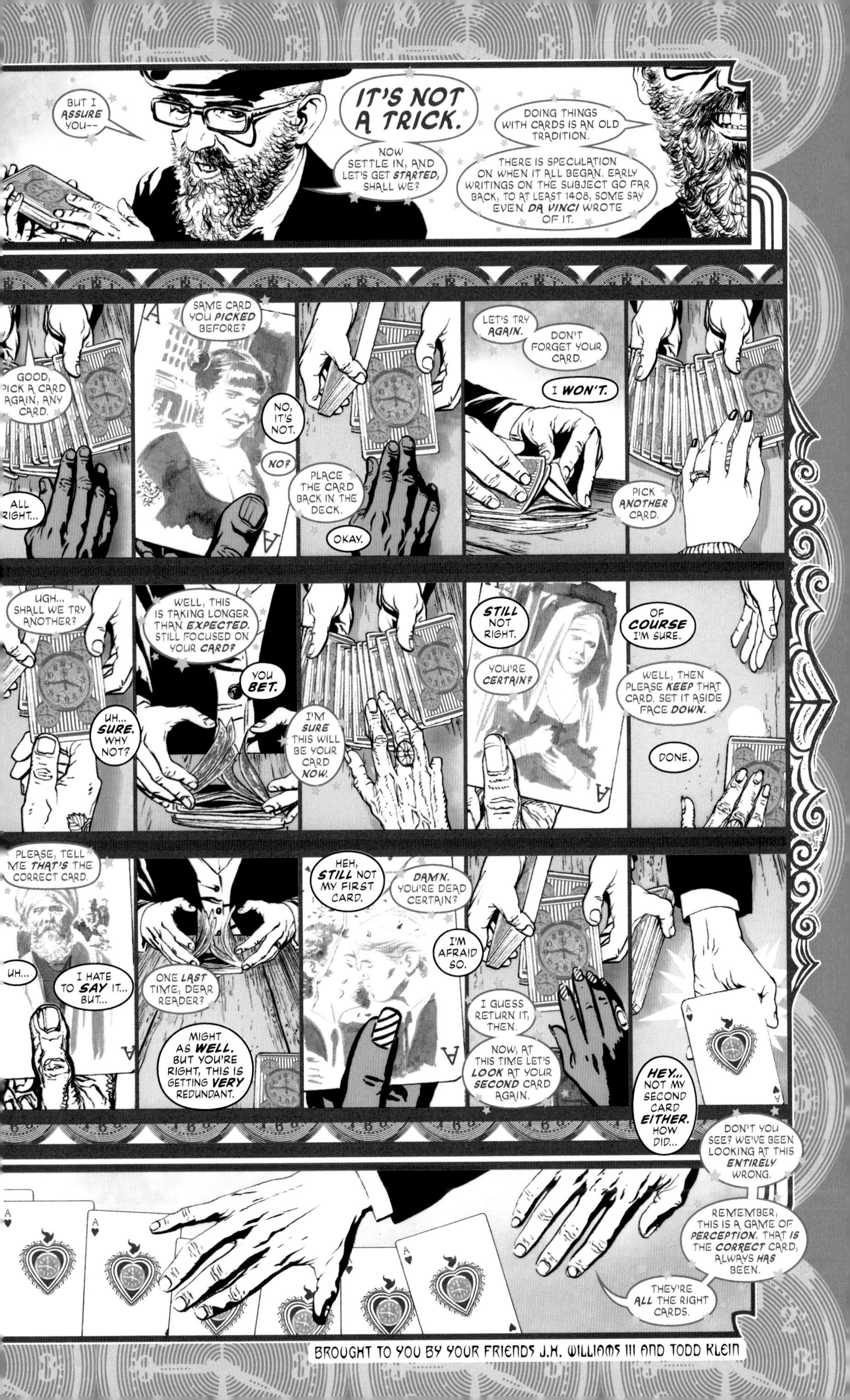

BUT I ASSURE YOU--
IT'S NOT A TRICK.
NOW SETTLE IN, AND LET'S GET STARTED, SHALL WE?
DOING THINGS WITH CARDS IS AN OLD TRADITION.
THERE IS SPECULATION ON WHEN IT ALL BEGAN. EARLY WRITINGS ON THE SUBJECT GO FAR BACK, TO AT LEAST 1408, SOME SAY EVEN DA VINCI WROTE OF IT.
GOOD, PICK A CARD AGAIN, ANY CARD.
ALL RIGHT...
SAME CARD YOU PICKED BEFORE?
NO, IT'S NOT.
NO?
PLACE THE CARD BACK IN THE DECK.
OKAY.
LET'S TRY AGAIN.
DON'T FORGET YOUR CARD.
I WON'T.
PICK ANOTHER CARD.
UGH... SHALL WE TRY ANOTHER?
UH... SURE. WHY NOT?
WELL, THIS IS TAKING LONGER THAN EXPECTED. STILL FOCUSED ON YOUR CARD?
YOU BET.
I'M SURE THIS WILL BE YOUR CARD NOW.
STILL NOT RIGHT.
YOU'RE CERTAIN?
OF COURSE I'M SURE.
WELL, THEN PLEASE KEEP THAT CARD. SET IT ASIDE FACE DOWN.
DONE.
PLEASE, TELL ME THAT'S THE CORRECT CARD.
UH...
I HATE TO SAY IT... BUT...
ONE LAST TIME, DEAR READER?
MIGHT AS WELL. BUT YOU'RE RIGHT, THIS IS GETTING VERY REDUNDANT.
HEH, STILL NOT MY FIRST CARD.
DAMN. YOU'RE DEAD CERTAIN?
I'M AFRAID SO.
I GUESS RETURN IT, THEN.
NOW, AT THIS TIME LET'S LOOK AT YOUR SECOND CARD AGAIN.
HEY... NOT MY SECOND CARD EITHER. HOW DID...
DON'T YOU SEE? WE'VE BEEN LOOKING AT THIS ENTIRELY WRONG.
REMEMBER, THIS IS A GAME OF PERCEPTION. THAT IS THE CORRECT CARD, ALWAYS HAS BEEN.
THEY'RE ALL THE RIGHT CARDS.
BROUGHT TO YOU BY YOUR FRIENDS J.H. WILLIAMS III AND TODD KLEIN

story by Kyle McCulloch

the light at the end of the tunnel

art by Dave Cooper

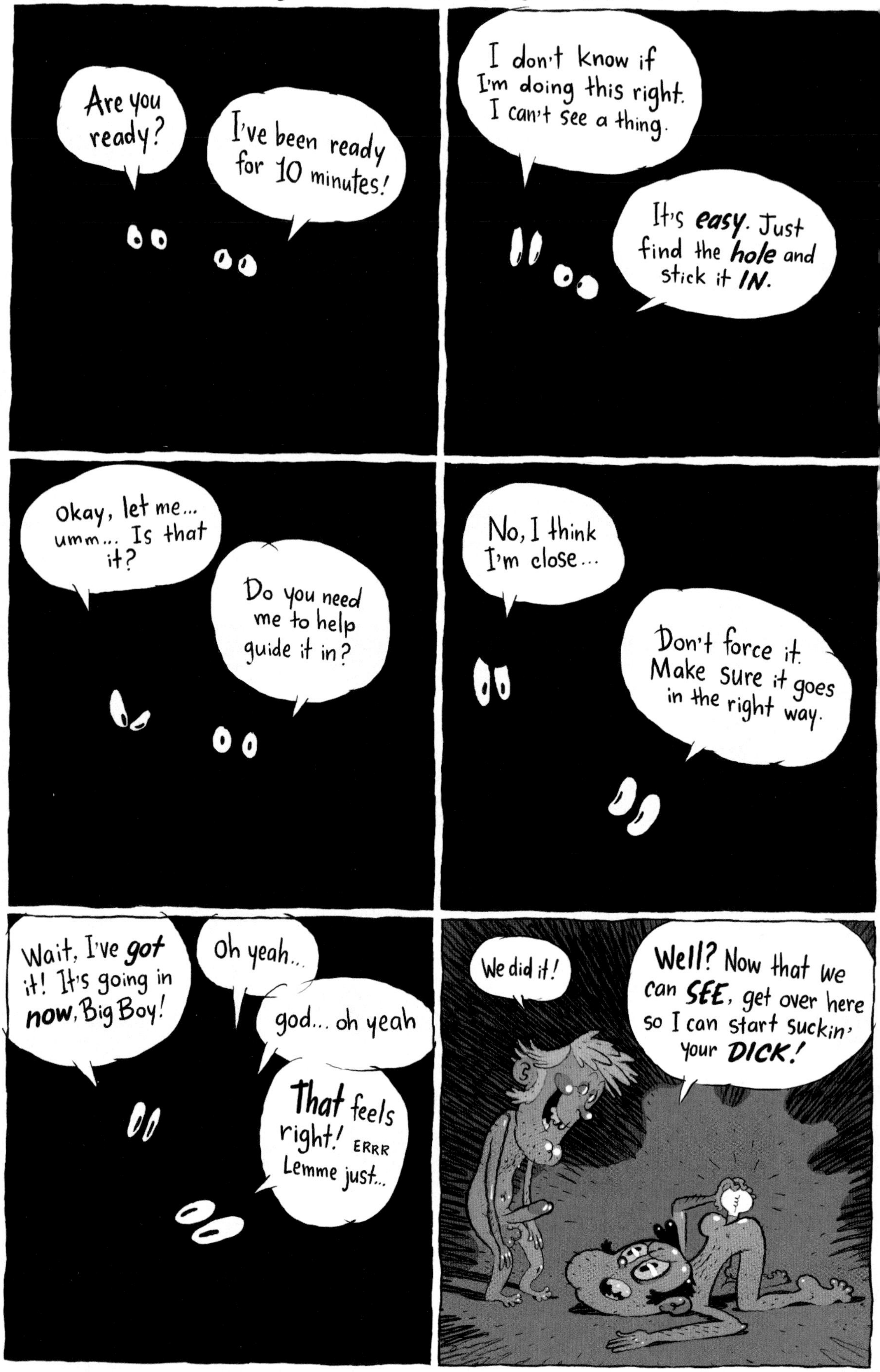

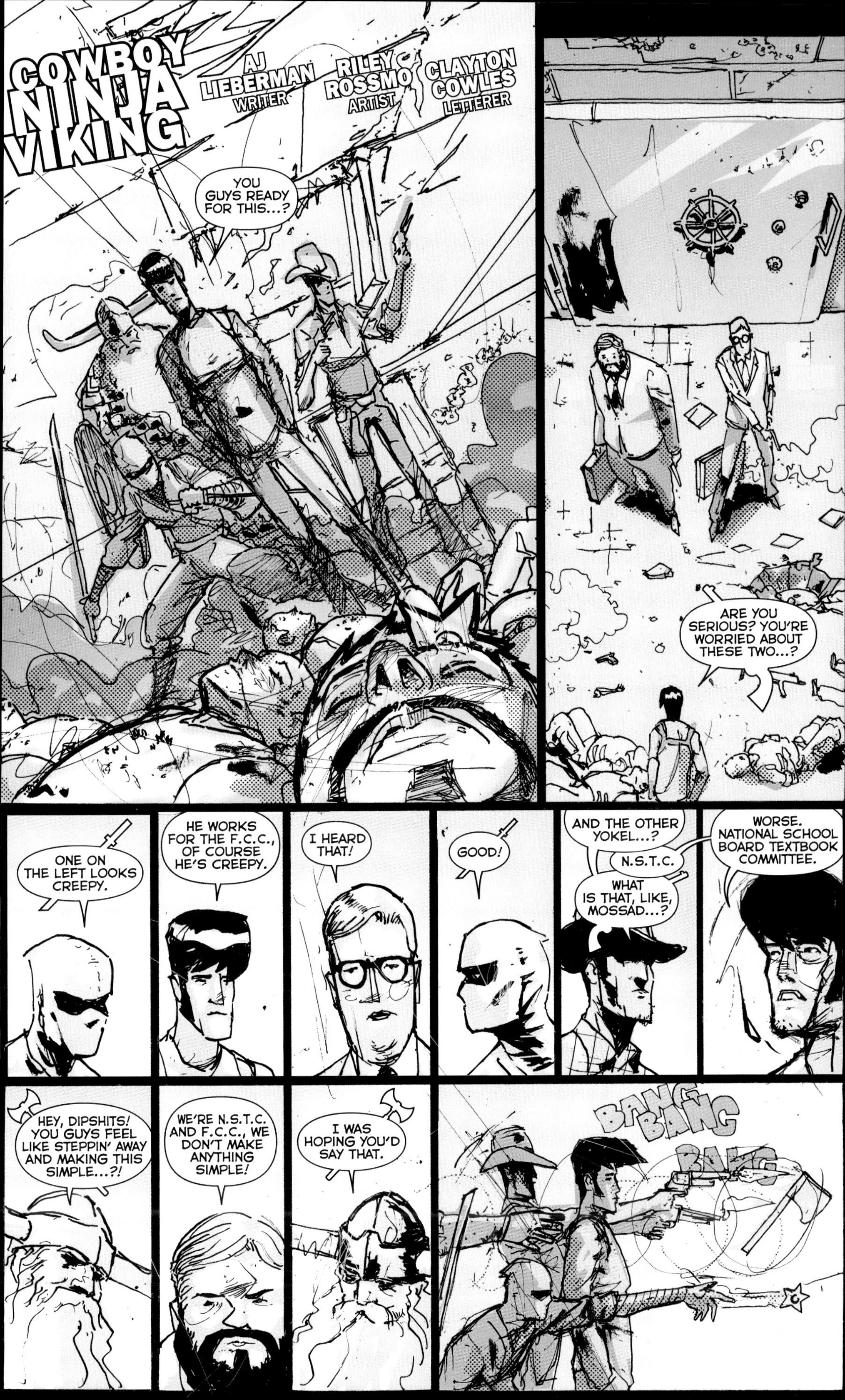
COWBOY NINJA VIKING
AJ LIEBERMAN WRITER
RILEY ROSSMO ARTIST
CLAYTON COWLES LETTERER
YOU GUYS READY FOR THIS...?
ARE YOU SERIOUS? YOU'RE WORRIED ABOUT THESE TWO...?
ONE ON THE LEFT LOOKS CREEPY.
HE WORKS FOR THE F.C.C., OF COURSE HE'S CREEPY.
I HEARD THAT!
GOOD!
AND THE OTHER YOKEL...?
N.S.T.C.
WHAT IS THAT, LIKE, MOSSAD...?
WORSE. NATIONAL SCHOOL BOARD TEXTBOOK COMMITTEE.
HEY, DIPSHITS! YOU GUYS FEEL LIKE STEPPIN' AWAY AND MAKING THIS SIMPLE...?!
WE'RE N.S.T.C. AND F.C.C., WE DON'T MAKE ANYTHING SIMPLE!
I WAS HOPING YOU'D SAY THAT.
BANG
BANG
BANG

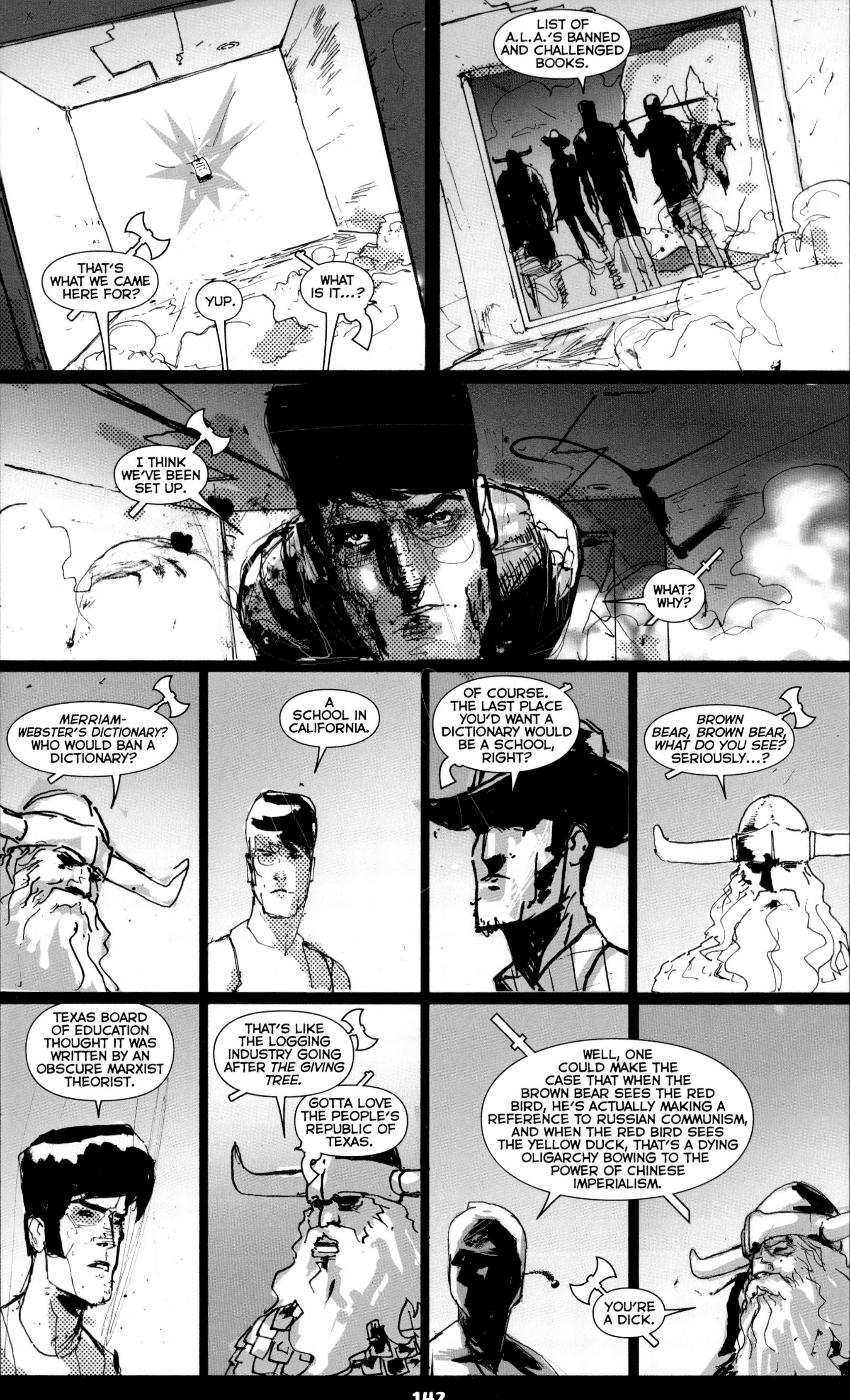
THAT'S WHAT WE CAME HERE FOR?
YUP.
WHAT IS IT...?
LIST OF A.L.A.'S BANNED AND CHALLENGED BOOKS.
I THINK WE'VE BEEN SET UP.
WHAT? WHY?
MERRIAM-WEBSTER'S DICTIONARY? WHO WOULD BAN A DICTIONARY?
A SCHOOL IN CALIFORNIA.
OF COURSE. THE LAST PLACE YOU'D WANT A DICTIONARY WOULD BE A SCHOOL, RIGHT?
BROWN BEAR, BROWN BEAR, WHAT DO YOU SEE? SERIOUSLY...?
TEXAS BOARD OF EDUCATION THOUGHT IT WAS WRITTEN BY AN OBSCURE MARXIST THEORIST.
THAT'S LIKE THE LOGGING INDUSTRY GOING AFTER *THE GIVING TREE.*
GOTTA LOVE THE PEOPLE'S REPUBLIC OF TEXAS.
WELL, ONE COULD MAKE THE CASE THAT WHEN THE BROWN BEAR SEES THE RED BIRD, HE'S ACTUALLY MAKING A REFERENCE TO RUSSIAN COMMUNISM, AND WHEN THE RED BIRD SEES THE YELLOW DUCK, THAT'S A DYING OLIGARCHY BOWING TO THE POWER OF CHINESE IMPERIALISM.
YOU'RE A DICK.

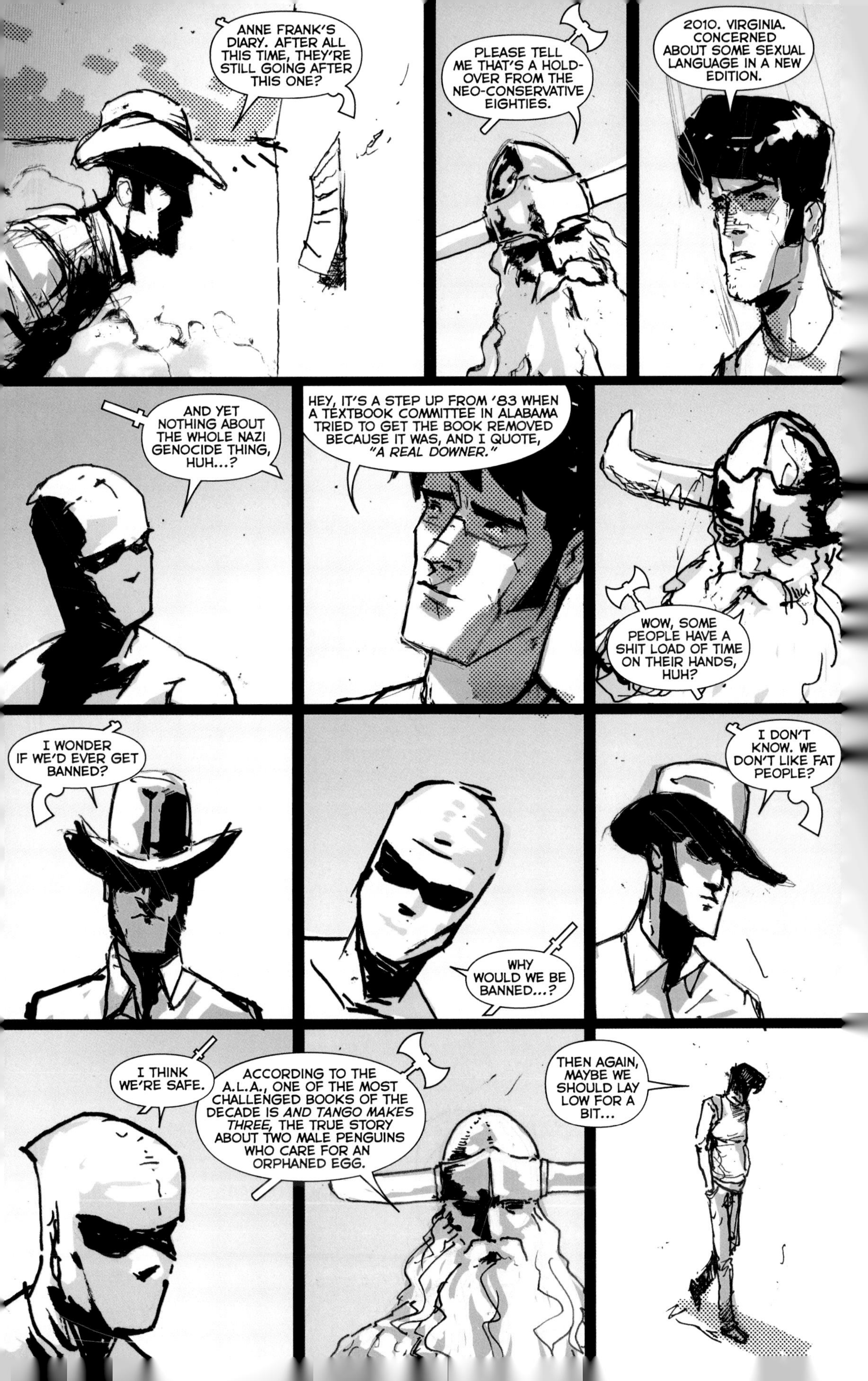
ANNE FRANK'S DIARY. AFTER ALL THIS TIME, THEY'RE STILL GOING AFTER THIS ONE?
PLEASE TELL ME THAT'S A HOLD-OVER FROM THE NEO-CONSERVATIVE EIGHTIES.
2010. VIRGINIA. CONCERNED ABOUT SOME SEXUAL LANGUAGE IN A NEW EDITION.
AND YET NOTHING ABOUT THE WHOLE NAZI GENOCIDE THING, HUH...?
HEY, IT'S A STEP UP FROM '83 WHEN A TEXTBOOK COMMITTEE IN ALABAMA TRIED TO GET THE BOOK REMOVED BECAUSE IT WAS, AND I QUOTE, "A REAL DOWNER."
WOW, SOME PEOPLE HAVE A SHIT LOAD OF TIME ON THEIR HANDS, HUH?
I WONDER IF WE'D EVER GET BANNED?
WHY WOULD WE BE BANNED...?
I DON'T KNOW. WE DON'T LIKE FAT PEOPLE?
I THINK WE'RE SAFE.
ACCORDING TO THE A.L.A., ONE OF THE MOST CHALLENGED BOOKS OF THE DECADE IS AND TANGO MAKES THREE, THE TRUE STORY ABOUT TWO MALE PENGUINS WHO CARE FOR AN ORPHANED EGG.
THEN AGAIN, MAYBE WE SHOULD LAY LOW FOR A BIT...

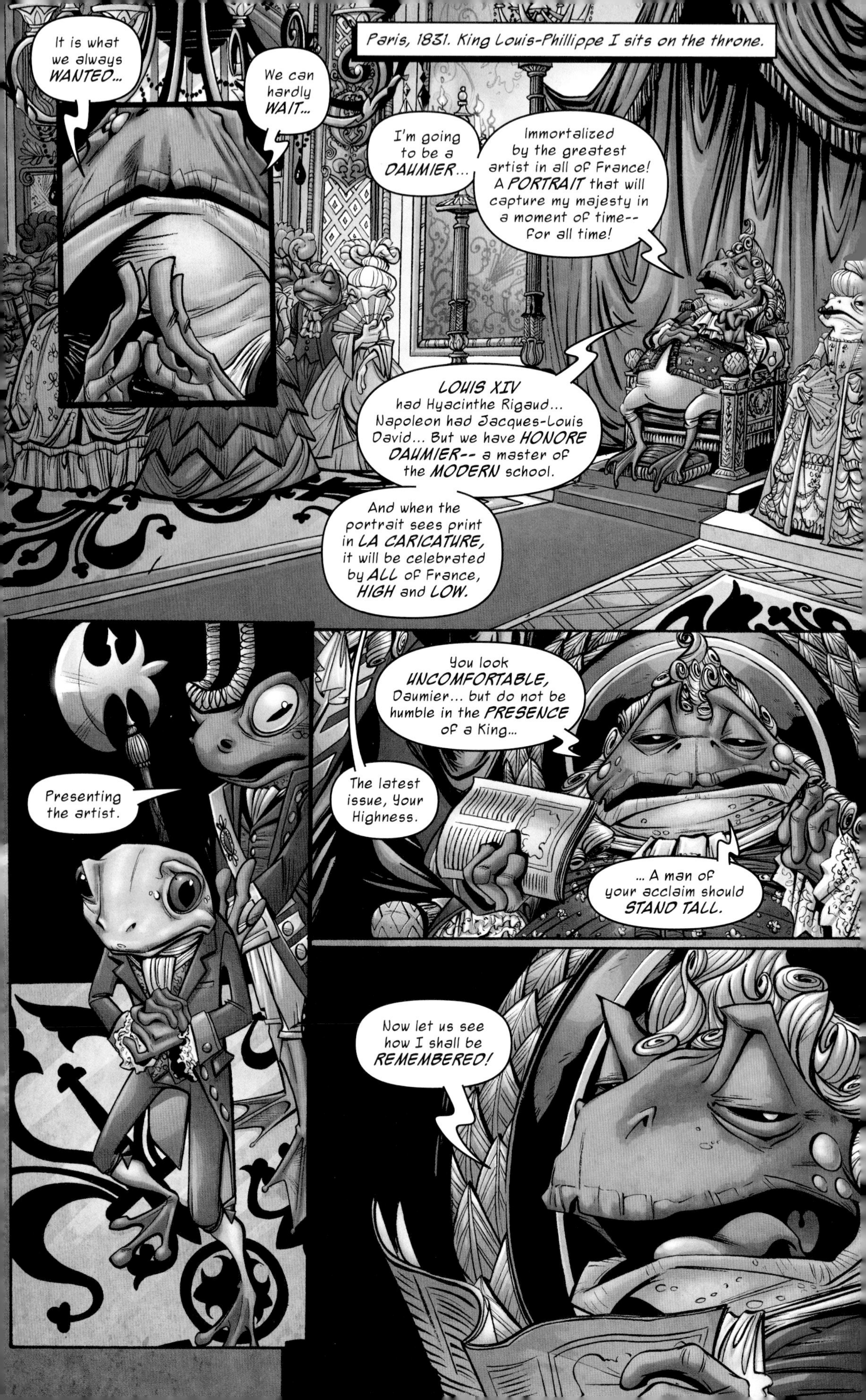
Paris, 1831. King Louis-Phillippe I sits on the throne.
It is what we always WANTED...
We can hardly WAIT...
I'm going to be a DAUMIER...
Immortalized by the greatest artist in all of France! A PORTRAIT that will capture my majesty in a moment of time-- for all time!
LOUIS XIV had Hyacinthe Rigaud... Napoleon had Jacques-Louis David... But we have HONORE DAUMIER-- a master of the MODERN school.
And when the portrait sees print in LA CARICATURE, it will be celebrated by ALL of France, HIGH and LOW.
Presenting the artist.
You look UNCOMFORTABLE, Daumier... but do not be humble in the PRESENCE of a King...
The latest issue, Your Highness.
... A man of your acclaim should STAND TALL.
Now let us see how I shall be REMEMBERED!

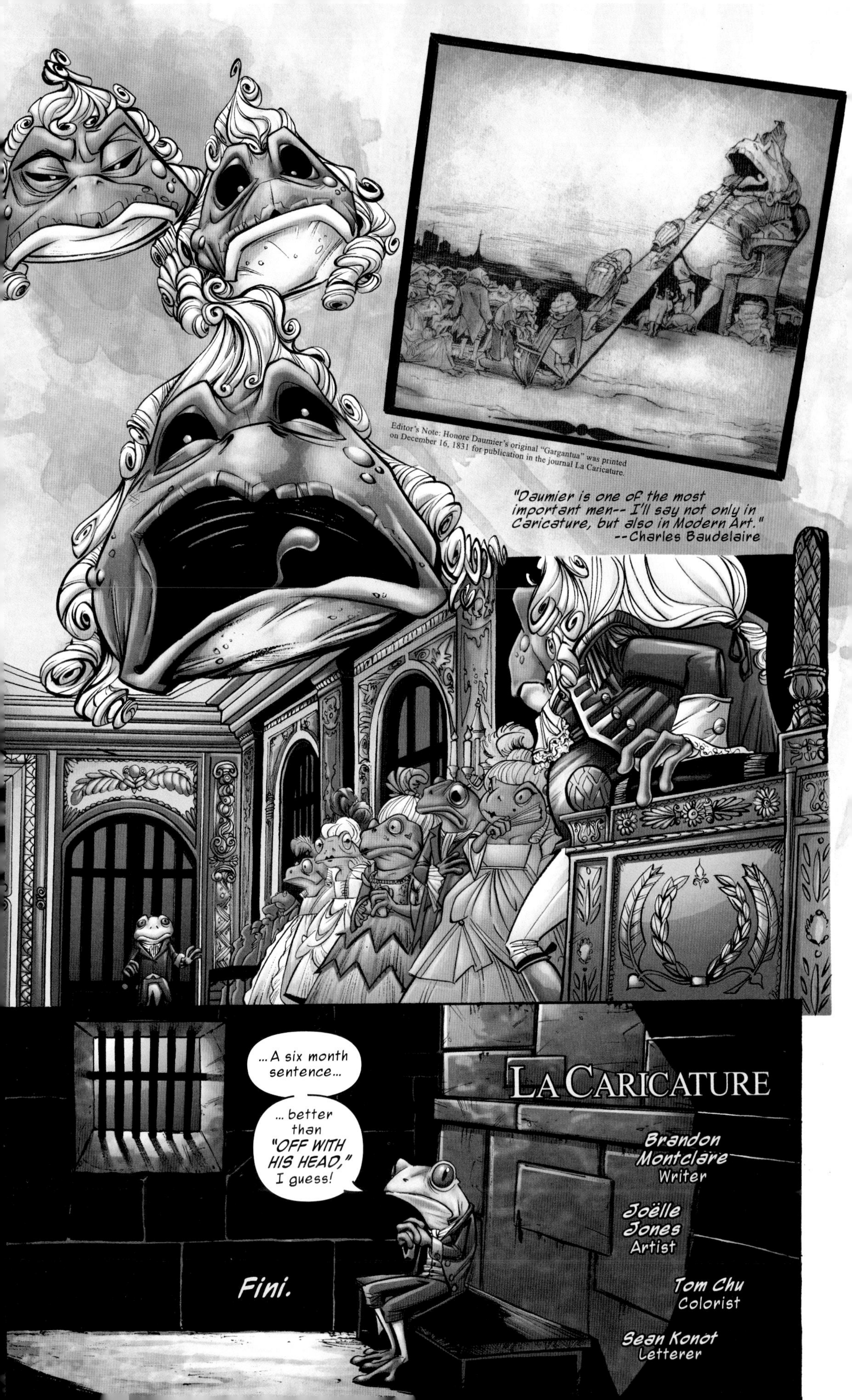

Editor's Note: Honore Daumier's original "Gargantua" was printed on December 16, 1831 for publication in the journal La Caricature.
"Daumier is one of the most important men-- I'll say not only in Caricature, but also in Modern Art."
--Charles Baudelaire
...A six month sentence...
...better than "OFF WITH HIS HEAD," I guess!
LA CARICATURE
Brandon Montclare Writer
Joëlle Jones Artist
Tom Chu Colorist
Sean Konot Letterer
Fini.

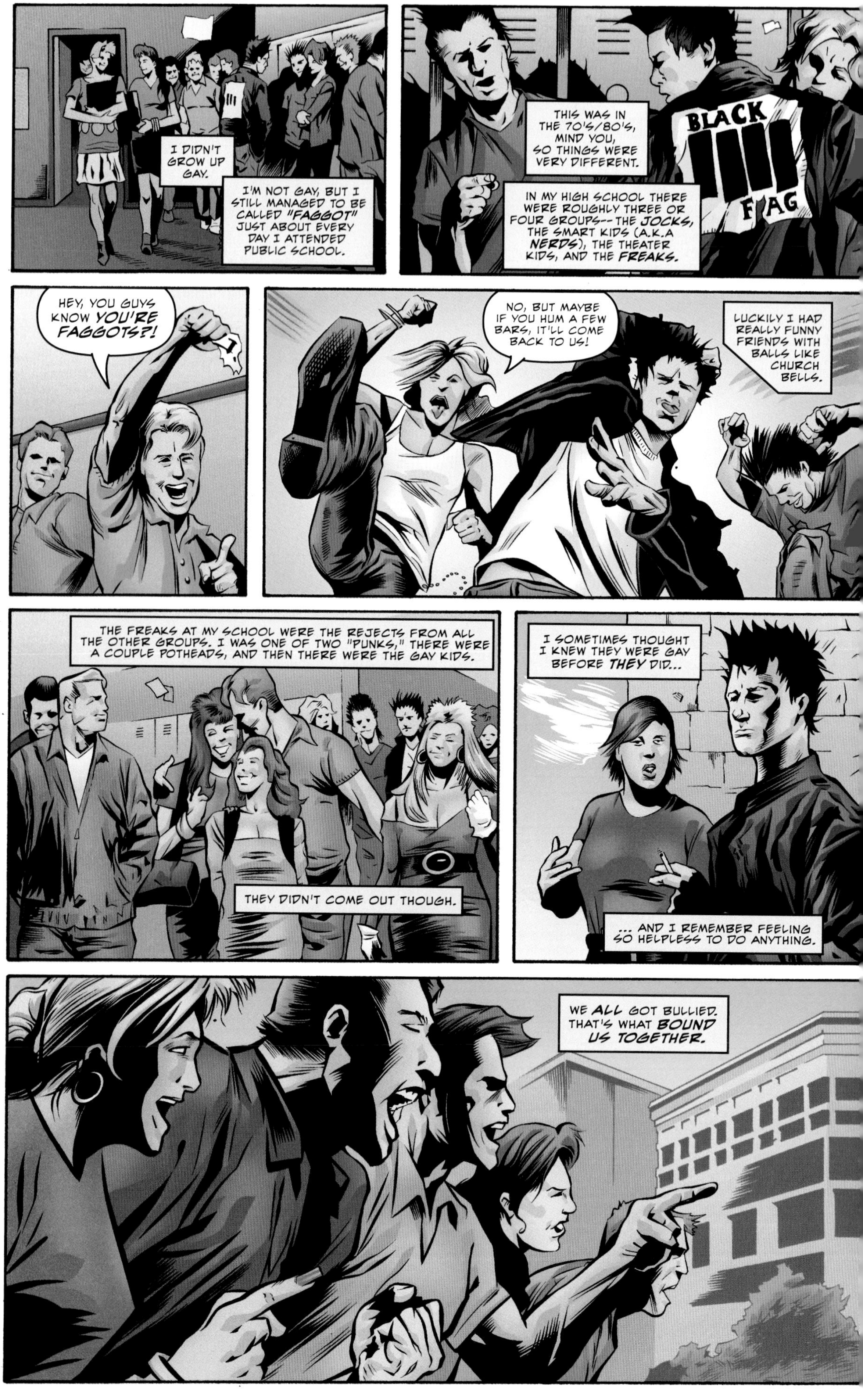

I DIDN'T GROW UP GAY.
I'M NOT GAY, BUT I STILL MANAGED TO BE CALLED "FAGGOT" JUST ABOUT EVERY DAY I ATTENDED PUBLIC SCHOOL.
THIS WAS IN THE 70'S/80'S, MIND YOU, SO THINGS WERE VERY DIFFERENT.
BLACK FLAG
IN MY HIGH SCHOOL THERE WERE ROUGHLY THREE OR FOUR GROUPS-- THE JOCKS, THE SMART KIDS (A.K.A NERDS), THE THEATER KIDS, AND THE FREAKS.
HEY, YOU GUYS KNOW YOU'RE FAGGOTS?!
NO, BUT MAYBE IF YOU HUM A FEW BARS, IT'LL COME BACK TO US!
LUCKILY I HAD REALLY FUNNY FRIENDS WITH BALLS LIKE CHURCH BELLS.
THE FREAKS AT MY SCHOOL WERE THE REJECTS FROM ALL THE OTHER GROUPS. I WAS ONE OF TWO "PUNKS," THERE WERE A COUPLE POTHEADS, AND THEN THERE WERE THE GAY KIDS.
THEY DIDN'T COME OUT THOUGH.
I SOMETIMES THOUGHT I KNEW THEY WERE GAY BEFORE THEY DID...
... AND I REMEMBER FEELING SO HELPLESS TO DO ANYTHING.
WE ALL GOT BULLIED. THAT'S WHAT BOUND US TOGETHER.

THEN SOMETHING HAPPENED TO ME THAT REALLY OPENED MY EYES.

MY OLDEST SISTER, THE ONE WHO TURNED ME ONTO EVERY HORROR MOVIE AND PUNK RECORD I EVER LOVED, CAME OUT OF THE CLOSET AND TOLD ME SHE WAS A LESBIAN.

SO, I'M ONLY GOING TO BE WITH WOMEN NOW, BUT THAT DOESN'T MEAN I HATE MEN, OKAY?

OKAY.

I REMEMBER FEELING *EXHILARATED,* THAT I'D SOMEHOW CONNECTED WITH SOME HOPE OUTSIDE THE SUBURBAN HELL I WAS TRAPPED IN.

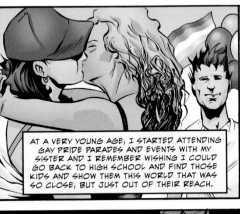

AT A VERY YOUNG AGE, I STARTED ATTENDING GAY PRIDE PARADES AND EVENTS WITH MY SISTER AND I REMEMBER WISHING I COULD GO BACK TO HIGH SCHOOL AND FIND THOSE KIDS AND SHOW THEM THIS WORLD THAT WAS SO CLOSE, BUT JUST OUT OF THEIR REACH.

SEE, BACK THEN, COMING OUT IN HIGH SCHOOL COULD GET YOU *HURT.*

TO THIS DAY, I STILL DON'T KNOW IF MY FRIENDS EVER CAME OUT OR DISCOVERED THE WORLD OUTSIDE THE IGNORANCE.

BECAUSE AS FUCKED UP AS THE WORLD STILL IS, AS FILLED WITH HATE AND IGNORANCE AS OUR LIVES STILL ARE, WE HAVE MADE *TREMENDOUS STRIDES.*

NOW THERE ARE CLUBS IN HIGH SCHOOLS FOR GAY STUDENTS AND EVEN THOUGH THEY STILL DEAL WITH ALL MANNER OF HARASS- MENT, THEY HAVE EACH OTHER.

THEY KNOW THEY'RE NOT *ALONE.*

I WISH I HAD THE *TIME MACHINE* SO I COULD SHOW MY FRIENDS BACK THEN THAT THINGS NOT ONLY GET BETTER AS YOU GET OLDER, BUT THERE ARE REAL SIGNS OF *HOPE* AND *GROWTH* IN THE WORLD WE LIVE IN TODAY.

I KNOW SOMETIMES, WHEN WE FIND OURSELVES FIGHTING FOR THE RIGHT FOR ALL HUMANS TO LOVE AND MARRY, IT SEEMS LIKE THINGS WILL NEVER CHANGE.

BUT THEY *HAVE* CHANGED, AND THEY WILL *CONTINUE* TO CHANGE.

THINGS REALLY DO GET BETTER.

INKER- JACK PURCELL
COLORIST- LOVERN KINDZIERSKI
LETTERER- SEAN KONOT

STEVE NILES
-WRITER
MICHAEL MONTENAT
-PENCILER

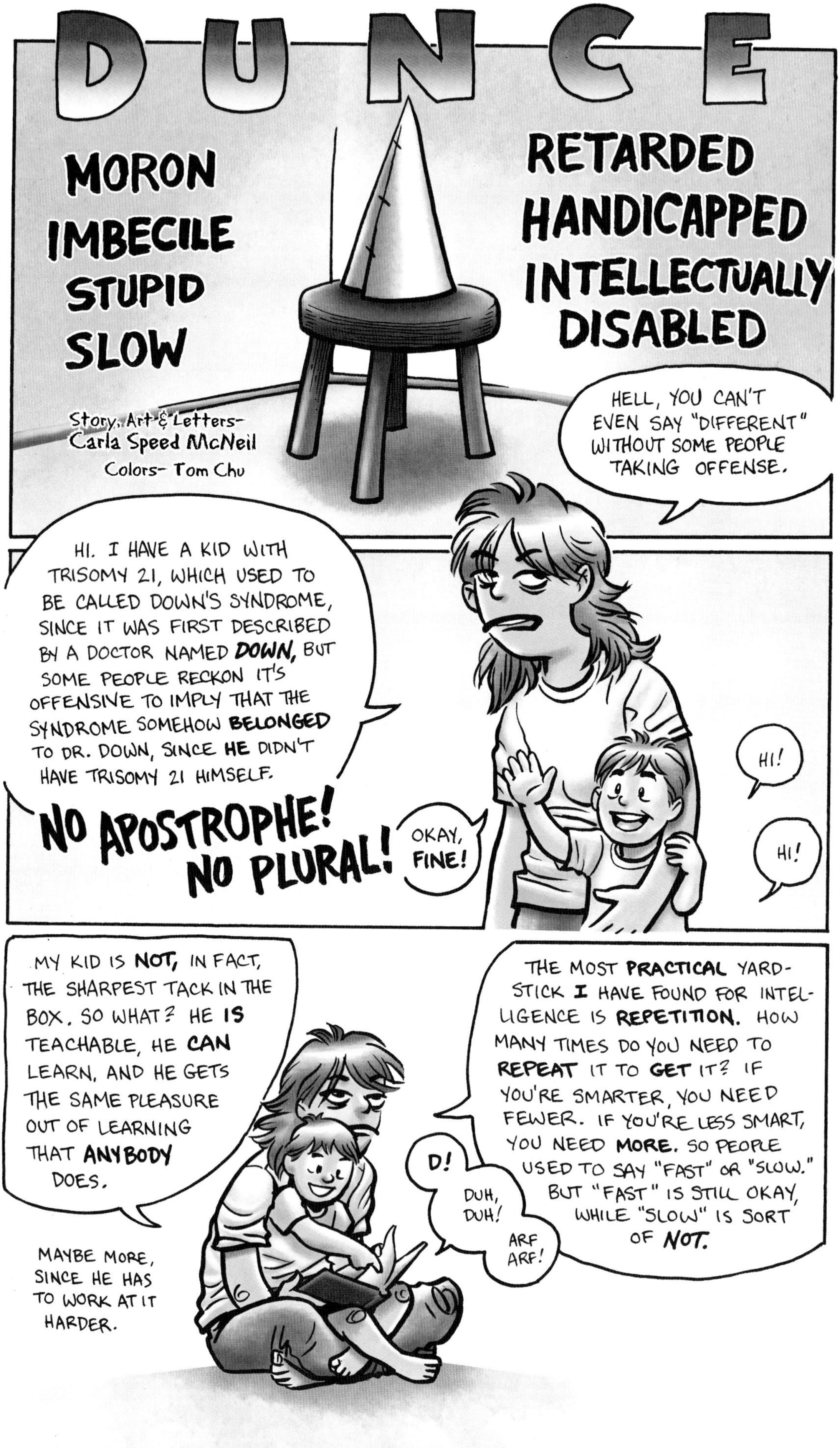
DUNCE
MORON
IMBECILE
STUPID
SLOW
RETARDED
HANDICAPPED
INTELLECTUALLY
DISABLED
Story, Art & Letters- Carla Speed McNeil
Colors- Tom Chu
HELL, YOU CAN'T EVEN SAY "DIFFERENT" WITHOUT SOME PEOPLE TAKING OFFENSE.
HI. I HAVE A KID WITH TRISOMY 21, WHICH USED TO BE CALLED DOWN'S SYNDROME, SINCE IT WAS FIRST DESCRIBED BY A DOCTOR NAMED DOWN, BUT SOME PEOPLE RECKON IT'S OFFENSIVE TO IMPLY THAT THE SYNDROME SOMEHOW BELONGED TO DR. DOWN, SINCE HE DIDN'T HAVE TRISOMY 21 HIMSELF.
NO APOSTROPHE! NO PLURAL!
OKAY, FINE!
HI!
HI!
MY KID IS NOT, IN FACT, THE SHARPEST TACK IN THE BOX. SO WHAT? HE IS TEACHABLE, HE CAN LEARN, AND HE GETS THE SAME PLEASURE OUT OF LEARNING THAT ANYBODY DOES.
MAYBE MORE, SINCE HE HAS TO WORK AT IT HARDER.
D!
DUH, DUH!
ARF ARF!
THE MOST PRACTICAL YARD-STICK I HAVE FOUND FOR INTEL-LIGENCE IS REPETITION. HOW MANY TIMES DO YOU NEED TO REPEAT IT TO GET IT? IF YOU'RE SMARTER, YOU NEED FEWER. IF YOU'RE LESS SMART, YOU NEED MORE. SO PEOPLE USED TO SAY "FAST" OR "SLOW." BUT "FAST" IS STILL OKAY, WHILE "SLOW" IS SORT OF NOT.

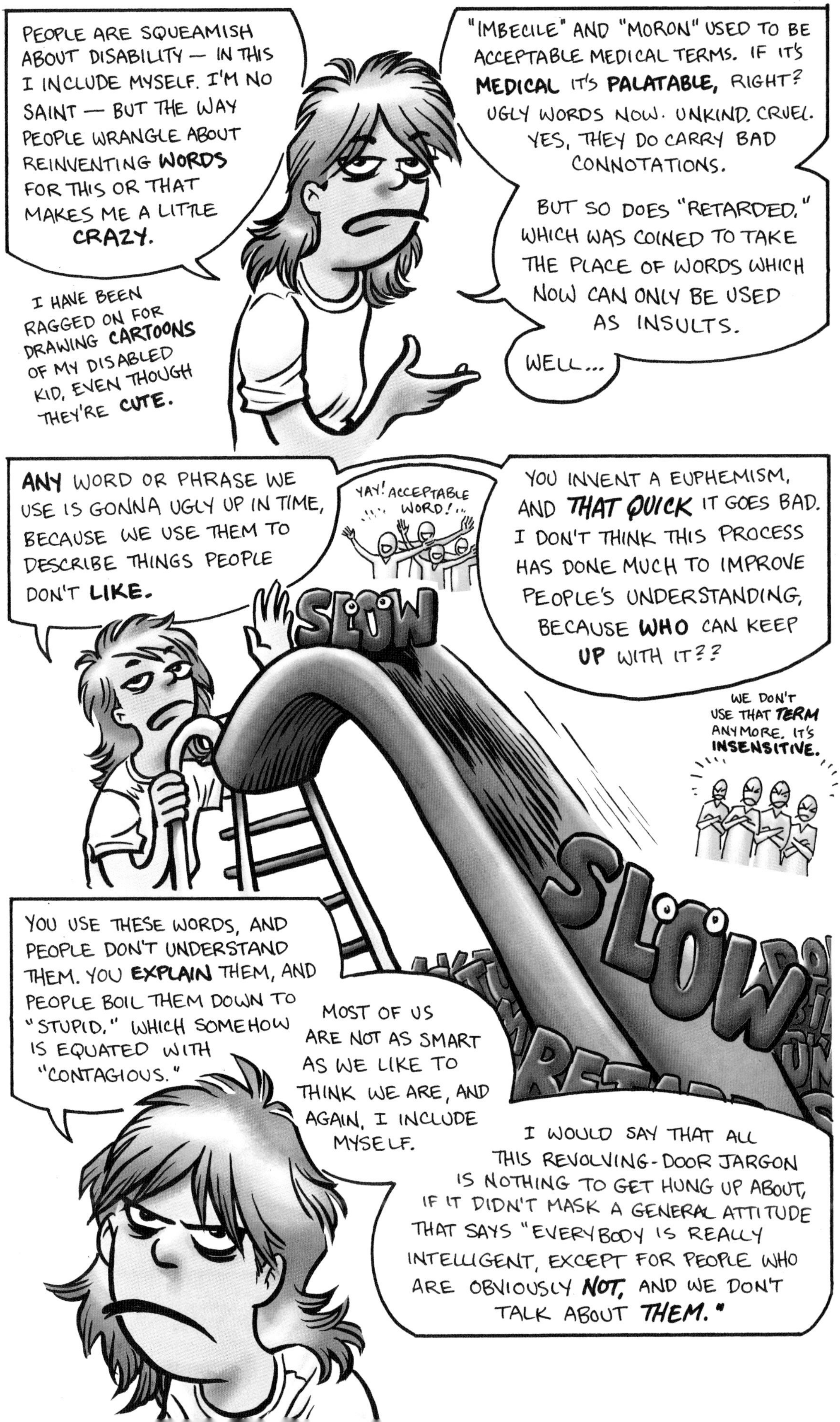
PEOPLE ARE SQUEAMISH ABOUT DISABILITY — IN THIS I INCLUDE MYSELF. I'M NO SAINT — BUT THE WAY PEOPLE WRANGLE ABOUT REINVENTING **WORDS** FOR THIS OR THAT MAKES ME A LITTLE **CRAZY**.
I HAVE BEEN RAGGED ON FOR DRAWING **CARTOONS** OF MY DISABLED KID, EVEN THOUGH THEY'RE **CUTE**.
"IMBECILE" AND "MORON" USED TO BE ACCEPTABLE MEDICAL TERMS. IF IT'S **MEDICAL** IT'S **PALATABLE,** RIGHT? UGLY WORDS NOW. UNKIND. CRUEL. YES, THEY DO CARRY BAD CONNOTATIONS.
BUT SO DOES "RETARDED," WHICH WAS COINED TO TAKE THE PLACE OF WORDS WHICH NOW CAN ONLY BE USED AS INSULTS.
WELL...
ANY WORD OR PHRASE WE USE IS GONNA UGLY UP IN TIME, BECAUSE WE USE THEM TO DESCRIBE THINGS PEOPLE DON'T **LIKE**.
YAY! ACCEPTABLE WORD!
SLOW
YOU INVENT A EUPHEMISM, AND ***THAT QUICK*** IT GOES BAD. I DON'T THINK THIS PROCESS HAS DONE MUCH TO IMPROVE PEOPLE'S UNDERSTANDING, BECAUSE **WHO** CAN KEEP **UP** WITH IT??
WE DON'T USE THAT ***TERM*** ANYMORE. IT'S **INSENSITIVE.**
SLOW
YOU USE THESE WORDS, AND PEOPLE DON'T UNDERSTAND THEM. YOU **EXPLAIN** THEM, AND PEOPLE BOIL THEM DOWN TO "STUPID," WHICH SOMEHOW IS EQUATED WITH "CONTAGIOUS."
MOST OF US ARE NOT AS SMART AS WE LIKE TO THINK WE ARE, AND AGAIN, I INCLUDE MYSELF.
I WOULD SAY THAT ALL THIS REVOLVING-DOOR JARGON IS NOTHING TO GET HUNG UP ABOUT, IF IT DIDN'T MASK A GENERAL ATTITUDE THAT SAYS "EVERYBODY IS REALLY INTELLIGENT, EXCEPT FOR PEOPLE WHO ARE OBVIOUSLY ***NOT,*** AND WE DON'T TALK ABOUT ***THEM.***"

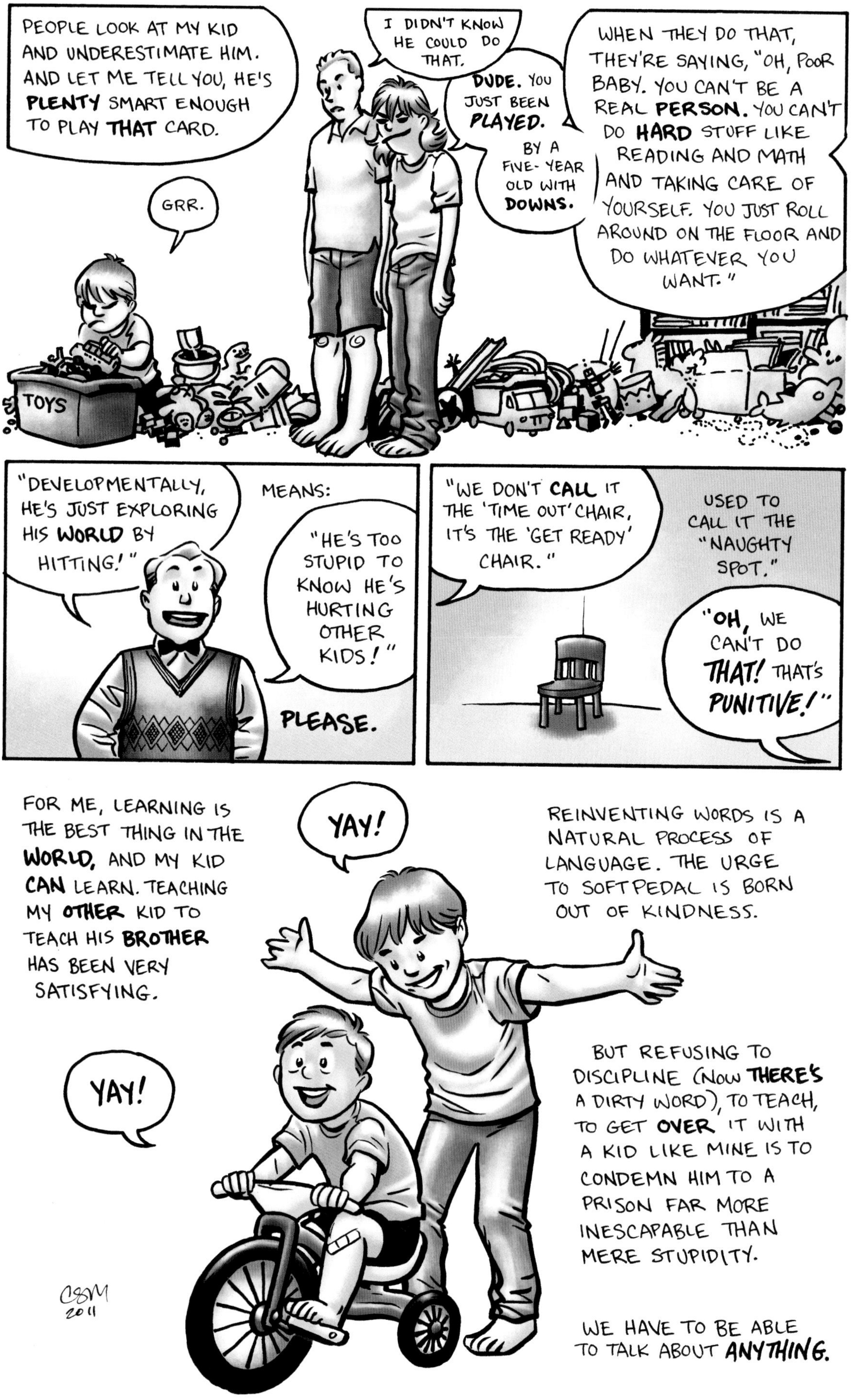
PEOPLE LOOK AT MY KID AND UNDERESTIMATE HIM. AND LET ME TELL YOU, HE'S **PLENTY** SMART ENOUGH TO PLAY **THAT** CARD.
GRR.
I DIDN'T KNOW HE COULD DO THAT.
DUDE. YOU JUST BEEN **PLAYED.**
BY A FIVE-YEAR OLD WITH **DOWNS.**
WHEN THEY DO THAT, THEY'RE SAYING, "OH, POOR BABY. YOU CAN'T BE A REAL **PERSON.** YOU CAN'T DO **HARD** STUFF LIKE READING AND MATH AND TAKING CARE OF YOURSELF. YOU JUST ROLL AROUND ON THE FLOOR AND DO WHATEVER YOU WANT."
TOYS
"DEVELOPMENTALLY, HE'S JUST EXPLORING HIS **WORLD** BY HITTING!"
MEANS:
"HE'S TOO STUPID TO KNOW HE'S HURTING OTHER KIDS!"
PLEASE.
"WE DON'T **CALL** IT THE 'TIME OUT' CHAIR, IT'S THE 'GET READY' CHAIR."
USED TO CALL IT THE "NAUGHTY SPOT."
"**OH,** WE CAN'T DO **THAT!** THAT'S **PUNITIVE!**"
FOR ME, LEARNING IS THE BEST THING IN THE **WORLD,** AND MY KID **CAN** LEARN. TEACHING MY **OTHER** KID TO TEACH HIS **BROTHER** HAS BEEN VERY SATISFYING.
YAY!
REINVENTING WORDS IS A NATURAL PROCESS OF LANGUAGE. THE URGE TO SOFTPEDAL IS BORN OUT OF KINDNESS.
YAY!
BUT REFUSING TO DISCIPLINE (NOW **THERE'S** A DIRTY WORD), TO TEACH, TO GET **OVER** IT WITH A KID LIKE MINE IS TO CONDEMN HIM TO A PRISON FAR MORE INESCAPABLE THAN MERE STUPIDITY.
WE HAVE TO BE ABLE TO TALK ABOUT **ANYTHING.**
CSM
2011

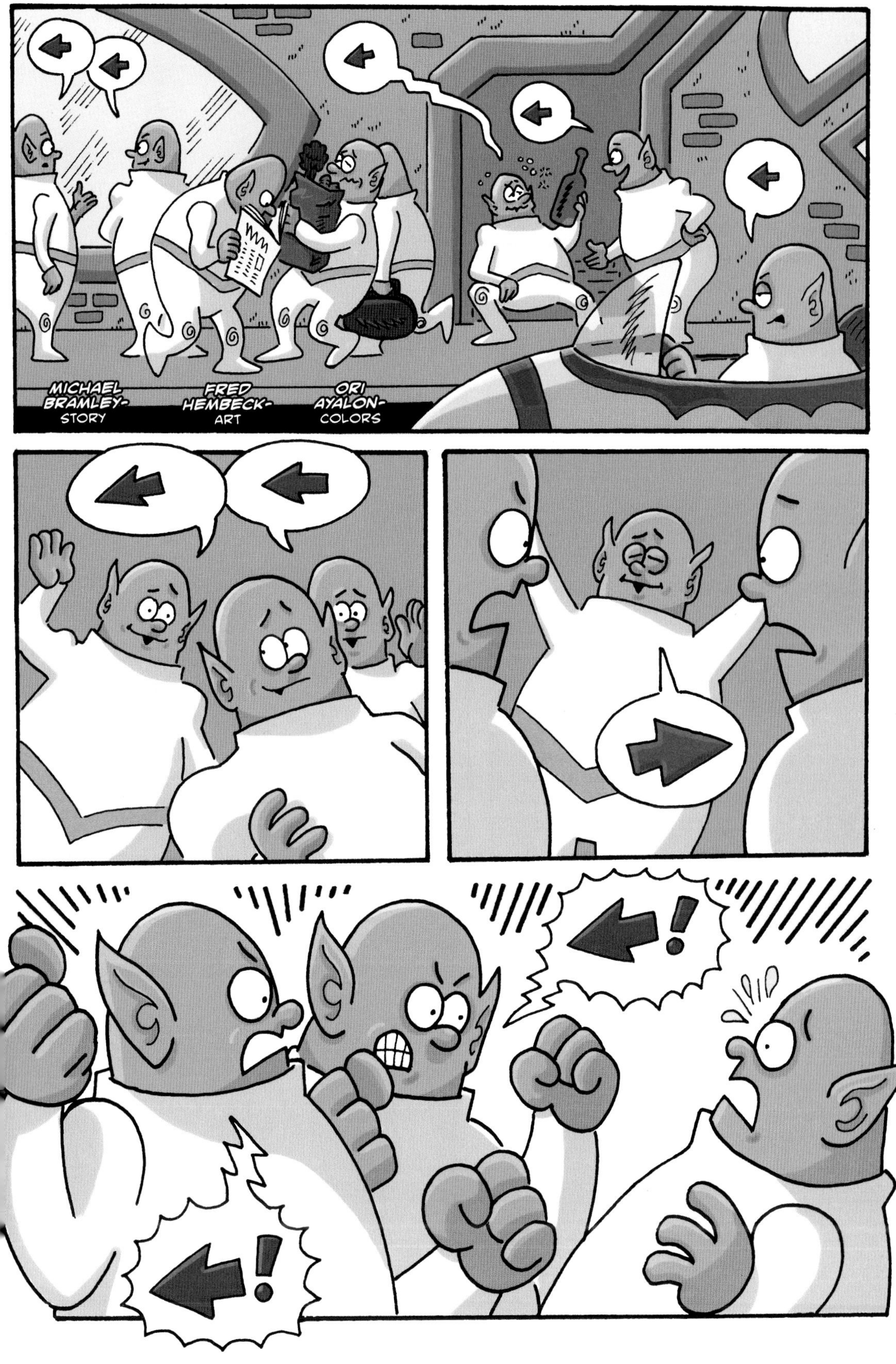
MICHAEL BRAMLEY- STORY
FRED HEMBECK- ART
ORI AYALON- COLORS
!
!

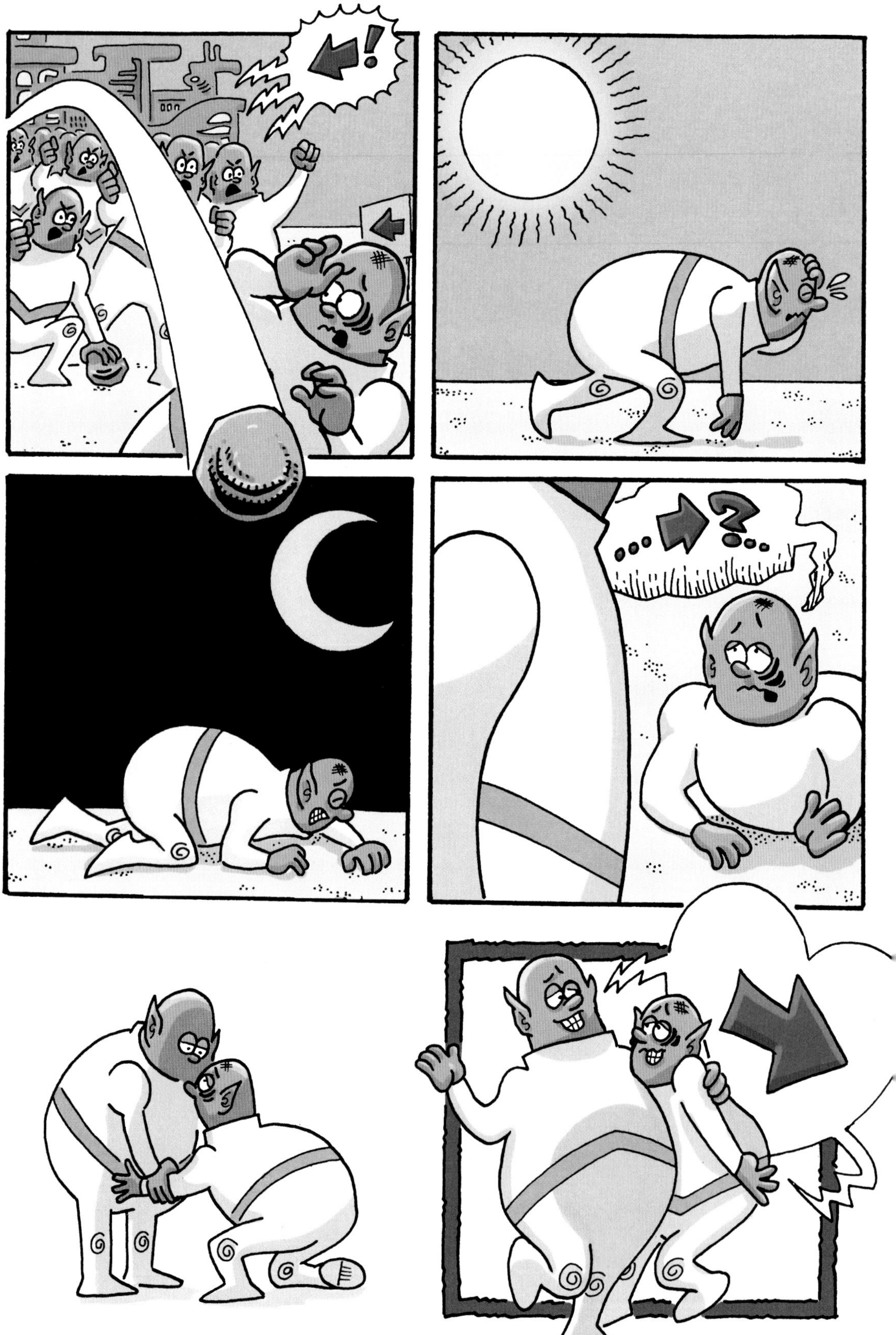

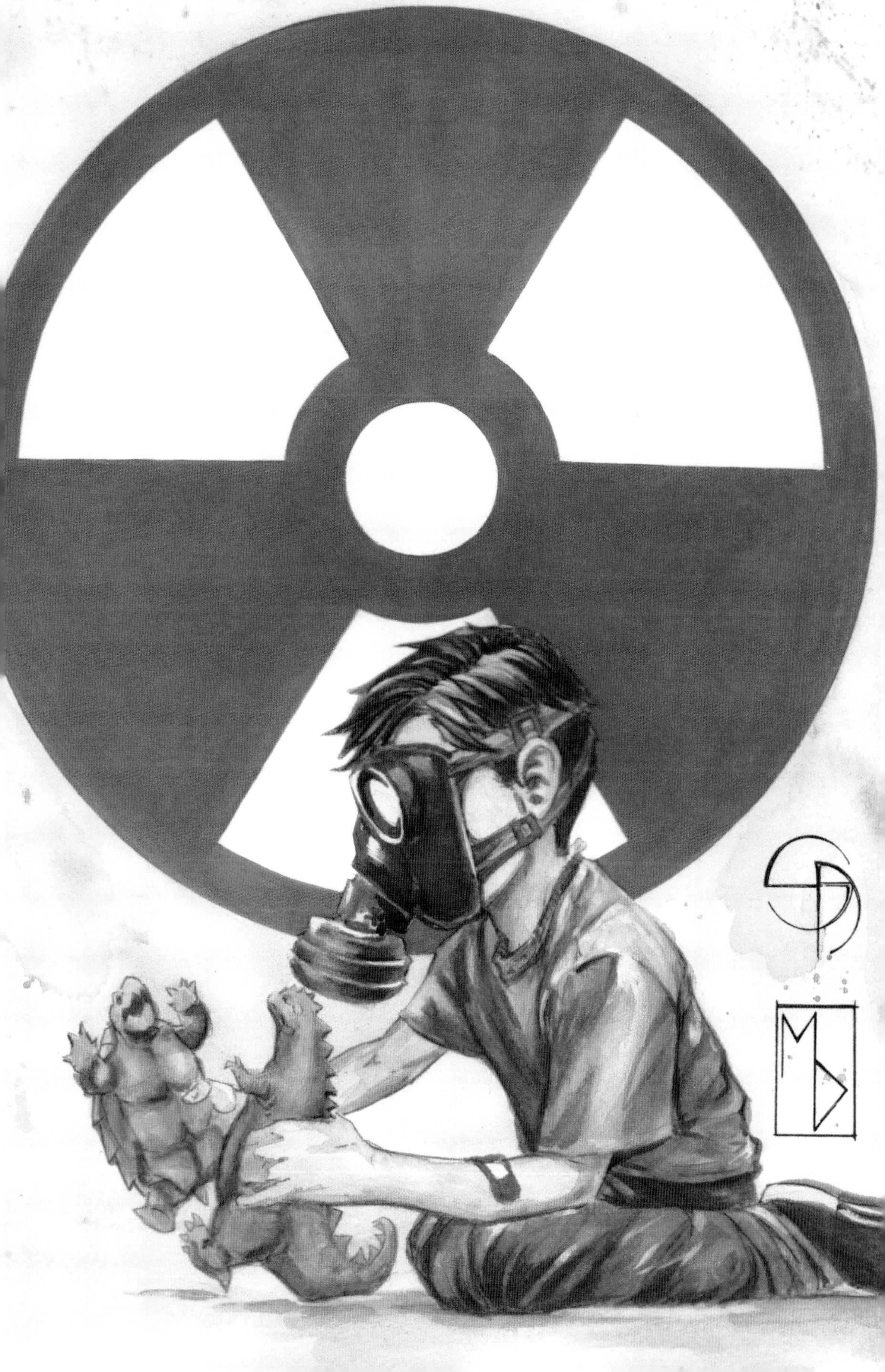

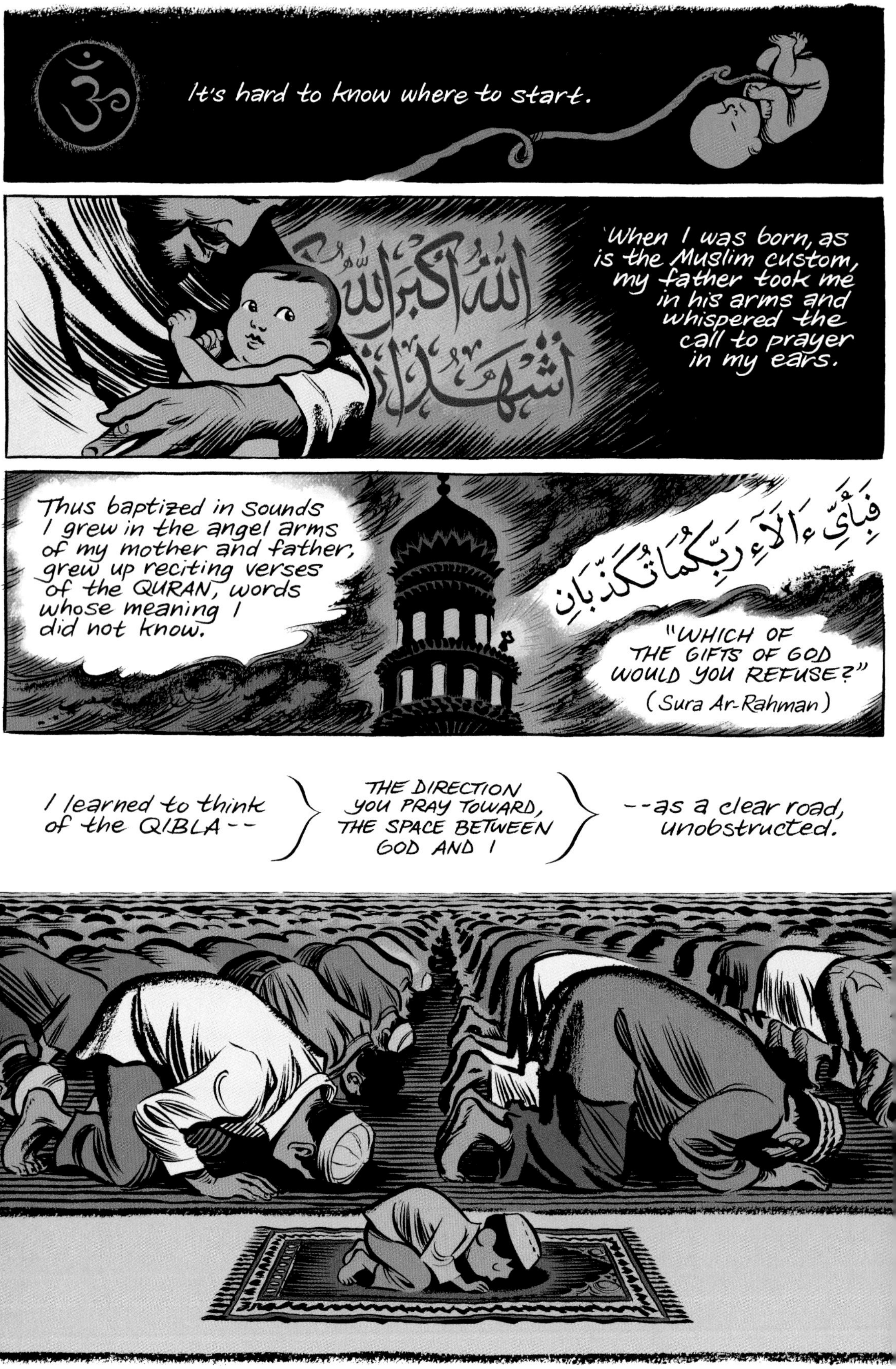
It's hard to know where to start.
'When I was born, as is the Muslim custom, my father took me in his arms and whispered the call to prayer in my ears.
الله أكبر الله
Thus baptized in sounds I grew in the angel arms of my mother and father, grew up reciting verses of the QURAN, words whose meaning I did not know.
فَبِأَيِّ ءَالَآءِ رَبِّكُمَا تُكَذِّبَانِ
"WHICH OF THE GIFTS OF GOD WOULD YOU REFUSE?"
(Sura Ar-Rahman)
I learned to think of the QIBLA--
THE DIRECTION YOU PRAY TOWARD, THE SPACE BETWEEN GOD AND I
--as a clear road, unobstructed.

WORDS : Kazim Ali
PICTURES : Craig Thompson
COLORS : Dave Stewart

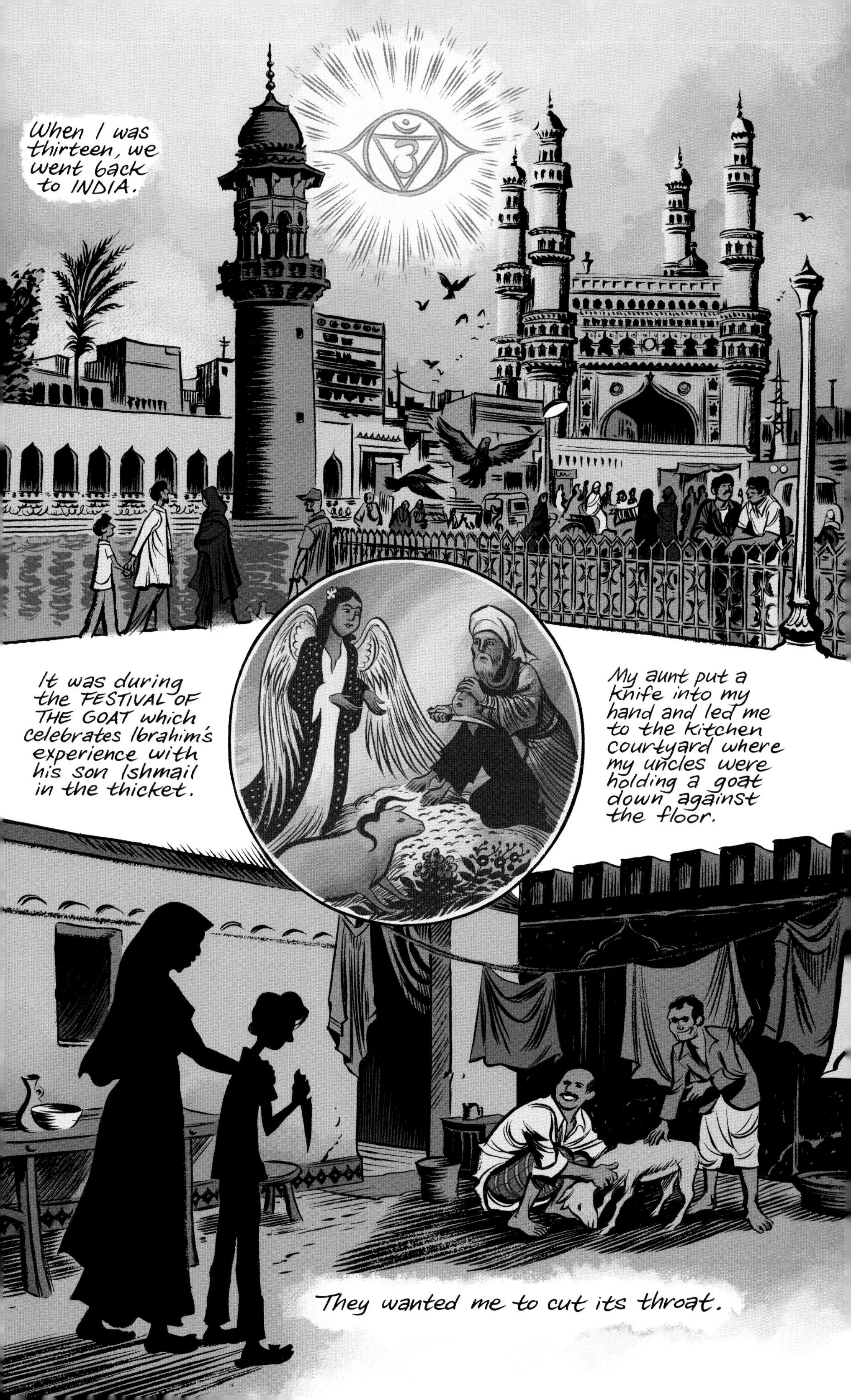
When I was thirteen, we went back to INDIA.
It was during the FESTIVAL OF THE GOAT which celebrates Ibrahim's experience with his son Ishmail in the thicket.
My aunt put a knife into my hand and led me to the kitchen courtyard where my uncles were holding a goat down against the floor.
They wanted me to cut its throat.

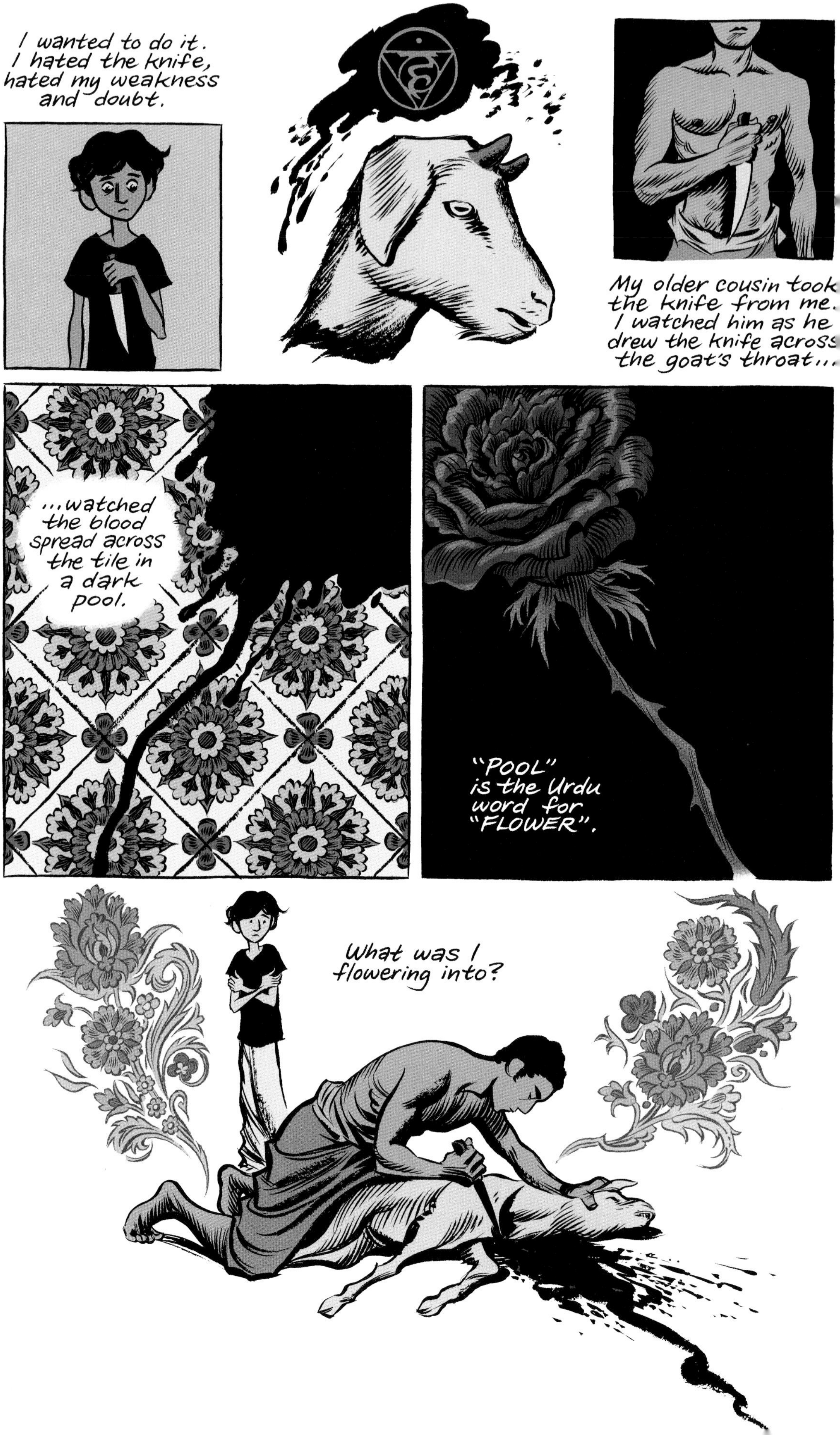
I wanted to do it. I hated the knife, hated my weakness and doubt.
My older cousin took the knife from me. I watched him as he drew the knife across the goat's throat...
...watched the blood spread across the tile in a dark pool.
"POOL" is the Urdu word for "FLOWER".
What was I flowering into?

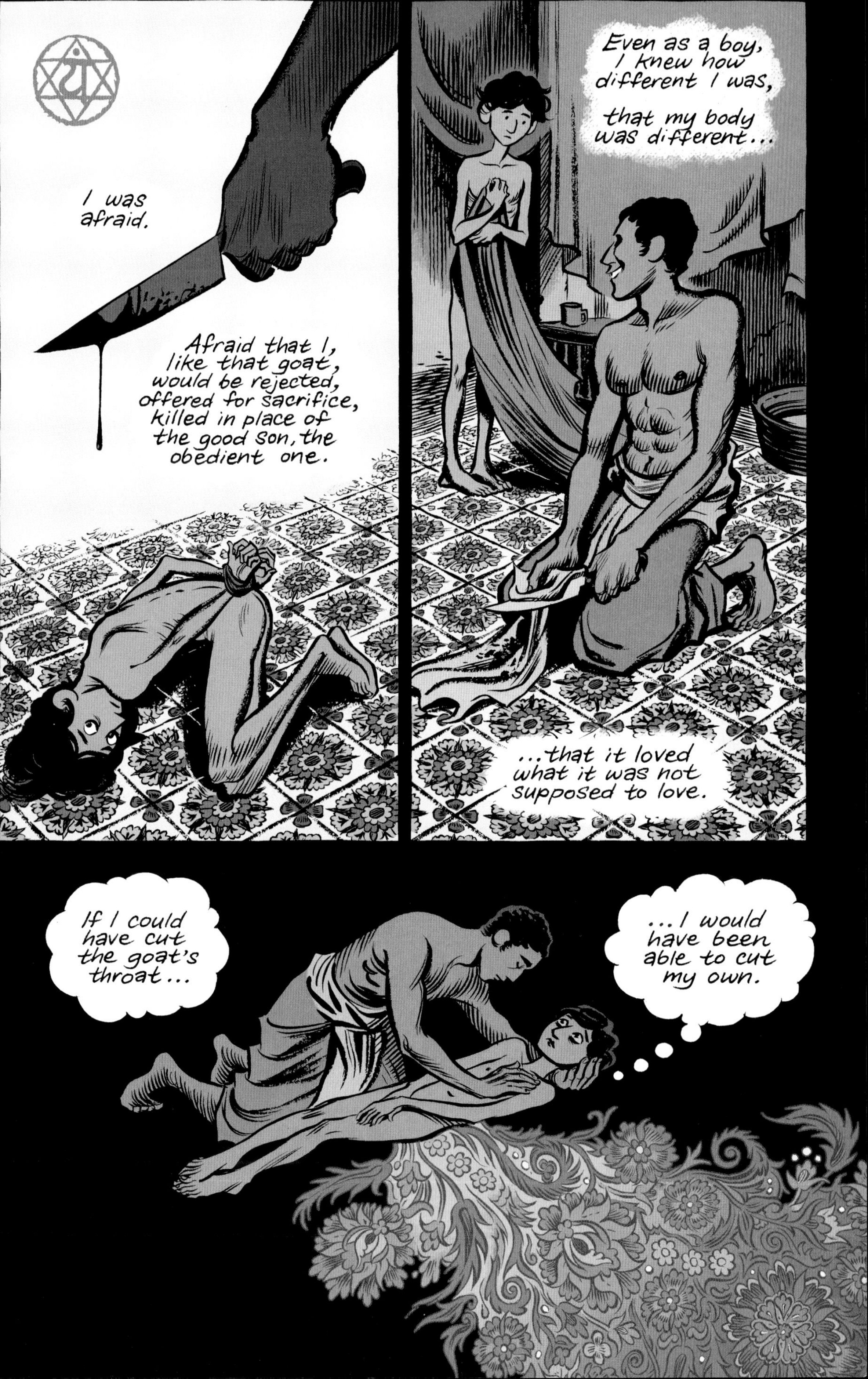
I was afraid.
Afraid that I, like that goat, would be rejected, offered for sacrifice, killed in place of the good son, the obedient one.
Even as a boy, I knew how different I was,
that my body was different...
...that it loved what it was not supposed to love.
If I could have cut the goat's throat...
...I would have been able to cut my own.

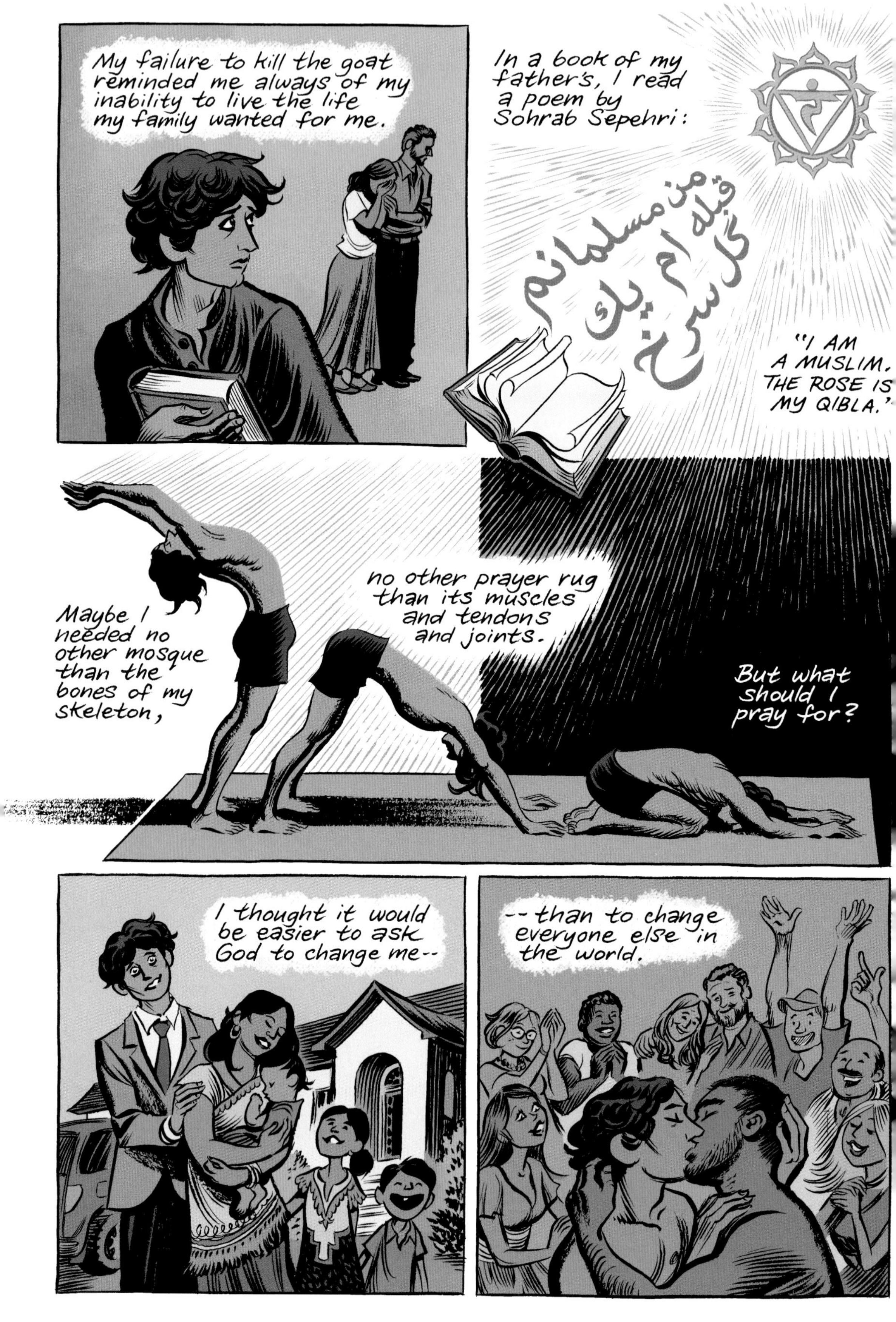

My failure to kill the goat reminded me always of my inability to live the life my family wanted for me.
In a book of my father's, I read a poem by Sohrab Sepehri:
من مسلمانم
قبله ام يك
گل سرخ
"I AM A MUSLIM. THE ROSE IS MY QIBLA."
Maybe I needed no other mosque than the bones of my skeleton,
no other prayer rug than its muscles and tendons and joints.
But what should I pray for?
I thought it would be easier to ask God to change me--
--than to change everyone else in the world.

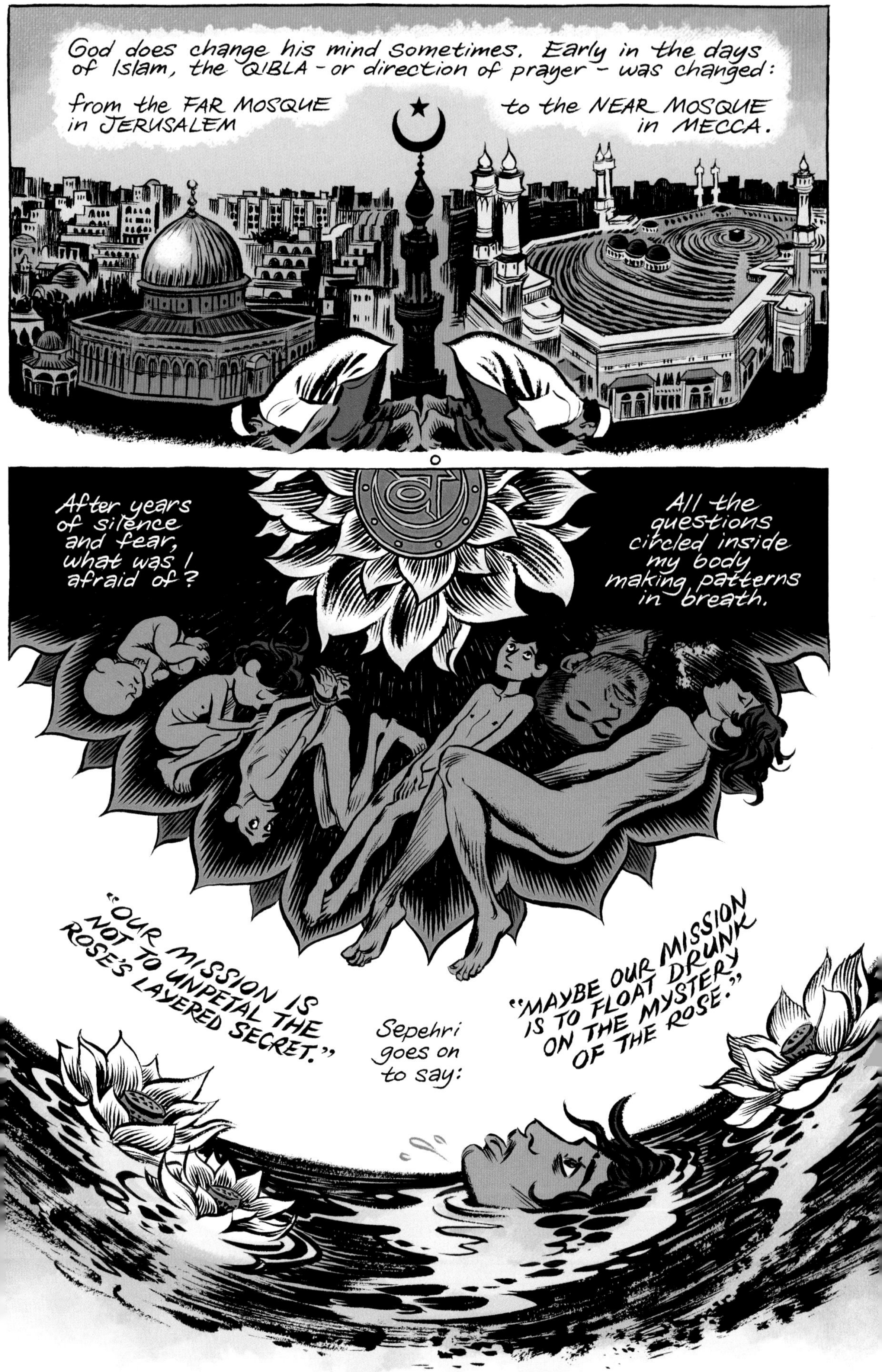

God does change his mind sometimes. Early in the days of Islam, the QIBLA - or direction of prayer - was changed:
from the FAR MOSQUE in JERUSALEM
to the NEAR MOSQUE in MECCA.
After years of silence and fear, what was I afraid of?
All the questions circled inside my body making patterns in breath.
"OUR MISSION IS NOT TO UNPETAL THE ROSE'S LAYERED SECRET."
Sepehri goes on to say:
"MAYBE OUR MISSION IS TO FLOAT DRUNK ON THE MYSTERY OF THE ROSE."

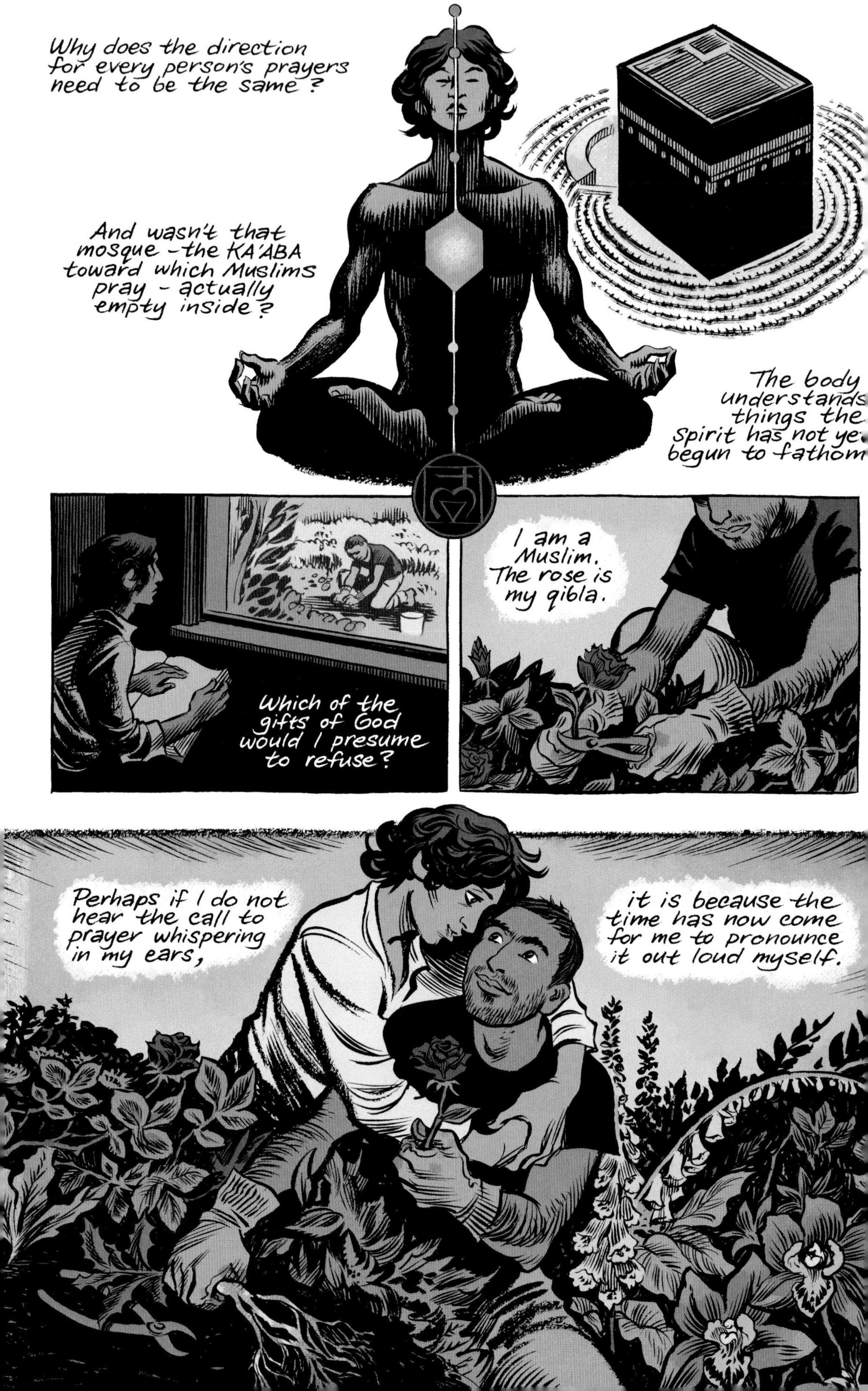
Why does the direction for every person's prayers need to be the same?
And wasn't that mosque - the KA'ABA toward which Muslims pray - actually empty inside?
The body understands things the spirit has not yet begun to fathom.
Which of the gifts of God would I presume to refuse?
I am a Muslim. The rose is my qibla.
Perhaps if I do not hear the call to prayer whispering in my ears,
it is because the time has now come for me to pronounce it out loud myself.

SEPARATION OF CHURCH AND STATE

"The best friend the Church ever had!"

BY J. MICHAEL STRACZYNSKI- WRITER & KEVIN SACCO- ARTIST

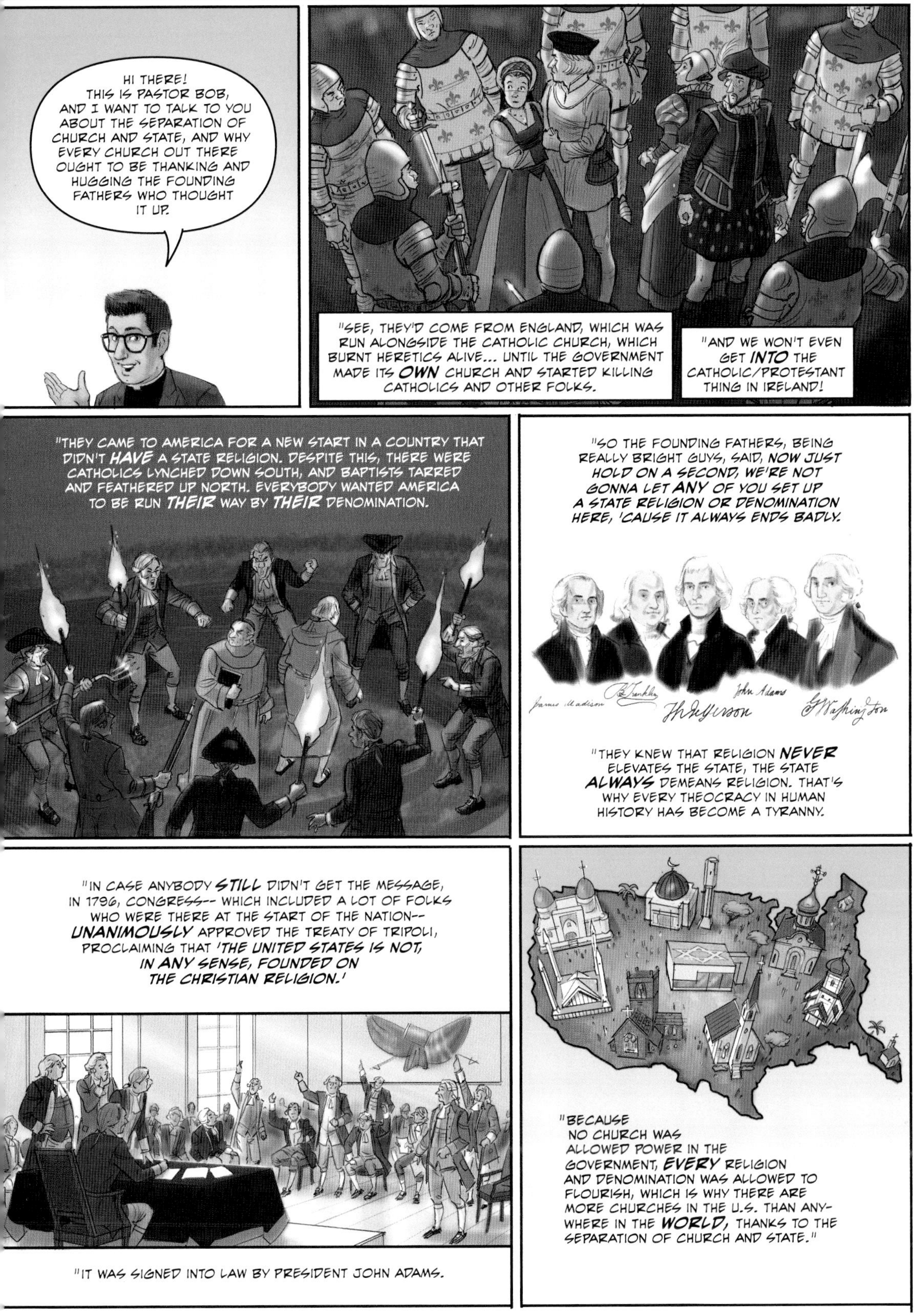
HI THERE! THIS IS PASTOR BOB, AND I WANT TO TALK TO YOU ABOUT THE SEPARATION OF CHURCH AND STATE, AND WHY EVERY CHURCH OUT THERE OUGHT TO BE THANKING AND HUGGING THE FOUNDING FATHERS WHO THOUGHT IT UP.
"SEE, THEY'D COME FROM ENGLAND, WHICH WAS RUN ALONGSIDE THE CATHOLIC CHURCH, WHICH BURNT HERETICS ALIVE... UNTIL THE GOVERNMENT MADE ITS OWN CHURCH AND STARTED KILLING CATHOLICS AND OTHER FOLKS.
"AND WE WON'T EVEN GET INTO THE CATHOLIC/PROTESTANT THING IN IRELAND!
"THEY CAME TO AMERICA FOR A NEW START IN A COUNTRY THAT DIDN'T HAVE A STATE RELIGION. DESPITE THIS, THERE WERE CATHOLICS LYNCHED DOWN SOUTH, AND BAPTISTS TARRED AND FEATHERED UP NORTH. EVERYBODY WANTED AMERICA TO BE RUN THEIR WAY BY THEIR DENOMINATION.
"SO THE FOUNDING FATHERS, BEING REALLY BRIGHT GUYS, SAID, NOW JUST HOLD ON A SECOND, WE'RE NOT GONNA LET ANY OF YOU SET UP A STATE RELIGION OR DENOMINATION HERE, 'CAUSE IT ALWAYS ENDS BADLY.
James Madison
John Adams
"THEY KNEW THAT RELIGION NEVER ELEVATES THE STATE, THE STATE ALWAYS DEMEANS RELIGION. THAT'S WHY EVERY THEOCRACY IN HUMAN HISTORY HAS BECOME A TYRANNY.
"IN CASE ANYBODY STILL DIDN'T GET THE MESSAGE, IN 1796, CONGRESS-- WHICH INCLUDED A LOT OF FOLKS WHO WERE THERE AT THE START OF THE NATION-- UNANIMOUSLY APPROVED THE TREATY OF TRIPOLI, PROCLAIMING THAT 'THE UNITED STATES IS NOT, IN ANY SENSE, FOUNDED ON THE CHRISTIAN RELIGION.'
"IT WAS SIGNED INTO LAW BY PRESIDENT JOHN ADAMS.
"BECAUSE NO CHURCH WAS ALLOWED POWER IN THE GOVERNMENT, EVERY RELIGION AND DENOMINATION WAS ALLOWED TO FLOURISH, WHICH IS WHY THERE ARE MORE CHURCHES IN THE U.S. THAN ANYWHERE IN THE WORLD, THANKS TO THE SEPARATION OF CHURCH AND STATE."

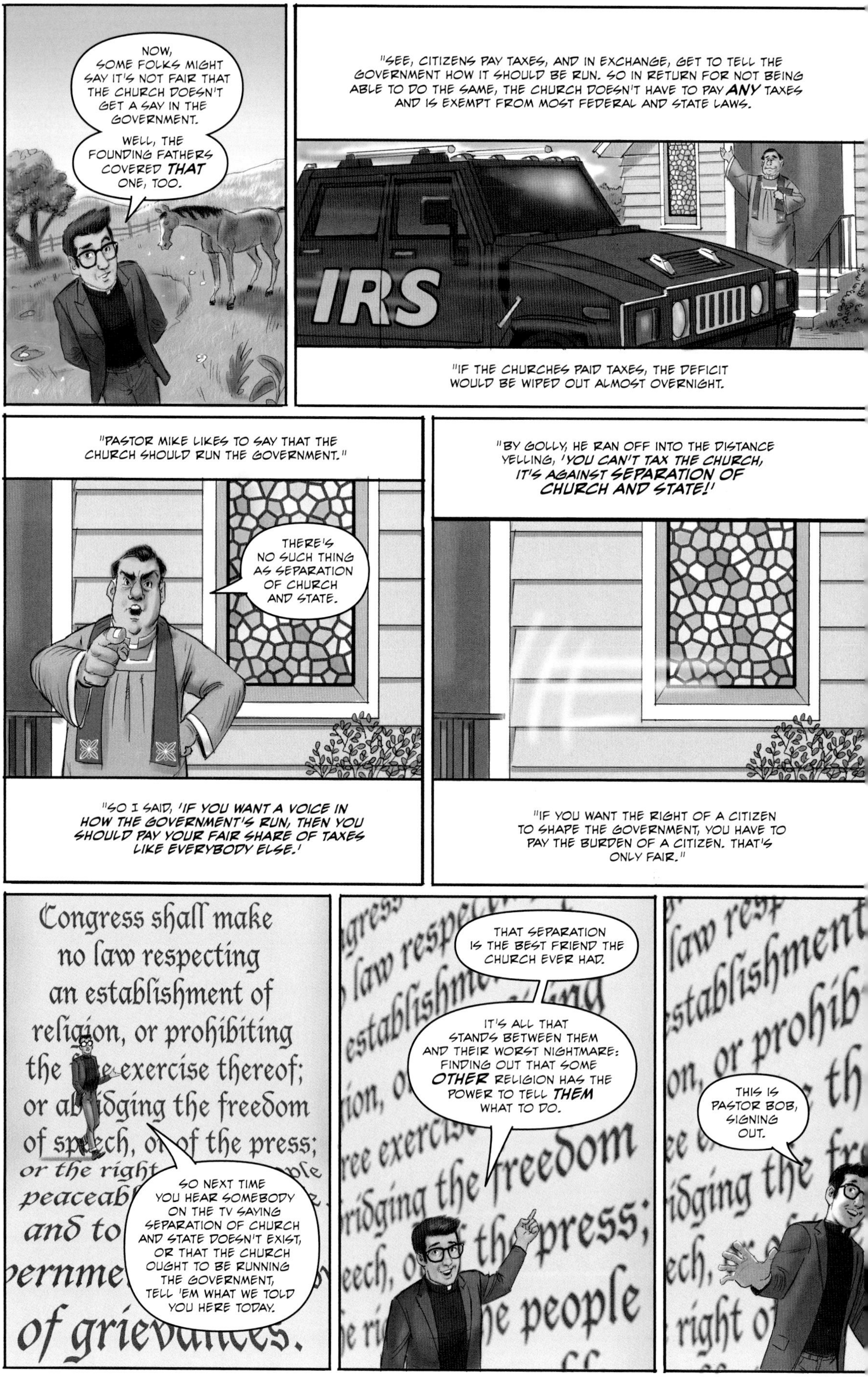
NOW, SOME FOLKS MIGHT SAY IT'S NOT FAIR THAT THE CHURCH DOESN'T GET A SAY IN THE GOVERNMENT.
WELL, THE FOUNDING FATHERS COVERED THAT ONE, TOO.
"SEE, CITIZENS PAY TAXES, AND IN EXCHANGE, GET TO TELL THE GOVERNMENT HOW IT SHOULD BE RUN. SO IN RETURN FOR NOT BEING ABLE TO DO THE SAME, THE CHURCH DOESN'T HAVE TO PAY ANY TAXES AND IS EXEMPT FROM MOST FEDERAL AND STATE LAWS.
IRS
"IF THE CHURCHES PAID TAXES, THE DEFICIT WOULD BE WIPED OUT ALMOST OVERNIGHT.
"PASTOR MIKE LIKES TO SAY THAT THE CHURCH SHOULD RUN THE GOVERNMENT."
THERE'S NO SUCH THING AS SEPARATION OF CHURCH AND STATE.
"SO I SAID, 'IF YOU WANT A VOICE IN HOW THE GOVERNMENT'S RUN, THEN YOU SHOULD PAY YOUR FAIR SHARE OF TAXES LIKE EVERYBODY ELSE.'
"BY GOLLY, HE RAN OFF INTO THE DISTANCE YELLING, 'YOU CAN'T TAX THE CHURCH, IT'S AGAINST SEPARATION OF CHURCH AND STATE!'
"IF YOU WANT THE RIGHT OF A CITIZEN TO SHAPE THE GOVERNMENT, YOU HAVE TO PAY THE BURDEN OF A CITIZEN. THAT'S ONLY FAIR."
Congress shall make no law respecting an establishment of religion, or prohibiting the free exercise thereof; or abridging the freedom of speech, or of the press;
or the right
peaceab
and to
vernme
of grievances.
SO NEXT TIME YOU HEAR SOMEBODY ON THE TV SAYING SEPARATION OF CHURCH AND STATE DOESN'T EXIST, OR THAT THE CHURCH OUGHT TO BE RUNNING THE GOVERNMENT, TELL 'EM WHAT WE TOLD YOU HERE TODAY.
THAT SEPARATION IS THE BEST FRIEND THE CHURCH EVER HAD.
IT'S ALL THAT STANDS BETWEEN THEM AND THEIR WORST NIGHTMARE: FINDING OUT THAT SOME OTHER RELIGION HAS THE POWER TO TELL THEM WHAT TO DO.
THIS IS PASTOR BOB, SIGNING OUT.

THERE'S BEEN A LOT OF TALK LATELY ABOUT "PUTTING PRAYER BACK INTO SCHOOLS," AND SIMILAR PLATITUDES.

NOW, I'LL BE THE FIRST TO ADMIT THAT I'M NOT A FAN OF ORGANIZED RELIGION, *ANY* OF THEM. BUT, I *AM* ALL FOR *FREEDOM OF RELIGION*.

THE GOVERNMENT SHOULDN'T *PREVENT* YOU FROM PRACTICING YOUR FAITH.

The Conversion

DARA NARAGHI - WRITER / CHRISTOPHER MITTEN - ARTIST
DOM REGAN - COLORIST / SEAN KONOT - LETTERER

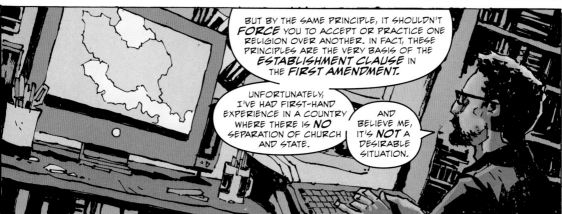

BUT BY THE SAME PRINCIPLE, IT SHOULDN'T *FORCE* YOU TO ACCEPT OR PRACTICE ONE RELIGION OVER ANOTHER. IN FACT, THESE PRINCIPLES ARE THE VERY BASIS OF THE *ESTABLISHMENT CLAUSE* IN THE *FIRST AMENDMENT*.

UNFORTUNATELY, I'VE HAD FIRST-HAND EXPERIENCE IN A COUNTRY WHERE THERE IS *NO* SEPARATION OF CHURCH AND STATE.

AND BELIEVE ME, IT'S *NOT* A DESIRABLE SITUATION.

I WAS BORN IN TEHRAN, IRAN.

PRIOR TO THE ISLAMIC REVOLUTION OF 1979, EVEN THOUGH A MAJORITY OF THE POPULATION WAS MUSLIM, THE GOVERNMENT WAS *SECULAR*.

BUT THAT ALL CHANGED WHEN THE *MULLAHS* CAME INTO POWER.

ISLAMIC DOCTRINE BECAME *LAW*, AND EVERYONE WAS FORCED TO OBEY IT, REGARDLESS OF THEIR PERSONAL BELIEFS.

INCIDENTALLY, THAT INCLUDED *MANDATORY* PRAYER IN SCHOOLS.

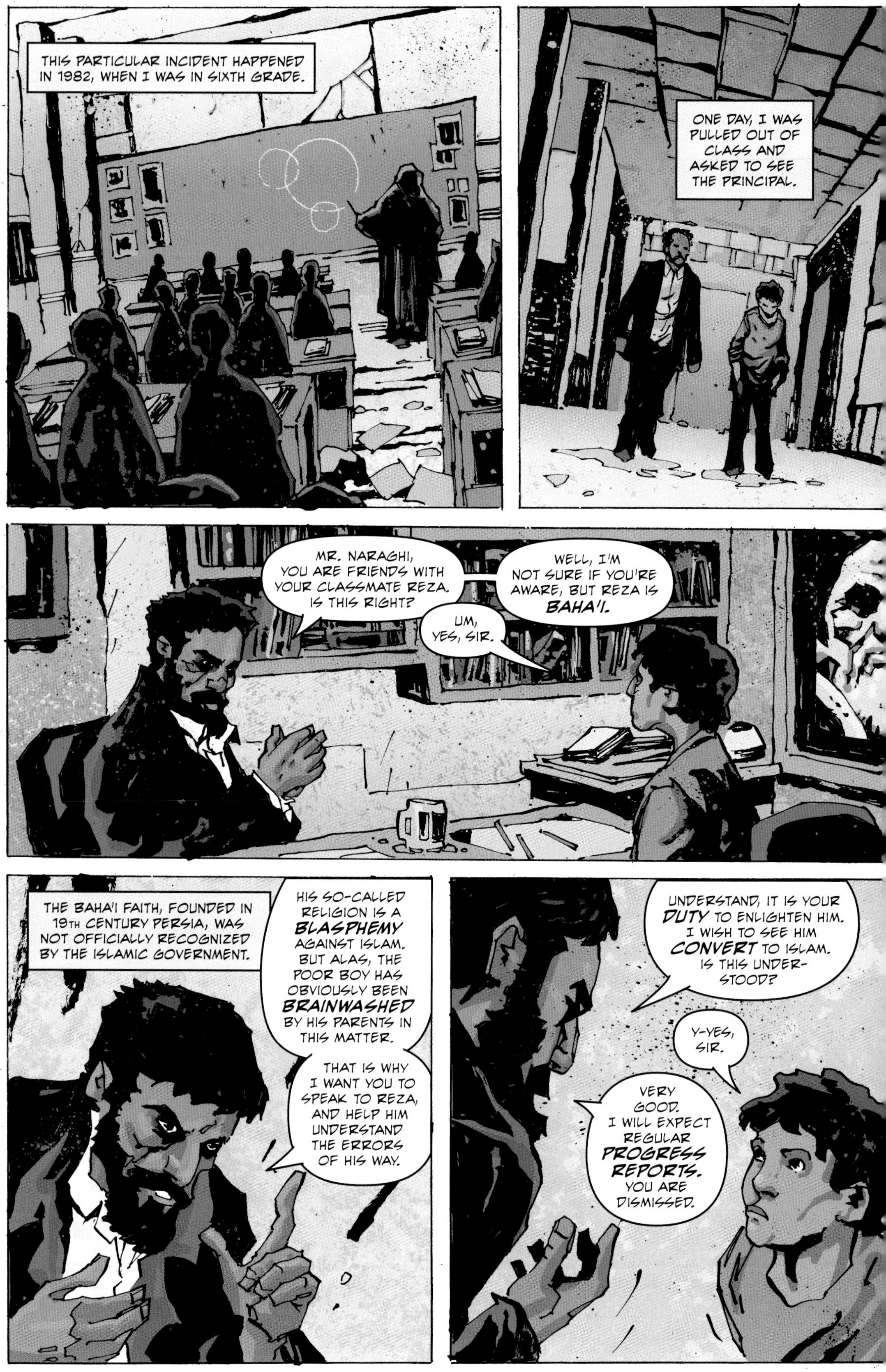
THIS PARTICULAR INCIDENT HAPPENED IN 1982, WHEN I WAS IN SIXTH GRADE.
ONE DAY, I WAS PULLED OUT OF CLASS AND ASKED TO SEE THE PRINCIPAL.
MR. NARAGHI, YOU ARE FRIENDS WITH YOUR CLASSMATE REZA. IS THIS RIGHT?
UM, YES, SIR.
WELL, I'M NOT SURE IF YOU'RE AWARE, BUT REZA IS BAHA'I.
THE BAHA'I FAITH, FOUNDED IN 19TH CENTURY PERSIA, WAS NOT OFFICIALLY RECOGNIZED BY THE ISLAMIC GOVERNMENT.
HIS SO-CALLED RELIGION IS A BLASPHEMY AGAINST ISLAM. BUT ALAS, THE POOR BOY HAS OBVIOUSLY BEEN BRAINWASHED BY HIS PARENTS IN THIS MATTER.
THAT IS WHY I WANT YOU TO SPEAK TO REZA, AND HELP HIM UNDERSTAND THE ERRORS OF HIS WAY.
UNDERSTAND, IT IS YOUR DUTY TO ENLIGHTEN HIM. I WISH TO SEE HIM CONVERT TO ISLAM. IS THIS UNDERSTOOD?
Y-YES, SIR.
VERY GOOD. I WILL EXPECT REGULAR PROGRESS REPORTS. YOU ARE DISMISSED.

AFTER SCHOOL THAT DAY, I WAS IN A *DAZE,* AND FELT QUEASY. I HAD NO INTENTION OF "CONVERTING" MY FRIEND, BUT AT THE SAME TIME, HOW COULD I GO AGAINST THE SCHOOL PRINCIPAL?

WHEN I TOLD MY PARENTS WHAT HAD HAPPENED, THEY WERE *LIVID.* BUT WHAT COULD THEY DO? EXPRESSING THEIR *OUTRAGE* AT THE PRINCIPAL WOULD ONLY GUARANTEE AN UNWELCOME VISIT FROM THE *"MORALITY POLICE."*

OR WORSE, THE *BASIJ*-- THE STATE-SANCTIONED MILITIA.

THEY CALLED REZA'S PARENTS, TO GIVE THEM A HEADS UP. THAT'S HOW THEY FOUND OUT THAT HE WAS SWITCHING SCHOOLS THE NEXT YEAR.

AND SINCE MY PARENTS WERE PLANNING ON MOVING *OUR FAMILY* TO THE U.S. SOON, THEY CAME UP WITH A PLAN TO GET ME THROUGH THE REMAINDER OF THE SCHOOL YEAR.

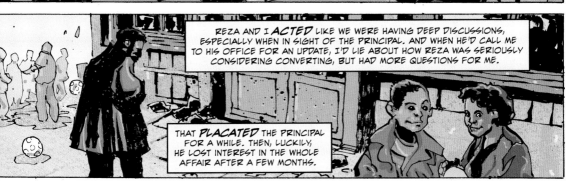

REZA AND I *ACTED* LIKE WE WERE HAVING DEEP DISCUSSIONS, ESPECIALLY WHEN IN SIGHT OF THE PRINCIPAL. AND WHEN HE'D CALL ME TO HIS OFFICE FOR AN UPDATE, I'D LIE ABOUT HOW REZA WAS SERIOUSLY CONSIDERING CONVERTING, BUT HAD MORE QUESTIONS FOR ME.

THAT *PLACATED* THE PRINCIPAL FOR A WHILE. THEN, LUCKILY, HE LOST INTEREST IN THE WHOLE AFFAIR AFTER A FEW MONTHS.

I'M ONE OF THE *LUCKY ONES* WHO WAS ABLE TO LEAVE THAT REGIME BEHIND, AND START A NEW LIFE IN AMERICA.

BUT FOR OVER THIRTY YEARS, PEOPLE IN IRAN HAVE BEEN FORCED TO LIVE UNDER GOVERNMENT-MANDATED RELIGION. AND THAT'S THE CASE IN DOZENS OF OTHER COUNTRIES, AS WELL.

NOBODY SHOULD HAVE TO LIVE LIKE THAT.

A GOVERNMENT'S JOB ISN'T TO *PUSH* RELIGION ON ITS CITIZENS, REGARDLESS OF WHETHER IT'S ISLAM, CHRISTIANITY, JUDAISM, OR SOME OTHER FAITH.

JUST AS IMPORTANT AS THE RIGHT TO FREE SPEECH, FREEDOM OF RELIGION IS *GUARANTEED* BY THE FIRST AMENDMENT OF OUR *CONSTITUTION.*

FAITH SHOULD BE A *PERSONAL* CHOICE FOR EACH INDIVIDUAL.

AFTER ALL, ISN'T THAT THE VERY DEFINITION OF *FREEDOM?*

End

—Chtapol

GREAT, UNSUNG MOMENTS *in the* HISTORY *of* FREE SPEECH

OVER THE COURSE OF HUMAN HISTORY, THERE HAVE BEEN NOT SO QUIET MOMENTS WHEN BRAVE INDIVIDUALS HAVE SPOKEN THEIR MINDS. UNFORTUNATELY, THESE COURAGEOUS STATEMENTS HAVE NEVER GOTTEN THE RECOGNITION THEY DESERVED. UNTIL NOW.

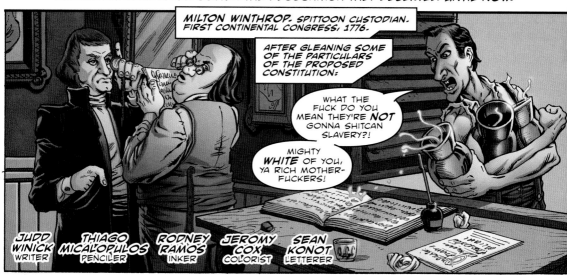

MILTON WINTHROP. SPITTOON CUSTODIAN. FIRST CONTINENTAL CONGRESS, 1776.

AFTER GLEANING SOME OF THE PARTICULARS OF THE PROPOSED CONSTITUTION:

WHAT THE FUCK DO YOU MEAN THEY'RE **NOT** GONNA SHITCAN SLAVERY?!

MIGHTY **WHITE** OF YOU, YA RICH MOTHER-FUCKERS!

JUDD WINICK WRITER   THIAGO MICAL'OPULOS PENCILER   RODNEY RAMOS INKER   JEROMY COX COLORIST   SEAN KONOT LETTERER

ALEXANDER FORREST. PERSONAL VALET TO FRANKLIN DELANO ROOSEVELT. 1943.

AFTER FIVE WHISKEY SOURS, HE SHARES HIS OPINION WITH THE PRESIDENT ON THE POWER OF ADOLF HITLER.

HE'S A PARANOID, RAT-FACED, **SATAN WORSHIPPER** WITH JUST **ONE NUT** LEFT IN HIS SACK!

A FUCKING CRIP LIKE **YOU** COULD KICK HIS ASS ALL BY YOUR LONESOME!

RIP HIM A NEW ONE, FRANKIE!!

JEROME HOTTLE. ELEVATOR OPERATOR. ST. FRANCIS HOTEL, SAN FRANCISCO, 1948.

UPON MEETING AL JOLSON.

FUCK YOU.

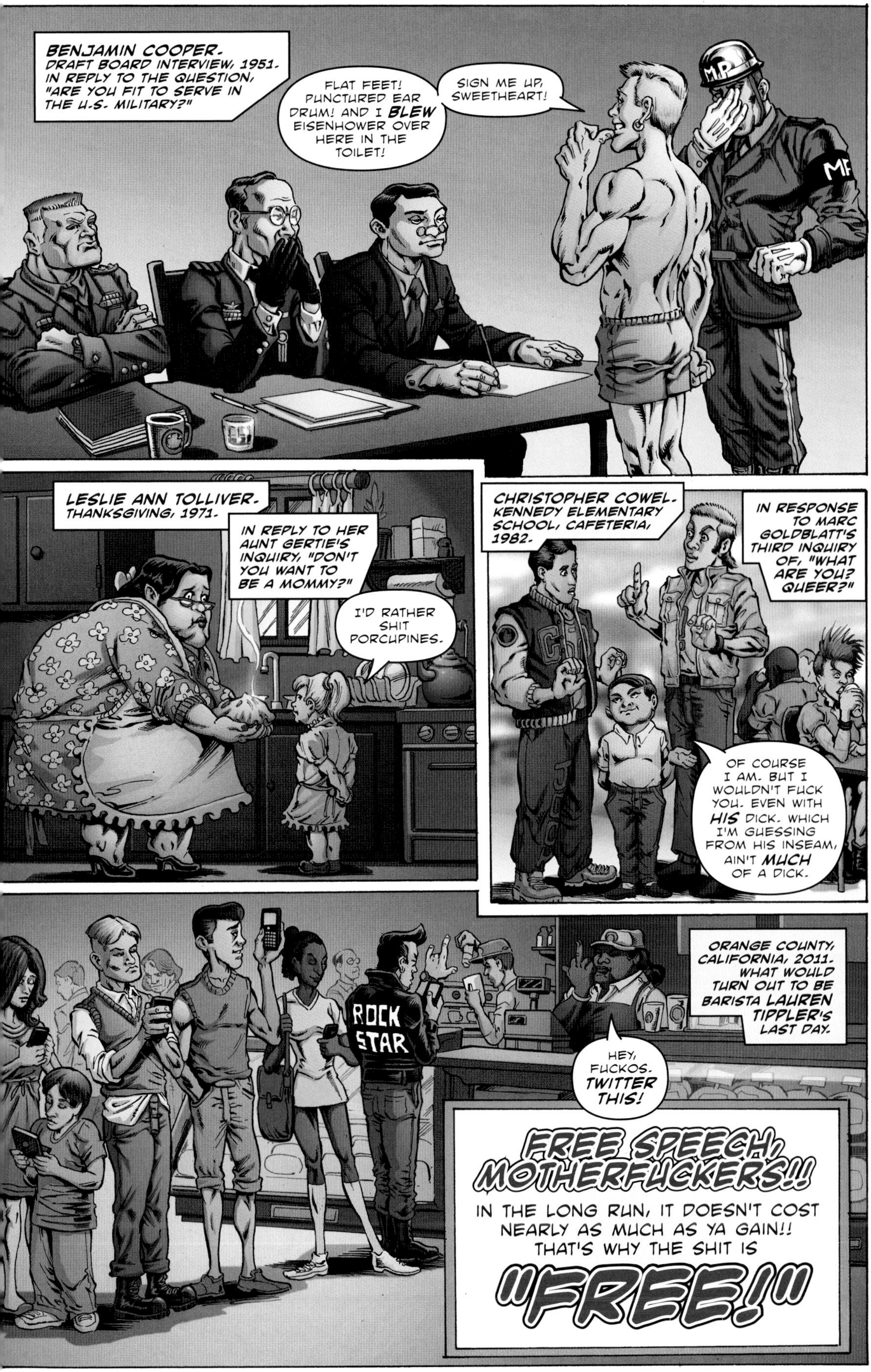
BENJAMIN COOPER. DRAFT BOARD INTERVIEW, 1951. IN REPLY TO THE QUESTION, "ARE YOU FIT TO SERVE IN THE U.S. MILITARY?"
FLAT FEET! PUNCTURED EAR DRUM! AND I BLEW EISENHOWER OVER HERE IN THE TOILET!
SIGN ME UP, SWEETHEART!
M.P.
MP
LESLIE ANN TOLLIVER. THANKSGIVING, 1971.
IN REPLY TO HER AUNT GERTIE'S INQUIRY, "DON'T YOU WANT TO BE A MOMMY?"
I'D RATHER SHIT PORCUPINES.
CHRISTOPHER COWEL. KENNEDY ELEMENTARY SCHOOL, CAFETERIA, 1982.
IN RESPONSE TO MARC GOLDBLATT'S THIRD INQUIRY OF, "WHAT ARE YOU? QUEER?"
OF COURSE I AM. BUT I WOULDN'T FUCK YOU. EVEN WITH HIS DICK. WHICH I'M GUESSING FROM HIS INSEAM, AIN'T MUCH OF A DICK.
ORANGE COUNTY, CALIFORNIA, 2011. WHAT WOULD TURN OUT TO BE BARISTA LAUREN TIPPLER'S LAST DAY.
ROCK STAR
HEY, FUCKOS. TWITTER THIS!
FREE SPEECH, MOTHERFUCKERS!!!
IN THE LONG RUN, IT DOESN'T COST NEARLY AS MUCH AS YA GAIN!! THAT'S WHY THE SHIT IS
"FREE!"

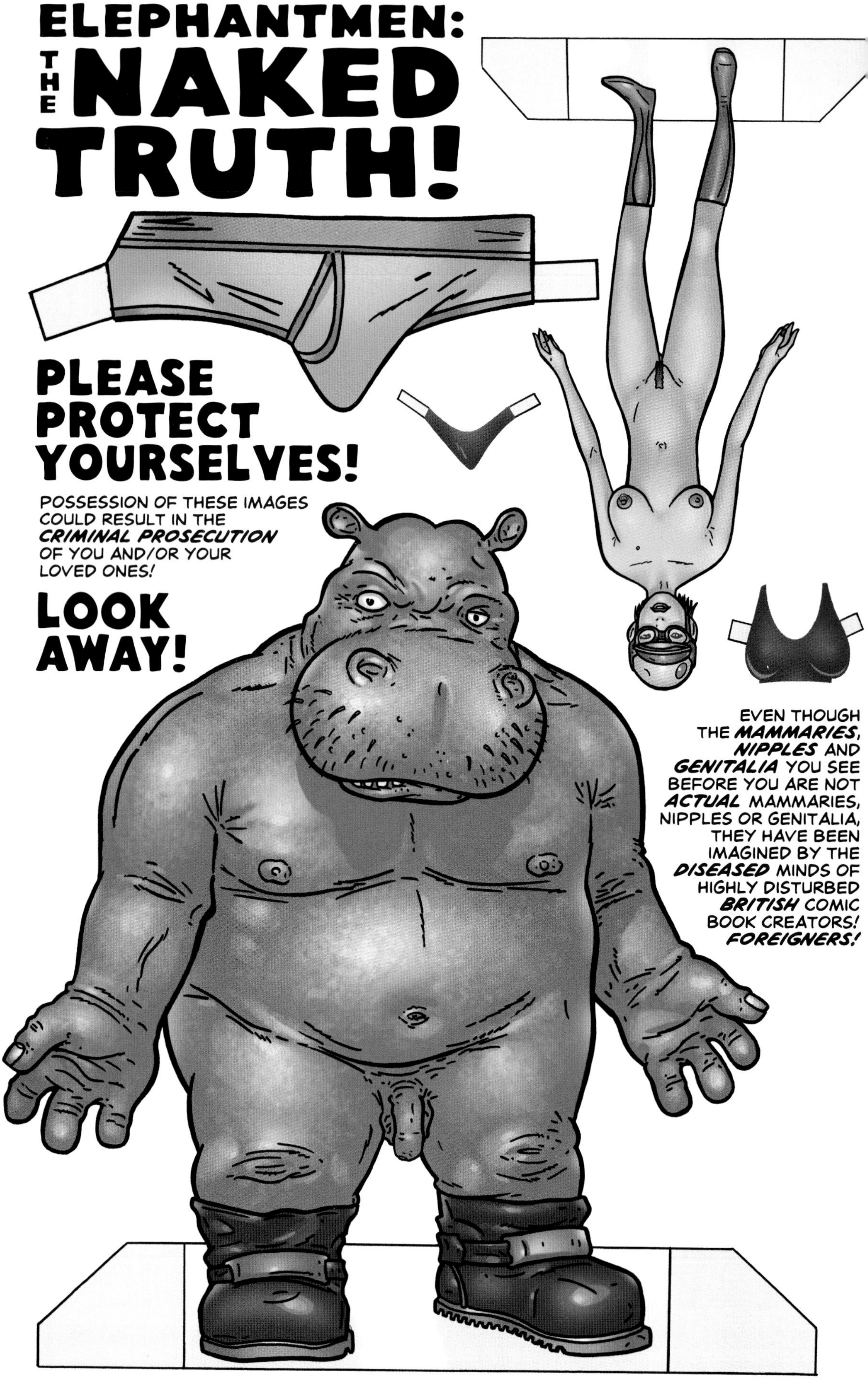
ELEPHANTMEN: THE NAKED TRUTH!
PLEASE PROTECT YOURSELVES!
POSSESSION OF THESE IMAGES COULD RESULT IN THE *CRIMINAL PROSECUTION* OF YOU AND/OR YOUR LOVED ONES!
LOOK AWAY!
EVEN THOUGH THE *MAMMARIES, NIPPLES* AND *GENITALIA* YOU SEE BEFORE YOU ARE NOT *ACTUAL* MAMMARIES, NIPPLES OR GENITALIA, THEY HAVE BEEN IMAGINED BY THE *DISEASED* MINDS OF HIGHLY DISTURBED *BRITISH* COMIC BOOK CREATORS! *FOREIGNERS!*

IT'S NOT TOO LATE!

CLIP OUT THE FIGURES AND THE UNDERWEAR YOU SEE HERE AND ***COVER UP*** THE UNFORTUNATE ELEPHANTMEN AND THE WOMEN THEY LOVE!

ANY ***DISGUSTING*** THOUGHTS YOU ARE CURRENTLY ENTERTAINING IN RESPONSE TO THESE IMAGES ARE ***NOT*** THE PUBLISHER'S RESPONSIBILITY. NO ONE AT ***IMAGE COMICS*** OR THE ***COMIC BOOK LEGAL DEFENSE FUND*** HAS ENJOYED LOOKING AT THESE DRAWINGS OR DESCRIBING THEM TO OFFICERS OF THE LAW!

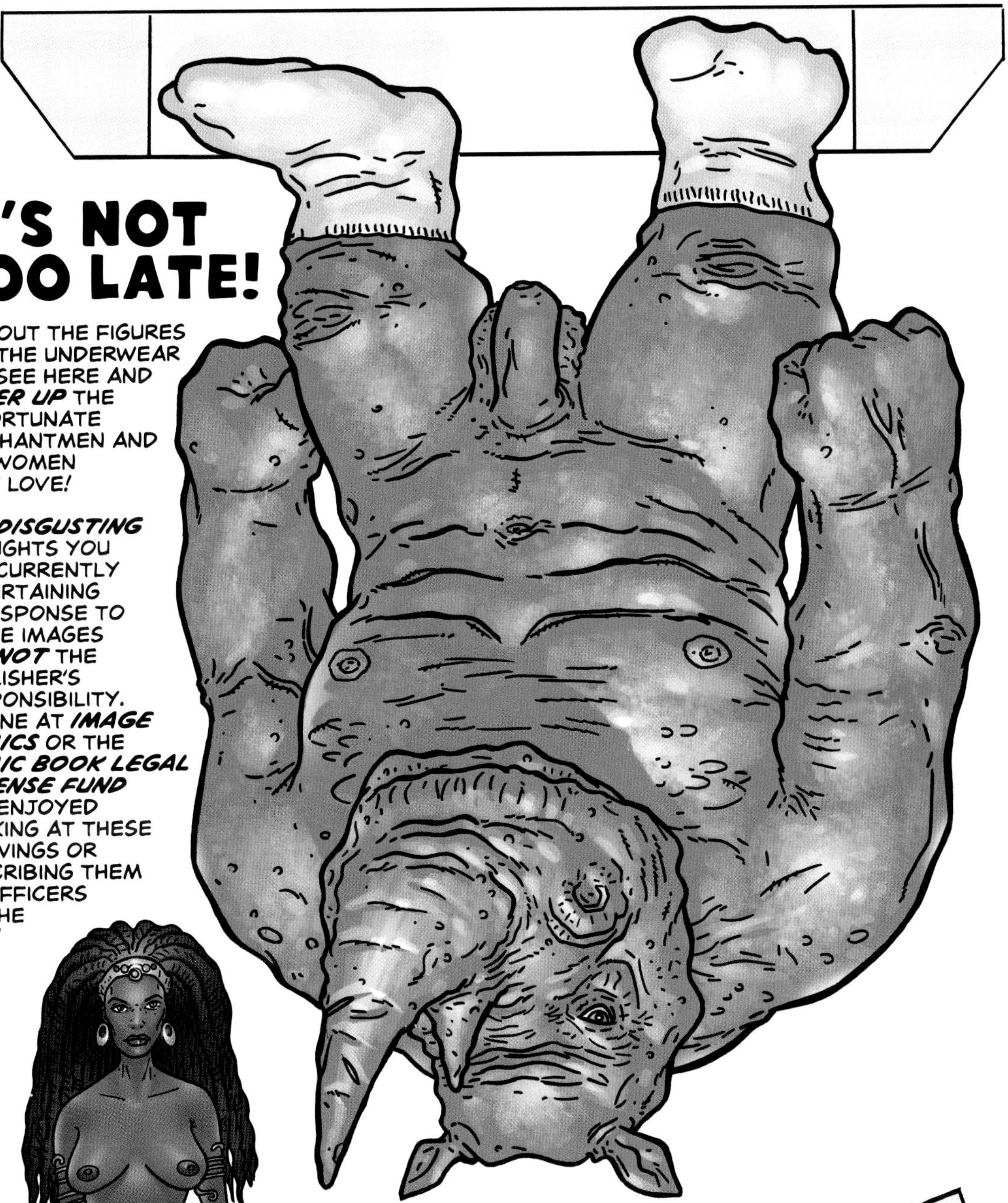

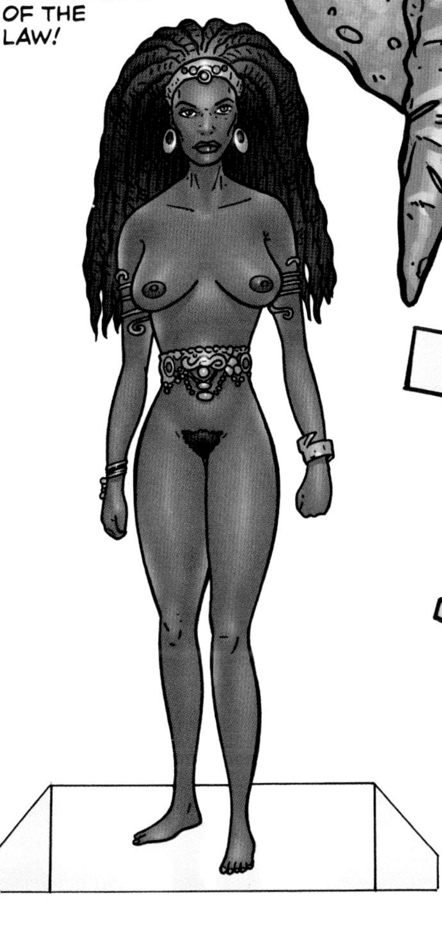

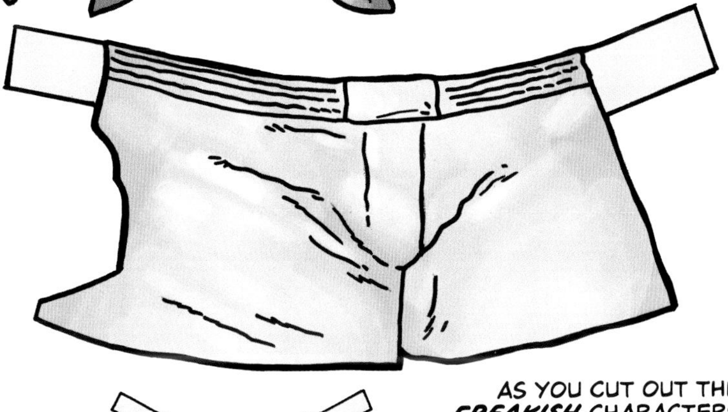

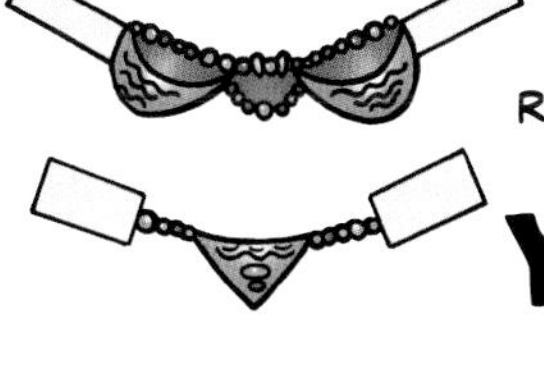

AS YOU CUT OUT THE ***FREAKISH*** CHARACTERS SHOWN HERE, WE STRONGLY RECOMMEND THAT YOU

CLOSE YOUR EYES!

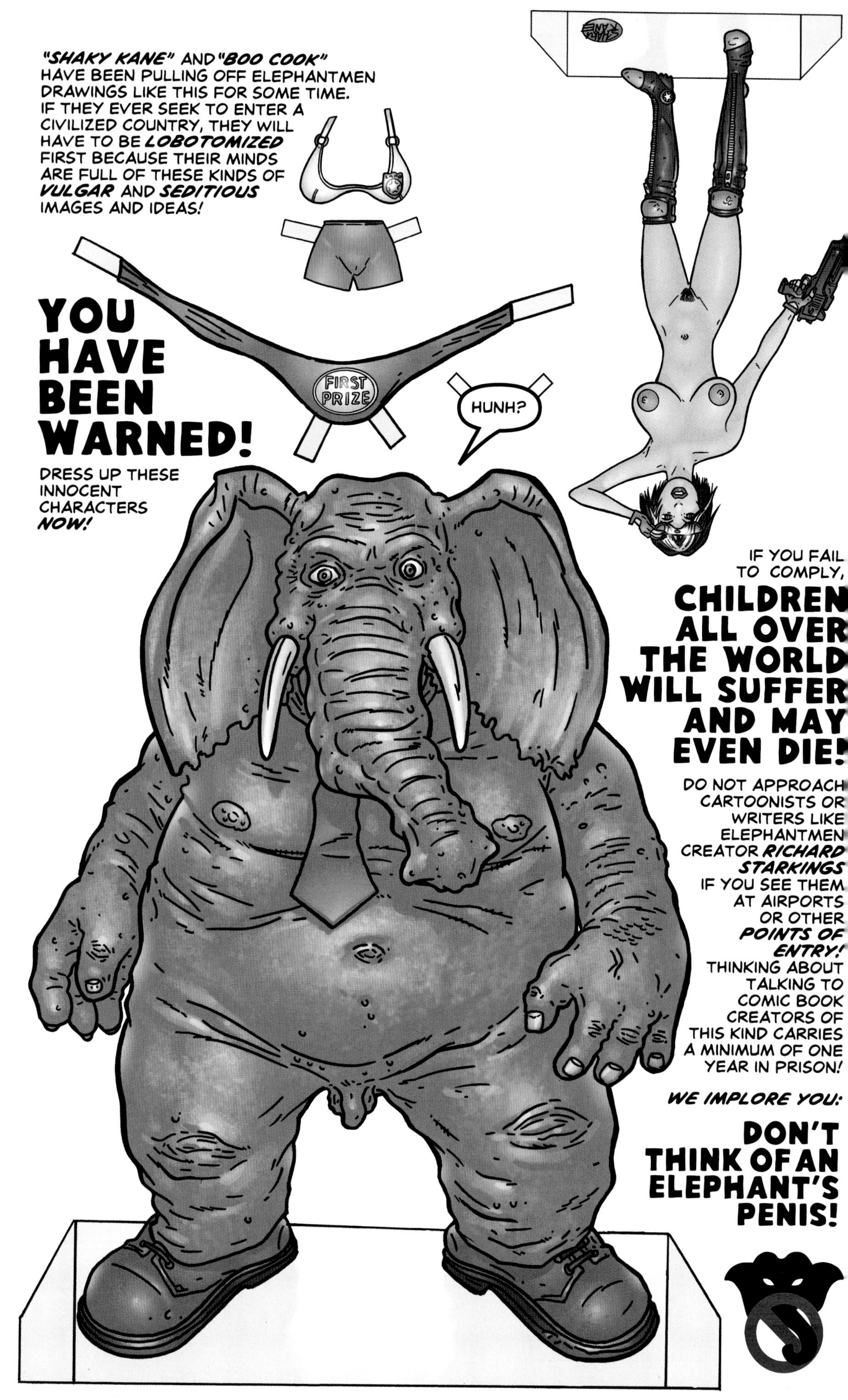
"SHAKY KANE" AND "BOO COOK" HAVE BEEN PULLING OFF ELEPHANTMEN DRAWINGS LIKE THIS FOR SOME TIME. IF THEY EVER SEEK TO ENTER A CIVILIZED COUNTRY, THEY WILL HAVE TO BE LOBOTOMIZED FIRST BECAUSE THEIR MINDS ARE FULL OF THESE KINDS OF VULGAR AND SEDITIOUS IMAGES AND IDEAS!
FIRST PRIZE
YOU HAVE BEEN WARNED!
DRESS UP THESE INNOCENT CHARACTERS NOW!
HUNH?
IF YOU FAIL TO COMPLY,
CHILDREN ALL OVER THE WORLD WILL SUFFER AND MAY EVEN DIE!
DO NOT APPROACH CARTOONISTS OR WRITERS LIKE ELEPHANTMEN CREATOR RICHARD STARKINGS IF YOU SEE THEM AT AIRPORTS OR OTHER POINTS OF ENTRY! THINKING ABOUT TALKING TO COMIC BOOK CREATORS OF THIS KIND CARRIES A MINIMUM OF ONE YEAR IN PRISON!
WE IMPLORE YOU:
DON'T THINK OF AN ELEPHANT'S PENIS!

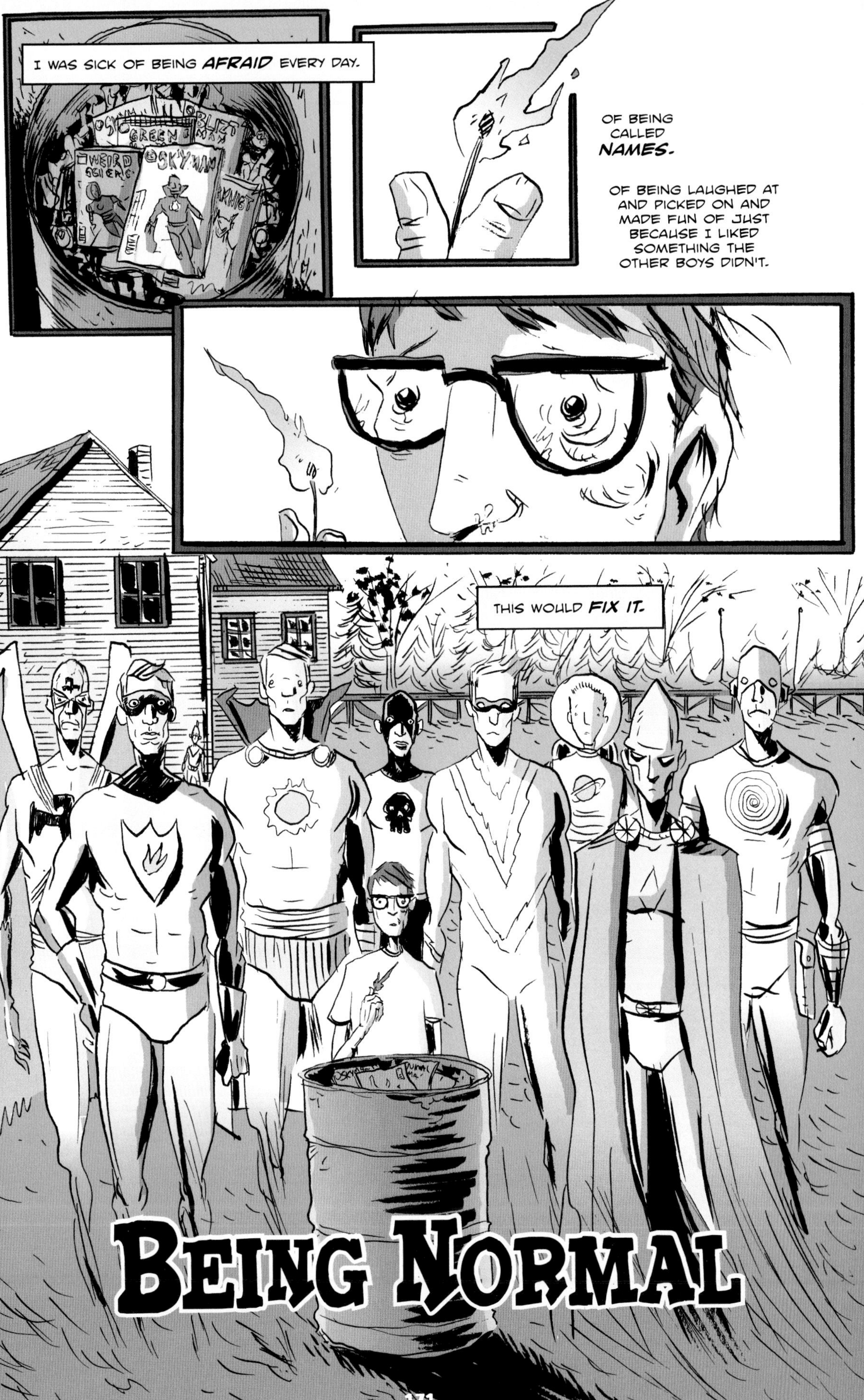
I WAS SICK OF BEING AFRAID EVERY DAY.
OF BEING CALLED NAMES.
OF BEING LAUGHED AT AND PICKED ON AND MADE FUN OF JUST BECAUSE I LIKED SOMETHING THE OTHER BOYS DIDN'T.
THIS WOULD FIX IT.
BEING NORMAL

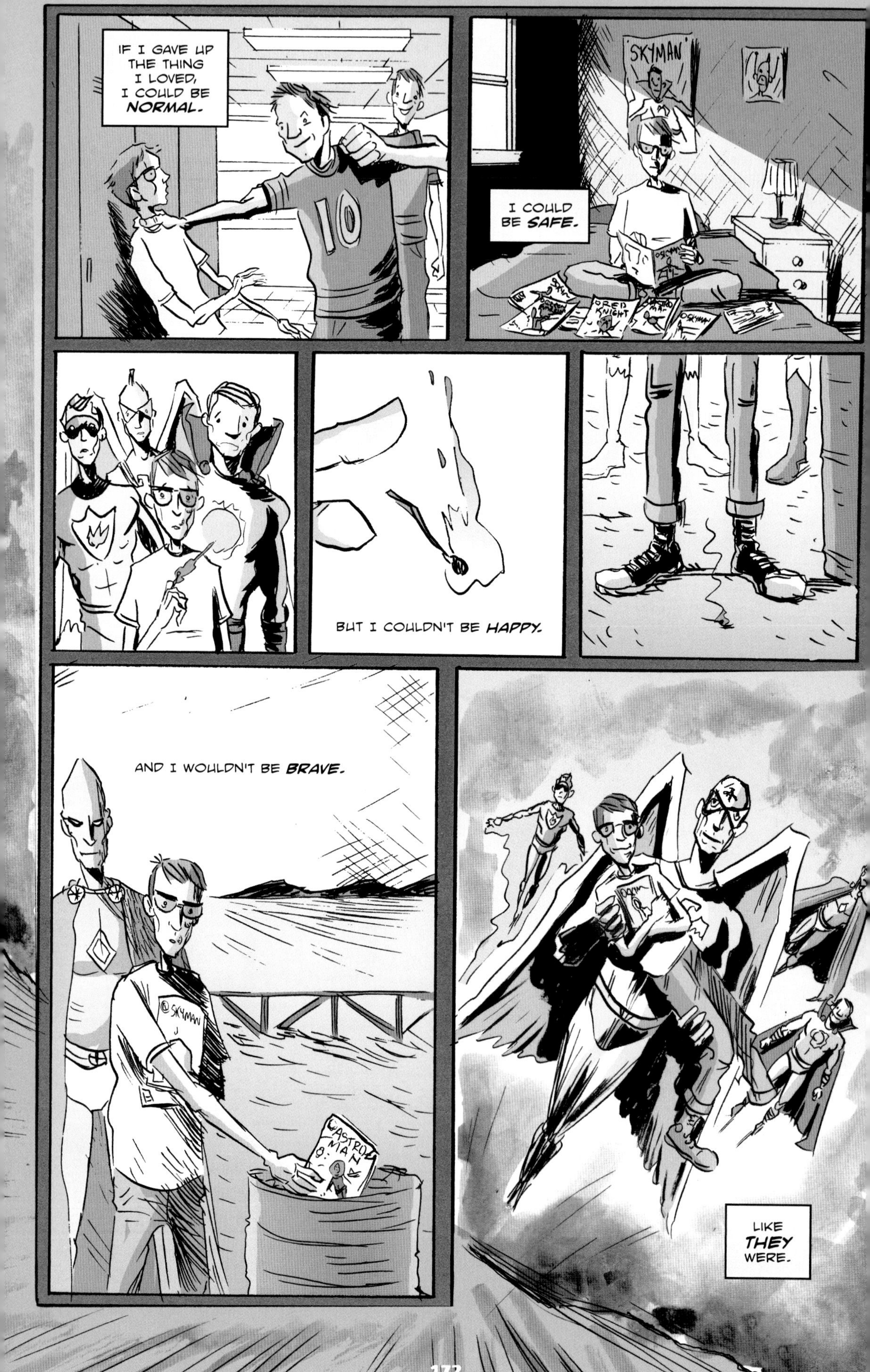
IF I GAVE UP THE THING I LOVED, I COULD BE NORMAL.
SKYMAN
I COULD BE SAFE.
RED KNIGHT
BUT I COULDN'T BE HAPPY.
AND I WOULDN'T BE BRAVE.
SKYMAN
ASTRO MAN
LIKE THEY WERE.

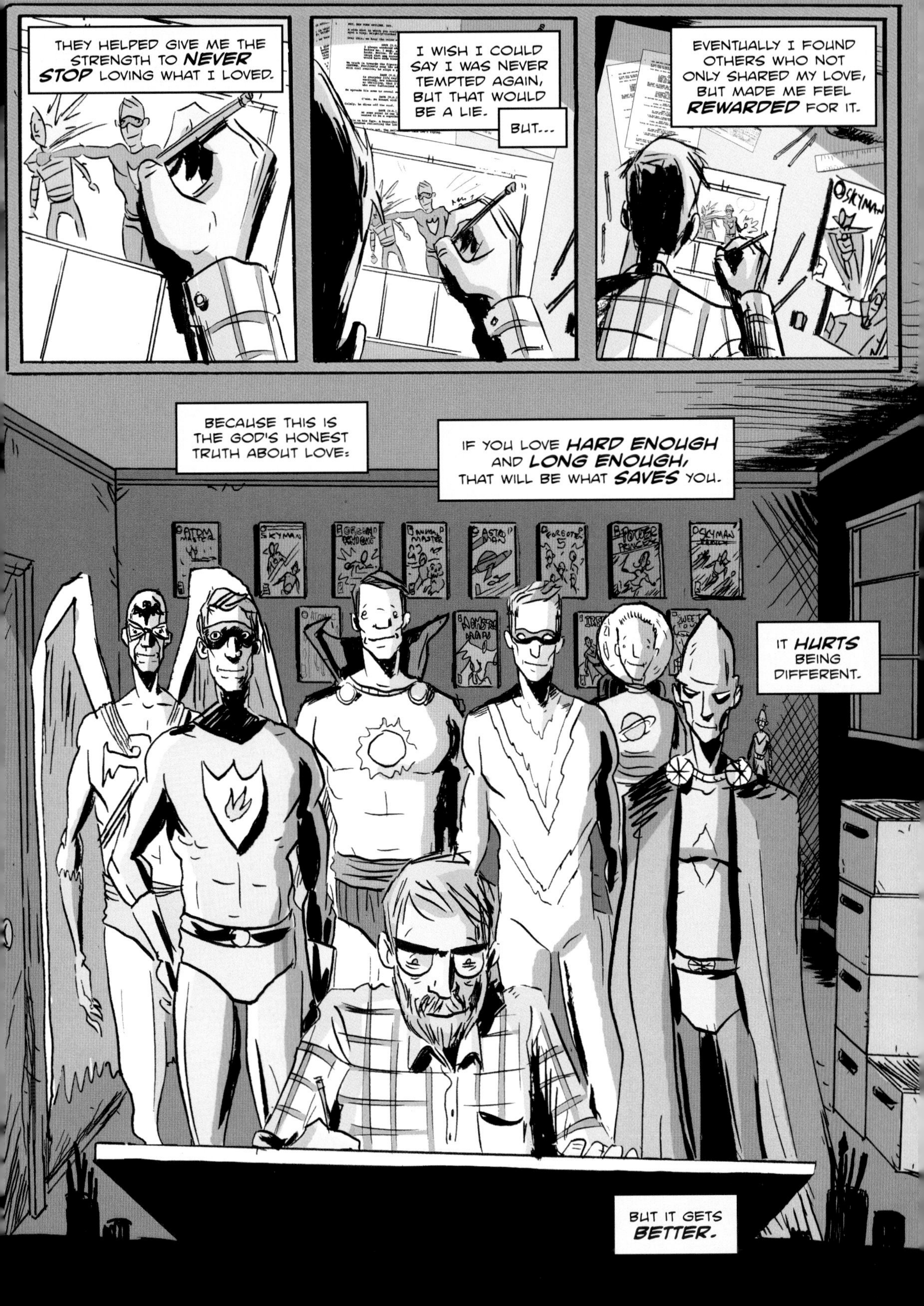
THEY HELPED GIVE ME THE STRENGTH TO NEVER STOP LOVING WHAT I LOVED.
I WISH I COULD SAY I WAS NEVER TEMPTED AGAIN, BUT THAT WOULD BE A LIE.
BUT...
EVENTUALLY I FOUND OTHERS WHO NOT ONLY SHARED MY LOVE, BUT MADE ME FEEL REWARDED FOR IT.
BECAUSE THIS IS THE GOD'S HONEST TRUTH ABOUT LOVE:
IF YOU LOVE HARD ENOUGH AND LONG ENOUGH, THAT WILL BE WHAT SAVES YOU.
IT HURTS BEING DIFFERENT.
BUT IT GETS BETTER.

MARK WAID WRITER

JEFF LEMIRE ARTIST

LEE LOUGHRIDGE COLORS

SEAN KONOT LETTERS

JL+MW

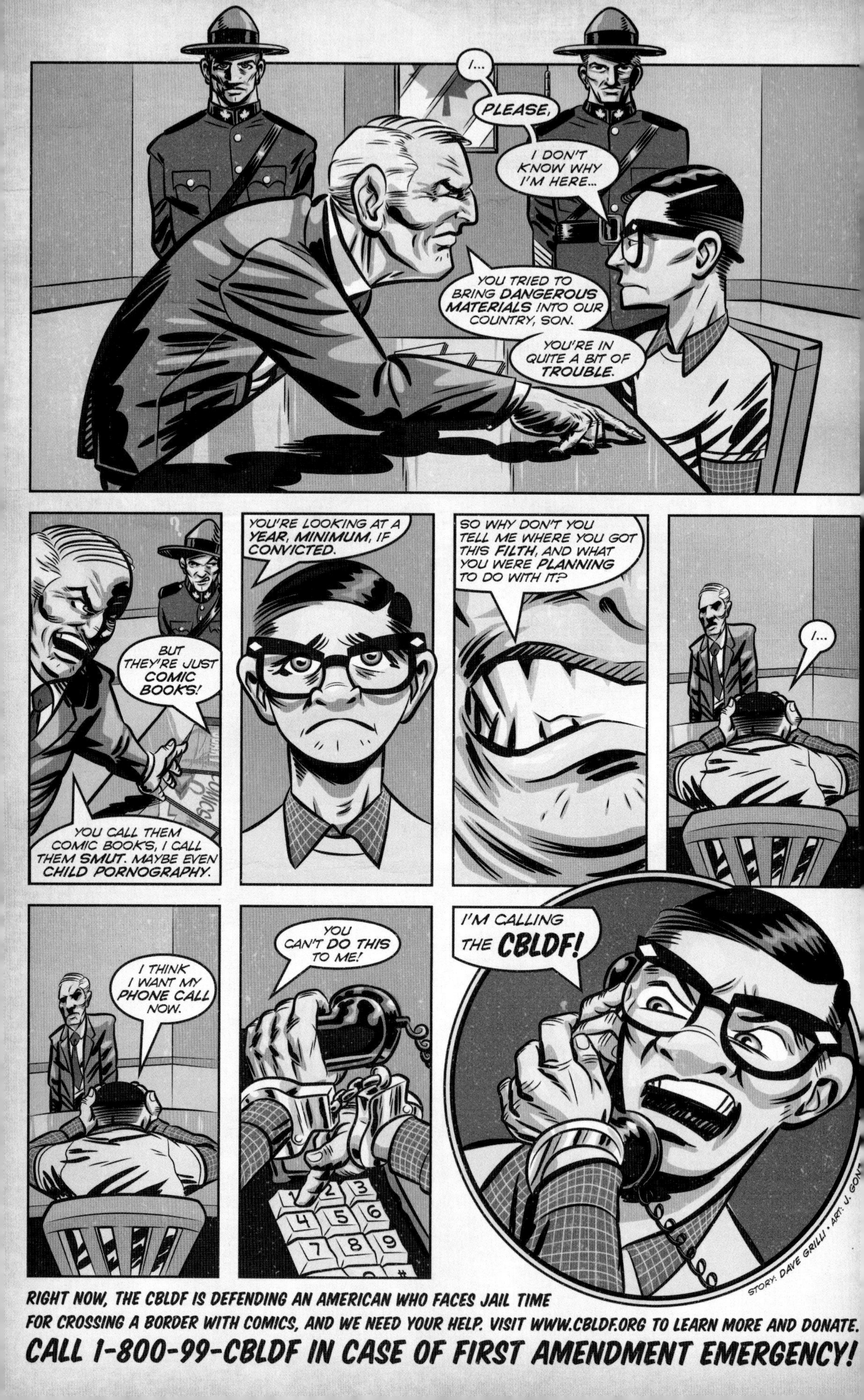
I...
PLEASE,
I DON'T KNOW WHY I'M HERE...
YOU TRIED TO BRING DANGEROUS MATERIALS INTO OUR COUNTRY, SON.
YOU'RE IN QUITE A BIT OF TROUBLE.
BUT THEY'RE JUST COMIC BOOKS!
YOU CALL THEM COMIC BOOKS, I CALL THEM SMUT. MAYBE EVEN CHILD PORNOGRAPHY.
YOU'RE LOOKING AT A YEAR, MINIMUM, IF CONVICTED.
SO WHY DON'T YOU TELL ME WHERE YOU GOT THIS FILTH, AND WHAT YOU WERE PLANNING TO DO WITH IT?
I...
I THINK I WANT MY PHONE CALL NOW.
YOU CAN'T DO THIS TO ME!
I'M CALLING THE CBLDF!

LIBERTY ANNUAL 2012

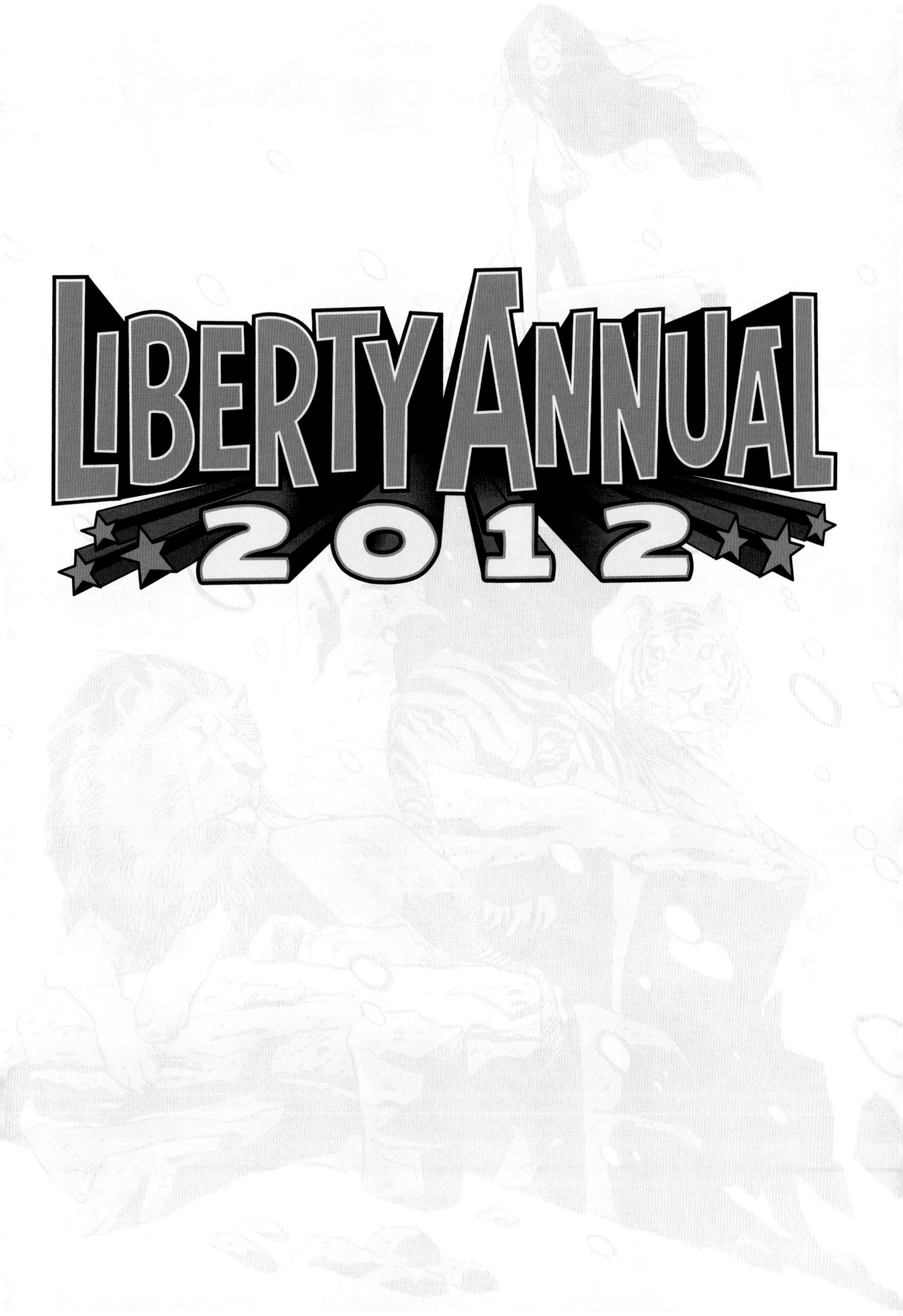

COVER BY GABRIEL BÁ

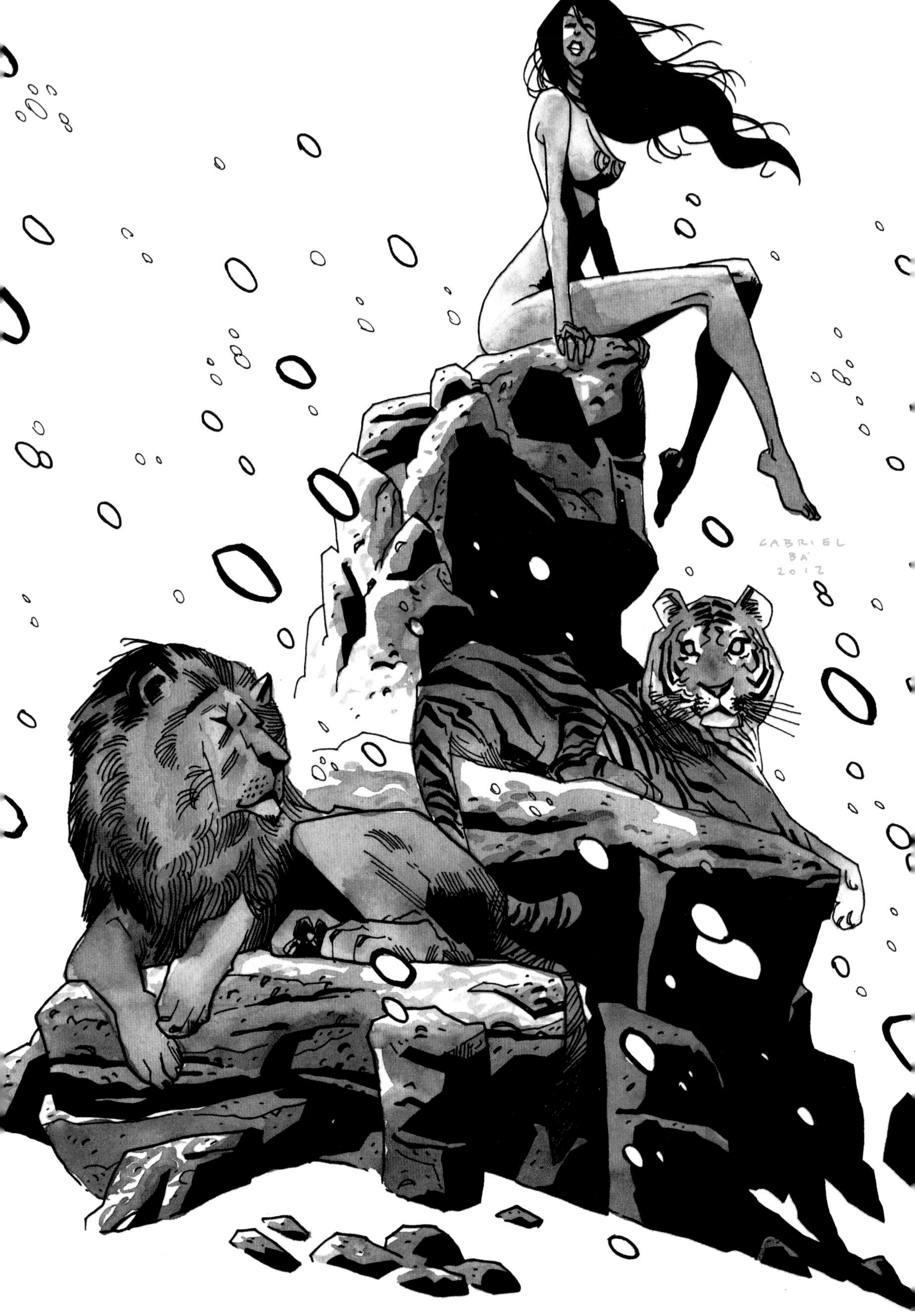
GABRIEL
BÁ
2012

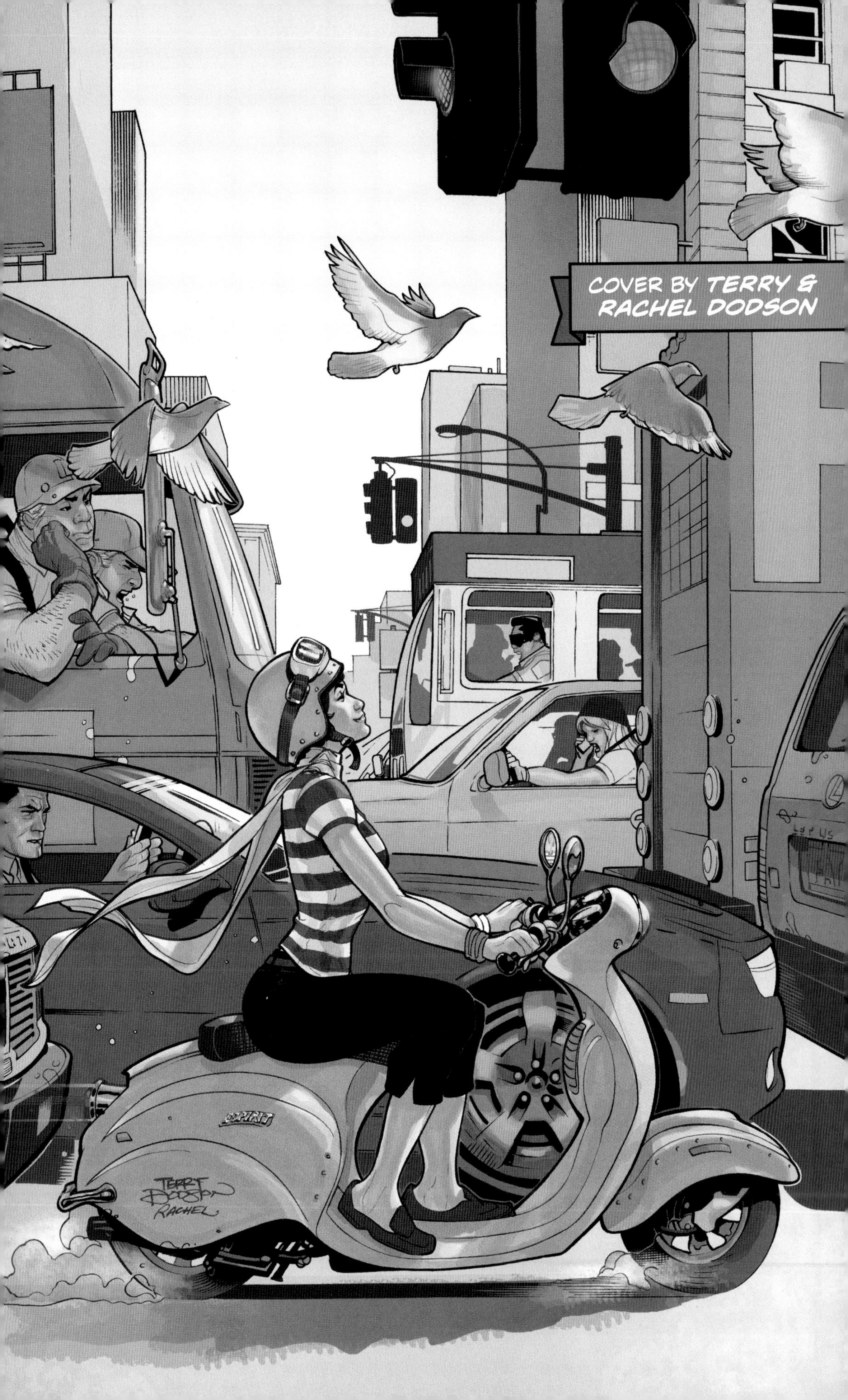
COVER BY TERRY & RACHEL DODSON

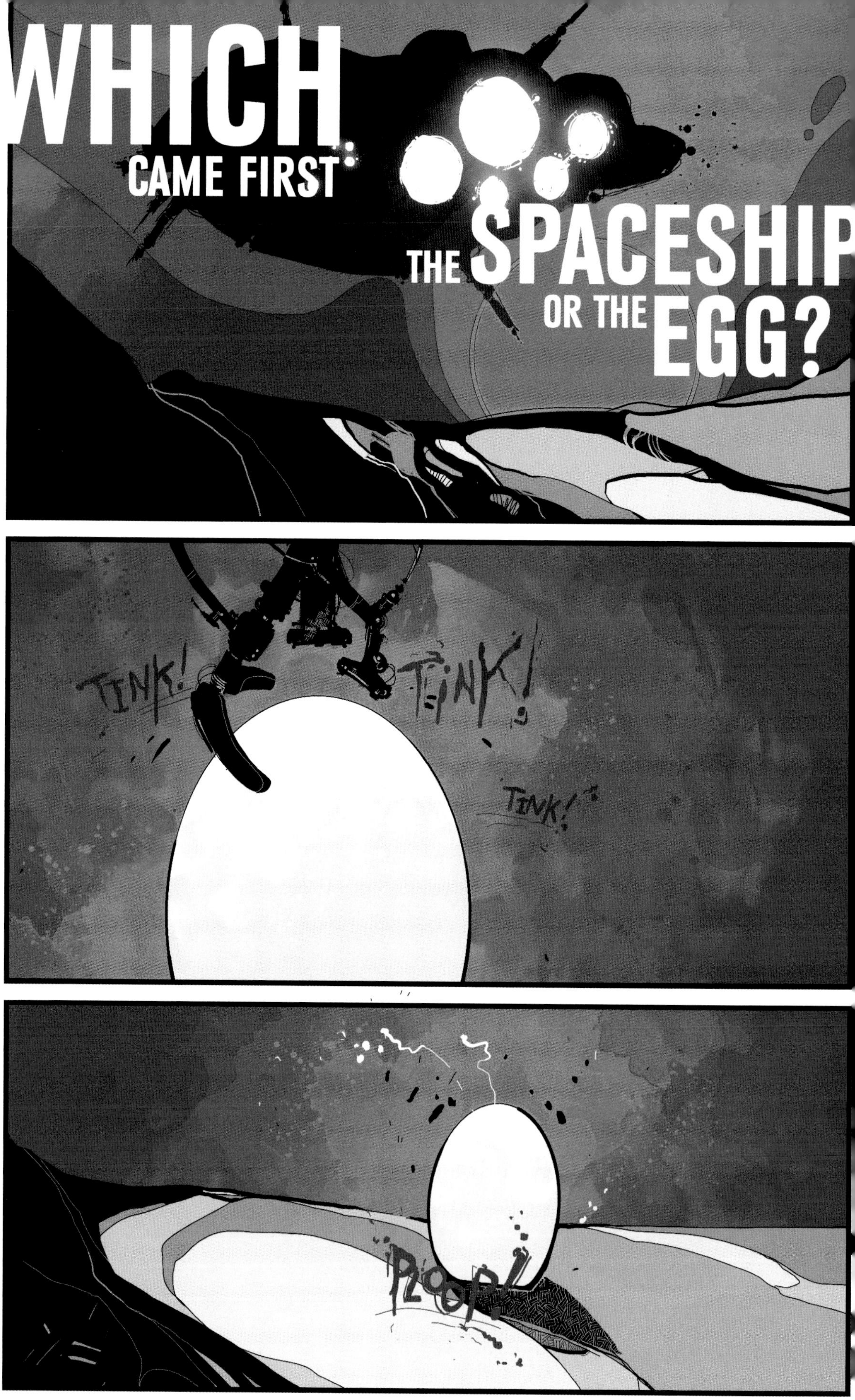
WHICH CAME FIRST
THE SPACESHIP OR THE EGG?
TINK!
TINK!
TINK!
PLOOP!

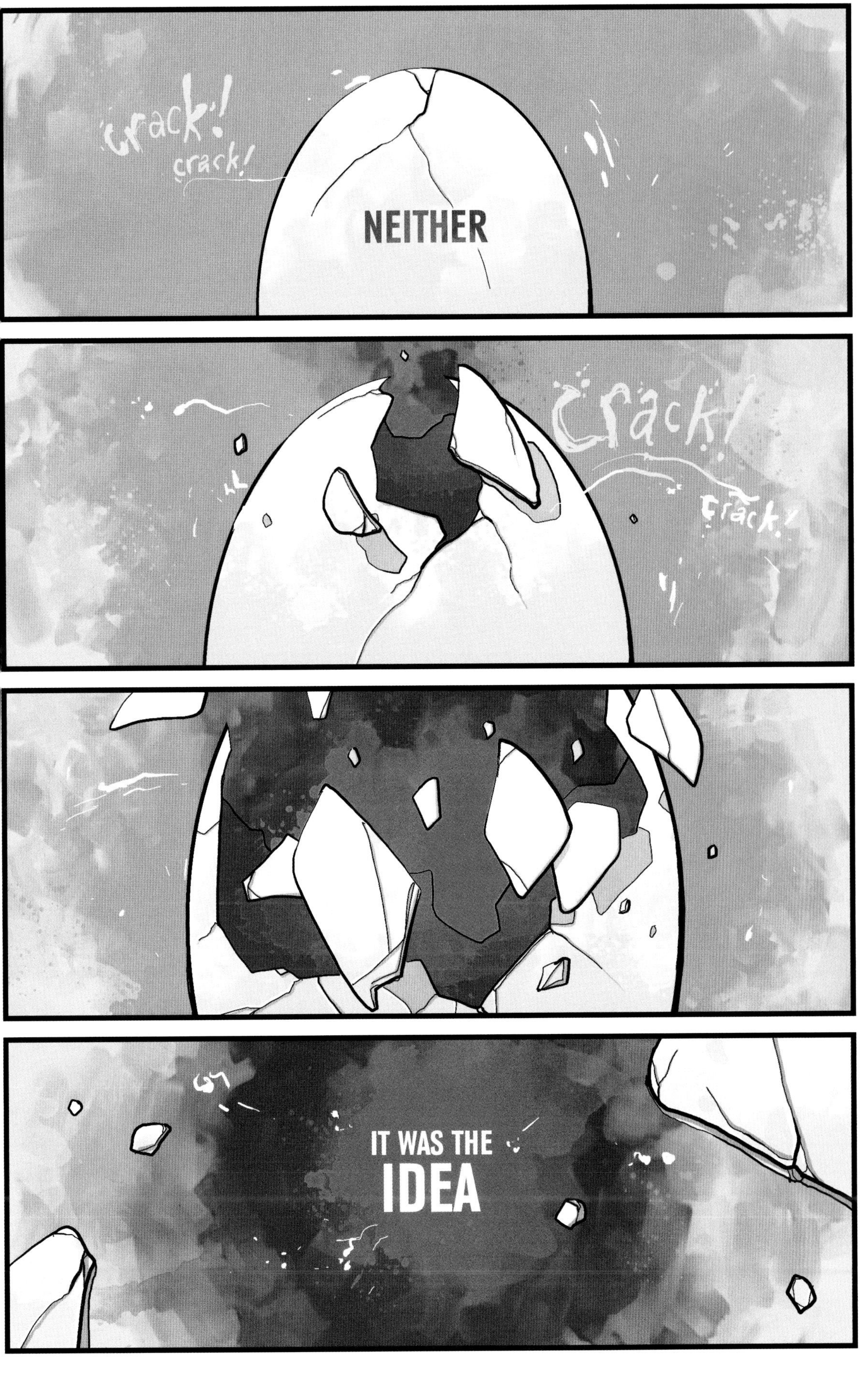
crack!
crack!
NEITHER
crack!
crack!
IT WAS THE
IDEA

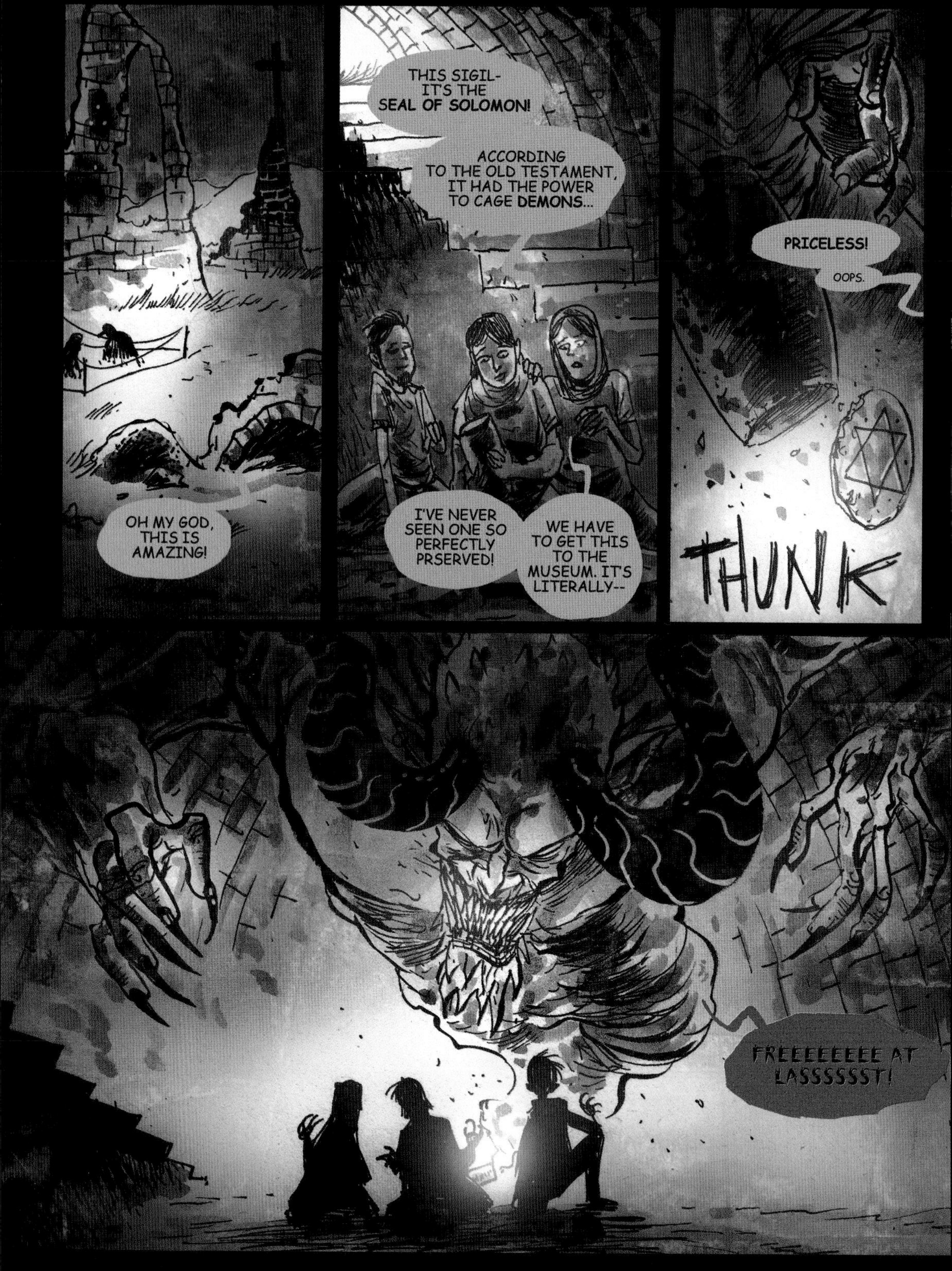
OH MY GOD, THIS IS AMAZING!
THIS SIGIL- IT'S THE SEAL OF SOLOMON!
ACCORDING TO THE OLD TESTAMENT, IT HAD THE POWER TO CAGE DEMONS...
I'VE NEVER SEEN ONE SO PERFECTLY PRSERVED!
WE HAVE TO GET THIS TO THE MUSEUM. IT'S LITERALLY--
PRICELESS!
OOPS.
THUNK
FREEEEEEEE AT LASSSSSST!

BARREN GROUND

BY ANDY DIGGLE & BEN TEMPLESMITH

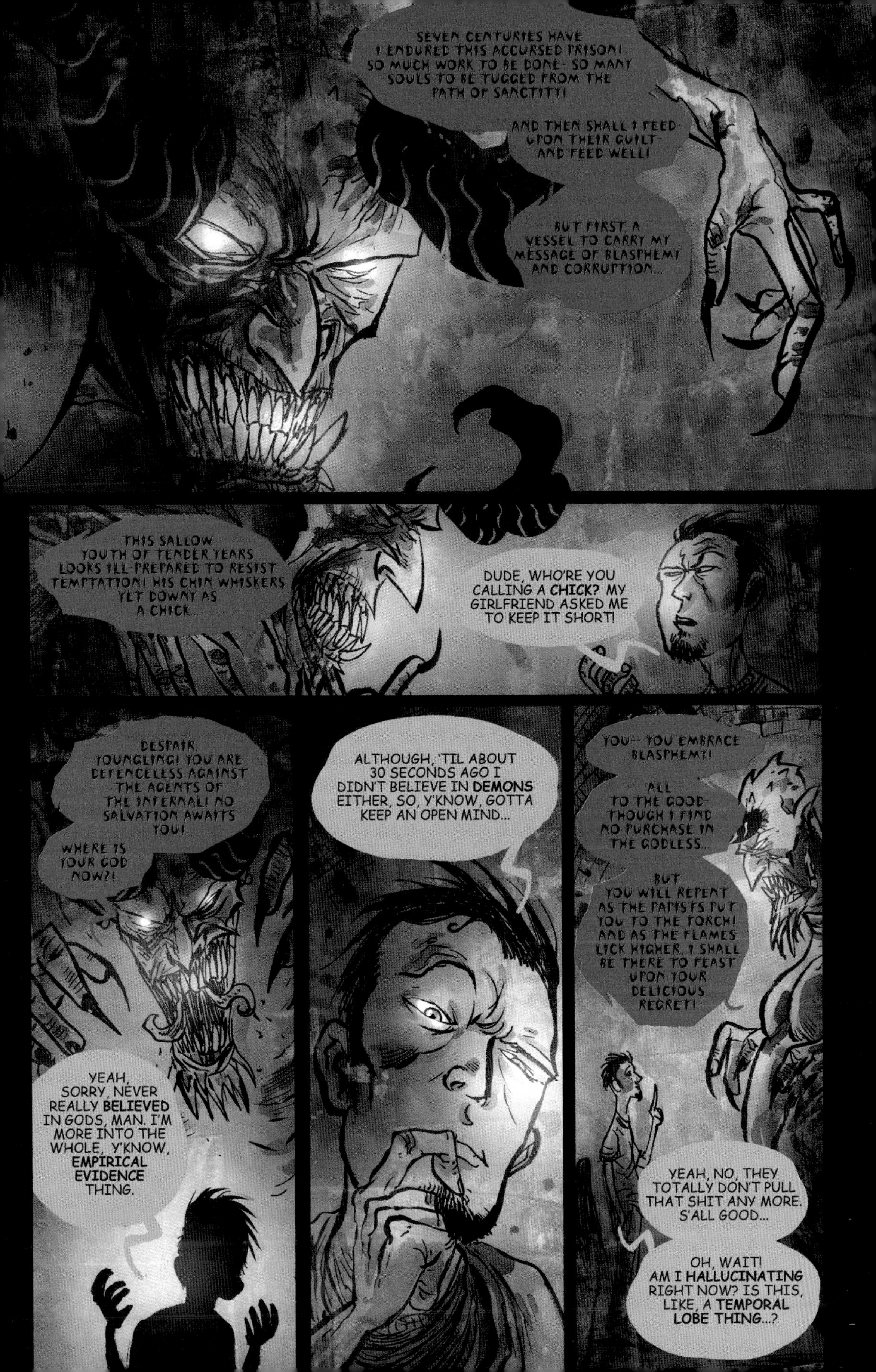
SEVEN CENTURIES HAVE I ENDURED THIS ACCURSED PRISON! SO MUCH WORK TO BE DONE- SO MANY SOULS TO BE TUGGED FROM THE PATH OF SANCTITY!
AND THEN SHALL I FEED UPON THEIR GUILT- AND FEED WELL!
BUT FIRST, A VESSEL TO CARRY MY MESSAGE OF BLASPHEMY AND CORRUPTION...
THIS SALLOW YOUTH OF TENDER YEARS LOOKS ILL-PREPARED TO RESIST TEMPTATION! HIS CHIN WHISKERS YET DOWNY AS A CHICK...
DUDE, WHO'RE YOU CALLING A CHICK? MY GIRLFRIEND ASKED ME TO KEEP IT SHORT!
DESPAIR, YOUNGLING! YOU ARE DEFENCELESS AGAINST THE AGENTS OF THE INFERNAL! NO SALVATION AWAITS YOU!
WHERE IS YOUR GOD NOW?!
YEAH, SORRY, NEVER REALLY BELIEVED IN GODS, MAN. I'M MORE INTO THE WHOLE, Y'KNOW, EMPIRICAL EVIDENCE THING.
ALTHOUGH, 'TIL ABOUT 30 SECONDS AGO I DIDN'T BELIEVE IN DEMONS EITHER, SO, Y'KNOW, GOTTA KEEP AN OPEN MIND...
YOU-- YOU EMBRACE BLASPHEMY!
ALL TO THE GOOD- THOUGH I FIND NO PURCHASE IN THE GODLESS...
BUT YOU WILL REPENT AS THE PAPISTS PUT YOU TO THE TORCH! AND AS THE FLAMES LICK HIGHER, I SHALL BE THERE TO FEAST UPON YOUR DELICIOUS REGRET!
YEAH, NO, THEY TOTALLY DON'T PULL THAT SHIT ANY MORE. S'ALL GOOD...
OH, WAIT! AM I HALLUCINATING RIGHT NOW? IS THIS, LIKE, A TEMPORAL LOBE THING...?

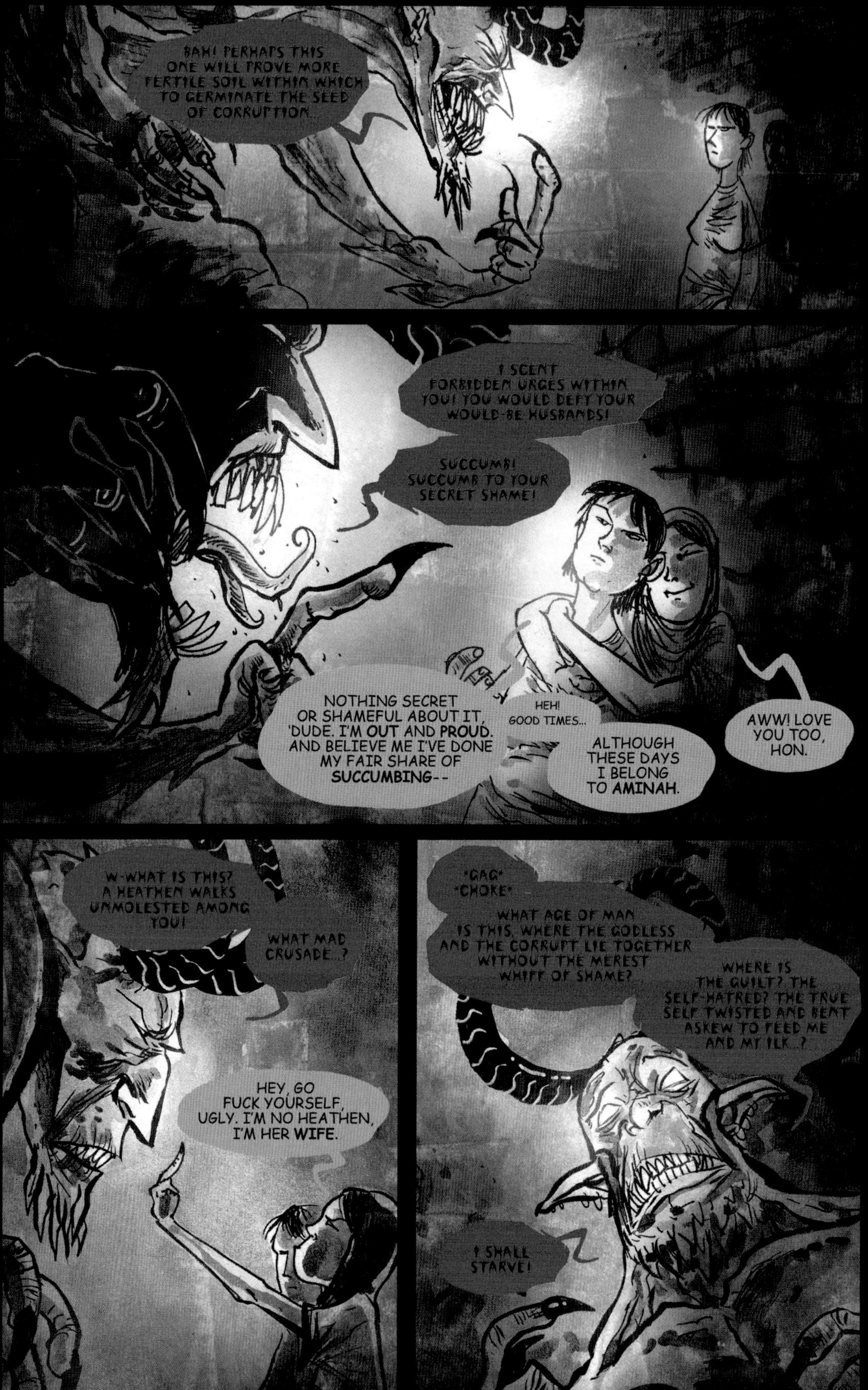
BAH! PERHAPS THIS ONE WILL PROVE MORE FERTILE SOIL WITHIN WHICH TO GERMINATE THE SEED OF CORRUPTION...
I SCENT FORBIDDEN URGES WITHIN YOU! YOU WOULD DEFY YOUR WOULD-BE HUSBANDS!
SUCCUMB! SUCCUMB TO YOUR SECRET SHAME!
NOTHING SECRET OR SHAMEFUL ABOUT IT, 'DUDE. I'M OUT AND PROUD. AND BELIEVE ME I'VE DONE MY FAIR SHARE OF SUCCUMBING--
HEH! GOOD TIMES...
ALTHOUGH THESE DAYS I BELONG TO AMINAH.
AWW! LOVE YOU TOO, HON.
W-WHAT IS THIS? A HEATHEN WALKS UNMOLESTED AMONG YOU!
WHAT MAD CRUSADE...?
HEY, GO FUCK YOURSELF, UGLY. I'M NO HEATHEN, I'M HER WIFE.
GAG *CHOKE*
WHAT AGE OF MAN IS THIS, WHERE THE GODLESS AND THE CORRUPT LIE TOGETHER WITHOUT THE MEREST WHIFF OF SHAME?
WHERE IS THE GUILT? THE SELF-HATRED? THE TRUE SELF TWISTED AND BENT ASKEW TO FEED ME AND MY ILK...?
I SHALL STARVE!

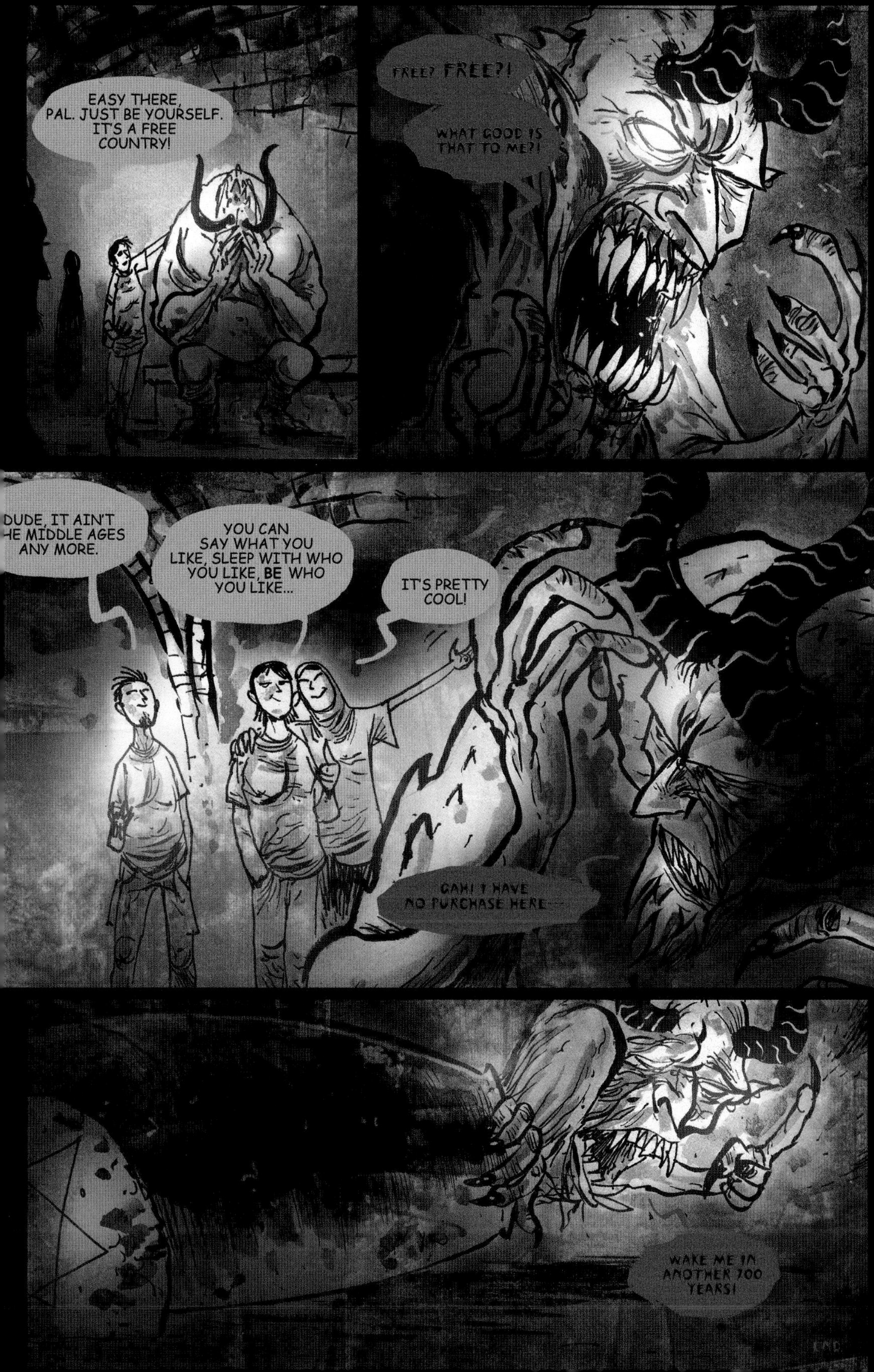
EASY THERE, PAL. JUST BE YOURSELF. IT'S A FREE COUNTRY!
FREE? FREE?!
WHAT GOOD IS THAT TO ME?!
DUDE, IT AIN'T HE MIDDLE AGES ANY MORE.
YOU CAN SAY WHAT YOU LIKE, SLEEP WITH WHO YOU LIKE, BE WHO YOU LIKE...
IT'S PRETTY COOL!
GAH! I HAVE NO PURCHASE HERE---
WAKE ME IN ANOTHER 700 YEARS!
END

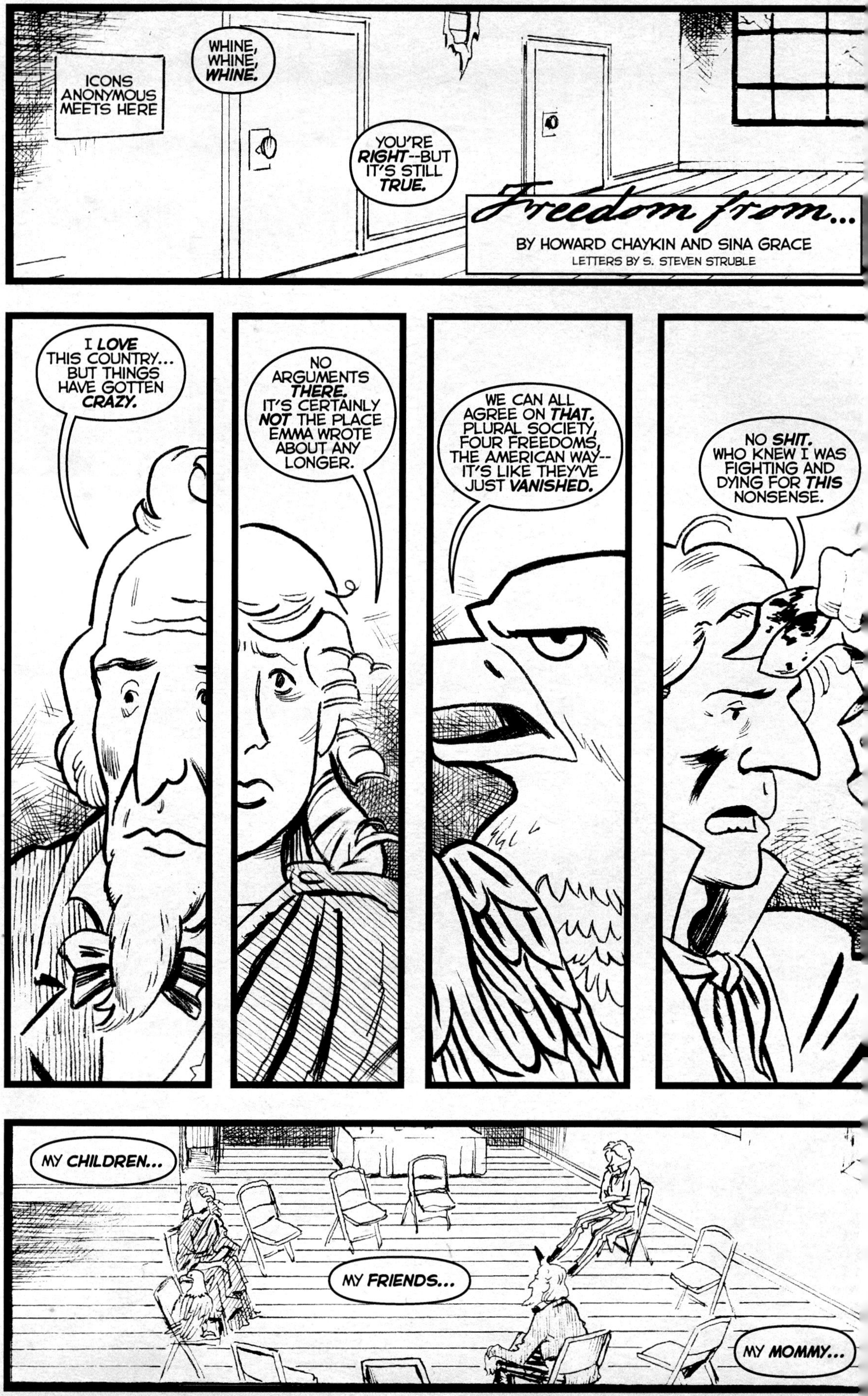
ICONS ANONYMOUS MEETS HERE
WHINE, WHINE, WHINE.
YOU'RE RIGHT--BUT IT'S STILL TRUE.
Freedom from...
BY HOWARD CHAYKIN AND SINA GRACE
LETTERS BY S. STEVEN STRUBLE
I LOVE THIS COUNTRY... BUT THINGS HAVE GOTTEN CRAZY.
NO ARGUMENTS THERE. IT'S CERTAINLY NOT THE PLACE EMMA WROTE ABOUT ANY LONGER.
WE CAN ALL AGREE ON THAT. PLURAL SOCIETY, FOUR FREEDOMS, THE AMERICAN WAY-- IT'S LIKE THEY'VE JUST VANISHED.
NO SHIT. WHO KNEW I WAS FIGHTING AND DYING FOR THIS NONSENSE.
MY CHILDREN...
MY FRIENDS...
MY MOMMY...

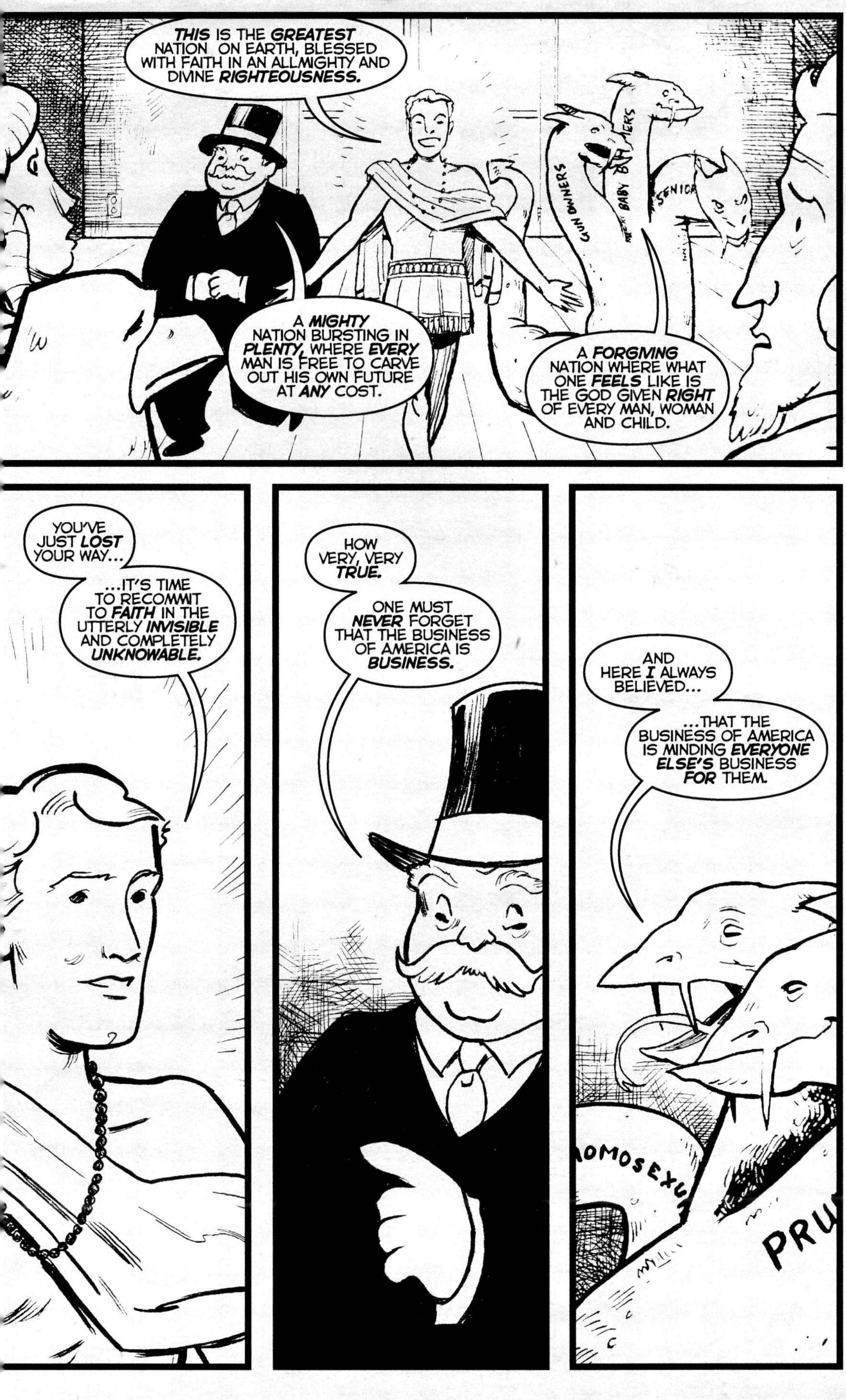
THIS IS THE GREATEST NATION ON EARTH, BLESSED WITH FAITH IN AN ALLMIGHTY AND DIVINE RIGHTEOUSNESS.
A MIGHTY NATION BURSTING IN PLENTY, WHERE EVERY MAN IS FREE TO CARVE OUT HIS OWN FUTURE AT ANY COST.
GUN OWNERS
BABY
SENIO
A FORGIVING NATION WHERE WHAT ONE FEELS LIKE IS THE GOD GIVEN RIGHT OF EVERY MAN, WOMAN AND CHILD.
YOU'VE JUST LOST YOUR WAY...
...IT'S TIME TO RECOMMIT TO FAITH IN THE UTTERLY INVISIBLE AND COMPLETELY UNKNOWABLE.
HOW VERY, VERY TRUE.
ONE MUST NEVER FORGET THAT THE BUSINESS OF AMERICA IS BUSINESS.
AND HERE I ALWAYS BELIEVED...
...THAT THE BUSINESS OF AMERICA IS MINDING EVERYONE ELSE'S BUSINESS FOR THEM.
OMOSEXU
PRU

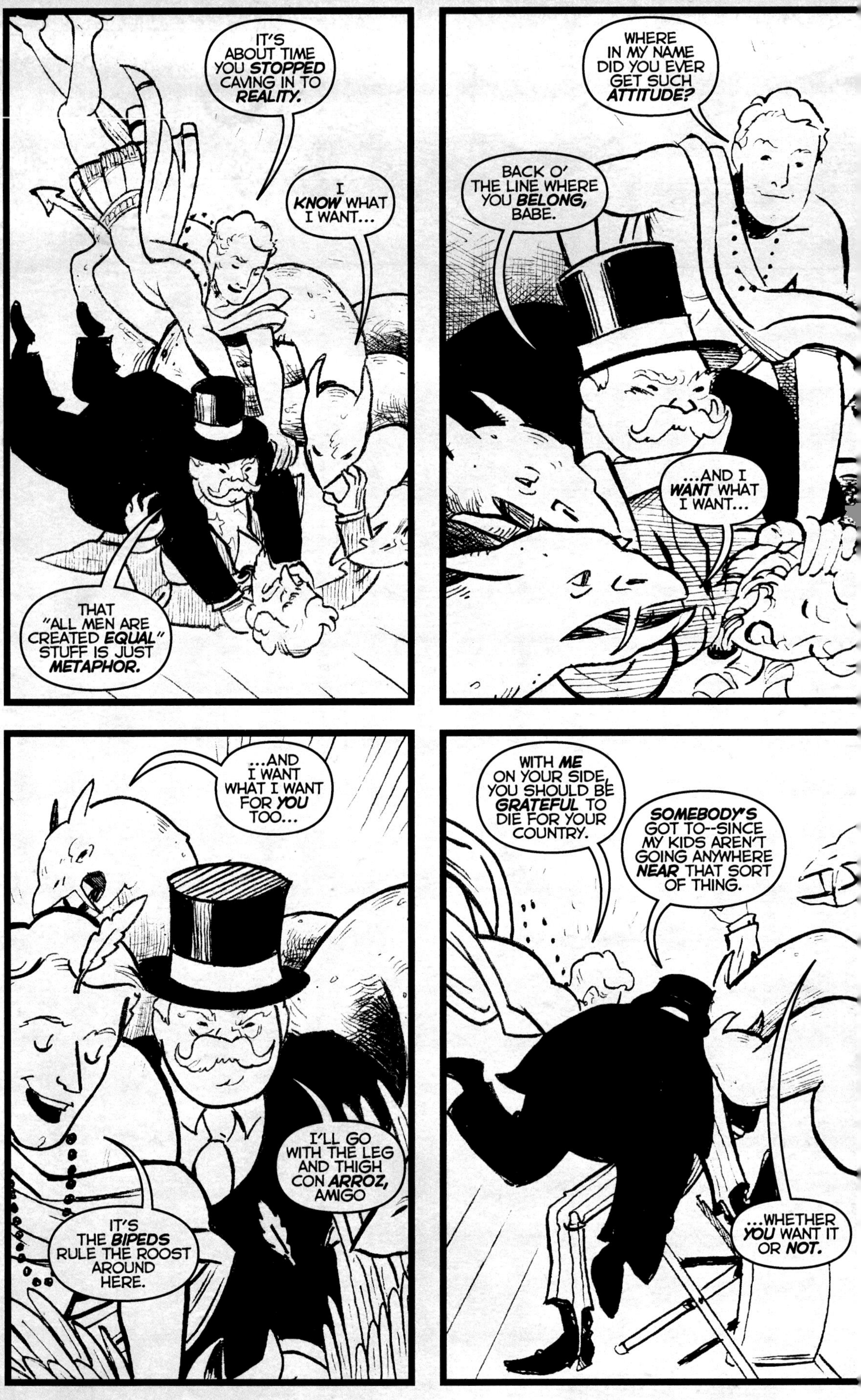
IT'S ABOUT TIME YOU STOPPED CAVING IN TO REALITY.
I KNOW WHAT I WANT...
THAT "ALL MEN ARE CREATED EQUAL" STUFF IS JUST METAPHOR.
WHERE IN MY NAME DID YOU EVER GET SUCH ATTITUDE?
BACK O' THE LINE WHERE YOU BELONG, BABE.
...AND I WANT WHAT I WANT...
...AND I WANT WHAT I WANT FOR YOU TOO...
I'LL GO WITH THE LEG AND THIGH CON ARROZ, AMIGO
IT'S THE BIPEDS RULE THE ROOST AROUND HERE.
WITH ME ON YOUR SIDE, YOU SHOULD BE GRATEFUL TO DIE FOR YOUR COUNTRY.
SOMEBODY'S GOT TO--SINCE MY KIDS AREN'T GOING ANYWHERE NEAR THAT SORT OF THING.
...WHETHER YOU WANT IT OR NOT.

I *BEG* YOUR PARDON.

HEY-- WE'RE *TALKING* HERE.

WAAHH!

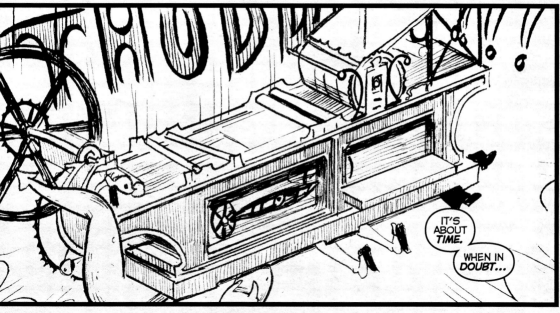

IT'S ABOUT *TIME.*

WHEN IN *DOUBT...*

...WE CAN ALWAYS *COUNT* ON FREEDOM OF THE *PRESS...*

...IN *THEORY,* ANYWAY.

THE END.

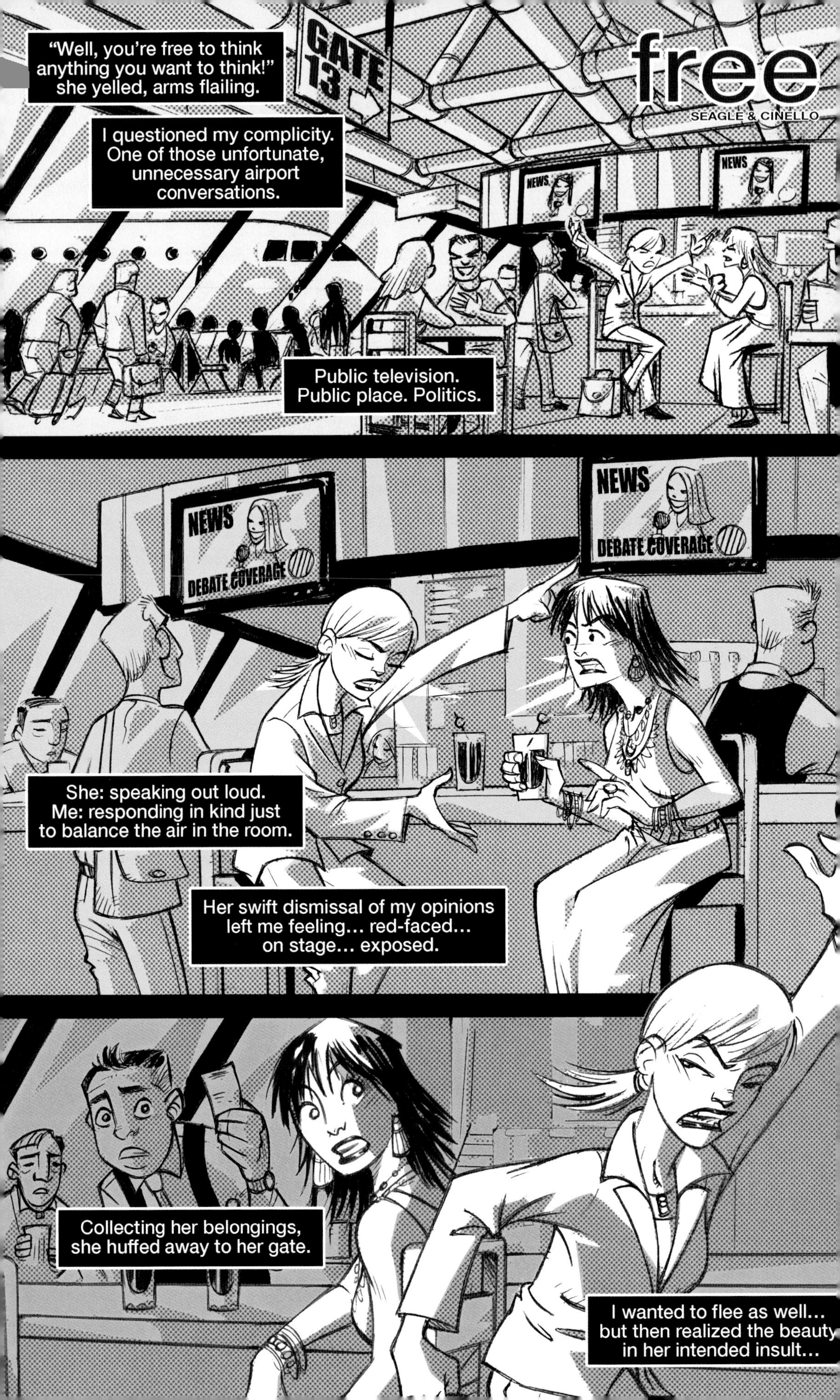
free
SEAGLE & CINELLO
"Well, you're free to think anything you want to think!" she yelled, arms flailing.
GATE 13
I questioned my complicity. One of those unfortunate, unnecessary airport conversations.
NEWS
NEWS
Public television. Public place. Politics.
NEWS
DEBATE COVERAGE
NEWS
DEBATE COVERAGE
She: speaking out loud. Me: responding in kind just to balance the air in the room.
Her swift dismissal of my opinions left me feeling... red-faced... on stage... exposed.
Collecting her belongings, she huffed away to her gate.
I wanted to flee as well... but then realized the beauty in her intended insult...

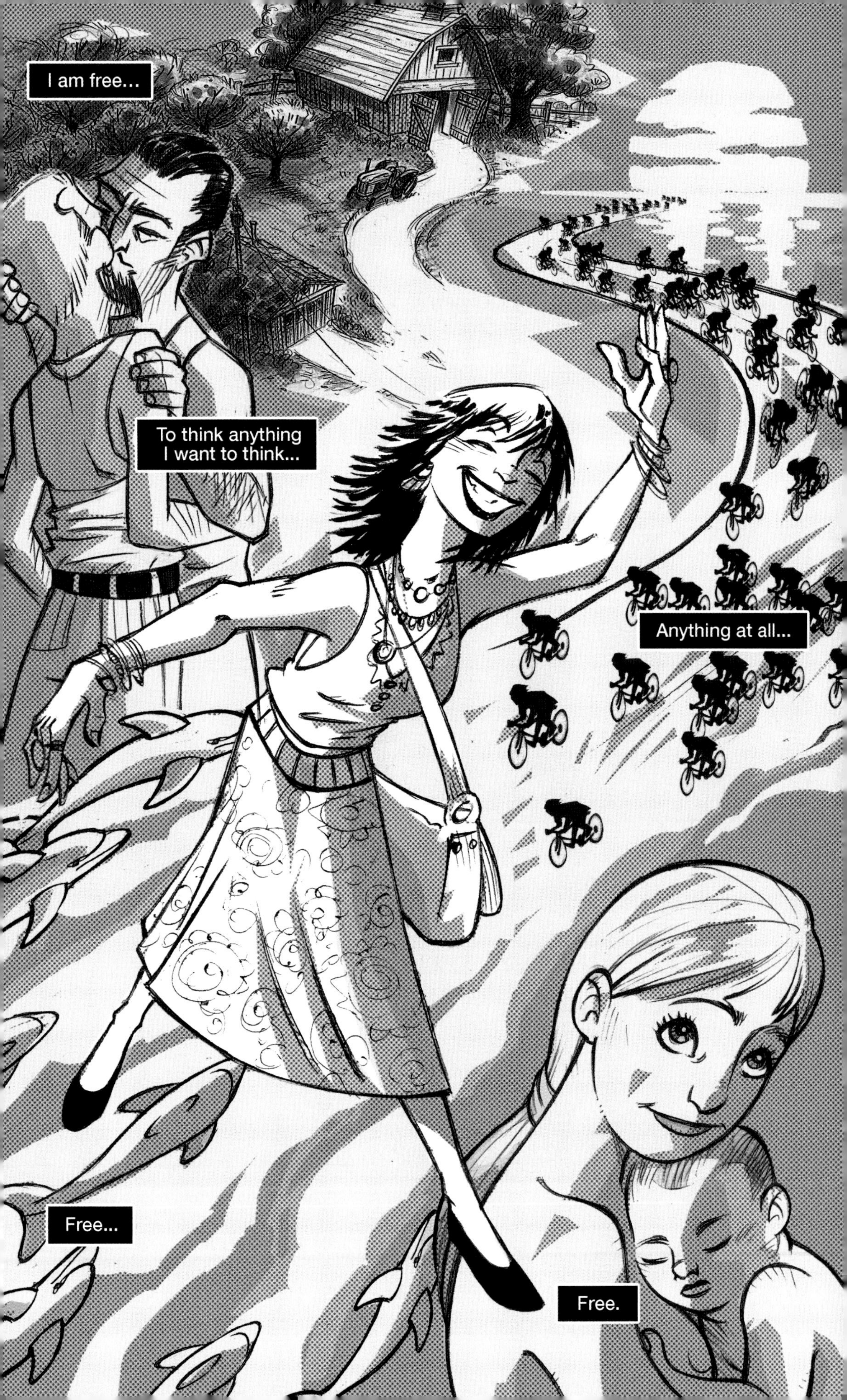
I am free...
To think anything
I want to think...
Anything at all...
Free...
Free.

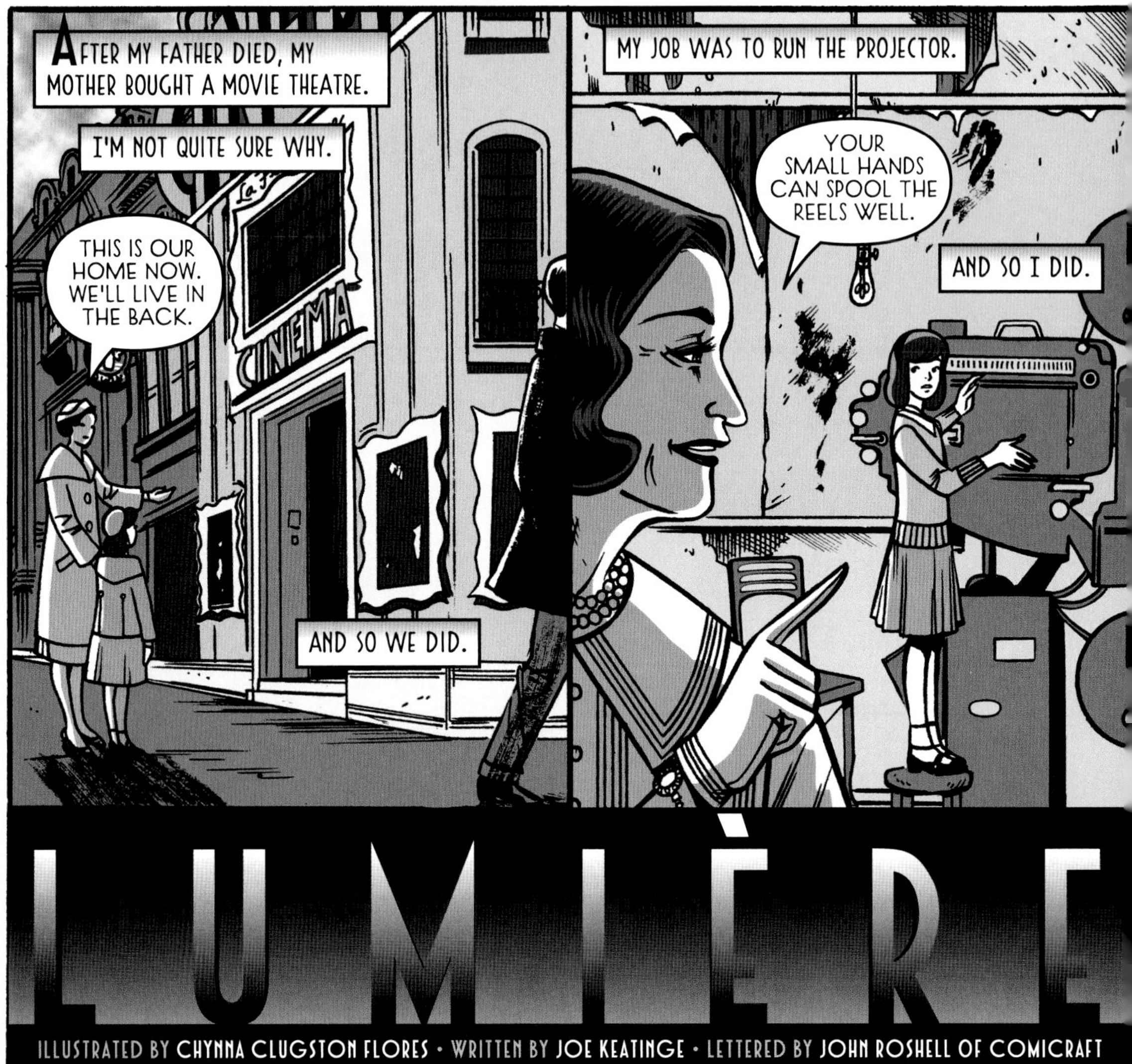
AFTER MY FATHER DIED, MY MOTHER BOUGHT A MOVIE THEATRE.
I'M NOT QUITE SURE WHY.
THIS IS OUR HOME NOW. WE'LL LIVE IN THE BACK.
AND SO WE DID.
CINEMA
MY JOB WAS TO RUN THE PROJECTOR.
YOUR SMALL HANDS CAN SPOOL THE REELS WELL.
AND SO I DID.

LUMIÈRE

ILLUSTRATED BY CHYNNA CLUGSTON FLORES • WRITTEN BY JOE KEATINGE • LETTERED BY JOHN ROSHELL OF COMICRAFT

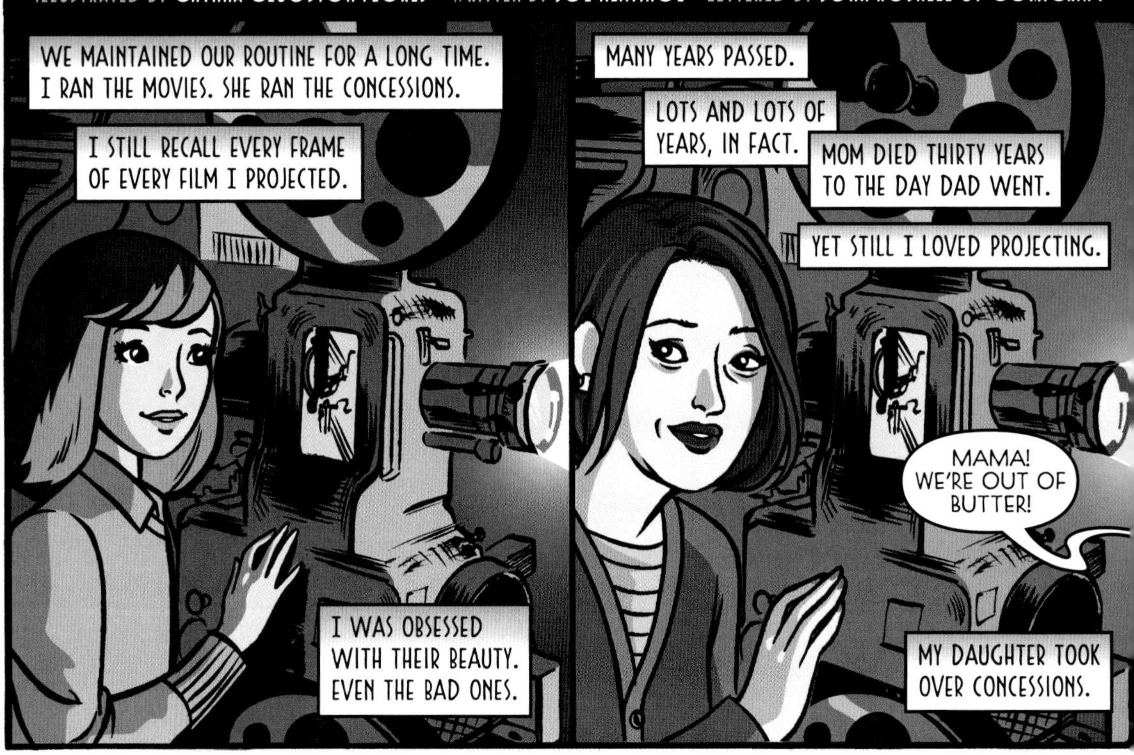
WE MAINTAINED OUR ROUTINE FOR A LONG TIME. I RAN THE MOVIES. SHE RAN THE CONCESSIONS.
I STILL RECALL EVERY FRAME OF EVERY FILM I PROJECTED.
I WAS OBSESSED WITH THEIR BEAUTY. EVEN THE BAD ONES.
MANY YEARS PASSED.
LOTS AND LOTS OF YEARS, IN FACT.
MOM DIED THIRTY YEARS TO THE DAY DAD WENT.
YET STILL I LOVED PROJECTING.
MAMA! WE'RE OUT OF BUTTER!
MY DAUGHTER TOOK OVER CONCESSIONS.

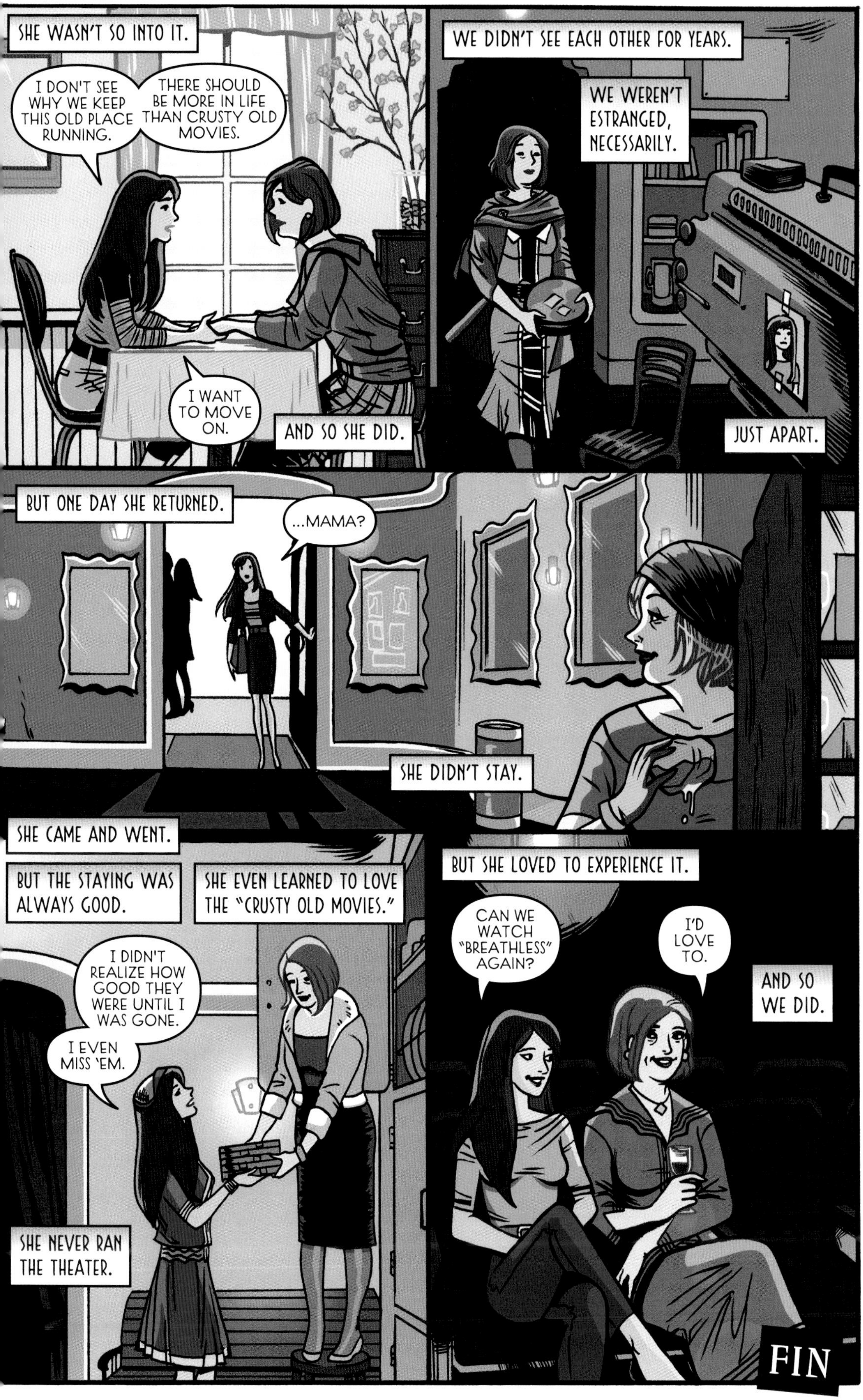
SHE WASN'T SO INTO IT.
I DON'T SEE WHY WE KEEP THIS OLD PLACE RUNNING.
THERE SHOULD BE MORE IN LIFE THAN CRUSTY OLD MOVIES.
I WANT TO MOVE ON.
AND SO SHE DID.
WE DIDN'T SEE EACH OTHER FOR YEARS.
WE WEREN'T ESTRANGED, NECESSARILY.
JUST APART.
BUT ONE DAY SHE RETURNED.
...MAMA?
SHE DIDN'T STAY.
SHE CAME AND WENT.
BUT THE STAYING WAS ALWAYS GOOD.
SHE EVEN LEARNED TO LOVE THE "CRUSTY OLD MOVIES."
I DIDN'T REALIZE HOW GOOD THEY WERE UNTIL I WAS GONE.
I EVEN MISS 'EM.
SHE NEVER RAN THE THEATER.
BUT SHE LOVED TO EXPERIENCE IT.
CAN WE WATCH "BREATHLESS" AGAIN?
I'D LOVE TO.
AND SO WE DID.
FIN

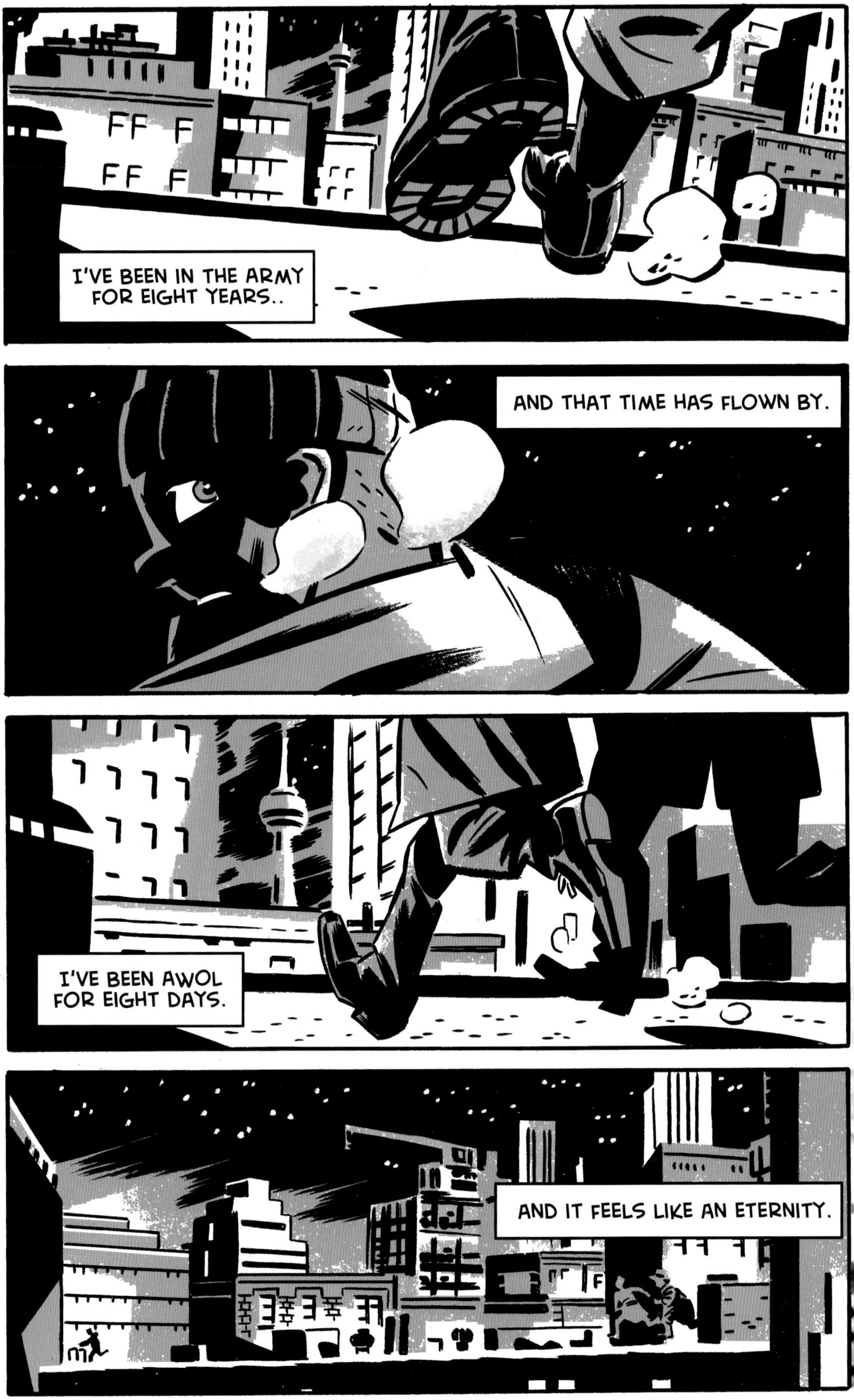
I'VE BEEN IN THE ARMY FOR EIGHT YEARS..
AND THAT TIME HAS FLOWN BY.
I'VE BEEN AWOL FOR EIGHT DAYS.
AND IT FEELS LIKE AN ETERNITY.

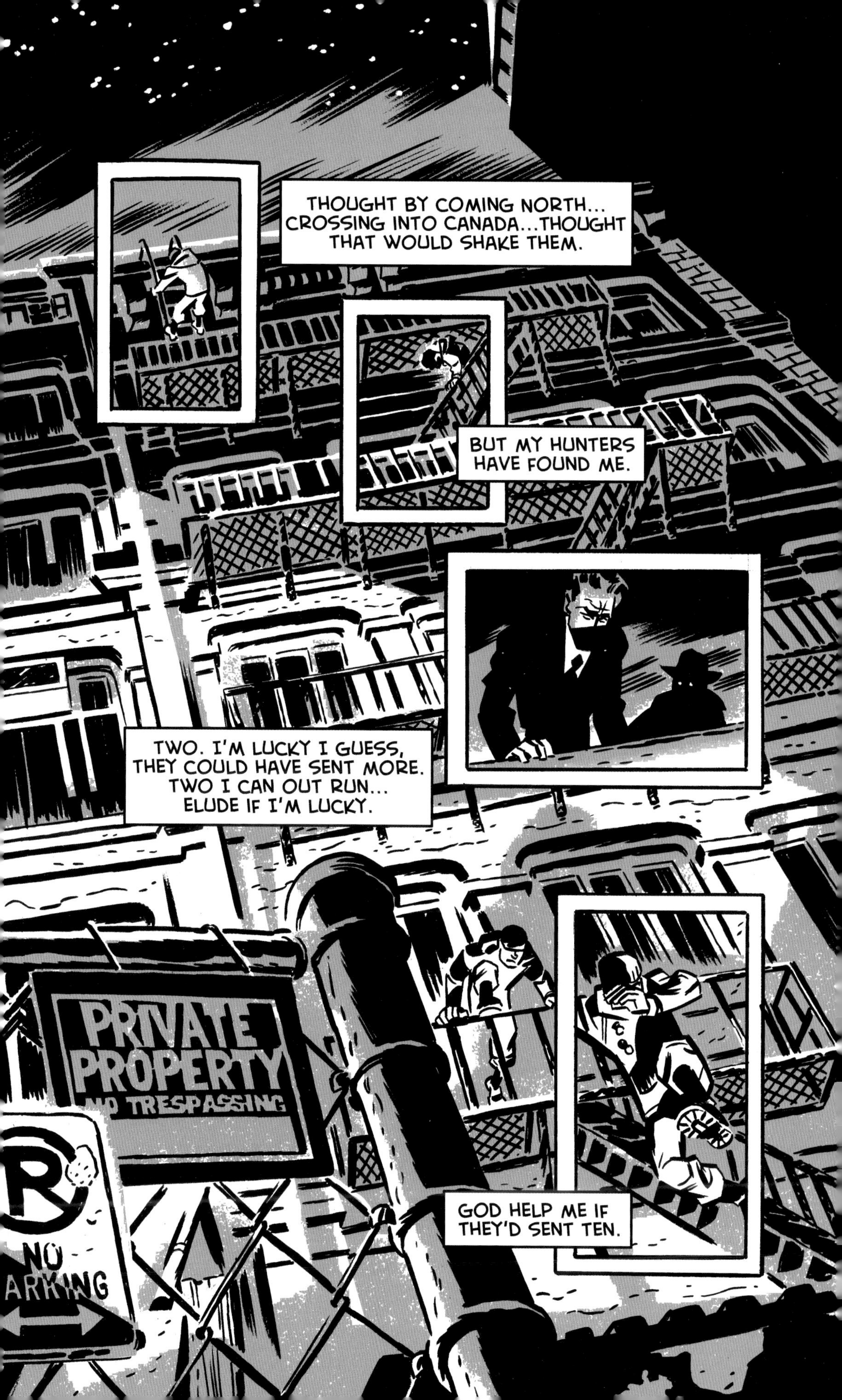
THOUGHT BY COMING NORTH... CROSSING INTO CANADA...THOUGHT THAT WOULD SHAKE THEM.
BUT MY HUNTERS HAVE FOUND ME.
TWO. I'M LUCKY I GUESS, THEY COULD HAVE SENT MORE. TWO I CAN OUT RUN... ELUDE IF I'M LUCKY.
PRIVATE PROPERTY
NO TRESPASSING
NO
ARKING
GOD HELP ME IF THEY'D SENT TEN.

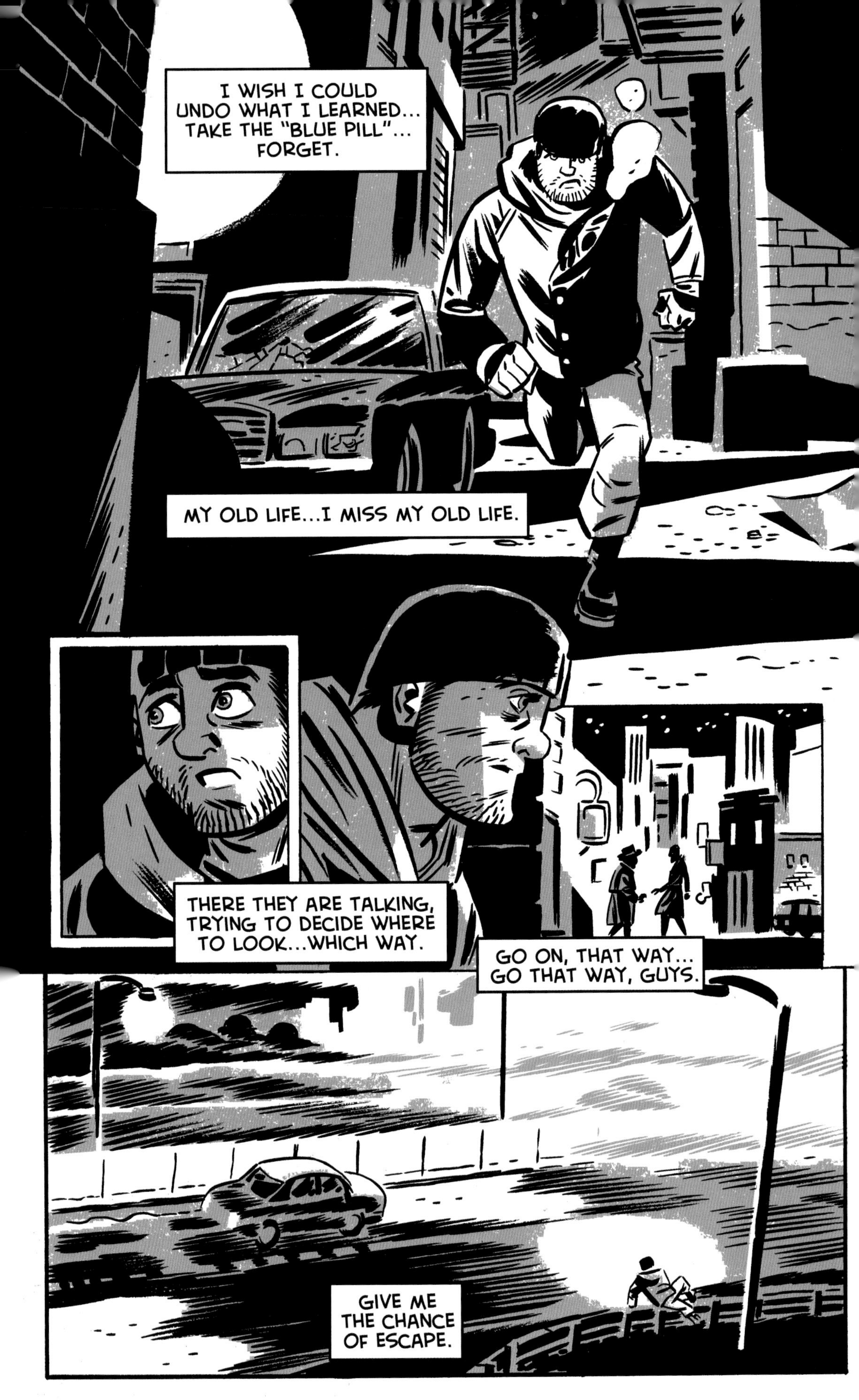
I WISH I COULD UNDO WHAT I LEARNED... TAKE THE "BLUE PILL"... FORGET.
MY OLD LIFE...I MISS MY OLD LIFE.
THERE THEY ARE TALKING, TRYING TO DECIDE WHERE TO LOOK...WHICH WAY.
GO ON, THAT WAY... GO THAT WAY, GUYS.
GIVE ME THE CHANCE OF ESCAPE.

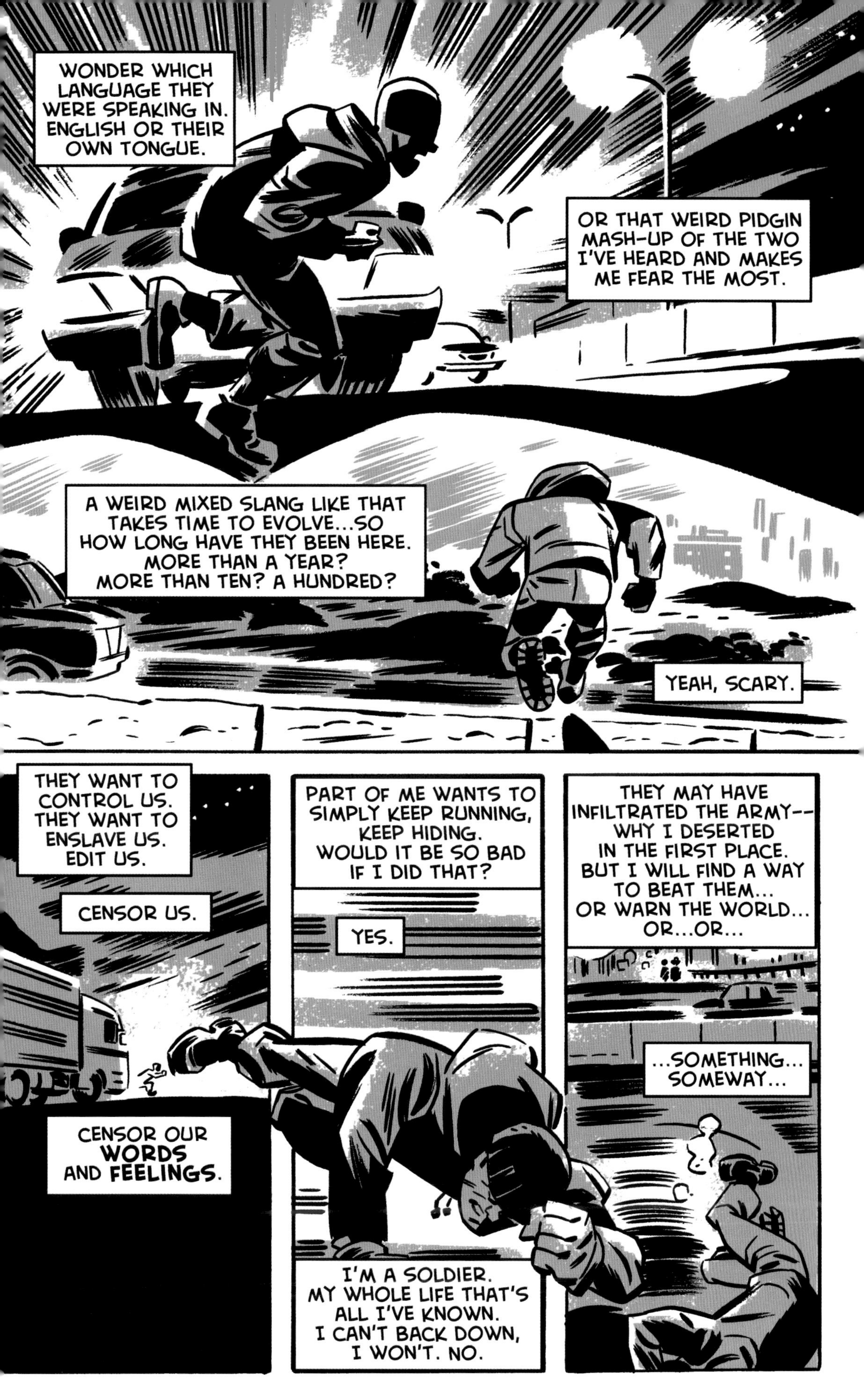

WONDER WHICH LANGUAGE THEY WERE SPEAKING IN. ENGLISH OR THEIR OWN TONGUE.
OR THAT WEIRD PIDGIN MASH-UP OF THE TWO I'VE HEARD AND MAKES ME FEAR THE MOST.
A WEIRD MIXED SLANG LIKE THAT TAKES TIME TO EVOLVE...SO HOW LONG HAVE THEY BEEN HERE. MORE THAN A YEAR? MORE THAN TEN? A HUNDRED?
YEAH, SCARY.
THEY WANT TO CONTROL US. THEY WANT TO ENSLAVE US. EDIT US.
CENSOR US.
CENSOR OUR **WORDS** AND **FEELINGS**.
PART OF ME WANTS TO SIMPLY KEEP RUNNING, KEEP HIDING. WOULD IT BE SO BAD IF I DID THAT?
YES.
I'M A SOLDIER. MY WHOLE LIFE THAT'S ALL I'VE KNOWN. I CAN'T BACK DOWN, I WON'T. NO.
THEY MAY HAVE INFILTRATED THE ARMY-- WHY I DESERTED IN THE FIRST PLACE. BUT I WILL FIND A WAY TO BEAT THEM... OR WARN THE WORLD... OR...OR...
...SOMETHING... SOMEWAY...

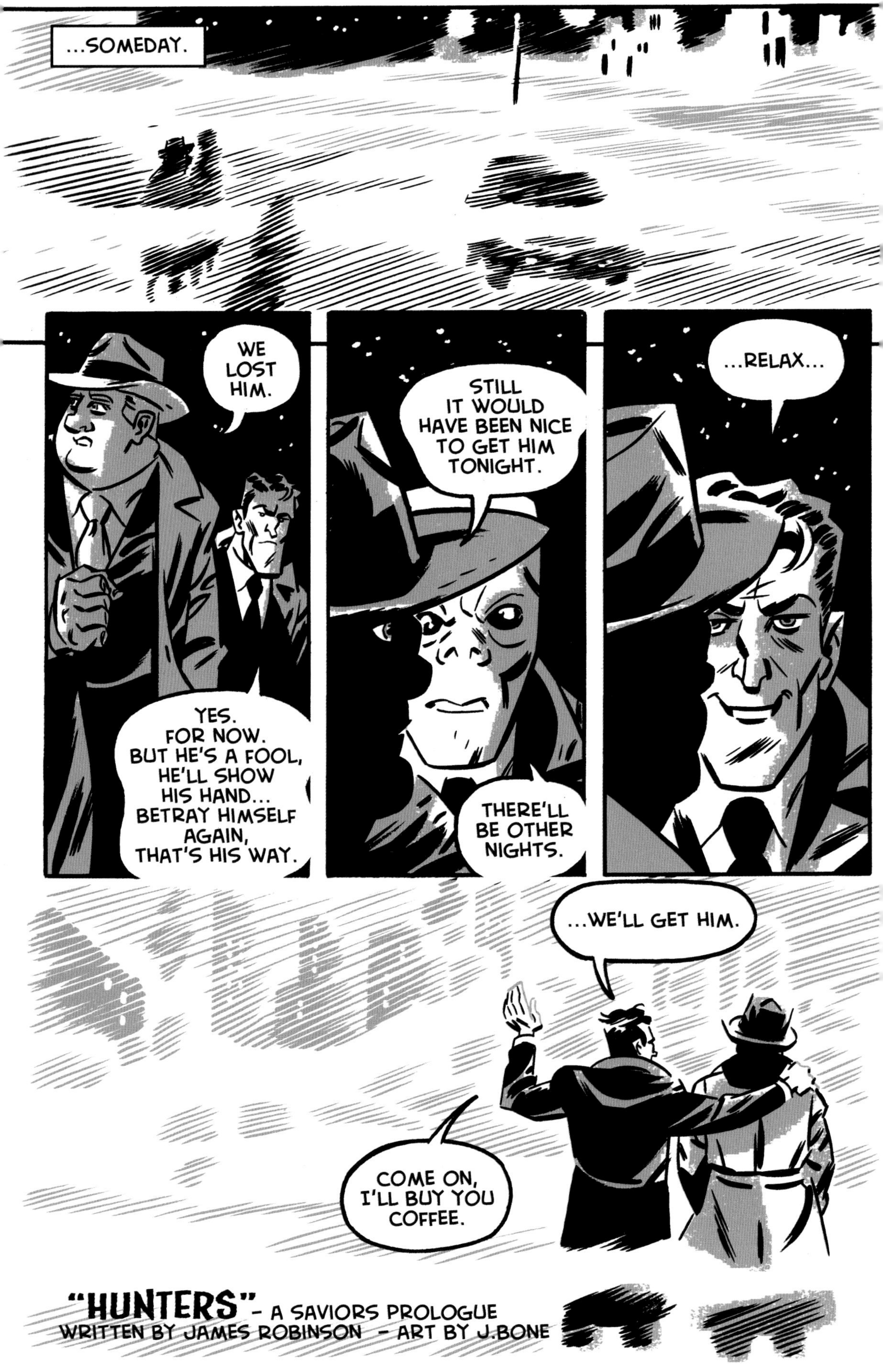
...SOMEDAY.
WE LOST HIM.
YES. FOR NOW. BUT HE'S A FOOL, HE'LL SHOW HIS HAND... BETRAY HIMSELF AGAIN, THAT'S HIS WAY.
STILL IT WOULD HAVE BEEN NICE TO GET HIM TONIGHT.
THERE'LL BE OTHER NIGHTS.
...RELAX...
...WE'LL GET HIM.
COME ON, I'LL BUY YOU COFFEE.
"HUNTERS" - A SAVIORS PROLOGUE
WRITTEN BY JAMES ROBINSON - ART BY J.BONE

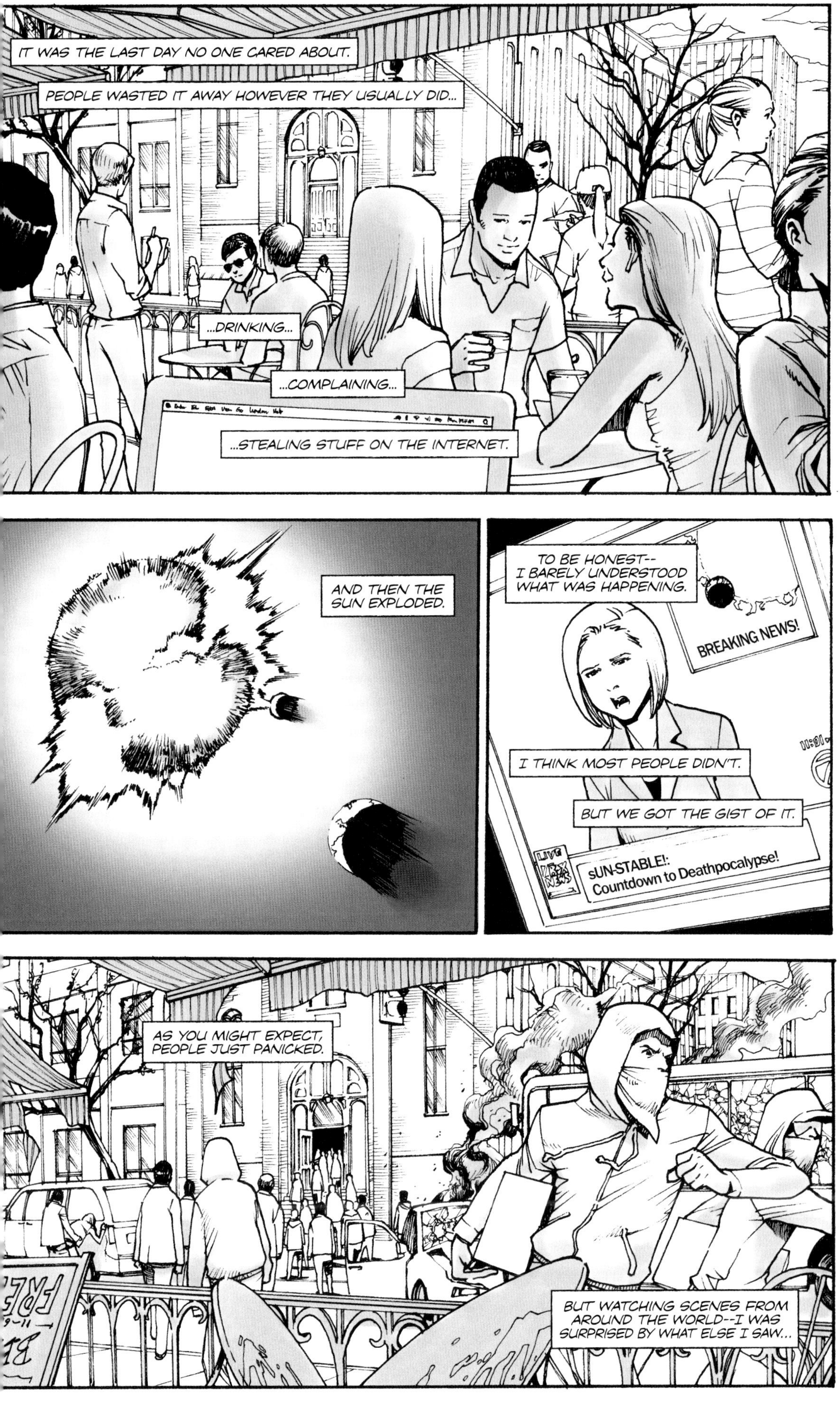
IT WAS THE LAST DAY NO ONE CARED ABOUT.
PEOPLE WASTED IT AWAY HOWEVER THEY USUALLY DID...
...DRINKING...
...COMPLAINING...
...STEALING STUFF ON THE INTERNET.
AND THEN THE SUN EXPLODED.
TO BE HONEST-- I BARELY UNDERSTOOD WHAT WAS HAPPENING.
BREAKING NEWS!
I THINK MOST PEOPLE DIDN'T.
BUT WE GOT THE GIST OF IT.
sUN-STABLE!: Countdown to Deathpocalypse!
AS YOU MIGHT EXPECT, PEOPLE JUST PANICKED.
BUT WATCHING SCENES FROM AROUND THE WORLD--I WAS SURPRISED BY WHAT ELSE I SAW...

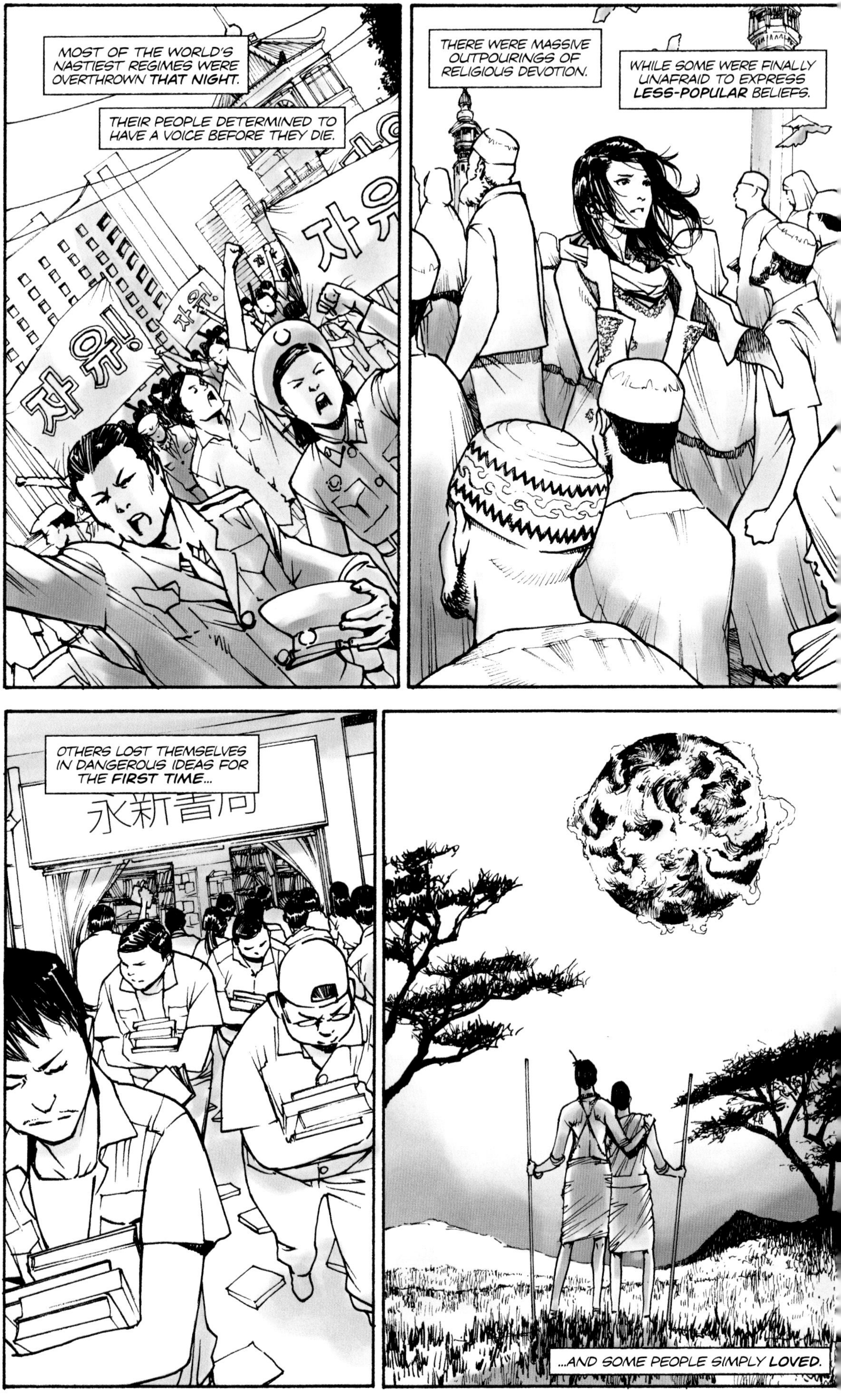
MOST OF THE WORLD'S NASTIEST REGIMES WERE OVERTHROWN THAT NIGHT.
THEIR PEOPLE DETERMINED TO HAVE A VOICE BEFORE THEY DIE.
자유!
자유!
자유
THERE WERE MASSIVE OUTPOURINGS OF RELIGIOUS DEVOTION.
WHILE SOME WERE FINALLY UNAFRAID TO EXPRESS LESS-POPULAR BELIEFS.
OTHERS LOST THEMSELVES IN DANGEROUS IDEAS FOR THE FIRST TIME...
永新書局
...AND SOME PEOPLE SIMPLY LOVED.

SEEING ALL THIS ON THE EVE OF THE END OF EVERYTHING...

...IT STRUCK ME FOR THE FIRST TIME.

JUST HOW MANY PEOPLE'S DYING WISHES...

...WERE FOR THE FREEDOMS I'D TAKEN FOR GRANTED.

SO WHEN THE END DID COME FOR ME...

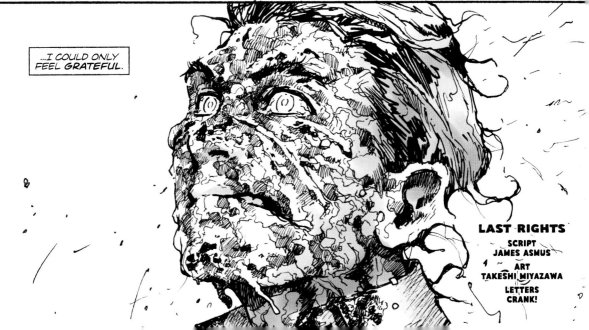

...I COULD ONLY FEEL GRATEFUL.

LAST RIGHTS

SCRIPT
JAMES ASMUS

ART
TAKESHI MIYAZAWA

LETTERS
CRANK!

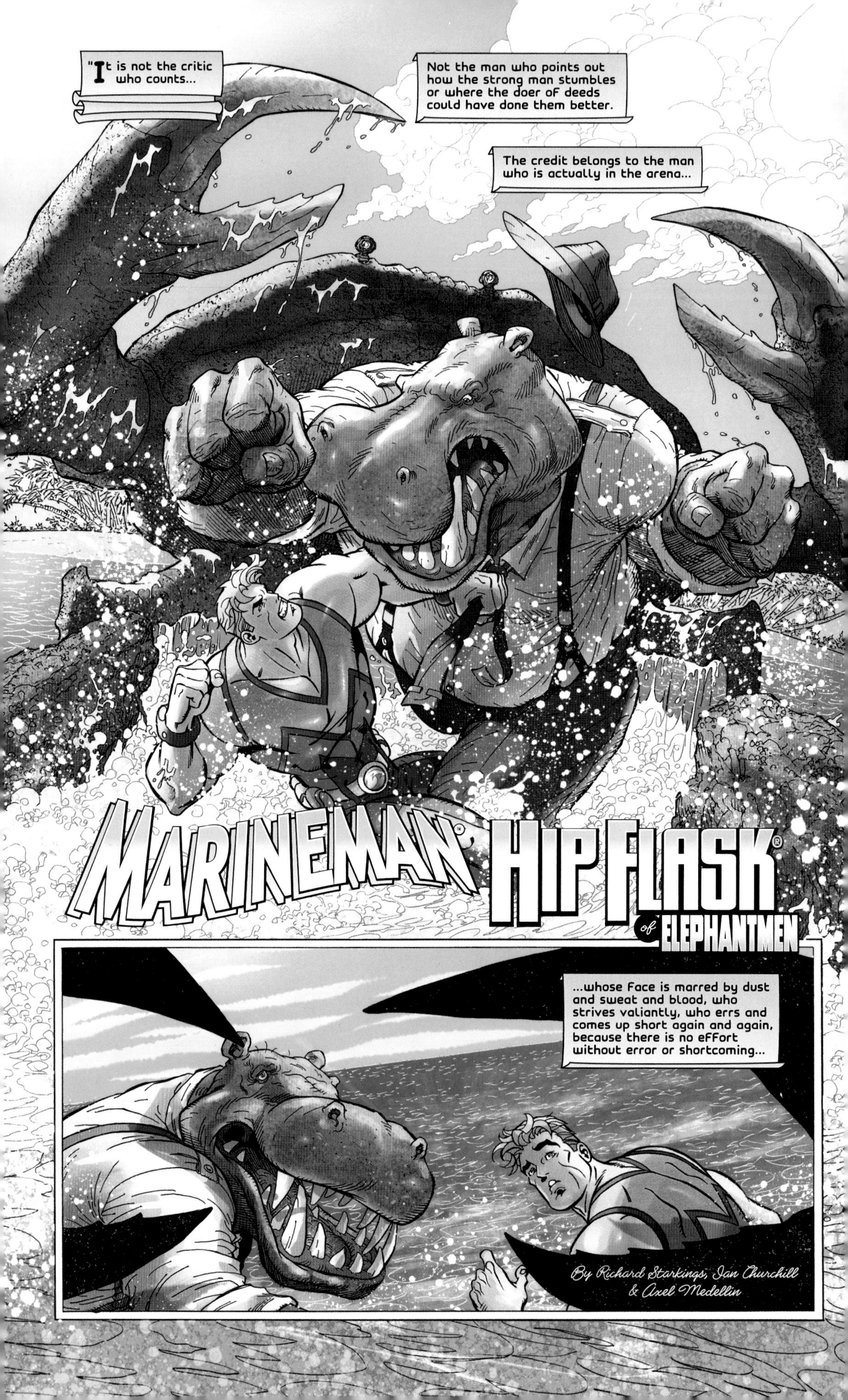
"It is not the critic who counts...
Not the man who points out how the strong man stumbles or where the doer of deeds could have done them better.
The credit belongs to the man who is actually in the arena...
MARINEMAN
HIP FLASK of ELEPHANTMEN
...whose face is marred by dust and sweat and blood, who strives valiantly, who errs and comes up short again and again, because there is no effort without error or shortcoming...
By Richard Starkings, Ian Churchill & Axel Medellin

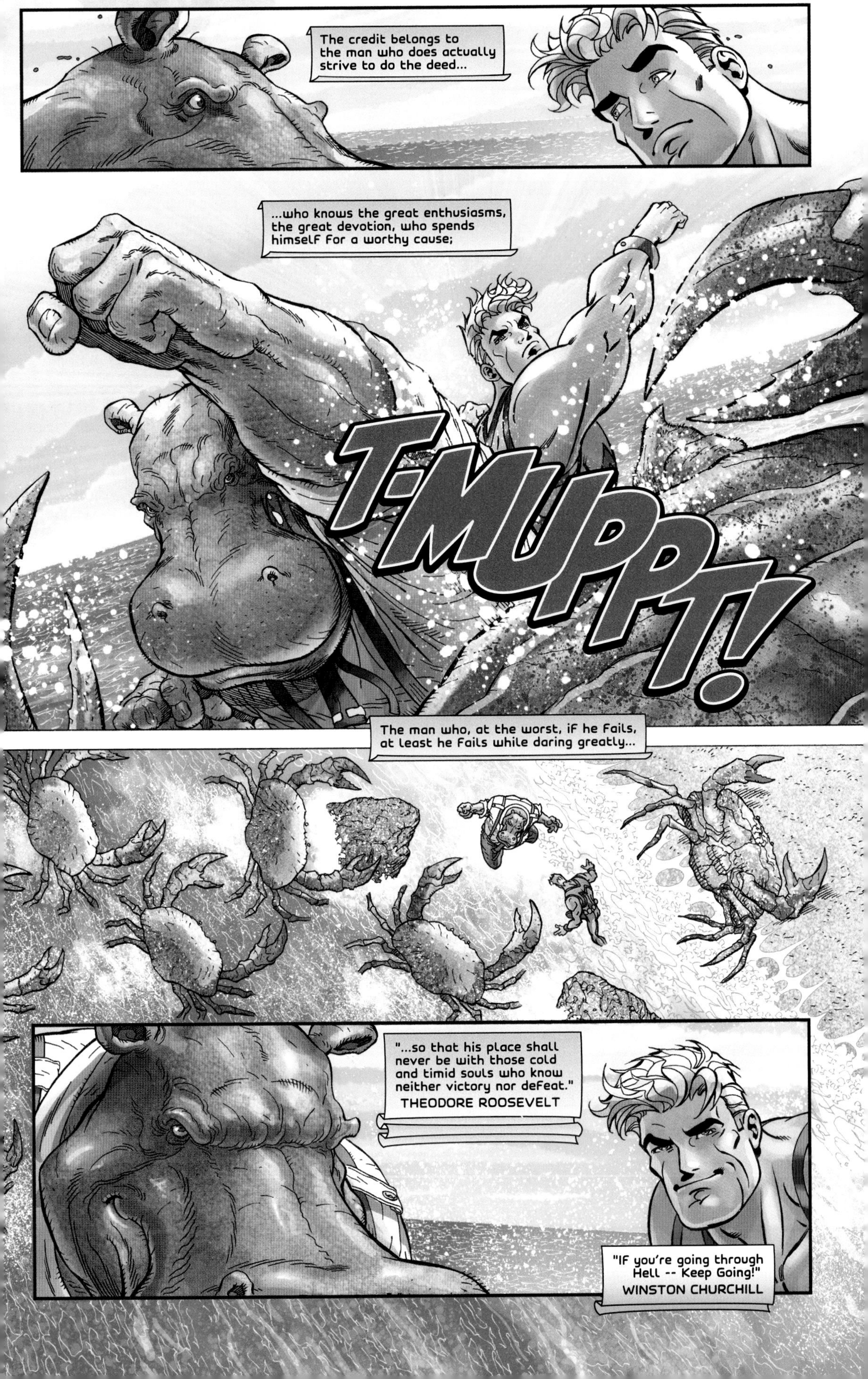
The credit belongs to the man who does actually strive to do the deed...
...who knows the great enthusiasms, the great devotion, who spends himself for a worthy cause;
T-MUPPT!
The man who, at the worst, if he fails, at least he fails while daring greatly...
"...so that his place shall never be with those cold and timid souls who know neither victory nor defeat."
THEODORE ROOSEVELT
"If you're going through Hell -- Keep Going!"
WINSTON CHURCHILL

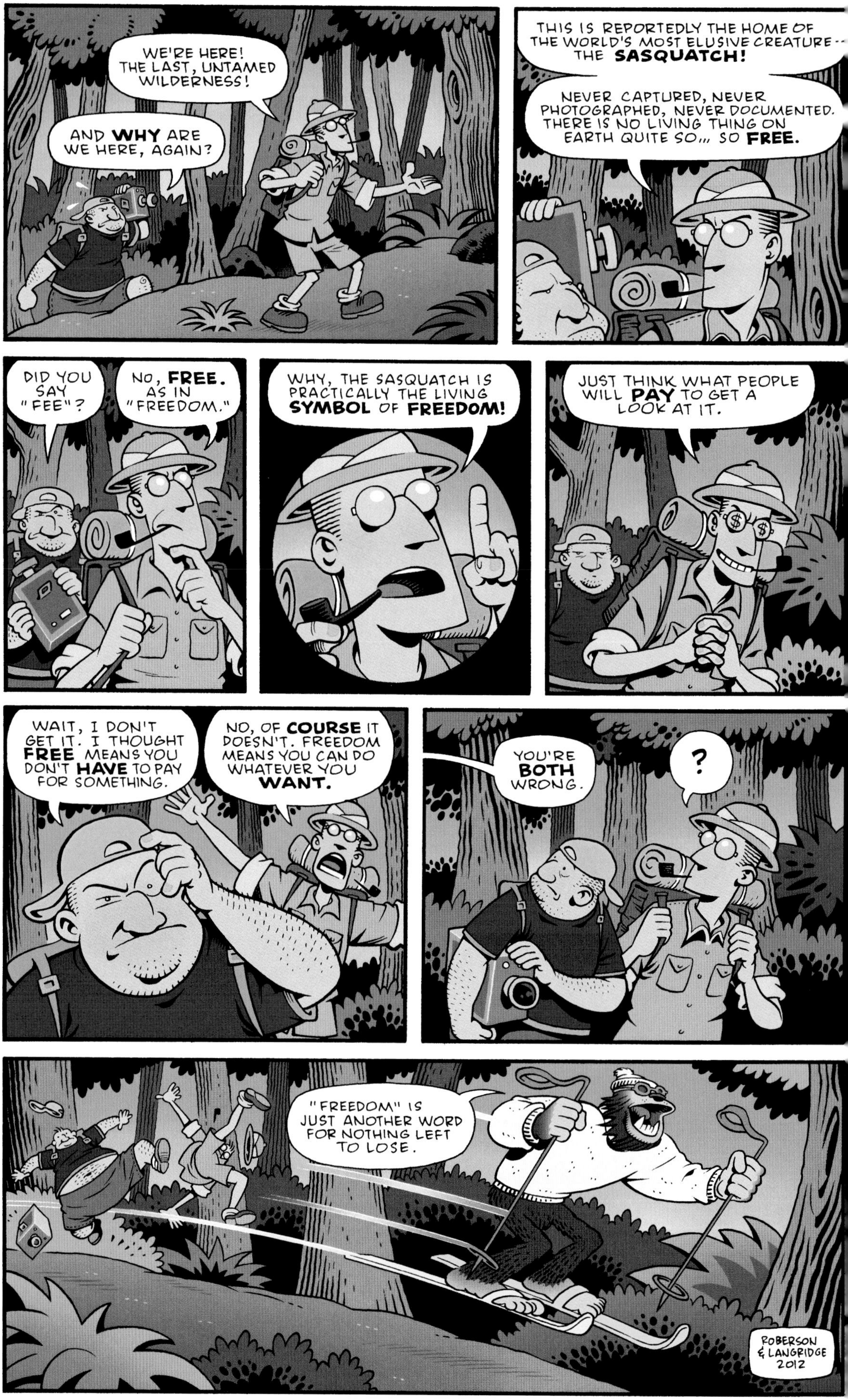
WE'RE HERE! THE LAST, UNTAMED WILDERNESS!
AND WHY ARE WE HERE, AGAIN?
THIS IS REPORTEDLY THE HOME OF THE WORLD'S MOST ELUSIVE CREATURE -- THE SASQUATCH!
NEVER CAPTURED, NEVER PHOTOGRAPHED, NEVER DOCUMENTED. THERE IS NO LIVING THING ON EARTH QUITE SO... SO FREE.
DID YOU SAY "FEE"?
NO, FREE. AS IN "FREEDOM."
WHY, THE SASQUATCH IS PRACTICALLY THE LIVING SYMBOL OF FREEDOM!
JUST THINK WHAT PEOPLE WILL PAY TO GET A LOOK AT IT.
WAIT, I DON'T GET IT. I THOUGHT FREE MEANS YOU DON'T HAVE TO PAY FOR SOMETHING.
NO, OF COURSE IT DOESN'T. FREEDOM MEANS YOU CAN DO WHATEVER YOU WANT.
YOU'RE BOTH WRONG.
?
"FREEDOM" IS JUST ANOTHER WORD FOR NOTHING LEFT TO LOSE.
ROBERSON & LANGRIDGE 2012

Common ComiConversation

by Chris Giarrusso

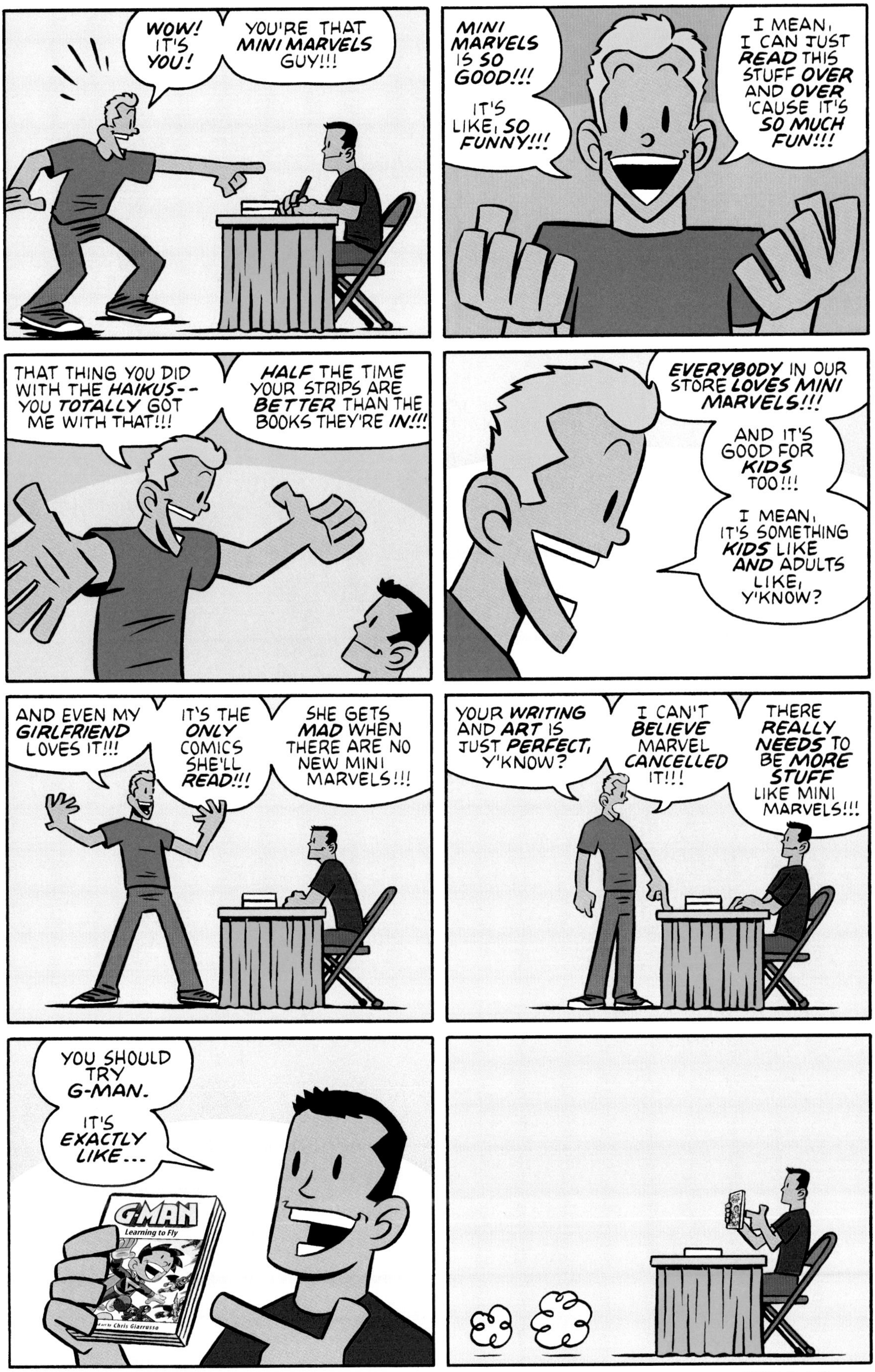

WOW! IT'S YOU!
YOU'RE THAT MINI MARVELS GUY!!!
MINI MARVELS IS SO GOOD!!!
IT'S LIKE, SO FUNNY!!!
I MEAN, I CAN JUST READ THIS STUFF OVER AND OVER 'CAUSE IT'S SO MUCH FUN!!!
THAT THING YOU DID WITH THE HAIKUS-- YOU TOTALLY GOT ME WITH THAT!!!
HALF THE TIME YOUR STRIPS ARE BETTER THAN THE BOOKS THEY'RE IN!!!
EVERYBODY IN OUR STORE LOVES MINI MARVELS!!!
AND IT'S GOOD FOR KIDS TOO!!!
I MEAN, IT'S SOMETHING KIDS LIKE AND ADULTS LIKE, Y'KNOW?
AND EVEN MY GIRLFRIEND LOVES IT!!!
IT'S THE ONLY COMICS SHE'LL READ!!!
SHE GETS MAD WHEN THERE ARE NO NEW MINI MARVELS!!!
YOUR WRITING AND ART IS JUST PERFECT, Y'KNOW?
I CAN'T BELIEVE MARVEL CANCELLED IT!!!
THERE REALLY NEEDS TO BE MORE STUFF LIKE MINI MARVELS!!!
YOU SHOULD TRY G-MAN.
IT'S EXACTLY LIKE...
G-MAN
Learning to Fly
Chris Giarrusso

WWW.CHRISGCOMICS.COM

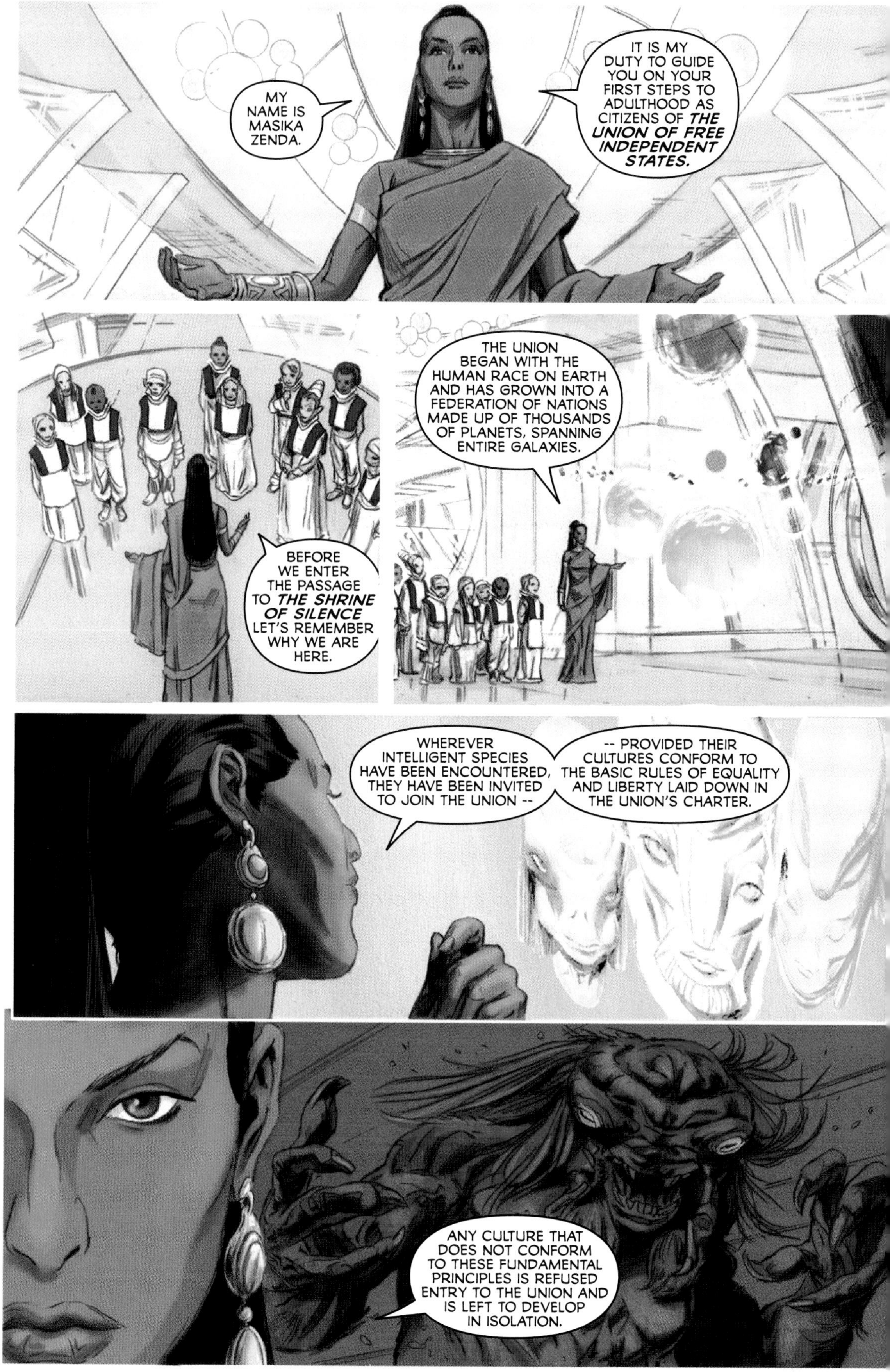

MY NAME IS MASIKA ZENDA.
IT IS MY DUTY TO GUIDE YOU ON YOUR FIRST STEPS TO ADULTHOOD AS CITIZENS OF ***THE UNION OF FREE INDEPENDENT STATES.***
BEFORE WE ENTER THE PASSAGE TO ***THE SHRINE OF SILENCE*** LET'S REMEMBER WHY WE ARE HERE.
THE UNION BEGAN WITH THE HUMAN RACE ON EARTH AND HAS GROWN INTO A FEDERATION OF NATIONS MADE UP OF THOUSANDS OF PLANETS, SPANNING ENTIRE GALAXIES.
WHEREVER INTELLIGENT SPECIES HAVE BEEN ENCOUNTERED, THEY HAVE BEEN INVITED TO JOIN THE UNION --
-- PROVIDED THEIR CULTURES CONFORM TO THE BASIC RULES OF EQUALITY AND LIBERTY LAID DOWN IN THE UNION'S CHARTER.
ANY CULTURE THAT DOES NOT CONFORM TO THESE FUNDAMENTAL PRINCIPLES IS REFUSED ENTRY TO THE UNION AND IS LEFT TO DEVELOP IN ISOLATION.

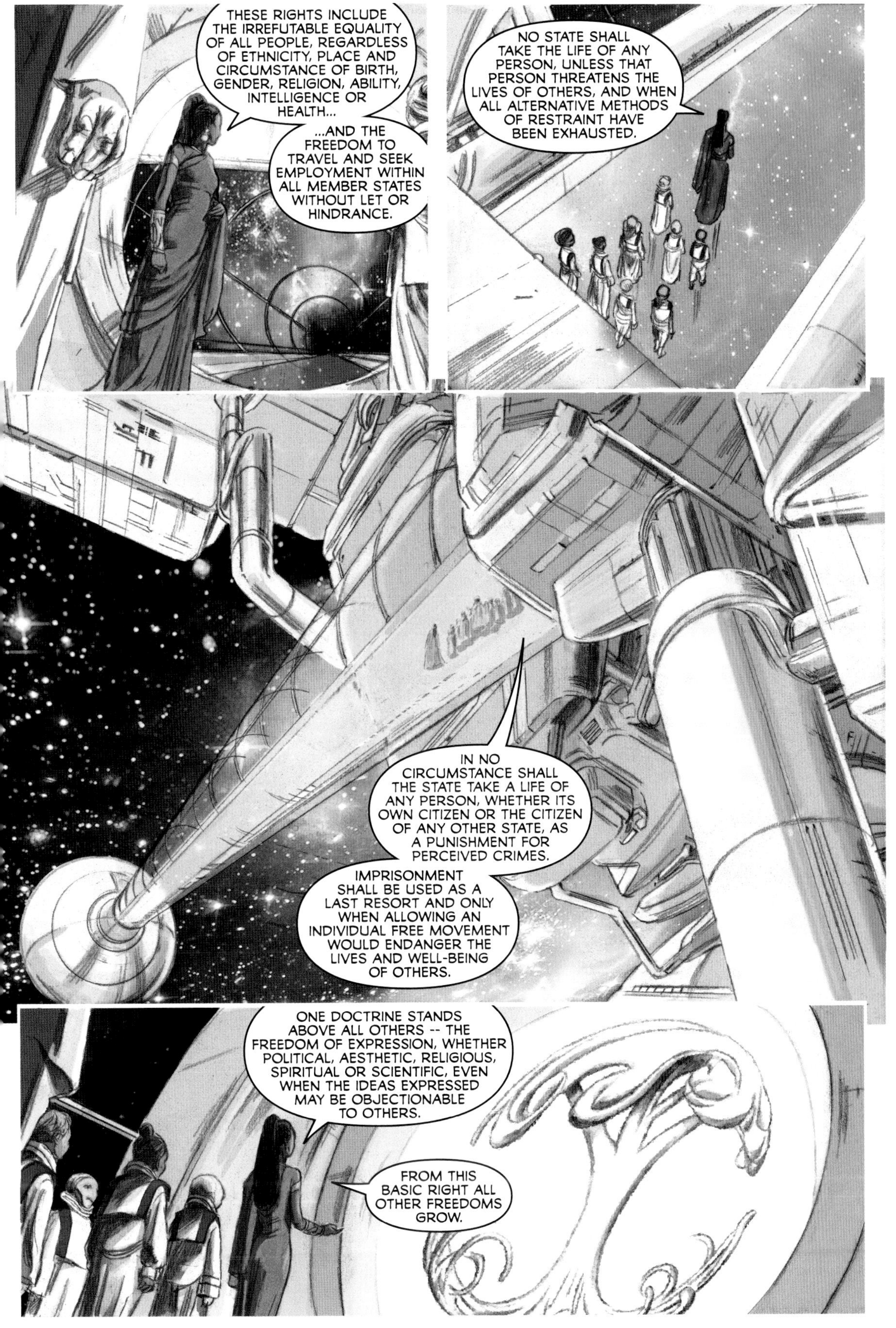
THESE RIGHTS INCLUDE THE IRREFUTABLE EQUALITY OF ALL PEOPLE, REGARDLESS OF ETHNICITY, PLACE AND CIRCUMSTANCE OF BIRTH, GENDER, RELIGION, ABILITY, INTELLIGENCE OR HEALTH...
...AND THE FREEDOM TO TRAVEL AND SEEK EMPLOYMENT WITHIN ALL MEMBER STATES WITHOUT LET OR HINDRANCE.
NO STATE SHALL TAKE THE LIFE OF ANY PERSON, UNLESS THAT PERSON THREATENS THE LIVES OF OTHERS, AND WHEN ALL ALTERNATIVE METHODS OF RESTRAINT HAVE BEEN EXHAUSTED.
IN NO CIRCUMSTANCE SHALL THE STATE TAKE A LIFE OF ANY PERSON, WHETHER ITS OWN CITIZEN OR THE CITIZEN OF ANY OTHER STATE, AS A PUNISHMENT FOR PERCEIVED CRIMES.
IMPRISONMENT SHALL BE USED AS A LAST RESORT AND ONLY WHEN ALLOWING AN INDIVIDUAL FREE MOVEMENT WOULD ENDANGER THE LIVES AND WELL-BEING OF OTHERS.
ONE DOCTRINE STANDS ABOVE ALL OTHERS -- THE FREEDOM OF EXPRESSION, WHETHER POLITICAL, AESTHETIC, RELIGIOUS, SPIRITUAL OR SCIENTIFIC, EVEN WHEN THE IDEAS EXPRESSED MAY BE OBJECTIONABLE TO OTHERS.
FROM THIS BASIC RIGHT ALL OTHER FREEDOMS GROW.

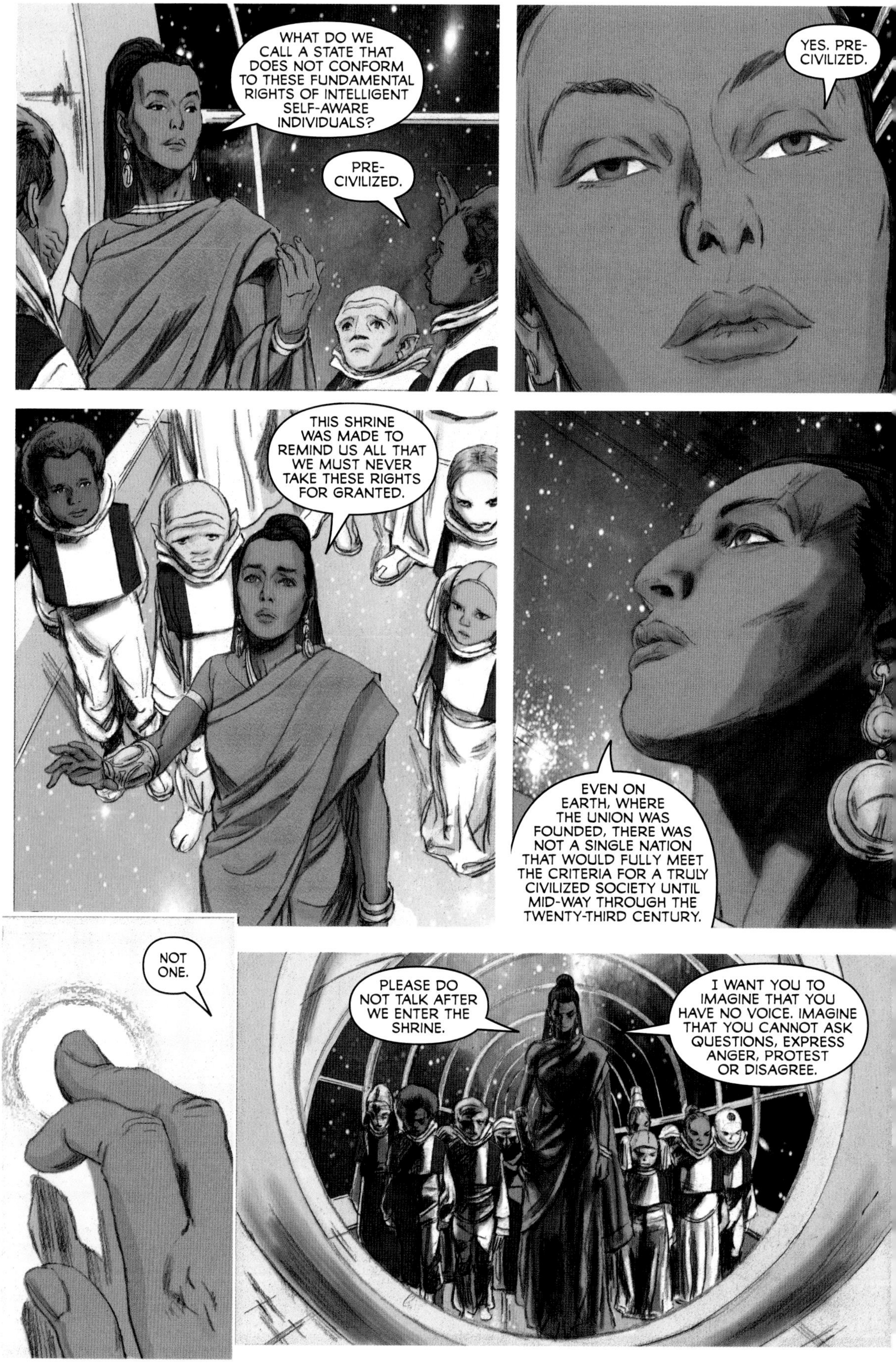
WHAT DO WE CALL A STATE THAT DOES NOT CONFORM TO THESE FUNDAMENTAL RIGHTS OF INTELLIGENT SELF-AWARE INDIVIDUALS?
PRE-CIVILIZED.
YES. PRE-CIVILIZED.
THIS SHRINE WAS MADE TO REMIND US ALL THAT WE MUST NEVER TAKE THESE RIGHTS FOR GRANTED.
EVEN ON EARTH, WHERE THE UNION WAS FOUNDED, THERE WAS NOT A SINGLE NATION THAT WOULD FULLY MEET THE CRITERIA FOR A TRULY CIVILIZED SOCIETY UNTIL MID-WAY THROUGH THE TWENTY-THIRD CENTURY.
NOT ONE.
PLEASE DO NOT TALK AFTER WE ENTER THE SHRINE.
I WANT YOU TO IMAGINE THAT YOU HAVE NO VOICE. IMAGINE THAT YOU CANNOT ASK QUESTIONS, EXPRESS ANGER, PROTEST OR DISAGREE.

IMAGINE SILENCE...

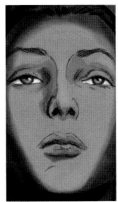

"ALL FREEDOMS GROW..."

FEATURING
MASIKA ZENDA
FROM

STORM DOGS

WORDS: DAVID HINE
ART: DOUG BRAITHWAITE
LETTERING: COMICRAFT

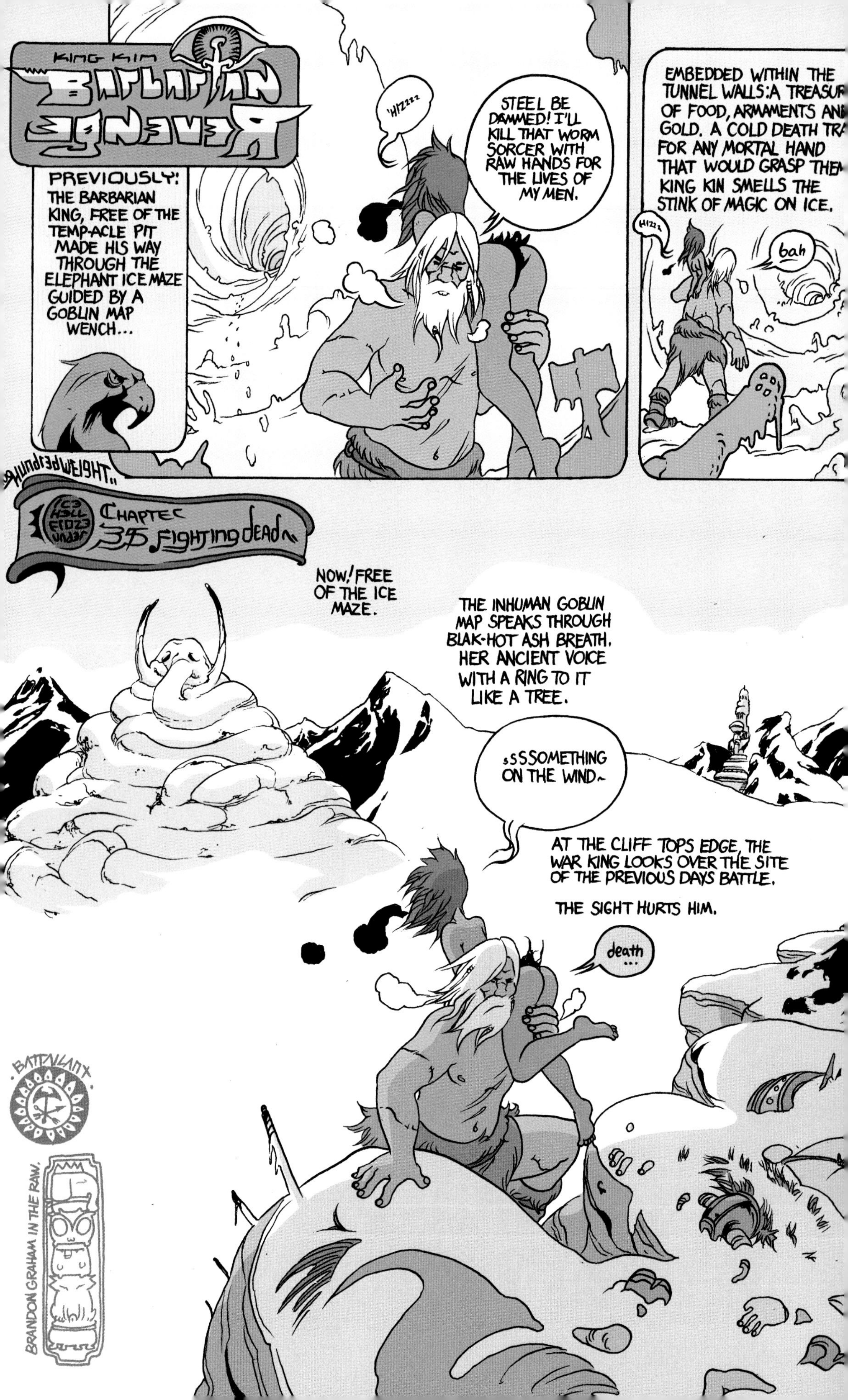

KING KIM
BARBARIAN REVENGE
PREVIOUSLY: THE BARBARIAN KING, FREE OF THE TEMP-ACLE PIT MADE HIS WAY THROUGH THE ELEPHANT ICE MAZE GUIDED BY A GOBLIN MAP WENCH...
'HIZzzz
STEEL BE DAMMED! I'LL KILL THAT WORM SORCER WITH RAW HANDS FOR THE LIVES OF MY MEN.
EMBEDDED WITHIN THE TUNNEL WALLS: A TREASUR OF FOOD, ARMAMENTS AN GOLD. A COLD DEATH TRA FOR ANY MORTAL HAND THAT WOULD GRASP THEM KING KIN SMELLS THE STINK OF MAGIC ON ICE.
HIZzz
bah
CHAPTER 35 FIGHTING DEAD
NOW! FREE OF THE ICE MAZE.
THE INHUMAN GOBLIN MAP SPEAKS THROUGH BLAK-HOT ASH BREATH. HER ANCIENT VOICE WITH A RING TO IT LIKE A TREE.
sSSSOMETHING ON THE WIND~
AT THE CLIFF TOPS EDGE, THE WAR KING LOOKS OVER THE SITE OF THE PREVIOUS DAYS BATTLE.
THE SIGHT HURTS HIM.
death...
BRANDON GRAHAM IN THE RAW.

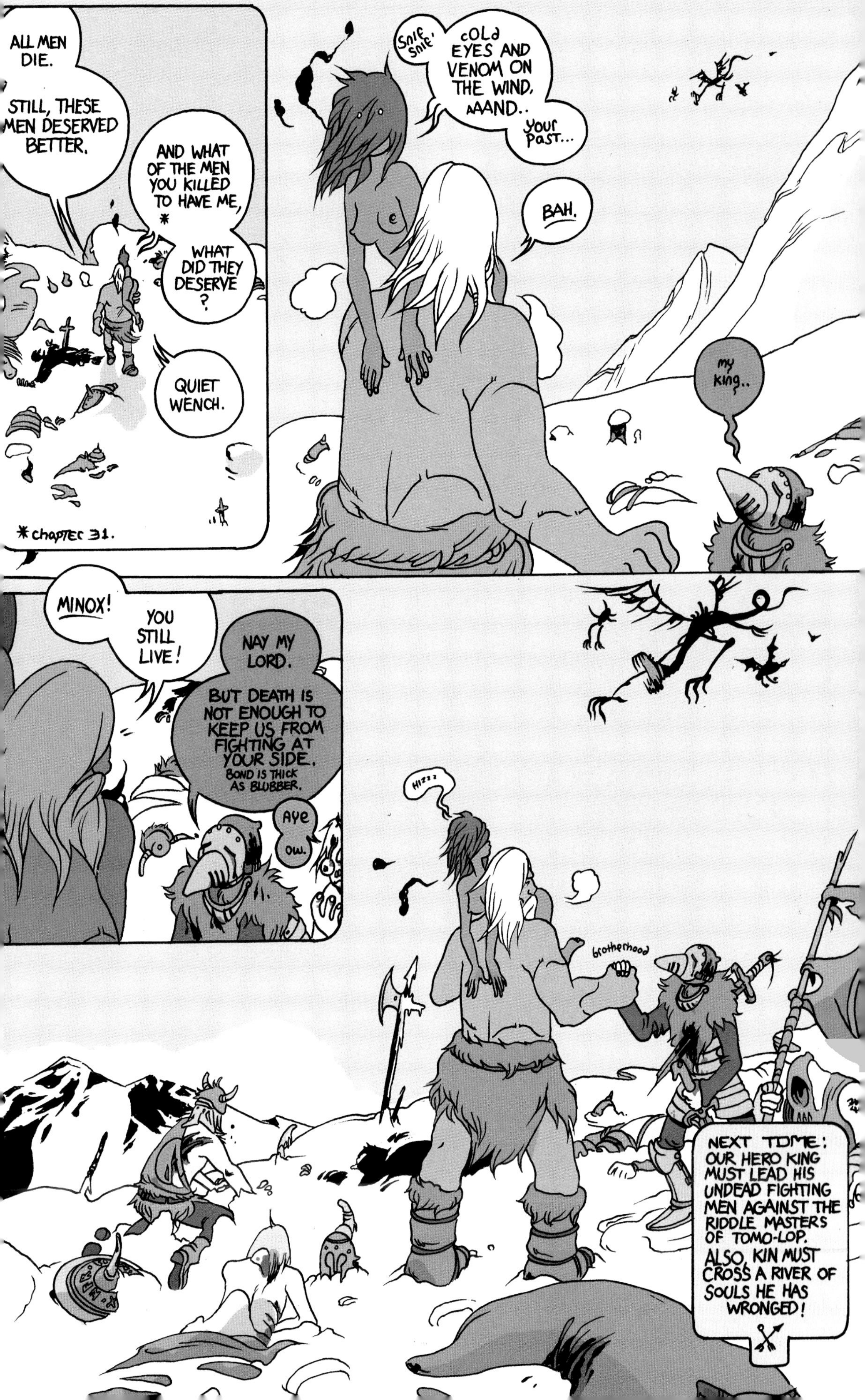
ALL MEN DIE.
STILL, THESE MEN DESERVED BETTER.
AND WHAT OF THE MEN YOU KILLED TO HAVE ME, *
WHAT DID THEY DESERVE ?
QUIET WENCH.
* chapter 31.
Snif snif
cOLd EYES AND VENOM ON THE WIND, AAAND..
your past...
BAH.
my king..
MINOX!
YOU STILL LIVE!
NAY MY LORD.
BUT DEATH IS NOT ENOUGH TO KEEP US FROM FIGHTING AT YOUR SIDE.
BOND IS THICK AS BLUBBER.
Aye
OW.
HIZZZ
brotherhood
NEXT TOME: OUR HERO KING MUST LEAD HIS UNDEAD FIGHTING MEN AGAINST THE RIDDLE MASTERS OF TOMO-LOP.
ALSO, KIN MUST CROSS A RIVER OF SOULS HE HAS WRONGED!

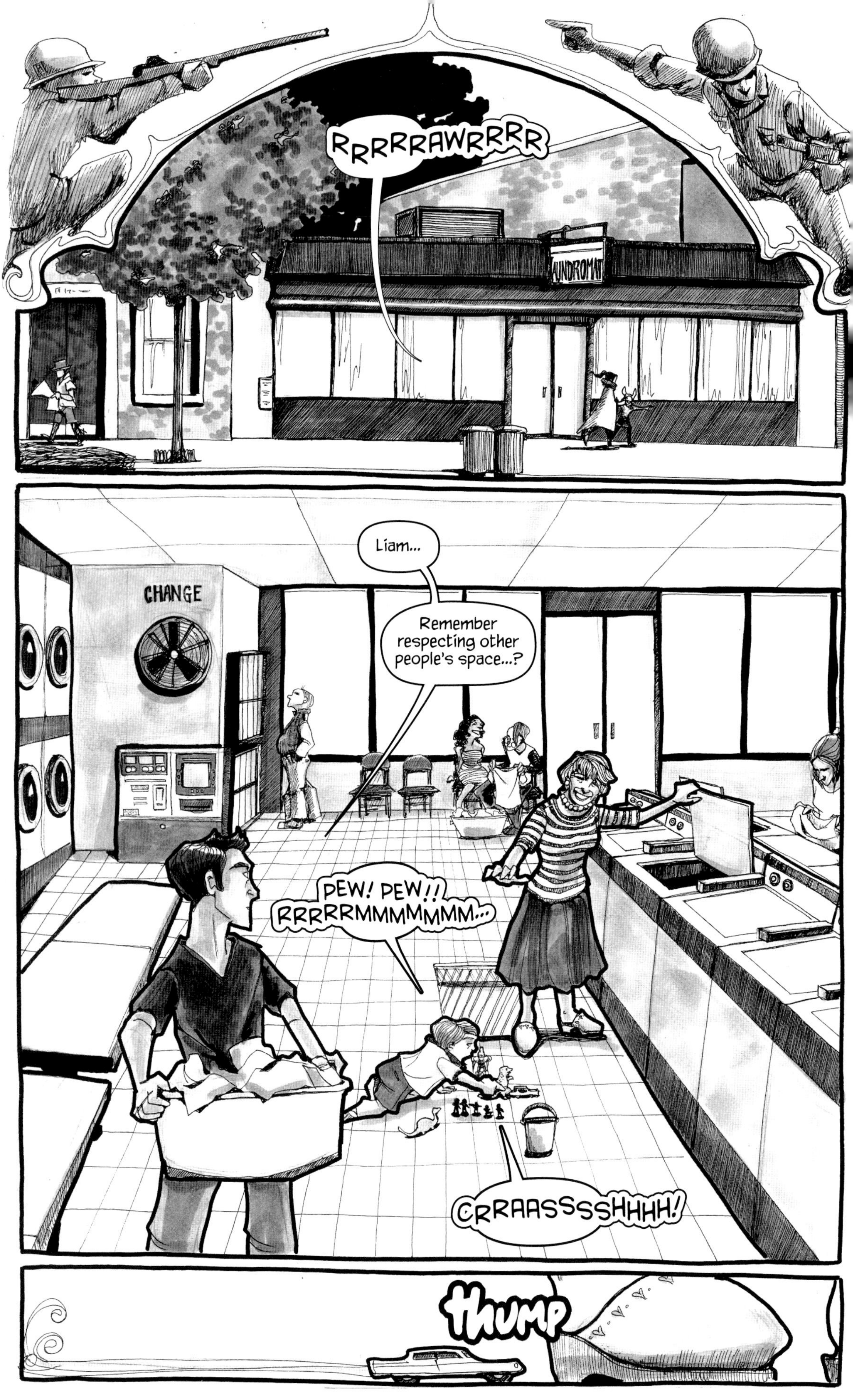
RRRRRAWRRRR
LAUNDROMAT
Liam...
Remember respecting other people's space...?
CHANGE
PEW! PEW!! RRRRRMMMMMMM...
CRRAASSSSHHHH!
thump

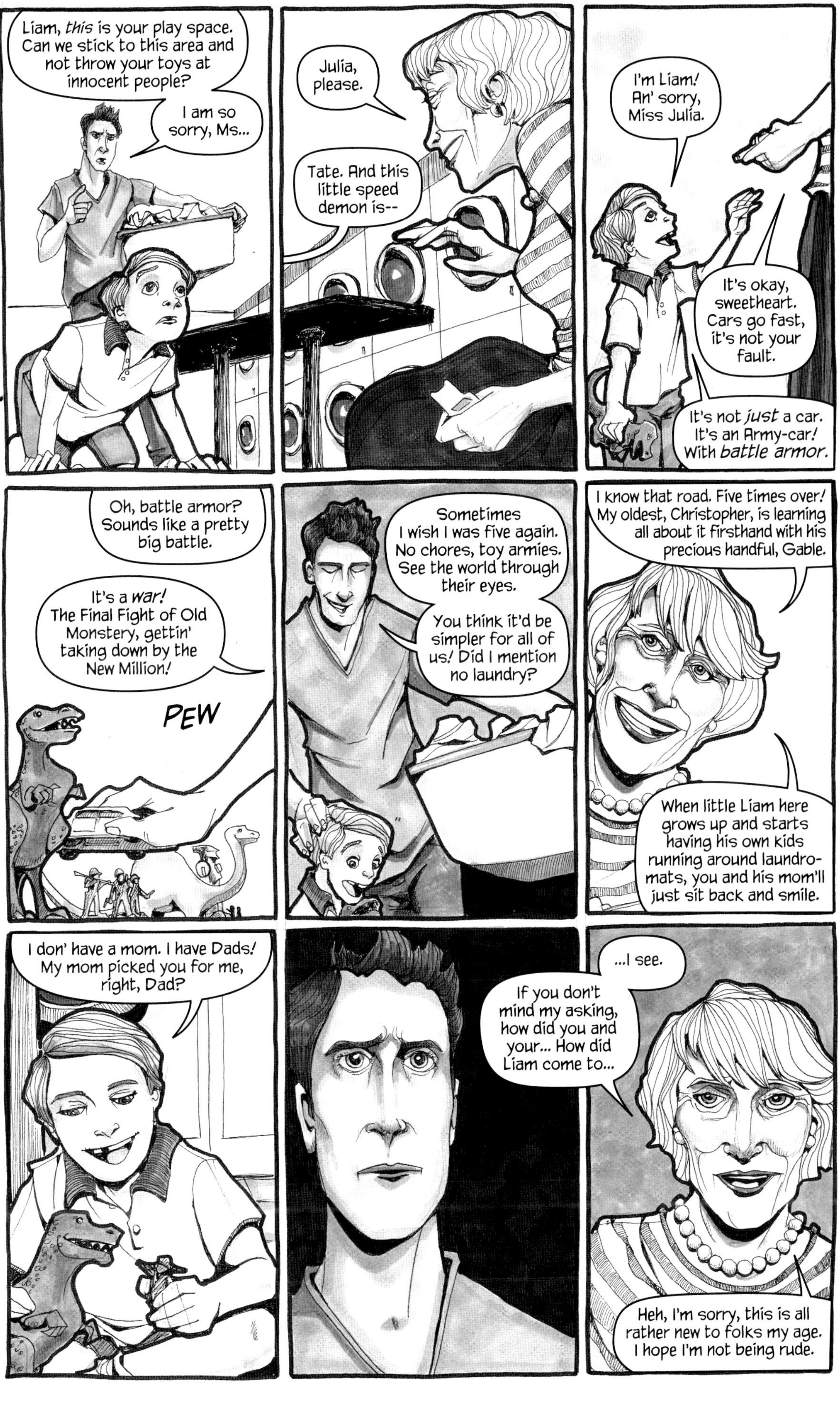

Liam, *this* is your play space. Can we stick to this area and not throw your toys at innocent people?
I am so sorry, Ms...
Julia, please.
Tate. And this little speed demon is--
I'm Liam! An' sorry, Miss Julia.
It's okay, sweetheart. Cars go fast, it's not your fault.
It's not *just* a car. It's an Army-car! With *battle armor*.
Oh, battle armor? Sounds like a pretty big battle.
It's a *war!* The Final Fight of Old Monstery, gettin' taking down by the New Million!
PEW
Sometimes I wish I was five again. No chores, toy armies. See the world through their eyes.
You think it'd be simpler for all of us! Did I mention no laundry?
I know that road. Five times over! My oldest, Christopher, is learning all about it firsthand with his precious handful, Gable.
When little Liam here grows up and starts having his own kids running around laundro-mats, you and his mom'll just sit back and smile.
I don' have a mom. I have Dads! My mom picked you for me, right, Dad?
...I see.
If you don't mind my asking, how did you and your... How did Liam come to...
Heh, I'm sorry, this is all rather new to folks my age. I hope I'm not being rude.

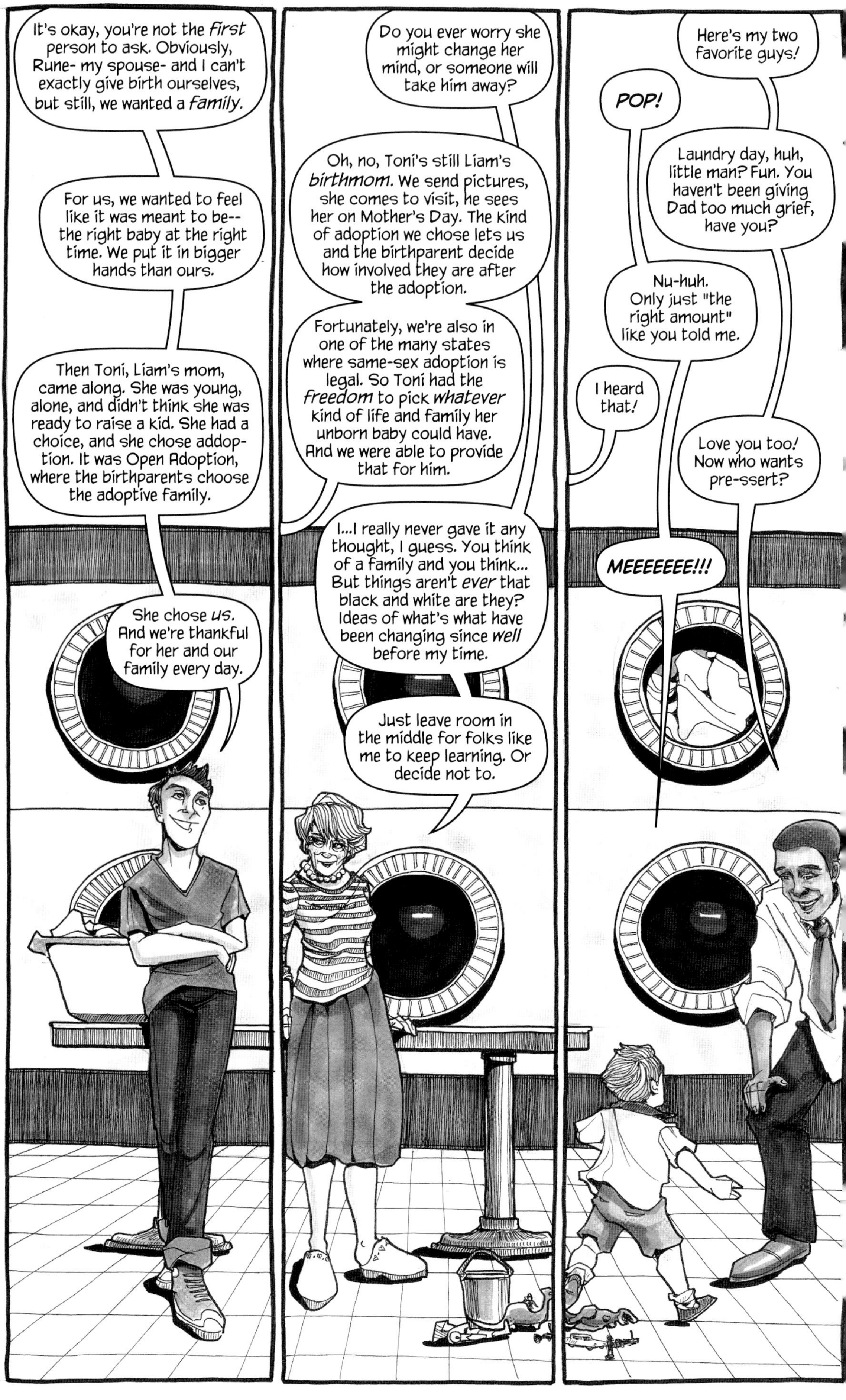

It's okay, you're not the *first* person to ask. Obviously, Rune- my spouse- and I can't exactly give birth ourselves, but still, we wanted a *family.*
For us, we wanted to feel like it was meant to be-- the right baby at the right time. We put it in bigger hands than ours.
Then Toni, Liam's mom, came along. She was young, alone, and didn't think she was ready to raise a kid. She had a choice, and she chose addop-tion. It was Open Adoption, where the birthparents choose the adoptive family.
She chose *us.* And we're thankful for her and our family every day.
Do you ever worry she might change her mind, or someone will take him away?
Oh, no, Toni's still Liam's *birthmom.* We send pictures, she comes to visit, he sees her on Mother's Day. The kind of adoption we chose lets us and the birthparent decide how involved they are after the adoption.
Fortunately, we're also in one of the many states where same-sex adoption is legal. So Toni had the *freedom* to pick *whatever* kind of life and family her unborn baby could have. And we were able to provide that for him.
I...I really never gave it any thought, I guess. You think of a family and you think... But things aren't *ever* that black and white are they? Ideas of what's what have been changing since *well* before my time.
Just leave room in the middle for folks like me to keep learning. Or decide not to.
Here's my two favorite guys!
POP!
Laundry day, huh, little man? Fun. You haven't been giving Dad too much grief, have you?
Nu-huh. Only just "the right amount" like you told me.
I heard that!
Love you too! Now who wants pre-ssert?
MEEEEEEE!!!

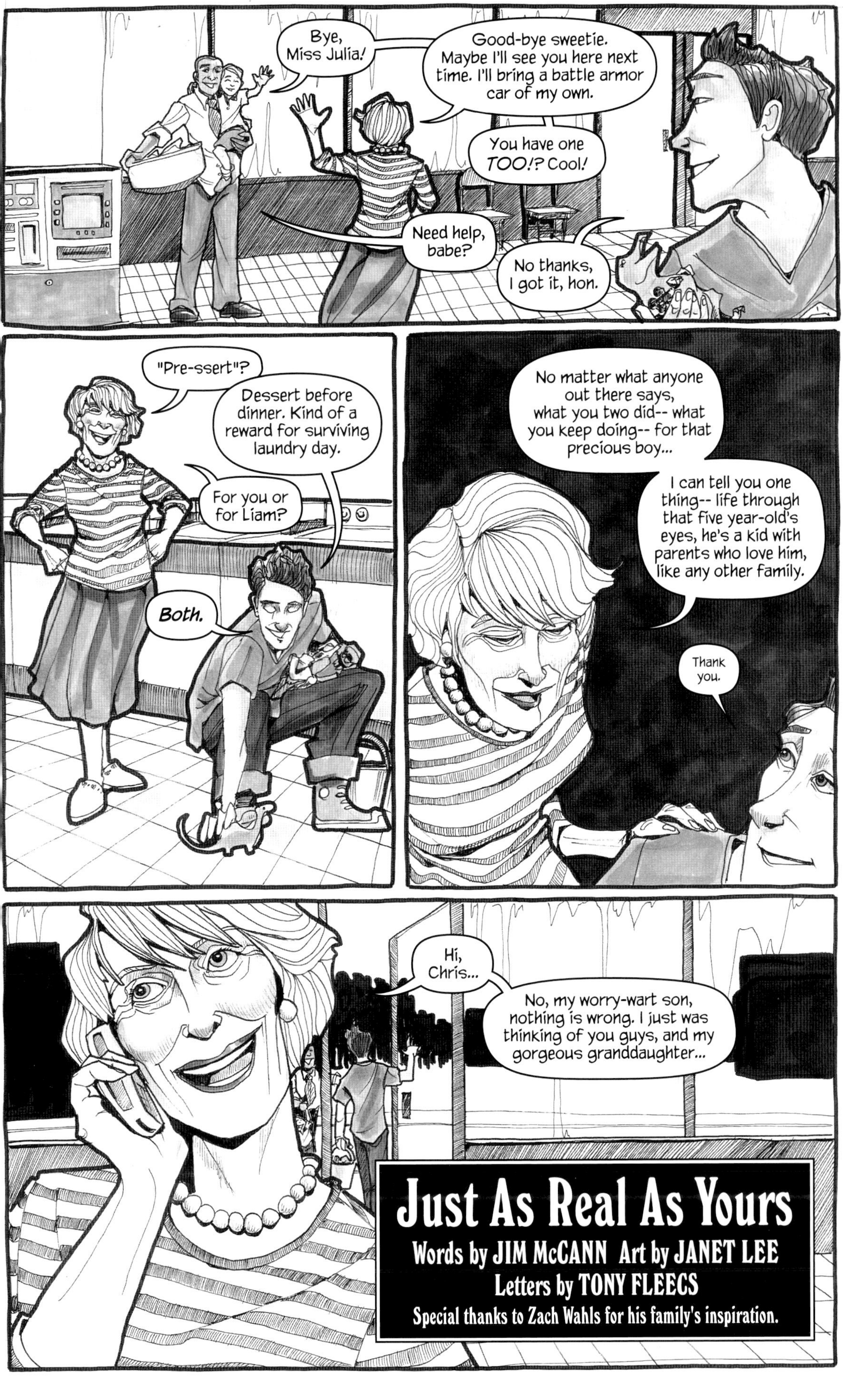
Bye, Miss Julia!
Good-bye sweetie. Maybe I'll see you here next time. I'll bring a battle armor car of my own.
You have one TOO!? Cool!
Need help, babe?
No thanks, I got it, hon.
"Pre-ssert"?
Dessert before dinner. Kind of a reward for surviving laundry day.
For you or for Liam?
Both.
No matter what anyone out there says, what you two did-- what you keep doing-- for that precious boy...
I can tell you one thing-- life through that five year-old's eyes, he's a kid with parents who love him, like any other family.
Thank you.
Hi, Chris...
No, my worry-wart son, nothing is wrong. I just was thinking of you guys, and my gorgeous granddaughter...
Just As Real As Yours
Words by JIM McCANN Art by JANET LEE
Letters by TONY FLEECS
Special thanks to Zach Wahls for his family's inspiration.

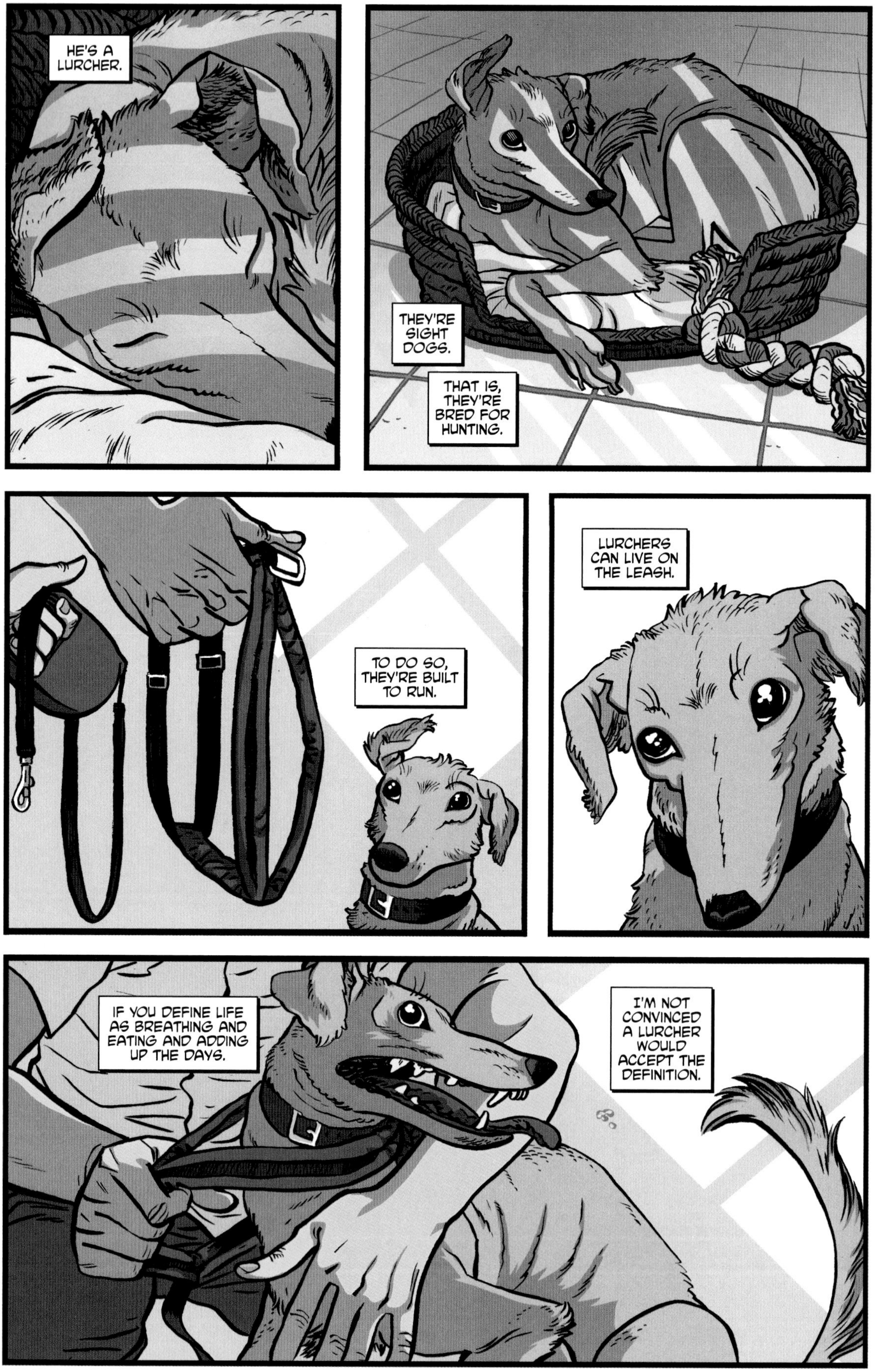
HE'S A LURCHER.
THEY'RE SIGHT DOGS.
THAT IS, THEY'RE BRED FOR HUNTING.
TO DO SO, THEY'RE BUILT TO RUN.
LURCHERS CAN LIVE ON THE LEASH.
IF YOU DEFINE LIFE AS BREATHING AND EATING AND ADDING UP THE DAYS.
I'M NOT CONVINCED A LURCHER WOULD ACCEPT THE DEFINITION.

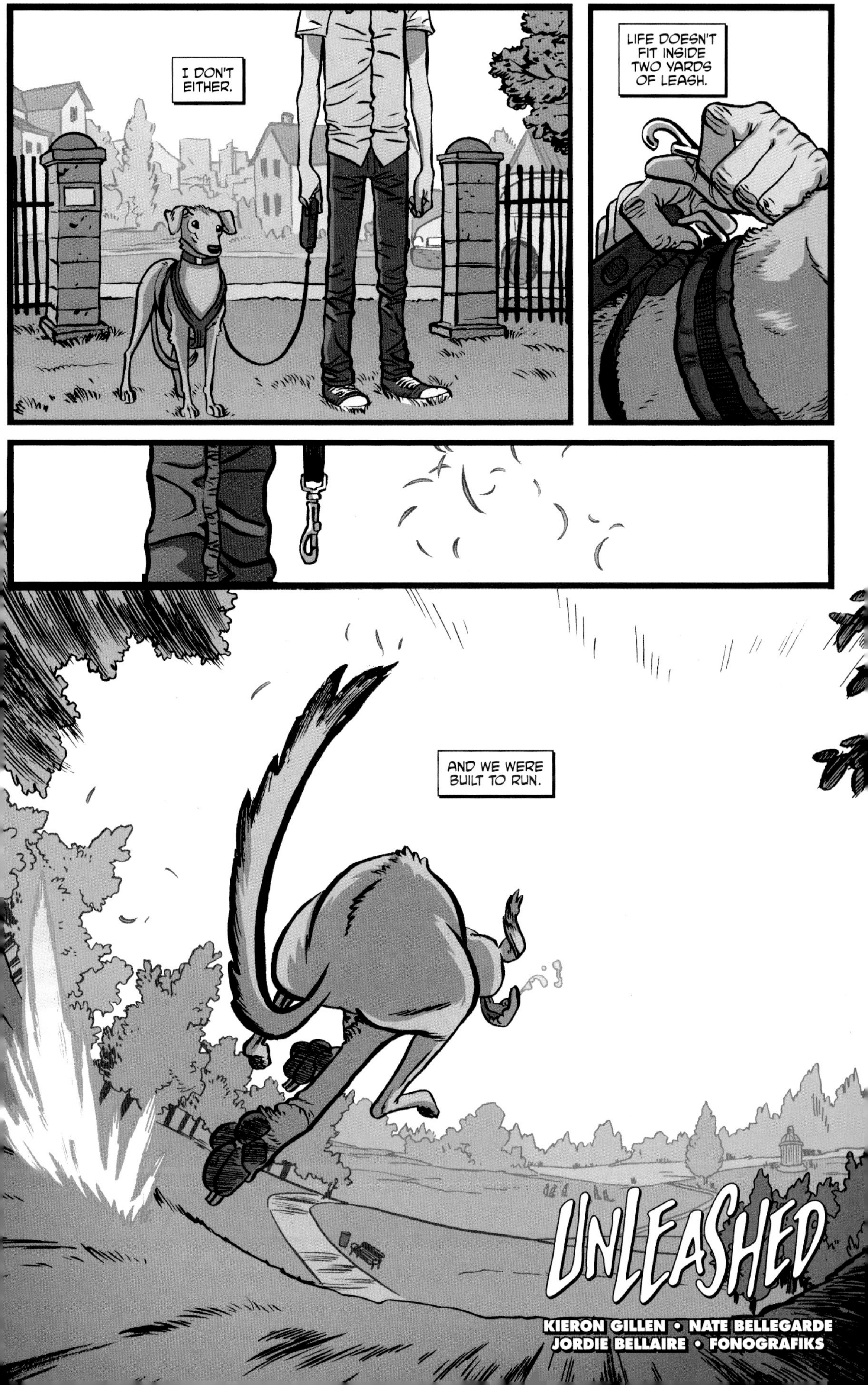
I DON'T EITHER.
LIFE DOESN'T FIT INSIDE TWO YARDS OF LEASH.
AND WE WERE BUILT TO RUN.
UNLEASHED
KIERON GILLEN • NATE BELLEGARDE
JORDIE BELLAIRE • FONOGRAFIKS

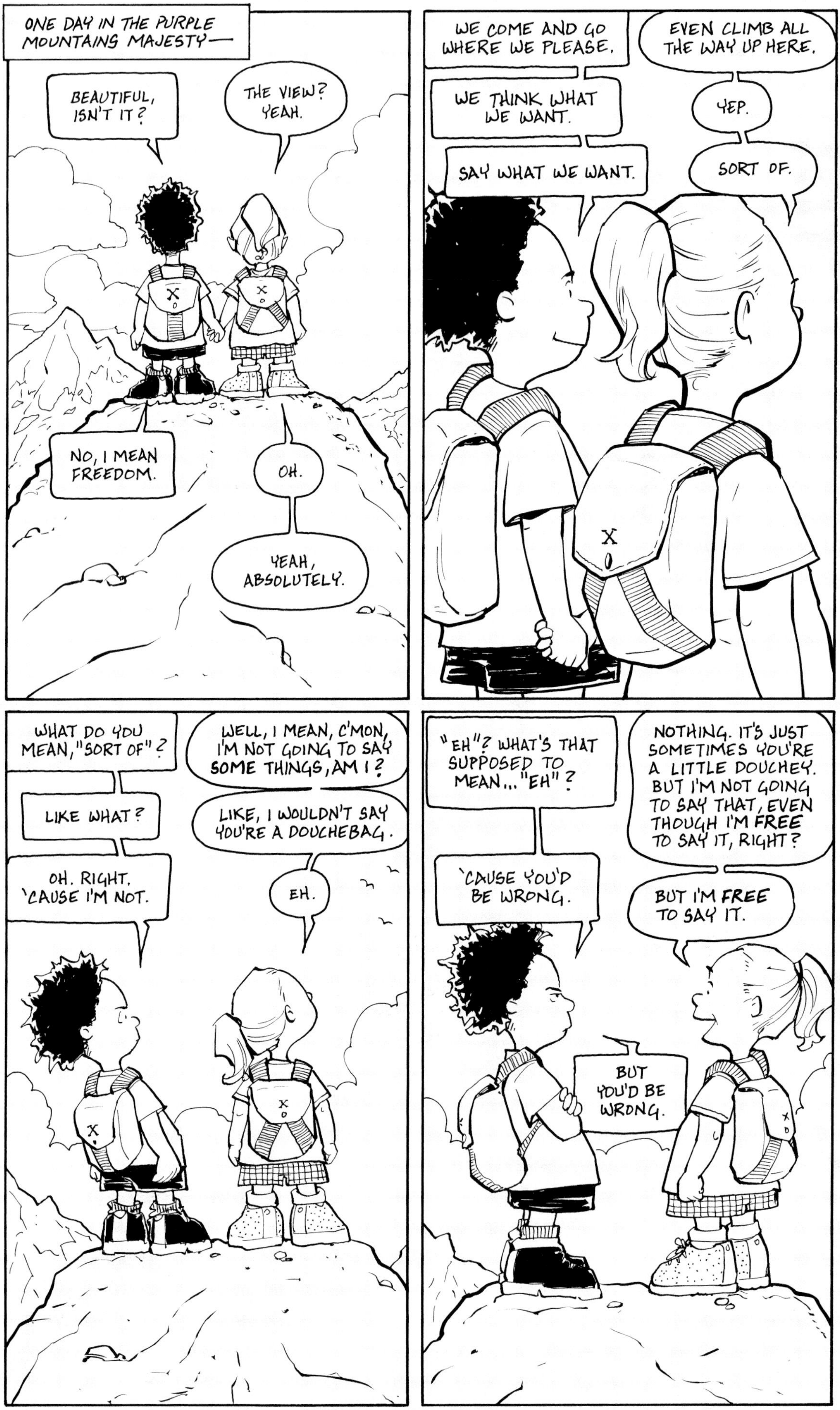
ONE DAY IN THE PURPLE MOUNTAINS MAJESTY—
BEAUTIFUL, ISN'T IT?
THE VIEW? YEAH.
NO, I MEAN FREEDOM.
OH.
YEAH, ABSOLUTELY.
WE COME AND GO WHERE WE PLEASE.
WE THINK WHAT WE WANT.
SAY WHAT WE WANT.
EVEN CLIMB ALL THE WAY UP HERE.
YEP.
SORT OF.
WHAT DO YOU MEAN, "SORT OF"?
LIKE WHAT?
OH. RIGHT. 'CAUSE I'M NOT.
WELL, I MEAN, C'MON, I'M NOT GOING TO SAY SOME THINGS, AM I?
LIKE, I WOULDN'T SAY YOU'RE A DOUCHEBAG.
EH.
"EH"? WHAT'S THAT SUPPOSED TO MEAN... "EH"?
'CAUSE YOU'D BE WRONG.
NOTHING. IT'S JUST SOMETIMES YOU'RE A LITTLE DOUCHEY. BUT I'M NOT GOING TO SAY THAT, EVEN THOUGH I'M FREE TO SAY IT, RIGHT?
BUT I'M FREE TO SAY IT.
BUT YOU'D BE WRONG.

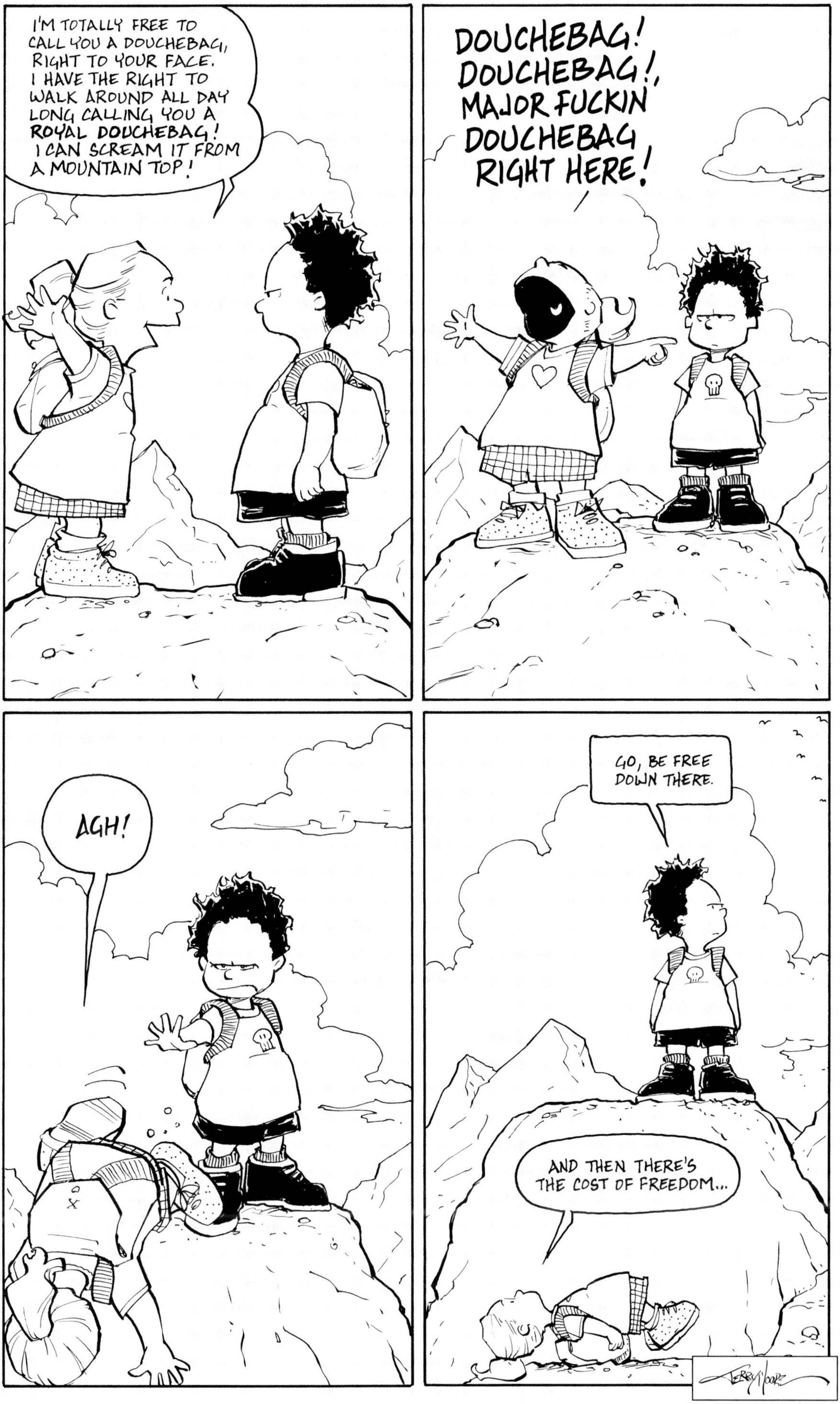
I'M TOTALLY FREE TO CALL YOU A DOUCHEBAG, RIGHT TO YOUR FACE. I HAVE THE RIGHT TO WALK AROUND ALL DAY LONG CALLING YOU A **ROYAL DOUCHEBAG**! I CAN SCREAM IT FROM A MOUNTAIN TOP!
DOUCHEBAG! DOUCHEBAG!, MAJOR FUCKIN DOUCHEBAG RIGHT HERE!
AGH!
GO, BE FREE DOWN THERE.
AND THEN THERE'S THE COST OF FREEDOM...
TERRY MOORE

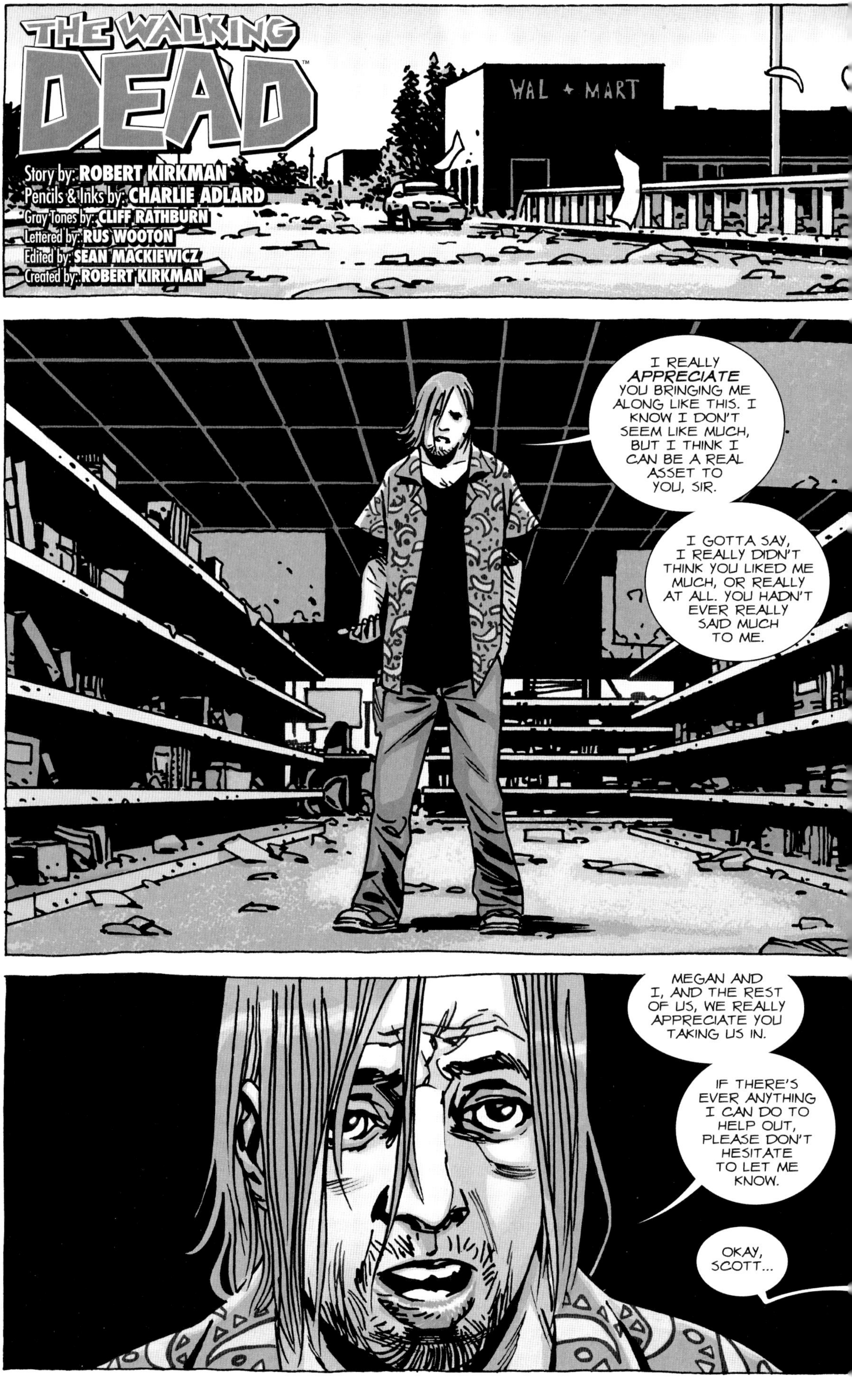
THE WALKING DEAD
Story by: ROBERT KIRKMAN
Pencils & Inks by: CHARLIE ADLARD
Gray Tones by: CLIFF RATHBURN
Lettered by: RUS WOOTON
Edited by: SEAN MACKIEWICZ
Created by: ROBERT KIRKMAN
WAL ✦ MART
I REALLY APPRECIATE YOU BRINGING ME ALONG LIKE THIS. I KNOW I DON'T SEEM LIKE MUCH, BUT I THINK I CAN BE A REAL ASSET TO YOU, SIR.
I GOTTA SAY, I REALLY DIDN'T THINK YOU LIKED ME MUCH, OR REALLY AT ALL. YOU HADN'T EVER REALLY SAID MUCH TO ME.
MEGAN AND I, AND THE REST OF US, WE REALLY APPRECIATE YOU TAKING US IN.
IF THERE'S EVER ANYTHING I CAN DO TO HELP OUT, PLEASE DON'T HESITATE TO LET ME KNOW.
OKAY, SCOTT...

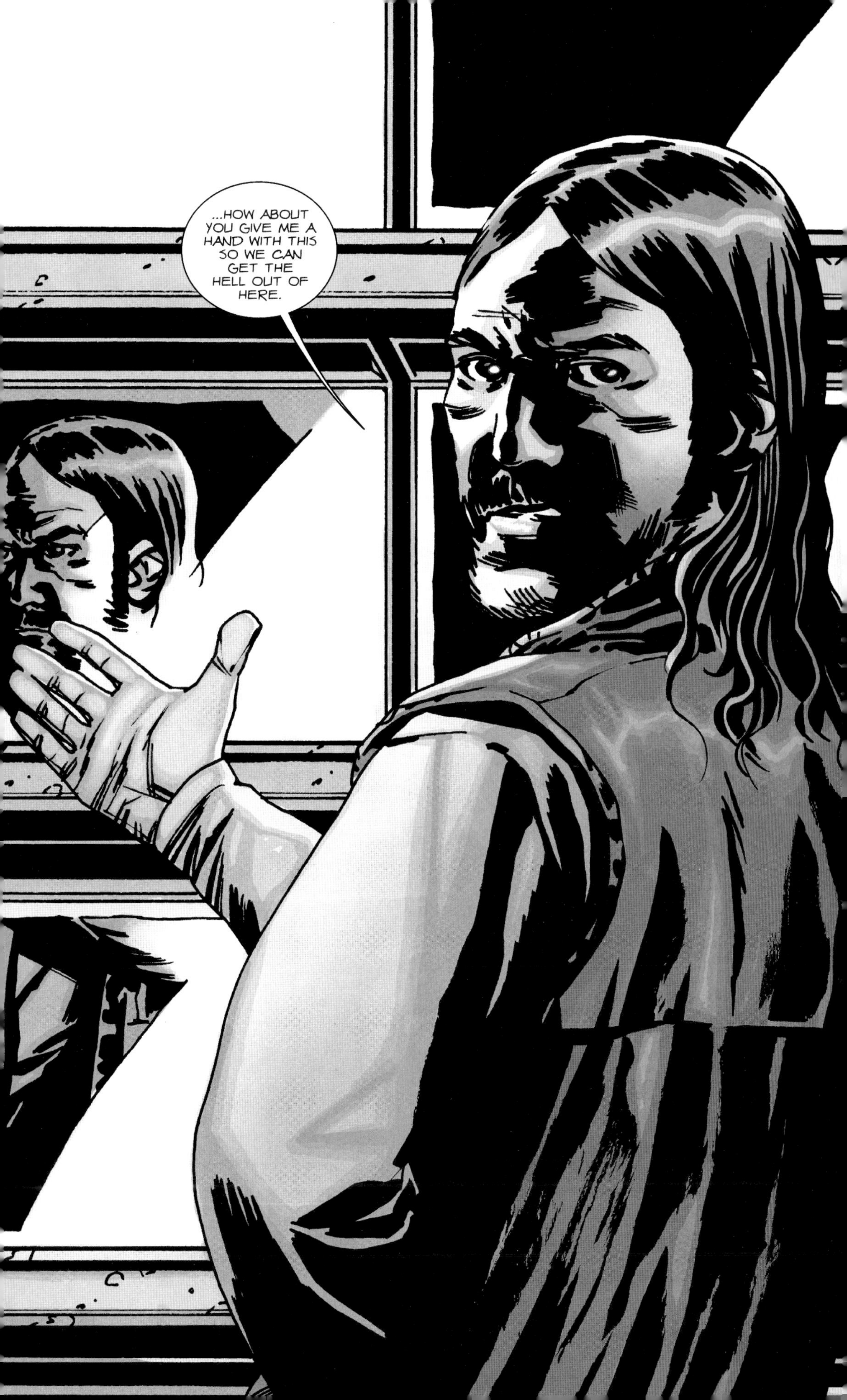
...HOW ABOUT YOU GIVE ME A HAND WITH THIS SO WE CAN GET THE HELL OUT OF HERE.

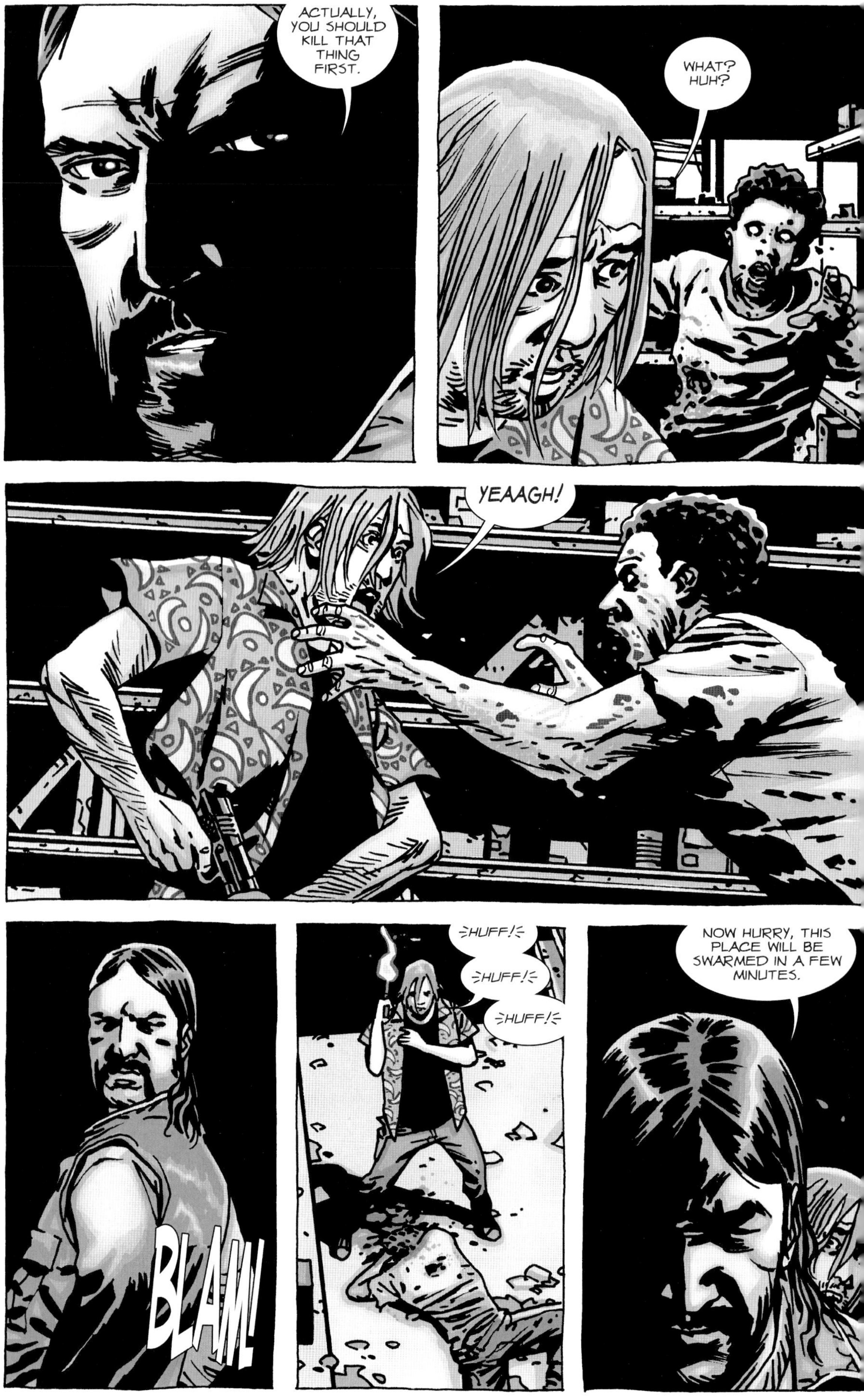
ACTUALLY, YOU SHOULD KILL THAT THING FIRST.
WHAT? HUH?
YEAAGH!
BLAM!
HUFF!
HUFF!
HUFF!
NOW HURRY, THIS PLACE WILL BE SWARMED IN A FEW MINUTES.

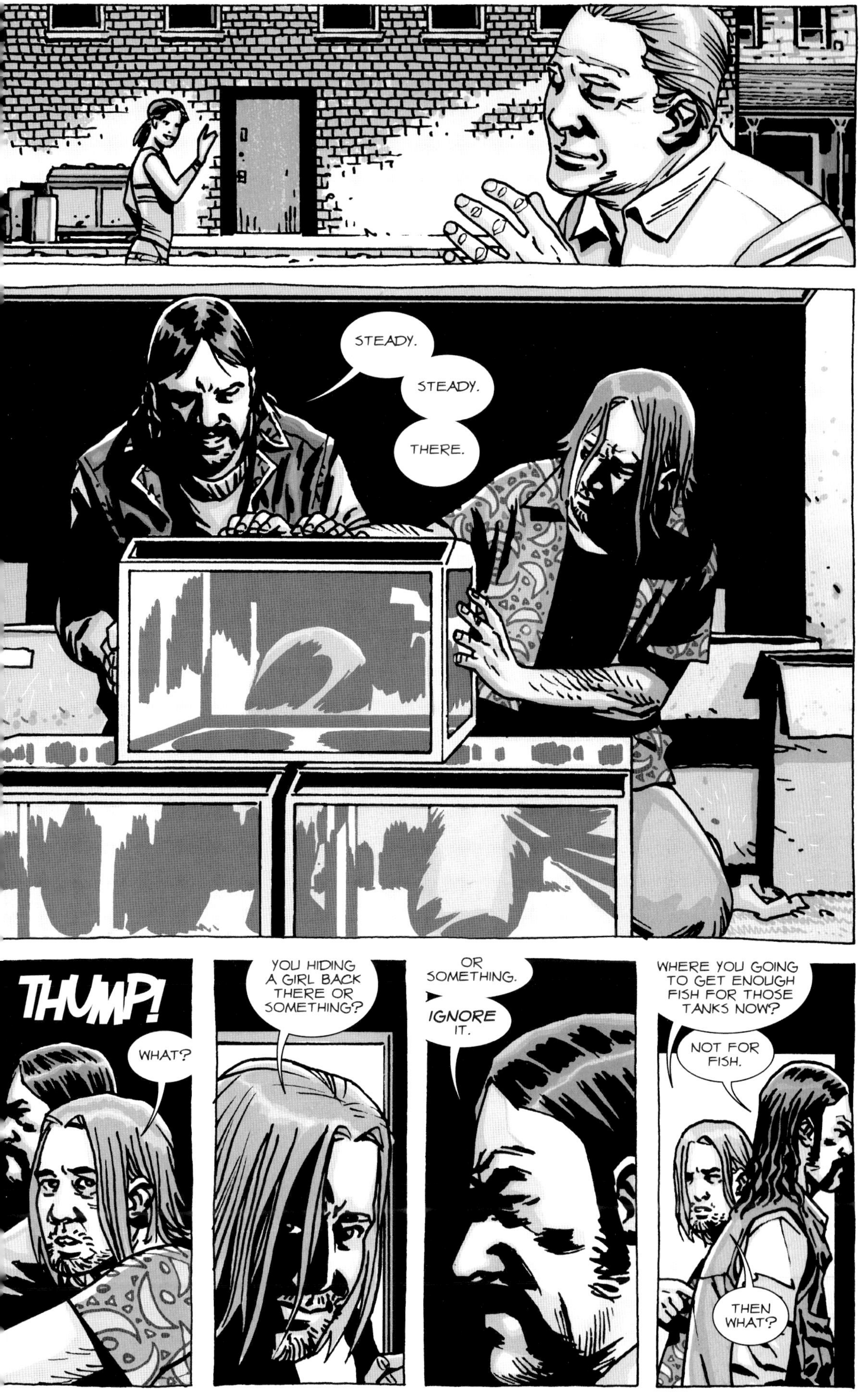
STEADY.
STEADY.
THERE.
THUMP!
WHAT?
YOU HIDING A GIRL BACK THERE OR SOMETHING?
OR SOMETHING.
IGNORE IT.
WHERE YOU GOING TO GET ENOUGH FISH FOR THOSE TANKS NOW?
NOT FOR FISH.
THEN WHAT?

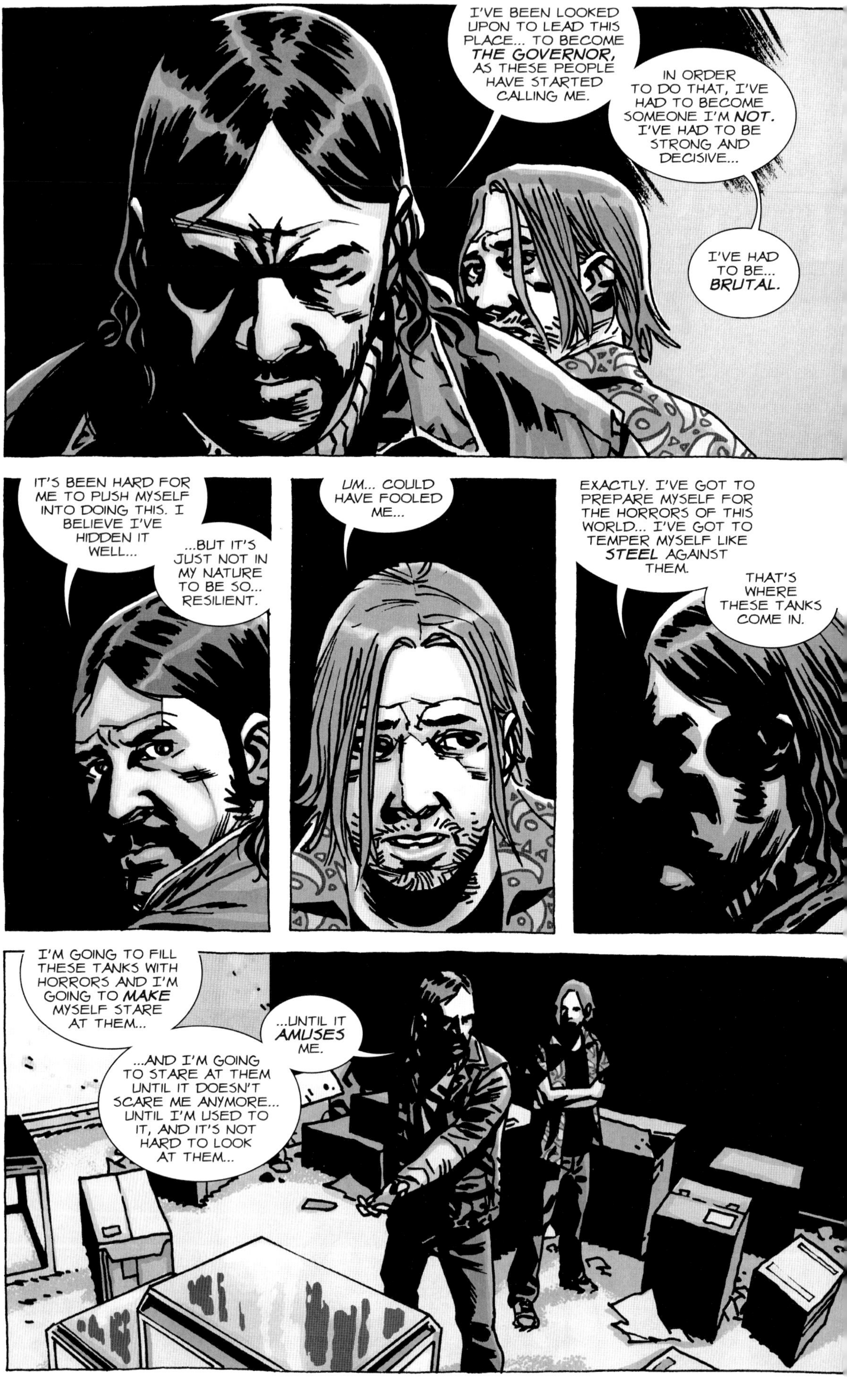

I'VE BEEN LOOKED UPON TO LEAD THIS PLACE... TO BECOME **THE GOVERNOR,** AS THESE PEOPLE HAVE STARTED CALLING ME.
IN ORDER TO DO THAT, I'VE HAD TO BECOME SOMEONE I'M **NOT.** I'VE HAD TO BE STRONG AND DECISIVE...
I'VE HAD TO BE... **BRUTAL.**
IT'S BEEN HARD FOR ME TO PUSH MYSELF INTO DOING THIS. I BELIEVE I'VE HIDDEN IT WELL...
...BUT IT'S JUST NOT IN MY NATURE TO BE SO... RESILIENT.
UM... COULD HAVE FOOLED ME...
EXACTLY. I'VE GOT TO PREPARE MYSELF FOR THE HORRORS OF THIS WORLD... I'VE GOT TO TEMPER MYSELF LIKE **STEEL** AGAINST THEM.
THAT'S WHERE THESE TANKS COME IN.
I'M GOING TO FILL THESE TANKS WITH HORRORS AND I'M GOING TO **MAKE** MYSELF STARE AT THEM...
...AND I'M GOING TO STARE AT THEM UNTIL IT DOESN'T SCARE ME ANYMORE... UNTIL I'M USED TO IT, AND IT'S NOT HARD TO LOOK AT THEM...
...UNTIL IT **AMUSES** ME.

THEN I'LL BE READY FOR THE WORLD OUTSIDE... AND WHATEVER I HAVE TO DO TO KEEP WOODBURY TOGETHER.

THEN I'LL LIVE UP TO MY NEW NAME.

SO, WHAT ARE YOU GOING TO PUT IN THEM THEN?

WELL, I WAS THINKING ABOUT SOMETHING ALONG THE LINES OF *SEVERED HEADS.*

...

STARTING WITH *YOURS.*